Instructional Leadership

A Learning-Centered Guide

Anita Woolfolk Hoy and Wayne Kolter Hoy

The Ohio State University

Boston   New York   San Francisco
Mexico City   Montreal   Toronto   London   Madrid   Munich   Paris
Hong Kong   Singapore   Tokyo   Cape Town   Sydney

Editor in Chief, Education: *Paul A. Smith*
Series Editor: *Arnis E. Burvikovs*
Editorial Assistant: *Matthew Forster*
Marketing Manager: *Tara Whorf*
Editorial Production Service: *Chestnut Hill Enterprises, Inc.*
Manufacturing Buyer: *JoAnne Sweeney*
Cover Administrator: *Kristina Mose-Libon*
Electronic Composition: *Omegatype Typography, Inc.*

Internet: www.ablongman.com

Between the time Website information is gathered and then published, it is not unusual for some sites to have closed. Also, the transcription of URLs can result in unintended typographical errors. The publisher would appreciate notification where these occur so that they may be corrected in subsequent editions.

Library of Congress Cataloging-in-Publication Data

Hoy, Anita Woolfolk
     Instructional leadership : a learning-centered guide / Anita Woolfolk
     Hoy and Wayne Kolter Hoy.
          p.   cm.
     Includes bibliographical references (p.) and index.
     ISBN 0-205-35497-1
     1. Educational leadership—Handbooks, manuals, etc.   2. School
     management and organization—Handbooks, manuals, etc.   3.
     Teaching—Handbooks, manuals, etc.   4. Learning—Handbooks, manuals,
     etc.   I. Hoy, Wayne K.   II. Title.

LB2805 .H713 2003
371.2–dc21   2002019379

Printed in the United States of America

10   9   8   7   6   5   4   3   2   1   07   06   05   04   03   02

CONTENTS

Preface   xi

1 Introduction to Teaching and Learning   1

The Role of Instructional Leader   2
Student Differences   3
Learning   4
Motivation   5
Teaching   6
Classroom Management   7
Assessing Student Learning   8
Assessing and Changing School Culture and Climate   10
Summary   12
Develop Your Portfolio   13
Instructional Leader's Toolbox   14

2 Students   16

Preview: Key Points   16
Leadership Challenge   17
Today's Multicultural Classrooms   18
    Cultural Diversity   18
    Language Differences in the Classroom   19
    Theory into Action Guidelines: Dialects   20
Creating Culturally Compatible Classrooms   21
    Social Organization   22
    Cognitive and Learning Styles   23
    Participation Structures   26
    Sources of Misunderstandings   26
    Theory into Action Guidelines: Culturally Compatible Classrooms   28
Gender Differences in the Classroom   27
    Gender Bias in the Curriculum   27
    Sex Discrimination in Classrooms   27
    Sex Differences in Mental Abilities   29
    Eliminating Gender Bias   30
    Theory into Action Guidelines: Avoiding Sexism   31
Individual Differences in Intelligence   30
    What Does Intelligence Mean?   30

What Does an IQ Score Mean?   36
Theory into Action Guidelines: Interpreting Intelligence Test Scores   37

Ability Differences in Teaching   38
Between-Class Ability Grouping   38
Within-Class Ability Grouping   39
Gifted and Talented   39
Theory into Action Guidelines: Ability Grouping   40

Students with Learning Challenges   42
Hyperactivity and Attention Disorders   42
Learning Disabilities   44
Integration, Mainstreaming, and Inclusion   46
Effective Teaching in Inclusion Classrooms   49
Theory into Action Guidelines: Productive Family Conferences   51

Summary   52
Key Terms   56
Some Ideas for Your Portfolio   57
Instructional Leader's Toolbox   57

3 Learning   60

Preview: Key Points   61
Leadership Challenge   61
What Is Learning?   62
Behavioral View of Learning   63
Types of Consequences   63
Antecedents and Behavior Change   65

Teaching Applications of Behavioral Theories   67
Contingency Contract Programs   67
Theory into Action Guidelines: Using Reinforcement and Punishment   69

Cognitive Views of Learning   70
Knowledge and Learning   72
An Information Processing Model   73
Sensory Memory   74
Working Memory   75
Theory into Action: Capturing Attention   76
Long-Term Memory   77
Storing and Retrieving Information in Long-Term Memory   79
Metacognition, Regulation, and Individual Differences   81
Theory into Action Guidelines: Applying Information Processing   82

Cognitive Contributions: Learning Strategies and Tactics   83
Deciding What Is Important   84
Visual Tools for Organizing   86
Mnemonics   87
Reading Strategies   88

Constructivist Theories of Learning   89
Constructivist Views of Learning   89
Theory into Action Guidelines: Learning Strategies   90
Is the World Knowable?   92
Knowledge: Situated or General?   93

Teaching Applications of Constructivist Perspectives   94
Elements of Constructivist Teaching   94
Inquiry Learning   97
Problem-Based Learning   99
Cognitive Apprenticeships   100
Group Work and Cooperation in Learning   101

Summary   105
Theory into Action Guidelines: Explaining Innovations   106

Key Terms   107
Some Ideas for Your Portfolio   107
Instructional Leader's Toolbox   108

4 Motivation   110

Preview: Key Points   111
Leadership Challenge   111
Motivation—A Definition   112
Intrinsic and Extrinsic Motivation   112
Four General Approaches to Motivation   113
Motivation to Learn in School   115

Goals and Motivation   116
Types of Goals   116
Goals: Lessons for Teachers and Principals   118

Needs and Motivation   118
Maslow's Hierarchy   118
Theory into Action Guidelines: Family and Community Partnerships   119
Achievement Motivation   120
The Need for Self-Determination   120
The Need for Social Support   121
Needs and Motivation: Lessons for Teachers and Principals   121
Theory into Practice Guidelines: Supporting Self-Determination   122

Attributions, Beliefs, and Motivation   123
Attribution Theory   123
Beliefs about Ability   126
Beliefs about Self-Efficacy   127
Attributions, Achievement Motivation, and Self-Worth   130
Attributions and Beliefs: Lessons for Teachers and Principals   131

Interests and Emotions   131

Theory into Action Guidelines: Encouraging Self-Worth and Self-Efficacy   132

Tapping Interests   132

Theory into Action Guidelines: Building on Students' Interests   133

Arousal: Excitement and Anxiety in Learning   134

Strategies to Encourage Motivation and Thoughtful Learning   137

Necessary Conditions in Classrooms   137

Theory into Action Guidelines: Dealing with Anxiety   138

Can I Do It? Building Confidence and Positive Expectations   139

Do I Want to Do It? Seeing the Value of Learning   140

What Do I Need to Do to Succeed? Staying Focused on the Task   142

How Do Beginning Teachers Motivate Students?   143

Summary   143

Key Terms   147

Some Ideas for Your Portfolio   147

Instructional Leader's Toolbox   147

5 Teaching   150

Preview: Key Points   150

Leadership Challenge   151

What Is a Good Teacher?   151

Inside Five Classrooms   151

Expert Teachers   153

Concerns of Teachers   155

The First Step: Planning   155

Objectives for Learning   156

Theory into Action Guidelines: Developing Objectives   159

Flexible and Creative Plans—Using Taxonomies   159

Another View: Planning from a Constructivist Perspective   162

Successful Teaching: Focus on the Teacher   164

Characteristics of Effective Teachers   165

Teacher Effects   167

Theory into Action Guidelines: Characteristics of Good Teachers   168

Teaching for Understanding: Focus on the Subject   171

Learning to Read and Write   171

Learning and Teaching Mathematics   173

Learning Science   176

A Model for Good Subject Matter Teaching   177

Theory into Action Guidelines: Conceptual Change Teaching   178

Criticisms of Constructivist Approaches to Subject Teaching   179

Beyond Models to Outstanding Teaching   180

Cautions: Where's the Learning?   181

Summary   182

Key Terms   184

Some Ideas for Your Portfolio   184

Instructional Leader's Toolbox   184

6   Classroom Management   187

Preview: Key Points   188

Leadership Challenge   188

Organizing the Learning Environment   189

The Basic Task: Gain Their Cooperation   189

Managing the Learning Environment   190

Creating a Positive Learning Environment: Some Research Results   192

Rules and Procedures   193

Theory into Action Guidelines: Rules and Procedures   194

Planning Spaces for Learning   197

Theory into Action Guidelines: Designing Learning Spaces   200

Getting Started: The First Weeks of Class   202

Effective Classroom Managers for Elementary Students   202

Effective Classroom Managers for Secondary Students   203

Creating a Learning Community   203

The Three Cs of Classroom Management   204

Getting Started on Community   205

Maintaining a Good Learning Environment   205

Encouraging Engagement   205

Theory into Action Guidelines: Encouraging Student Accountability   206

Prevention Is the Best Medicine   207

Dealing with Discipline Problems   208

Special Problems with Secondary Students   209

Theory into Action Guidelines: Penalties   210

Special Programs for Classroom Management   211

The Need for Communication   213

Message Sent—Message Received   213

Diagnosis: Whose Problem Is It?   213

Counseling: The Student's Problem   214

Confrontation and Assertive Discipline   215

Student Conflicts and Confrontations   217

Communicating with Families about Classroom Management   219

Designing Motivating Learning Environments on Target for Learning   220

Theory into Action Guidelines: Working with Families   220

Authentic Tasks   221

Supporting Autonomy   221

Recognizing Accomplishment   225
Grouping   225
Evaluation   227
Time   228

Summary   228

Key Terms   230

Some Ideas for Your Portfolio   230

Instructional Leader's Toolbox   231

7 Assessing Student Learning   233

Preview: Key Points   233

Leadership Challenge   234

Evaluation, Measurement, and Assessment   234
Norm-Referenced Tests   235
Criterion-Referenced Tests   236

What Do Test Scores Mean?   236
Basic Concepts   237
Types of Scores   238
Interpreting Test Scores   242

Types of Standardized Tests   244
Achievement Tests: What Has the Student Learned?   244
Diagnostic Tests: What Are the Student's Strengths and Weaknesses?   247
Aptitude Tests: How Well Will the Student Do in the Future?   248

Issues in Standardized Testing   249
The Uses of Testing in American Society   249
Theory into Action Guidelines: Family Partnerships for Using Test Results   250
Advantages in Taking Tests—Fair and Unfair   252

New Directions in Standardized Testing and Classroom Assessment   255
Theory into Action Guidelines: Becoming an Expert Test-Taker   256
Authentic Assessment   257
Authentic Classroom Tests   258
Performance in Context: Portfolios and Exhibitions   258
Theory into Action Guidelines: Student Portfolios   261
Evaluating Portfolios and Performances   262
Theory into Action Guidelines: Developing a Rubric   265
Getting the Most from Traditional Tests   265

Effects of Grades and Grading on Students   266
Effects of Failure   267
Effects of Feedback   268
Grades and Motivation   268
Theory into Action Guidelines: Grading   269

Summary   269

Key Terms   271

Some Ideas for Your Portfolio   271

Instructional Leader's Toolbox   272

8 Assessing and Changing School Culture and Climate   274

Preview: Key Points   274

Leadership Challenge   275

The School Workplace   275

Organizational Culture   276

Levels of Culture   276

Functions of Culture   281

Common Elements of Culture   281

Some General Propositions about School Culture   281

Organizational Climate   283

Organizational Climate: Open to Closed   283

A Revised OCDQ   284

Climate Types   287

The OCDQ: Some Implications   289

Organizational Climate: Healthy To Unhealthy   290

Dimensions of Organizational Health   291

Organizational Health Inventory (OHI-S)   293

The OHI: Some Implications   295

Collective Efficacy   296

Changing School Climate   299

Some Assumptions about Change in Schools   299

The Case of Martin Luther King, Jr. High School: An Example   300

A Problem   301

An Organizational Development Model   302

Back to Martin Luther King, Jr. High School   302

Summary   309

Key Terms   310

Some Ideas for Your Portfolio   310

Instructional Leader's Toolbox   311

Appendices   312

Index   363

PREFACE

Instructional Leadership is predicated on the assumption that teachers and principals need to work together as colleagues to improve teaching and learning in schools. Traditional supervision in which the principal rates the effectiveness of teachers is an outmoded concept, one that was always more ritual than reality. We believe that this is the first text of its kind, one written for principals to help them understand current theories of teaching and learning as well as the practical applications of these perspectives. The text uses a learning-centered approach, one that emphasizes making decisions based upon what supports student learning.

We don't believe that instructional supervision can be effective unless the parties involved have a good understanding of how students learn. Although principals may take the lead in cooperative and professional endeavors, in the end it is the teachers who determine their success. Perhaps just as important as taking the lead in instructional matters is to develop a school climate where instructional leadership flourishes and emerges spontaneously from teachers themselves.

The text addresses the critical aspects of the teaching–learning process—student differences, learning, student motivation, teaching, classroom management, assessing student learning, and assessing and changing school climate and culture. Each chapter is grounded in the latest research and theory in that area and provides specific suggestions for applying that knowledge to practice. After the Introduction, each chapter begins with a ***Preview of Key Points*** and a ***Leadership Challenge,*** an actual teaching problem, and ends with suggestions of projects to relate theory to practice in the form of professional ***Portfolio*** exercises. Moreover, throughout the chapters, ***Theory into Action Guidelines*** provide concrete suggestions. Also, each chapter includes an ***Instructional Leader's Toolbox,*** a collection of contemporary readings, useful web sites, and helpful organizations. Finally, the text concludes with ***Appendices,*** which include a series of instruments for assessing your school learning environment as well as the standards of the Interstate School Leaders Licensure Consortium (ISLLC).

Our colleagues and students are important sources of ideas and criticism. We would like to thank and acknowledge them for their suggestions and encouragement in this project:

Michael DiPaola, College of William & Mary,
Megan Tschannen-Moran, College of William & Mary
Pamela J. Gaskill, The Ohio State University
P. Karen Murphy, The Ohio State University
James Sinden, The Ohio State University
Jana Alig-Mielcarek, The Ohio State University
Page A. Smith, The University of Texas, San Antonio

Scott R. Sweetland, The Ohio State University
Franklin B. Walter, The University of Texas, San Antonio
Rhonda Burke-Spero, University of Miami
Roger D. Goddard, University of Michigan
C. John Tarter, St. John's University
Harry Galinsky, Superintendent, Paramus, NJ

In addition, we thank the following reviewers for their helpful suggestions: Nancy Nestor-Baker, University of Cincinnati; Robert J. Hanny, College of William and Mary; and Linda J. Naimi, Chicago State University.

AWH

WKH

1 Introduction to Teaching and Learning

The Role of Instructional Leader

Student Differences

Learning

Motivation

Teaching

Classroom Management

Assessing Student Learning

Assessing and Changing School Culture and Climate

Summary

Develop Your Portfolio

Instructional Leader's Toolbox
  Readings
  Websites
  Organizations

Schools are about teaching and learning; all other activities are secondary to these basic goals. Teaching and learning are elaborate and complex processes that need careful attention and study. If they are to help teachers improve, school administrators must first understand, but there are neither quick fixes nor easy answers to the improvement of teaching and learning. This book is about understanding teaching and learning. It is not a book about administration, but it is a book for administrators because the fundamental purpose of schooling is student learning. School leaders are responsible for creating learning organizations. Even though we focus on principals, this text is for all school leaders who are interested in improving teaching and learning whether they are teachers, curriculum and instructional specialists, or administrators; in the end, instructional leadership is a shared responsibility.

The centrality of student learning in the school is irrefutable; in fact, preparation standards for school leaders embrace this fundamental fact in their second standard as follows (Council of Chief State School Officers, 1996, p. 12):

> A school administrator is an educational leader who promotes the success of all students by advocating, nurturing, and sustaining a school culture and instructional program conducive to student learning and staff professional growth.

We argue that school leaders cannot achieve this purpose without a clear and deep understanding of teaching, learning, motivation, and a nurturing school culture.

The Role of Instructional Leader

A critical role for all principals is that of instructional leader. We are not suggesting that the principal alone is responsible for leadership in instruction. Clearly that is not the case. Leadership in instructional matters should emerge freely from both the principal and teachers. After all, teachers deliver the instruction in the classroom; they have expertise in curriculum and teaching, and they have mastered a substantive body of knowledge. The principal, however, is responsible for developing a school climate that is conducive to providing the very best instructional practices. Thus, it is the principal who should forge a partnership with teachers with the primary goal of the improvement of teaching and learning.

There is no one way to engage in such cooperation, but instructional leaders need to spend time in classrooms as colleagues and engage teachers in conversations about learning and teaching. Improvement of teaching and learning is a continuous process, not merely a ritual observation that principals make once or twice a year. Professional conversations and professional development should revolve around the improvement of instruction, how students learn, and appropriate teaching strategies for different situations. Cooperation, colleagueship, expertise, and teamwork are hallmarks of successful improvement and are substitutes for traditional supervision.

Although principals may take the lead in cooperative and professional endeavors, in the end it is the teachers who determine their success. Perhaps just as important as taking the lead in instructional matters is developing a school climate where instructional leadership flourishes and emerges spontaneously from teachers themselves. Above all, the principal must communicate a clear vision of instructional excellence and continuous professional development consistent with the goal of the improvement of teaching and learning. What does this mean? How does it get translated into action?

■ First, academic excellence should be a strong motivating force in the school. Increasingly the research is affirming that a school's academic emphasis is critical to student achievement (Goddard, Sweetland, & Hoy, 2000; Hoy & Sabo, 1998; and Hoy, Tarter, & Kottkamp, 1991). The instructional leader should ensure a learning environment that is orderly, serious, and focused on high but achievable academic goals. The principal must demonstrate in both words and action a belief that all students can achieve, while developing a school culture in which teachers and students alike respect hard work and academic success.

■ Second, instructional excellence and continuous improvement are ongoing and cooperative activities by instructional leaders and teachers. Activities such as student growth and achievement, school climate, teacher and student motivation, and faculty morale should be monitored and assessed regularly with the aim of improvement.

■ Third, teachers are at the center of the instructional improvement; in the end, only the teachers themselves can change and improve their instructional practice in the classroom; hence, teacher motivation and self-regulation are critical to improvement. Teachers must decide that they want to improve.

■ Fourth, principals must provide constructive support and obtain the resources and materials necessary for teachers to be successful in the classroom; indeed, resource support is a basic principal role.

- Fifth, principals should be intellectual leaders who keep abreast of the latest developments in teaching, learning, motivation, classroom management, and assessment, and share best practices in each area with teachers.
- Finally, the principal should take the lead in recognizing and celebrating academic excellence among students and teachers because such activities reinforce a vision and culture of academic excellence.

Wang, Haertal, and Walberg (1993, 1997) did a meta-analysis of more than 10,000 statistical findings on the most significant influences on learning and found a reasonable consensus; in general, direct influences have a greater impact on student learning than indirect ones. Fifty years of research contradicts the current reliance on school restructuring as the key to school reform. Classroom management, student metacognitive and cognitive processes (e g., study skills, background knowledge, work habits), instruction, motivation, and assessment have a greater impact on learning than indirect influences such as restructuring, district policy, and school policy. One exception to the general finding was school culture. School culture does seem to make an important difference by providing a school context that reinforces important teaching and learning practices. Increasingly the research suggests that the key to improving student learning rests with what happens in the classroom: the teacher is critical. Instructional leadership calls for the principal to work with teacher colleagues in the improvement of instruction by providing a school culture and climate where change is linked to the best knowledge about student learning.

Student Differences

We begin our analysis of teaching and learning with the students and the broad range of differences that they bring to the school and the classroom. Students differ in intelligence, emotion, learning styles, gender, and culture. Each of these differences has implications for teaching and learning. For example, beliefs about intelligence influence the structure and design of the curriculum. Administrators invariably confront such practical issues of ability grouping and programs for the gifted as they try to organize the school for effective learning.

Although students have different cognitive styles and learning styles, the consequences of these styles for teaching and learning are not clear; in fact, popular programs have far outrun what we know about how to deal with such differences. It is much easier to grasp at the latest fad than it is to examine the research before making a decision. Indeed, the research may give one pause.

Gender differences and sex stereotyping are two other problems that face most teachers and administrators. Gender bias in the curriculum, sex discrimination in the classroom, as well as gender differences in math and science are just a few of the challenges facing school leaders. To act wisely is to first understand the facts and consequences.

Finally, in less than two decades over half of the students in public schools will be students of color, many of whom will speak a language that is different from the teacher's. Teachers and administrators will have to work together to create classrooms that are good for all students. The challenge will be creating tolerance, respect, and understanding among a diverse student and teacher school community. This formidable task will be complicated by laws that mandate the inclusion of students with learning and behavior problems in the classroom who once were taught in separate classes.

Learning

Learning occurs when there is a stable change in an individual's skill, knowledge, or behavior. Most experts on learning would agree with this general definition of learning, but some would emphasize behavior and skills; others, cognition and knowledge. Because learning is a complex cognitive process, there is no single best explanation of learning. Different theories of learning offer more or less useful explanations depending on what is to be explained. We examine three general theories of learning—behavioral, cognitive, and constructivist—each with a different focus.

Behavioral theories of learning stress observable changes in behaviors, skills, and habits. Attention is clearly on behavior. Learning is seen as a change in behavior brought about by experience with virtually no concern for the mental or internal processes of thinking. Behavior is what people do. The intellectual underpinnings of behavioral theory rest with Skinner's (1950) operant conditioning; learning objectives, mastery learning, direct instruction, and basic skills are all teaching strategies that evolved from this perspective. When specific skills and behaviors need to be learned, teaching approaches consistent with behavioral learning theory are quite effective.

Cognitive theories of learning deal with thinking, remembering, creating, and problem solving. How information is remembered and processed as well as how individuals use their own knowledge to regulate their thinking are critical in this perspective. Some of the most important teaching applications of cognitive theories are teaching students how to learn and remember by using learning tactics such as note taking, mnemonics, and visual organizers. Teaching strategies based on cognitive views of learning, particularly on information processing, highlight the importance of attention, organization, practice, and elaboration in learning. They also provide ways to give students more control over their own learning by developing and improving their own self-regulated learning strategies. The emphasis of the cognitive approach is on what is happening "inside the head" of the learner.

Constructivist theories of learning are concerned with how individuals make meaning of events and activities; hence, learning is seen as the construction of knowledge. In general, constructivism assumes that people create and construct knowledge rather than internalize it from the external environment, but there are a variety of different approaches to constructivism. Some constructivist views emphasize the shared and social construction of knowledge while others see social forces as less important. Constructivist perspectives on learning and teaching, which are increasingly influential today, are grounded in the research of Piaget, Bruner, Dewey, and Vygotsky. Inquiry and problem-based learning, cooperative learning, and cognitive apprenticeships are typical teaching strategies that are consistent with constructivist approaches. The essence of the constructivist approach is that it places the students' own efforts at the center of the educational process—thus the notion of student-centered teaching.

Each of these approaches to learning has much to offer; in fact, each brings with it advantages and disadvantages. It is not sufficient to know one perspective; indeed, knowledgeable teachers and administrators should know, understand, and apply all of these perspectives appropriately. Administrators, particularly school principals, have the added responsibility of developing school climates and cultures that are conducive to student learning—climates that focus on academic achievement, support learning, and are open, healthy, and efficacious. This aspect of instructional leadership will be the focus of Chapter 8.

Motivation

Effective teaching and learning are dependent upon motivated students; hence, teachers must know how to stimulate, direct, and maintain high levels of interest among students. Teachers can create intrinsic motivation by stimulating the students' curiosity and making them feel more competent as they learn, but that is easier said than done because some tasks simply are not inherently interesting. Teachers cannot count on intrinsic motivation to energize all their students all of the time. There are times when incentives and external supports are necessary. Teachers inevitably must use such extrinsic means to motivate students without undermining intrinsic aspects of learning. To do this, teachers need to know the factors that influence motivation. Four approaches to motivation are important in this regard.

Behaviorists explain motivation with concepts such as "reward" and "incentive." A reward is an attractive object or event supplied as a consequence of a particular behavior. An incentive is an object or event that encourages or discourages behavior—the promise of a reward. Thus, according to the behavioral view, understanding of student motivation begins with a careful analysis of the incentives and rewards present in the classroom. Providing grades, stars, and so on for learning—or demerits for misbehavior—are attempts to motivate students by extrinsic means of incentives, rewards, and punishments. Of course, in any individual case, many other factors will affect how a person behaves. There is much more to motivating students than manipulating rewards and incentives.

In fact, proponents of humanistic psychology such as Carl Rogers argued that such behavioral explanations did not adequately explain why people act as they do. Humanistic interpretations of motivation emphasize such intrinsic sources of motivation as a person's needs for "self-actualization" (Maslow, 1968, 1970) and the need for "self-determination" (Deci, Vallerand, Pelletier, & Ryan, 1991). These humanistic explanations are based upon the belief that people are continually motivated by the inborn need to fulfill their potential. Thus, from the humanistic perspective, to motivate means to encourage peoples' inner resources—their sense of competence, self-esteem, autonomy, and self-actualization. When we examine the role of needs in motivation, we will see two examples of the humanistic approach—Maslow's theory of the hierarchy of needs and Deci's self-determination theory.

Cognitive explanations of motivation also developed as a reaction to behavioral views. These perspectives argue that our behavior is determined by our thinking, not simply by whether we have been rewarded or punished for the behavior in the past. Behavior is initiated and regulated by an individual's plans, goals, schemas, expectations, and attributions. A central assumption in cognitive approaches is that people respond not to external events, but rather to their interpretations of these events. People are seen as active and curious, searching for information to solve personally relevant problems; the focus of motivation is internal and personal.

Social learning theories of motivation are integrations of behavioral and cognitive approaches: They take into account both the behaviorists' concern with the effects or outcomes of behavior and the cognitivists' interest in the impact of individual beliefs and expectations. Many influential social learning explanations view motivation as the product of two main forces, the individual's expectation of reaching a goal and the value of that goal to him or her. In other words, the important questions are, "If I try hard, can I succeed?" and "If I succeed, will the outcome be valuable or rewarding to me?"

Teachers and administrators must understand all these perspectives if they are to be effective in improving student learning. The implications for teaching and learning are varied. For example, goals that are specific, challenging, and realistic are effective in motivating students, as are goals that focus on learning rather than performance. Motivation is affected by such individual needs as self-esteem and achievement, but students have different needs at different times. Motivation is also affected by students' beliefs about the causes of successes and failures; for example, when students believe effort can improve their ability, they persist longer and reach higher levels of achievement. In fact, simply believing that they have the ability to be successful is a strong motivator.

In sum, student motivation to learn is enhanced when teachers use strategies that help students develop confidence in their ability to learn, see the value of the learning, and stay focused on learning without resorting to self-protective and self-defeating beliefs and actions. We will explore both the current explanations of motivation as well as the development of strategies to enhance motivation and performance.

Teaching

Good teaching is *sine qua non* of schooling; in fact, good teaching is what instructional leadership is about—finding ways to improve teaching and learning. There are no simple answers to what good teaching is, but we know it is anchored in expertise. Expert teachers work from integrated sets of principles instead of dealing with each new event as a new problem. They have broad professional knowledge in academic subjects, teaching strategies, curriculum, student characteristics, learning contexts, teaching goals, and pedagogical content knowledge. We will exam successful teachers from a variety of settings, trying to describe their similarities and differences.

Effective teachers are creative and organized and the basis for their organization is planning. Planning influences what students will learn because planning transforms the available time and curriculum materials into activities, assignments, and tasks for students. Plans reduce—but do not eliminate—uncertainty in teaching, but even the best plans cannot control everything that happens in class; thus, planning must allow for flexibility and creativity. There is, however, no one model for effective planning. For experienced teachers, planning is a creative problem-solving process of determining how to accomplish many lessons and segments of lessons. Experienced teachers know what to expect and how to proceed, so they don't necessarily follow the detailed lesson-planning models that are so useful for beginning teachers. For all teachers, regardless of experience, clear objectives—both cognitive and affective—are a key to successful planning.

Effective teachers are also warm and enthusiastic in their teaching. Warmth, friendliness, and understanding seem to be the teacher traits most strongly related to student attitudes. In other words, teachers who are warm and friendly tend to have students who like them and the class in general, but being warm, friendly, and enthusiastic is not enough to guarantee student achievement. Research has identified teacher knowledge, clarity, and organization as important characteristics of effective teachers. We will examine the practical implications of these findings for the classroom.

Learning to read and write involves both phonics and whole-language approaches to teaching. The "reading wars" have raged for years—phonics versus whole language. Again, there are no simple solutions, but we will examine the research and propose some sensible suggestions about the teaching of reading and writing. There is enough excellent research to make some clear recommendations.

Some of the most compelling support for constructivist approaches to teaching comes from mathematics education. Critics of direct instruction believe that traditional mathematics instruction often has unintended consequences—students don't understand mathematics, or worse, they decide that mathematics doesn't have to make sense, you just have to memorize the formulas. In science, as in mathematics, for students to learn and understand, they must go through a number of stages: initial discomfort with their own beliefs, attempts to explain away inconsistencies between their understandings and evidence, attempts to adjust observations to fit personal explanations, doubt, vacillation, and finally conceptual change and understanding.

In the end students have to do the learning, but teachers can create situations that guide, support, stimulate, and encourage learning, just as administrators can do the same for teachers. We will examine teaching from the perspectives of the teacher, the subject, and the student. In spite of the debates and different viewpoints, it remains clear that there is no one best way to teach. Different goals require different methods. Teacher-centered instruction leads to better performance on achievement tests, whereas the open, informal methods like discovery learning or inquiry approaches are associated with better performance on tests of creativity, abstract thinking, and problem solving. In addition, open methods are better for improving attitudes toward school and for stimulating curiosity, cooperation among students, and lower absence rates. Our goal is to help teachers and administrators understand the complexities of teaching and learning so that they can make better, more reasoned decisions in these areas.

Classroom Management

Classrooms are distinctive environments that affect participants regardless of how students are organized for learning or what educational philosophy the teacher espouses (Doyle, 1986). Classrooms are crowded with people, tasks, and time pressures. There are many students—all with differing goals, preferences, and abilities—who must share resources, accomplish various tasks, and use and reuse materials. In addition, actions typically have multiple effects. Calling on low-ability students may encourage their participation and thinking, but it also may slow the discussion and lead to management problems if the students cannot answer. Moreover, events occur simultaneously—everything happens at once and the pace is fast. Teachers have literally hundreds of exchanges with students during a single day. In this rapid-fire existence, events are unpredictable.

Even when plans are carefully made, a burned-out projector bulb or a loud, angry discussion right outside the classroom can still interrupt the lesson. The public nature of the classroom also means that the way the teacher handles these unexpected intrusions is seen and judged by all. Students have a keen sense of fairness. Finally, classrooms have histories. The meaning of a particular action depends in part on what has happened before. The 10th time a student arrives late requires a different response from the teacher than the first tardiness. Moreover, the history of the first few weeks of school affects life in the classroom all year. To manage a classroom is a challenge for all, but an especially major one for beginning teachers.

No productive activity can take place in a group without the cooperation of members; hence, a main task of teaching is to enlist students' cooperation in activities that will lead to learning, and the first step in achieving cooperation is to organize the learning environment in a productive way. Indeed, the aim of classroom management is to maintain a positive, productive learning environment. But order for its own sake is a hollow ritual. There are at least three reasons why classroom management is important—to make more time for learning, to develop effective participation structures, and to develop systems that help students better manage their own learning.

Research on effective elementary and secondary classroom managers shows that these teachers have carefully planned rules and procedures (including consequences) for their classes; they teach these rules and procedures early using explanations, examples, practice, correction, and student involvement. In fact, getting started with a careful system of rules and procedures the first week of school sets the tone for the rest of the year. Teachers need to establish a climate of trust and respect to create a positive community for learning. At the heart of a learning community is the idea of positive interdependence—individuals working together to achieve mutual goals.

To create supportive learning contexts, teachers need to design flexible room arrangements that match their teaching goals and the learning activities of the class. Once a good classroom environment is established, it must be maintained by encouraging student engagement and by preventing management problems. "Withitness," overlapping, group focus, and movement management are the skills of good preventers of problems. For special or more difficult situations, group consequences, token systems, or contingency contracts are strategies that are often helpful in preventing disruptive classroom episodes.

Even with the best prevention, there will be discipline problems in the classroom. When conflicts arise, teachers can deal more effectively with the situation if they first determine who "owns" the problem, then respond appropriately with empathetic listening or problem solving. Conflicts between students, though potentially dangerous, can be the occasions for learning conflict-negotiation and peer-mediation strategies. Establishing a positive learning context also includes attention to the factors that support motivation to learn, such as tasks, autonomy, recognition, grouping, evaluation, and time. Effective teaching and learning are not likely to occur unless the appropriate classroom climate is developed and maintained, and our goal is to give teachers and principals the tools to succeed in that endeavor.

Assessing Student Learning

The teaching–learning cycle is not complete until evaluation and assessment of student learning outcomes have been made; in fact, all teaching involves assessing and evaluating learning. At the heart of assessment is judgment, making decisions based on values. In the process of evaluation, we compare outcomes and information to some set of criteria and then make judgments. Teachers must make all kinds of judgments. Increasingly, evaluation and measurement specialists are using the term "assessment" to describe the process of gathering information about student learning. Assessment is broader than testing and measurement. Assessments can be designed by classroom teachers or by local, state, or national agencies such as school districts or the Educational Testing Service. Today's assessments can go well beyond paper-and-pencil exercises to observations of performances and the development of portfolios and artifacts.

Teachers and administrators are increasingly being called upon to make assessments of student learning and interpret the results of tests. Hence, they need to know the difference between norm-referenced and criterion-referenced tests. They must understand the concepts and language of test makers—sample, mean, mode, median, standard deviation, reliability, validity, normal distribution, percentile scores, standard scores, grade-equivalent scores—because they will be called upon to interpret test results to parents and policymakers.

Several kinds of standardized tests are used in schools today. If you have seen the cumulative folders that include testing records for individual students over several years, then you know the many ways students are tested in this country. There are three broad categories of standardized tests: achievement, diagnostic, and aptitude (including interest). Principals and teachers will probably encounter achievement and aptitude tests most frequently because they are important tools for diagnosing learning problems and measuring the success of schooling.

Today, many important decisions about students, teachers, and schools are based in part on the results of standardized tests. Test scores may affect admission to first grade, promotion from one grade to the next, high school graduation, access to special programs, placement in special education classes, teacher certification and tenure, and school funding. Because the decisions affected by test scores are so critical, many educators call this process *high-stakes testing;* in fact, most states have statewide mandated testing for public school students. Some groups are working to increase the role of testing   by establishing national standards, for example—while others are working to cut back the use of standardized tests in schools. We will consider a number of critical questions about standardized tests. For example, what role should testing play in making decisions about people? Do some students have an unfair advantage in taking tests? We will also explore the pros and cons of so-called "authentic assessment."

Although standardized tests are important and will likely increase in their significance, most tests given to students to evaluate their performance are teacher-made tests. In the end, teachers are the ones who give grades and decide who will be promoted and who will repeat, and what and how to teach. Teachers are concerned with formative assessment, that is, diagnosing the strengths and weaknesses of students so they can build an instructional program that will be effective. Teachers also must make summative assessments at the end of instruction to determine the level of accomplishment.

Teachers and administrators need to know the strengths and weaknesses of such traditional assessment approaches as objective and essay tests. But today objective and essay exams have been complemented with a few new approaches to classroom assessment. One of the main criticisms of standardized tests—that they control the curriculum, emphasizing recall of facts instead of thinking and problem solving—is a major criticism of classroom tests as well. Few teachers would dispute these criticisms. Even if you follow the guidelines we propose, traditional testing can be limiting. What can be done? One proposed solution to the testing dilemma is to apply the concept of authentic assessment to classroom testing.

Authentic tests ask students to apply skills and abilities as they would in real life. For example, they might use fractions to design a floor plan for a student lounge. If our instructional goals for students include the abilities to write, speak, listen, create, think critically, solve problems, or apply knowledge, then our tests should ask students to write, speak, listen, create, think, solve, and apply. The concern with authentic assessment has led to the development of several new approaches based on the goal of *performance in context*. Instead of circling answers to "factual" questions on nonexistent situations, students are required to solve real problems. Facts are used in a context where they apply—for example, the student uses grammar facts to write a persuasive letter to a software company requesting donations for the class computer center.

Portfolios and exhibitions are two new approaches to assessment that require performance in context. With these new approaches, it is difficult to tell where instruction stops and assessment starts because the two processes are interwoven. A portfolio is a purposeful collection of student work that demonstrates the student's efforts, progress, and achievements. The collection should include student participation in selecting contents, the criteria for judging merit, and evidence of student self-reflection. Portfolios often include work in progress, revisions, student self-analyses, and reflections on what the student has learned.

An exhibition is a performance test that has two additional features. First, it is public, so students preparing exhibitions must take the audience into account; communication and understanding are essential. Second, an exhibition often requires many hours of preparation, because it is the culminating experience of a whole program of study. Ted Sizer (1984) proposed that "exhibitions of mastery" replace traditional tests in determining graduation or course completion requirements. Grant Wiggins (1989) believes that an exhibition of mastery "is meant to be more than a better test. Like the thesis and oral examination in graduate school, it indicates whether a student has earned a diploma, is ready to leave high school" (p. 47).

Finally, it is important to consider the effects of grades and grading on students. It may sound as though low grades and failure should be avoided in school. But the situation is not that simple. After reviewing many years of research on the effects of failure, Margaret Clifford (1990, 1991) concluded that failure could have both positive and negative effects on subsequent performance, depending on the situation and the personality of the students involved. Perhaps it is time for educators to replace easy success with challenge, that is, encourage students to reach beyond their intellectual grasp and allow them the opportunity to learn and grow from mistakes. Teachers and administrators need to learn how to take advantage of the positive functions of grading and feedback while avoiding their negative consequences. That is no mean feat, but it is possible.

Assessing and Changing School Culture and Climate

The school is a complex social system. Teachers teach in classrooms, but classrooms are only a part of the broader social system of the school. Just as a positive classroom climate is critical for effective teaching and learning so too are the culture and climate of the school. The concepts of culture and climate are two ways to capture the feel or atmosphere of the school workplace. These two approaches to examining the collective identity of the workplace, its culture and climate, come from different intellectual traditions. Scholars of organizational culture tend to use the qualitative and ethnographic techniques of anthropology and sociology to examine the character or atmosphere of organizations. In contrast, scholars of climate use quantitative techniques and multivariate analyses to find patterns of perceived behavior in organizations. Both perspectives, climate and culture, are attempts to understand the influence of social context on school life. Thus, both should be useful to teachers and principals as they grapple with how social conditions in the school affect teaching and learning.

Organizational culture is a pattern of shared orientations that binds the unit together and gives it a distinctive identity. A school's culture can be examined at four levels—artifacts, shared norms, core values, and tacit assumptions. Although artifacts are the most concrete, they often are the most difficult to decipher. At the other extreme, tacit assumptions are abstract and can be very difficult to identify, but they most clearly capture the meanings of events and relationships in organizations. Shared norms and core values are at the middle range of abstraction and give meaning and understanding to the culture of the school. A thorough understanding of culture requires a comprehension of all four levels. In other words, to understand the culture of a school, one must comprehend the meanings and the shared orientations of the school—its artifacts, norms, values, and tacit assumptions.

Although there is no one culture that is best for every school, there are some tacit assumptions that facilitate the process of supervision as improvement of instruction. Consider the following set of basic assumptions that Schein (1992) labels the heart of a learning culture.

- Teachers and students are proactive problem solvers and learners.
- Solutions to problems derive from a pragmatic search; knowledge is found in many forms—scientific research, experience, trial and error, and clinical research in which teachers and supervisors work things out together.
- Teachers are basically good and are amenable to change and improvement.
- Creativity and innovation are central to learning.
- Both individualism and teamwork are important aspects of human interaction.
- Diversity is a resource that has the potential to enhance learning.

Schools anchored with such assumptions have created learning cultures that encourage learning and improvement among all participants—students, teachers, and administrators.

Another aspect of the school context that sets the scene for effective teaching and learning is organizational climate. Teachers' performance in schools is in part determined by the climate in which they work. Climate is a general concept that refers to teachers' perceptions of the school's work environment; it is affected by the formal organization, informal organization, and politics, all of which, including climate, affect the motivations and behavior of teachers. School climate is a relatively enduring quality of the school environment that is experienced by teachers, influences their behavior, and is based on their collective perceptions. Climate is to a school what personality is to an individual.

We examine organizational climate from several perspectives. First, we look at school climate in terms of its openness, that is, the extent to which behaviors in the school are authentic and real. Then we explore the health of the interpersonal dynamics among the students, teachers, and principal, for example, the extent to which the principal is collegial in his or her leadership, the extent to which teachers treat each others as professionals, and the extent to which the school emphasizes the primacy of teaching and learning. Finally, we explore the collective efficacy of the school, that is, the extent to which the teachers as a group believe that they have the ability to organize and teach such that the school can overcome extant student difficulties and help students achieve academically. Each of these climate perspectives brings with it a set of reliable and valid measures that teachers and principals can use to assess the functionality of the climate of their school.

Organizations are in a constant state of flux. Their change can be progressive, regressive, or aimless. Schools can develop their own learning procedures to solve their problems. They can become places where teachers and principals can continually expand their capacity to create the results that they desire, where emergent patterns of thinking are nurtured, where collective aspiration is liberated and where people are constantly learning how to learn (Senge, 1990). We will illustrate how teachers and administrators can use the climate framework and its measures as bases for organizational change. Using an organizational development approach, we will demonstrate how one school identified a climate problem, established a problem-solving team, diagnosed potential causes of the problem, developed an action plan, and set the stage for improving teaching and learning.

Summary

This is a book about understanding and improving teaching and learning. This chapter has provided an overview of our strategy for accomplishing that goal. We began with a discussion of the role of instructional leadership. Then we turned to the student—how they differ in intelligence, emotion, learning styles, gender, and race. Each of these differences has implications for teaching and learning that is examined carefully in some detail (Chapter 2). Most experts agree that learning occurs when there is a stable change in an individual's skill, knowledge, or behavior, but some emphasize behavior and skills while others emphasize cognition and knowledge. Because learning is a complex cognitive process, there is no single best explanation of learning. Different perspectives are more or less useful depending on what kind of learning is to be explained. We examine three general explanations of learning—behavioral, cognitive, and constructivist—each with a different focus and each with different consequences (Chapter 3).

Effective teaching and learning depend on motivated students; hence, teachers must know how to stimulate, direct, and maintain high levels of student engagement. Motivation to learn is enhanced when teachers use strategies that help students develop confidence in their ability to learn, see the value of the learning, and stay focused on learning without resorting to self-protective and self-defeating beliefs and actions. Four approaches to motivation are important in this regard—behavioral, humanistic, cognitive, and social learning theories. Each perspective has something to offer to improve teaching and learning (Chapter 4). In the end, students have to do the learning, but teachers must create situations that guide, support, stimulate, and encourage learning. Good teaching is critical to student learning, but there is no one best way to teach. Different goals require different methods—teacher-centered, student-centered, discovery, and inquiry are all more or less effective depending on the task and goal (Chapter 5).

Teachers not only have to motivate and teach, they must also be able to manage the classroom. Inevitably there will be discipline problems in the classroom. When conflicts arise, teachers can deal more effectively with the situation if they first determine who "owns" the problem, then respond appropriately with empathetic listening and problem solving. Establishing a positive learning context also includes attention to the factors that support motivation to learn, such as tasks, autonomy, recognition, grouping, evaluation, and time (Chapter 6). All teaching involves assessing and evaluating learning. Assessment involves standardized and teacher-made tests, objective and essay tests, local and national tests, reliability and validity, traditional and innovative tests, and portfolios and exhibitions. Appropriate assessment is becoming increasingly more important for teachers and administrators as pressure mounts for school accountability (Chapter 7).

Finally, teaching and learning are affected by the organizational context—the culture and climate of the school. Open, healthy, and efficacious school environments are pivotal in improving teaching and learning. Administrators and teachers need to assess their school environment and then work together to develop and improve the learning environment (Chapter 8).

In sum, we will address the critical aspects of the teaching–learning process—student differences, learning, student motivation, teaching, classroom management, assessing student learning, and assessing and changing school climate and culture. Each chapter is grounded in the latest research and theory in that area and provides specific ideas for applying that knowledge to practice, including many *Theory into Action* guidelines with concrete suggestions. The following chapters begin with a *Preview of Key Points* and a *Leadership Challenge,* an actual school problem. They conclude with suggestions of projects to relate theory to practice in the form of professional *Portfolio* exercises and an *Instructional Leader's Toolbox,* a collection of contemporary readings, useful websites, and helpful organizations.

Finally, included in the *Appendices* you will find the Interstate School Leaders Licensure Consortium (ISLLC) Standards and a series of instruments for assessing your school learning environment. For example, we provide measures of school climate, collective efficacy, teacher efficacy, and student motivation to learn, as well as self-assessments and guidelines for developing and evaluating student assessments.

Develop Your Portfolio

Portfolios are increasingly being used for the licensure, hiring, and evaluation of principals; thus portfolios serve many purposes. There are two major uses for portfolios. The first is for the professional growth and reflection of the individual who is developing the portfolio. The second is as an assessment for external audiences—college and university programs, state licensure boards, and districts who are hiring principals.

At the end of every chapter in this book you will read suggestions for possible entries into your professional portfolio. Each idea asks you to create a product that incorporates the knowledge from the chapter into a plan, newsletter, presentation, or policy statement. A portfolio is not a scrapbook of clippings, notes, transcripts, and awards. A portfolio is a planful collection that reveals your philosophy, skills, and accomplishments. Often portfolios are developed to demonstrate competence in the Interstate School Leaders Licensure Consortium (ISLLC) Standards: development and implementation of a vision of learning; creation of a school culture that supports student learning; management of a safe, efficient, and effective learning environment; appropriate collaboration with families and the community; ethical practice; and understanding of the larger context of schooling. The exercises in this book will help you especially with the first two standards.

For your first exercise, decide how you will organize your portfolio. Examine other principal portfolios and develop ideas for your own.

INSTRUCTIONAL LEADER'S TOOLBOX

Readings

Alexander, P. A., & Murphy, P. K. (1998). The research base for APA's Learner-Centered Psychological Principles. In N. Lambert & B. McCombs (Eds.) *How students learn: Reforming schools through learner-centered education.* Washington, DC: American Psychological Association.

Dietz, M. E. (2001). *Designing the school leader's portfolio.* Arlington Heights, IL: Skylight Professional Development.

Good, T. L., & Brophy, J. E. (1997). *Looking in classrooms* (7th ed.). New York: Longman.

Meece, J. L. (1997). *Child and adolescent development for educators.* New York: McGraw-Hill.

Slavin, R. E., & Olatokunbo, S. F. (1998). *Show me the evidence: Proven and promising programs for American's schools.* Thousand Oaks, CA: Corwin Press.

Speaking of Teaching. (1996, Spring). *Stanford University Newsletter on Teaching, (7)*3.

Barrett, H. C. (1999). *Electronic teaching portfolios.* ERIC/AE, Washington, DC. (ERIC Document Reproduction Service No. ED 432 265).

Burke, K. (1997). *Designing professional portfolios for change.* Arlington Heights, IL: IRI/Skylight Training and Publishing.

Burke, K., Fogarty, R., & Belgrad, S. (1994). *The Portfolio Connection.* Arlington Heights, IL: IRI/Skylight Training and Publishing.

Campbell, D. M., Cignetti, P. B., Melenyzer, B. J., Nettles, D. H., & Wyman, R. M. (1997) *How to Develop a Professional Portfolio.* Boston: Allyn & Bacon.

Seldin, P. (2000). Portfolios: A positive appraisal. *Academe, (86)* 1, 36–44.

Tuttle, H. G. (1997, January/February). Electronic portfolios. *Multimedia Schools.* 33–37.

Websites

The Vent—a discussion group for new teachers	www.proteacher.com
Barrett, H. C. (2000). Create your own portfolio: Using off the-shelf software to showcase your own student work. Anchorage: University of Alaska-Anchorage	http://transition.alaska.edu/www/portfolios/iste2k.html
Using Technology to Support Alternative Assessment and Electronic Portfolios	http://transition.alaska.edu/www/portfolios.html
Graphics and Images	http://animatedgifs.simplenet.com/

The contact information and website address for every state's Department of Education	http://www.ed.gov/Programs/bastmp/SEA.htm
National Commission on Teaching and Learning	http://www.tc.columbia.edu/~teachcomm/

Organizations

Association for Supervision and Curriculum Development (ASCD)	http://ascd.org
Council of Chief State School Officers	http://www.ccsso.org
Institute for Educational Leadership	http://www.iel.org
National Association of Secondary School Principals	http://www.nassp.org
National Association of Elementary School Principals	http://www.naesp.org

2 Students

Preview: Key Points

Leadership Challenge

Today's Multicultural Classrooms
Cultural Diversity
Language Differences in the Classroom
Theory into Action Guidelines: Dialects

Creating Culturally Compatible Classrooms
Social Organization
Cognitive and Learning Styles
Participation Structures
Sources of Misunderstandings
Theory into Action Guidelines: Culturally
Compatible Classrooms

Gender Differences in the Classroom
Gender Bias in the Curriculum
Sex Discrimination in Classrooms
Sex Differences in Mental Abilities
Eliminating Gender Bias
Theory into Action Guidelines: Avoiding Sexism

Individual Differences in Intelligence
What Does Intelligence Mean?
What Does an IQ Score Mean?
Theory into Action Guidelines: Interpreting
Intelligence Test Scores

Ability Differences in Teaching
Between-Class Ability Grouping
Within-Class Ability Grouping
Gifted and Talented
Theory into Action Guidelines: Ability Grouping

Students with Learning Challenges
Hyperactivity and Attention Disorders
Learning Disabilities
Integration, Mainstreaming, and Inclusion
Theory into Action Guidelines: Productive
Family Conferences
Effective Teaching in Inclusion Classrooms

Summary

Key Terms

Some Ideas for Your Portfolio

Instructional Leader's Toolbox
Readings
Videos
Websites
Organizations

Preview: Key Points

- By the year 2020 more than half of the students in public school classrooms will be children of color, many of whom will speak a dialect or language that differs from the teacher's.
- Creating culturally compatible classrooms will require that teachers know, respect, and effectively teach all their students.
- There appear to be some gender differences in spatial and mathematical abilities, but these do not hold in all cultures and situations.

- Teachers are in a position to reinforce or challenge gender stereotypes through their choice of materials and interactions with students.
- Over the years there have been many theories about intelligence, but most current views emphasize abstract thinking, reasoning, and problem solving; some interpretations of intelligence emphasize multiple abilities while others stress the processes of analytical, creative, and practical thinking.
- Grouping students by ability seems to be advantageous for high achievers, but other approaches such as heterogeneous and cross-age grouping work better for other students.
- Teachers are not always successful at identifying gifted students, but once identified both acceleration and enrichment may be necessary to give highly gifted students an appropriate education.
- Students may have different cognitive styles (preferred ways of processing information) and different learning preferences; the research on learning preferences is weak.
- Legal changes since the mid-1970s mean that regular teachers will be responsible for more students with learning and behavior problems; the largest group represented are students with learning disabilities.
- In order to provide students with disabilities with the least restrictive placement and an individual educational program, the students may be taught in inclusion classrooms using collaborative or cooperative teaching models.

Leadership Challenge

You are the principal of a fairly homogeneous elementary school. In fact, most of your students are middle or upper-middle class and white. In January, a new student enters your school—the daughter of an African American professor who recently moved to the nearby college. After a few weeks, one of your third-grade teachers comes to you with a potential problem. She has noticed that the new student is not being included in many activities. She sits alone in the library and plays alone at recess. All these things are troubling to your teacher, but most disturbing of all is that yesterday the teacher overheard two of her higher achieving girls talking about their "White Girls Club." Your teacher is shocked and has turned to you for advice.

- Would you investigate to learn more about this "Club"? How?
- What advice do you give this teacher?
- Should you formulate a plan of action? What should you do? What should the teacher do?
- If you find that the students have created a club that excludes nonwhite students, what would you do?
- Do you need a school policy on this matter? If so, what should the policy be? If not, why not?

Schools and instructional leaders today must deal with a wealth of student differences. These differences pose challenges (as evident in the situation above) and provide opportunities as well. This chapter examines student differences in culture, gender, intelligence, and learning abilities. We begin with the differences that the principal faces in dealing with the "White Girls Club."

Today's Multicultural Classrooms

Who are the students in American classrooms today? Here are a few statistics:

- One in 4 Americans under the age of 18 lives in poverty. For children under age 3, the number is 1 in 3.
- The number of children in poverty in the United States is almost 50% higher than in *any other developed Western* nation and 5 to 8 times higher than in many prominent industrialized nations.
- Nearly 50 percent of all African American children are poor.
- One in 3 children lives with a single parent, usually a working mother.
- In 1986, 15% of the children entering school were immigrants who spoke little or no English; 10% had poorly educated or illiterate parents.
- By the year 2020, about 46% of all students in the United States will be students of color, many the children of new immigrants.
- By 2050, there will be no *majority* race or ethnicity in the United States; every American will be a member of a minority group (Banks, 1997; Grant & Sleeter, 1989; Halford, 1999; McLoyd, 1998; Payne & Biddle, 1999; *Teacher Magazine,* April 1991).

Cultural Diversity

There are many definitions of culture. Most include the knowledge, rules, traditions, attitudes, and values that guide behavior in a particular group of people (Betancourt & Lopez, 1993). The group creates a culture—a program for living—and communicates the culture to members. Cultural groups can be defined along regional, ethnic, religious, racial, gender, social class, or other lines. Each of us is a member of many groups, so we all are influenced by many different cultures. Sometimes the influences are incompatible or even contradictory. For example, if you are a feminist but also a Roman Catholic, you might have trouble reconciling the two different cultures' beliefs about the ordination of women as priests. Your personal belief on the issue will be based, in part, on how strongly you identify with each group (Banks, 1994).

There are many different cultures, of course, in every modern country. In the United States, students growing up in a small rural town in the Deep South are part of a cultural group that is very different from that of students in a large urban center or students in a West Coast suburb. In Canada, students living in the suburbs of Toronto certainly differ in a number of ways from students growing up in a Montreal high-rise apartment or on a farm in Quebec. Within those small towns in the Deep South or Quebec, the child of a gas station attendant grows up in a different culture from the child of the town doctor or dentist. Individuals of African, Asian, Hispanic, Native American, or European descent have distinctive histories and traditions. The experiences of males and females are different in most ethnic and economic groups. Everyone living within a particular country shares many common experiences and values, especially because of the influence of the mass media. But other experiences are not common to all, so we should be cautious in making assumptions based on cultural memberships:

> Although membership in a gender, racial, ethnic, social-class, or religious group can provide us with important clues about an individual's behavior, it cannot enable us to predict behavior.... Membership in a particular group does not determine behavior but makes certain types of behavior more probable. (Banks, 1993, pp. 13–14)

The information we will examine reflects tendencies and probabilities. It does not tell you about a specific person. Each person is a unique product of many influences, a member of a variety of groups.

Language Differences in the Classroom

In the classroom, quite a bit happens through language. In this section, we will examine two kinds of language differences—dialect differences and bilingualism. A **dialect** is a language variation spoken by a particular ethnic, social, or regional group. The rules for a language define how words should be pronounced, how meaning should be expressed, and the ways the basic parts of speech should be put together to form sentences. Dialects appear to differ in their rules in these areas, but it is important to remember that these differences are not errors. Each dialect within a language is just as logical, complex, and rule-governed as the standard form of the language (often called standard speech). An example of this is the use of the double negative. In Standard English the redundancy of the double negative is not allowed. But in many dialects, just as in many other languages (for instance, Russian, French, Spanish, and Hungarian), the double negative is required by the grammatical rules. To say "I don't want anything" in Spanish, you must literally say, "I don't want nothing," or "*No quiero nada.*"

Dialects and Teaching.   Although the various dialects of a language may be equally logical, complex, and rule-governed, should teachers make learning easier for children by teaching in the dialect of the majority of students? To do this would show respect for the children's language, but the children would be robbed of the opportunity to learn the standard speech of the dominant culture. Being able to communicate effectively in standard speech allows adults to take advantage of many social and occupational opportunities.

The best teaching approach seems to be to focus on understanding the children and to accept their dialect as a valid and correct language system, but to teach Standard English (or whatever the dominant language is in your country) as an alternative. Learning standard speech is easy for most children whose original language is a dialect, as long as they have good models. How can teachers cope with linguistic diversity in the classroom? First, they can be sensitive to their own possible negative stereotypes about children who speak a different dialect. Taylor (1983) found that teachers who held negative attitudes toward "Black English" gave lower ratings for reading comprehension to students using that dialect, even when the accuracy of the students' performance was the same as that of speakers of Standard English. Second, principals and teachers can ensure comprehension by repeating instructions using different words and by asking students to paraphrase instructions or give examples. The Theory into Action Guidelines give more ideas.

Bilingualism.   The topic of **bilingualism** sparks heated debates and touches many emotions. One reason is the changing demographics mentioned earlier in this chapter. In the past 10 years there has been a 65% increase in the number of Spanish-speaking students and almost a 100% increase in students who speak Asian languages. In some states almost

---

THEORY INTO ACTION GUIDELINES

Dialects

1. Become familiar with features of the students' dialect. This will allow you to understand students better and to distinguish a reading miscue (a noncomprehension feature) from a comprehension error. Students should not be interrupted during the oral reading process. Correction of comprehension features is best done after the reading segment.

2. Allow students to listen to a passage or story first. This can be done in two ways: (a) finish the story and then ask comprehension questions, or (b) interrupt the story at key comprehension segments and ask students to predict the outcome.

3. Use predictable stories, which can be familiar episodes in literature, music, or history. They can be original works or experiential readers.

4. Use visual aids to enhance comprehension. Visual images, whether pictures or words, will aid word recognition and comprehension.

5. Use "cloze procedure" deletions to focus on vocabulary and meaning. Cloze procedures are selected deletions of words from a passage in order to focus on a specific text feature. *Examples:* (a) The little red hen found

an ear of corn. The little red _____ said, "Who will dry the ear of _____?" (vocabulary focus) (b) Today I feel like a (*noun*). (grammar focus) (c) There was a (*pain*) in the pit of his stomach. (semantic focus)

6. Allow students to retell the story or passage in various speech styles. Have students select different people to whom they would like to retell the story (family member, principal, friend), and assist them in selecting synonyms most appropriate to each audience. This allows both teacher and student to become language authorities.

7. Integrate reading, speaking, and writing skills whenever possible.

8. Use the computer (if available) as a time-on-task exercise. The microcomputer can effectively assist in teaching the reading techniques of skimming (general idea), scanning (focused reference), reading for comprehension (mastery of total message), and critical reading (inference and evaluation).

9. Teach students directly how to switch between home and school dialects.

10. Give practice with feedback and correction in using school dialect. All learning takes practice.

Source: Adapted from Christine I. Bennett, *Comprehensive Multicultural Education, Theory and Practice* (2nd ed.), pp. 234–235. Copyright © 1990 by Allyn & Bacon and Ogbu, J. U. (1999). Beyond language: Ebonics, proper English, and identity in a Black-American speech community. *American Educational Research Journal, 36,* p. 178. Reprinted by permission.

one-fourth of all students speak a first language other than English—usually Spanish (Gersten, 1996a). By 2050, about one fourth of the United States population is expected to be Latina/o (Yetman, 1999).

Two terms that you will see associated with bilingualism are **English as a second language (ESL),** describing classes for students whose primary language is not English, and **limited English proficiency (LEP),** referring to students whose English skills are limited. Proficiency in a second language has two separate aspects: face-to-face communication (known as "contextualized language skills") and academic uses of language like reading and doing grammar exercises ("decontextualized language skills") (Snow, 1987). It takes students about two years in a good program to be able to communicate face-to-face in a second language, but mastering decontextualized, academic language skills in the new language takes five to seven years. So students who seem in conversation to "know" a second language may still have great difficulty with complex schoolwork in that language (Cummins, 1994; Ovando, 1989).

Research on Bilingual Programs.   It is difficult to separate politics from practice in the debate about bilingual education. It is clear that high-quality bilingual education programs can have positive results. Students improve in the subjects that were taught in their native language, in their mastery of English, and in self-esteem as well (Hakuta & Gould, 1987; Willig, 1985; Wright & Taylor, 1995). English as a second language (ESL) programs seem to have positive effects on reading comprehension (Fitzgerald, 1995). But attention today is shifting from debate about general approaches to a focus on effective teaching strategies. As you will see many times in this book, the combination of clarity of learning goals, direct instruction in needed skills (including learning strategies and tactics), teacher- or peer-guided practice leading to independent practice, authentic and engaging tasks, interactions and conversations that are academically focused, and warm encouragement from the teacher seems to be effective (Chamot & O'Malley, 1996; Gersten, 1996b, Goldenberg, 1996). Table 2.1 on page 22 is a set of constructs for promoting learning and language acquisition that capture many of theses ideas for effective instruction. We will revisit many of these ideas in later chapters.

We have touched on a wide range of differences in this chapter. How can schools provide an appropriate education for all their students? One response is to make the classroom compatible with the students' cultural heritage. Such a classroom is described as being *culturally compatible.*

Creating Culturally Compatible Classrooms

The goal of creating culturally compatible classrooms is to eliminate racism, sexism, and ethnic prejudice while providing equal educational opportunities for all students. Roland Tharp (1989) states that "two decades of data on cultural issues in classroom interactions and school outcomes have accumulated. When schools are changed, children's experiences and achievement also change" (p. 349). Tharp outlines several dimensions of classrooms that can be tailored to fit the needs of students. Three dimensions are social organization, learning style, and participation structures.

TABLE 2.1   Ideas for Promoting Learning and Language Acquisition

Effective teaching for students in bilingual and ESL classrooms combines many strategies—direct instruction, mediation, coaching, feedback, modeling, encouragement, challenge, and authentic activities.

1. Structures, frameworks, scaffolds, and strategies
   - Provide support to students by "thinking aloud," building on and clarifying input of students
   - Use visual organizers, story maps, or other aids to help students organize and relate information
2. Relevant background knowledge and key vocabulary concepts
   - Provide adequate background knowledge to students and informally assess whether students have background knowledge
   - Focus on key vocabulary words and use consistent language
   - Incorporate students' primary language meaningfully
3. Mediation/feedback
   - Give feedback that focuses on meaning, not grammar, syntax, or pronunciation
   - Give frequent and comprehensible feedback
   - Provide students with prompts or strategies
   - Ask questions that press students to clarify or expand on initial statements
   - Provide activities and tasks that students can complete
   - Indicate to students when they are successful
   - Assign activities that are reasonable, avoiding undue frustration
   - Allow use of native language responses (when context is appropriate)
   - Be sensitive to common problems in second language acquisition
4. Involvement
   - Ensure active involvement of all students, including low-performing students
   - Foster extended discourse
5. Challenge
   - Implicit (cognitive challenge, use of higher-order questions)
   - Explicit (high but reasonable expectations)
6. Respect for—and responsiveness to—cultural and personal diversity
   - Show respect for students as individuals, respond to things students say, show respect for culture and family, and possess knowledge of cultural diversity
   - Incorporate students' experiences into writing and language arts activities
   - Link content to students' lives and experiences to enhance understanding
   - View diversity as an asset, reject cultural deficit notions

Source: From "Literacy Instruction for Language-Minority Students: The Transition Years," by R. Gersten, 1996, *The Elementary School Journal, 96,* pp. 241–242. Copyright © 1996 by the University of Chicago Press. Adapted with permission.

Social Organization

Tharp states that "a central task of educational design is to make the organization of teaching, learning, and performance compatible with the social structures in which students are most productive, engaged, and likely to learn" (p. 350). Social organization in this context means the ways people interact to accomplish a particular goal. For example, the social organization of Hawaiian society depends heavily on collaboration and cooperation. Children play together in groups of friends and siblings, with older children often caring for the younger ones. When cooperative work groups of four or five boys and girls were established in Hawaiian classrooms, student learning and participation improved (Au, 1980). The teacher worked intensively with one group while the children in the remaining groups helped each other. But when the same structure was tried in a Navajo classroom, students would not work together. These students are socialized to be more solitary and not to play with the opposite sex. By setting up same-sex working groups of only two or three Navajo students, teachers encouraged them to help each other.

Cognitive and Learning Styles

Some psychologists have found ethnic group differences in students' **cognitive styles**—the ways that individuals typically process information. These differences also have been called **learning styles.** Be aware that you may hear these terms used interchangeably. In general, educators prefer the term learning styles, and include many kinds of differences in this broad category. Psychologists tend to prefer the term cognitive styles, and to limit their discussion to differences in the ways people process information (Bjorklund, 1989).

Cognitive Styles.   The notion of cognitive styles is fairly new. It grew out of research on how people perceive and organize information from the world around them. Results from these studies suggest that individuals differ in how they approach a task, but these variations do not reflect levels of intelligence or patterns of special abilities. Instead, they have to do with "characteristic modes of perceiving, remembering, thinking, problem solving, and decisions making, reflective of information-processing regularities that develop... around underlying personality trends" (Messick, 1994, p. 122). For example, certain individuals respond very quickly in most situations. Others are more reflective and slower to respond, even though both types of people may be equally knowledgeable about the task at hand.

Field Dependence and Field Independence.   In the early 1940s, Herman Witkin became intrigued by the observation that certain airline pilots would fly into a bank of clouds and fly out upside down, without realizing that they had changed position. His interest led to a great deal of research on how people separate one factor from the total visual field. Based on his research, Witkin identified the cognitive styles of field dependence and field independence (Davis, 1991; Witkin, Moore, & Goodenough, 1977). People who are field dependent tend to perceive a pattern as a whole, not separating one element from the total visual field. They have difficulty focusing on one aspect of a situation, picking out important details, analyzing a pattern into different parts, or monitoring their use of strategies to solve problems. They tend to work well in groups, have a good memory for social information, and prefer subjects such as literature and history. Field-independent people, on the other hand, are more likely to monitor their own information processing. They perceive separate parts of a total pattern and are able to analyze a pattern according to its components. They are not as attuned to social relationships as field-dependent people, but they do well in math and science where their analytical abilities pay off.

Although teachers will not necessarily be able to determine all the variations in their students' cognitive styles, they should be aware that students approach problems in different ways. Some may need help learning to pick out important features and to ignore irrelevant details. They may seem lost in less structured situations and need clear, step-by-step instructions. Other students may be great at organizing but less sensitive to the feelings of others and not as effective in social situations. Some authors claim that Mexican American, African American and Native American students tend to have a more field-dependent learning style.

Impulsive and Reflective Cognitive Styles. Another aspect of cognitive style is impulsivity versus reflectiveness. An impulsive student works very quickly but makes many mistakes. The more reflective student, on the other hand, works slowly and makes fewer errors. As with field dependence/independence, impulsive and reflective cognitive styles are not highly related to intelligence within the normal range. However, as children grow older, they generally become more reflective, and for school-age children, being more reflective does seem to improve performance on school tasks such as reading (Kogan, 1983; Smith & Caplan, 1988).

Students can learn to be more reflective, however, if they are taught specific strategies. One possibility is scanning strategies. For example, students taking multiple-choice tests might be encouraged to cross off each alternative as they consider it, so that no possibilities will be ignored. They might work in pairs and talk about why each possibility is right or wrong. In math classes, impulsive children need to be given specific strategies for checking their work. Just slowing down is not enough. These students must be taught effective strategies for solving the problem at hand by considering each reasonable alternative.

Learning Styles and Preferences. The way a person approaches learning and studying is his or her learning style. Although many different learning styles have been described, one theme that unites most of the styles is differences between deep and surface approaches to processing information in learning situations (Snow, Corno, & Jackson, 1996). Individuals who have a deep-processing approach to learning see the learning materials or activities as a means for understanding some underlying concepts or meanings. These students tend to learn for the sake of learning and are less concerned about how their performance is evaluated, so motivation plays a role as well. Students who take a surface-processing approach focus on memorizing the learning materials, not understanding them. These students tend to be motivated by rewards, grades, external standards, and the desire to be evaluated positively by others. Of course, the situation can encourage deep or surface processing, but there is evidence that individuals have tendencies to approach learning situations in characteristic ways (Pintrich & Schrauben, 1992; Tait & Entwistle, in press). There appear to be no ethnic differences in this dimension of learning style.

Since the late 1970s, a great deal has been written about differences in students' **learning preferences** (Dunn, 1987; Dunn & Dunn, 1978, 1987; Gregorc, 1982; Keefe, 1982). Workshops and in-service training sessions around the country focus on this topic. Learning preferences are usually called learning styles in these workshops, but we believe preferences is a more accurate label. Learning preferences are individual preferences for particular learning environments. They could be preferences for where, when, with whom, or with what lighting, food, or music you like to study. There are a number of instruments for assessing students' learning preferences—for example, The Learning Style Inventory (Renzulli & Smith, 1978), The Learning Style Inventory (Dunn, Dunn, & Price, 1984), and the Learning Style Profile (Keefe & Monk, 1986). Tests of learning style have been criticized for lacking evidence of reliability and validity. This led Snider (1990) to conclude,

> "People are different, and it is good practice to recognize and accommodate individual differences. It is also good practice to present information in a variety of ways through more than one modality, but it is not wise to categorize learners and prescribe methods solely on the basis of tests with questionable technical qualities.... The idea of learning styles is appealing, but a critical examination of this approach should cause educators to be skeptical" (p. 53).

The same is true for the claims that we should teach to both sides of the brain. Recent research on brain functioning makes it clear that "the practice of teaching to 'different sides of the brain' is not supported by the neuroscientific research" (Byrnes & Fox, 1998, p. 310). So beware of educational approaches based on simplistic views of brain functioning—what Keith Stanovich (1998) has called "the left-brain–right-brain nonsense that has inundated education through workshop, in-services, and the trade publications" (p. 420).

Misuses and Uses of Learning-Styles Research.

In considering this research on learning styles, you should keep two points in mind. First, the validity of some of the learning styles research has been strongly questioned. Second, there is a heated debate today about whether identifying ethnic group differences in learning styles and preferences is a dangerous, racist, sexist exercise. In our society we are quick to move from the notion of "difference" to the idea of "deficit." Information about the "typical" learning styles of a given ethnic group can become just one more basis for stereotyping (Gordon, 1991; O'Neil, 1990). If used with caution and common sense, these general guidelines can help teachers be more sensitive to individual and group differences. It is dangerous and incorrect, however, to assume that every individual in a group shares the same learning style. Get to know the individual.

Instead of stereotyping students, how can your teachers respond to the learning-styles claims. Schools can make learning options available. Having quiet, private corners as well as large tables for working; comfortable cushions as well as straight chairs; brightly lighted desks along with darker areas; headphones for listening to music as well as earplugs; structured as well as open-ended assignments; information available on films and tapes as well as in books—all these options will allow students to work and learn in their preferred mode at least some of the time.

Will making these alterations lead to greater learning? Here the answer is not clear. Results of some research indicate that students learn more when they study in their preferred setting and manner (Dunn, Beaudry, & Klavas, 1989; Dunn & Dunn, 1987), but generally there are more claims than hard evidence. Very bright students appear to need less structure and prefer quiet, solitary learning (Torrance, 1986). But before you encourage your teachers to accommodate all your students' learning styles, remember that students, especially younger ones, may not be the best judges of how they should learn. Preference for a particular style may not always guarantee that using the style will be effective. Sometimes students, particularly poorer students, prefer what is easy and comfortable; real learning can be hard and uncomfortable. Sometimes students prefer to learn in a certain way because they have no alternatives; it is the only way they know how to approach the task. These students may benefit from developing new—and perhaps more effective—ways to learn.

Participation Structures

Sociolinguistics is the study of "the courtesies and conventions of conversation across cultures" (Tharp, 1989, p. 351). A knowledge of sociolinguistics will help you and your teachers understand why communication sometimes breaks down in classrooms. The classroom is a special setting for communicating; it has its own set of rules for when, how, to whom, about what subject, and in what manner to use language. In order to be successful, students must know these communication rules. This is not such an easy task. As class activities change, rules change. Sometimes you have to raise your hand (during the teacher's presentation), but sometimes you don't (during storytime on the rug). Sometimes it is good to ask a question (during discussion), but other times it isn't so good (when the teacher is scolding you). The differing activity rules are called **participation structures.** These structures define appropriate participation for each class activity. Most classrooms have many different participation structures.

To be competent communicators in the classroom, students sometimes have to read very subtle, nonverbal cues telling them which participation structures are currently in effect. For example, in one classroom, when the teacher stood in a particular area of the room, put her hands on her hips, and leaned forward at the waist, the children in the class were signaled to "stop and freeze," look at the teacher, and anticipate an announcement (Shultz & Florio, 1979).

Sources of Misunderstandings

Some children are simply better than others at reading the classroom situation because the participation structures of the school match the structures they have learned at home. The communication rules for most school situations are similar to those in middle class homes, so children from these homes often appear to be more competent communicators. They know the unwritten rules. Students from different cultural backgrounds may have learned participation structures that conflict with the behaviors expected in school. For example, one study found that the home conversation style of Hawaiian children is to chime in with contributions to a story. In school, however, this overlapping style is seen as "interrupting." When the teachers in one school learned about these differences and made their reading groups more like their students' home conversation groups, the young Hawaiian children in their classes improved in reading (Au, 1980; Tharp, 1989).

The source of misunderstanding can be a subtle sociolinguistic difference, such as how long the teacher waits to react to a student's response. White and Tharp (1988) found that when Navajo students in one class paused in giving a response, their Anglo teacher seemed to think that they were finished speaking. As a result, the teacher often unintentionally interrupted students. In another study, researchers found that Pueblo Indian students participated twice as much in classes where teachers waited longer to react. Waiting longer also helps girls to participate more freely in math and science classes (Grossman & Grossman, 1994).

So it seems that even students who speak the same language as their teachers may still have trouble communicating, and thus learning school subjects, if their knowledge of participation structures does not fit the school situation. What should principals and teachers do?

Especially in the early grades, you and your teachers should make communication rules for activities clear and explicit. Do not assume students know what to do. Use cues to signal students when changes occur. Explain and demonstrate appropriate behavior. We have seen teachers show young children how to "talk in your inside voice" or "whisper so you won't disturb others." One teacher said and then demonstrated, "If you have to interrupt me while I'm working with other children, stand quietly beside me until I can help you." The Theory into Action Guidelines give more ideas for creating culturally compatible classrooms.

Gender Differences in the Classroom

Through their interactions with family, peers, teachers, and the environment in general, children begin to form **gender schemas,** or organized networks of knowledge about what it means to be male or female. These schemas help the children make sense of the world and guide their behavior. So a young girl whose schema for "girls" includes "girls play with dolls and not with trucks" or "girls can't be scientists" will pay attention to, remember, and interact more with dolls than trucks, and she may avoid science activities (Liben & Signorella, 1993; Martin & Little, 1990).

Gender Bias in the Curriculum

Most of the textbooks produced for the early grades before 1970 portrayed both males and females in sexually stereotyped roles. Materials for the later grades often omitted women altogether from illustrations and text. In a study of 2,760 stories in 134 books from 16 publishers, a group called Women on Words and Images (1975) found the total number of stories dealing with males or male animals to be four times greater than the number of stories dealing with females or female animals. They also found that females tended to be shown in the home, behaving passively and expressing fear or incompetence. Males were usually more dominant and adventurous; they often rescued the females.

In recent years textbook publishers have recognized these problems to some extent and established guidelines to prevent them. It still makes sense to check your teaching materials for such stereotypes, however. When Purcell and Stewart (1990) used the same design as Women on Words and Images to analyze 62 elementary readers, they found that the numbers of male and female characters were about equal. Girls were shown in a wide range of activities, but were still portrayed as more helpless than boys. And don't assume that books for older children are free of sexual stereotypes. Despite new publishers' guidelines, problems have not disappeared entirely (Powell, Garcia, & Denton, 1985).

Sex Discrimination in Classrooms

There has been quite a bit of research on teachers' treatment of male and female students. One of the best-documented findings of the past 20 years is that teachers interact more with boys than with girls. This is true from preschool to college. Teachers ask more questions of males, give males more feedback (praise, criticism, and correction), and give more specific and valuable comments to boys. As girls move through the grades, they have less

THEORY INTO ACTION GUIDELINES

Culturally Compatible Classrooms

Experiment with different grouping arrangements to encourage cooperation.

Examples
1. Try "study buddies" and pairs.
2. Organize heterogeneous groups of four or five.
3. Establish larger teams for older students.

Provide a range of ways to learn material to accommodate a range of learning styles.

Examples
1. Give students verbal materials at different reading levels.
2. Offer visual materials—charts, diagrams, models.
3. Provide tapes for listening and viewing.
4. Set up activities and projects.

Teach classroom procedures directly, even ways of doing things that you thought everyone would know.

Examples
1. Tell students how to get the teacher's attention.
2. Explain when and how to interrupt the teacher if students need help.
3. Show which materials students can take and which require permission.
4. Demonstrate acceptable ways to disagree with or challenge another student.

Learn the meaning of different behaviors for your students.

Examples
1. Ask students how they feel when you correct or praise them. What gives them this message?

2. Talk to family and community members and other teachers to discover the meaning of expressions, gestures, or other responses that are unfamiliar to you.

Emphasize meaning in teaching.

Examples
1. Make sure students understand what they read.
2. Try storytelling and other modes that don't require written materials.
3. Use examples that relate abstract concepts to everyday experiences; for instance, relate negative numbers to being overdrawn in your checkbook.

Get to know the customs, traditions, and values of your students.

Examples
1. Use holidays as a chance to discuss the origins and meaning of traditions.
2. Analyze different traditions for common themes.
3. Attend community fairs and festivals.

Help students detect racist messages.

Examples
1. Analyze curriculum materials for biases.
2. Make students "bias detectives," reporting comments from the media.
3. Discuss the ways that students communicate biased messages about each other and what should be done when this happens.
4. Discuss expressions of prejudice such as anti-Semitism.

---

and less to say. By the time students reach college, men are twice as likely to initiate comments as women (Bailey, 1993; Sadker & Sadker, 1985, 1986; Serbin & O'Leary, 1975; Wingate, 1986). The effect of these differences is that from preschool through college, girls on the average receive 1,800 fewer hours of attention and instruction than boys (Sadker, Sadker, & Klein, 1991). Of course, these differences are not evenly distributed. Some boys, generally high-achieving white students, receive more than their share. Minority-group boys, like girls, tend to receive much less attention from the teacher. The imbalances of teacher attention given to boys and girls are particularly dramatic in science classes. In one study, boys were questioned on the subject matter 80 percent more often than girls (Baker, 1986). Boys also dominate the use of equipment in science labs, often dismantling the apparatus before the girls in the class have a chance to perform the experiments (Rennie & Parker, 1987).

Stereotypes are perpetuated in many ways, some obvious, some subtle. Guidance counselors, parents, and teachers often do not protest at all when a bright girl says she doesn't want to take any more math or science courses, but when a boy of the same ability wants to forget about math or science, they will object. In these subtle ways, students' stereotyped expectations for themselves can be reinforced (Sadker & Sadker, 1985, 1996).

Sex Differences in Mental Abilities

From infancy through the preschool years, most studies find few differences between boys and girls in overall mental and motor development or in specific abilities. During the school years and beyond, psychologists find no differences in general intelligence on the standard measures—these tests have been designed and standardized to minimize sex differences. However, scores on some tests of specific abilities show sex differences. In the concluding article of a special issue on sex differences in cognition in the journal *Learning and Individual Differences,* Diane Halpern (1996) summarized the research:

> The data presented here and in other sources clearly show that there are some areas of cognition in which there are no male–female differences, others where the differences are small, and others where the differences are large, some favoring females and some favoring males. The "on-the-average" differences show that females excel in reading comprehension, production of written and oral language, and computation (to name a few); whereas the constellation of mathematical, mechanical, and visual information processing is often accomplished either more accurately or more quickly by males. In addition we know that there is much overlap between the sexes in these ability areas, and everyone can improve in any area with appropriate education and practice. (p. 75)

Also, the scores of males tend to be more variable in general, so there are more males than females with very high *and* very low scores on tests (Willingham & Cole, 1997).

There is a caution, however. In most studies of sex differences, race and socioeconomic status are not taken into account. When racial groups are studied separately, African American females outperform African American males in high school mathematics, while there is little or no difference in the performance of Asian American girls and boys in math or science (Grossman & Grossman, 1994; Yee, 1992).

What is the basis for the differences? The answers are complex. For example, males on average are better on tests that require mental rotation of a figure in space, prediction of the trajectories of moving objects, and navigating. Some researchers argue that evolution has favored these skills in males (Buss, 1995; Geary, 1995b, 1999) but others relate these skills to males' more active play styles and to their participation in athletics (Linn & Hyde, 1989; Newcombe & Baenninger, 1990; Stumpf, 1995).

Eliminating Gender Bias

There is some evidence that teachers treat girls and boys differently in mathematics classes. For example, some elementary school teachers spend more academic time with boys in math and with girls in reading. In one study, high school geometry teachers directed most of their questions to boys, even though the girls asked questions and volunteered answers more often. Several researchers have found that some teachers tend to accept wrong answers from girls, saying, in effect, "Well, at least you tried." But when boys give the wrong answer, the teachers are more likely to say, "Try harder! You can figure this out." These messages, repeated time and again, can convince girls that they just aren't cut out for mathematics (Horgan, 1995). If you are like a few of the student teachers I have supervised who "really hate math," please don't pass this attitude on. You may have been the victim of sex discrimination yourself.

Patricia Casserly of the Educational Testing Service studied 20 high schools where no sex differences in mathematics performance were found. Even though the schools were not alike in all ways, they shared several common features. The teachers had strong backgrounds in mathematics, engineering, or science, not just in general education. They were enthusiastic about mathematics. The brightest students, male and female, were grouped together for instruction in math, and there was heavy emphasis on reasoning in the classes (Kolata, 1980). The activities used to teach math may make a difference as well. Elementary school girls may do better in math if they learn in cooperative as opposed to competitive activities (Fennema & Peterson, 1988). Certainly it makes sense to balance both cooperative and competitive approaches so that students who learn better each way have equal opportunities. The Theory into Action Guidelines gives ideas for your school about how to avoid sexism.

The most important individual differences for schools are the differences in students' academic abilities. These also are complex and often misunderstood.

Individual Differences in Intelligence

Because the concept of intelligence is so important in education, so controversial, and so often misunderstood, we will spend quite a few pages discussing it. Let us begin with a basic question.

What Does Intelligence Mean?

The idea that people vary in what we call **intelligence** has been with us for a long time. Plato discussed similar variations over 2,000 years ago. Most early theories about the nature of intelligence involved one or more of the following three themes: (1) the capacity to learn; (2) the total knowledge a person has acquired; and (3) the ability to adapt successfully to new situations and to the environment in general.

In this century, there has been considerable controversy over the meaning of intelligence. In 1986 at a symposium on intelligence, 24 psychologists offered 24 different views about the nature of intelligence (Neisser et al., 1996; Sternberg & Detterman, 1986). Over

THEORY INTO ACTION GUIDELINES

Avoiding Sexism

Check to see if textbooks and other materials you are using present an honest view of the options open to both males and females.

Examples
1. Are both males and females portrayed in traditional and nontraditional roles at work, at leisure, and at home?
2. Discuss your analyses with teachers, and ask them to help you find sex role biases in other materials—magazine advertising, TV programs, news reporting, for example.

Watch for any unintended biases in your teachers' classroom practices.

Examples
1. Do teachers group students by sex for certain activities? Is the grouping appropriate?

2. Do teachers call on one sex or the other for certain answers—boys for math and girls for poetry, for example?

Look for ways in which your school may be limiting the options open to male or female students.

Examples
1. What advice is given by guidance counselors to students in course and career decisions?
2. Is there a good sports program for both girls and boys?

---

half of the experts did mention higher-level thinking processes such as abstract reasoning, problem solving, and decision making as important aspects of intelligence, but they disagreed about the structure of intelligence—is it a single ability or many separate abilities (Gustafsson & Undheim, 1996).

Intelligence: One Ability or Many?   Some theorists believe intelligence is a basic ability that affects performance on all cognitively oriented tasks. An "intelligent" person will do well in computing mathematical problems, analyzing poetry, taking history essay examinations, and solving riddles. Evidence for this position comes from correlational evaluations of intelligence tests. In study after study, moderate to high positive correlations are found among all the different tests that are designed to measure separate intellectual abilities (McNemar, 1964; Sattler, 2001). What could explain these results?

Charles Spearman (1927) suggested there is one factor or mental attribute, which he called *g* or general intelligence, that is used to perform any mental test, but that each test also requires some specific abilities in addition to *g*. For example, performance on a test of memory for numbers probably involves both *g* and some specific ability for immediate recall of what is heard. Spearman assumed that individuals vary in both general intelligence and specific abilities, and that together these factors determine performance on mental tasks. A current version of the general and specific abilities theory is John Carroll's (1993) work identifying a few broad abilities and at least 70 specific abilities.

Multiple Intelligences.   In spite of the correlations among the various tests of "specific abilities," some psychologists insist that there several separate "primary mental abilities." Years ago, Thurstone (1938) listed verbal comprehension, memory, reasoning, ability to visualize spatial relationships, numerical ability, word fluency, and perceptual speed as the major mental abilities underlying intellectual tasks. J. P. Guilford (1988) and Howard Gardner (1983, 1993, 1998) are the most prominent modern proponents of the concept of multiple cognitive abilities.

Guilford suggests that there are three basic categories, or faces of intellect: *mental operations,* or the processes of thinking; *contents,* or what we think about; and *products,* or the end results of our thinking. According to this view, carrying out a cognitive task is essentially performing a mental operation on some specific content to achieve a product. For example, listing the next number in the sequence 3, 6, 12, 24,…requires a convergent operation (there is only one right answer—48) with symbolic content (numbers) to achieve a relationship product (each number is double the one before). There are 180 combinations of operations, contents, and products—6 × 5 × 6. Guilford's ideas have been used to develop diagnostic tests for students and instructional methods for teachers.

According to Gardner's (1983, 1993) **theory of multiple intelligences,** there are at least eight separate intelligences: linguistic (verbal), musical, spatial, logical-mathematical, bodily-kinesthetic (movement), interpersonal (understanding others), intrapersonal (understanding self), and naturalist (observing and understanding natural and human-made patterns and systems) (see Figure 2.1). Gardner stresses that there may be more kinds of intelligence—eight is not a magic number. In the past few years he has speculated that there may be a ninth—*existential intelligence* or the ability to ask big questions about the meaning of life (Gardner, 1999). Gardner bases his notion of separate abilities in part on evidence that brain damage (from a stroke, for example) often interferes with functioning in one area, such as language, but does not affect functioning in other areas. Also, individuals may excel in one of these eight or nine areas but have no remarkable abilities in the other seven. Still, these "separate abilities" may not be so separate after all. Recent evidence linking musical and spatial abilities has prompted Gardner to consider that there may be connections among the intelligences (Gardner, 1998). Stay tuned for more developments.

What are these intelligences? Gardner (1998, 1999) contends that an intelligence is the ability to solve problems and create products or outcomes that are valued by a culture. Varying cultures and eras of history have placed different values on the eight intelligences. A naturalist intelligence is critical in farming cultures, whereas verbal and mathematical intelligences are important in technological cultures. In addition, Gardner (1998) believes that intelligence has a biological basis. Intelligence "is a biological and psychological potential; that potential is capable of being realized to a greater or lesser extent as a consequence of the experiential, cultural, and motivational factors that affect a person" (p. 62). Some critics suggest that Gardner's multiple intelligences are really multiple talents (Sternberg, 1985). But Gardner rejects the distinction between talent and intelligence. He believes that our common notion of intelligence "is simply a certain set of talents in the linguistic and/or logical-mathematical spheres" (1998, p. 63).

Gardner (1998) has identified a number of myths and misconceptions about multiple intelligence theory and schooling. One is that intelligences are the same as learning styles; Gardner doesn't believe that people actually have consistent learning styles. Another

Intelligence	End States	Core Components
Logical-mathematical	Scientist Mathematician	Sensitivity to, and capacity to discern, logical or numerical patterns; ability to handle long chains of reasoning.
Linguistic	Poet Journalist	Sensitivity to the sounds, rhythms, and meanings of words; sensitivity to the different functions of language.
Musical	Composer Violinist	Abilities to produce and appreciate rhythm, pitch, and timbre; appreciation of the forms of musical expressiveness.
Spatial	Navigator Sculptor	Capacities to perceive the visual-spatial world accurately and to perform transformations on one's initial perceptions.
Bodily-kinesthetic	Dancer Athlete	Abilities to control one's body movements and to handle objects skillfully.
Interpersonal	Therapist Salesman	Capacities to discern and respond appropriately to the moods, temperaments, motivations, and desires of other people.
Intrapersonal	Person with detailed, accurate self-knowledge	Access to one's own feelings and the ability to discriminate among them and draw on them to guide behavior; knowledge of one's own strengths, weaknesses, desires, and intelligence.
Naturalist	Botanist Farmer Hunter	Abilities to recognize plants and animals, to make distinctions in the natural world, to understand systems and define categories (perhaps even categories of intelligence).

FIGURE 2.1 Eight Intelligences   Howard Gardner's theory of multiple intelligences suggests that there are eight kinds of human abilities. An individual might have strengths or weaknesses in one or several areas.

Source: From "Multiple Intelligences Go to School," by H. Gardner and T. Hatch, 1989, *Educational Research, 18*(8), Figure p. 6. Copyright © 1989 by the American Educational Research Association. Reprinted with permission of the publisher. "Are There Additional Intelligences? The Case for the Naturalist, Spiritual, and Existential Intelligences," by H. Gardner (1999) in J. Kane (Ed.), *Educational Information and Transformation,* Saddle River, NJ: Prentice-Hall, Inc.

misconception is that multiple intelligence theory disproves the idea of *g*. Gardner does not deny the existence of a general ability, but he does question how useful *g* is as an explanation for human achievements.

Multiple Intelligences Go to School.   An advantage of the multiple intelligences perspective is that it expands teachers' thinking about abilities and avenues for teaching, but the theory has been misused. Some teachers embrace a simplistic version of Gardner's theory. They include every "intelligence" in every lesson, no matter how inappropriate. Table 2.2 lists some misuses and positive applications of Gardner's work.

Many educators and schools have embraced Gardner's ideas. But there is not yet strong research evidence that adopting a multiple intelligences approach will enhance

---

TABLE 2.2   Misuses and Applications of Multiple Intelligence Theory

Recently Howard Gardner described these negative and positive applications of his theory. The quotes are his words on the subject.

Misuses:

1. **Trying to teach all concepts or subjects using all intelligences:** "There is no point in assuming that every subject can be effectively approached in at least seven ways, and it is a waste of effort and time to attempt to do this."
2. **Assuming that it is enough just to apply a certain intelligence, no matter how you use it:** For bodily-kinesthetic intelligence, for example, "random muscle movements have nothing to do with the cultivation of the mind."
3. **Using an intelligence as a background for other activities,** such as playing music while students solve math problems. "The music's function is unlikely to be different from that of a dripping faucet or humming fan."
4. **Mixing intelligences with other desirable qualities:** For example, interpersonal intelligence "is often distorted as a license for cooperative learning," and intrapersonal intelligence "is often distorted as a rationale for self-esteem programs."
5. **Direct evaluation or even grading of intelligences without regard to context:** "I see little point in grading individuals in terms of how 'linguistic' or how 'bodily-kinesthetic' they are."

Good uses:

1. **The cultivation of desired capabilities:** "Schools should cultivate those skills and capabilities that are valued in the community and in the broader society."
2. **Approaching a concept, subject matter, discipline in a variety of ways:** Schools try to cover too much. "It makes far more sense to spend a significant amount of time on key concepts, generative ideas, and essential questions and to allow students to become familiar with these notions and their implications."
3. **The personalization of education:** "At the heart of the MI perspective—in theory and in practice—inheres in taking human difference seriously."

Source: "Reflections on Multiple Intelligences: Myths and Messages," by H. Gardner, 1998. In A. Woolfolk (Ed.), *Readings in Educational Psychology* (2nd ed.) (pp. 64–66), Boston: Allyn & Bacon. Used by permission of Howard Gardner, Harvard University.

learning. In one of the few carefully designed evaluations, Callahan, Tomlinson, and Plucker (1997) found no significant gains in either achievement or self-concept for students who participated in START, a multiple intelligences approach to identifying and promoting talent in students who were at risk of failing. Learning is still hard work, even if there are multiple paths to knowledge.

Emotional Intelligence.   We all know people who are academically or artistically talented, but unsuccessful. They have problems in school, in relationships, and on the job but can't improve the situations. According to some psychologists, the source of the difficulties may be a lack of **emotional intelligence,** defined as a set of capabilities to "monitor one's own and others' feelings and emotions, to discriminate among them and to use this information to guide one's thinking and actions" (Salovey & Mayer, 1990, p. 189). Daniel Goleman (1995) popularized the idea of emotional intelligence or **EQ** in his best-selling book on the subject. Extending the work of Peter Salovey and John Mayer (1990; Mayer & Salovey, 1993, 1997), Goleman identified five aspects of emotional intelligence. Using Gardner's categories, three of these aspects involve intrapersonal abilities and two are interpersonal.

At the center of emotional intelligence is the intrapersonal ability to *know your own emotions.* If you can't recognize what you are feeling, how can you make good choices about jobs, relationships, time management, or even entertainment (Baron, 1998)? If you don't know your own emotions, how can you communicate your feelings to others accurately? Friends keep asking, "What's wrong?" and you keep saying, "Nothing!" The second aspect of EQ is *managing your emotions,* particularly negative emotions such as anger or depression. It is useful to know you are angry, but if anger leads to rage and temper tantrums, then success in school and life is more difficult. The goal is not to suppress feelings, but not to be overwhelmed by them either. The third aspect is *self-motivation*—the ability to focus energy, persist, control impulses, and delay immediate gratification in order to reach important goals. Self-motivation is critical in school. For example, compared to 4-year-old students who act on their impulses immediately, 4-year-old children who can delay instant gratification to work toward a goal are much better students in high school (Shoda, Mischel, & Peake, 1990).

The two interpersonal aspects of EQ are *recognizing emotions in others* and *handling relationships.* People who can recognize emotions in others (usually by reading the nonverbal cues) and can respond appropriately are more successful in working with people and often emerge as leaders (Wood & Wood, 1999).

Some researchers have criticized the notion of EQ, saying that emotional intelligence is not a cluster of capabilities but a rather set of personality traits (Nestor-Baker, 1999). Does intelligence inform emotion so we are "smart" about managing our feelings and impulses or does emotion inform intelligence so we make good decision and understand other people? Probably both are true. The major point is that success in life requires more that cognitive skills and schools are important in helping students develop all of their capabilities.

Intelligence as a Process.   As you can see, the theories of Spearman, Thurstone, Guilford, and Gardner tend to describe how individuals differ in the content of intelligence—the different abilities. Recent work in cognitive psychology has emphasized instead the thinking processes that may be common to all people. How do humans gather and use information to solve problems and behave intelligently? New views of intelligence are growing out of this work.

Robert Sternberg's (1985, 1990) **triarchic theory of intelligence** is an example of a cognitive process approach to understanding intelligence. As you might guess from the name, this theory has three parts—analytic, creative, and practical. Analytic intelligence involves the mental processes of the individual that lead to more or less intelligent behavior. Some processes are specific; that is, they are necessary for only one kind of task, such as solving analogies. Other processes such as monitoring progress are very general and may be necessary in almost every cognitive task.

The second part of Sternberg's theory, creativity, involves coping with new experiences. Intelligent behavior is marked by two characteristics: (1) *insight,* or the ability to deal effectively with novel situations, and (2) *automaticity*—the ability to become efficient and automatic in thinking and problem solving. The third part, practical intelligence, highlights the importance of choosing an environment in which a person can succeed, adapting to that environment, and reshaping it if necessary. People who are successful often seek situations in which their abilities will be valuable, then work hard to capitalize on those abilities and compensate for any weaknesses. Thus, intelligence in this third sense involves practical matters such as career choice or social skills (Sternberg, Wagner, Williams, & Horvath, 1995).

Principals, teachers, and parents are most familiar with intelligence as a number or score on an IQ test. Let's consider an important question:

What Does an IQ Score Mean?

Most intelligence tests are designed so that they have certain statistical characteristics. For example, the average score is 100. Fifty percent of the people from the general population who take the tests will score 100 or above, and 50 percent will score below 100. About 68 percent of the general population will earn IQ scores between 85 and 115. Only about 16 percent of the population will receive scores below 85, and only 16 percent will score above 115. Note, however, that these figures hold true for white, native-born Americans whose first language is Standard English. Whether IQ tests should even be used with ethnic minority group students is hotly debated.

Group versus Individual IQ Tests.   Individual intelligence tests (such as the Standford-Binet or Wechsler scales) have to be administered to one student at a time by a trained psychologist and take about two hours. Most of the questions are asked orally and do not require reading or writing. A student usually pays closer attention and is more motivated to do well when working directly with an adult. Psychologists also have developed group tests that can be given to whole classes or schools. Compared to an individual test, a group test is much less likely to yield an accurate picture of any one person's abilities. When students take tests in a group, they may do poorly because they do not understand the instructions, because their pencils break, because they are distracted by other students, or because they do not shine on paper-and-pencil tests. As an instructional leader you should be very wary of IQ scores based on group tests. The Theory into Action Guidelines give ideas for helping teachers and parents interpret scores from intelligence tests.

THEORY INTO ACTION GUIDELINES

Interpreting Intelligence Test Scores

Check to see if the score is based on an individual or a group test. Be wary of group test scores.

Examples

1. Individual tests include the Wechsler Scales (WPPSI–R, WISC-III, WAIS-III), the Stanford-Binet, the McCarthy Scales of Children's Abilities, the Woodcock-Johnson Psycho-Educational Battery, and the Kaufman Assessment Battery for Children.
2. Group tests include the Lorge-Thorndike Intelligence Tests, the Analysis of Learning Potential, the Kuhlman-Anderson Intelligence Tests, the Otis-Lennon Mental Abilities Tests, and the School and College Ability Tests (SCAT).

Remember that IQ tests are only estimates of general aptitude for learning.

Examples

1. Ignore small differences in scores among students.
2. Bear in mind that even an individual student's scores may change over time for many reasons, including measurement error.

3. Be aware that a total score is usually an average of scores on several kinds of questions. A score in the middle or average range may mean that the student performed at the average on every kind of question or that the student did quite well in some areas (for example, on verbal tasks) and rather poorly in other areas (for example, on visual–spatial tasks).

Remember that IQ scores reflect a student's past experiences and learning.

Examples

1. Consider these scores as predictors of school abilities, not measures of innate intellectual abilities.
2. If a student is doing well in your school, do not change your opinion or lower your expectations just because one score seems low.
3. Be wary of IQ scores for minority students and for students whose first language was not English. Even scores on "culture-free" tests are lower for disadvantaged students.

Intelligence and Achievement. Intelligence test scores predict achievement in schools quite well, at least for large groups. For example, the correlation is about .65 between school achievement and scores on a popular individual intelligence test, the revised Wechsler Intelligence Scale for Children (WISC-III) (Sattler, 2001). This isn't surprising because the tests were designed to predict school achievement. In designing the first intelligence test in France, Binet threw out test items that did not discriminate between good and poor students.

But do people who score high on IQ tests achieve more in life? Here the answer is less clear. There is evidence that *g,* or general intelligence, correlates with real-world academic, social, and occupational accomplishments (Ceci, 1991), but there is great debate about the size and meaning of these correlations (*Current Directions in Psychological Science,* Special Section: Controversies, February 1993; McClelland, 1993). People with higher intelligence-test scores tend to complete more years of school and to have higher-status jobs. However, when the number of years of education is held constant, IQ scores and school achievement are not highly correlated with income and success in later life. Other factors like motivation, social skills, and luck may make the difference (Neisser et al., 1996; Sternberg & Wagner, 1993).

Intelligence: Heredity or Environment?   Nowhere, perhaps, has the nature-versus-nurture debate raged so hard as in the area of intelligence. Should intelligence be seen as a potential, limited by our genetic makeup, that once fulfilled cannot be exceeded? Or does intelligence simply refer to an individual's current level of intellectual functioning, as fed and influenced by experience and education? In fact, it is almost impossible to separate intelligence "in the genes" from intelligence "due to experience." Today, most psychologists believe that differences in intelligence are due to both heredity and environment, probably in about equal proportions for children. "Genes do not fix behavior. Rather they establish a range of possible reactions to the range of possible experiences that the environment can provide" (Weinberg, 1989, p. 101). And environmental influences include everything from the health of a child's mother during pregnancy to the amount of lead in the child's home to the quality of teaching a child receives.

It is especially important for educators to realize that cognitive skills, like any other skills, are always improvable. Intelligence is a current state of affairs, affected by past experiences and open to future changes. Even if intelligence is a limited potential, the potential is still quite large, and a challenge to all teachers. For example, Japanese and Chinese students know much more mathematics than American students, but their intelligence test scores are quite similar. This superiority in math probably is due to differences in the way mathematics is taught and studied in the three countries (Stevenson & Stigler, 1992).

Ability Differences in Teaching

In the early 1900s, before group intelligence tests were readily available, teachers dealt with student achievement differences by promoting students who performed adequately and holding back others. This worked well for those promoted, but not for those who failed. The idea of social promotion was introduced to keep age-mates together, but then teaching had to change. When intelligence tests became available, one solution was to promote all students, but group them by intelligence within their grade level. Ability grouping was the basis of many studies in the 1930s, but then fell from favor until 1957 and the era of Sputnik, when concern grew about developing talent in math and science and ability grouping was seen as a path to higher student achievement. Again, in the 1960s and 1970s, ability grouping was criticized, based in part on the self-fulfilling prophecy research of Rosenthal and Jacobson (1968). Today, teachers are encouraged to use forms of cooperative learning and heterogeneous grouping to deal with ability differences in their classes (Hilgard, 1996). In this section we consider how to handle differences in academic ability. Is ability grouping a solution to the challenge of ability differences? If so, when and for whom?

Between-Class Ability Grouping

When whole classes are formed based on ability, the process is called **between-class ability grouping** or **tracking**—a common practice in secondary schools and some elementary schools as well. Most high schools have "college prep" courses and "general" courses or, for example, high-, middle-, and low-ability classes in a particular subject. Although this seems on the surface to be an efficient way to teach, research has consistently shown that segregation by ability may benefit high-ability students but causes problems for low-ability students (Garmon, Nystrand, Berends, & LePore, 1995; Good & Marshall, 1984; Slavin, 1987, 1990).

Low-ability classes seem to receive lower-quality instruction in general. Teachers tend to emphasize lower-level objectives and routine procedures, with less academic focus. Often there are more management problems and, with these problems, increased stress and decreased enthusiasm. These differences in instruction and the teachers' negative attitudes may mean that low expectations are communicated to the students. Attendance may drop. The lower tracks often have a disproportionate number of minority group and economically disadvantaged students, so ability grouping, in effect, becomes resegregation in school. Possibilities for friendships become limited to students in the same ability range. Assignments to classes are often made on the basis of group IQ tests instead of tests in the subject area itself. Yet group IQ tests are not good guides for what someone is ready to learn in a particular subject area (Corno & Snow, 1986; Garmon, Nystrand, Berends, & LePore, 1995; Good & Brophy, 1994; Kulik & Kulik, 1982; Slavin, 1987, 1990; Slavin & Karweit, 1985).

There are two exceptions to the general finding that between-class ability grouping leads to lower achievement. The first is found in honors or gifted classes, where high-ability students tend to perform better than comparable students in regular classes. The second exception is the nongraded elementary school. In this arrangements, students are grouped by ability in particular subjects, regardless of their age or grade. A reading class might therefore have students from several grades, all working on the same level on reading. This *cross-grade grouping* seems to be effective for students of all abilities as long as the grouping allows teachers to give more direct instruction to the groups. When cross-age grouping is used to implement individualized instruction, the effects are much less positive, probably because many individualized instruction programs leave students on their own too much of the time. Many students (of all ages) are not able to manage their own time without some supervision (Gutierrez & Slavin, 1992).

Within-Class Ability Grouping

A second method, within-class ability grouping, clustering students by ability within the same class, is another story. Many elementary school classes are grouped for reading, and some are grouped for math, even though there is no clear evidence that this approach is superior to other approaches. If you use homogeneous small groups in your school, the following Theory into Action Guidelines on page 40 should help your teachers make the approach more effective (Good & Brophy, 1994; Slavin, 1987).

What should instructional leaders do when they face more extreme differences in student ability? We turn to this question next.

Gifted and Talented

There is a growing recognition that gifted students are being poorly served by most public schools. A national survey found that more than one half of all gifted students do not achieve in school at a level equal to their ability (Tomlinson-Keasey, 1990).

THEORY INTO ACTION GUIDELINES

Ability Grouping

Form and reform groups on the basis of students' current performance in the subject being taught.

Examples

1. Use scores on the most recent reading assessments to establish reading groups, and rely on current math performance to form math groups.
2. Change group placement frequently when students' achievement changes.

Discourage comparisons between groups and encourage students to develop a whole-class spirit.

Examples

1. Don't seat groups together outside the context of their reading or math group.
2. Avoid naming ability groups—save names for mixed-ability or whole-class teams

Group by ability for one or, at the most, two subjects.

Examples

1. Make sure there are many lessons and projects that mix members from the groups.

2. Experiment with learning strategies in which cooperation is stressed (described in Chapter 3).
3. Keep the number of groups small (two or three at most) so that you can provide as much direct teaching as possible—leaving students alone for too long leads to less learning.

Make sure teachers, methods, and pace are adjusted to fit the needs of the group.

Examples

1. Organize and teach groups so that low achieving students get appropriate extra instruction—not just the same material again.
2. Experiment with alternatives to grouping. There are alternatives to within-class grouping that appear more effective for some subjects. Mason and Good (1993) found that supplementing whole-class instruction in math with remediation and enrichment for students when they needed it worked better than dividing the class into two ability groups and teaching these groups separately.

Who Are the Gifted?   There is no agreement about what constitutes a gifted student. Individuals can have many different gifts. Remember that Gardner (1983) identified seven or eight separate kinds of "intelligences," and Guilford (1988) claims there are 180. Renzulli and Reis (1991) have defined giftedness as a combination of three basic characteristics: above-average general ability, a high level of creativity, and a high level of task commitment or motivation to achieve in certain areas. Truly gifted children are not the students who simply learn quickly with little effort. The work of gifted students is original, extremely advanced for their age, and potentially of lasting importance.

Identifying a gifted child is not always easy. Many parents provide early educational experiences for their children. A preschool or primary student coming to your school may read above grade level, play an instrument quite well, or whiz through every assignment. But even very advanced reading in the early grades does not guarantee that students will still be outstanding readers years later (Mills & Jackson, 1990). How do you separate gifted students from hardworking or parentally pressured students? In middle school and high school, some very able students deliberately earn lower grades, making their abilities even harder to recognize.

Teachers are successful only about 10% to 50% of the time in picking out the gifted children in their classes (Fox, 1981). One reason identification can be difficult is because some students with intellectual gifts and talents also have learning problems such as difficulties hearing, learning disabilities, or attention deficit disorders and their talents will be missed if the abilities as well as the problems are not properly assessed. In fact, Whitmore and Maker (1985) estimated that least 2% of the children with disabilities, excluding those with mental retardation, have exceptional abilities as well. These seven questions, taken from an early study of gifted students, are still good guides today (Walton, 1961):

- Who learns easily and rapidly?
- Who uses a lot of common sense and practical knowledge?
- Who retains easily what he or she has heard?
- Who knows about many things that the other children don't?
- Who uses a large number of words easily and accurately?
- Who recognizes relations and comprehends meanings?
- Who is alert and keenly observant and responds quickly?

Based on Renzulli and Reis's (1991) definition of giftedness, we might add:

- Who is persistent and highly motivated on some tasks?
- Who is creative, often has unusual ideas, or makes interesting connections?

Giftedness and Formal Testing.   The best single predictor of academic giftedness is still the individual IQ test, but these tests are costly and time-consuming—and far from perfect. Group achievement and intelligence tests tend to underestimate the IQs of very bright children. Group tests may be appropriate for screening, but they are not appropriate for making placement decisions. One answer is a case study approach to identifying gifted students. This means gathering many kinds of information, test scores, grades, examples of work, projects and portfolios, letters or ratings from teachers, self-ratings, and so on (Renzulli & Reis, 1991; Sisk, 1988). Especially for recognizing artistic talent, experts in the field can be called in to judge the merits of a child's creations. Science projects, exhibitions, performances, auditions, and interviews are all possibilities. Creativity tests may identify some children not picked up by other measures, particularly minority students who may be at a disadvantage on the other types of tests (Maker, 1987).

Teaching Gifted Students.   Some educators believe that gifted students should be accelerated—moved quickly through the grades or through particular subjects. Other educators prefer enrichment—giving the students additional, more sophisticated, and more thought-provoking work, but keeping them with their age-mates in school. Actually, both may be appropriate (Torrance, 1986).

Many people object to acceleration, but most careful studies indicate that truly gifted students who begin primary, elementary, junior high, high school, college, or even graduate school early do as well as, and usually better than, nongifted students who are progressing at the normal pace. Social and emotional adjustment does not appear to be impaired. Gifted students tend to prefer the company of older playmates and may be miserably bored if kept with children of their own age. Skipping grades may not be the best solution for a particular student, but it does not deserve the bad name it has received (Jones & Southern, 1991; Kulik & Kulik, 1984; Richardson & Benbow, 1990). An alternative to skipping grades is to accelerate students in one or two particular subjects but keep them with peers for most classes (Reynolds & Birch, 1988). For students who are extremely advanced intellectually (for example, those scoring 160 or higher on an individual intelligence test), the only practical solution may be to accelerate their education (Gross, 1992; Keogh & MacMillan, 1996).

Teaching methods for gifted students should encourage abstract thinking, creativity, and independence, not just the learning of greater quantities of facts. In working with gifted and talented students, a teacher must be imaginative, flexible, and unthreatened by the capabilities of these students. Instructional leaders must ask, What does this child need most? What is she or he ready to learn? Who can help me to help? Answers might come from faculty members at nearby colleges, retired professionals, books, museums, or older students. Strategies might be as simple as letting the child do math with the next grade. Increasingly, more flexible programs are being devised for gifted students: summer institutes; courses at nearby colleges; classes with local artists, musicians, or dancers; independent research projects; selected classes in high school for younger students; honors classes; and special-interest clubs. All are options for offering gifted students appropriate learning experiences (Mitchell, 1984).

We have spent quite a bit of time considering differences in cognitive ability. However, there are many more differences among students that have implications for student learning. We turn to these next.

Students with Learning Challenges

Thus far we have focused mostly on schools' responses to the varying abilities and styles of students. For the rest of the chapter we will consider problems that can interfere with learning. It is beyond this book to discuss all the exceptionalities, but there are two that are the source of much confusion in teaching—attention deficit disorder and learning disabilities.

Hyperactivity and Attention Disorders

You have probably heard and may even have used the term hyperactivity. The notion is a modern one; there were no hyperactive children 30 to 40 years ago. Today, if anything, the term is applied too often and too widely. Hyperactivity is not one particular condition; it is "a set of behaviors—such as excessive restlessness and short attention span—that are quantitatively and qualitatively different from those of children of the same sex, mental age, and SES [socioeconomic status]" (O'Leary, 1980, p. 195). Today most psychologists agree that the main problem for children labeled hyperactive is directing and maintaining attention, not simply controlling their restlessness and physical activity. The American

Psychiatric Association has established a diagnostic category called **attention deficit-hyperactive disorder (ADHD)** to identify children with this problem. Table 2.3 lists some indicators of ADHD used by this group.

Hyperactive children are not only more physically active and inattentive than other children, they also have difficulty responding appropriately and working steadily toward goals (even their own goals), and they may be impulsive and unable to control their behavior on command, even for a brief period. The problem behaviors are generally evident in all situations and with every teacher. It is difficult to know how many children should be classified as hyperactive. The most common estimate is 3% to 5% of the elementary school population (Berk, 2002). More boys than girls are identified as hyperactive. Just a few years ago, most psychologists thought that ADHD diminished as children entered adolescence, but now there are some researchers who believe that the problems can persist into

TABLE 2.3   Indicators of ADHD: Attention Deficit-Hyperactivity Disorder

Do any of your students show these signs? They could be indications of ADHD.

Problems with *Inattention*
- Fails to give close attention to details or makes careless mistakes
- Has difficulty sustaining attention in tasks or play activities
- Does not seem to listen when spoken to directly
- Does not follow through on instructions and fails to finish schoolwork (not due to oppositional behavior or failure to understand instructions)
- Has difficulty organizing tasks or activities
- Avoids, dislikes, or is reluctant to engage in tasks that require sustained mental effort (such as schoolwork or homework)
- Loses things necessary for tasks or activities
- Is easily distracted by extraneous stimuli
- Is forgetful in daily activities

Problems with *Impulse Control*
- Blurts out answers before questions have been completed
- Has difficulty awaiting his/her turn
- Interrupts or intrudes on others in conversations or games

Hyperactivity
- Fidgets with hands or feet or squirms in seat
- Leaves seat in classroom or in other situations in which remaining seated is expected
- Runs about or climbs excessively in situations in which it is inappropriate (in adolescents may be limited to subjective feelings of restlessness)
- Has difficulty playing or engaging in leisure activities quietly
- Talks excessively
- Acts as if "driven by a motor" and cannot remain still

Source: Reprinted with permission from *Diagnostic Statistical Manual of Mental Disorders (DSM-IV-TR),* Fourth Edition. Text revision, 1994, Washington DC: American Psychiatric Association. Copyright © 2000 American Psychiatric Association.

adulthood (Hallowell & Ratey, 1994). Today there is an increasing reliance on drug therapy such as ritalin for ADHD. In fact, from 1990 to 1998, there was a 700% increase in the production of ritalin in the United States (Diller, 1998).

Ritalin and other prescribed drugs such as Dexedrine and Cylert are stimulants, but in particular dosages they tend to have paradoxical effects on many ADHD children: short-term effects include possible improvements in social behaviors such as cooperation, attention, and compliance. Research suggests that about 70% of hyperactive children are more manageable when on medication. But for many there are negative side effects such as increased heart rate and blood pressure, interference with growth rate, insomnia, weight loss, and nausea (Panksepp, 1998; Weiss & Hechtman, 1993). In addition, little is known about the long-term effects of drug therapy. There also is no evidence that the drugs lead to improvement in academic learning or peer relationships, two areas where hyperactive children have great problems. Because students appear to improve dramatically in their behavior, parents, teachers, and principals, relieved to see change, may assume the problem has been cured. It hasn't. The students still need special help in learning.

The methods that have proved most successful in helping students with attention deficits are based on the behavioral principles described in Chapter 3. One promising approach combines instruction in learning and memory strategies with motivational training. The goal is to give students the "skill and will" (Paris, 1988) to improve their achievement. Students learn how and when to apply learning strategies and study skills. They are also encouraged to be persistent and to see themselves as "in control" (Reid & Borkowski, 1987). These methods should be thoroughly tested with the student before drugs are used. Even if students in your school are on medication, it is critical that they also learn the academic and social skills they will need to survive. Again, this will not happen by itself, even if behavior improves with medication

Learning Disabilities

How do you explain what is wrong with a student who is not mentally retarded, emotionally disturbed, or educationally deprived; who has normal vision, hearing, and language capabilities; and who still cannot learn to read, write, or compute? One explanation is that the student has a **learning disability.** This is a relatively new and controversial category of exceptional students. There is no fully agreed upon definition. In fact, Cartwright, Cartwright, and Ward (1989) list 38 different definitions. A group of parents and professionals, the National Joint Committee on Learning Disabilities (1989), proposes the following definition:

> Learning disabilities is a general term that refers to a heterogeneous group of disorders manifest by significant difficulties in the acquisition and use of listening, speaking, reading, writing, reasoning, or mathematical abilities. These disorders are intrinsic to the individual, presumed to be due to central nervous system dysfunction, and may occur across the life span. (p. 1)

This definition eliminates references to older terms such as brain injury or minimal brain dysfunction, and indicates that learning disabilities may pose a lifelong challenge. Most definitions agree that students with learning disabilities are at least average in intelligence, but have significant academic problems and perform well below what would be expected.

Some educators and psychologists believe the learning disability label is overused, even abused. Almost half of all students receiving some kind of special education services in the public schools are diagnosed as having learning disabilities. This is by far the largest category of disabled student. Some researchers have suggested that many of the students considered to have learning disabilities are really slow learners in average schools, average learners in high-achieving schools, students with second-language problems, or that they may simply be behind in their work because they are absent frequently or have to change schools often (Gartner & Lipsky, 1987).

Students with Learning Disabilities.   Students with learning disabilities are not all alike. The most common characteristics are: specific difficulties in one or more academic areas; poor fine motor coordination; problems paying attention; hyperactivity and impulsivity; problems organizing and interpreting visual and auditory information; disorders of thinking, memory, speech, and hearing; and difficulties making and keeping friends (Hallahan & Kauffman, 2000). As you can see, many students with other disabilities (such as attention deficit disorder) and many normal students may have some of the same characteristics. To complicate the situation even more, not all students with learning disabilities will have these problems, and few will have all of the problems. These students may be well below average in some academic areas, but average or strong in others.

Most students with learning disabilities have difficulties reading. Table 2.4 on page 46 lists some of the most common problems and signs. These difficulties appear to be due to problems with relating sounds to letters that make up words, making spelling hard as well (Stanovich, 1991). Math, both computation and problem solving, is the second most common problem for learning-disabled students. The writing of some learning-disabled students is virtually unreadable, and their spoken language can be halting and disorganized. Many researchers trace some of these problems to the students' inability to use effective learning strategies, which we discuss in Chapter 3. Students with learning disabilties often lack effective ways to approach academic tasks. They don't know how to focus on the relevant information, get organized, apply learning strategies and study skills, change strategies when one isn't working, or evaluate their learning. They tend to be passive learners, in part because they don't know how to learn. Working independently is especially trying, so homework and seatwork are often left incomplete (Hallahan & Kauffman, 2000; Hallahan, Kauffman, & Lloyd, 1999).

Early diagnosis is important so that students with learning disabilities do not become terribly frustrated and discouraged or develop bad habits in an attempt to compensate. The students themselves do not understand why they are having such trouble, and they may become victims of **learned helplessness.** This condition was first identified in learning experiments with animals. The animals were put in situations where they received punishment (electric shocks) that they could not control. Later, when the situation was changed and they could have escaped the shocks or turned them off, the animals didn't even bother trying (Seligman, 1975). They had learned to be helpless victims. Learning-disabled students may also come to believe that they cannot control or improve their own learning. This is a powerful belief. The students never exert the effort to discover that they can make a difference in their own learning, so they remain passive and helpless.

TABLE 2.4   Reading Habits and Errors of Students with Learning Disabilities

Do any of your students show these signs? They could be indications of learning disabilities.

Poor Reading Habits

- Frequently loses his or her place
- Jerks head from side to side
- Expresses insecurity by crying or refusing to read
- Prefers to read with the book held within inches from face
- Shows tension while reading; such as reading in a high-pitched voice, biting lips, and fidgeting

Word Recognition Errors

- Omitting a word (e.g., "He came to the park," is read, "He came to park")
- Inserting a word (e.g., "He came to the [beautiful] park")
- Substituting a word for another (e.g., "He came to the *pond*")
- Reversing letters or words (e.g., *was* is read *saw*)
- Mispronouncing words (e.g., *park* is read *pork*)
- Transposing letters or words (e.g., "The dog ate fast," is read, "The dog fast ate")
- Not attempting to read an unknown word by breaking it into familiar units
- Slow, laborious reading, less than 20 to 30 words per minute

Comprehension Errors

- Recalling basic facts (e.g., cannot answer questions directly from a passage)
- Recalling sequence (e.g., cannot explain the order of events in a story)
- Recalling main theme (e.g., cannot give the main idea of a story)

Source: From *Child and Adolescent Development for Educators* (p. 400), by J. L. Meece, 1997, New York: McGraw-Hill. Copyright © 1997 by McGraw-Hill Companies. Adapted with permission.

Teaching Students with Learning Disabilities.   There is controversy over how best to help these students. A promising approach seems to be to emphasize study skills and methods for processing information in a given subject like reading or math. Many of the principles of cognitive learning discussed in Chapter 3 can be applied to help all students improve their attention, memory, and problem-solving abilities (Sawyer, Graham, & Harris, 1992). The Kansas Learning Strategies Curriculum is one example of this approach (Deshler & Schumaker, 1986). No set of teaching techniques will be effective for every student with learning disabilities. Principals and teachers should work with the special education teachers in the school to design appropriate instruction for individual students. Table 2.5 summarizes problem areas and the most effective teaching approaches for students with learning disabilities across the life span.

Integration, Mainstreaming, and Inclusion

No matter what grade or subject you supervise, your teachers will work with exceptional students in their classrooms. The trend to integrate exceptional students into regular education

TABLE 2.5 Learning Disabilities across the Life Span

Learning disabilities are not limited to the school years. This table lists the problems that may occur during different phases of life and the treatments that have the strongest support from research or from expert teachers in the field.

	Preschool	Grades K–1	Grades 2–6	Grades 7–12	Adult
Problem Areas	Delay in developmental milestones (e.g., walking) Receptive language Expressive language Visual perception Auditory perception Short attention span Hyperactivity	Academic readiness skills (e.g., alphabet knowledge, quantitative concepts, directional concepts, etc.) Receptive and expressive language Visual and auditory perception Gross and fine motor skills Attention/Hyperactivity Social skills	Reading skills Arithmetic skills Written expression Verbal expression Receptive language Attention span Hyperactivity Social-emotional	Reading skills Arithmetic skills Written expression Verbal expression Listening skills Study skills (metacognition) Social-emotional delinquency	Reading skills Arithmetic skills Written expression Verbal expression Listening skills Study skills Social-emotional
Treatments with Most Research and/or Expert Support	Direct instruction in language skills Behavioral management Parent training	Direct instruction in academic and language areas Behavioral management Parent training	Direct instruction in academic areas Behavioral management Self-control training Parent training	Direct instruction in academic areas Tutoring in subject areas Direct instruction in learning strategies (study skills) Self-control training Curriculum alternatives	Direct instruction in academic areas Tutoring in subject (college) or job area Compensatory instruction (i.e., using aids such as tape recorder, calculator, computer, dictionary)

Source: From *Students with Learning Disabilities* (5th ed.) (p. 50), by C. D. Mercer, © 1996. Reprinted by permission of Pearson Education, Upper Saddle River, NJ.

began in the 1960s and led to legal actions in the 1970s. In 1975 a law was passed that began revolutionary changes in the education of children with disabilities. The Education for All Handicapped Children Act (Public Law 94-142) required states to provide "a free, appropriate public education for every child between the ages of 3 and 21 (unless state law does not provide free public education to children 3 to 5 or 18 to 21 years of age) regardless of how, or how seriously, he may be handicapped." In 1986, PL 99-457 extended the requirement for a free, appropriate education to all children with disabilities ages 3 to 5, even in states that do not have public schooling for children this age. Also in the mid-1980s, some special educators and educational policymakers suggested that regular and special education should be merged so that regular teachers would have to take even more responsibility for the education of exceptional students. This movement is called the **regular education initiative.**

In 1990, PL 94-142 was amended by the Individuals with Disabilities Education Act (IDEA). This legislation replaced the word "handicapped" with "disabled," and expanded the services for disabled students. Also in 1990, the **Americans with Disabilities Act (ADA)** extended civil rights protection in employment, transportation, public accommodations, state and local government, and telecommunications to people with disabilities. In 1997, IDEA was reauthorized (see www.ed.gov/offices/OSERS/IDEA for current information).

Let's examine the requirements in these laws. There are three major points of interest to principals and teachers: the concept of "least restrictive placement"; the individualized education program (IEP); and the protection of the rights of students with disabilities and of their parents.

Least Restrictive Placement.   The laws require states to develop procedures for educating each child in the **least restrictive placement.** This means a setting that is as close to the general education class setting as possible. Earlier interpretations of this requirement led to **mainstreaming**—bringing exceptional students into general educational settings when they could meet expectations for that setting—for example allowing them to participate in recess or art or music (Friend & Bursuck, 2002). In most schools severely disabled students were not integrated into regular classes; but in some districts there is a movement toward **inclusion**—integrating all students, even those with severe disabilities, into regular classes. Advocates of inclusion believe that disabled students can benefit from involvement with their nondisabled peers and should be educated with them in their regular home-district school, even if doing so calls for changes in educational requirements, special aids, services, and training or consultation for the regular teaching staff (Stainback & Stainback, 1992). But some researchers caution that inclusion classrooms are not the best placement for every child. For example, Naomi Zigmond and her colleagues (1995) report that in their study of six elementary schools that had implemented full inclusion, only about half of the learning disabled students in these schools were able to benefit.

The Rights of Students and Parents.   Several stipulations in these laws protect the rights of parents and students. Schools must have procedures for maintaining the confidentiality of school records. Testing practices must not discriminate against students from different cultural backgrounds. Parents have the right to see all records relating to the testing, placement, and teaching of their child. If they wish, parents may obtain an independent evaluation of their child. Parents may bring an advocate or representative to the meeting at which the IEP is developed. Students whose parents are unavailable must be assigned a surrogate parent to participate in the planning. Parents must receive written notice (in their native language) before any evaluation or change in placement is made. Finally, parents have the right to challenge the program developed for their child, and are protected by due process of law. Because principals and teachers often have conferences with these families, we have provided some Theory into Action Guidelines to make the meetings more effective, but be aware that guidelines apply to all students and their parents.

THEORY INTO ACTION GUIDELINES

Productive Family Conferences

Plan and prepare for a productive conference.

Examples

1. Have a clear purpose and gather the needed information. If you want to discuss student progress, have work samples.
2. Send home a list of questions and ask families to bring the information to the conference. Sample questions from Friend and Bursuck (2002) are:
   - What is your child's favorite class activity?
   - Does your child have worries about any class activities? If so, what are they?
   - What are your priorities for your child's education this year?
   - What questions do you have about your child's education in my class this year?
   - How could we at school help make this the most successful year ever for your child?
   - Are there any topics you want to discuss at the conference that I might need to prepare for? If so, please let me know.
   - Would you like other individuals to participate in the conference? If so, please give me a list of their names.
   - Is there particular school information you would like me to have available? If so, please let me know. (p. 100)

During the conference, create and maintain an atmosphere of collaboration and respect.

Examples

1. Arrange the room for private conversation. Put a sign on your door to avoid interruptions. Meet around a conference table for better collaboration. Have tissues available.
2. Address families as "Mr." and "Ms.," not "Mom" and "Dad" or "Grandma." Use students' names.
3. Listen to families' concerns and build on their ideas for their children.

After the conference, keep good records and follow up on decisions.

Examples

1. Make notes to yourself and keep them organized.
2. Summarize any actions or decisions in writing and send a copy to the family and any other teachers or professionals involved.
3. Communicate with families on other occasions, especially when there is good news to share.

FIGURE 2.2 An Excerpt from an Individualized Educational Program (IEP)

This IEP was developed for a 9-year-old girl. This section of the plan focuses on following the teacher's directions and on reading.

Student: _____Amy North_____ Age: ___9___ Grade: ___1___ Date: _Oct. 17, 1995_

1. Unique Characteristics or Needs: Noncompliance

Frequently noncompliant with teacher's instructions.

1. Present Levels of Performance
Complies with about 50% of teacher requests/commands.

2. Special Education, Related Services, and Modifications
Implemented immediately, strong reinforcement for compliance with teacher's instructions (Example: "Sure I will!" plan including precision requests and reinforcer menu for points earned for compliance, as described in The Tough Kid Book, by Rhode, Jenson, and Reavis, 1992); within 3 weeks, training of parents by school psychologist to use precision requests and reinforcement at home.

3. Objectives (Including Procedures, Criteria, and Schedule)
Within one month, will comply with teacher requests/commands 90% of the time; compliance monitored weekly by the teacher.

4. Annual Goals
Will become compliant with teacher's requests/commands.

2. Unique Characteristics or Needs: Reading

2a. Very slow reading rate   2c. Limited phonics skills
2b. Poor comprehension   2d. Limited sight-word vocabulary

1. Present Levels of Performance
2a. Reads stories of approximately 100 words of first-grade level at approximately 40 words per min.
2b. Seldom can recall factual information about stories immediately after reading them.
2c. Consistently confuses vowel sounds, often misidentifies consonants, and does not blend sounds.
2d. Has sight-word vocabulary of approximately 150 words.

2. Special Education, Related Services, and Modifications
2a–2c. Direct instruction 30 minutes daily in vowel discrimination, consonant identification, and sound blending: begin immediately, continue throughout schoolyear.
2a & 2d. Sight word drill 10 minutes daily in addition to phonics instruction and daily practice; 10 minutes practice in using phonics and sight-word skills in reading story at her level; begin immediately, continue for schoolyear.

3. Objectives (Including Procedures, Criteria, and Schedule)
2a. Within 3 months, will read stories on her level at 60 words per minute with 2 or fewer errors per story; within six months, 80 words with 2 or fewer errors; performance monitored daily by teacher or aide.
2b. Within 3 months will answer oral and written comprehension questions requiring recall of information from stories she has just read with 90% accuracy (e.g., Who is in the story? What happened? When? Why?) and be able to predict probably outcomes with 80% accuracy; performance monitored daily by teacher or aide.
2c. Within 3 months, will increase sight-word vocabulary to 200 words, within 6 months to 250 words, assessed by flashcard presentation.

4. Annual Goals
2a–2c. Will read fluently and with comprehension at beginning-second-grade level.

Source: From *Exceptional Learners: Introduction to Special Education* (7th ed.) (p. 37), by D. P. Hallahan and J. M. Kauffman, 1997, Boston: Allyn & Bacon. Copyright © 1997 by Allyn & Bacon. Reprinted with permission of Allyn & Bacon.

Individual Education Program.   The drafters of the laws recognized that each student is unique and may need a specially tailored program to make progress. The individualized education program, or IEP, is written by a team that includes the student's teacher or teachers, at least one general education teacher, a qualified school psychologist or special education supervisor, the parent(s) or guardian(s), and (when possible) the student. The program must be updated each year and must state in writing:

1. The student's present level of functioning.
2. Goals for the year and short-term measurable instructional objectives leading to those goals.
3. A list of specific services to be provided to the student and details of when those services will be initiated.
4. A description of how fully the student will participate in the regular school program.
5. A schedule telling how the student's progress toward the objectives will be evaluated and approximately how long the services described in the plan will be needed.
6. Beginning at age 16 (and as young as 14 for some students), a statement of needed transitional services to move the student toward further education or work in adult life.

Figure 2.2 is an excerpt from the IEP of a 9-year-old girl with mild retardation. This section of the IEP focuses on one behavior problem and on reading.

Effective Teaching in Inclusive Classrooms

Effective teaching for exceptional students is not a unique set of skills. It is a combination of good teaching practices and sensitivity to students. Students with disabilities need to learn the academic material, and they need to be full participants in the day-to-day life of the classroom. To accomplish the first goal of academic learning, Larrivee (1985) concluded that effective teachers of mainstreamed students do the following: Use time efficiently by having smooth management routines, avoiding discipline problems, and planning carefully. Ask questions at the right level of difficulty. Give supportive, positive feedback to students, helping them figure out the right answer if they are wrong but on the right track.

To accomplish the second goal of integrating disabled students into the day-to-day life of the classroom, Ferguson, Ferguson, and Bogdan (1987) give the following guidelines:

1. Mix students with disabilities into groups with nondisabled students. Avoid resegregating the disabled students into separate groups.
2. Instead of sending students out for special services like speech therapy, remedial reading, or individualized instruction, try to integrate the special help into the class setting, perhaps during a time when the other students are working independently too.
3. Make sure your language and behavior with disabled students is a good model for everyone.
4. Teach about differences among people as part of the curriculum. Let students become familiar with aids for people with disabilities, such as hearing aids, sign language, communication boards, and so on.

5. Have students work together in cooperative groups or on special projects such as role playing, biographical interviews, or lab assignments.
6. Try to keep the schedules and activity patterns of disabled and nondisabled students similar.

Collaborative Consultation and Cooperative Teaching.   Increasingly, special and regular educators are working together, collaborating to assume equal responsibility for the education of students with disabilities. The collaboration may work through consultation, planning, and problem solving about how to teach specific students or the special education teacher might work directly alongside the regular teacher in a class made up of students with and without disabilities. The latter is called cooperative teaching. The teachers assume different roles, depending on the age of the students and their needs. For example, in a secondary class the regular teacher might be responsible for academic content, while the special instructor teaches study skills and learning strategies. In another classroom the regular teacher might deal with core content, while the special teacher provides remediation, enrichment, or reteaching when necessary. The two teachers might also try team teaching, where each is responsible for different parts of the lesson.

In using cooperative teaching, it is important that students with or without disabilities aren't resegregated in the class, with the regular teacher always working with the "regular" students and the special teacher always working with the "mainstreamed" students. Figure 2.3 shows different ways to implement cooperative teaching.

Making a Referral.   At times, your teachers may need help in referring one of their students for an evaluation. Table 2.6 on page 54 guides you and them through the referral process.

Summary

Statistics point to increasing cultural diversity in American society. Everyone is a member of many cultural groups, defined in terms of geographic region, nationality, ethnicity, race, gender, social class, and religion. Membership in a particular group does not determine behavior or values but makes certain values and kinds of behavior more likely. Wide variations exist within each group.

Language differences among students include dialects, bilingualism, and culture-based communication styles. Dialects are not inferior languages and should be respected, but Standard English should be taught for academic contexts. Bilingual students may have some degree of limitation in English proficiency, and also must often struggle with social adjustment problems relating to biculturalism. While there is much debate over the best way to help bilingual students master English, studies show it is best if they are not forced to abandon their first language. The more proficient students are in their first language, the faster they will master the second. Mastering academic language skills in any new language takes five to seven years.

Cognitive styles are characteristic modes of perceiving, remembering, thinking, problem solving, and decision making. They reflect information-processing regularities that develop around underlying personality trends. Field dependence versus field indepen-

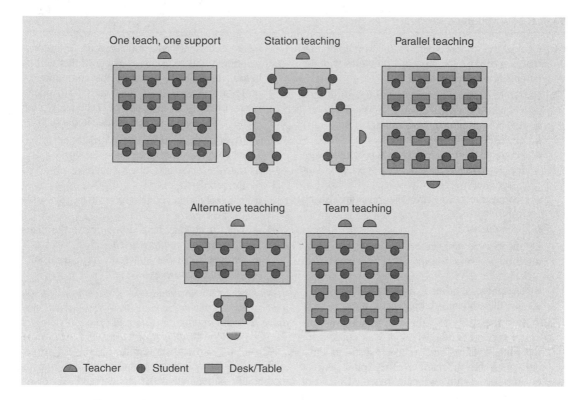

One teach, one support   Station teaching   Parallel teaching

Alternative teaching   Team teaching

△ Teacher   ● Student   ▭ Desk/Table

FIGURE 2.3   Cooperative and Co-Teaching Approaches   There are many ways for teachers
to work together in inclusion classrooms.

Source: From *Including Students with Special Needs: A Practical Guide for Classroom Teachers* (p. 87), by M.
Friend and W. Bursuck, Boston: Allyn & Bacon. Copyright © 1996 by Allyn & Bacon. Reprinted with permission of Allyn & Bacon.

dence and impulsive versus reflective cognitive styles are examples of these differences.
Learning preferences are individual preferences for particular learning modes and environments. They could be preferences for where, when, with whom, or with what lighting,
food, or music you like to study. While cognitive styles and learning preferences are not
related to intelligence or effort, they may affect school performance.

Some educators suggest that students learn more when they study in their preferred
setting and manner. But sometimes students, particularly poorer students, prefer what is
easy and comfortable; real learning can be hard and uncomfortable. Sometimes students
prefer to learn in a certain way because they have no alternatives; it is the only way they
know how to approach the task. These students may benefit from developing new—and
perhaps more effective—ways to learn.

Culturally compatible classrooms are free of racism, sexism, and ethnic prejudice and
provide equal educational opportunities for all students. Dimensions of classroom life that

TABLE 2.6   Making a Referral

1. Contact the student's parents. It is very important that you discuss the student's problems with the parents *before* you refer.

2. Before making a referral, check *all* the student's school records. Has the student ever:
   - had a psychological evaluation?
   - qualified for special services?
   - been included in other special programs (e.g., for disadvantaged children; speech or language therapy)?
   - scored far below average on standardized tests?
   - been retained?

   Do the records indicate:
   - good progress in some areas, poor progress in others?
   - any physical or medical problem?
   - that the student is taking medication?

3. Talk to the student's other teachers and professional support personnel about your concern for the student. Have other teachers also had difficulty with the student? Have they found ways of dealing successfully with the student? Document the strategies that you have used in your class to meet the student's educational needs. Your documentation will be useful as evidence that will be helpful to or be required by the committee of professionals who will evaluate the student. Demonstrate your concern by keeping written records. Your notes should include items such as:
   - exactly what you are concerned about
   - why you are concerned about it
   - dates, places, and times you have observed the problem
   - precisely what you have done to try to resolve the problem
   - who, if anyone, helped you devise the plans or strategies you have used
   - evidence that the strategies have been successful or unsuccessful

Remember that you should refer a student only if you can make a convincing case that the student may have a handicapping condition and probably cannot be served appropriately without special education. Referral for special education begins a time-consuming, costly, and stressful process that is potentially damaging to the student and has many legal ramifications.

Source: From *What Should I Know about Special Education? Answers for Classroom Teachers,* by P. L. Pullen & J. M. Kauffman, 1987. Used with permission of the authors.

can be modified to that end are social organization, learning-style formats, and participation structures. Teachers, however, must avoid stereotypes of culture-based learning styles and must not assume that every individual in a group shares the same style. Communication may break down in classrooms because of differences in sociolinguistic styles and skills. Teachers can directly teach appropriate participation structures and be sensitive to culture-based communication rules. To help create compatible multicultural classrooms, teachers must know and respect all their students, have high expectations of them, and teach them what they need to know to succeed.

Educational equity for females and males is also an issue. Research shows that gender-role stereotyping begins in the preschool years and continues through gender bias in the school curriculum and sex discrimination in the classroom. Teachers often unintentionally perpetuate these problems. Some measures on IQ and SAT tests have shown small sex-linked differences, especially in spatial abilities and mathematics. Research on the causes of these differences has been inconclusive, except to indicate that academic socialization and teachers' treatment of male and female students in mathematics classes do play a role. Teachers can use many strategies for reducing gender bias.

Spearman suggested there is one mental attribute, which he called g or *general intelligence,* that is used to perform on any mental test, but that each test also requires some specific abilities in addition to g. A current version of the general plus specific abilities theory is Carroll's work identifying a few broad abilities (such as learning and memory, visual perception, verbal fluency) and at least 70 specific abilities. Gardner contends that an intelligence is a biological and psychological potential to solve problems and create products or outcomes that are valued by a culture. There are at least eight separate intelligences: linguist, musical, spatial, logical-mathematical, bodily-kinesthetic, interpersonal, intrapersonal (these last two are similar to the idea of emotional intelligence), naturalist, and perhaps existential. Gardner does not deny the existence of a general ability, but does question how useful g is as an explanation for human achievements.

Sternberg's triarchic theory of intelligence is a cognitive process approach to understanding intelligence that has three parts—analytic, creative, and practical. Analytic/componential intelligence involves the mental processes that lead to more or less intelligent behavior. Creative/experiential intelligence involves coping with new experiences through insight, or the ability to deal effectively with novel situations, and automaticity, or the ability to become efficient and automatic in thinking and problem solving. The third part is practical/contextual intelligence—choosing to live and work in a context where success is likely, adapting to that context, and reshaping it if necessary.

Intelligence is measured through individual tests (Stanford-Binet, Wechsler, Woodcock-Johnston, etc.) and group tests (Lorge-Thorndike, Analysis of Learning Potential, Otis-Lennon Mental Abilities Tests, School and College Ability Tests, etc.). Compared to an individual test, a group test is much less likely to yield an accurate picture of any one person's abilities. The average score is 100; 50% of the people from the general population who take the tests will score 100 or above, and 50% will score below 100. About 68% of the general population will earn IQ scores between 85 and 115. Only about 16% of the population will receive scores below 85, and only 16% will score above 115. These figures hold true for white, native-born Americans whose first language is Standard English. Intelligence predicts success in school, but is less predictive of success in life when level of education is taken into account.

Academic ability groupings can have both disadvantages and advantages for students and teachers. Low-ability classes seem to receive lower-quality instruction in general. Teachers tend to emphasize lower-level objectives and routine procedures, with less academic focus. Often there are more student behavior problems and, along with these problems, increased teacher stress and decreased enthusiasm. Low expectations may be communicated to the students. Attendance may drop. The lower tracks often have a disproportionate number of minority group and economically disadvantaged students, so ability grouping becomes segregation in school. Cross-age grouping by subject can be an effective way to deal with ability differences in nongraded elementary schools. Within-class ability grouping, if handled sensitively and flexibly, can have positive effects, but alternatives such as cooperative learning are also possible.

Ability grouping has benefits for gifted students, as does acceleration. Many people object to acceleration, but most careful studies indicate that truly gifted students who are accelerated do as well as, and usually better than, nongifted students who are progressing at the normal pace. Gifted students tend to prefer the company of older playmates and may be bored if kept with children of their own age. Skipping grades may not be the best solution for a particular student, but for students who are extremely advanced intellectually (160 or higher on an individual intelligence test), the only practical solution may be to accelerate their education

Two common learning problems in the schools are attention deficit disorders and learning disabilities. Attention deficit-hyperactivity disorder (ADHD) is the term used to describe individuals of any age with hyperactivity and attention difficulties. Use of medication to address ADHD is controversial, but currently on the rise. About 70% of children with ADHD are more manageable when on medication. But for many there are negative side effects. In addition, little is known about the long-term effects of drug therapy. There also is no evidence that the drugs lead to improvement in academic learning or peer relationships, two areas where children with ADHD have great problems. Two promising approaches are behavior modification and techniques that combine instruction in learning and memory strategies with motivational training.

Specific learning disabilities involve significant difficulties in the acquisition and use of listening, speaking, reading, writing, reasoning, or mathematical abilities. These disorders are intrinsic to the individual, presumed to be due to central nervous system dysfunction, and may occur across the life span. Students with learning disabilities may become victims of learned helplessness when they come to believe that they cannot control or improve their own learning and therefore cannot succeed. A focus on learning strategies often helps students with learning disabilities.

Public Law 94-142 (1975) requires that each exceptional learner or special needs student be educated in the least restrictive environment according to an individualized education program. The law also protects the rights of special needs students and their parents. Public Law 99-457 extends PL 94-142 to preschool-age children, and IDEA, the Individuals with Disabilities Education Act, extends services to include transition programming for exceptional learners 16 years old and older. The regular education initiative calls for regular classroom teachers to receive training in teaching exceptional learners.

KEY TERMS

Americans with Disabilities Act
   (ADA)   (48)
attention deficit-hyperactive disorder (ADHD)   (43)
between-class ability grouping;
   tracking   (38)
bilingualism   (20)
cognitive styles   (23)
dialect   (19)
emotional intelligence
   (EQ)   (35)

English as a second language
   (ESL)   (21)
g   (31)
gender schemas   (27)
inclusion   (48)
intelligence   (30)
learned helplessness   (45)
learning disability   (44)
learning preferences   (24)
learning styles   (23)
least restrictive placement   (48)

limited English proficiency
   (LEP)   (21)
mainstreaming   (48)
participation structures   (26)
regular education initiative   (48)
theory of multiple
   intelligences   (32)
triarchic theory of
   intelligence   (36)
tracking   (38)

SOME IDEAS FOR YOUR PORTFOLIO

1. Develop a position statement and action plan on the appropriate use of school-level student groupings.

   - What is your philosophy about ability grouping and tracking? Be sure to support your perspective with the available research.

   - What will you do? Develop a plan for implementing this philosophy in your school.

   - How will you do it? Develop a realistic implementation strategy.

2. Develop a position statement and action plan on inclusion that complies with PL 94-142 and the subsequent modifications and extensions of the law.

   - What is your philosophy about mainstreaming and inclusion? Be sure to support your perspective with the available research and the law.

   - Develop a plan for implementing this philosophy in your school. Be sure to include how you will comply with the "least restrictive placement" and other provisions of PL 94-142 as well as your district's policies on inclusion. Does the district policy facilitate or hinder your philosophy about inclusion? How?

   - Develop a framework and checklist to insure that your school is in compliance with the relevant laws.

3. Develop a school policy on the use of results from intelligence tests. What sort of testing should be done? Who should have access? How should scores be used to support students' learning? Buttress your positions with current research and theory on intelligence.

INSTRUCTIONAL LEADER'S TOOLBOX

Readings

Campbell, L., Campbell, B., & Dickinson, D. (1999). *Teaching and learning through multiple intelligences* (2nd ed.). Boston: Allyn & Bacon.

Halpern, D. F. (1996). Changing data, changing minds: What the data on cognitive sex differences tell us and what we hear. *Learning and Individual Differences, 8,* 73–82.

Ladson-Billings, G. (1995). But that is just good teaching! The case for culturally relevant pedagogy. *Theory Into Practice, 34,* 161–165.

Loveless, T. (1999). Will tracking reform promote social equity? *Educational Leadership, 56*(7), 28–32.

Panksepp, J. (1998). Attention deficit hyperactivity disorders, psychostimulants, and intolerance of playfulness: A tragedy in the making? *Current Directions in Psychological Science, 7,* 91–98

Williams, W., Blythe, T., White, N., Li, J., Sternberg, R., & Gardner, H. (1996). *Practical intelligence in school.* New York: HarperCollins.

Education week article on inclusion: http://www.edweek.org/context/topics/include.htm

Videos

An excellent listing of videotapes on disabilities can be found at http://www.state.nh.us/nhsl/frc/vid3.htm.

See http://teach.virginia.edu/curry/dept/cise/ose/new.html for a listing of films depicting a special needs individual.

Educating Everybody's Children. The three-tape series shows how teachers set high expectations for learning, respond to the cultural differences of students, and create classroom environments that serve diverse learning styles. (ASCD videos, 2000) Three 20- to 25-minute videotapes and a 92-page Facilitator's Guide. Order from: Association for Supervision and Curriculum Development (ASCD), 125 N. West St., Alexandria, VA 22314-2798. Telephone: (703) 549-9110; FAX: (703) 549-3891. http://shop.ascd.org/category.cfm?categoryid=video

Websites

A collection of child development websites	http://www.ume.maine.edu/~cofed/eceol/guide.html
Listing of technical assistance documents from the Office of Special Education	http://www.state.sd.us/state/executive/deca/special/taguide.htm
Introduction to multiple intelligences	http://edweb.gsn.org/edref.mi.intro.html
Project Zero	http://pzweb.harvard.edu
Teaching to the 7 Multiple Intelligences	http://ns1.iols.net/users/berolart/GRPWEBPG.HTM
Emotional Intelligence: Popular or scientific psychology	http://www.apa.org/monitor/sep99/sp.html
National Education Association's Policy on Inclusion	http://www.nea.org/publiced/idea/ideaplcy.html
IDEA law (Individuals with Disabilities Education Act)	http://www.ed.gov/offices/OSERS/IDEA/the law.html
Profiles of Children with Disabilities	http://www.nces.ed.gov/pubs97/97254.html
Disability-Related Resources on the Web	http://www.thearc.org/misc/dislnkin.html
Clearing House for Multicultural and Bilingual Education	http://www.weber.edu/MBE/htmls/MBE-resources.html
Community Learning Network: is a Canadian site with information on multiculturalism	http://www.cln.org/
Multicultural curriculum and instructional resources	http://www.cln.org/subkects/mc.html
Modified Fennema-Sherman Attitude: assessment of attitudes towards mathematics	http://www.woodrow.org/teachers/math/gender/08scale.html
Resources on Women and Mathematics	http://www.forum.swarthmore.edu/library/ed topics/equity women/

Organizations

The Office of Special Education: You can find information on new legislation, new resources on this site. This is an excellent general resource.	http://teach.virginia.edu/curry/dept/cise/ose/new.html

The National Academy of Child Development: NACD is an international organization of parents and professionals dedicated to helping children and adults reach their full potential. The site includes resources for parents and links to research articles.	http://www.nacd.org/
American Academy of Child and Adolescent Psychiatry: This organization helps families understand the developmental, emotional, and behavioral disorders affecting children and adolescents.	http://www. aacap.org/
National Multicultural Institute: The mission of this institute is to increase knowledge, awareness, and respect among people of different racial, ethnic and cultural backgrounds.	http://www.nmci.org/index.htm
Al-Anon/Alateen: This organization provides support for the family members of alcoholics.	http://www.al-anon.org
National Association for Attention Deficit Disorder	http://www.add.org/
Learning Disabilities Association	http://www.ldanatl.org/
Children and Adults with Attention Deficit Disorders (C.H.A.D.D.).	http://www.chadd.org/
National Multicultural Institute: The mission of this institute is to increase knowledge, awareness, and respect among people of different racial, ethnic and cultural backgrounds.	http://www.nmci.org/index.htm

CHAPTER

3 Learning

Preview: Key Points

Leadership Challenge

What Is Learning?

Behavioral View of Learning
Types of Consequences
Antecedents and Behavior Change
Theory into Action Guidelines: Using
Reinforcement and Punishment

Teaching Applications of Behavioral Theories
Contingency Contract Programs

Cognitive Views of Learning
Knowledge and Learning
An Information Processing Model
Sensory Memory
Working Memory
Theory into Action: Capturing Attention
Long-Term Memory
Storing and Retrieving Information in Long-Term
Memory
Metacognition, Regulation, and Individual
Differences
Theory into Action Guidelines: Applying
Information Processing

**Cognitive Contributions: Learning Strategies
and Tactics**
Deciding What Is Important
Visual Tools for Organizing

Mnemonics
Reading Strategies
Theory into Action Guidelines: Learning
Strategies

Constructivist Theories of Learning
Constructivist Views of Learning
Is the World Knowable?
Knowledge: Situated or General?

**Teaching Applications of Constructivist
Perspectives**
Elements of Constructivist Teaching
Inquiry Learning
Problem-Based Learning
Cognitive Apprenticeships
Group Work and Cooperation in Learning
Theory into Action Guidelines: Explaining
Innovations

Summary

Key Terms

Some Ideas for Your Portfolio

Instructional Leader's Toolbox
Readings
Videos
Websites
Organizations

PREVIEW: KEY POINTS

- Learning occurs when experience leads to a relatively permanent change in an individual's knowledge or behavior.
- There are many explanations for learning, but the most useful are the behavioral, cognitive, and constructivist perspectives.
- Behavioral explanations of learning emphasize the importance of antecedents (cues and prompts) and consequences (reinforcement and punishment) in shaping behavior.
- Learning objectives (clear descriptions of teachers' educational goals for students) and contingency contracts.
- Cognitive explanations of learning highlight the importance of prior knowledge in focusing attention, making sense of new information, and supporting memory.
- Information processing is a cognitive theory of memory that describes how information is taken in; processed (combined with prior knowledge); stored in long-term memory in the forms of episodes, productions, images and schemas; and retrieved.
- Learning strategies (overall plans for learning) and learning tactics such as underlining, highlighting, and graphing are applications of the cognitive approach.
- Constructivist views of learning explain learning in terms of the individual and social construction of knowledge; knowledge is judged not so much by its accuracy as by its usefulness.
- Situated learning emphasizes the idea that learning is specific to the situation in which it is learned and that it is difficult to transfer.
- Features of constructivist applications include complex real-life tasks, social interaction and shared responsibility, multiple representations of content, and student-centered teaching.
- Three promising applications of the constructivist approach are inquiry or problem-based learning, cognitive apprenticeships, and cooperative learning.

Leadership Challenge

Your school's social studies department is highly regarded for its innovative approach to teaching. The program is oriented toward inquiry as a process, rather than the retention of historical fact. Typically, curriculum is developed by the department. The teachers are enthusiastic about their program and it is well received by the students. You do not always agree with the direction of the curriculum, but there is little question that this is a highly skilled and professional group of teachers whom you respect.

Recent reform in the state has argued for back to basics and the use of curricular materials that stress recall of specific persons, places, and events in state and national history. The reform is supported by a battery of state tests. Although the state maintained that no invidious comparisons would be made, your community has made them. The superintendent has her feet to the fire on this issue, and now you too are feeling the heat. Recent test scores show that your students are not doing nearly as well in history as they are in science and mathematics. The superintendent has "requested" that you integrate the state curricular materials into the history program to correct the current deficiencies. Your history faculty, on the other hand, claim that this is exactly the wrong tack to take to develop inquiring minds. They are not overly concerned with the students' performance on the state tests because they claim the tests measure the wrong thing. Parents, however, cannot understand why their children are not doing as well in history as they are in math and science; in fact, at the last board meeting the superintendent promised that the history scores would rise.

- What do students need to "know" about history?
- What is the role of rote memory in learning?
- What do the behavioral, cognitive, and constructivist perspectives on learning have to offer?
- How does one achieve the right balance of teaching facts and teaching for discovery and understanding?

Source: The above situation has been adapted from W. K. Hoy and C. J. Tarter's (1995), *Administrators solving the problems of practice: Decision making, concepts, cases, and consequences.* Allyn & Bacon: Boston.

What Is Learning?

Learning is at the center of schooling. Learning is a goal and a process—a noun and a verb. As a goal, learning (new knowledge and skills) is the outcome instructional leaders work toward as they interact with teachers. Learning is the teachers' goal with their students. But learning is also a process. In order to design useful learning environments in schools and classrooms, we must understand how people learn. Methods of teaching that are incompatible with the ways students learn are not likely to succeed. The purpose of this chapter is to examine briefly what is known about learning so that your work with teachers and their work with students can be informed by and compatible with the ways that people learn. We will examine the contemporary contributions to education of three major perspectives on learning: behavioral, cognitive, and constructivist, noting specific strategies for teaching that are consistent with each perspective. Our goal is not to pick the "best" or most popular explanation of learning, but instead to use the best from each explanation, because each tells us something different and useful about the complex phenomenon that is human learning.

When we hear the word "learning," most of us think of studying and school. We think about subjects or skills we intend to master, such as algebra, history, chemistry, or karate. But learning is not limited to school. We learn every day of our lives. Babies learn to kick their legs to make the mobile above their cribs move, teenagers learn the lyrics to all their favorite songs, and every few years we all learn to find a new style of dress attractive when the old styles go out of fashion. This last example shows that learning is not always intentional. We don't try to like new styles and dislike old; it just seems to happen that way. So what is this powerful phenomenon called learning?

In the broadest sense, **learning** occurs when experience causes a relatively permanent change in an individual's knowledge or behavior. The change may be deliberate or unintentional, for better or for worse. To qualify as learning, this change must be brought about by experience—by the interaction of a person with his or her environment. Changes due simply to maturation, such as growing taller or turning gray, do not qualify as learning. Temporary changes due to illness, fatigue, or hunger are also excluded from a general definition of learning. A person who has gone without food for two days does not learn to be hungry, and a person who is ill does not learn to run more slowly. Of course, learning plays a part in how we respond to hunger or illness.

Our definition specifies that the changes resulting from learning are in the individual's knowledge or behavior. Although most learning theorists would agree with this statement, some tend to emphasize the change in knowledge, others the change in behavior.

- Behavioral psychologists emphasize observable changes in behaviors, skills, and habits.
- Cognitive psychologists, who focus on changes in knowledge, believe learning is an internal mental activity that cannot be observed directly. Cognitive psychologists studying learning are interested in unobservable mental activities such as thinking, remembering, and solving problems (Schwartz & Reisberg, 1991).
- Constructivist psychologists, more commonly known as constructivists, are interested in how people make meaning—learning is seen as the construction of knowledge.

Different theories of learning have had different impacts on education and have supported different practices. In the 1960s and early 70s, behavioral views of learning dominated education. But beginning in the 1980s, cognitive and constructivist explanations became more prevalent. Even though there are differences in these explanations, each provides insights about some aspect of learning, in part because they focus on different kinds of outcomes. Each perspective provides instructional leaders with tools for improving instruction. We begin our explorations of learning with the behavioral perspective.

Behavioral View of Learning

The behavioral approach to learning developed out of work by Skinner and others who emphasized the role of antecedents and consequences in behavior change. Learning was defined as a change in behavior brought about by experience, with little concern for the mental or internal aspects of learning. Behavior, like response or action, is simply a word for what a person does in a particular situation. Conceptually, we may think of a behavior as sandwiched between two sets of environmental influences: those that precede it (its antecedents) and those that follow it (its consequences) (Skinner, 1950). This relationship can be shown very simply as antecedent–behavior–consequence, or A–B–C. As behavior is ongoing, a given consequence becomes an antecedent for the next ABC sequence. Research shows that behavior can be altered by changes in the antecedents, the consequences, or both. Early work focused on consequences.

Types of Consequences

According to the behavioral view, consequences determine to a great extent whether a person will repeat the behavior that led to the consequences. The type and timing of consequences can strengthen or weaken behaviors. Consequences that strengthen behaviors are called *reinforcers*.

Reinforcement.   Although reinforcement is commonly understood to mean "reward," this term has a particular meaning in learning theory. A **reinforcer** is any consequence that strengthens the behavior it follows. So, by definition, reinforced behaviors increase in frequency or duration. The **reinforcement process** can be diagrammed as follows:

CONSEQUENCE   EFFECT

behavior $\rightarrow$ reinforcer $\rightarrow$ strengthened or repeated behavior

We can be fairly certain that food will be a reinforcer for a hungry animal, but what about people? It is not clear why an event acts as a reinforcer for an individual, but there are many theories about why reinforcement works. For example, some psychologists suggest that reinforcers satisfy needs, while other psychologists believe that reinforcers reduce tension or stimulate a part of the brain (Rachlin, 1991). Whether the consequences of any action are reinforcing probably depends on the individual's perception of the event and the meaning it holds for her or him. For example, students who repeatedly get themselves sent to the principal's office for misbehaving may be indicating that *something* about this consequence is reinforcing for them, even if it doesn't seem desirable to their teachers. We once worked with a principal in a middle school who was concerned about a student. The boy had lost his father a few years earlier and was having trouble in a number of subjects, especially math. The student was sent to the office from math at least twice a week. When he arrived, the boy got the principal's undivided attention for at least 10 minutes. After a scolding they talked sports because the principal liked the student and was concerned that he had no male role models. It is easy to spot the reinforcers in this situation, even though the principal did not mean to be part of the problem.

There are two types of reinforcement. The first, called **positive reinforcement,** occurs when the behavior produces a new stimulus. Examples include wearing a new outfit producing many compliments, or, for a student, falling out of the chair producing cheers and laughter from classmates. When teachers claim that a student misbehaves "just to get attention" the teachers are applying a behavioral explanation based on positive reinforcement— assuming that attention is a positive reinforcer for the student.

Notice that positive reinforcement can occur even when the behavior being reinforced (falling out of a chair or disrupting math class) is not "positive" from the teacher's point of view. In fact, positive reinforcement of inappropriate behaviors occurs unintentionally in many classrooms. Teachers and principals help maintain problem behaviors by inadvertently reinforcing them.

When the consequence that strengthens a behavior is the appearance (addition) of a new stimulus, (an object or event) the situation is defined as positive reinforcement. In contrast, when the consequence that strengthens a behavior is the disappearance (subtraction) of a stimulus, the process is called **negative reinforcement.** If a particular action leads to stopping, avoiding, or escaping an aversive situation, that action is likely to be repeated in a similar situation. A common example is the car seat belt buzzer. As soon as you attach your seat belt, the irritating buzzer stops. You are likely to *repeat* this action in the future (so the process is *reinforcement*) because the behavior made an aversive stimulus *disappear* (so the kind of reinforcement is *negative*). Consider students who continually "get sick" right before a test and are sent to the nurse's office. The behavior allows the students to escape aversive situations—tests—so getting "sick" is being maintained, in part, through negative reinforcement. It is negative because something (the test) is *escaped* or *avoided;* it is reinforcement because the behavior that caused the test to disappear (getting "sick") increases or repeats. The student who was repeatedly sent to the principal's office from math class not only spent time with the principal talking sports (positive reinforcement), he also escaped math class (negative reinforcement). Whatever the student did to get kicked out of math class is likely to continue (and it did) because the behavior led to both positive and negative reinforcers.

The "negative" in negative reinforcement does not imply that the behavior being reinforced is necessarily bad. The meaning is closer to that of "negative" numbers—something is subtracted. Associate positive and negative reinforcement with adding or subtracting something following a behavior, leading to an increase in that behavior.

Punishment.   Negative reinforcement is often confused with punishment. In fact, when you understand the difference between negative reinforcement and punishment, you will know more than most of your colleagues. The process of reinforcement (positive or negative) always involves strengthening behavior. **Punishment,** on the other hand, involves decreasing or suppressing behavior. A behavior followed by a "punisher" is *less* likely to be repeated in similar situations in the future. Again, it is the effect that defines a consequence as punishment, and different people have different perceptions of what is punishing. One student may find suspension from school punishing, while another student wouldn't mind at all. The process of punishment is diagrammed as follows:

CONSEQUENCE   EFFECT

behavior → punisher → weakened or decreased behavior

Like reinforcement, punishment may take one of two forms. The first type has been called Type I punishment, but this name isn't very informative, so we use the term **presentation punishment.** It occurs when the appearance of a stimulus following the behavior suppresses or decreases the behavior. When teachers assign demerits, extra work, running laps, and so on, they are using presentation punishment. The other type of punishment (Type II punishment) we call **removal punishment** because it involves removing a stimulus. When teachers or parents take away privileges after a young person has behaved inappropriately, they are applying removal punishment. With both types, the effect is to decrease or slow down the behavior that led to the punishment. Figure 3.1 on page 66 summarizes the processes of reinforcement and punishment we have just discussed.

Antecedents and Behavior Change

Antecedents.   The events preceding behaviors, the **antecedents,** provide information about which behaviors will lead to positive consequences and which to negative. We all learn to discriminate—to read situations. When should a principal ask the board for additional resources, after a budget cut or when a good story about the school has appeared in the local paper? The antecedent cue of a school principal standing in the hall helps students discriminate the probable consequences of running or attempting to break into a locker. We often respond to such antecedent cues without fully realizing that they are influencing our behavior. But we can use cues deliberately.

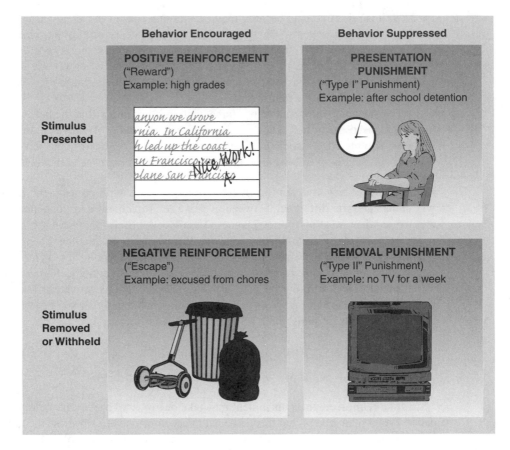

FIGURE 3.1   Kinds of Reinforcement and Punishment   Negative reinforcements and punishment are often confused. It may help you to remember that reinforcement is always associated with increases in behaviors, and punishment always involves decreasing or suppressing behavior.

Source: From Anita Woolfolk, *Educational Psychology,* 8/e. Copyright © 2001. Reprinted by permission of Allyn & Bacon.

Cueing.   By definition, **cueing** is the act of providing an antecedent stimulus just before a particular behavior is to take place. Cueing is particularly useful in setting the stage for behaviors that must occur at a specific time but are easily forgotten. In working with young people, teachers often find themselves correcting behaviors after the fact. For example, they may ask students, "When are you going to start remembering to…?" But the mistake is already made, and the young person is left with only two choices, to promise to try harder or to say, "Why don't you leave me alone?" Neither response is very satisfying. Presenting a nonjudgmental cue, such as a checklist, can help prevent these negative confrontations. When a student performs the appropriate behavior after a cue, the teacher can reinforce the student's accomplishment instead of punishing the student's failure.

Prompting.   Sometimes students need help in learning to respond to a cue in an appropriate way. One approach is to provide an additional cue, called a *prompt,* following the first cue. There are two principles for using a cue and a prompt to teach a new behavior (Becker, Engelmann, & Thomas, 1975). First, make sure the environmental stimulus that you want to become a cue occurs immediately before the prompt you are using, so students will learn to respond to the cue and not rely only on the prompt. Second, fade the prompt as soon as possible so students do not become dependent on it.

An example of cueing and prompting is providing students with a checklist or reminder sheet. Figure 3.2 is a checklist for the steps in peer tutoring. Working in pairs is the cue; the checklist is the prompt. As students learn the procedures, the teacher may stop using the checklist, but may remind the students of the steps. When no written or oral prompts are necessary, the students have learned to respond appropriately to the environmental cue of working in pairs—they have learned how to behave in tutoring situations. But the teacher should continue to monitor the process, recognize good work, and correct mistakes. Before a tutoring session, the teacher might ask students to close their eyes and "see" the checklist, focusing on each step. As students work, the teacher could listen to their interactions and continue to coach students as they improve their tutoring skills.

Principals and teachers can make good use of behavioral principles, particularly in their wise and caring applications of reinforcement and punishment. The Theory into Action Guidelines on page 69 gives examples that will help your teachers apply the behavioral theory described above. Instructional leaders not only need to know the theory; they must be able to demonstrate and apply it as they work with their teachers.

Teaching Applications of Behavioral Theories

The behavioral approach to learning has made several important contributions to instruction, including systems for specifying learning objectives (we will look at this topic in Chapter 5 when we discuss planning and teaching) and class management systems such as group consequences, token economies, contingency contracts. These approaches are especially useful when the goal is to learn explicit information or change behaviors and when the material is sequential and factual. As an example of a teaching approach, let's consider contingency contracts.

Contingency Contract Programs

In a **contingency contract** program, the teacher draws up an individual contract with each student, describing exactly what the student must do to earn a particular privilege or reward. For example, we devised a contract with the student who kept being sent to the principal's office from math class. The student, teacher, and principal agreed on specific improvements in student behavior that would allow the student to earn time with the principal. Then when the student arrived in the office, the principal could congratulate instead of criticize.

In some programs, students participate in deciding on the behaviors to be reinforced and the rewards that can be gained. The negotiating process itself can be an educational

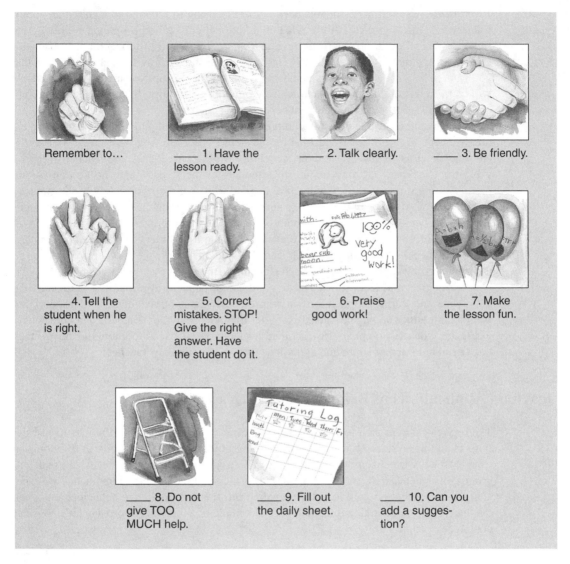

Remember to…   _____ 1. Have the lesson ready.   _____ 2. Talk clearly.   _____ 3. Be friendly.

_____ 4. Tell the student when he is right.   _____ 5. Correct mistakes. STOP! Give the right answer. Have the student do it.   _____ 6. Praise good work!   _____ 7. Make the lesson fun.

_____ 8. Do not give TOO MUCH help.   _____ 9. Fill out the daily sheet.   _____ 10. Can you add a suggestion?

FIGURE 3.2   Written Prompts: A Peer-Tutoring Checklist   By using this checklist, students are reminded how to be effective tutors. As they become more proficient, the checklist may be less necessary.

Source: From *Achieving Educational Excellence: Behavior Analysis for School Personnel* (Figure, p. 89), by B. Sulzer-Azaroff and G. R. Mayer, 1994, San Marcos, CA: Western Image, P.O. Box 427. Copyright © 1994 by Beth Sulzer-Azaroff and G. Roy Mayer. Reprinted by permission of the authors.

experience, as students learn to set reasonable goals and abide by the terms of a contract. An example of a contract for completing assignments that is appropriate for intermediate and upper-grade students is presented in Figure 3.3 (page 71). This chart serves as a contract, assignment sheet, and progress record. The few paragraphs devoted here to contingency

THEORY INTO ACTION GUIDELINES

Using Reinforcement and Punishment

Associate positive, pleasant events with learning tasks.

Examples
1. Emphasize group competition and cooperation over individual competition. Many students have negative emotional responses to individual competition that may generalize to other learning.
2. Make division drills fun by having students decide how to divide refreshments equally, then letting them eat the results.
3. Make voluntary reading appealing by creating a comfortable reading corner with pillows, colorful displays of books, and reading props such as puppets (see Morrow & Weinstein, 1986, for more ideas).

Help students to risk anxiety-producing situations voluntarily and successfully.

Examples
1. Assign a shy student the responsibility of teaching two other students how to distribute materials for map study.
2. Devise small steps toward a larger goal. For example, give ungraded practice tests daily, and then weekly, to students who tend to "freeze" in test situations.
3. If a student is afraid of speaking in front of the class, let the student read a report to a small group while seated, then read it while standing, then give the report from notes instead of reading it verbatim. Next, move in stages toward having the student give a report to the whole class.

Be clear, systematic, and genuine in giving praise.

Examples
1. Make sure praise is tied directly to appropriate behavior.
2. Make sure the student understands the specific action or accomplishment that is being praised. Say, "You returned this poster on time and in good condition," not, "You were very responsible."
3. Tie praise to students' improving competence or to the value of their accomplishment. Say, "I noticed that you double-checked all your problems. Your score reflects your careful work."

Attribute the student's success to effort and ability so the student will gain confidence that success is possible again.

Examples
1. Don't imply that the success may be based on luck, extra help, or easy material.
2. Ask students to describe the problems they encountered and how they solved them.

When students are tackling new material or trying new skills, give plenty of reinforcement.

Examples
1. Find and comment on something right in every student's first life drawing.
2. Reinforce students for encouraging each other. "French pronunciation is difficult and awkward at first. Let's help each other by eliminating all giggles when someone is brave enough to attempt a new word."

After new behaviors are established, give reinforcement on an unpredictable schedule to encourage persistence.

Examples
1. Offer surprise rewards for good participation in class.
2. Start classes with a short, written extra-credit question. Students don't have to answer, but a good answer will add points to their total for the semester.
3. Make sure the good students get compliments for their work from time to time. Don't take them for granted.

(continued)

Continued

Make sure all students, even those who often cause problems, receive some praise, privileges, or other rewards when they do something well.

Examples

1. Review your class list occasionally to make sure all students are receiving some reinforcement.
2. Set standards for reinforcement so that all students will have a chance to be rewarded.
3. Let students suggest their own reinforcers or choose from a "menu" of reinforcers with "weekly specials."

Be consistent in your application of punishment.

Examples

1. Avoid inadvertently reinforcing the behavior you are trying to punish. Keep confrontations private, so that students don't become heroes for standing up to the teacher in a public showdown.
2. Let students know in advance the consequences of breaking the rules by posting major class rules for younger students or outlining rules and consequences in a course syllabus for older students.
3. Tell students they will receive only one warning before punishment is given. Give the warning in a calm way, then follow through.
4. Make punishment as unavoidable and immediate as is reasonably possible.

Focus on the students' actions, not on the students' personal qualities.

Examples

1. Reprimand in a calm but firm voice.
2. Avoid vindictive or sarcastic words or tones of voice. You might hear your own angry words later when students imitate your sarcasm.
3. Stress the need to end the problem behavior instead of expressing any dislike you might feel for the student.

Adapt the punishment to the infraction.

Examples

1. Ignore minor misbehaviors that do not disrupt the class, or stop these misbehaviors with a disapproving glance or a move toward the student.
2. Don't use homework as a punishment for misbehaviors like talking in class.
3. When a student misbehaves to gain peer acceptance, removal from the group of friends can be effective, since this is really time out from a reinforcing situation.
4. If the problem behaviors continue, analyze the situation and try a new approach. Your punishment may not be very punishing, or you may be inadvertently reinforcing the misbehavior.

---

contracts can offer only an introduction to these programs. If you want to set up a large-scale reward program in your school, the school psychologist often can help. In addition, remember that, applied inappropriately, external rewards can undermine the students' motivation to learn (Deci, 1975; Lepper & Greene, 1978).

Cognitive Views of Learning

The cognitive perspective is both the oldest and youngest explanation of learning. It is old because discussions of the nature of knowledge, the value of reason, and the contents of the mind date back at least to the ancient Greek philosophers (Hernshaw, 1987). From the late

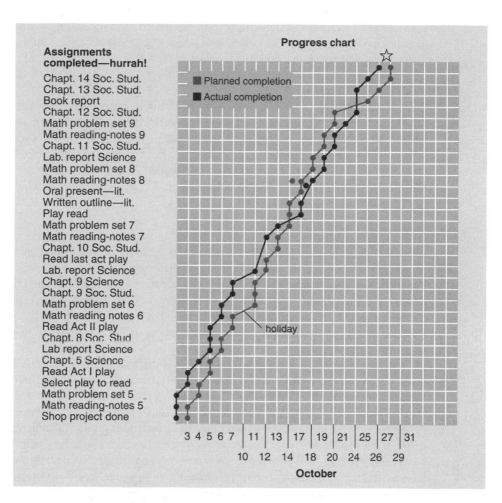

Progress chart

Assignments completed—hurrah!

Chapt. 14 Soc. Stud.
Chapt. 13 Soc. Stud.
Book report
Chapt. 12 Soc. Stud.
Math problem set 9
Math reading-notes 9
Chapt. 11 Soc. Stud.
Lab. report Science
Math problem set 8
Math reading-notes 8
Oral present—lit.
Written outline—lit.
Play read
Math problem set 7
Math reading-notes 7
Chapt. 10 Soc. Stud.
Read last act play
Lab. report Science
Chapt. 9 Science
Chapt. 9 Soc. Stud.
Math problem set 6
Math reading notes 6
Read Act II play
Chapt. 8 Soc. Stud.
Lab report Science
Chapt. 5 Science
Read Act I play
Select play to read
Math problem set 5
Math reading-notes 5
Shop project done

■ Planned completion
■ Actual completion

holiday

3 4 5 6 7 11 13 17 19 21 25 27 31
10 12 14 18 20 24 26 29
October

FIGURE 3.3   A Contingency Contract for Completing Assignments   The teacher and student agree on the due dates for each assignment, marking them in gray on the chart. Each time an assignment is turned in, the date of completion is marked in black on the chart. As long as the actual completion line is above the planned completion line, the student earns free time or other contracted rewards.

Source: From *Achieving Educational Excellence: Behavior Analysis for School Personnel* (Figure, p. 89), by B. Sulzer-Azaroff and G. R. Mayer, 1994, San Marcos, CA: Western Image, P.O. Box 427. Copyright © 1994 by Beth Sulzer-Azaroff and G. Roy Mayer. Reprinted with permission of Beth Sulzer-Azaroff.

1800s until a few decades ago, however, cognitive studies fell from favor and behaviorism thrived. Then, research during World War II on the development of complex human skills, the computer revolution, and breakthroughs in understanding language development all stimulated a resurgence in cognitive research. Evidence accumulated indicating that people do more than simply respond to reinforcement and punishment. For example, we plan our responses, use systems to help us remember, and organize the material we are learning in our own unique ways (Miller, Galanter, & Pribram, 1960; Shuell, 1986). With the growing realization that learning is an active mental process, educational psychologists became interested in how people think, learn concepts, and solve problems (e.g., Ausubel, 1963; Bruner, Goodnow, & Austin, 1956).

Interest in concept learning and problem solving soon gave way, however, to interest in how knowledge is represented in the mind and particularly how it is remembered. Remembering and forgetting became major topics for investigation in cognitive psychology in the 1970s and 80s, and the information processing model of memory dominated research. Today, there are other models of memory besides information processing. In addition, many cognitive theorists have a renewed interest in learning, thinking, and problem solving.

Knowledge and Learning

Current cognitive approaches suggest that one of the most important elements in the learning process is what the individual brings to the learning situation. What we already know determines to a great extent what we will pay attention to, perceive, learn, remember, and forget (Alexander, 1996; Greeno, Collins, & Resnick, 1996; Resnick, 1981; Shuell, 1986). Pat Alexander (1996) notes that what we already know—our knowledge base—"is a scaffold that supports the construction of all future learning" (p. 89). Thus knowledge is more than the end product of previous learning; it also guides new learning.

A study by Recht and Leslie (1988) shows the importance of knowledge in understanding and remembering new information. These researchers identified junior high school students who were either very good or very poor readers. They tested the students on their knowledge of baseball and found that knowledge of baseball was not related to reading ability. So the researchers were able to identify four groups of students: good readers/high baseball knowledge, good readers/low baseball knowledge, poor readers/high baseball knowledge, and poor readers/low baseball knowledge. Then all the subjects read a passage describing a baseball game and were tested in a number of ways to see if they understood and remembered what they had read.

The results demonstrated the power of knowledge. Poor readers who knew baseball remembered more than good readers with little baseball knowledge and almost as much as good readers who knew baseball. Poor readers who knew little about baseball remembered the least of what they had read. So a good basis of knowledge can be more important than good learning strategies in understanding and remembering—but extensive knowledge plus good strategies are even better.

There are different kinds of knowledge. Some is general—it applies to many different situations. For example, general knowledge about how to read or write or use a word processor is useful in and out of school. **Domain-specific knowledge,** on the other hand, pertains to a particular task or subject. For example, knowing that the shortstop plays between second and third base is specific to the domain of baseball. Another way of categorizing knowledge is as declarative, procedural, or conditional (Paris & Cunningham, 1996; Paris, Lipson, & Wixson, 1983). **Declarative knowledge** is "knowledge that can be declared, usually in words, through lectures, books, writing, verbal exchange, Braille, sign language, mathematical notation, and so on" (Farnham-Diggory, 1994, p. 468). Declarative knowledge is "knowing that" something is the case. The range of declarative knowledge is tremendous. You can know very specific facts (the atomic weight of gold is 196.967), or generalities (leaves of some trees change color in autumn), or personal preferences (I don't like lima beans), or personal events (what happened at the last faculty meeting), or rules (to divide fractions, invert the divisor and multiply). Small units of declarative knowledge can be organized into larger units; for example, principles of reinforcement and punishment can be organized in your thinking into a theory of behavioral learning (Gagné, Yekovich, & Yekovich, 1993).

Procedural knowledge is "knowing how" to do something such as divide fractions or clean a carburetor—procedural knowledge must be demonstrated. Notice that repeating the rule "to divide fractions, invert the divisor and multiply" shows declarative knowledge—the student can state the rule. But to show procedural knowledge, the student must act. When faced with a fraction to divide, the student must divide correctly. Students or teachers demonstrate procedural knowledge when they translate a passage into Spanish or correctly categorize a geometric shape or craft a coherent paragraph.

Conditional knowledge is "knowing when and why" to apply your declarative and procedural knowledge. Given many kinds of math problems, it takes conditional knowledge to know when to apply one procedure and when to apply another to solve each problem. It takes conditional knowledge to know when to read every word in a text and when to skim or when to intervene when new teachers are struggling and when to hold back and let the teachers work it out for themselves. For many people, conditional knowledge is a stumbling block. They have the facts and can do the procedures, but they don't seem to apply what they know at the appropriate time. Table 3.1 shows that we can combine our two systems for describing knowledge. Declarative, procedural, and conditional knowledge can be either general or domain-specific.

To be used, knowledge must be remembered. What do we know about memory?

An Information Processing Model

One widely used cognitive model of the structure and processes of memory is the information processing model, based on the analogy between the mind and the computer. This model (see Figure 3.4) includes three storage systems: the sensory register, working

TABLE 3.1   Kinds of Knowledge

	General Knowledge	Domain-Specific Knowledge
Declarative	Hours the library is open Rules of grammar	The definition of "hypotenuse" The lines of the poem "The Raven"
Procedural	How to use your word processor How to drive	How to solve an oxidation-reduction equation How to throw a pot on a potter's wheel
Conditional	When to give up and try another approach When to skim and when to read carefully	When to use the formula for calculating volume When to rush the net in tennis

Source: From Anita Woolfolk, *Educational Psychology, 8/e,* Copyright © 2001. Reprinted by permission of Allyn & Bacon.

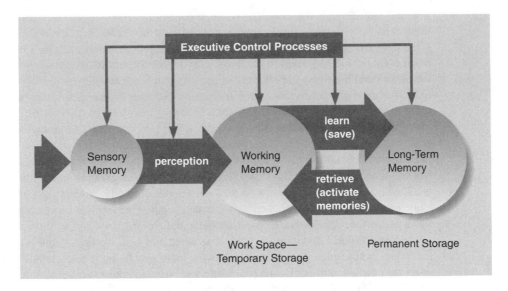

FIGURE 3.4   The Information Processing System   Information is encoded in the sensory register where perception determines what will be held in working memory for further use. Thoroughly processed information becomes part of long-term memory and can be activated at any time to return to working memory.

Source: From Anita Woolfolk, *Educational Psychology, 8/e.* Copyright © 2001. Reprinted by permission of Allyn & Bacon.

memory (also called short-term memory), and long-term memory. Working memory holds five to nine bits of information at a time for up to about 20 seconds—long enough for processing to occur. Long-term memory seems to hold an unlimited amount of information permanently. Information may be coded only verbally or both verbally and visually. In long-term memory, bits of information may be stored and interrelated in terms of images and schemas—data structures that allow us to represent large amounts of complex information, make inferences, and understand new information.

Information is retrieved from long-term memory through the spread of activation, as one memory activates other related information. Remembering is a reconstruction process leading to accurate, partly accurate, or inaccurate recall. Accurate retrieval depends in part on how the information was learned in the first place. Let's look at this system in more depth.

Sensory Memory

The meaning we attach to the raw information received through our senses is called perception. This meaning is constructed based on both objective reality and our existing knowledge. For example, consider these marks: **I3**. If asked what the letter is, you would say "B." If asked what the number is, you would say "13." The actual marks remain the same; the perception of them—their meaning—changes in keeping with your expectation to recognize a number or a letter. To a child without appropriate knowledge to perceive either a number or a letter, the marks would probably be meaningless (Smith, F., 1975). To recognize patterns rapidly, in addition to noting specific features, we use what we already know about the situation—what we know about words or pictures or the way the world generally operates.

If every variation in color, movement, sound, smell, temperature, and so on had to be perceived, life would be impossible. By paying attention to certain stimuli and ignoring others, we select what we will process from all the possibilities. But attention is a very limited resource. We can pay attention to only one demanding task at time (Anderson, 1995). For example, if you learned to drive a stick shift, there probably was a time when you couldn't listen to the radio and drive at the same time. After some practice, you could listen, but might turn the radio off when traffic was heavy. After years of practice, some people shave or put on make-up as they drive. This is because many processes that initially require attention and concentration become automatic with practice. Actually, automaticity probably is a matter of degree—we are not completely automatic but rather more or less automatic in our performances depending on how much practice we have had (Anderson, 1995).

The first step in learning is paying attention. Students cannot process something that they do not recognize or perceive. Many factors in the classroom influence student attention. Eye-catching or startling displays or actions can draw attention at the beginning of a lesson. A teacher might begin a science lesson on air pressure by blowing up a balloon until it pops. Bright colors, underlining, highlighting of written or spoken words, calling students by name, surprise events, intriguing questions, variety in tasks and teaching methods, and changes in voice level, lighting, or pacing can all be used to gain attention. And students have to maintain attention—they have to stay focused on the important features of the learning situation. How can instructional leaders help teachers develop strategies for capturing and maintaining students' attention? The following Theory into Action Guidelines provides some concrete examples.

Working Memory

Once noticed and transformed into patterns, the information in sensory memory is available for further processing. **Working memory** is the "workbench" of the memory system, the component of memory where new information is held temporarily and combined with knowledge from long-term memory. Working memory is like the workspace or screen of a computer: Its content is activated information—what you are thinking about at the moment. For this reason, some psychologists consider the working memory to be synonymous with "consciousness."

Capacity and Contents.   Working memory capacity is limited. In experimental situations it appears that the capacity of working memory is only about five to nine separate new items at once (Miller, 1956). For example, if you get a phone number from information, you can remember it long enough to dial the number, but would you try to remember two numbers? Two new phone numbers (14 digits) probably cannot be stored simultaneously. We are discussing the recall of *new* information. In daily life we certainly can hold more than five to nine bits of information at once. While you are dialing that seven-digit phone number you

THEORY INTO ACTION GUIDELINES

Capturing Attention

Use Signals.

Examples
1. Develop a signal that tells students to stop what they are doing and focus on you. Some teachers move to a particular spot in the room, flick the lights, or play a chord on the class piano.
2. Avoid distracting behaviors such as tapping a pencil that interfere with both signals and attention to learning.
3. Give short, clear directions before, not during, transitions.

Make sure the purpose of the lesson or assignment is clear to students.

Examples
1. Write the goals or objectives on the board and discuss them with students before starting. Ask students to summarize or restate the goals.
2. Explain the reasons for learning, and ask students for examples of how they will apply their understanding of the material.
3. Tie the new material to previous lessons— show an outline or map of how the new topic fits with previous and upcoming material.

Emphasize variety, curiosity, and surprise.

Examples
1. Arouse curiosity with questions such as "What would happen if…?"

2. Create shock by staging an unexpected event such as a loud argument just before a lesson on communication.
3. Alter the physical environment by changing the arrangement of the room or moving to a different setting.
4. Shift sensory channels by giving a lesson that requires students to touch, smell, or taste.
5. Use movements, gestures, and voice inflection—walk around the room, point, and speak softly and then more emphatically. (The second author has been known to jump up on his desk to make an important point in his college classes!)

Ask questions and provide frames for answering.

Examples
1. Ask students why the material is important, how they intend to study, and what strategies they will use.
2. Give students self-checking or self-editing guides that focus on common mistakes or have them work in pairs to improve each other's work—sometimes it is difficult to pay attention to your own errors.

just found, you are bound to have other things "on your mind" (in your memory), such as how to use a telephone, whom you are calling, and why. You don't have to pay attention to these things; they are not new knowledge. Some of the processes, such as dialing the phone, have become automatic. However, because of the working memory's limitations, if you were in a foreign country and were attempting to use an unfamiliar telephone system, you might very well have trouble remembering the phone number because you were trying to figure out the phone system at the same time.

Some psychologists argue that working memory is limited not by the number of bits of information it can store, but by the amount of information we can rehearse (repeat to ourselves) in about 1.5 seconds (Baddeley, 1986). The seven-digit telephone number fits this limitation. Recent theories suggest that there are actually two working memory systems—one for language-based information and another for nonverbal, spatial, visual information (Baddeley, 1986; Jurden, 1995).

It is clear that the duration of information in working memory is short, about 5 to 20 seconds. This is why working memory has been called short-term memory. It may seem to you that a memory system with a 20-second time limit is not very useful. But without this system, you would have already forgotten what you read in the first part of this sentence before you came to these last few words. This would clearly make understanding sentences difficult.

Retaining Information in Working Memory.   Because information in working memory is fragile and easily lost, it must be kept activated to be retained. When activation fades, forgetting follows. To keep information activated in working memory for longer than 20 seconds, most people keep rehearsing the information mentally.

There are two types of rehearsal (Craik & Lockhart, 1972). **Maintenance rehearsal** involves repeating the information in your mind. As long as you repeat the information, it can be maintained in working memory indefinitely. Maintenance rehearsal is useful for retaining something you plan to use and then forget, like a phone number. **Elaborative rehearsal** involves connecting the information you are trying to remember with something you already know, that is, with information from long-term memory. For example, if you meet someone at a party whose name is the same as yours, you don't have to repeat the name to keep it in memory, you just have to make the association. This kind of rehearsal not only retains information in working memory but helps move information from short-term to long-term memory. Rehearsal is thus an *executive control process* that affects the flow of information through the information processing system.

The limited capacity of working memory can also be somewhat circumvented by the control process of **chunking.** Because the number of bits of information, not the size of each bit, is the limitation for working memory, you can retain more information if you can group individual bits of information. For example, if you have to remember the six digits 3, 5, 4, 8, 7, and 0, it is easier to put them together into three chunks of two digits each (35, 48, 70) or two chunks of three digits each (354, 870). With these changes, there are only two or three bits of information rather than six to hold at one time. Chunking helps you remember a telephone number or a Social Security number.

Long-Term Memory

Working memory holds the information that is currently activated, such as a telephone number you have just found and are about to dial. Long-term memory holds the information that is well learned, such as all the other telephone numbers you know.

Capacity and Duration of Long-Term Memory.   Information enters working memory very quickly. To move information into long-term storage requires more time and a bit of effort. Whereas the capacity of working memory is limited, the capacity of long-term memory appears to be, for all practical purposes, unlimited. In addition, once information is securely stored in long-term memory, it can remain there permanently. Theoretically, we should be able to remember as much as we want for as long as we want. Of course, the problem is finding the right information when it is needed. Our access to information in working memory is immediate because we are thinking about the information at that very moment. But access to information in long-term memory requires time and effort.

Contents of Long-Term Memory.   Most cognitive psychologists distinguish three categories of long-term memory: episodic, procedural, and semantic. Memory for information tied to a particular place and time, especially information about the events of your own life, is called episodic memory. **Episodic memory** keeps track of the order of things, so it is also a good place to store jokes, gossip, or plots from films. Memory for how to do things is called **procedural memory.** It may take a while to learn a procedure—such as how to ski, serve a tennis ball, or factor an equation—but once learned, this knowledge tends to be remembered for a long time. Procedural memories are represented as condition–action rules, sometimes called *productions*. Productions specify what to do under certain conditions: if A occurs, then do B. A production might be something like, "If you want to snow ski faster, lean back slightly," or "If your goal is to increase student attention, and a student has been paying attention a bit longer than usual, then praise the student." People can't necessarily state all their condition–action rules, but they act on them nevertheless. The more practiced the procedure, the more automatic the action (Anderson, 1995). **Semantic memory** is memory for meaning. Two important ways that these memories are stored are images and schemas. Because these are very important concepts for teaching, we will spend some extra time on them.

Images are representations based on perceptions—on the structure or appearance of the information (Anderson, 1995). As we form images we try to remember or recreate the physical attributes and spatial structure of information. For example, when asked how many windowpanes are in their living room, most people call up an image of the windows "in their mind's eye" and count the panes—the more panes, the longer it takes to respond (Mendell, 1971). Images are useful in making many practical decisions such as how a sofa might look in your living room or how to line up a golf shot. Images may also be helpful in abstract reasoning. Physicists, such as Faraday and Einstein, report creating images to reason about complex new problems (Gagné, Yekovich, & Yekovich, 1993).

Schemas (sometimes called "schemata") are abstract knowledge structures that organize vast amounts of information. A schema (the singular form) is a pattern or guide for understanding an event, a concept, or a skill.

The schema tells you what features are typical of a category, what to expect. The schema is like a pattern, specifying the "standard" relationships in an object or situation. The pattern has "slots" that are filled with specific information as we apply the schema in a particular situation. And schemas are individual. For example, a museum curator and a salesperson may have very different schemas about antiques.

Another type of schema, a *story grammar* (sometimes called a schema for text or story structure) helps students to understand and remember stories (Gagné, Yekovich, & Yekovich, 1993; Rumelhart & Ortony, 1977). A story grammar could be something like this: murder discovered, search for clues, murderer's fatal mistake identified, trap set to trick suspect into confessing, murderer takes bait…mystery solved! In other words, a story grammar is a typical general structure that could fit many specific stories. To comprehend a story, we select a schema that seems appropriate. Then we use this framework to decide which details are important, what information to seek, and what to remember. It is as though the schema is a theory about what should occur in the story. The schema guides us in "interrogating" the text, filling in the specific information we expect to find so that the story makes sense. If we activate our "murder mystery schema" we may be alert for clues or a murderer's fatal mistake (Resnick, 1981). Without the appropriate schema, trying to understand a story, textbook, or classroom lesson is a very slow, difficult process, something like finding your way through a new town without a map.

A schema representing the typical sequence of events in an everyday situation is called a *script* or an *event schema.* Children as young as 3 have basic scripts for the familiar events in their lives (Nelson, 1986).

Storing and Retrieving Information in Long-Term Memory

Just what is done to "save" information permanently—to create semantic, episodic, or procedural, memories? How can we make the most effective use of our practically unlimited capacity to learn and remember? The way you learn information in the first place—the way you process it at the outset—seems to affect its recall later. One important requirement is that you integrate new material with information already stored in long-term memory as you construct an understanding. Here elaboration, organization, and context play a role.

Elaboration is the addition of meaning to new information through its connection with already existing knowledge. In other words, we apply our schemas and draw on already existing knowledge to construct an understanding and often change our existing knowledge in the process. We often elaborate automatically. For example, a paragraph about an historic figure in the 17th century tends to activate our existing knowledge about that period; we use the old knowledge to understand the new.

Material that is elaborated when first learned will be easier to recall later. First, as we saw earlier, elaboration is a form of rehearsal. It keeps the information activated in working memory long enough to have a chance for permanent storage in long-term memory. Second, elaboration builds extra links to existing knowledge. The more one bit of information or knowledge is associated with other bits, the more routes there are to follow to get to the original bit. To put it another way, you have several "handles," or retrieval cues, by which you can recognize or "pick up" the information you might be seeking (Schunk, 2000). The more students elaborate new ideas, the more they "make them their own," the deeper their understanding and the better their memory for the knowledge. We help students to elaborate when we ask them to translate information into their own words, create examples, explain to a peer, draw the relationships, or apply the information to solve new problems. Of course, if students elaborate new information by making incorrect connections or developing misguided explanations, these misconceptions will be stored and remembered too.

Organization is a second element of processing that improves learning. Material that is well organized is easier to learn and to remember than bits and pieces of information, especially if the information is complex or extensive. Placing a concept in a structure will help you learn and remember either general definitions or specific examples. The structure serves as a guide back to the information when you need it. For example, Table 3.1 (on page 73) organizes information about kinds of knowledge.

Context is a third element of processing that influences learning. Aspects of physical and emotional context—places, rooms, how we are feeling on a particular day, who is with us—are learned along with other information (Ashcraft, 2002). Later, if you try to remember the information, it will be easier if the current context is similar to the original one. So studying for a test under "testlike" conditions may result in improved performance. Of course, you can't always go back to the same place you learned in order to recall something. But you can picture the setting, the time of day, and your companions, and you may eventually reach the information you seek.

Craik and Lockhart (1972) suggested that what determines how long information is remembered is how completely the information is analyzed and connected with other information. The more completely information is processed, the better our chances of remembering it. For example, according to the levels of processing theory, if you were asked to sort pictures of dogs based on the color of their coats, you might not remember many of the pictures later. But if asked to rate each dog on how likely it is to chase you as you jog, you probably would remember more of the pictures. To rate the dogs as dangerous you must pay attention to details in the pictures, relate features of the dogs to characteristics associated with danger, and so on. This rating procedure requires "deeper" processing and more focus on the meaning of the features in the photos.

Retrieving Information from Long-Term Memory.

When we need to use information from long-term memory, we search for it. Sometimes the search is conscious, as when you see a friend approaching and you search for her name. At other times locating and using information from long-term memory is automatic, as when you call your home or solve a math problem without having to search for each step. Think of long-term memory as a huge shelf full of tools and supplies ready to be brought to the workbench of working memory to accomplish a task. The shelf (long-term memory) stores an incredible amount, but it may be hard to quickly find what you are looking for. The workbench (working memory) is small, but anything on it is immediately available. Because it is small, however, supplies (bits of information) sometimes are lost when the workbench overflows or when one bit of information covers (interferes with) another (Gagné, 1985).

The size of the long-term memory network is huge, but only one small area is activated at any one time. Only the information we are currently thinking about is in working memory. Information is retrieved in this network through the spread of activation. When particular information is active—when we are thinking about it—other closely associated knowledge can be activated as well, and activation can spread through the network (Anderson, 1993; Gagné, Yekovich, & Yekovich, 1993). Thus, as you focus on the thought, "I'd like to go for a drive to see the fall leaves today," related ideas such as, "I should rake leaves," and "The car needs an oil change," come to mind. As activation spreads from the "car trip" to the "oil change," the original thought, or active memory, disappears from working memory because of the limited space.

In long-term memory the information is still available, even when it is not activated, even when you are not thinking about it at the moment. If spreading activation does not "find" the information we seek, then we might still come up with the answer through *reconstruction,* a problem-solving process that makes use of logic, cues, and other knowledge to construct a reasonable answer by filling in any missing parts. Sometimes reconstructed recollections are incorrect. For example, in 1932, F. C. Bartlett conducted a series of famous studies on remembering stories. He read a complex, unfamiliar Native American tale to students at England's Cambridge University and after various lengths of time, asked the students to recall the story. Students' recalled stories were generally shorter than the original and were translated into the concepts and language of the Cambridge student culture. The story told of a seal hunt, for instance, but many students remembered "a fishing trip," an activity closer to their experiences and more consistent with their schemas.

Forgetting and Long-Term Memory.   Information lost from working memory truly disappears. No amount of effort will bring it back. But information stored in long-term memory may be available, given the right cues. Some researchers believe that nothing is ever lost from long-term memory; but research casts doubts on this assertion (Schwartz & Reisberg, 1991). Information appears to be lost from long-term memory through time decay and interference. For example, memory for Spanish–English vocabulary decreases for about 3 years after a person's last course in Spanish, then stays level for about 25 years, then drops again for the next 25 years. One explanation for this decline is that neural connections, like muscles, grow weak without use (Anderson, 1995). Finally, newer memories may interfere with or obscure older memories, and older memories may interfere with memory for new material.

Even with decay and interference, long-term memory is remarkable. In a review of almost 100 studies of memory for knowledge taught in school, Semb and Ellis (1994) concluded that, "contrary to popular belief, students retain much of the knowledge taught in the classroom" (p. 279). It appears that teaching strategies that encourage student engagement and lead to higher levels of initial learning (such as frequent reviews and tests, elaborated feedback, high standards, mastery learning, and active involvement in learning projects) are associated with longer retention. What can instructional leaders do to use the principles of information processing to improve instruction? See the Theory into Action Guidelines suggestions on the next page.

Metacognition Regulation, and Individual Differences

One question that intrigues many educators and cognitive psychologists is why some people learn and remember more than others. For those who hold an information processing view, part of the answer lies in the executive control processes shown earlier in Figure 3.4. **Executive control processes** guide the flow of information through the information processing system. We have already discussed a number of control processes, including selective attention, maintenance rehearsal, elaborative rehearsal, organization, and elaboration. These executive control processes are sometimes called metacognitive skills, because the processes can be intentionally used to regulate cognition.

Metacognitive Knowledge and Regulation.   Donald Meichenbaum and his colleagues describe **metacognition** as people's "awareness of their own cognitive machinery and how the machinery works" (Meichenbaum, Burland, Gruson, & Cameron, 1985, p. 5). Metacognition literally means cognition about cognition—or knowledge about knowledge. This

THEORY INTO ACTION GUIDELINES

Applying Information Processing

Make sure you have the students' attention.

Examples

1. Develop a signal that tells students to stop what they are doing and focus on you. Make sure students respond to the signal—don't let them ignore it. Practice using the signal.
2. Move around the room, use gestures, and avoid speaking in a monotone.
3. Begin a lesson by asking a question that stimulates interest in the topic.
4. Regain the attention of individual students by walking closer to them, using their names, or asking them a question.

Help students separate essential from nonessential details and focus on the most important information.

Examples

1. Summarize instructional objectives to indicate what students should be learning. Relate the material you are presenting to the objectives as you teach: "Now I'm going to explain exactly how you can find the information you need to meet Objective One on the board—determining the tone of the story."
2. When you make an important point, pause, repeat, ask a student to paraphrase, note the information on the board in colored chalk, or tell students to highlight the point in their notes or readings.

Help students make connections between new information and what they already know.

Examples

1. Review prerequisites to help students bring to mind the information they will need to understand new material: "Who can tell us the definition of a quadrilateral? Now, what is a rhombus? Is a square a quadrilateral? Is a square a rhombus? What did we say yes-

terday about how you can tell? Today we are going to look at some other quadrilaterals."
2. Use an outline or diagram to show how new information fits with the framework you have been developing. For example, "Now that you know the duties of the FBI, where would you expect to find it in this diagram of the branches of the U.S. government?
3. Give an assignment that specifically calls for the use of new information along with information already learned.

Provide for repetition and review of information.

Examples

1. Begin the class with a quick review of the homework assignment.
2. Give frequent, short tests.
3. Build practice and repetition into games, or have students work with partners to quiz each other.

Present material in a clear, organized way.

Examples

1. Make the purpose of the lesson very clear.
2. Give students a brief outline to follow. Put the same outline on an overhead so you can keep yourself on track. When students ask questions or make comments, relate these to the appropriate section of the outline.
3. Use summaries in the middle and at the end of the lesson.

Focus on meaning, not memorization.

Examples

1. In teaching new words, help students associate the new word to a related word they already understand: "*Enmity* is from the same base as *enemy.*..."
2. In teaching about remainders, have students group 12 objects into sets of 2, 3, 4, 5, 6, and ask them to count the "leftovers" in each case.

knowledge is used to monitor and regulate cognitive processes—reasoning, comprehension, problem solving, learning, and so on. Because people differ in their metacognitive knowledge and skills, they differ in how well and how quickly they learn (Brown, Branford, Ferra, & Campione, 1983; Morris, P. F., 1990).

There are three essential metacognitive skills: planning, monitoring, and evaluation (Brown, 1987; Nelson, 1996). *Planning* involves deciding how much time to give to a task, which strategies to use, how to start, what resources to gather, what order to follow, what to skim and what to give intense attention, and so on. *Monitoring* is the on-line awareness of "how I'm doing." Monitoring means asking, "Is this making sense? Am I trying to go too fast? Have I studied enough? *Evaluation* involves making judgments about the processes and outcomes of thinking and learning. Should I change strategies? Get help? Give up for now? Is this report (proposal, painting, formula, model, poem, dance, plan, etc.) finished yet or does it need more work? Many planning, monitoring, and evaluation processes are not necessarily conscious. Especially in adults, these processes can be automatic. Experts in a field may plan, monitor, and evaluate as second nature— they have difficulty describing their metacognitive knowledge and skills (Schraw & Moshman, 1995).

Individual Differences in Metacognition.   Some differences in metacognitive abilities are due to development. Metacognitive abilities begin to develop around ages 5 to 7 and improve throughout school. Most children go through a transitional period when they can apply a particular strategy if reminded, but will not apply it on their own (Flavell, 1985; Flavell, Green, & Flavell, 1995; Garner, 1990). Nancy Perry found that asking students two questions helped them become more metacognitive. The questions were: "What did you learn about yourself as a reader/writer today?" and "What did you learn that you can do again and again and again?" When teachers asked these questions regularly during class, even young students demonstrated fairly sophisticated levels of metacognitive understanding and action (Perry, VandeKamp, & Mercer, 2000).

Not all differences in metacognitive abilities have to do with age or maturation. Some individual differences probably are caused by biological differences or by variations in learning experiences. In fact, many students diagnosed as having learning disabilities actually have attention disorders (Hallahan & Kauffman, 2000), particularly with long tasks (Pelham, 1981). Thus there is great variability even among students of the same developmental level, but these differences do not appear to be related to intellectual abilities. In fact, superior metacognitive skills can compensate for lower levels of ability, so these metacognitive skills can be especially important for students who often have trouble in school (Swanson, 1990).

Cognitive Contributions: Learning Strategies and Tactics

One of the most important applications of cognitive theories is teaching students how to learn and remember by using learning strategies and tactics. Learning strategies are ideas for accomplishing learning goals, a kind of overall plan of attack. Learning tactics are the specific techniques that make up the plan (Derry, 1989). For example, if you are reading this chapter for a graduate class, your strategy for learning the material might include the tactics of using mnemonics to remember key terms, skimming the chapter to identify the organization, and then writing sample answers to possible essay questions. But do teachers actually focus on teaching students how to learn? Research indicates such instruction seldom is provided. As Norman (1982) pointed out:

> It is strange that we expect students to learn yet seldom teach them about learning. We expect students to solve problems yet seldom teach them about problem solving. And, similarly, we sometimes require students to remember a considerable body of material yet seldom teaching them the art of memory.... We need to develop the general principles of how to learn, how to remember, how to solve problems, and then to develop applied courses, and then to establish the place of these methods in the academic curriculum. (p. 209)

Several principles have been identified for teaching learning strategies.

- Students must be exposed to a number of *different strategies,* not only general learning strategies but also very specific tactics, such as the graphic strategies described later in this chapter.
- *Teach conditional knowledge* about when, where, and why to use various strategies (Pressley, 1986). Although this may seem obvious, teachers often neglect this step, either because they do not realize its significance or because they assume students will make inferences on their own. A strategy is more likely to be maintained and employed if students know when, where, and why to use it.
- Students may know when and how to use a strategy, but unless they also *develop the desire to employ these skills,* general learning ability will not improve. Several learning strategy programs (Borkowski, Johnston, & Reid, 1986; Dansereau, 1985) include a motivational training component.
- *Direct instruction in schematic knowledge* is often an important component of strategy training. In order to identify main ideas—a critical skill for a number of learning strategies—students must have an appropriate schema for making sense of the material. Table 3.2 summarizes several tactics for learning declarative (verbal) knowledge and procedural skills (Derry, 1989).

Deciding What Is Important

As indicated in the first entry in Table 3.2, learning begins with focusing attention—deciding what is important. But distinguishing the main idea from less important information is not always easy. Often students focus on the "seductive details" or the concrete examples, perhaps because they are more interesting (Dole, Duffy, Roehler, & Pearson, 1991; Gardner, Brown, Sanders, & Menke, 1992). Finding the central idea is especially difficult if you lack prior knowledge in an area and the amount of new information provided is extensive. Teachers can give students practice in using signals in texts such as headings, bold words, outlines, or other indicators to identify key concepts and main ideas. Teaching students to summarize material can be helpful too.

TABLE 3.2 Examples of Learning Tactics

	Examples	Use When?
Tactics for Learning Verbal Information	**1.** Attention Focusing	
	■ Making outlines, underlining	With easy, structured materials; for good readers
	■ Looking for headings and topic sentences	For poorer readers; with more difficult materials
	2. Schema Building	
	■ Story grammars	With poor text structure, goal is to encourage active comprehension
	■ Theory schemas	
	■ Networking and mapping	
	3. Idea Elaboration	
	■ Self-questioning	To understand and remember specific ideas
	■ Imagery	
Tactics for Learning Procedural Information	**1.** Pattern Learning	
	■ Hypothesizing	To learn attributes of concepts
	■ Identifying reasons for actions	To match procedures to situations
	2. Self-instruction	
	■ Comparing own performance to expert model	To tune, improve complex skills
	3. Practice	
	■ Part practice	When few specific aspects of a performance need attention
	■ Whole practice	To maintain and improve skill

Source: Based on "Putting Learning Strategies to Work," by S. Derry, 1989, *Educational Leadership, 47*(5), pp. 5–6.

Summaries.   Creating summaries can help students learn, but students have to be taught how to summarize (Byrnes, 1996; Dole et al., 1991; Palincsar & Brown, 1989). Jeanne Ormrod (1999, p. 333) summarizes these suggestions for helping students create summaries:

- Begin doing summaries of short, easy, well-organized readings. Introduce longer, less organized and more difficult passages gradually.
- For each summary, ask students to find or write a *topic sentence* for each paragraph or section, identify *big ideas* that cover several specific points, find some *supporting information* for each big idea, and delete any *redundant information* or unnecessary details.
- Ask students to compare their summaries and discuss what ideas they thought were important and why—what's their evidence?

Two other study strategies that are based on identifying key ideas are *underlining* texts and *taking notes*.

Underlining and Highlighting.   Underlining and note taking are probably two of the most commonly used strategies among high school and college students. Yet few students receive any instruction in the best ways to take notes or underline, so it is not surprising that many students use ineffective strategies.

One common problem is that students underline or highlight too much. It is far better to be selective. In studies that limit how much students can underline—for example, only one sentence per paragraph—learning has improved (Snowman, 1984). In addition to being selective, students also should actively transform the information into their own words as they underline or take notes. Teach students not to rely on the words of the book. Encourage them to note connections between what they are reading and other things that they already know. Draw diagrams to illustrate relationships. Finally, look for organizational patterns in the material and use them to guide underlining or note taking (Irwin, 1991; Kiewra, 1988).

Taking Notes.   Research indicates that taking notes serves at least two important functions:

- Taking notes focuses attention during class and helps encode information so it has a chance of making it to long-term memory. In order to record key ideas in your own words, you have to translate, connect, elaborate, and organize. Of course, if taking notes distracts them from actually listening to and making sense of the lecture, then note taking may not be effective (DiVesta & Gray, 1972, Kiewra, 1989; Van Meter, Yokoi, & Pressley, 1994).
- Notes provide extended external storage that allows students to return and review. Students who use their notes to study tend to perform better on tests, especially if they take many high quality notes—more is better as long as the students are capturing key ideas, concepts, and relationships, not just intriguing details (Kiewra, 1985, 1989).

To help students organize their note taking, some teachers provide matrices or maps, such as the one in Figure 3.5. When students are first learning to use these maps, teachers often fill in some of the spaces for them. Also, it is helpful for students to exchange their filled-in maps and explain their thinking to each other.

Visual Tools for Organizing

To use underlining and note taking effectively, students must identify main ideas. In addition, effective use of underlining and note taking depends on an understanding of the organization of the text or lecture—the connections and relationships among ideas. Some visual strategies have been developed to help students with this key element. There is evidence that creating graphic organizers such as maps or charts is more effective than outlining when learning from texts (Robinson, 1998; Robinson & Kiewra, 1995). Armbruster and Anderson (1981) taught students specific techniques for diagramming relationships among ideas presented in a text. "Mapping" these relationships by noting causal connections, comparison/contrast connections, and examples improved recall. There are other

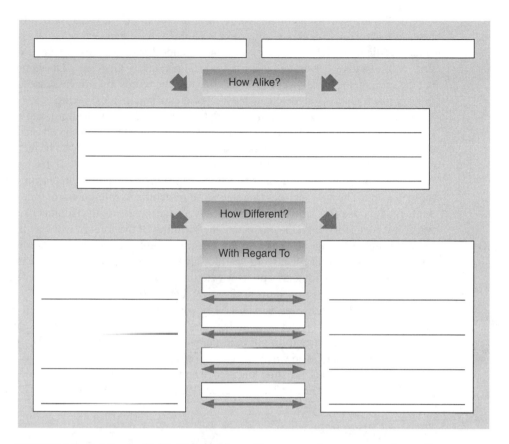

FIGURE 3.5   A Map to Guide Note Taking   The compare/contrast map above allows students to organize their listening or reading as they consider two ideas, concepts, time periods, authors, experiments, theories, and so on.

Source: From *Organizing Thinking: Book 1,* by S. Parks and H. Black, 1992, Critical Thinking Books and Software. Copyright © 1992 Critical Thinking Books and Software. 1-800-458-4849 (www.ciricalthinking.com). All rights reserved.

ways to visualize organization such as Venn diagrams showing how ideas or concepts overlap or tree diagrams showing how ideas branch off of each other. Timelines organize information in sequence and are useful in classes such as history or geology. Using any of these visual tools, students compare one another's drawings and discuss the differences.

Mnemonics

Mnemonics are systematic procedures for improving memory—a strategy many medical students count on to learn the names of all the bones, muscles, and other human body parts. Many mnemonic strategies use imagery (Atkinson et al., 1999; Levin, 1994; McCormick & Levin, 1987). If students need to remember information for long periods of time, an acronym may be the answer. An acronym is a form of abbreviation—a word formed from the first letter of each word in a phrase, for example HOMES to remember the Great Lakes (Huron, Ontario, Michigan, Erie, Superior). Another method forms phrases or sentences out of the first letter of each word or item in a list, for example, Every Good Boy Does Fine to remember the lines on the G clef—E, G, B, D, F. Because the words must make sense as a sentence, this approach also has some characteristics of chain mnemonics, methods that connect the first item to be memorized with the second, the second item with the third, and so on. In one type of chain method, each item on a list is linked to the next through some visual association or story. Another chain-method approach is to incorporate all the items to be memorized into a jingle like "i before e except after c."

The mnemonic system that has been most extensively applied in teaching is the keyword method. The approach has two stages. To remember a foreign word, for example, students first choose an English word, preferably a concrete noun, that sounds like the foreign word or a part of it. Next, they associate the meaning of the foreign word with the English word through an image or sentence. For example, the Spanish word *carta* (meaning "letter") sounds like the English word "cart." Cart becomes the keyword: students imagine a shopping cart filled with letters on its way to the post office, or make up a sentence such as "The cart full of letters tipped over" (Pressley, Levin, & Delaney, 1982).

One problem, however, is that the keyword method does not work well if it is difficult to identify a keyword for a particular item. Many words and ideas that students need to remember are abstract and do not lend themselves to associations with keywords (Hall, 1991; Pressley, 1991). And when the teacher provides the memory links, these associations may not fit the students' existing knowledge and may be forgotten or confused later, so remembering suffers (Wang & Thomas, 1995; Wang, Thomas, & Ouelette, 1992).

Reading Strategies

Effective learning strategies and tactics should help students focus attention, invest effort (elaborate, organize, summarize, connect, translate) so they process information deeply, and monitor their understanding. A number of strategies have been developed to support these processes in reading. Many use mnemonics to help students remember the steps involved. For example, one strategy for 4th grade or above is READS:

R   *Review* headings and subheadings.
E   *Examine* boldface words.
A   *Ask,* "What do I expect to learn?"
D   *Do* it—Read!
S   *Summarize* in you own words. (Friend & Bursuck, 2002).

A strategy that can be use in reading literature is CAPS:

C   Who are the *characters*?
A   What is the *aim* of the story?
P   What *problem* happens?
S   How is the problem *solved*?

There are literally hundreds of strategies that can be taught. Ours has been a brief and selective look. The point for teachers is to teach subject-appropriate learning strategies directly and support strategic learning through coaching and guided practice. Teaching strategies based on cognitive views of learning, particularly information processing, highlights the importance of attention, organization, rehearsal (practice), and elaboration in learning and provide ways to give students more control over their own learning by developing and improving their own metacognitive learning strategies. The focus is on what is happening "inside the head" of the learner. Using the cognitive theory just explicated, principals can give their teachers hands-on examples to develop more effective ways to teach learning strategies. The Theory into Action Guidelines on page 90 illustrates both the principles and practices of such strategies for students.

Constructivist Theories of Learning

In this section we look beyond the individual to expand our understanding of learning and teaching. Consider this situation:

> A young child who has never been to the hospital is in her bed in the pediatric wing. The nurse at the station down the hall calls over the intercom above the bed, "Hi Chelsea, how are you doing? Do you need anything?" The girl looks puzzled and does not answer. The nurse repeats the question with the same result. Finally, the nurse says emphatically, "Chelsea, are you there? Say something!" The little girl responds tentatively, "Hello, Wall—I'm here."

Chelsea encountered a new situation—a talking wall. The wall is persistent. It sounds like a grown-up wall. She shouldn't talk to strangers, but she is not sure about walls. She uses what she knows and what the situation provides to *construct* meaning and to act. Constructivist theories of learning focus on how people make meaning.

Constructivist Views of Learning

Constructivism, that "vast and woolly area in contemporary psychology, epistemology, and education" (von Glaserfeld, 1997, p. 204), is a broad term used by philosophers, curriculum designers, psychologists, educators, and others. Most people who use the term emphasize "the learner's contribution to meaning and learning through both individual and social activity" (Bruning, Schraw, & Ronning, 1999, p. 215). Constructivist perspectives are grounded in the research of Piaget, Vygotsky, the Gestalt psychologists (e.g., Kohler and Duncker) Bartlett, and Bruner as well as the educational philosophy of John Dewey, to mention just a few intellectual roots.

There is no one constructivist theory of learning. Most of the theories in cognitive science include some kind of constructivism because these theories assume that individuals construct their own cognitive structures as they interpret their experiences in particular situations (Palincsar, 1998). There are constructivist approaches in science and mathematics education, in educational psychology and anthropology, and in computer-based education. But

THEORY INTO ACTION GUIDELINES

Learning Strategies

Make sure you have the necessary declarative knowledge (facts, concepts, ideas) to understand new information.

Examples

1. Keep definitions of key vocabulary available as you study.
2. Review required facts and concepts before attempting new material.

Find out what type of test the teacher will give (essay, short answer), and study the material with that in mind.

Examples

1. For a test with detailed questions, practice writing answers to possible questions.
2. For a multiple-choice test, use mnemonics to remember definitions of key terms.

Make sure you are familiar with the organization of the materials to be learned.

Examples

1. Preview the headings, introductions, topic sentences, and summaries of the text.
2. Be alert for words and phrases that signal relationships, such as *on the other hand, because, first, second, however, since.*

Know your own cognitive skills and use them deliberately.

Examples

1. Use examples and analogies to relate new material to something you care about and understand well, such as sports, hobbies, or films.
2. If one study technique is not working, try another—the goal is to stay involved, not to use any particular strategy.

Study the right information in the right way.

Examples

1. Be sure you know exactly what topics and readings the test will cover.
2. Spend your time on the important, difficult, and unfamiliar material that will be required for the test or assignment.
3. Keep a list of the parts of the text that give you trouble and spend more time on those pages.
4. Process the important information thoroughly by using mnemonics, forming images, creating examples, answering questions, making notes in your own words, and elaborating on the text. Do not try to memorize the author's words—use your own.

Monitor your own comprehension.

Examples

1. Use questioning to check your understanding.
2. When reading speed slows down, decide if the information in the passage is important. If it is, note the problem so you can reread or get help to understand. If it is not important, ignore it.
3. Check your understanding by working with a friend and quizzing one another.

Source: Adapted from B. B. Armbruster and T. H. Anderson. "Research synthesis on study skills." *Educational Leadership, 39,* pp. 154–156. Reprinted by permission of the Association for Supervision and Curriculum Development. Copyright © 1981 by ASCD. All rights reserved.

even though many psychologists and educators use the term "constructivism," they often mean very different things (Marshall, 1996; Phillips, 1997). Some constructivist views focus on how individuals make meaning; others emphasize the *shared, social construction of knowledge*. (Driscoll, 1994; Iran-Nejad, 1990; Spiro, Feltovich, Jacobson, & Coulson, 1991; Tobin, 1990; von Glaserfeld, 1990; Wittrock, 1992). In fact, one way to organize constructivist views is to talk about two forms of constructivism, psychological and social (Palincsar, 1998; Phillips, 1997).

Psychological/Individual Constructivism.   The **psychological constructivists** "are concerned with how *individuals* build up certain elements of their cognitive or emotional apparatus" (Phillips, 1997, p. 153). These constructivists might be interested in individual knowledge, beliefs, self-concept, or identity, so they are sometimes called *individual* constructivists; they all focus on the inner psychological life of people. Using these standards, the most recent information processing theories are constructivist (Mayer, 1996). Information processing approaches to learning regard the human mind as a symbol-processing system. The outside world is seen as a source of input, but once the sensations are perceived and enter working memory, the important work is assumed to be happening "inside the head" of the individual (Schunk, 2000; Vera & Simon, 1989).

Even though information processing theorists talk about meaning and knowledge construction, many psychologists believe that information processing is "trivial constructivism" because the individual's only constructive contribution is to build accurate representations of the outside world (Derry, 1992; Garrison, 1995; Marshall, 1996). In contrast, Piaget's psychological constructivist perspective is less concerned with "correct" representations and more interested in meaning as constructed by the individual. Piaget proposed a sequence of cognitive stages that all human pass through. Thinking at each stage builds on and incorporates previous stages as it becomes more organized and adaptive and less tied to concrete events. Piaget's special concern was with logic and the construction of universal knowledge that cannot be learned directly from the environment—knowledge such as conservation or reversibility (Miller, 2002). Such knowledge comes from reflecting on and coordinating our own thoughts, not from mapping external reality. Piaget saw the social environment as an important factor in development, but did not believe that social interaction was the main mechanism for changing thinking (Moshman, 1997).

Vygotsky's Social Constructivism.   Vygotsky believed that social interaction, cultural tools, and activity shape individual development and learning. By participating in a broad range of activities with others, learners appropriate (take for themselves) the outcomes produced by working together; that is, "they acquire new strategies and knowledge of the world and culture" (Palincsar, 1998, pp. 351–352). Some theorists categorize Vygotsky as a psychological constructivist because he was primarily interested in development within the individual (Moshman, 1997; Phillips, 1997). But because his theory relies heavily on social interactions and the cultural context to explain learning, most psychologists classify Vygotsky as a **social constructivist** (Palincsar, 1998, Prawat, 1996). In a sense, he is both. One advantage of his theory of learning is that it gives us a way to consider both the psychological and the social—he bridges both camps. For example, Vygotsky's concept of the zone of proximal development—the area where a child can solve a problem with the help (scaffolding) of an adult or more able peer—has been called a place where culture and cognition create each other (Cole, 1985). Culture creates cognition when the adult uses tools and practices from the culture (language, maps, computers, looms, music, etc.) to steer the child toward goals the culture values (reading, writing, weaving, dance). Cognition creates culture as the adult and child together generate new practices and problem solutions to add to the cultural group's repertoire (Serpell, 1993).

The term constructivism is sometimes used to talk about how public knowledge is created. Although this is not our main concern, it is worth a quick look.

Sociological Constructivism.   Sociological constructivists (sometimes called construc-*tionists*) do not focus on individual learning. Their concern is how public knowledge in disciplines such as science, math, economics, or history is constructed. Beyond this kind of academic knowledge, sociological constructivists also are interested in how common-sense ideas, everyday beliefs, and commonly held understandings about the world are communicated to new members of a sociocultural group (Gergen, 1997; Phillips, 1997). Questions raised might be who determines what constitutes history or the proper way to behave in public or how to get elected class president. There is no true knowledge, according to these theorists. All of knowledge is socially constructed and more important, some people have more power than others do in defining what constitutes such knowledge. Relationships between and among teachers, students, families, and the community are the central issues. Collaboration to understand diverse viewpoints is encouraged and traditional bodies of knowledge often are challenged (Gergen, 1997). Vygotsky's theory, with its attention to how cognition creates culture, has some elements in common with sociological constructivism.

These different perspectives on constructivism raise some general questions and disagree on the answers. These questions can never be fully resolved, but different theories tend to favor different positions.

Is the World Knowable?

Most constructivists believe that people cannot perceive the world directly, but must filter it through their understandings, like Chelsea did when she answered the wall. But some perspectives, such as information processing, assume the world is knowable. There is an objective reality "out there," and an individual can grasp it, even though knowledge constructions are personal and may include misconceptions about how the world operates. For example, young children sometimes construct a subtraction procedure that says, "subtract the smaller number from the larger number, no matter which number in a problem is on top." Other constructivists, including Piaget and Vygotsky, don't talk about accurate conceptions but instead about logical or sound interpretations. Still, they believe that we can know about the world because knowledge construction is a rational process and some constructions are better than others—more logical, justifiable, or defensible, for example (Moshman, 1997).

Many of the more extreme constructivist perspectives, on the other hand, do not assume that the world is knowable. These theorists, often called **radical constructivists,** suggest that all knowledge is individually constructed within cultural and social contexts.

Radical constructivists are not concerned with accurate, "true" representations of the world.

> Radical constructivists hold that we live in a relativistic world that can only be understood from individually unique perspectives, which are constructed through experimental activity in the social/physical world. No individual's viewpoint thus constructed should be viewed as inherently distorted or less correct than another's, although it is certainly true that one individual perspective can be more useful than another. (Derry, 1992, p. 415)

Social constructivists add that what is true in one time and place—such as the "fact" before Columbus's time that the Earth was flat—becomes false in another time and place. Particular ideas may be useful within a specific community of practice, such as fifteenth-century navigation, but useless outside that community. What counts as new knowledge is determined in part by how well the new idea fits with current accepted practice. Over time, the current practice may be questioned and even overthrown, but until such major shifts occur, current practice will shape what is considered useful.

A difficulty with this position is that, when pushed to the extreme of relativism, all knowledge and beliefs are equal because all are constructed. There are problems with this thinking for educators. First, teachers have a professional responsibility to emphasize some values, such as honesty or justice, over others such as bigotry. All beliefs are not equal. As educators, we ask students to work hard to learn. If learning cannot advance understanding because all understandings are equally good, then, as Moshman (1997) notes, "we might just as well let students continue to believe whatever they believe" (p. 230). Also, it appears that some knowledge, such as counting and one-to-one correspondence, is not constructed but universal. Knowing one-to-one correspondence is part of being human (Geary, 1995a; Schunk, 2000).

Knowledge: Situated or General?

A second question that cuts across many constructivist perspectives is whether knowledge is internal, general, and transferable or bound to the time and place in which it is constructed. Psychologists who emphasize the social construction of knowledge and **situated learning** affirm Vygotsky's notion that learning is inherently social and embedded in a particular cultural setting (Cobb & Bowers, 1999). Learning in the real world is not like studying in school. It is more like an apprenticeship where novices, with the support of an expert guide and model, take on more and more responsibility until they are able to function independently. For those who take a situated learning view, this explains learning in factories, around the dinner table, in high school halls, in street gangs, in the business office, and on the playground.

Situated learning is often described as "enculturation," or adopting the norms, behaviors, skills, beliefs, language, and attitudes of a particular community. The community might be mathematicians or gang members or writers or students in your eighth-grade classes or soccer players—any group that has particular ways of thinking and doing. Knowledge is seen *not* as individual cognitive structures but as a creation of the community over time. The practices of the community—the ways of interacting and getting things done, as well as the tools the community has created—constitute the knowledge of that community. Learning means becoming more able to participate in those practices and use the tools (Cognition and Technology Group at Vanderbilt University, 1990, 1993; Derry, 1992; Garrison, 1995; Greeno, Collins, & Resnick, 1996).

At the most basic level, "situated learning…emphasizes the idea that much of what is learned is specific to the situation in which it is learned" (Anderson, Reder, & Simon, 1996, p. 5). Thus, some would argue, learning to do calculations in school may help students do more school calculations, but may not help them balance a checkbook, because the skills can be applied only in the context in which they were learned, namely school (Lave, 1988; Lave & Wenger, 1991). There is evidence that much learning is tied to the situation in which it was learned. But it also appears that knowledge and skills can be applied across contexts that were not part of the initial learning situation, as when you use your ability to read and calculate to do your income taxes, even though income tax forms were not part of your high school curriculum (Anderson, Reder, & Simon, 1996). So learning that is situated in school does not have to be doomed or irrelevant.

Much of the work within constructivist perspectives has focused on teaching. Many of the new standards for teaching, such as the National Council of Teacher of Mathematics' Curriculum and Evaluation Standards for School Mathematics (NCTM, 1989) and the American Association for the Advancement of Science's Benchmarks for Science Literacy (AAAS, 1993) are based on constructivist assumptions and methods. Many of the efforts to reform and restructure schools are attempts to apply constructivist perspectives on teaching and learning to the curriculum and organization of entire schools. Table 3.3 presents the behavioral and selected constructivist perspectives on learning.

Teaching Applications of Constructivist Perspectives

As we have seen, there are several interpretations of what constructivist theory means, but most educators would agree "that it involves a dramatic change in the focus of teaching, putting the students' own efforts to understand at the center of the educational enterprise" (Prawat, 1992, p. 357).

Elements of Constructivist Teaching

Even though there is no single constructivist theory, many constructivist teaching approaches recommend:

- authentic tasks and complex, challenging learning environments;
- social negotiation and shared responsibility as a part of learning;
- multiple representations of content;
- understanding that knowledge is constructed;
- student-centered instruction (Driscoll, 1994; Marshall, 1992).

Let's look more closely at these dimensions of constructivist teaching.

TABLE 3.3 Four Views of Learning

There are variations within each of these views of learning that differ in emphasis.
There is also an overlap in constructivist views.

| | Cognitive | | Constructivist | |
| | Behavioral | Information Processing | Psychological/Individual | Social/Situated |
	Skinner	J. Anderson	Piaget	Vygotsky
Knowledge	Fixed body of knowledge to acquire	Fixed body of knowledge to acquire	Changing body of knowledge, individually constructed in social world	Socially constructed knowledge
	Stimulated from outside	Stimulated from outside Prior knowledge influences how information is processed	Built on what learner brings	Built on what participants contribute, construct together
Learning	Acquisition of facts, skills, concepts	Acquisition of facts, skills, concepts, and strategies	Active construction, restructuring prior knowledge	Collaborative construction of socially defined knowledge and values
	Occurs through drill, guided practice	Occurs through the effective application of strategies	Occurs through multiple opportunities and diverse processes to connect to what is already known	Occurs through socially constructed opportunities
Teaching	Transmission Presentation (Telling)	Transmission Guide students toward more "accurate" and complete knowledge	Challenge, guide thinking toward more complete understanding	Co-construct knowledge with students
Role of Teacher	Manager, supervisor	Teach and model effective strategies	Facilitator, guide	Facilitator, guide Co-participant
	Correct wrong answers	Correct misconceptions	Listen for student's current conceptions, ideas, thinking	Co-construct different interpretation of knowledge; listen to socially constructed conceptions

(continued)

95

TABLE 3.3 Continued

| | Behavioral | Cognitive | Constructivist | |
| | | | Psychological/Individual | Social/Situated |
	Skinner	**J. Anderson**	**Piaget**	**Vygotsky**
Role of Peers	Not usually considered	Not necessary but can influence information processing	Not necessary but can stimulate thinking, raise questions	Ordinary part of process of knowledge construction
Role of Student	Passive reception of information Active listener, direction-follower	Active processor of information, strategy user Organizer and reorganizer of information Rememberer	Active construction (within mind) Active thinker, explainer, interpreter, questioner	Active co-construction with others and self Active thinker, explainer, interpreter, questioner Active social participant

Source: From *Reconceptualizing Learning for Restructured Schools* by H. H. Marshall. Paper presented at the Annual Meeting of the American Educational Research Association, April 1992. Copyright © Hermine H. Marshall. Adapted with permission.

Authentic Tasks.   Constructivists believe that students should not be given stripped down, simplified problems and basic skills drills, but instead should deal with complex situations and "fuzzy," ill-structured problems. The world beyond school presents few simplified problems or step-by-step directions, so schools should be sure that every student has experience solving complex problems. These problems should be embedded in authentic tasks and activities, the kinds of situations that students will face as they apply what they are learning to real-world problems (Needles & Knapp, 1994; Resnick, 1987).

Social Negotiation.   Many constructivists share Vygotsky's belief that higher mental processes develop through social interaction, so collaboration in learning is valued. The Language Development and Hypermedia Group (1992) suggests that a major goal of teaching is to develop students' abilities to establish and defend their own positions while respecting the positions of others. To accomplish this exchange, students must talk and listen to each other.

Multiple Representations.   When students encounter only one representation of content—one model, analogy, or way of understanding complex content, they often oversimplify as they try to apply that one approach to every situation. Rand Spiro and his colleagues (1991) suggest that "revisiting the same material, at different times, in rearranged contexts, for different purposes, and from different conceptual perspectives is essential for attaining the goals of advanced knowledge acquisition" (p. 28). This idea is not entirely new. Years ago Jerome Bruner (1966) described the advantages of a spiral curriculum. This is a way of teaching that introduces the fundamental structure of all subjects—the "big ideas"—early in the school years, then revisits the subjects in more and more complex forms over time.

Understanding Knowledge Construction.   The assumptions we make, our beliefs, and experiences shape what each of us comes to "know" about the world. Different assumptions and different experiences lead to different knowledge. Constructivists stress the importance of understanding the knowledge construction process so that students will be aware of the influences that shape their thinking; thus they will be able to choose, develop, and defend positions in a self-critical way while respecting the positions of others.

Student-Centered Instruction.   The last characteristic of constructivist teaching listed by Driscoll (1994) is student-centered instruction. Following are four examples of student-centered instruction that are consistent with the other dimension of constructivist teaching as well—inquiry learning, problem-based learning, cognitive apprenticeships, and cooperative learning.

Inquiry Learning

John Dewey described the basic **inquiry learning** format in 1910. There have been many adaptations of this strategy, but the form usually includes the following elements (Pasch, Sparks-Langer, Gardner, Starko, & Moody, 1991): The teacher presents a puzzling event, question, or problem. The students:

- formulate hypotheses to explain the event or solve the problem
- collect data to test the hypotheses

- draw conclusions
- reflect on the original problem and on the thinking processes needed to solve it.

Shirley Magnusson and Annemarie Palincsar have developed a teachers' guide for planning, implementing, and assessing different phases of inquiry science units (Palincsar, Magnusson, Marano, Ford, & Brown, 1998). The model, called *Guided Inquiry Supporting Multiple Literacies* or GIsML, is shown in Figure 3.6.

The teacher first identifies a curriculum area and some general guiding questions, puzzles, or problems. For example, an elementary teacher chooses communication as the area and asks this general question: "How and why do humans and animals communicate?" Next several specific focus questions are posed. "How do whales communicate? How do gorillas communicate?" The focus questions have to be carefully chosen to guide students toward important understandings. One key idea in understanding animal communication is the relationship between the animal's structures, survival functions, and habitat. Animals have specific *structures* such as large ears or echo-locators, that *function* to find food or attract mates or identify predators, and these structures and functions are related to the animals' *habitats.* So focus questions must ask about animals with different structures for communication, different functional needs for survival, and different habitats. Questions about animals with the same kinds of structures or the same habitats would not be good focus points for inquiry (Magnusson & Palincsar, 1995).

The next phase is to engage students in the inquiry, perhaps by playing different animal sounds, having students make guesses and claims about communication, and

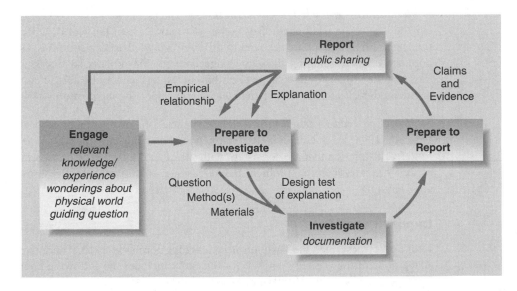

FIGURE 3.6   Learning Community: Program of Study

Source: From "Designing a Community of Practice: Principles and Practices of the GIsML Community," by A. S. Palincsar, S. J. Magnuson, N. Marano, D. Ford, and N. Brown, 1998, *Teaching and Teacher Education, 14,* p. 12. Adapted with permission.

asking the students questions about their guesses and claims. Then the students conduct both first-hand and second-hand investigations. *First-hand investigations* are direct experiences and experiments, for example, measuring and size of bats' eyes and ears in relation to their bodies (using pictures or videos—not real bats!). In *second-hand investigations,* students consult books, the Internet, interviews with experts, and so on to find specific information or get new ideas. As part of investigating, the students begin to identify patterns. The curved line in Figure 3.6 shows that cycles can be repeated. In fact, students might go through several cycles of investigation, pattern identification, and reporting results before moving on to constructing explanations and making final reports. Another possible cycle is to evaluate explanations before reporting by making and then checking predictions, applying the explanation to new situations.

Inquiry teaching allows students to learn content and process at the same time. In the examples above, students learned about the animal communication and habitats. In addition, they learned the inquiry process itself—how to solve problems, evaluate solutions, and think critically. Inquiry has much in common with guided discovery learning in that inquiry methods require great preparation, organization, and monitoring to be sure everyone is engaged and challenged (Kindsvatter, Wilen, & Ishler, 1988).

Problem-Based Learning

In **problem-based learning,** students are confronted with a real problem that has meaning for them. This problem launches their inquiry as they collaborate to find solutions. In true problem-based learning, the problem is real and the students' actions matter. For example, one teacher capitalized on current affairs to encourage student reading, writing, and social studies problem solving:

> Cathie's elementary class learned about the Alaskan oil spill. She brought a newspaper article to class that sequenced in logbook fashion the events of the oil spill in Prince William Sound. To prepare her students to understand the article, she had her students participate in several background-building experiences. First, they used a world map, an encyclopedia, and library books to gather and share relevant information. Next, she simulated an oil spill by coating an object with oil. By then, the class was eager to read the article. (Espe, Worner, & Hotkevich, 1990, p. 45)

After they read and discussed the newspaper article, the teacher asked the class to imagine how the problem might have been prevented. Students had to explain and support their proposed solutions. The next week the students read another newspaper article about how people in their state were helping with the cleanup efforts in Alaska. The teacher asked if the students wanted to help, and they replied with an enthusiastic "Yes!" The students designed posters and made speeches requesting donations of towels to be used to clean the oil-soaked animals in Prince William Sound. The class sent four large bags of towels to Alaska to help in the cleanup. The teacher's and the students' reading, writing, research, and speaking were directed toward solving a real-life problem (Espe, Worner, & Hotkevich, 1990). Other authentic problems that might be the focus for student projects are pollution in local rivers, student conflicts in school, raising money for the school computer lab, or building a playground for young children.

Some problems are not authentic (they do not affect the students' lives), but they are engaging. For example, the Cognition and Technology Group at Vanderbilt University (CTGV, 1990, 1993) has developed a videodisc-based learning environment for the fifth and sixth grades that focuses on mathematics instruction. The series, called *The Adventures of Jasper Woodbury,* presents students with complex situations that require problem finding; subgoal setting; and the application of mathematics, science, history, and literature concepts to solve problems. Even though the situations are complex and lifelike, the problems can be solved using data embedded in the stories presented. For example, in one adventure, Jasper sets out in a small motorboat, headed to Cedar Creek to inspect an old cruiser he is thinking of buying. Along the way Jasper has to consult maps, use his marine radio, deal with fuel and repair problems, buy the cruiser, and finally determine if he has enough fuel and time to sail his purchase home before sundown. Often the adventures have real-life follow-up problems that build on the knowledge developed. For example, after designing a playground for a hypothetical group of children in one Jasper adventure, students can tackle building a real playhouse for a preschool class.

There are 12 different adventures. Research indicates that students as young as fourth grade and as old as high school can work with the adventures (CTGV, 1990). Students are highly motivated as they work in groups to solve the problems; even group members with limited math skill can contribute to the solutions because they might notice key information in the videotape or suggest innovative ways to approach the situation

The Vanderbilt group calls its problem-based approach **anchored instruction.** The *anchor* is the rich, interesting situation. This anchor provides a focus—a reason for setting goals, planning, and using mathematical tools to solve problems. The intended outcome is to develop knowledge that is useful and flexible, not inert. Inert knowledge is information that is memorized but seldom applied (CTVG, 1996; Whitehead, 1929). The teacher's role in problem-based learning is summarized in Table 3.4.

Cognitive Apprenticeships

Over the centuries, apprenticeships have proved to be an effective form of education. By working alongside a master and perhaps other apprentices, young people have learned many skills, trades, and crafts. Why are they so effective? Apprenticeships are rich in information because the master knows a great deal about the subject. Working with more knowledgeable guides provides models, demonstrations, and corrections, as well as a personal bond that is motivating. The performances required of the learner are real and important and grow more complex as the learner becomes more competent (Collins, Brown, & Holum, 1991; Collins, Brown, & Newman, 1989).

Collins and his colleagues (1989) suggest that knowledge and skills learned in school have become too separated from their use in the world beyond school. To correct this imbalance, some educators recommend that schools adopt many of the features of apprenticeships. But rather than learning to sculpt or dance or build a cabinet, apprenticeships in school would focus on cognitive objectives such as reading comprehension or writing or mathematical problem solving. There are many **cognitive apprenticeship** models, but most share six features:

■ Students observe an expert (usually the teacher) model the performance.
■ Students get external support through coaching or tutoring (including hints, feedback, models, reminders).

TABLE 3.4   The Teacher's Role in Problem-Based Learning

Phase	Teacher Behavior
Phase 1 Orient students to the problem	Teacher goes over the objectives of the lesson, describes important logistical requirements, and motivates students to engage in self-selected problem-solving activity.
Phase 2 Organize students for study	Teacher helps students define and organize study tasks related to the problem.
Phase 3 Assist independent and group investigation	Teacher encourages students to gather appropriate information, conduct experiments, and search for explanations and solutions.
Phase 4 Develop and present artifacts and exhibits	Teacher assists students in planning and preparing appropriate artifacts such as reports, videos, and models and helps them share their work with others.
Phase 5 Analyze and evaluate the problem-solving process	Teacher helps students to reflect on their investigations and the processes they used

Source: From *Classroom Instruction and Management* (p. 161), by R. I. Arends, New York: McGraw-Hill. Copyright © 1997 McGraw Hill. Reprinted with permission.

- Conceptual scaffolding (in the form of outlines, explanations, notes, definitions, formulas, procedures, etc.) is provided and then gradually faded as the student becomes more competent and proficient.
- Students continually articulate their knowledge—putting into words their understanding of the processes and content being learned.
- Students reflect on their progress, comparing their problem solving to an expert's performance and to their own earlier performances.
- Students are required to explore new ways to apply what they are learning—ways that they have not practiced at the master's side.

Group Work and Cooperation in Learning

Clearly, collaboration and cooperation are important in many visions of innovation and school reform. Teachers are expected to collaborate with parents, administrators, and each other. Cooperative learning structures and approaches are seen as valuable; interdependence, reciprocal learning, and learning communities are mentioned often as desirable features of teaching and learning. For example, the second of three recommendations for strengthening middle grades teacher preparation published by the National Middle School Association (Scales & McEwin, 1994) is "greater variety of developmentally responsive teaching and assessment techniques, especially cooperative learning, interdisciplinary curriculum and team teaching, student exhibitions, and portfolios" (p. 5).

The History of Cooperative Learning.   Collaboration and cooperative learning have a long history in American education. In the early 1900s, John Dewey criticized the use of competition in education and encouraged educators to structure schools as democratic learning communities. These ideas fell from favor in the 1940s and 1950s, replaced by a resurgence of competition. In the 1960s, there was a swing back to individualized and cooperative learning structures, stimulated in part by concern for civil rights and interracial relations (Webb & Palincsar, 1996).

Today, evolving constructivist perspectives on learning fuel interest in collaboration and cooperative learning. Two characteristics of constructivist teaching—complex, real-life learning environments and social interaction (Driscoll, 1998)—are consistent with the use of cooperative learning structures. As educators focus on learning in real contexts, "there is a heightened interest in situations where elaboration, interpretation, explanation, and argumentation are integral to the activity of the group and where learning is supported by other individuals" (Webb & Palincsar, 1996, p. 844).

Theoretical Underpinnings of Cooperative Learning.   Advocates of different theories of learning find value in cooperative learning, but not for the same reasons.

In terms of *academic/cognitive goals,* information processing theorists suggest that group discussion can help participants rehearse, elaborate, and expand their knowledge. As group members question and explain, they have to organize their knowledge, make connections, and review—all processes that support information processing and memory. Advocates of a Piagetian perspective assert that the interactions in groups can create the cognitive conflict and disequilibrium that lead an individual to question his or her understanding and try out new ideas—or, as Piaget (1985) said, "to go beyond his current state and strike out in new directions" (p. 10). Educators who favor Vygotsky's theory suggest that social interaction is important for learning because higher mental functions such as reasoning, comprehension, and critical thinking originate in social interactions and are then internalized by individuals. Students can accomplish mental tasks with social support before they can do them alone. Thus cooperative learning provides the social support and scaffolding that students need to move learning forward. Table 3.5 summarizes the functions of cooperative learning from different perspectives, and describes some of the elements of each kind of group.

In terms of *interpersonal/social goals,* research indicates that cooperative learning has a positive impact on interracial friendships, prejudice reduction, acceptance of disabled students, self-esteem, peer support for academic goals, altruism, empathy, social perspective-taking, liking fellow classmates and feeling liked, sense of responsibility and control over learning, and time on task. Positive effects often are attributed to the process of working toward common goals as equals, which was shown in laboratory studies to increase liking and respect among individuals from different racial or social groups (Allport, 1954). The motivation growing from the praise and encouragement of peers working toward a common goal also brings positive effects (Deutsch, 1949). Thus cooperative strategies have been touted as particularly useful in combating the detrimental social effects of cliques in middle school and high schools, the negative effects of competition on student self-esteem, and the alienation of students who are not members of popular social groups (Aronson, in press; Aronson & Patnoe, 1997).

TABLE 3.5 Different Forms of Cooperative Learning for Different Purposes

Different forms of cooperative learning (Elaboration, Piagetian, and Vygotskian) fit different purposes, need different structures, and have their own potential problems and possible solutions.

Considerations	Elaboration	Piagetian	Vygotskian
Group size	Small (2–4)	Small	Dyads
Group composition	Heterogeneous/ homogeneous	Homogeneous	Heterogeneous
Tasks	Rehearsal/integrative	Exploratory	Skills
Teacher role	Facilitator	Facilitator	Model/guide
Potential problems	Poor help-giving	Inactive	Poor help-giving
	Unequal participation	No cognitive conflict	Providing adequate time/ dialogue
Averting Problems	Direct instruction in help-giving	Structuring controversy	Direct instruction in help-giving
	Modeling help-giving		Modeling help-giving
	Scripting interaction		

Source: From "Learning from Peers: Beyond the Rhetoric of Positive Results," by A. M. O'Donnell and J. O'Kelly, 1994, *Educational Psychology Review,* 6, p. 327. Reprinted with permission of Kluwer Academic/ Plenum Publishers and Angela O'Donnell.

Elements of Cooperative Learning. David and Roger Johnson (1994) list five elements that define true **cooperative learning** groups. Students *interact face-to-face* and close together, not across the room. Group members experience *positive interdependence*—they need each other for support, explanations, and guidance. Even though they work together and help each other, members of the group must ultimately demonstrate learning on their own—they are held *individually accountable* for learning, often through individual tests or other assessments. *Collaborative skills* are necessary for effective group functioning. Often these skills, such as giving constructive feedback, reaching consensus, and involving every member, must be taught and practiced before the groups tackle a learning task. Finally, members monitor *group processes* and relationships to make sure the group is working effectively and to learn about the dynamics of groups. They take time to ask, "How are we doing as a group? Is everyone working together?"

Setting Up Cooperative Groups. O'Donnell & O'Kelly (1994) note that determining the size of a group depends in part on the purpose of the group activity. If the purpose is for the group members to review, rehearse information, or practice, larger groups (about four to five or six students) are useful. But if the goal is to encourage each student to participate in discussions, problem solving, or computer learning, then groups of two to four members work best. Also some research indicates that when there are just a few girls in a group, they tend to be left out of the discussions unless they are the most able or assertive members. By contrast, when there are only one or two boys in the group, they tend to dominate and be "interviewed" by the girls unless these boys are less able than the girls or are very shy. In general, for very shy and introverted students, individual learning may be a better approach (Webb, 1985; Webb & Palincsar, 1996).

In practice, the effects of learning in a group vary, depending on what actually happens in the group and who is in it. If only a few people take responsibility for the work, these people will learn, but the nonparticipating members probably will not. Students who ask questions, get answers, and attempt explanations are more likely to learn than students whose questions go unasked or unanswered. In fact, there is evidence that the more a student provides elaborated, thoughtful explanations to other students in a group, the more the *explainer* learns. Giving good explanations appears to be even more important for learning than receiving explanations (Webb & Palincsar, 1996). In order to explain, students have to organize the information, put it into their own words, think of examples and analogies (which forges connections between prior knowledge and new information), and test understanding by answering questions. These are excellent learning strategies (King, 1990; O'Donnell & O'Kelly, 1994).

Some teachers assign roles such as reporter or discussion manager to students to encourage cooperation and full participation. Such roles should be assigned with engagement and learning in mind. In groups that focus on practice, review, or mastery of basic skills, roles should support persistence, encouragement, and participation. In groups that focus on higher-order problem solving or complex learning, roles should encourage thoughtful discussion, sharing of explanations and insights, probing, brainstorming, and creativity. Teachers must be careful, however, not to communicate to students that the major purpose of the groups is simply to do the roles, in order to avoid having roles become ends in themselves (Woolfolk Hoy & Tschannen-Moran, 1999).

Jigsaw.   An early format for cooperative learning, **Jigsaw** emphasized high interdependence. This structure was invented by Elliot Aronson and his graduate students in 1971 in Austin, Texas: "…as a matter of absolute necessity to help defuse a highly explosive situation" (Aronson, in press). The Austin schools had just been desegregated by court order. White, African American, and Hispanic students were together in classrooms for the first time. Hostility and turmoil ensued with fistfights in corridors and classrooms. Aronson's answer was the Jigsaw classroom.

In Jigsaw, each group member was given part of the material to be learned by the whole group and became an "expert" on his or her piece. Students had to teach each other, so everyone's contribution was important. A more recent version, Jigsaw II, adds expert groups where the students who have the same material from each learning group confer to make sure they understand their assigned part and then plan ways to teach the information to their learning group members. Next, students return to their learning groups, bringing their expertise to the sessions. In the end, students take an individual test covering all the material and earn points for their learning team score. Teams can work for rewards or simply for recognition (Aronson & Patnoe, 1997; Slavin, 1995).

In his first test of Jigsaw, Aronson reports that teachers "spontaneously told us of their great satisfaction with the way the atmosphere of their classrooms had been transformed. Adjunct visitors (such as music teachers and the like) were little short of amazed at the dramatically changed atmosphere in the classroom" (Aronson, in press). Students expressed less prejudice, were more confident, liked school better, and had higher scores on objective examinations. The overall improvements in test scores came mostly from increases in minority group children—Anglo students maintained their previous levels of performance. These findings are consistent with recent research on cooperative learning, as reviewed by Slavin (1995).

There are many other forms of cooperative learning used in schools today. It would be difficult to complete a teacher preparation program without encountering encouragement to use these methods. Kagan (1994) and Slavin (1995) have written extensively on the subject and developed many formats. No matter what the format, however, the key to learning in groups appears to be the *quality of the discussions* among the students. Talk that is interpretive—that analyses and discusses explanations, evidence, reasons, and alternatives—is more valuable than talk that is merely descriptive. And teachers play an important role; they cannot leave the students unguided, but rather have to seed the discussion with ideas and alternatives that push and prod student thinking (Palincsar, 1998). Tschannen-Moran and Woolfolk Hoy (2001) have written a guide for teacher decision making in designing cooperative learning.

Sometimes when schools adopt innovative teaching practices there are objections from families. On the next page are guidelines for principals and teachers about working with families and the community when schools adopt innovations.

Summary

Although theorists disagree about the definitions of learning, most would agree that learning occurs when experience causes a change in a person's knowledge or behavior. Behavioral views of learning focus on the role of external events—antecedents and consequences—in changing observable behaviors. Consequences that increase behaviors are called reinforcers and consequences that decrease behaviors are called punishers.

Contingency contracts are an application of behavioral learning. The teacher draws up an individual contract with each student, describing exactly what the student must do to earn a particular privilege or reward. In some programs, students participate in deciding on the behaviors to be reinforced and the rewards that can be gained. A teacher must use these programs with caution, emphasizing learning and not just "good" behavior.

Cognitive views of learning focus on the human mind's active attempts to make sense of the world. Knowledge is a central force in cognitive perspectives. The individual's prior knowledge affects what he or she will pay attention to, recognize, understand, remember, and forget. Knowledge can be general or domain-specific and declarative, procedural, or conditional, but to be useful, knowledge must be remembered. One influential model of memory is information processing, which describes how information moves from sensory memory (which holds a wealth of sensations and images very briefly) to working memory (where the information is elaborated and connected to existing knowledge) to long-term memory (where the information can be held for a long time, depending on how well it was learned in the first place and how interconnected it is to other information). People vary in how well they learn and remember based in part on their metacognitive knowledge—their

THEORY INTO ACTION GUIDELINES

Explaining Innovations

Be confident and honest.

Examples

1. Write out your rationale for the methods you are using—consider likely objections and craft your responses.
2. Admit mistakes or oversights—explain what you have learned from them.

Treat parents as equal partners.

Examples

1. Listen carefully to parents' objections, take notes, and follow up on requests or suggestions—remember, you both want the best for the child.
2. Give parents the telephone number of an administrator who will answer their questions about a new program or initiative.
3. Invite families to visit your room or assist in the project in some way.

Communicate effectively.

Examples

1. Use plain language and avoid jargon. If you must use a technical term, define it in accessible ways. Use your best teaching skills to educate parents about the new approach.

2. Encourage local newspapers or television stations to do stories about the "great learning" going on in your classroom or school.
3. Create a lending library of articles and references about the new strategies.

Have examples of projects and assignments available for parents when they visit your class.

Examples

1. Encourage parents to try math activities. If they have trouble, show them how your students (and their child) are successful with the activities and highlight the strategies the students have learned.
2. Keep a library of students' favorite activities to demonstrate for parents.

Develop family involvement packages.

Examples

1. Once a month, send families, via their children, descriptions and examples of the math, science, or language to be learned in the upcoming unit. Include activities children can do with their parents
2. Make the family project count, for example, as a homework grade.

Source: From M. Meyer, M. Delgardelle, and J. Middleton. "Addressing parents' concerns over curriculum reform." *Educational Leadership, 53*(7), p. 57. Adapted by permission of the Association for Supervision and Curriculum Development. Copyright © 1996 by ASCP. All rights reserved.

abilities to plan, monitor, and regulate their own thinking. There are many teaching applications of cognitive views including mnemonics, imagery, and other learning strategies to help organize and elaborate material.

Constructivist views of learning emphasize the importance of students' construction of knowledge; however, there are many different constructivist explanations of learning. Psychological constructivists are concerned with how *individuals* make sense of their worlds. These constructivists might be interested in individual knowledge, beliefs, self-concept, or identity, so they are sometimes called *individual* constructivists; they all focus on the inner psychological life of people. Social constructivists believe that social interaction, cultural tools, and activity shape individual development and learning. By participating in a broad range of activities with others, learners appropriate (take for themselves) the outcomes produced by working together; they acquire new strategies and knowledge of their world. Finally, sociological constructivists are interested in how public knowledge in disciplines such as science, math, economics, or history is constructed as well as how everyday beliefs and commonly held understandings about the world are communicated to new members of a sociocultural group.

Constructivist approaches to teaching recommend: complex, challenging learning environments; social negotiation and collaboration; multiple representations of content; understanding that knowledge is a human construction; and student-centered methods such as inquiry, problem-based learning, cognitive apprenticeships, and cooperative learning.

KEY TERMS

anchored instruction   (100)
antecedents   (65)
chunking   (77)
cognitive apprenticeship   (100)
conditional knowledge   (73)
constructivism   (89)
contingency contract   (67)
cooperative learning   (103)
cueing   (66)
declarative knowledge   (72)
domain-specific knowledge   (72)
elaboration   (79)
elaborative rehearsal   (77)

episodic memory   (78)
executive control processes   (81)
inquiry learning   (97)
Jigsaw   (104)
learning   (62)
maintenance rehearsal   (77)
metacognition   (81)
mnemonics   (87)
negative reinforcement   (64)
positive reinforcement   (64)
presentation punishment   (65)
problem-based learning   (99)
procedural knowledge   (73)

procedural memory   (78)
psychological
    constructivists   (91)
punishment   (65)
reinforcement process   (64)
reinforcer   (63)
removal punishment   (65)
radical constructivists   (92)
schemas   (78)
semantic memory   (78)
situated learning   (93)
social constructivist   (91)
working memory   (75)

SOME IDEAS FOR YOUR PORTFOLIO

1. As principal, you have decided that your elementary school needs a writing program that is a good balance of skills and composition. Prepare a short position paper on the advantages and disadvantages of each approach. Then prepare a plan that incorporates the best of both approaches. Support your argument with current research and theory on learning.

2. Prepare a power point presentation on the strengths and weaknesses of each of the learning perspectives discussed in this chapter—behavioral, cognitive, and constructivist. Be sure to discuss the situations for which each perspective is most appropriate. For example,

list the tasks or situations for which the behavioral approach is best. Give at least one example for each approach.

3. Reread the Principals' Casebook at the beginning of this chapter and assume you are the principal in that school.

   ■ Develop a plan for working with the history department to resolve the issue such that both extremes (the traditionalists and the constructivists) are satisfied.

   ■ Consult the Guidelines (p. 106) about explaining innovations and devise a process for introducing the new plan to the community.

INSTRUCTIONAL LEADER'S TOOLBOX

Readings

Perkins, D. (1992). *Smart schools: From training memories to education minds.* New York: Free Press.

Phillips, D. (1995). The good, the bad, and the ugly: The many faces of constructivism. *Educational Researcher, 24*(7), 5–12.

John-Steiner, V., & Mahn, H. (1996). Sociocultural approaches to learning and development; A Vygotskian framework. *Educational Psychologist, 31,* 191–206.

Videos

Memory: Fabric of the mind. 28 minutes. What kind of brain chemistry can explain memory? Are different types of memory located at different areas of the brain? What is the process of forgetting? Is it possible to improve memory? This program seeks answers to these and other fascinating questions about the brain and memory at several internationally renowned memory-research labs. Order from Films for the Humanities & Sciences, Inc. P.O. Box 2053, Princeton, NJ, 08543, or 800-257-5126.

Websites

Metacognition and Reading to Learn.	http://www.ed.gov/databases/ERIC_Digests/ed376427.html
Metacomprehension	http://www.ed.gov/databases/ERIC_Digests/ed250670.html
Overview of metacognition.	http://www.ncrel.org/skrs/areas/issues/students/learning/lrlmetn.htm
Improving the Quality of Student Notes	http://www.ed.gov/databases/ERIC_Digests/ed366645.html
Problem Solving in Early Childhood Classrooms	http://www.ed.gov/databases/ERIC_Digests/ed355040.html
Critical Thinking in the Social Studies	http://www.ed.gov/databases/ERIC_Digests/ed272432.html
Teaching Problem Solving—Secondary School Science	http://www.ed.gov/databases/ERIC_Digests/ed309049.html
Learning Strategies Matrix	http://edweb.sdsu.edu/Courses/ET650_OnLine/MAPPS/Stras.html
Learn To: provides thousands of step by step tutorials on a variety of skills.	www.learn2.com
Mindtools	http://www.psychwww.com/mtsite/

Organizations

Wolf Trap Institute for Early Learning Through the Arts: organization to help early childhood professionals use the arts as part of their care and instruction of young children. The Institute is accessible on the Web by going to the main site for Wolf Trap and then selecting education.	http://www.wolf-trap.org/
An interactive site sponsored by Wolf-Trap called *Artsplay*	http://www.wolf-trap.org/

CHAPTER

4 Motivation

Preview: Key Points

Leadership Challenge

Motivation—A Definition
Intrinsic and Extrinsic Motivation
Four General Approaches to Motivation
Motivation to Learn in School

Goals and Motivation
Types of Goals
Goals: Lessons for Teachers and Principals
Theory into Action Guidelines: Family and
Community Partnerships

Needs and Motivation
Maslow's Hierarchy
Achievement Motivation
The Need for Self-Determination
The Need for Social Support
Needs and Motivation: Lessons for Teachers
and Principals
Theory into Practice Guidelines: Supporting
Self-Determination

Attributions, Beliefs, and Motivation
Attribution Theory
Beliefs about Ability
Beliefs about Self-Efficacy
Attributions, Achievement Motivation,
and Self-Worth
Attributions and Beliefs: Lessons for Teachers
and Principals
Theory into Action Guidelines: Encouraging
Self-Worth and Self-Efficacy

Interests and Emotions
Tapping Interests
Theory into Action Guidelines: Building on
Students' Interests
Arousal: Excitement and Anxiety in Learning
Theory into Action Guidelines: Dealing
with Anxiety

**Strategies to Encourage Motivation and
Thoughtful Learning**
Necessary Conditions in Classrooms
Can I Do It? Building Confidence and Positive
Expectations
Do I Want to Do It? Seeing the Value
of Learning
What Do I Need to Do to Succeed? Staying
Focused on the Task
How Do Beginning Teachers Motivate Students?

Summary

Key Terms

Some Ideas for Your Portfolio

Instructional Leader's Toolbox
Readings
Videos
Websites
Organizations

PREVIEW: KEY POINTS

- Motivation is the spring of action—an internal state that arouses, directs, and maintains behavior.
- Whether motivation is intrinsic or extrinsic is determined by the individual's perception of causality for the action: internal causality → intrinsic motivation; external causality → extrinsic motivation.
- Four major approaches to motivation are behavioral (rewards and incentives); humanistic (self-actualization); cognitive (beliefs, attributions, and expectations); and social learning (outcomes combined with beliefs).
- Goals that are specific, moderately challenging, and can be reached in the near future with reasonable effort are the most motivating goals; in schools, goals that focus on learning (not performance) are the most powerful.
- Motivation is affected by the individual's need for safety, self-esteem, connections to others, self-determination, achievement, and self-actualization; people have different needs at different times.
- Motivation also is affected by the individual's beliefs about the causes of successes and failures and whether ability can improve; believing that effort can improve ability leads to greater persistence and achievement in school.
- Self-efficacy, the belief that you have the ability to orchestrate the actions to manage a particular situation, is a significant source of motivation.
- Anxiety can interfere with motivation and learning by affecting attention, information processing, and performance.
- Motivation to learn is enhanced when teachers employ strategies that help students have confidence in their abilities to learn, see the value of the learning task, and stay focused on learning without resorting to self-protective and self-defeating beliefs and actions.

Leadership Challenge

For some reason this year, many of the students in your middle school classes seem defeated about learning. At a recent faculty meeting, teachers started to complain about their students: "They look at an assignment and protest—This is too long (too hard, too much)!" and "We can't do this by tomorrow (Monday, next week)!" Because they don't exert much effort, of course, they prove themselves right every time—they can't do the work. Your teachers claim that neither pep talks nor punishments for incomplete work are making a dent in the students' defeatist attitudes. And the "I can't" attitude seems contagious. Even the better students are starting to drag their feet, protest longer assignments, and invest minimal effort in class. Teachers also maintain that more students have started to cheat on tests to save their sinking grades. A few teachers blame the negative attitudes on students from the "projects" who are in school this year because the other middle school in the district was closed and those students had to be redistributed. A cloud of despair seems to be hovering over the whole school. You are starting to dread Mondays. You need to show some leadership, and you begin by asking yourself these questions:

- Are these students "unmotivated"?
- Why might they be so pessimistic about learning?

- How can you help your teachers get a handle on this problem?
- What can you and your teachers do to change student attitudes toward their school work?
- How can teachers get students to believe in themselves?
- What perspectives on motivation seem most useful?

Motivation—A Definition

Motivation is usually defined as *an internal state that arouses, directs, and maintains behavior.* Psychologists studying motivation have focused on five basic questions. First, what choices do people make about their behavior. Why do some students, for example, focus on their homework while others watch television? Second, having made a decision, how long is it before the person actually gets started? Why do some students start their homework right away, while others procrastinate? Third, what is the intensity or level of involvement in the chosen activity? Once the book bag is opened, is the student absorbed and focused or just going through the motions? Fourth, what causes a person to persist or to give up? Will a student read the entire Shakespeare assignment or just a few pages? Finally, what is the individual thinking and feeling while engaged in the activity? Is the student enjoying Shakespeare, worrying about an upcoming test, or daydreaming (Graham & Weiner, 1996; Pintrich, Marx, & Boyle, 1993)?

Intrinsic and Extrinsic Motivation

We all know how it feels to be motivated, to move energetically toward a goal. We also know what it is like to work hard, even if we are not fascinated by the task. What energizes and directs our behavior? The explanation could be drives, needs, incentives, fears, goals, social pressure, self-confidence, interests, curiosity, beliefs, values, expectations, and more. Some psychologists have explained motivation in terms of personal *traits* or individual characteristics. Certain people, so the theory goes, have a strong need to achieve, a fear of tests, or an enduring interest in art, so they behave accordingly. They work hard to achieve, avoid tests, or spend hours in art galleries. Other psychologists see motivation more as a *state,* a temporary situation. If, for example, you are reading this paragraph because you have an examination tomorrow, you are motivated (at least for now) by the situation. Of course, the motivation we experience at any given time usually is a combination of trait and state.

As you can see, some explanations of motivation rely on internal, personal factors such as needs, interests, curiosity, and enjoyment. Other explanations point to external, environmental factors—rewards, social pressure, punishment, and so on. Motivation that stems from factors such as interest or curiosity is called **intrinsic motivation.** Intrinsic motivation is the natural tendency to seek out and conquer challenges as we pursue personal interests and exercise capabilities (Deci & Ryan, 1985; Reeve, 1996). When we are intrinsically motivated, we do not need incentives or punishments, because the activity itself is rewarding. James Raffini (1996) states simply that intrinsic motivation is "…what motivates us to do something when we don't have to do anything" (p. 3). In contrast, when we do something in order to earn a merit increase, avoid criticism from parents, please the superintendent, or for some other reason that has very little to do with the task itself, we experience **extrinsic motivation.** We are not really interested in the activity for its own sake; we care only about what it will gain us.

It is impossible to tell just by looking if a behavior is intrinsically or extrinsically motivated. The essential difference between the two types of motivation is the person's reason for acting, that is, whether the **locus of causality** for the action (the location of the cause) is internal or external. Students who read or practice their backstroke or paint may be reading, stroking, or painting because they freely chose the activity based on personal interests (internal locus of causality/intrinsic motivation), or because someone or something else outside is influencing them (external locus of causality/extrinsic motivation).

Is your motivation for reading this page intrinsic or extrinsic? Is your locus of causality internal or external? As you try to answer this question, you probably realize that the dichotomy between intrinsic and extrinsic motivation is too simple—too all-or-nothing. Human activities fall along a continuum from fully self-determined (internal causality/intrinsic motivation) to fully determined by others (external causality/extrinsic motivation). For example, teachers may freely choose to work hard on activities that they don't find particularly enjoyable, because they know the activities are important in reaching a valued goal—like spending hours studying preparing a portfolio in order to earn National Board Certification. Is this intrinsic or extrinsic motivation? Actually it is in between—the person is freely choosing to respond to outside causes such as certification requirements. The person has *internalized* an external cause.

In school, both intrinsic and extrinsic motivation are important. Many activities are, or could be, interesting to students. Teaching can create intrinsic motivation by stimulating the students' curiosity and making them feel more competent as they learn. But you know this won't work all the time. Did you find long division or grammar inherently interesting? Was your curiosity piqued by the states and their capitals? If teachers count on intrinsic motivation to energize all their students all of the time, they will be disappointed. There are situations when incentives and external supports are necessary. Principals and teachers must encourage and nurture intrinsic motivation while making sure that extrinsic motivation supports learning (Brophy, 1988; Ryan & Deci, 1996). To do this, they need to know about the factors that influence motivation.

Four General Approaches to Motivation

Motivation is a vast and complicated subject with many theories developed in laboratories, through games and simulations, and in clinical or industrial settings. Our examination of the field will be selective, otherwise we would never finish the topic. As with learning, there are several general explanations for motivation. Each has something to offer principals and teachers.

Behavioral Approaches to Motivation.   Behaviorists explain motivation with concepts such as "reward" and "incentive." A **reward** is an attractive object or event supplied as a consequence of a particular behavior. An **incentive** is an object or event that encourages or discourages behavior—the promise of a reward. Thus, according to the behavioral view, understanding motivation begins with a careful analysis of the incentives and rewards present in the school and classroom. Providing grades, stickers, certificates, and so on for learning—or demerits for misbehavior—are attempts to motivate students by extrinsic means of incentives, rewards, and punishments. Of course, in any individual case, many other factors will affect how a person behaves.

For years educators and psychologists have debated whether students should be rewarded for schoolwork and academic accomplishments. In the early 1990s, Paul Chance and Kohn exchanged opinions in several issues of *Phi Delta Kappan* (March 1991; November 1992; June, 1993). What are the arguments? Kohn (1993) argues that "Applied behaviorism, which amounts to saying, 'do this and you'll get that,' is essentially a technique for controlling people. In the classroom it is a way of doing things *to* children rather than working *with* them" (p. 784). He contends that rewards are ineffective because when the praise and prizes stop, the behaviors stop too. But Chance (1993) disagrees:

> Skinner, unlike Kohn, understood that people learn best in a responsive environment. Teachers who praise or otherwise reward student performance provide such an environment.... If it is immoral to let students know they have answered questions correctly, to pat students on the back for a good effort, to show joy at a student's understanding of a concept, or to recognize the achievement of a goal by providing a gold star or a certificate—if this is immoral, then count me a sinner. (p. 788)

Do rewards undermine interest? Even psychologists such as Edward Deci (1975) and Mark Lepper (1988) who suggest that rewards might undermine intrinsic motivation agree that rewards can also be used positively. When rewards provide students with information about their growing mastery of a subject or when the rewards show appreciation for a job well done, then the rewards bolster confidence and make the task more interesting to the students, especially students who lacked ability or interest in the task initially. Nothing succeeds like success. If students master reading or mathematics with the support of rewards, they will not forget what they have learned when the praise stops. Would they have learned without the rewards? Some would, but some might not. Would you continue working for a school that didn't pay you, even though you liked the work? Will freelance writer Alfie Kohn, for that matter, lose interest in writing because he gets paid fees and royalties?

Humanistic Approaches to Motivation. In the 1940s, proponents of humanistic psychology such as Carl Rogers argued that neither of the dominant schools of psychology, behavioral or Freudian, adequately explained why people act as they do. Humanistic interpretations of motivation emphasize such intrinsic sources of motivation as a person's needs for "self-actualization" (Maslow, 1968, 1970), the inborn "actualizing tendency" (Rogers & Freiberg, 1994), or the need for "self-determination" (Deci, Vallerand, Pelletier, & Ryan, 1991). What these theories have in common is the belief that people are continually motivated by the inborn need to fulfill their potential. So from the humanistic perspective, to motivate means to encourage peoples' inner resources—their sense of competence, self-esteem, autonomy, and self-actualization. When we examine the role of needs in motivation, we will see two examples of the humanistic approach, Maslow's theory of the hierarchy of needs and Deci's self-determination theory.

Cognitive Approaches to Motivation. In many ways, cognitive theories of motivation also developed as a reaction to the behavioral views. Cognitive theorists believe that behavior is determined by our thinking, not simply by whether we have been rewarded or punished for the behavior in the past (Stipek, 2002). Behavior is initiated and regulated by plans (Miller, Galanter, & Pribram, 1960), goals (Locke & Latham, 1990), schemas (Ortony, Clore, & Collins, 1988), expectations (Vroom, 1964), and attributions (Weiner, 1992). One of the central assumptions in cognitive approaches is that people respond not to external events or physical conditions like hunger, but rather to their interpretations of these events. In cognitive theories, people are seen as active and curious, searching for information to solve personally relevant problems. Thus, cognitive theorists emphasize intrinsic motivation. We will see examples of cognitive theories of motivation when we examine Bernard Weiner's attribution theory.

Social Learning Approaches to Motivation. Social learning theories of motivation are integrations of behavioral and cognitive approaches: They take into account both the behaviorists' concern with the consequences of behavior and the cognitivists' interest in the impact of individual beliefs and expectations. Many influential social learning explanations of motivation can be characterized as **expectancy-value theories.** This means that motivation is seen as the product of two main forces, the individual's expectation of reaching a goal and the value of that goal to him or her. In other words, the important questions are, "If I try hard, can I succeed?" and "If I succeed, will the outcome be valuable or rewarding to me?" Bandura's self-efficacy theory, discussed later in this chapter, is an example of an expectancy-value approach to motivation (Pintrich & Schunk, 2002).

The behavioral, humanistic, cognitive, and social learning approaches to motivation are summarized in Table 4.1. These theories differ in their answers to the question "What is motivation?" but each contributes in its own way to a comprehensive understanding of human motivation.

Motivation to Learn in School

Instructional leaders are concerned about developing a particular kind of motivation in their schools—the motivation to learn. Jere Brophy (1988) describes student **motivation to learn** as "...a student tendency to find academic activities meaningful and worthwhile and

TABLE 4.1   Four Views of Motivation

	Behavioral	**Humanistic**	**Cognitive**	**Sociocultural**
Source of Motivation	Extrinsic	Intrinsic	Intrinsic	Intrinsic
Important Influences	Reinforcers, rewards, incentives, and punishers	Need for self-esteem, self-fulfillment, and self-determination	Beliefs, attributions for success and failure, expectations	Engaged participation in learning communities; maintaining identity through participation in activities of group
Key Theorists	Skinner	Maslow Deci	Weiner Graham	Lave Wenger

to try to derive the intended academic benefits from them" (p. 205). Motivation to learn can be construed as both a general trait and a situation-specific state.

Many elements make up the motivation to learn. These include planning, concentration on the goal, metacognitive awareness of what you intend to learn and how you intend to learn it, the active search for new information, clear perceptions of feedback, pride and satisfaction in achievement, and no anxiety or fear of failure (Johnson & Johnson, 1985). Motivation to learn thus involves more than wanting or intending to learn. It includes the quality of the person's mental efforts. For example, reading a text ten times may indicate persistence, but motivation to learn implies more thoughtful, active study strategies, like summarizing, elaborating the basic ideas, outlining in your own words, drawing graphs of the key relationships, and so on (Brophy, 1988).

It would be wonderful if all students came to school filled with the motivation to learn, but they don't. And even if they did, schoolwork might still seem boring or unimportant to some students some of the time. Instructional leaders have three major goals. The first is to get students productively involved with the work of the class; in other words, to create a *state* of motivation to learn. Second, teachers want students to move beyond simple participation to cognitive engagement—to think deeply about what they study. Finally, the long-term goal is to develop in students the *trait* of being motivated to learn so they will be able to educate themselves for their entire lives (Blumenfeld, Puro, & Mergendoller, 1992).

As you can already see, motivation is a vast and complex subject. But principals and teachers need working knowledge. What can they do to support motivation to learn in their schools and classrooms? We will draw from a number of theories to examine four key elements that "build" motivation to learn: *goals, needs, beliefs,* and *emotions.* By keeping in mind these four important aspects of motivation, you can greatly enhance learning in your school.

Goals and Motivation

A **goal** is what an individual is striving to accomplish. Goals motivate people to act in order to reduce the discrepancy between "where they are" and "where they want to be." There are four main reasons why goal setting improves performance. First, goals direct our attention to the task at hand. Second, goals mobilize effort. (The harder the goal, to a point, the greater the effort.) Third, goals increase persistence. (When we have a clear goal we are less likely to be distracted or to give up until we reach the goal.) Finally, goals promote the development of new strategies when old strategies fall short (Locke & Latham, 1990).

Types of Goals

The types of goals we set influence the amount of motivation we have to reach them. Goals that are specific, moderately difficult, and likely to be reached in the near future tend to enhance motivation and persistence (Pintrich & Schunk, 2002; Stipek, 1996). Specific goals provide clear standards for judging performance. If performance falls short, we keep going. Moderate difficulty provides a challenge, but not an unreasonable one. Finally, goals that can be reached fairly soon are not likely to be pushed aside by more immediate concerns.

Groups like Alcoholics Anonymous show they are aware of the motivating value of short-term goals when they encourage their members to stop drinking "one day at a time."

In classrooms there are four main categories of *goal orientations*—learning goals, performance goals, work-avoidance goals, and social goals (Murphy & Alexander, 2000). The most common distinction in research on students' goals is between learning goals (also referred to as task goals or mastery goals) and performance goals (also called ability goals or ego goals). The point of a **learning goal** is to improve, to learn, no matter how many mistakes you make or how awkward you appear. Students who set learning goals tend to seek challenges and persist when they encounter difficulties. Nicholls and Miller (1984) call these students **task-involved learners** because they are concerned with mastering the task and are not worried about how their performance "measures up" compared to others in the class. We often say that these people "get lost in their work." In addition, task-involved learners are more likely to seek appropriate help, use deeper cognitive processing strategies, and apply better study strategies (Butler & Neuman, 1995; Young, 1997).

The second kind of goal is a **performance goal.** Students with performance goals care about demonstrating their ability to others. They may be focussed on getting good test scores and grades or they may be more concerned with winning and beating other students (Wolters, Yu, & Pintrich, 1996). Students whose goal is outperforming others may do things to look smart, such as reading easy books in order to "read the most books" (Young, 1997). If winning is impossible, they may adopt defensive, failure-avoiding strategies—they pretend not to care, make a show of "not really trying," or cheat (Jagacinski & Nicholls, 1987; Pintrich & Schunk, 1996). The evaluation of their performance by others, not what they learn or how hard they try, is what matters. Nicholls and Miller (1984) refer to these students as **ego-involved learners** because they are preoccupied with themselves. Deborah Stipek (2002) lists these behaviors as indicative of a student who is ego-involved with classwork:

- Cheats/copies from classmates' papers
- Seeks attention for good performance
- Only works hard on graded assignments
- Is upset by and hides papers with low grades
- Compares grades with classmates
- Chooses tasks that are most likely to result in positive evaluations
- Is uncomfortable with assignments that have unclear evaluation criteria

Some students don't want to learn or to look smart, they just want to avoid work. These students try to complete assignments and activities as quickly as possible without exerting much effort (Pintrich & Schunk, 2002). Nicholls called these **work-avoidant learners**—they feel successful when they don't have to try hard, when the work is easy, or when they can "goof off."

A final category of goals becomes more important as students get older—**social goals.** As students move into adolescence, their social networks change to include more peers. Nonacademic activities such as athletics, dating, and "hanging out" compete with schoolwork (Urdan & Maehr, 1995). Social goals include a wide variety of needs and motives with different relationships to learning—some help but some hinder learning. For example, adolescents' goal of maintaining friendly relations in a cooperative learning group can get in the way of learning when group members don't challenge wrong answers or misconceptions because they are afraid to hurt members' feelings (Anderson, Holland, & Palincsar, 1997). Certainly, pursuing goals such as having fun with friends or avoiding being labeled a "nerd" can get in the way of learning. But goals of bringing honor to your family or team by working hard can support learning (Urdan & Maehr, 1995).

We talk about goals in separate categories, but students have to coordinate their goals so they can make decisions about what to do and how to act. As noted above, sometimes social and academic goals are incompatible. For example, academic failure may be interpreted positively by some minority group students because noncompliance with the majority culture's norms and standards is seen as an accomplishment. Thus it would be impossible to simultaneously succeed in school and in the peer group (Ogbu, 1987; Wentzel, 1999).

Goals: Lessons for Teachers and Principals

Students and teachers are more likely to work toward goals that are clear, specific, reasonable, moderately challenging, and attainable within a relatively short period of time. If teachers focus on student performance, high grades, competition, and achievement, they may encourage students to set performance goals. This will undermine the students' ability to learn and encourage cheating or self-defeating actions (Anderman & Maehr, 1994). If any reward or incentive systems are used, make sure participants (teachers or students) understand that the goal is to learn and improve in some area, not just to perform well or look smart. And be sure the goal is not too difficult. Individual students or teachers may not yet be expert at setting their own goals or keeping the goal in mind, so encouragement and accurate feedback are necessary. The Theory into Action Guidelines give ideas to principals and teachers for involving families in goal setting in schools.

Needs and Motivation

A **need** can be defined as "…a biological or psychological requirement; a state of deprivation that motivates a person to take action toward a goal" (Darley, Glucksberg, & Kinchla, 1991, p. 743). Our needs are seldom satisfied completely and perfectly; improvement is always possible. People are thus motivated by the tensions the needs create to move toward goals that could satisfy the needs. Let's look at one very influential humanistic theory of motivation that deals with this central concept.

Maslow's Hierarchy

Abraham Maslow has had a great impact on the psychology of motivation. Maslow (1970) suggested that humans have a **hierarchy of needs** ranging from lower-level needs for survival and safety to higher-level needs for intellectual achievement and finally self-actualization. **Self-actualization** is Maslow's term for self-fulfillment, the realization of personal potential.

THEORY INTO ACTION GUIDELINES

Family and Community Partnerships

Understand family goals for children.

Examples

1. In an informal setting, around a coffee pot or snacks, meet with families individually or in small groups to listen to what they want for their children.
2. Mail out questionnaires or send response cards home with students, asking what skills the families believe their children most need to work on. Pick one goal for each child and develop a plan for working toward the goal both inside and outside school. Share the plan with the families and ask for feedback.

Identify student and family interests that can be related to goals.

Examples

1. Ask a member of the family to share a skill or hobby with the class.

2. Identify "family favorites"—favorite foods, music, vacations, sports, colors, activities, hymns, movies, games, snacks, recipes, memories. Tie class lessons to interests.

Give families a way to track progress toward goals.

Examples

1. Provide simple "progress charts" or goal cards that can be posted on the refrigerator.
2. Ask for feedback (and mean it) about parents' perceptions of your effectiveness in helping students reach goals.

Maslow (1968) called the four lower-level needs—survival, safety, belonging, and self-esteem—**deficiency needs.** When these needs are satisfied, the motivation for fulfilling them decreases. He labeled the three higher-level needs—intellectual achievement, aesthetic appreciation, and self-actualization—**being needs.** When they are met, a person's motivation does not cease; instead, it increases to seek further fulfillment. For example, the more successful you are in your efforts to develop professionally, the harder you are likely to strive for even greater improvement. Unlike the deficiency needs, these being needs can never be completely filled. The motivation to achieve them is endlessly renewed.

Maslow's theory has been criticized for the very obvious reason that people do not always appear to behave as the theory would predict. Most of us move back and forth among different types of needs and may even be motivated by many different needs at the same time. Some people deny themselves safety or friendship in order to achieve knowledge, understanding, or greater self-esteem.

Criticisms aside, Maslow's theory does give us a way of looking at the whole person, whose physical, emotional, and intellectual needs are all interrelated. This has important implications for education. A child whose feelings of safety and sense of belonging are threatened by divorce may have little interest in learning to divide fractions. If a school is a fearful, unpredictable place where neither teachers nor students know where they stand, they are likely to be more concerned with security and less with learning or teaching. Maslow's hierarchy can provide other insights into students' behavior. Students' desires to fill lower-level needs may at times conflict with a teacher's desire to have them achieve higher-level goals. Belonging to a social group and maintaining self-esteem within that group, for example, are important to students. If doing what the teacher says conflicts with group rules, students may choose to ignore the teacher's wishes or even defy the teacher.

A great deal has been written about needs and motivation. For teaching, the most fully developed and relevant work involves the need to achieve.

Achievement Motivation

David McClelland and John Atkinson were among the first to concentrate on the study of achievement motivation (McClelland, Atkinson, Clark, & Lowell, 1953). People who strive for excellence in a field for the sake of achieving, not for some reward, are considered to have a high need for achievement. There are two general explanations for the source of achievement motivation (Stipek, 2002). Some psychologists see achievement motivation as a stable and unconscious trait—something the individual has more or less of. The origins of high achievement motivation are assumed to be in the family and cultural group of the child. If achievement, initiative, and competitiveness are encouraged and reinforced in the home, and if parents let children solve problems on their own without becoming irritated by the children's initial failures, children are more likely to develop a high need for achievement (McClelland & Pilon, 1983). Children who see that their actions can have an impact and who are taught how to recognize a good performance are more likely to grow up with the desire to excel (Schunk, 2000).

Other theorists see achievement motivation as a set of conscious beliefs and values shaped mainly by recent experiences with success and failure and by factors in the immediate situation such as the difficulty of the task or the incentives available. Thus you might have high achievement motivation when working with teachers in one subject because you know it well and value it, but low achievement motivation when working in another area because you are less familiar with that subject and you question the real value of the material (Stipek, 2002).

Atkinson (1964) added a new consideration to the theory of achievement need when he noted that all people have a need to avoid failure as well as a need to achieve. If the need to avoid failure is greater than the need to achieve in a particular situation, the risk will be threatening rather than challenging, and the resultant motivation will be to avoid the situation. If students' motivation to achieve is greater than their motivation to avoid failure, a moderate amount of failure can often enhance their desire to pursue a problem. They are determined to achieve, so they try again. On the other hand, success gained too easily can actually decrease motivation for those with high achievement needs. In contrast, students motivated by the need to avoid failure are usually discouraged by failure and encouraged by success.

The Need for Self-Determination

Self-determination is the need to experience choice—to have our own wishes, rather than external rewards or pressures, determine what we do and how we do it (Deci & Ryan,

1985; Deci, Vallerand, Pelletier, & Ryan, 1991). People constantly struggle against pressure from external controls such as the rules, schedules, deadlines, orders, and limits imposed by others. Sometimes even help is rejected so that the individual can remain in command—a possible problem for principals striving to be instructional leaders.

To capture the difference between self- and other-determination, deCharms used the metaphor of people as "origins" and "pawns." Origins perceive themselves as the origin or source of their intention to act in a certain way. But pawns see themselves as powerless participants in a game controlled by others. When people feel like pawns, play becomes work, leisure feels like obligation, and intrinsic motivation becomes extrinsic motivation (Lepper & Greene, 1978). As origins, students are active and responsible, but as pawns they are passive and they take little responsibility for school work. DeCharms developed programs to help teachers support student self-determination. The programs emphasized setting realistic goals, personal planning of activities to reach the goals, personal responsibility for actions, and feelings of self-confidence. Results of some studies show that when students feel more like origins and less like pawns, they have higher self-esteem, feel more competent and in charge of their learning, score higher on standardized tests, and are absent less (deCharms, 1976; Ryan & Grolnick, 1986).

The Need for Social Support

Humans need to establish close emotional bonds and attachments with others to be emotionally connected to the important people in their lives (Ryan, 1991). This has been labeled the *need for relatedness*. When teachers and parents are responsive and demonstrate that they care about the children's interests and well-being, the children show high intrinsic motivation. But, when children are denied the interpersonal involvement they seek from adults—when adults, for example, are unresponsive to their needs—the children lose intrinsic motivation (Grolnick, Ryan, & Deci, 1991). In addition, emotional and physical problems—ranging from eating disorders to suicide—are more common among people who lack social relationships (Baumeister & Leary, 1995).

Relatedness has two components, *involvement* and *autonomy support*. Involvement is the degree to which teachers and parents are interested in and knowledgeable about their children's activities and experiences and devote time to them. When students feel a sense of belonging and personal support from their teachers, they are more interested in class work and find it more valuable (Goodenow, 1993; Stipek, 1996). Autonomy support is the degree to which teachers and parents encourage children to make their own choices rather than applying pressure to control the children's behavior. When teachers and parents show high involvement and autonomy support, children show greater competence, academic achievement, and responsibility, as well as less aggression (Grolnick & Ryan, 1989; Grolnick, Ryan, & Deci, 1991).). The Theory into Practice Guidelines on page 122 give principals and teachers ideas about how to support students' self-determination and autonomy.

Needs and Motivation: Lessons for Teachers and Principals

All people need to feel safe, secure, accepted, competent, effective, connected, and in charge of their own behavior. Some people may have developed a particularly strong need

THEORY INTO PRACTICE GUIDELINES

Supporting Self-Determination

Allow and encourage students to make choices.

Examples

1. Design several different ways to meet a learning objective (e.g., a paper, a compilation of interviews, a test, a news broadcast) and let students choose one. Encourage them to explain the reasons for their choice.
2. Appoint student committees to make suggestions about streamlining procedures such as caring for class pets or distributing equipment.
3. Provide time for independent and extended projects.

Help students plan actions to accomplish self-selected goals.

Examples

1. Experiment with goal cards. Students list their short- and long-term goals and then record three or four specific actions that will move them toward the goals. Goal cards are personal—like credit cards.
2. Encourage middle school and high school students to set goals in each subject area, record them in a goal book or on a floppy disk, and check progress toward the goals on a regular basis.

Hold students accountable for the consequences of their choices.

Examples

1. If students choose to work with friends and do not finish a project because too much time was spent socializing, grade the project as it deserves and help the students see the connection between lost time and poor performance.
2. When students choose a topic that captures their imagination, discuss the connections between their investment in the work and the quality products that follow.

Provide rationales for limits, rules, and constraints.

Examples

1. Explain reasons for rules.
2. Respect rules and constraints in your own behavior.

Acknowledge that negative emotions are valid reactions to teacher control.

Examples

1. Communicate that it is OK (and normal) to feel bored waiting for a turn, for example.
2. Communicate that sometimes important learning involves frustration, confusion, weariness.

Use noncontrolling, positive feedback.

Examples

1. See poor performance or behavior as a problem to be solved, not a target of criticism.
2. Avoid controlling language, "should," "must," "have to."

Source: Adapted from J. P. Raffini (1996). *150 ways to increase intrinsic motivation in the classroom.* Boston: Allyn & Bacon, and J. Reeve (1996). *Motivating others: Nurturing inner motivational resources.* Boston: Allyn & Bacon, pp. 29–31.

to achieve. Most people are more motivated when they are involved with tasks that give them a sense of achievement and a chance to form positive relationships with others. No one enjoys failure, and for some people it is crushing. Students, like adults, are unlikely to stick with tasks or respond well to teachers who make them feel insecure or incompetent. They are less likely to take responsibility for learning if they feel like pawns rather than origins in the classroom or if they believe that the teacher doesn't really care about them. The same can be said for teachers—if they feel like pawns or if they believe that the principal doesn't really care about them or their problems, they are not likely to respond well to help.

Attributions, Beliefs, and Motivation

Thus far, we have talked about goals and needs, but there is another factor that must be considered in explaining motivation to learn. Success will not encourage motivation if you believe it was "just lucky" and probably won't happen again. Failure is not threatening unless you believe that it implies something is "wrong" with you. In other words, our beliefs and attributions about what is happening and why—about why we succeed and why we fail—affect motivation.

Attribution Theory

Cognitive explanations of motivation, called **attribution theories,** begin with the assumption that we all ask "Why?" in our attempts to understand our successes and failures. Attribution theories of motivation describe how the individual's explanations, justifications, and excuses influence motivation.

Dimensions: Locus, Stability, Responsibility.   Bernard Weiner is one of the main educational psychologists responsible for relating attribution theory to school learning (Weiner, 1979, 1986, 1992, 1994; Weiner & Graham, 1989). According to Weiner, most of the causes to which students attribute their successes or failures can be characterized in terms of three dimensions: locus (location of the cause internal or external to the person), stability (whether the cause stays the same or can change), and responsibility (whether the person can control the cause). Table 4.2 shows how a student might explain failing a test using the eight possible combinations of these dimensions as causes.

Weiner (1992, 1994) believes that these three dimensions have important implications for motivation. The internal/external locus, for example, seems to be closely related to feelings of self-esteem (Weiner, 1980). If success or failure is attributed to internal factors, success will lead to pride and increased motivation, whereas failure will diminish self-esteem. The stability dimension seems to be closely related to expectations about the future. If, for example, students attribute their success (or failure) to stable factors such as the difficulty of the subject, they will expect to succeed (or fail) in that subject in the future. But if they attribute the outcome to unstable factors such as mood or luck, they will expect (or hope for) changes in the future when confronted with similar tasks. The responsibility dimension is related to emotions such as anger, pity, gratitude, or shame. If we fail at something that we believe is controllable, we may feel guilt; if we succeed, we may feel proud.

TABLE 4.2   Weiner's Theory of Causal Attribution

There are many explanations students can give for why they fail a test. Below are eight reasons representing the eight combinations of locus, stability, and responsibility in Weiner's model of attributions.

Dimension Classification	Reason for Failure
Internal-stable-uncontrollable	Low aptitude
Internal-stable-controllable	Never studies
Internal-unstable-uncontrollable	Sick the day of the exam
Internal-unstable-controllable	Did not study for this particular test
External-stable-uncontrollable	School has hard requirements
External-stable-controllable	Instructor is biased
External-unstable-uncontrollable	Bad luck
External-unstable-controllable	Friends failed to help

Source: From *Human Motivation: Metaphors, Theories and Research* (p. 253), by B. Weiner, 1992, Newbury Park, CA: Sage Publications. Copyright © 1992 by Sage Publications. Adapted with permission of Sage Publications.

Failing at an uncontrollable task may lead to shame or to anger toward the person or institution in control, while succeeding leads to feeling lucky or grateful. Also, feeling in control of your own learning seems to be related to choosing more difficult academic tasks, putting out more effort, and persisting longer in school work (Schunk, 2000; Weiner, 1994).

Weiner (1994) summarizes the sequence of motivation when failure is attributed to lack of ability and ability is considered uncontrollable:

> Failure → lack of ability → uncontrollable → not responsible → shame and embarrassment → performance declines in future

When failure is attributed to lack of effort, the sequence is:

> Failure → lack of effort → controllable → responsible → guilt → performance improves in future

Weiner's locus and responsibility dimensions are closely related to locus of causality and deCharm's origin/pawn distinction, discussed earlier.

Learned Helplessness.   Whatever the label, most theorists agree that a sense of choice, control, and self-determination is critical if people are to feel intrinsically motivated. When people come to believe that the events and outcomes in their lives are mostly uncontrollable, they have developed **learned helplessness** (Seligman, 1975). To understand the power of learned helplessness, consider this experiment (Hiroto & Seligman, 1975). Subjects receive either solvable or unsolvable puzzles. In the next phase of the experiment, all subjects are given a series of solvable puzzles. The subjects who struggled with unsolvable problems in the first phase of the experiment usually solve significantly fewer puzzles in the second phase. They have learned that they cannot control the outcome, so why should they even try?

Learned helplessness appears to cause three types of deficits: motivational, cognitive, and affective. Students who feel hopeless will be unmotivated and reluctant to attempt work. They expect to fail so why even try—thus motivation suffers. Because they are pessimistic about learning, these students miss opportunities to practice and improve skills and abilities, so they develop cognitive deficits. Finally, they often suffer from affective problems such as depression, anxiety, and listlessness (Alloy & Seligman, 1979). Once established, it is very difficult to reverse the effects of learned helplessness. Learned helplessness is a particular danger for students with learning disabilities and students who are the victims of discrimination.

Attributions and Student Motivation. Most students try to explain their failures to themselves. When usually successful students fail, they often make internal, controllable attributions: they misunderstood the directions, lacked the necessary knowledge, or simply did not study hard enough, for example. When students see themselves as capable and attribute failure to lack of effort or insufficient knowledge—controllable causes—they usually focus on strategies for succeeding next time. This is an adaptive, mastery-oriented response, one that often leads to achievement, pride, a greater feeling of control, and a sense of self-determination (Ames, 1992).

The greatest motivational problems arise when students attribute failures to stable, uncontrollable causes. Such students may seem resigned to failure, depressed, and helpless—what we generally call "unmotivated" (Weiner, 1994; Weiner, Russell, & Lerman, 1978). These students respond to failure by focusing even more on their own inadequacy; their attitudes toward schoolwork may deteriorate even further (Ames, 1992). Apathy is a logical reaction to failure if students believe the causes are stable, unlikely to change, and beyond their control. In addition, students who view their failures in this light are less likely to seek help—they believe nothing and no one can help (Ames & Lau, 1982).

Cues about Causes. How do students determine the causes of their successes and failures? The behavior of their teachers is one cue. When teachers assume that student failure is attributable to forces beyond the students' control, they tend to respond with sympathy and to avoid giving punishments. If, however, the failures are attributed to a controllable factor such as lack of effort, the teacher's response is more likely to be anger, and punishments may follow. These tendencies seem to be consistent across time and cultures (Weiner, 1986).

What do students make of these reactions from their teachers? Graham (1991, 1996) gives some surprising answers. There is evidence that when teachers respond to students' mistakes with pity, praise for a "good try," or unsolicited help, the students are more likely to attribute their failure to an uncontrollable cause—usually lack of ability. Does this mean that teachers should be critical and withhold help? Of course not! But it is a reminder that "praise as a consolation prize" for failing (Brophy, 1985) or oversolicitous help can give unintended messages. Graham (1991) suggests that many minority group students could be the victims of well-meaning pity from teachers. Seeing the very real problems that the students face, teachers may "ease up" on requirements so the students will "experience success" and "feel good about themselves." But a subtle communication may accompany the pity, praise, and extra help: "You don't have the ability to do this, so I will overlook your failure." Graham says, "The...pertinent question for blacks is whether their own history of academic failure makes them more likely to be the targets of sympathetic feedback from teachers and thus the recipients of low-ability cues" (1991, p. 28). This kind of sympathetic feedback, even if well-intended, can be a subtle form of racism.

Beliefs about Ability

As you can see, some of the most powerful attributions affecting motivation in school are beliefs about ability. Adults use two basic concepts of ability. An **entity view** of ability assumes that ability is a stable, uncontrollable trait—a characteristic of the individual that cannot be changed. According to this view, some people have more ability than others, but the amount each person has is set. An **incremental view** of ability, on the other hand, suggests that ability is unstable and controllable—"...an ever-expanding repertoire of skills and knowledge" (Dweck & Bempechat, 1983, p. 144). By hard work, study, or practice, knowledge can be increased and thus ability can be improved. Table 4.3 shows how these two conceptions of ability would fit into Weiner's model of causal attribution (Table 4.2).

Young children tend to hold an exclusively incremental view of ability (Nicholls & Miller, 1984). Through the early elementary grades, most students believe that effort is the same as intelligence. Smart people try hard and trying hard makes you smart. If you fail, you aren't smart and you didn't try hard; if you succeed, you must be a smart, hard worker (Stipek, 2002). Children are age 11 or 12 before they can differentiate among effort, ability, and performance. About this time, they come to believe that someone who succeeds without working at all must be really smart. This is when beliefs about ability begin to influence motivation (Anderman & Maehr, 1994).

Students who hold an entity view of intelligence tend to set performance goals. They seek situations where they can look smart and protect their self-esteem. They keep doing what they can do well without expending too much effort or risking failure, because either one—working hard or failing—indicates (to them) low ability. And to work hard but still fail would be a devastating blow to their sense of competence. Another strategy is to make a point of not trying at all. If you don't try and then fail, no one can accuse you of being

TABLE 4.3   A Revised View of the Internal Attribution Model with Two Kinds of Ability

	Internal Attribution	
	Stable	**Unstable**
Controllable	Never studies	Did not study for this particular test *Incremental ability*
Uncontrollable	*Entity ability*	Sick day of exam

dumb. Just before a test a student might say, "I didn't study at all!" or "All I want to do is pass." Then, any grade above passing is a success. Procrastination is another self-protective strategy. Low grades do not imply low ability if the student can claim, "I did okay considering I didn't start the term paper until last night." Some evidence suggests that blaming anxiety for poor test performance can also be a self-protective strategy (Covington & Omelich, 1987). Of course, even though these strategies may help students avoid the negative implications of failure, very little learning is going on.

Students who have an incremental notion of ability, in contrast, tend to set learning goals and seek situations in which they can improve their skills, because improvement means getting smarter. Failure is not devastating; it simply indicates more work is needed, as the best athletic coaches know well. Ability is not threatened when failure signals simply that more effort is needed. Incremental theorists tend to set moderately difficult goals, the kind we have seen are the most motivating.

Beliefs about Self-Efficacy

Albert Bandura (1986, 1997) suggests that critical sources of motivation are predictions about possible outcomes of behavior. "Will I succeed or fail? Will I be liked or laughed at?" We imagine future consequences based on past experiences and our observations of others. These predictions are affected by **self-efficacy**—our beliefs about our personal competence or effectiveness *in a given area.* Bandura (1997) defines self-efficacy as "beliefs in one's capabilities to organize and execute the courses of action required to produce given attainments" (p. 3).

Self-Efficacy, Self-Concept, and Self-Esteem.   Most people assume self-efficacy is the same as self-concept or self-esteem, but it isn't. Self-efficacy is distinct from other conceptions of self, in that it involves judgments of capabilities *specific to a particular task.* Self-efficacy is "a context-specific assessment of competence to perform a specific task" (Pajares, 1997, p. 15). Self-concept is a more global construct that contains many perceptions about the self, including self-efficacy. Self-concept is developed as a result of external and internal comparisons, using others people or other aspects of the self as frames of reference. But self-efficacy focuses on your ability to successfully accomplish a particular task with no need for comparisons—the question is can *you* do it, not would others be successful (Marsh, Walker, & Debus, 1991). Also, efficacy beliefs are strong predictors of behavior, but self-concept has weaker predictive power (Bandura, 1997).

Compared to self-esteem, self-efficacy is concerned with judgments of personal capabilities; self-esteem is concerned with judgments of self-worth. There is no direct relationship between self-esteem and self-efficacy. It is possible to feel highly efficacious in one area and still not have a high level of self-esteem, or vice versa. For example, if you have very low self-efficacy for singing, your self-esteem as an instructional leader probably won't be affected unless you believe that singing is a critical skill for educational administrators.

Sources of Efficacy.   Bandura identified four sources of efficacy expectations: mastery experiences, physiological and emotional arousal, vicarious experiences, and social persuasion. **Mastery experiences** are our own direct experiences—the most powerful source of efficacy information. Successes raise efficacy beliefs while failures lower efficacy. *Level of arousal* affects efficacy, depending on how the arousal is interpreted. As you face the task, are you anxious and worried (lowers efficacy) or excited and "psyched" (raises efficacy) (Bandura, 1997; Pintrich & Schunk, 2002).

In **vicarious experiences,** accomplishments are modeled by someone else. The more closely the observer identifies with the model, the greater the impact on efficacy. When the model performs well, the observer's efficacy is enhanced, but when the model performs poorly, efficacy expectations decrease. Although mastery experiences generally are acknowledged as the most influential source of efficacy beliefs in adults, Keyser and Barling (1981) found that children (sixth graders in this study) rely more on modeling as a source of self-efficacy information.

Social persuasion may be a "pep talk" or specific performance feedback. Social persuasion alone can't create enduring increases in self-efficacy, but a persuasive boost in self-efficacy can lead a student or teacher to make an effort, attempt new strategies, or try hard enough to succeed (Bandura, 1982). Social persuasion can counter occasional setbacks that might have instilled self-doubt and interrupted persistence. The potency of persuasion depends on the credibility, trustworthiness, and expertise of the persuader (Bandura, 1986).

Efficacy and Motivation.   Greater efficacy leads to greater effort and persistence in the face of setbacks. Efficacy also influences motivation through goal setting. If we have a high sense of efficacy in a given area, we will set higher goals, be less afraid of failure, and find new strategies when old ones fail. If our sense of efficacy is low, however, we may avoid a task altogether or give up easily when problems arise (Bandura, 1993, 1997; Zimmerman, 1995).

Self-efficacy and attributions affect each other. If success is attributed to internal or controllable causes such as ability or effort, then self-efficacy is enhanced. But if success is attributed to luck or the intervention of others, then self-efficacy may not be strengthened. And efficacy affects attributions too. People with a strong sense of self-efficacy for a given task ("I'm good at math") tend to attribute their failures to lack of effort ("I should have double-checked my work"). But people with a low sense of efficacy ("I'm terrible at math") tend to attribute their failures to lack of ability ("I'm just dumb"). So having a strong sense of efficacy for a certain task encourages controllable attributions and controllable attributions increase efficacy. You can see that if a student held an *entity view* (ability cannot be changed) and a *low sense of self-efficacy,* motivation would be destroyed when failures were attributed to lack of ability ("I just can't do this and I'll never be able to learn") (Bandura, 1997; Pintrich & Schunk, 2002).

There is evidence that a high sense of self-efficacy supports motivation, even when the efficacy is unrealistically high. Children and adults who are optimistic about the future, who believe that they can be effective, and who have high expectations are more mentally and physically healthy, less depressed, and more motivated to achieve (Flammer, 1995). After examining almost 140 studies of motivation, Sandra Graham concluded that these qualities characterize many African Americans. She found that the African Americans studied had strong self-concepts and high expectations, even in the face of difficulties (Graham, 1994, 1995).

Research on self-efficacy and achievement suggests that performance in school is improved and self-efficacy is increased when students (a) adopt short-term goals so it is easier to judge progress; (b) are taught to use specific learning strategies such as outlining or summarizing that help them focus attention; and (c) receive rewards based on quality of performance, not just engagement, because the former signal increasing competence (Graham & Weiner, 1996). Table 4.4 shows how the different elements we have been discussing combine to support motivation to learn.

Teacher Efficacy.   Much of our own research has focused on a particular kind of self-efficacy—sense of efficacy in teaching (Hoy & Woolfolk, 1990, 1993; Tschannen-Moran, Woolfolk Hoy, & Hoy, 1998; Woolfolk & Hoy, 1990; Woolfolk, Rosoff, & Hoy, 1990). **Teaching efficacy,** a teacher's belief that he or she can reach even difficult students to help them learn, appears to be one of the few personal characteristics of teachers that is correlated with student achievement. Self-efficacy theory predicts that teachers with a high sense of efficacy work harder and persist longer even when students are difficult to teach, in part because these teachers believe in themselves and in their students.

TABLE 4.4   Building a Concept of Motivation to Learn

Motivation to learn is encouraged when the sources of motivation are intrinsic, the goals are personally challenging, and the individual is focused on the task, has a mastery orientation, attributes successes and failures to controllable causes, and believes ability can be improved.

	Optimum Characteristics of Motivation to Learn	**Characteristics That Diminish Motivation to Learn**
Source of Motivation	INTRINSIC: Personal factors such as needs, interests, curiosity, enjoyment	EXTRINSIC: Environmental factors such as rewards, social pressure, punishment
Type of Goal Set	LEARNING GOAL: Personal satisfaction in meeting challenges and improving; tendency to choose moderately difficult and challenging goals	PERFORMANCE GOAL: Desire for approval for performance in others' eyes; tendency to choose very easy or very difficult goals
Type of Involvement	TASK-INVOLVED: Concerned with mastering the task	EGO-INVOLVED: Concerned with self in others' eyes.
Achievement Motivation	Motivation to ACHIEVE: mastery orientation	Motivation to AVOID FAILURE: prone to anxiety
Likely Attributions	Successes and failures attributed to CONTROLLABLE effort and ability	Success and failures attributed to UNCONTROLLABLE causes
Beliefs about Ability	INCREMENTAL VIEW: Belief that ability can be improved through hard work and added knowledge and skills	ENTITY VIEW: Belief that ability is a stable, uncontrollable trait

Source: From Anita Woolfolk, *Educational Psychology, 8/e.* Copyright © 2001. Reprinted by permission of Allyn & Bacon.

We have found that prospective teachers tend to increase in their personal sense of efficacy as a consequence of completing student teaching. Teachers' sense of personal efficacy is higher in schools where the other teachers and administrators have high expectations for students and where teachers receive help from their principals in solving instructional and management problems (Hoy & Woolfolk, 1993). Another important research conclusion is that efficacy grows from real success with students, not just from the moral support or cheerleading of professors and colleagues. Any experience or training that helps teachers succeed in the day-to-day tasks of teaching will give them a foundation for developing a sense of efficacy in their career.

Attributions, Achievement Motivation, and Self-Worth

What are the connections between need for achievement, attributions for success and failure, beliefs about ability, self-efficacy, and self-worth? Covington and his colleagues suggest that these factors come together in three kinds of motivational sets: mastery-oriented, failure-avoiding, and failure-accepting, as shown in Table 4.5 (Covington, 1992; Covington & Omelich, 1984, 1987).

Mastery-oriented students tend to value achievement and see ability as improvable, so they focus on learning goals in order to increase their skills and abilities. They are not fearful of failure, because failing does not threaten their sense of competence and self-worth. This allows them to set moderately difficult goals, take risks, and cope with failure constructively. They generally attribute success to their own effort, and so they assume responsibility for learning and have a strong sense of self-efficacy. They perform best in competitive situations, learn fast, have more self-confidence and energy, are more aroused, welcome concrete feedback (it does not threaten them), and are eager to learn "the rules of

TABLE 4.5   Mastery-Oriented, Failure-Avoiding, and Failure-Accepting Students

	Attitude toward Failure	Goals Set	Attributions	View of Ability	Strategies
Mastery-Oriented	Low fear of failure	Learning goals: moderately difficult and challenging	Effort, use of right strategy, sufficient knowledge is cause of success	Incremental; improvable	Adaptive strategies; e.g., try another way, seek help, practice/study more
Failure-Avoiding	High fear of failure	Performance goals; very hard or very easy	Lack of ability is cause of failure	Entity; set	Self-defeating strategies; e.g., make a feeble effort, pretend not to care
Failure-Accepting	Expectation of failure; depression	Performance goals or no goals	Lack of ability is cause of failure	Entity; set	Learned helplessness; likely to give up

Source: From Anita Woolfolk, *Educational Psychology, 8/e.* Copyright © 2001. Reprinted by permission of Allyn & Bacon.

the game" so that they can succeed. All of these factors make for persistent, successful learning for teachers or students (Alderman, 1985; McClelland, 1985; Morris, 1991).

Failure-avoiding students tend to hold an entity view of ability, so they set performance goals. They lack a strong sense of their own competence and self-worth separate from their performance. In other words, they feel only as smart as their last test grade or performance evaluation, so they never develop a solid sense of self-efficacy. In order to feel competent, they must protect themselves (and their self-images) from failure. If they have been generally successful, they may avoid failure simply by taking few risks and "sticking with what they know." If, on the other hand, they have experienced some successes but also a good bit of failure, they may adopt the strategies we discussed earlier—procrastination, feeble efforts, setting very low or ridiculously high goals, or claiming not to care.

Unfortunately, as we have seen, failure-avoiding strategies are self-defeating, generally leading to the very failure the person was trying to avoid. If failures continue and excuses wear thin, the students or teachers may finally decide that they are incompetent. This is what they feared in the first place, but they come to accept it. Their sense of self-worth and self-efficacy deteriorate. They give up and thus become **failure-accepting.** They are convinced that their problems are due to low ability, and they can no longer protect themselves from this conclusion. As we saw earlier, those students who attribute failure to low ability and believe ability is set are likely to become depressed, apathetic, and helpless.

Teachers may be able to prevent some failure-avoiding students from becoming failure-accepting by helping them to find new and more realistic goals. Also, some students may need support in aspiring to higher levels in the face of sexual or ethnic stereotypes about what they "should" want or what they "should not" be able to do well. This kind of support could make all the difference. Instead of pitying or excusing these students, teachers and schools can teach them how to learn and then hold them accountable.

Attributions and Beliefs: Lessons for Teachers and Principals

At the heart of attribution theory is the notion of individual perception. If students believe they lack the ability to deal with higher mathematics, they will probably act on this belief even if their actual abilities are well above average. These students are likely to have little motivation to tackle calculus, because they expect to do poorly in these areas. If students believe that failing means they are stupid, they are likely to adopt many self-protective, but also self-defeating, strategies. Just telling students to "try harder" is not particularly effective. Students need real evidence that effort will pay off, that setting a higher goal will not lead to failure, that they can improve, and that abilities can be changed. The Theory into Action Guidelines on page 132 should help instructional leaders suggest ideas for teachers to encourage student self-worth and self-efficacy.

Interests and Emotions

How do you feel about learning? Excited, bored, curious, fearful? Today, researchers emphasize that learning is not only about the *cold cognition* of reasoning and problem solving.

T H E O R Y   I N T O   A C T I O N   G U I D E L I N E S

Encouraging Self-Worth and Self-Efficacy

Emphasize students' progress in a particular area.

Examples
1. Return to earlier material in reviews and show how "easy" it is now.
2. Encourage students to improve projects when they have learned more.
3. Keep examples of particularly good work in portfolios.

Make specific suggestions for improvement, and revise grades when improvements are made.

Examples
1. Return work with comments noting what the students did right, what they did wrong, and why they might have made the mistakes.
2. Experiment with peer editing.
3. Show students how their revised, higher grade reflects greater competence and raises their class average.

Stress connections between past efforts and past accomplishments.

Examples
1. Have individual goal-setting and goal-review conferences with students, in which you ask students to reflect on how they solved difficult problems.
2. Confront self-defeating, failure-avoiding strategies directly.

Set learning goals for your students, and model a mastery orientation for them.

Examples
1. Recognize progress and improvement.
2. Share examples of how you have developed your abilities in a given area and provide other models of achievement who are similar to your students—no supermen or women whose accomplishment seem unattainable.
3. Read stories about students who overcame physical, mental, or economic challenges.
4. Don't excuse failure because a student has problems outside school. Help the student succeed inside school.

Learning and information processing also are influenced by emotion, so *hot cognition* plays a role in learning as well (Miller, 1993; Pintrich, Marx, & Boyle, 1993). Students are more likely to pay attention to, learn, and remember events, images, and readings that provoke emotional responses (Alexander & Murphy, 1998; Cowley & Underwood, 1998; Reisberg & Heuer, 1992) or that are related to their personal interests (Renninger, Hidi, & Krapp, 1992). How can we use these findings to support learning in school?

Tapping Interests

When Walter Vispoel and James Austin (1995) asked over 200 middle school students to rate reasons for their successes and failures in different school subjects, lack of interest in the topic received the highest rating as an explanation for failures. Interest was second only to effort as a choice for explaining successes. It seems logical that learning experiences should be related to the interests of the students. And interests increase when students feel competent, so even if students are not initially interested in a subject or activity, they may develop interests as they experience success (Stipek, 2002).

One source of interest is fantasy. For example, Cordova and Lepper (1996) found that students learned more math facts during a computer exercise when they were challenged, as captains of star ships, to navigate through space by solving math problems. The students got to name their ships, stock the (imaginary) galley with their favorite snacks, and name all the crew members after their friends. Principals can use the Theory into Action Guidelines below to give teachers other ideas.

However, there are cautions in responding to students' interests. Ruth Garner (1992) and her colleagues found that the presence of "seductive details" can hinder learning. Seductive details are interesting bits of information that are not central to the learning, but

---

THEORY INTO ACTION GUIDELINES

Building on Students' Interests

Relate content objectives to student experiences.

Examples

1. With a teacher in another school, establish pen pals across the classes. Through writing letters, students exchange personal experiences, photos, drawings, written work, and ask and answer questions ("Have you learned cursive writing yet?" "What are you doing in math now?" "What are you reading?"). Letters can be mailed in one large mailer to save stamps.
2. Identify classroom experts for different assignments or tasks. Who knows how to use the computer for graphics? How to search the Net? How to cook? How to use an index?
3. Have a "Switch Day" when students exchange roles with a school staff or support person. Students must research the role by interviewing their staff member, prepare for the job, dress the part for the day they take over, and then evaluate their success after the switch.

Identify student interests, hobbies, and extracurricular activities that can be incorporated into class lessons and discussions.

Examples

1. Have students design and conduct interviews and surveys to learn about each other's interests.
2. Keep the class library stocked with books that connect to students' interests and hobbies.

Support instruction with humor, personal experiences, and anecdotes that show the human side of the content.

Examples

1. Share your own hobbies, interests, and favorites.
2. Tell students there will be a surprise visitor, then dress up as the author of a story and tell about "yourself" and your writing.

Source: Adapted from J. P. Raffini (1996). *150 ways to increase intrinsic motivation in the classroom.* Boston: Allyn & Bacon.

distract from it. Some examples might be interesting puzzles or other manipulatives that don't connect with important learning objectives but are intriguing to students or details about the life of a scientist that do not help you understand her theories. So if you dress up like the author of the book and visit a teacher's class, as described in the Guidelines, make sure that the details you share about "your" life are connected to the teacher's learning objectives.

Arousal: Excitement and Anxiety in Learning

Just as we all know how it feels to be motivated, we all know what it is like to be aroused. **Arousal** involves both psychological and physical reactions—changes in brain wave patterns, blood pressure, heart rate, and breathing rate. We feel alert, wide-awake, even excited. To understand the effects of arousal on motivation, think of two extremes. The first is late at night. You are trying for the third time to finish reading materials for a meeting tomorrow, but you are so sleepy. Your attention drifts as your eyes droop, even though you have not finished your preparation. At the other extreme, imagine that you have a television interview tomorrow—one that is sure to be watched by many parents in your district. You feel tremendous pressure from everyone to do well. You know that you need a good night's sleep, but you are wide awake. In the first case arousal is too low and in the second, too high.

There appears to be an optimum level of arousal for most activities, as shown in Figure 4.1 (Yerkes & Dodson, 1908). Generally speaking, a higher level of arousal is helpful on simple tasks like organizing files, but lower levels of arousal are better for complex tasks such as taking the GRE. Let's look for a moment at how to increase arousal by arousing curiosity.

Curiosity: Novelty and Complexity. Over 30 years ago, psychologists suggested that individuals are naturally motivated to seek novelty, surprise, and complexity (Berlyne, 1966). Research on teaching has found that variety in teaching approaches and tasks can support learning (Brophy & Good, 1986; Stipek, 1996). For younger students, the chance to manipulate and explore objects relevant to what is being studied may be the most effective way to keep curiosity stimulated. For older students, well-constructed questions, logical puzzles, and paradoxes can have the same effect. Example: ranchers in an area killed the wolves on their land. The following spring they noticed that the deer population was much smaller. How could this be, since wolves hunt the deer and fewer wolves should mean more deer? In searching for a solution, students learn about ecology and the balance of nature: without wolves to eliminate the weaker and sicker deer, the deer population expanded so much that the winter food supply could not sustain the herds and many deer died of starvation.

George Lowenstein (1994) suggests that curiosity arises when attention is focused on a gap in knowledge "Such information gaps produce the feeling of deprivation labeled *curiosity.* The curious person is motivated to obtain the missing information to reduce or eliminate the feeling of deprivation" (p. 87). This idea, similar to Piaget's concept of disequilibrium, has a number of implications for teaching. First, students need some base of knowledge before they can experience gaps in knowledge leading to curiosity. Second, students must be aware of the gaps in order for curiosity to result. Asking students to make guesses, then providing feedback can be helpful. Also, mistakes, properly handled, can

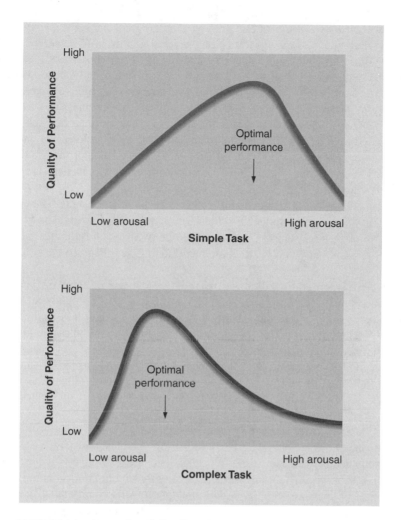

FIGURE 4.1   Arousal and Quality of Performance   On a simple or well-practiced task, the best performance occurs when arousal is moderately high. But on a complex task, lower arousal leads to better performance—as long as the arousal isn't *too* low.

Source: From Anita Woolfolk, *Educational Psychology,* 8/e. Copyright © 2001. Reprinted by permission of Allyn & Bacon.

stimulate curiosity by pointing to missing knowledge. Finally, the more we learn about a topic, the more curious we may become about that subject. As Maslow (1970) predicted, fulfilling the need to know and understand increases, not decreases, the need to know more.

As we discussed earlier, sometimes arousal is too high, not too low. Because schools are places where students are tested and graded, anxiety can become a factor in classroom motivation.

Anxiety in the Classroom.   At one time or another, everyone has experienced **anxiety,** or "general uneasiness, a sense of foreboding, a feeling of tension" (Hansen, 1977, p. 91). The effects of anxiety on school achievement are clear. "From the time of the earliest work on this problem, starting with the pioneering work of Yerkes and Dodson (1908), to the present day, researchers have consistently reported a negative correlation between virtually every aspect of school achievement and a wide range of anxiety measures" (Covington & Omelich, 1987, p. 393). Anxiety can be both a cause and an effect of school failure— students do poorly because they are anxious, and their poor performance increases their anxiety. Anxiety probably is both a trait and a state. Some students tend to be anxious in many situations (*trait anxiety*), but some situations are especially anxiety-provoking (*state anxiety*) (Covington, 1992).

Anxiety seems to have both cognitive and affective components. The cognitive side includes worry and negative thoughts—thinking about how bad it would be to fail and worrying that you will, for example. The affective side involves physiological and emotional reactions such as sweaty palms, upset stomach, racing heartbeat, or fear (Schunk, 2000; Zeidner, 1995).

In the classroom, the conditions surrounding a test can influence the performance of highly anxious individuals. For example, Hill and Eaton (1977) found that very anxious fifth and sixth graders worked as quickly and accurately as their less-anxious classmates when there was no time limit for solving arithmetic problems. With a time limit, however, the very anxious students made three times as many errors as their classmates, spent about twice as much time on each problem, and cheated twice as often as the less-anxious group. Whenever there are pressures to perform, severe consequences for failure, and competitive comparisons among students, anxiety may be encouraged (Wigfield & Eccles, 1989).

How Does Anxiety Interfere with Achievement?   Sigmund Tobias (1985) suggests a model to explain how anxiety interferes with learning and test performance at three points in the learning and performance cycle. When students are learning new material, they must pay attention to it. Highly anxious students evidently divide their attention between the new material and their preoccupation with how nervous they are feeling. Instead of concentrating on a lecture or on what they are reading, they keep noticing the tight feelings in their chest, thinking, "I'm so tense, I'll never understand this stuff!" Much of their attention is taken up with negative thoughts about performing poorly, being criticized, and feeling embarrassed. From the beginning, anxious students may miss much of the information they are supposed to learn because their thoughts are focused on their own worries (Hill & Wigfield, 1984; Paulman & Kennelly, 1984).

But the problems do not end here. Even if they are paying attention, many anxious students have trouble learning material that is somewhat disorganized and difficult—material that requires them to rely on their memory. Unfortunately, much material in school could be described this way. Anxious students may be more easily distracted by irrelevant or incidental aspects of the task at hand. They seem to have trouble focusing on the significant details (Hill & Wigfield, 1984). In addition, many highly anxious students have poor study habits. Simply learning to be more relaxed will not automatically improve these students' performance; their learning strategies and study skills must be improved as well (Naveh-Benjamin, 1991).

Finally, anxious students often know more than they can demonstrate on a test. They may lack critical test-taking skills, or they may have learned the materials but "freeze and forget" on tests. So anxiety can interfere at one or all three points—attention, learning, and testing (Naveh-Benjamin, McKeachie, & Lin, 1987).

Coping with Anxiety.   When students face stressful situations such as tests, they can use three kinds of coping strategies—*problem solving, emotional management,* and *avoidance.* Problem-focused strategies might include planning a study schedule, borrowing good notes, or finding a protected place to study. Emotion-focused strategies are attempts to reduce the anxious feelings, for example, by using relaxation exercises or describing the feelings to a friend. Of course, the latter might become an avoidance strategy, along with going out for pizza or suddenly launching an all out desk-cleaning attack (can't study till you get organized). Different strategies are helpful at different points—for example, problem solving before and emotion management during an exam. Different strategies fit different people and situations (Zeidner, 1995).

Teachers should help highly anxious students to set realistic goals, because these individuals often have difficulty making wise choices. They tend to select either extremely difficult or extremely easy tasks. In the first case, they are likely to fail, which will increase their sense of hopelessness and anxiety about school. In the second case, they will probably succeed on the easy tasks, but they will miss the sense of satisfaction that could encourage greater effort and ease their fears about schoolwork. Anxious students may need a good deal of guidance in choosing both short- and long-term goals. Goal cards, progress charts, or goal planning journals may help here. We have developed some guidelines for principals to help teachers deal with anxious students, as you can see on page 138.

Now that we have a picture of some important building blocks of motivation, let's consider how to put this knowledge to work in classrooms. How will you help teachers deal with one of their greatest challenges—motivating their students?

Strategies to Encourage Motivation and Thoughtful Learning

Until four basic conditions are met, no motivational strategies will succeed. So your first step as an instructional leader working with teachers to improve their students' motivation is to determine if these basic conditions are met in your school. Once these requirements are in place, there are many strategies to help students gain confidence, value learning, and stay involved with the task (Brophy, 1988; Lepper, 1988).

Necessary Conditions in Classrooms

First, the classroom must be relatively organized and free from constant interruptions and disruptions. (Chapter 6 will give you the information you need to make sure this requirement is met.) Second, the teacher must be a patient, supportive person who never embarrasses students for making mistakes. Everyone in the class should see mistakes as opportunities for learning (Clifford, 1990, 1991). Third, the work must be challenging but

THEORY INTO ACTION GUIDELINES

Dealing with Anxiety

Use competition carefully.

Examples

1. Monitor activities to make sure no students are being put under undue pressure.
2. During competitive games, make sure all students involved have a reasonable chance of succeeding.
3. Experiment with cooperative learning activities.

Avoid situations in which highly anxious students will have to perform in front of large groups.

Examples

1. Ask anxious students questions that can be answered yes or no, or some other brief reply.
2. Give anxious students practice in speaking before smaller groups.

Make sure all instructions are clear. Uncertainty can lead to anxiety.

Examples

1. Write test instructions on the board or on the test itself instead of giving them orally.
2. Check with students to make sure they understand. Ask several students how they would do the first question of an exercise or the sample question on a test. Correct any misconceptions.

3. If you are using a new format or starting a new type of task, give students examples or models to show how it is done.

Avoid unnecessary time pressures.

Examples

1. Give occasional take-home tests.
2. Make sure all students can complete classroom tests within the period given.

Remove some of the pressures from major tests and exams.

Examples

1. Teach test-taking skills; give practice tests; provide study guides.
2. Avoid basing most of a report-card grade on one test.
3. Make extra-credit work available to add points to course grades.
4. Use different types of items in testing because some students have difficulty with certain types.

Develop alternatives to written tests.

Examples

1. Try oral, open-book, or group tests.
2. Have students do projects, organize portfolios of their work, make oral presentations, or create a finished product.

---

reasonable. If work is too easy or too difficult, students will have little motivation to learn. They will focus on finishing, not on learning. Finally, the learning tasks must be authentic and not just busywork (Brophy, 1983; Brophy & Kher, 1986; Stipek, 2002).

Once these four basic conditions are met, the influences on students' motivation to learn in a particular situation can be summarized in three basic questions: Can I succeed at this task? Do I want to succeed? What do I need to do to succeed? (Eccles & Wigfield, 1985). As reflected in these questions, we want students to have confidence in their ability so they will approach learning with energy and enthusiasm. We want them to see the value of the tasks involved and work to learn, not just try to get the grade or get finished. We want students to believe that success will come when they apply good learning strategies instead of believing that their only option is to use self-defeating, failure-avoiding, face-saving strategies. When things get difficult, we want students to try to solve the problem and stay focused on the task, not get so worried about failure that they "freeze" with anxiety. Table 4.6 summarizes the basic requirements and strategies for encouraging student motivation to learn, all of which are discussed at length in the next few pages.

Can I Do It? Building Confidence and Positive Expectations

Let's assume the four basic conditions are met in a your school. What's next? One of the most important factors in building expectations for success is past success. No amount of encouragement or "cheerleading" will substitute for real accomplishment. To ensure genuine progress, teachers in your school should be encouraged to:

1. *Begin work at the students' level and move in small steps.* The pace should be brisk, but not so fast that students have to move to the next step before they understand the previous one. This may require assigning different tasks to different students. One possibility is

TABLE 4.6   Strategies to Encourage Motivation to Learn

This table refers to the entire Strategies to Encourage Motivation and Thoughtful Learning section of the text.

Fulfill basic requirements
- Provide an organized class environment
- Be a supportive teacher
- Assign challenging work, but not too difficult
- Make tasks worthwhile

Build confidence and positive expectations
- Begin work at the students' level
- Make learning goals clear, specific, and attainable
- Stress self-comparison, not competition
- Communicate that academic ability is improvable
- Model good problem solving

Show the value of learning
- Connect the learning task to the needs of the students
- Tie class activities to the students' interests

- Arouse curiosity
- Make the learning task fun
- Make use of novelty and familiarity
- Explain connections between present learning and later life
- Provide incentives and rewards, if needed
- Use ill-structured problems and authentic tasks

Help students stay focused on the task
- Give students frequent opportunities to respond
- Provide opportunities for students to create a finished product
- Avoid heavy emphasis on grading
- Reduce task risk without oversimplifying the task
- Model motivation to learn
- Teach learning tactics

Source: From Anita Woolfolk, *Educational Psychology, 8/e.* Copyright © 2001. Reprinted by permission of Allyn & Bacon.

to have very easy and very difficult questions on every test and assignment, so all students are sure to pass some questions and fail others. This provides both success and challenge for everyone. When grades are required, make sure all the students in class have a chance to make at least a C if they work hard.

2. *Make sure learning goals are clear, specific, and possible to reach in the near future.* When long-term projects are planned, break the work into subgoals and help students feel a sense of progress toward the long-term goal. For example, a big research paper could be broken down into identifying a topic and a few basic references, doing an outline, taking notes, finding additional references and learning the form for a bibliography, writing an introduction, doing a first draft, and finally writing the polished paper. If possible, give students a range of goals at different levels of difficulty and let them choose.

3. *Stress self-comparison, not comparison with others.* Help students see the progress they are making by showing them how to use self-management strategies. Give specific feedback and corrections. Tell students what they are doing right as well as what is wrong and *why* it is wrong. Periodically, give students a question or problem that was once hard for them but now seems easy. Point out how much they have improved. Show the connections between their efforts and their accomplishments.

4. *Communicate to students that academic ability is improvable* and specific to the task at hand. In other words, the fact that a student has trouble in algebra doesn't necessarily mean that geometry will be difficult or that he or she is a bad English student. Even when a task is hard, students can improve if they stick with it. Don't undermine efforts to stress improvement by displaying only the A+ papers on the bulletin board.

5. *Model good problem solving,* Students need to see that learning is not smooth and error-free, even for the teacher.

Do I Want to Do It? Seeing the Value of Learning

We can think of a task as having three kinds of value to the students (Eccles & Wigfield, 1985). *Attainment value* is the importance of doing well on the task. This aspect of value is closely tied to the needs of the individual (for example, the need to be competent, well-liked, masculine, etc.) and the meaning of success to that person. A second kind of value is intrinsic or *interest value.* This is simply the enjoyment one gets from the activity itself. Some people like the experience of learning. Others enjoy the feeling of hard physical effort or of solving puzzles. Finally, tasks have *utility value;* that is, they help us achieve a short-term or long-term goal.

Principals and teachers can use intrinsic and extrinsic motivation strategies to help students see the value of the learning task. In this process the age of the student must be considered. For young children, interest value is a greater determinant of motivation than attainment or utility value. Because younger students have a more immediate, concrete focus, they have trouble seeing the value of an activity that is linked to distant goals such as getting a good job—or even preparing for the next grade. Older students, on the other hand, have the cognitive ability to think more abstractly and connect what they are learning now with goals and future possibilities, so utility value becomes important to these students (Eccles & Wigfield, 1985).

Attainment and Intrinsic Value. To establish attainment value, we must connect the learning task with the needs of the students. First, it must be possible for students to meet their needs for safety, belonging, and achievement in our schools. The classroom should not be a frightening or lonely place. Second, we must be sure that sexual or ethnic stereotypes do not interfere with motivation. For example, if students subscribe to rigid notions of masculinity and femininity, we must make it clear that both women and men can be high achievers in all subjects and that no subjects are the territory of only one sex. It is not "unfeminine" to be strong in mathematics, science, shop, or sports. It is not "unmasculine" to be good in literature, art, music, or French. There are many strategies for encouraging intrinsic (interest) motivation. Several of the following are taken from Brophy (1988).

1. *Tie class activities to student interests* in sports, music, current events, pets, common problems or conflicts with family and friends, fads, television and cinema personalities, or other significant features of their lives (Schiefele, 1991). When possible, give students choices of research papers or reading topics so they can follow their own interests.

2. *Arouse curiosity.* Point out puzzling discrepancies between students' beliefs and the facts. For example, Stipek (2002) describes a teacher who asked her fifth-grade class if there were "people" on some of the other planets. When the students said yes, the teacher asked if people needed oxygen to breathe. Since the students had just learned this fact, they responded yes to this question also. Then the teacher told them that there is no oxygen in the atmosphere of the other planets. This surprising discrepancy between what the children knew about oxygen and what they believed about life on other planets led to a rousing discussion of the atmospheres of other planets, the kinds of beings that could survive in these atmospheres, and so on. A straight lecture on the atmosphere of the planets might have put the students to sleep, but this discussion led to real interest in the subject.

3. *Make the learning task fun.* Many lessons can be taught through simulations or games. Computers, problem-based learning, cable TV, and Web connections are just a few possibilities. Students can create newspapers, videotaped debates, or learning materials for younger students

4. *Make use of novelty and familiarity.* Don't overuse a few teaching approaches or motivational strategies. We all need some variety. Varying the goal structures of tasks (cooperative, competitive, individualistic) can help, as can using different teaching media. When the material being covered in class is abstract or unfamiliar to students, try to connect it to something they know and understand. For example, talk about the size of a large area, such as the Acropolis in Athens, in terms of football fields. Brophy (1988) describes one teacher who read a brief passage from *Spartacus* to personalize the unit on slavery in the ancient world.

Instrumental Value. Sometimes it is difficult to encourage intrinsic motivation, and so teachers must rely on the utility or "instrumental" value of tasks. That is, it is important to learn many skills because they will be needed in more advanced classes or because they are necessary for life outside school.

1. When these connections are not obvious, educators should *explain the connections to their students.* Jeanette Abi-Nader (1991) describes one project, the PLAN program, that makes these connections come alive for Hispanic high school students. The three major strategies used in the program to focus students' attention on their future are: (1) working with mentors and models—often PLAN graduates—who give advice about how to choose courses, budget time, take notes, and deal with cultural differences in college; (2) storytelling about the achievements of former students—sometimes the college term papers of former students are posted on PLAN bulletin boards; and (3) filling the classroom with future-oriented talk such as "When you go to college, you will encounter these situations…" or, "You're at a parents' meeting—you want a good education for your children—and you are the ones who must speak up; that's why it is important to learn public speaking skills" (p. 548).

2. In some situations educators need to *provide incentives and rewards for learning.* Remember, though, that giving rewards when students are already interested in the activity may undermine intrinsic motivation. As Stipek (2002) has noted, if teachers began testing and grading students on their memory of the television programs they watched the previous evening, even television viewing would lose some of its intrinsic appeal.

3. *Use ill-structured problems and authentic tasks* in teaching. Connect problems in school to real problems outside—helping the homeless, improving traffic problems, protecting endangered species, creating safe playgrounds for children, or any current community concern.

What Do I Need to Do to Succeed? Staying Focused on the Task

When students encounter difficulties, as they must if they are working at a challenging level, they need to keep their attention on the task. If the focus shifts to worries about performance, fear of failure, or concern with looking smart, then motivation to learn is lost. Here are some ideas principals can suggest to teachers for keeping the focus on learning.

1. *Give students frequent opportunities to respond* through questions and answers, short assignments, or demonstrations of skills. Make sure you check the students' answers so you can correct problems quickly. You don't want students to practice errors too long. Computer learning programs give students the immediate feedback they need to correct errors before they become habits.

2. When possible, *have students create a finished product.* They will be more persistent and focused on the task when the end is in sight. We all have experienced the power of the need for closure.

3. *Avoid heavy emphasis on grades and competition.* Competition will force students to be ego-involved rather than task-involved. Anxious students are especially hard hit by highly competitive evaluation.

4. *Reduce task risk without oversimplifying the task.* When tasks are risky (failure is likely and the consequences of failing are grave), student motivation suffers. For difficult, complex, or ambiguous tasks, provide students with plenty of time, support, resources, help, and the chance to revise or improve work.

5. *Model motivation to learn for students.* Teachers can talk about their interest in the subject and how they deal with difficult learning problems.

6. *Teach the particular learning tactics* that students will need to master the material being studied. Show students how to learn and remember so they won't be forced to fall back on self-defeating strategies or rote memory.

Table 4.6 on page 139 summarizes these ideas for helping students to have confidence in their abilities, value learning, and stay focused on the right task.

How Do Beginning Teachers Motivate Students?

Timothy Newby (1991) trained classroom observers to record the motivational strategies of 30 first-year elementary school teachers over a 16-week period. He found that the teachers used about 10 different strategies per hour—half were rewards and punishments. Figure 4.2 on the next page gives examples of the four types of strategies used by these beginning teachers. As you can see, commenting on the relevance of the lessons and building student confidence each accounted for about 7 percent of strategies, focusing student attention made up 27 percent, and rewards and punishments accounted for 58 percent. Another interesting finding is that commenting on relevance was positively correlated with students being on task, while using rewards/punishments was negatively correlated. So beginning teachers tended to use less effective strategies more often. It may be that these new teachers turned to extrinsic reinforcement (rewards and punishments) only when it became difficult to keep the students interested in their work.

Summary

Motivation is an internal state that arouses, directs, and maintains behavior. The study of motivation focuses on how and why people initiate actions directed toward specific goals, how intensively they are involved in the activity, how persistent they are in their attempts to reach these goals, and what they are thinking and feeling along the way. Explanations of motivation include both personal and environmental factors as well as intrinsic and extrinsic sources of motivation.

Intrinsic motivation is the natural tendency to seek out and conquer challenges as we pursue personal interests and exercise capabilities—it is motivation to do something when we don't have to. Extrinsic motivation is based on factors not related to the activity itself. We are not really interested in the activity for its own sake; we care only about what it will gain us. The essential difference between the intrinsic and extrinsic motivation is the person's reason for acting, that is, whether the locus of causality for the action (the location of the cause) is internal or external—inside or outside the person. If the locus in internal, the motivation is intrinsic and if the locus is external, the motivation is extrinsic. Most motivation has elements of both.

Behaviorists tend to emphasize extrinsic motivation caused by incentives, rewards, and punishment. Humanistic views stress the intrinsic motivation created by the need for

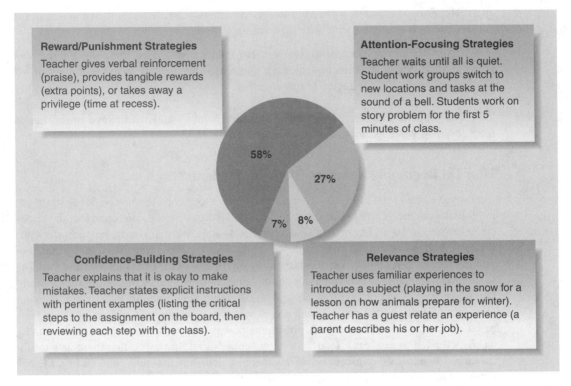

Reward/Punishment Strategies

Teacher gives verbal reinforcement (praise), provides tangible rewards (extra points), or takes away a privilege (time at recess).

Attention-Focusing Strategies

Teacher waits until all is quiet. Student work groups switch to new locations and tasks at the sound of a bell. Students work on story problem for the first 5 minutes of class.

58%

27%

7%   8%

Confidence-Building Strategies

Teacher explains that it is okay to make mistakes. Teacher states explicit instructions with pertinent examples (listing the critical steps to the assignment on the board, then reviewing each step with the class).

Relevance Strategies

Teacher uses familiar experiences to introduce a subject (playing in the snow for a lesson on how animals prepare for winter). Teacher has a guest relate an experience (a parent describes his or her job).

FIGURE 4.2   Motivational Strategies of Beginning Teachers   First-year teachers tend to rely on reward and punishment strategies to motivate students, even though these are not necessarily the most effective approaches.

Source: From "Classroom Motivation: Strategies of First-Year Teachers," by T. J. Newby, 1991, *Journal of Educational Psychology, 83,* pp. 195–200. Copyright © 1991 by the American Psychological Association. Adapted with permission.

personal growth, fulfillment, and self-determination. Cognitive psychologists stress a person's active search for meaning, understanding, and competence, and the power of the individual's beliefs and interpretations. Social learning views suggest that motivation to reach a goal is the product of our expectations for success and the value of the goal to us. If either is zero, our motivation is zero also. This general approach is called the expectancy—× value theory of motivation.

Teachers are interested in a particular kind of motivation—student motivation to learn. Student motivation to learn is both a trait and a state. It involves taking academic work seriously, trying to get the most from it, and applying appropriate learning strategies in the process. In order to encourage motivation to learn, instructional leaders can create environments that give students *goals* for learning, meet students' basic and higher-level *needs,* help students and teachers have *beliefs* that support learning, and arouse *interest* while avoiding *anxiety* in learning.

Many theories of motivation feature a prominent role for goals. Goals increase motivation if they are specific, moderately difficult, and able to be reached in the near future. Four kinds of goals influence classroom activities. A learning goal is the intention to gain knowledge and master skills. Students who set learning goals tend to seek challenges and persist when they encounter difficulties. They are not too concerned with setbacks because they are focused on the task. A performance goal is the intention get good grades or to appear smarter or more capable than others. Students who set performance goals are preoccupied with themselves and how they appear. Work-avoidant learners simply want to find the easiest way to handle the situation. Students with social goals can be supported or hindered in their learning, depending on the specific goal (i.e., have fun with friends or bring honor to the family). In order for goal setting to be effective in the classroom, students need accurate feedback about their progress toward goals and they must accept the goals rather than reject them.

Needs are also an important component of many theories of motivation. Maslow has suggested that people are motivated by a hierarchy of needs, beginning with basic physiological requirements and moving up to the need for self-fulfillment. Lower-level needs must be met before higher-level needs can influence motivation. The need for achievement has been viewed as a personal characteristic nurtured by early experiences in the family and as a reaction to recent experiences with success or failure. The need to achieve is balanced by the need to avoid failure. Together, these are strong motivating forces. Several theorists emphasize the role of choice and self-determination in motivation and the need for positive relations with others. When students experience self-determination, they are intrinsically motivated—they are more interested in their work, have a greater sense of self-esteem, and learn more. Whether students experience self-determination depends in part on if the teacher's communications with students provide information or seek to control them. In addition, teachers must acknowledge the students' perspective, offer choices, provide rationales for limits, and treat poor performance as a problem to be solved rather than a target for criticism.

The attribution theory of motivation suggests that the explanations people give for behavior, particularly their own successes and failures, have strong influences on future plans and performance. One of the important features of an attribution is whether it is internal and within a person's control or external and beyond control. Teachers may cue attributions by the way they respond to students' work. Surprisingly, praise, sympathy, and unsolicited help can communicate to students that they lack the ability to do the work. When people believe that ability is fixed, they tend to set performance goals and strive to protect themselves from failure. When they believe ability is improvable, however, they tend to set appropriate learning goals and handle failure constructively.

Bandura suggests that sense of self-efficacy, the belief that you will be effective in a given situation, is a powerful influence on motivation. If an individual has a strong sense of self-efficacy, he or she tends to set more challenging goals and to persist even when obstacles are encountered. Self-efficacy is distinct from other conceptions of self, in that it involves judgments of capabilities *specific to a particular task*. Self-concept is a more global construct that contains many perceptions about the self, including self-efficacy. Self-concept is developed as a result of external and internal comparisons, using others people or other aspects of the self as frames of reference. Compared to self-esteem, self-efficacy is concerned with judgments of personal capabilities; self-esteem is concerned with judgments of self-worth.

Attributions and beliefs about self come together in three possible student orientations. Mastery-oriented students tend to value achievement and see ability as improvable, so they focus on learning goals in order to increase their skills and abilities. They are not fearful of failure, because failing does not threaten their sense of competence and self-worth. They attribute failure to controllable causes. This allows them take risks and cope with failure constructively. A low sense of self-worth seems to be linked with the failure-avoiding and failure-accepting strategies intended to protect the individual from the consequences of failure. These strategies may seem to help in the short term, but are damaging to motivation and self-esteem in the long run.

Learning and information processing are influenced by emotion. Students are more likely to pay attention to, learn, and remember events, images, and readings that provoke emotional responses or that are related to their personal interests. However, there are cautions in responding to students' interests. "Seductive details"—interesting bits of information that are not central to the learning but distract from it—can hinder learning.

There appears to be an optimum level of arousal for most activities. Generally speaking, a higher level of arousal is helpful on simple tasks, but lower levels of arousal are better for complex tasks. When arousal is too low, teachers can stimulate curiosity by pointing out gaps in knowledge or use variety in activities. Severe anxiety is an example of arousal that is too high for optimal learning. Anxiety can be the cause or the result of poor performance; it can interfere with attention to, learning of, and retrieval of information. Many anxious students need help in developing effective test-taking and study skills.

What can teachers do to motivate students? Before any strategies to encourage motivation can be effective, four conditions must exist in the classroom. The classroom must be organized and free from constant disruption, the teacher must be a supportive person who never embarrasses students for making mistakes, the work must be neither too easy nor too difficult, and finally, the tasks set for students must be authentic—not busywork.

Once these conditions are met, teachers can use strategies that help students feel confident in their abilities to improve (e.g., set challenging but reachable goals, stress self—not other—comparisons, communicate the belief that ability is improvable), strategies that highlight the value the learning tasks (e.g., tie tasks to student interests, arouse curiosity, show connections to the future and to real-world problems, provide incentives), and strategies that help students stay involved in the learning process without being threatened by fear of failure (e.g., provide opportunities to create a finished product, teach learning tactics, model motivation to learn for students, avoid emphasizing grades, reduce risk without oversimplifying the task).

New teachers do not always use the best strategies for motivating students. In one study, commenting on the relevance of the lessons (showing value) accounted for 8% of strategies and building student confidence accounted for 7% of strategies, focusing student attention made up 27%, and rewards and punishments accounted for 58%. Commenting on relevance was positively correlated with students being on task, while using rewards/punishments was negatively correlated. Thus, beginning teachers tended to use less effective strategies more often. These findings do suggest that it is wise to develop a repertoire of strategies in addition to rewards and punishments.

KEY TERMS

anxiety   (136)
arousal   (134)
attribution theories   (123)
being needs   (119)
deficiency needs   (119)
ego-involved learners   (117)
entity view   (126)
expectancy-value theories   (115)
extrinsic motivation   (113)
failure-accepting   (131)
failure-avoiding students   (131)
goal   (116)

hierarchy of needs   (118)
incentive   (113)
incremental view   (126)
intrinsic motivation   (112)
learned helplessness   (124)
learning goal   (117)
locus of causality   (113)
mastery experience   (128)
mastery-oriented students   (130)
motivation   (112)
motivation to learn   (115)
need   (118)

performance goal   (117)
reward   (113)
self-actualization   (118)
self-determination   (120)
self-efficacy   (127)
social goals   (117)
social persuasion   (128)
task-involved learners   (117)
teaching efficacy   (129)
vicarious experience   (128)
work-avoidant learners   (117)

SOME IDEAS FOR YOUR PORTFOLIO

1. As principal of your school, outline a one-day inservice program to help your teachers understand student motivation so they can apply it in the classroom.

   - What motivational theories will be discussed? Why? How?
   - What hands-on approaches to motivation will be demonstrated and discussed? Why? How?
   - How will you and your teachers decide on a motivational program to be implemented in your school? Consider the pros and cons of various approaches, then develop a rationale for your choice(s).

2. Describe how you and your teachers will develop and design a comprehensive plan for working with parents and families to improve motivation and instruction in your school.

   - Of what utility are the various motivation theories? Which theories seem most promising given the make-up of your student body?

   - How can parents and teachers work cooperatively to set goals?
   - Consider plans that have both intrinsic and extrinsic rewards.

3. Develop a 45-minute power point presentation to explain your three favorite motivation theories.

   - What theories would you select? Why?
   - What are the strengths and weaknesses of each theory?
   - What are the practical applications of each perspective? Give some hands-on examples of each.
   - Develop a series of questions for your teachers to discuss about student motivation? What end products do you expect from your teachers?

INSTRUCTIONAL LEADER'S TOOLBOX

Readings

Butterworth, B., & Weinstein, R. S. Enhancing motivational opportunity in elementary schooling: A case study of the ecology of principal leadership. *The Elementary School Journal, 97,* 57–80.

Childress, H. (1998). Seventeen reasons why football is better than high school. *Phi Delta Kappan, 79,* 616–619.

Johnson, D., & Johnson, R. (1999). *Learning together and alone: Cooperation, competition, and individualization* (5th ed.). Boston: Allyn & Bacon.

Maehr, M. L., & Anderman, E. M. (1993). Reinventing schools for early adolescents: Emphasizing task goals. *The Elementary School Journal, 93,* 593–610.

Raffini, J. P. (1996). *150 ways to increase intrinsic motivation in the classroom.* Boston: Allyn & Bacon.

Stipek, D. (2002). *Motivation to Learn.* (4th ed.). Boston: Allyn & Bacon.

Paul Chance and Alfie Kohn exchanged opinions in several issues of *Phi Delta Kappan:*

Kohn, A. (1991, March). Caring kids: The role of the schools. *Phi Delta Kappan.*

Chance, P. (1991, June). Backtalk: A gross injustice. *Phi Delta Kappan.*

Chance, P. (1992, November). The rewards of learning. *Phi Delta Kappan.*

Kohn, A. (1993, June). Rewards versus learning: A response to Paul Chance. *Phi Delta Kappan.*

Chance, P. (1993, June). Sticking up for rewards. *Phi Delta Kappan.*

Videos

What I learned from not learning, 12 minutes. An insightful examination of what really goes on in a classroom: teachers present accurate information in unintelligible ways to uninterested students or irrelevant answers to appropriate questions. Teachers may be so intent on what they are teaching that they are unable to distinguish between students who already know what they are being taught and those who are only pretending to understand. To purchase: #CC-1915. Order from Films for the Humanities & Sciences, Inc. P.O. Box 2053, Princeton, NJ, 08543, or (800)-257-5126.

Head of the class, 14 minutes. This story aroused tremendous interest when it was broadcast on *60 Minutes.* It reveals the high pressure of the Japanese educational system, where the goal is to gain admission to the university. American educators must decide which elements of the Japanese educational system they should draw upon to improve their own. Order from Films for the Humanities & Sciences, Inc. P.O. Box 2053, Princeton, NJ, 08543, or (800)-257-5126.

Websites

Comparison of Incentive Reading Programs	http://www.consunion.org/other/captivekids/SEMs_incentives.htm
Reading Incentive Program from Pizza Hut to encourage K–6 students to read	http://www.bookitprogram.com/adults.html
Herzberg's Theory of Motivation and Maslow's Hierarchy of Needs	http://www.ed.gov/databases/ERIC_Digests/ed421486.html
Motivating Low Performing Adolescent Readers	http://www.ed.gov/databases/ERIC_Digests/ed396265.html
Creating Learning Centered Classrooms—What Does Learning Theory Have To Say? (talks about self-efficacy)	http://www.ed.gov/databases/ERIC_Digests/ed422777.html
Motivation and Middle School Students	http://www.ed.gov/databases/ERIC_Digests/ed421281.html
Student Motivation to Learn	http://www.ed.gov/databases/ERIC_Digests/ed370200.html

The following websites have interesting content that can be used for a variety of purposes related to motivation and instruction.

History: The History House	www.historyhouse.com
Science: The Particle Adventure	www.particleadventure.org
The Why Files	http://whyfiles.news.wisc.edu/

Organizations

Success for All Foundation	www.successforall.net
International Association for the Study of Cooperation in Education	http://miavx1.muohio.edu/~iascecwis

Preview: Key Points

Leadership Challenge

What is a Good Teacher?
Inside Five Classrooms
Expert Teachers
Concerns of Teachers

The First Step: Planning
Objectives for Learning
Theory into Action Guidelines: Developing
Objectives
Flexible and Creative Plans—Using Taxonomies
Another View: Planning from a Constructivist
Perspective

Successful Teaching: Focus on the Teacher
Characteristics of Effective Teachers
Teacher Effects
Theory into Action Guidelines: Characteristics
of Good Teachers

Teaching for Understanding: Focus on the Subject
Learning to Read and Write
Learning and Teaching Mathematics

Learning Science
A Model for Good Subject Matter Teaching
Theory into Action Guidelines: Conceptual
Change Teaching
Criticisms of Constructivist Approaches to
Subject Teaching

Beyond Models to Outstanding Teaching

Cautions: Where's the Learning?

Summary

Key Terms

Some Ideas for Your Portfolio

Instructional Leader's Toolbox
Readings
Videos
Websites
Organizations

PREVIEW: KEY POINTS

- Expert teachers work from integrated sets of principles instead of dealing with each new event as a new problem.
- Shulman's seven areas of professional knowledge include academic subjects, teaching strategies, curriculum materials, student characteristics, learning settings, teaching goals, and pedagogical content knowledge.
- There is no one model for effective planning, but having clear objectives is important.
- Using taxonomies of objectives improves planning; a new taxonomy in the cognitive domain has just been developed.

- Constructivist planning often involves themes and integrated units.
- Characteristics of effective teaching include organization, clarity, warmth, and enthusiasm.
- A balanced approach to reading, including both phonics and whole language, is effective.
- Constructivist theories have inspired new ways of teaching mathematics and science.
- There is no one best way to teach; different goals and students require different approaches.

Leadership Challenge

Your school district has adopted a whole-language, integrated curriculum approach for grades K through six. Quite a bit of time and money was spent on workshops for teachers; buying big books and multiple copies of good children's literature; developing manipulatives for mathematics; building comfortable reading corners; making costumes, puppets, and other reading props; designing science projects; and generally supporting the innovations. Students and teachers are mostly pleased with the program. There seems to be more reading and more enjoyment of reading, at least for many children—but some students seem lost. The students' written work is longer and more creative. However, standardized tests indicate a drop in scores. As principal you are getting worried—after all it was your big project and you had worked hard to sell it to members of the PTA and school board. But now some parents of students in your school are complaining that they have had to hire tutors or buy commercial programs to teach their children to read.

- What would you do about the parents' complaints?
- What would you advise your teachers to do about such complaints?
- Are changes necessary? How can you find out?
- What information do you need to make good decisions?
- Who should be involved in these decisions?
- What is your stance on phonics versus whole language? Can you support your position?

What Is a Good Teacher?

There are hundreds of answers to this question, including ideas based on your own experience. This question has been examined by educators, psychologists, philosophers, novelists, journalists, mathematicians, scientists, historians, policymakers, and parents, to name only a few groups. And good teachers are not confined to classrooms—they are found in homes and hospitals, museums and sales meetings, therapists' offices and summer camps.

Inside Five Classrooms

To begin our examination of good teachers, let's step inside the classrooms of several outstanding teachers. All the situations that follow are real. The first two are elementary teachers described by Weinstein & Mignano (1997). The next three are secondary school teachers who have been studied by other researchers.

A Bilingual First Grade.   There are 25 students in Viviana's class. Most have recently emigrated from the Dominican Republic; the rest come from Nicaragua, Mexico, Puerto Rico, and Honduras. Even though the children speak little or no English when they begin school, by the time they leave in June, Viviana has helped them master the normal first-grade curriculum for their district. She accomplishes this by teaching in Spanish early in the year to aid understanding, then gradually introducing English as the students are ready. Viviana does not want her students segregated or labeled as disadvantaged. She encourages them to take pride in their Spanish-speaking heritage while using every available opportunity to support their developing English proficiency.

Viviana's expectations for her students are high, and she makes sure the students have the resources they need. She provides materials—pencils, scissors, colors—so no child lacks the means to learn. And she supplies constant encouragement. "Viviana's commitment to her students is evident in her first-grade bilingual classroom. With an energy level that is rare, she motivates, prods, instructs, models, praises, and captivates her students.... The pace is brisk and Viviana clearly has a flair for the dramatic; she uses music, props, gestures, facial expressions, and shifts in voice tone to communicate the material" (Weinstein & Mignano, 1997, p. 13). Viviana's expectations for herself are high as well. She continually expands her knowledge of teaching through graduate work and participation in special training programs. To know more about her students each year, she spends hours in their homes. For Viviana, teaching is a not just a job; it is a way of life.

A Suburban Sixth Grade.   Ken teaches sixth grade in a suburban elementary school in central New Jersey. Ken emphasizes "process writing." His students complete first drafts, discuss them with others in the class, revise, edit, and "publish" their work. The students also keep daily journals and often use these to share personal concerns with Ken. They tell him of problems at home, fights, and fears; he always takes the time to respond in writing. The study of science is also placed in the context of the real world. The students use a National Geographic Society computer network to link with other schools in order to identify acid rain patterns around the world. For social studies, the class play two simulation games focusing on the first half of the 1800s. They "lived" as trappers collecting animal skins and as pioneers heading west to search for gold.

Throughout the year Ken is very interested in the social and emotional development of his students—he wants them to learn about responsibility and fairness as well as science and social studies. This concern is evident in the way he develops his class rules at the beginning of the year. Rather than specifying dos and don'ts, Ken and his students devise a "Bill of Rights" for the class, describing the rights of the students and of the teacher. These rights cover most of the situations that might need a "rule."

An Inner-City Middle School.   Another excellent teacher is described in the *Harvard Education Letter.*

> Robert Moses, founder of the Algebra Project at the Martin Luther King School in Cambridge, Massachusetts, teaches students the concept of number and sign through a physical event: they go for a ride on a subway. Choosing one subway stop as a starting point, students relate inbound and outbound to positive and negative numbers. They translate their subway ride into mathematical language by considering both the number of stops and their direction.

By giving students such experiences before introducing the formal language of algebra, Moses…has made math more enjoyable and accessible. (Ruopp & Driscoll, 1990, p. 5)

Two Advanced Math Classes. Hilda Borko and Carol Livingston (1989) describe two expert secondary school mathematics teachers. In one lesson for her advanced mathematics class, Ellen had her students identify any three problems about ellipses from their text. She asked if there were any questions or uncertainties about these problems. Ellen answered student questions, worked two of the problems, and then used the three problems to derive all the concepts and equations the students needed to understand the material. Ellen's knowledge of the subject and of her students was so thorough that she could create the explanations and derive the formulas on the spot, no matter which problems the students chose.

Another teacher, Randy, worked with his students' confusion to construct a review lesson about strategies for doing integrals. When one student said that a particular section in the book seemed "haphazard," Randy led the class through a process of organizing the material. He asked the class for general statements about useful strategies for doing integrals. He clarified their suggestions, elaborated on some, and helped students improve others. He asked the students to tie their ideas to passages in the text. Even though he accepted all reasonable suggestions, he listed only the key strategies on the board. By the end of the period, the students had transformed the disorganized material from the book into an ordered and useful outline to guide their learning. They also had a better idea about how to read and understand difficult material.

What do you see in these classrooms? The teachers are committed to their students. They must deal with a wide range of student abilities and challenges: different languages, different home lives, different needs. These teachers must understand their subjects and their students' thinking so well that they can spontaneously create new examples and explanations when students are confused. They must make the most abstract concepts, such as negative numbers, real and understandable for their particular students. And then there is the challenge of new technologies and techniques. The teachers must use them appropriately to accomplish important goals and not just to entertain the students. The whole time that these experts are navigating through the academic material, they also are taking care of the emotional needs of their students, propping up sagging self-esteem and encouraging responsibility. If we followed these individuals from the first day of class, we would see that they carefully plan and teach the basic procedures for living and learning in their classes. They can efficiently collect and correct homework, regroup students, give directions, distribute materials, collect lunch money, and deal with disruptions—while also making a mental note to check why one of their students is so tired.

Viviana, Ken, Robert, Ellen, and Randy are examples of expert teachers—the focus of much recent research in education and psychology. For another perspective on the question "What is a good teacher?" let's examine this research on expertise in teaching.

Expert Teachers

What do expert teachers know that allows them to be so successful? How do they differ from beginners? Researchers are investigating how expert teachers think about their students, the subjects they teach, and the process of teaching itself.

Experts work from integrated sets of principles instead of dealing with each new event as a new problem. They look for patterns revealing similarities in situations that seem quite different at first glance. Experts focus more than beginners on analyzing a problem and mentally applying different principles to develop a solution. In one study of solutions to discipline problems, the expert teachers spent quite a bit of time framing each problem, forming questions, deciding what information was necessary, and considering alternatives (Swanson, O'Conner, & Cooney, 1990).

Expert teachers have a sense of what is typical in classrooms, of what to expect during certain activities or times of the day. They also have a good sense of what students in their grade and school are like—their background, needs, concerns, abilities, and problems. Many of their teaching routines have become automatic—they don't even have to think about how to distribute materials, take roll, move students in and out of groups, or assign grades. This gives the teachers more mental and physical energy for being creative and focusing on their students' progress. For example, one study found that expert math teachers could go over the previous day's work with the class in 2 or 3 minutes, compared to 15 minutes for novices (Leinhardt, 1986).

We saw with Ellen and Randy that expert teachers can improvise explanations and create new examples on the spot. They can turn students' confusion into understanding by helping the students organize and expand upon what they know. Expert teachers are not bound by their plans, but can follow the needs of the students. They begin teaching by assessing what their students know and need to know. Their starting point is not where the book starts or where the last teacher left off, but instead where the students are. Expert teachers read student cues as information for instruction whereas novices read student cues in terms of classroom management issues. Experts are less likely to take student misbehavior personally and are confident that they can handle most classroom interactions. Finally, many experts continue their education, adding to their knowledge (Borko & Livingston, 1989; Sabers, Cushing, & Berliner, 1991; Tochon & Munby, 1993).

So it seems that expert teachers, like expert dancers or gymnasts, have mastered a number of moves or routines that they can perform easily, almost without thinking. But they also know a great deal about their subject, so they can create new moves, improvise, and avoid trouble. And they are analytical; they can take a situation apart, diagnose the source of the problem, consider alternatives, and make decisions about what will work.

Expert teachers have more elaborate systems of knowledge for understanding problems in teaching. For example, when a beginning teacher is faced with students' wrong answers on math or history tests, all the wrong answers may seem about the same—simply wrong. The inexperienced teacher may have trouble connecting other facts or ideas with the students' wrong answers. But for an expert teacher, wrong answers are part of a rich system of knowledge that could include how to recognize several types of wrong answers, the misunderstanding or lack of information behind each kind of mistake, the best way to reteach and correct the misunderstanding, materials and activities that have worked in the past, and several ways to test whether the reteaching was successful (Leinhardt, 1988; Floden & Klinzing, 1990). Peterson and Comeaux (1989) argue that it is the quality of teachers' professional knowledge and their ability to be aware of their own thinking that makes them expert. One goal for instructional leaders is to help teachers develop this wide range of knowledge as they gain experience. In working with teachers, it makes sense to be aware of their perspectives and concerns.

Concerns of Teachers

Beginning teachers everywhere share many concerns. A review of studies conducted around the world found that beginning teachers regard maintaining classroom discipline, motivating students, accommodating differences among students, evaluating student work, and dealing with parents as the most serious challenges they face. Many teachers also experience what has been called "reality shock" when they take their first job and confront the "harsh and rude reality of everyday classroom life" (Veenman, 1984, p. 143). One source of shock may be that teachers really cannot ease into their responsibilities. On the first day of their first job, beginning teachers face the same tasks as teachers with years of experience. Student teaching, while a critical experience, does not really prepare prospective teachers for starting off a school year with a new class. When schools give beginning teachers a lighter load and limit outside class assignments, new teachers say that they do a better job of learning to teach. But schools seldom allow these arrangements. In addition, a full school day usually offers little chance for helpful contact between novice and experienced teachers, making mutual support and assistance difficult (Calderhead & Robson, 1991; Cooke & Pang, 1991; Duke, 1993; Veenman, 1984).

With experience, however, most teachers meet the challenges that seem difficult for beginners. They have more time to experiment with new methods or materials. Finally, as confidence grows, seasoned teachers can focus on the students' needs. Are my students learning? Are they developing positive attitudes? Is this the best way to teach the slower learners to write a persuasive essay? At this advanced stage teachers judge their success by the successes of their students (Feiman-Nemser, 1983; Fuller, 1969). So advanced teachers need a different kind of support that gives them the tools to teach and assess students.

For the remainder of the chapter we will look at the research on good teaching, beginning with planning.

The First Step: Planning

In the past few years, educational researchers have become very interested in teachers' planning. They have interviewed teachers about how they plan, asked teachers to "think out loud" while planning or to keep journals describing their plans, and even studied teachers intensively for months at a time. What have they found?

First, planning influences what students will learn, because planning transforms the available time and curriculum materials into activities, assignments, and tasks for students. When a teacher decides to devote 7 hours to language arts and 15 minutes to science in a given week, the students in that class will learn more language than science. In fact, differences as dramatic as this do occur. Nancy Karweit (1989) reported that in one school the time allocated to mathematics ranged from 2 hours and 50 minutes a week in one class to 5 hours and 55 minutes a week in a class down the hall (Clark & Peterson, 1986; Clark & Yinger, 1988; Doyle, 1983).

Second, teachers engage in several levels of planning—by the year, term, unit, week, and day. All the levels must be coordinated. Accomplishing the year's plan requires breaking the work into terms, the terms into units, and the units into weeks and days. Planning done at the beginning of the year is particularly important, because many routines and patterns are established early. For experienced teachers, unit planning seems to be the most important level, followed by weekly and then daily planning (Clark & Peterson, 1986; Clark & Yinger, 1988).

Third, plans reduce—but do not eliminate—uncertainty in teaching. Even the best plans cannot (and should not) control everything that happens in class; planning must allow flexibility (Calderhead, 1996). There is some evidence that when teachers "overplan"—fill every minute and stick to the plan no matter what—their students do not learn as much as students whose teachers are flexible (Shavelson, 1987). Beginning teachers may need to be reminded that they should not proceed with a scheduled new unit if their in-class review shows that many students still don't understand the material in the current unit.

In order to plan creatively and flexibly, teachers need to have wide-ranging knowledge about students, their interests, and abilities; the subjects being taught; alternative ways to teach and assess understanding; working with groups; the expectations and limitations of the school and community; how to apply and adapt materials and texts; and how to pull all this knowledge together into meaningful activities. The plans of beginning teachers sometimes don't work because they lack knowledge about the students or the subject—they can't estimate how long it will take students to complete an activity, for example, or they stumble when asked for an explanation or a different example (Calderhead, 1996).

Finally, there is no one model for effective planning. For experienced teachers, planning is a creative problem-solving process (Shavelson, 1987). Experienced teachers know how to accomplish many lessons and segments of lessons. They know what to expect and how to proceed, so they don't necessarily continue to follow the detailed lesson-planning models they learned during their teacher preparation programs. Planning is more informal—"in their heads." But many experienced teachers think it was helpful to learn this detailed system as a foundation (Clark & Peterson, 1986).

No matter how your teachers plan, they must have a learning goal in mind. In the next section we consider the range of goals for your students.

Objectives for Learning

We hear quite a bit today about visions, goals, outcomes, and standards. At a very general, abstract level are the grand goals society may have for graduates of public schools such as, "All children will start school ready to learn," one of the eight goals for U.S. education in *Goals 2000*. But very general goals are meaningless as potential guidelines for instruction. States may turn these grand goals into standards, such as the South Carolina standard that students will, "Develop the concept of fractions, mixed numbers, and decimals and use models to relate fractions to decimals and to find equivalent fractions." Sometimes the standards are turned into indicators such as "representing equivalent fractions." At this level, the indicators are close to being instructional objectives (Airasian, 2001).

An **instructional objective** is a clear and unambiguous description of educational intentions for students. Norman Gronlund (2000) defines instructional objectives as "intended learning outcomes…the types of performance students are expected to demonstrate at the end of instruction to show that they have learned what was expected of them" (p. 4). Although there are many different approaches to writing objectives, each assumes that the first step in teaching is to decide what changes should take place in the learner—what is the goal of teaching. Objectives written by people with behavioral views focus on observable and measurable changes in the learner. **Behavioral objectives** use terms such as *list, define, add,* or *calculate.* **Cognitive objectives,** on the other hand, emphasize thinking and comprehension, so they are more likely to include words such as *understand, recognize, create,* or *apply.* Let's look at one well-developed method of writing instructional objectives.

Mager: Start with the Specific.   Robert Mager has developed a very influential system for writing instructional objectives. Mager's idea is that objectives ought to describe what students will be doing when demonstrating their achievement and how you will know they are doing it (Mager, 1975). Mager's objectives are generally regarded as *behavioral.* According to Mager, a good objective has three parts. First, it describes the intended student behavior—what must the student do? Second, it lists the conditions under which the behavior will occur—how will this behavior be recognized or tested? Third, it gives the criteria for acceptable performance on the test. Figure 5.1 shows how the system works. This system, with its emphasis on final behavior, requires a very explicit statement. Mager contends that often students can teach themselves if they are given well-stated objectives.

Gronlund: Start with the General.   Norman Gronlund (2000) offers a different approach, often used for writing cognitive objectives. He believes that an objective should be stated first in general terms (*understand, solve, appreciate,* etc.). Then the teacher should clarify by listing a few sample behaviors that would provide evidence that the student has attained the objective. Look at the example in Table 5.1. The goal here really is presenting

Part	Central Question	Example
Student behavior	Do what?	Mark statements with an *F* for fact or an *O* for opinion
Conditions of performance	Under what conditions?	Given an article from a newspaper
Performance criteria	How well?	75% of the statements are correctly marked

FIGURE 5.1 Mager's Three-Part System   Robert Mager believes that a good learning objective has three parts: the student behavior, the conditions under which the behavior will be performed, and the criteria for judging a performance.

TABLE 5.1   Gronlund's Combined Method for Creating Objectives

General Objective

Presents and defends the research project before a group.

Specific Examples

1. Describes the project in a well-organized manner.
2. Summarizes the findings and their implications.
3. Uses display materials to clarify ideas and relationships.
4. Answers group members' questions directly and completely.
5. Presents a report that reflects careful planning.
6. Displays sound reasoning ability through presentation and answers to questions.

Source: Adapted from *How to Write and Use Instructional Objectives* (6th ed.) (pp. 74–75), by N. E. Gronlund, © 1999. Reprinted by permission of Pearson Education, Inc., Upper Saddle River, NJ.

and defending a research project. The teacher does not want the student to stop with describing, summarizing, answering questions, and so on. Instead, the teacher looks at performance on these sample tasks to decide if the student can effectively present and defend. The teacher could just as well have chosen six different indicators.

Gronlund's emphasis on specific objectives as samples of more general student ability is important. A teacher could never list all the behaviors that might be involved in solving problems in the subject area, but stating an initial, general objective makes it clear that the ability to solve problems is the purpose. The most recent research on instructional objectives tends to favor approaches similar to Gronlund's. It seems reasonable to state a few central objectives in general terms and clarify them with samples of specific behaviors, as in Table 5.1 (Hamilton, 1985; Popham, 1993).

Are Objectives Useful?   Providing objectives for student learning can promote learning with loosely organized and less-structured activities such as lectures, films, and research projects. If the importance of some information is not clear from the learning materials and activities themselves, instructional objectives will probably help focus students' attention and thus increase achievement (Duchastel, 1979). But when the task involves simply getting the gist of the passage or transferring the information to a new situation, it is better to use questions that focus on meaning, inserting the questions right before the passage to be read (Hamilton, 1985).

If the objectives are supplied in advance—and especially if students have a role designing objectives—both students and teacher will know what the performance criteria are. In thinking about objectives, both teachers and students must consider what is important, what is worth learning. Teachers who have clear, appropriate goals for every student often are successful in helping the students learn. Finally, many school districts still require teachers to complete lesson plans that include learning objectives. The Theory into Action Guidelines should help your teachers whether they decide to make thorough use of objectives or just to prepare them for certain assignments.

THEORY INTO ACTION GUIDELINES

Developing Objectives

Avoid "word magic"—phrases that sound noble and important but say very little, such as "Students will become deep thinkers."

Examples

1. Keep the focus on specific changes that will take place in the students' knowledge of skills.
2. Ask students to explain the meaning of the objectives. If they can't give specific examples of what you mean, the objectives are not communicating your intentions to your students.

Suit the activities to the objectives.

Examples

1. If the goal is the memorization of vocabulary, give the students memory aids and practice exercises.

2. If the goal is the ability to develop well-thought-out positions, consider position papers, debates, projects, or mock trials.
3. If you want students to become better writers, give many opportunities for writing and rewriting.

Make sure your tests are related to your objectives.

Examples

1. Write objectives and rough drafts for tests at the same time—revise these drafts of tests as the units unfold and objectives change.
2. Weight the tests according to the importance of the various objectives and the time spent on each.

Flexible and Creative Plans—Using Taxonomies

Several decades ago, a group of experts in educational evaluation led by Benjamin Bloom set out to improve college and university examinations. The impact of their work has touched education at all levels around the world (Anderson & Sosniak, 1994). Bloom and his colleagues developed a **taxonomy,** or classification system, of educational objectives. Objectives were divided into three domains: *cognitive, affective,* and *psychomotor.* A handbook describing the objectives in each area was eventually published. In real life, of course, behaviors from these three domains occur simultaneously. While students are writing (psychomotor), they are also remembering or reasoning (cognitive), and they are likely to have some emotional response to the task as well (affective).

The Cognitive Domain.   The most well known and widely used taxonomy is in the **cognitive domain.** Six basic objectives are listed in this thinking or cognitive domain (Bloom, Engelhart, Frost, Hill, & Krathwohl, 1956):

1. *Knowledge:* Remembering or recognizing something without necessarily understanding, using, or changing it.
2. *Comprehension:* Understanding the material being communicated without necessarily relating it to anything else.

3. *Application:* Using a general concept to solve a particular problem.
4. *Analysis:* Breaking something down into its parts.
5. *Synthesis:* Creating something new by combining different ideas.
6. *Evaluation:* Judging the value of materials or methods as they might be applied in a particular situation.

It is common in education to consider these six kinds of objectives as a hierarchy, each skill building on the previous ones, but this is not entirely accurate (Seddon, 1978). Some subjects, such as mathematics, do not fit this structure very well (Kreitzer & Madaus, 1994). Still, you will hear many references to *lower-level* and *higher-level objectives,* with knowledge, comprehension, and application considered lower level and the other categories considered higher level. As a rough way of thinking about objectives, this can be helpful (Gronlund, 2000).

The taxonomy of objectives can also be helpful in planning assessments because different procedures are appropriate for objectives at the various levels. Gronlund (2000) suggests that factual knowledge objectives can best be measured by true-false, short-answer, matching, or multiple-choice tests. Such tests will also work with the comprehension, application, and analysis levels of the taxonomy. For measuring synthesis and evaluation objectives, however, essays, reports, projects, and portfolios are more appropriate. Essay tests will also work at the middle levels of the taxonomy.

Bloom 2001. Bloom's taxonomy guided educators for over 40 years. It is considered one of the most significant educational writings of the 20th century (Anderson & Sosniak, 1994). In 1995, a group of educational researchers met to discuss revising the taxonomy. The outcome of that project (Anderson & Krathwohl, 2001) is now available. The taxonomy revisers have retained the six basic levels, but they have changed the names of three to indicate the cognitive processes involved and altered the order slightly. The six cognitive processes of the revised taxonomy are *remembering* (knowledge), *understanding* (comprehension), *applying, analyzing, evaluating,* and *creating* (synthesizing). In addition, the revisers have added a new dimension to the taxonomy to recognize that cognitive processes must process something—you have to remember or understand or apply some form of knowledge. If you look at Table 5.2 you will see the result. We now have six processes or verbs—the cognitive acts of remembering, understanding, applying, analyzing, evaluating, and creating. These processes act on four kinds of knowledge—factual, conceptual, procedural, and metacognitive.

Consider how this revised taxonomy might suggest objectives for a social studies/language arts class. An objective that targets *analysis of conceptual knowledge* is:

> After reading an historical account of the battle of the Alamo, the student will be able to recognize the author's point of view or bias.

An objective for *evaluating metacognitive knowledge* might be:

> Students will explain their strategies for identifying the biases of the author.

Certain processes are more likely to be paired with certain kinds of knowledge. For example, remembering is most often used with factual and conceptual knowledge and metacognitive

TABLE 5.2 A Revised Taxonomy in the Cognitive Domain

	The Cognitive Process Dimension					
The Knowledge Dimension	**1.** Remember	**2.** Understand	**3.** Apply	**4.** Analyze	**5.** Evaluate	**6.** Create
A. Factual Knowledge						
B. Conceptual Knowledge						
C. Procedural Knowledge						
D. Metacognitive Knowledge						

Source: From *A Taxonomy of Teaching and Learning: A Revision of Bloom's Taxonomy of Educational Objectives* by L. Anderson & D. Krathwohl (Eds.) (2000). Copyright © 2000. Adapted by permission of Allyn & Bacon.

knowledge is more likely to be applied and analyzed than remembered. In two books, a complete and an abridged version, Anderson and Krathwohl (2001) describe the new taxonomy and give many examples of using this revised version to design lessons and assessments.

The Affective Domain. The objectives in the taxonomy of the **affective domain,** or domain of emotional response, run from least committed to most committed (Krathwohl, Bloom, & Masia, 1964). At the lowest level, a student would simply pay attention to a certain idea. At the highest level, the student would adopt an idea or a value and act consistently with that idea. There are five basic objectives in the affective domain.

1. *Receiving:* Being aware of or attending to something in the environment. This is the I'll-listen-to-the-concert-but-I-won't-promise-to-like-it level.
2. *Responding:* Showing some new behavior as a result of experience. At this level a person might applaud after the concert or hum some of the music the next day.
3. *Valuing:* Showing some definite involvement or commitment. At this point a person might choose to go to a concert instead of a film.
4. *Organization:* Integrating a new value into one's general set of values, giving it some ranking among one's general priorities. This is the level at which a person would begin to make long-range commitments to concert attendance.
5. *Characterization by value:* Acting consistently with the new value. At this highest level, a person would be firmly committed to a love of music and demonstrate it openly and consistently.

Like the basic objectives in the cognitive domain, these five objectives are very general. To write specific learning objectives, you must state what students will actually be doing when they are receiving, responding, valuing, and so on. For example, an objective for a nutrition class at the valuing level (showing involvement or commitment) might be stated:

> After completing the unit on food contents and labeling, at least 50% of the class will commit to the junk-food boycott project by giving up snack foods for a month.

The Psychomotor Domain.   James Cangelosi (1990) provides a useful way to think about objectives in the psychomotor domain as either voluntary muscle capabilities that require endurance, strength, flexibility, agility, or speed; or the ability to perform a specific skill. Objectives in the **psychomotor domain** should be of interest to a wide range of educators, including those in fine arts, vocational-technical education, and special education. Many other subjects, such as chemistry, physics, and biology, also require specialized movements and well-developed hand and eye coordination. Using lab equipment, the "mouse" on a computer, or art materials means learning new physical skills. Here are two psychomotor objectives:

> Four minutes after completing a one-mile run in eight minutes or under, your heart rate will be below 120.

> Use a computer mouse effectively to "drag and drop" files.

Another View: Planning from a Constructivist Perspective

Traditionally, it has been the teacher's responsibility to do most of the planning for instruction, but new ways of planning are developing. Like many recent educational innovations, these new models of planning have not been tested in large-scale carefully designed studies, but you should be aware of the possibilities. Your new teachers will certainly have studied these models in their teacher preparation programs.

In **constructivist approaches,** planning is shared and negotiated. The teacher and students together make decisions about content, activities, and approaches. Rather than having specific student behaviors and skills as objectives, the teacher has overarching goals—"big ideas"—that guide planning. These goals are understandings or abilities that the teacher returns to again and again.

An Example of Constructivist Planning.   Vito Perrone (1994) has these goals for his secondary history students. He wants his student to be able to:

- Use primary sources, formulate hypotheses, and engage in systematic study
- Handle multiple points of view
- Be close readers and active writers
- Pose and solve problems

The next step in the planning process is to create a learning environment that allows students to move toward these goals in ways that respect their individual interests and abilities. Perrone (1994) suggests identifying "those ideas, themes, and issues that provide the depth and variety of perspective that help students develop significant understandings" (p. 12). For a secondary history course, a theme might be "democracy and revolution," "fairness," or "slavery." In math or music a theme might be "patterns"; in literature, "personal identity" might be the theme. Perrone suggests mapping the topic as a way of thinking about how the theme can generate learning and understanding. An example of a topic map, using the theme of "Immigrants in the United States," is shown in Figure 5.2.

With this topic map as a guide, teacher and students can work together to identify activities, materials, projects, and performances that will support the development of the students' understanding and abilities—the overarching goals of the class. The teacher spends less time planning specific presentations and assignments and more time gathering a variety

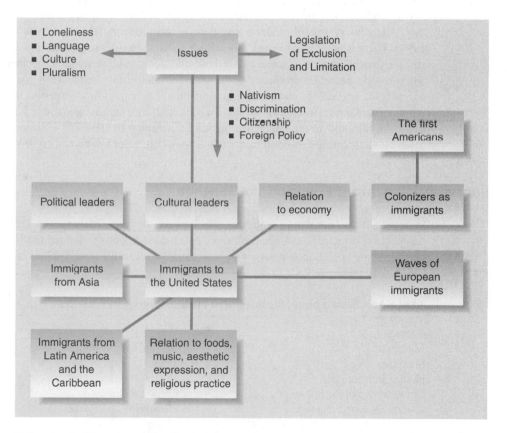

FIGURE 5.2 Planning with a Topic Map With this map of the topic, "Immigrants to the United States," a history teacher can identify themes, issues, and ideas for study. Rather than "cover" the whole map, a few areas are examined in depth.

Source: From "How to Engage Students in Learning," by V. Perrone, 1994, *Educational Leadership, 51*(5), p. 13. Copyright 1994 by the Association for Supervision and Curriculum Development. Reprinted with permission. All rights reserved.

of resources and facilitating students' learning. The focus is not so much on students' products as on the processes of learning and the thinking behind the products.

Integrated and Thematic Plans.   Perrone's planning map shows a way to use the theme of immigrants to the United States to integrate issues in a history class. Today, teaching with themes and integrated content are major elements in planning and designing lessons and units, from kindergarten (Roskos & Neuman, 1995) through high school (Clarke & Agne, 1997). For example, a college professor and two middle school teachers (Pate, McGinnis, & Homestead, 1995) designed a unit on "Human Interactions" that included studying racism, world hunger, pollution, and air and water quality. Students researched issues by reading textbooks and outside sources, learning to use databases, interviewing local officials, and inviting guest speakers into class. Students had to develop knowledge in science, mathematics, and social studies. They learned to write and speak persuasively, and in the process, raised money for hunger relief in Africa.

Elementary school students can benefit form integrated planning too (Thompson, 1991). There is no reason to work on spelling skills, then listening skills, then writing skills, and then social studies or science. All these abilities can be developed together if students work to solve authentic problems. Some ideas for integrating themes with younger children are people, friendship, communications, habitats, communities, patterns, and roots and wings (Thompson, 1991). Possibilities for older children are given in Table 5.3.

We turn now to the interactive phase of teaching—the lesson itself. Here much good research has identified some elements of teaching that make a difference in student learning.

Successful Teaching: Focus on the Teacher

How would you go about identifying the keys to effective teaching? You might ask students, other principals, college professors of education, or experienced teachers to list the characteristics of good teachers. Or you could do intensive case studies of a few class-

TABLE 5.3   Some Themes for Integrated Planning for Older Children

Courage	Time and Space
Mystery	Groups and Institutions
Survival	Work
Human Interaction	Motion
Communities of the Future	Cause and Effect
Communication/Language	Probability and Prediction
Human Rights and Responsibilities	Change and Conservation
Identity/Coming of Age	Diversity and Variation
Interdependence	Autobiography

Source: Adapted from *Toward a Coherent Curriculum* by J. A. Beane (Ed.), 1995, Alexandria, VA: Association for Supervision and Curriculum Development; *Interdisciplinary High School Teaching* by J. H. Clarke and R. M. Agne, 1997, Boston: Allyn & Bacon; and *Teaching through Themes* by G. Thompson, 1991, New York: Scholastic.

rooms over a long period. You might observe classrooms, rate different teachers on certain characteristics, and then see which characteristics were associated with teachers whose students either achieved the most or were the most motivated to learn. (To do this, of course, you would have to decide how to assess achievement and motivation.) You could identify teachers whose students, year after year, learned more than students working with other teachers; then you could watch the more successful teachers, and note what they do. You might also train teachers to apply several different strategies to teach the same lesson and then determine which strategy led to the greatest student learning. You could videotape teachers, then ask them to view the tapes and report what they were thinking about as they taught and what influenced their decisions while teaching. You might study transcripts of classroom dialogue to learn what helped students understand.

All these approaches and more have been used to investigate teaching. Often researchers conduct a series of studies by making careful observations and identifying relationships between teaching and learning. The researchers then use these relationships as the basis for developing teaching approaches and testing these approaches in design experiments (Brown, 1992; Greeno, Collins, & Resnick, 1996). Let's examine some of the specific knowledge about teaching gained from these projects.

Characteristics of Effective Teachers

Some of the earliest research on effective teaching focused on the personal qualities of the teachers themselves. Researchers thought that the key to success in teaching must lie in the characteristics of teachers (Medley, 1979). Although this assumption proved incorrect—or at least incomplete—it did teach us some lessons about three teacher characteristics: knowledge, clarity, and warmth.

Teachers' Knowledge.   Do teachers who know more about their subject have a more positive impact on their students? When we look at teachers' knowledge of facts and concepts, as measured by test scores and college grades, the relationship to student learning is unclear and may be indirect. Teachers who know more facts about their subject do not necessarily have students who learn more. But teachers who know more may make clearer presentations and recognize student difficulties more readily. They are ready for any student questions and do not have to be evasive or vague in their answers. So knowledge is necessary but not sufficient for effective teaching—but being more knowledgeable helps teachers be clearer and more organized.

Clarity and Organization.   Students discussing a teacher are likely to say things like, "Oh, she can really explain," or "He's so confusing!" When Barak Rosenshine and Norma Furst (1973) reviewed about 50 studies of teaching, they concluded that clarity was the most promising teacher behavior for future research on effective teaching. Recent studies confirm the importance of clarity. Teachers who provide clear presentations and explanations tend to have students who learn more and who rate their teachers more positively (Hines, Cruickshank, & Kennedy, 1982, 1985; Land, 1987). Teachers with more knowledge of the subject tend to be less vague in their explanations to the class. The less vague the teacher, the more the students learn (Land, 1987).

Planning for Clarity.   Research offers guidelines for greater clarity in teaching (Berliner, 1987; Evertson et al., 2000; Hines, Cruickshank, & Kennedy, 1982, 1985). When planning a lesson, teachers should try to anticipate the problems students will have with the material. Teachers' manuals and experienced teachers can help new teachers with this. You might also encourage your teachers to do the written parts of the lesson themselves to identify potential problems. Have definitions ready for new terms, and prepare several relevant examples for concepts. Think of analogies that will make ideas easier to understand. Organize the lesson in a logical sequence; include checkpoints that incorporate oral or written questions or problems to make sure the students are following the explanations.

Plan a clear introduction to the lesson. Tell students what they will be learning and how they could approach it. Often teachers are vague about both the "what" and the "how." For example, in a study by Duffy, Roehler, Meloth, and Vavrus (1986), an ineffective reading teacher began her lesson on using context in reading by saying

> Today we are going to learn about context. This skill will help you in your reading. (p. 206)

This is a vague and general statement of "what" the students will learn. An effective teacher in the same study began her lesson with an explicit, precise description:

> At the end of today's lesson, you will be able to use the other words in a sentence to figure out the meaning of an unknown word. The skill is one that you use when you come to a word that you don't know and you have to figure out what the word means. (p. 206)

Being precise about "how" to do the work is even harder. One study found that teachers seldom, if ever, explain the cognitive processes they want their students to practice in a seatwork activity. Bright students figure out the right process, but slower students often guess or give up. For example, an *ineffective* teacher might introduce a seatwork activity on words with prefixes by saying, "Here are some words with prefixes. Write the meaning of each in the blanks." An *effective* teacher, on the other hand, would demonstrate how to divide the words into a prefix and a root; how to determine the meaning of the root and the prefix; and how to put the two meanings together to make sense of the whole word (Berliner, 1987).

Clarity During the Lesson.   As you observe teachers, do they make clear connections between facts or concepts by using **explanatory links** such as because, if...then, or therefore? For example, when a teacher says, "The Northern economy was based on manufacturing and the North had an advantage in the Civil War," students are given two facts, but no connection between them. If there is a relationship between the two ideas, it should be indicated with an explanatory link as in, "The North had an advantage in the Civil War because its economy was based on manufacturing." Explanatory links tie ideas together and make them easier to learn (Berliner, 1987). Explanatory links are also helpful in labeling visual material such as graphs, concept maps, or illustrations.

Teachers also should signal transitions from one major topic to another with phrases such as "The next area...," "Now we will turn to...," or "The second step is..." Teachers might help students follow the lesson by outlining topics, listing key points, or drawing concept maps on the board or on an overhead projector. Continually monitor the group to see if everyone is following the lesson. Look for confident nods or puzzled stares. Throughout the lesson, choose words that are familiar to the students. Define new terms and relate them to what the students already know.

Vagueness is the enemy of understanding. Encourage teachers and students to be precise. Avoid vague words and ambiguous phrases: steer clear of "the somes": something, someone, sometime, somehow; "the not verys": not very much, not very well, not very hard, not very often; and other unspecific fillers, such as most, not all, sort of, and so on, of course, as you know, I guess, in fact, or whatever, and more or less. Use specific (and, if possible, colorful) names instead of it, them, and thing. Also, refrain from using pet phrases such as you know, like, and Okay? Another idea is to have teachers record a lesson on tape to check themselves for clarity.

Warmth and Enthusiasm.   As you are well aware, some teachers are much more enthusiastic than others. Studies have found that ratings of teachers' enthusiasm for their subject are correlated with student achievement gains (Rosenshine & Furst, 1973). Warmth, friendliness, and understanding seem to be the teacher traits most strongly related to student attitudes (Murray, 1983; Ryans, 1960; Soar & Soar, 1979). In other words, teachers who are warm and friendly tend to have students who like them and the class in general. But notice, these are correlational studies. The results do not tell us that teacher enthusiasm causes student learning or that warmth causes positive attitudes, only that the two variables tend to occur together. Teachers trained to demonstrate their enthusiasm have students who are more attentive and involved but not necessarily more successful on tests of content (Gillett & Gall, 1982).

The research we have looked at has identified teacher knowledge, clarity, organization, warmth, and enthusiasm as important characteristics of effective teachers. The Theory into Action Guidelines on the next page summarize the practical implications that principals and teachers can use to improve learning and teaching.

Teacher Effects

What else can the teacher do to increase student learning? Two decades of research on teacher effects points to five keys, summarized by Brophy and Good (1986).

1. Teachers do make a difference. Some teachers, year after year, have students who learn more and do better on standardized tests.

2. Teachers who make a difference take responsibility for their students learning. These teachers have a strong sense of efficacy. They believe that they can get through to the most difficult students. If one approach doesn't work, the teachers try another way—no excuses, no giving up for teacher or student.

3. These teachers make sure that class time is not wasted or lost on empty "fun" activities or unnecessary housekeeping tasks. Class management and organization make time for learning. In the next chapter we see how important time is and how to create learning environments that minimize distractions and maximize learning.

THEORY INTO ACTION GUIDELINES

Characteristics of Good Teachers

Organize your lessons carefully.

Examples

1. Provide objectives that help students focus on the purpose of the lesson.
2. Begin lessons by writing a brief outline on the board, or work on an outline with the class as part of the lesson.
3. If possible, break the presentation into clear steps or stages.
4. Review periodically.

Strive for clear explanations.

Examples

1. Use concrete examples or analogies that relate to the students' own lives. Have several examples for particularly difficult points.
2. Give explanations at several levels so all students, not just the brightest, will understand.
3. Focus on one idea at a time and avoid digressions.

Communicate an enthusiasm for your subject and the day's lesson.

Examples

1. Tell students why the lesson is important. Have a better reason than "This will be on the test" or "You will need to know it next year." Emphasize the value of the learning itself.
2. Make eye contact with the students.
3. Vary your pace and volume in speaking. Use silence for emphasis.

4. Teaching is active with a great deal of time devoted to teacher–student interaction, explanation, and questioning. Less time is spent in independent seatwork or unsupervised worksheets.

5. Even though the academic focus is clear, the class environment is friendly and supportive. The teacher's enthusiasm about learning and respect for students is contagious (Brophy, 1997).

These keys have been associated with the term **direct instruction.** Weinert and Helmke describe direct instruction as having the following features:

(a) the teachers' classroom management is especially effective and the rate of student interruptive behaviors is very low; (b) the teacher maintains a strong academic focus and uses available instructional time intensively to initiate and facilitate students' learning activities; (c) the teacher insures that as many students as possible achieve good learning progress by carefully choosing appropriate tasks, clearly presenting subject-matter information and solution strategies, continuously diagnosing each student's learning progress and learning difficulties, and providing effective help through remedial instruction. (1995, p. 138)

You can see that direct instruction applies best to the teaching of basic skills—clearly structured knowledge and essential skills, such as science facts, mathematics computations, reading vocabulary, and grammar rules (Rosenshine & Stevens, 1986). These skills involve tasks that are relatively unambiguous; they can be taught step by step and tested by standardized tests. The teaching approach described above are not necessarily appropriate for objectives such as helping students to write creatively, solve complex problems, or mature emotionally. How would a teacher turn these themes into actions?

Rosenshine's Six Teaching Functions. Rosenshine and his colleagues (Rosenshine, 1988; Rosenshine & Stevens, 1986) have identified six teaching functions based on the research on effective instruction. These could serve as a checklist or framework for teaching basic skills.

1. *Review and check the previous day's work.* Reteach if students misunderstood or made errors.

2. *Present new material.* Make the purpose clear, teach in small steps, provide many examples and nonexamples.

3. *Provide guided practice.* Question students, give practice problems, and listen for misconceptions and misunderstandings. Reteach if necessary. Continue guided practice until students answer about 80% of the questions correctly.

4. *Give feedback and correctives* based on student answers. Reteach if necessary.

5. *Provide independent practice.* Let students apply the new learning on their own, in seatwork, cooperative groups, or homework. The success rate during independent practice should be about 95%. This means that students must be well prepared for the work by the presentation and guided practice and that assignments must not be too difficult. The point is for the students to practice until the skills become overlearned and automatic—until the students are confident. Hold students accountable for the work they do—check it.

6. *Review weekly and monthly* to consolidate learning. Include some review items as homework. Test often, and reteach material missed on the tests.

These six functions are not steps to be followed in a particular order, but all of them are elements of effective instruction. For example, feedback, review, or reteaching should occur whenever necessary and should match the abilities of the students. There are several other models of direct instruction, but most share the elements presented in Table 5.4 on page 170 showing the Hunter Mastery Teaching Program (Hunter, 1995).

Why Does Direct Instruction Work? What aspects of direct instruction might explain its success? Linda Anderson (1989b) suggests that lessons that help students perceive links among main ideas will help them construct accurate understandings. Well-organized presentations, clear explanations, the use of explanatory links, and reviews can all help students perceive connections among ideas. If done well, therefore, a direct instruction lesson could be a resource that students use to construct understanding. For example, reviews activate prior knowledge so the student is ready to understand. Brief, clear presentations and guided practice avoid overloading the students' information processing systems and taxing their working memories. Numerous examples and explanations give many pathways and associations for building networks of concepts. Guided practice can also give the teacher a

TABLE 5.4 The Hunter Mastery Teaching Program: Selected Principles

Get students set to learn.

- Make the best use of the prime time at the beginning of the lesson.
- Give students a review question or two to consider while you call the roll, pass out papers, or do other "housekeeping" chores. Follow up—listen to their answers, and correct if necessary.
- Create an *anticipatory set* to capture the students' attention. This might be an advance organizer, an intriguing question, or a brief exercise. For example, at the beginning of a lesson on categories of plants you could ask, "How is pumpkin pie similar to cherry pie but different from sweet potato pie?" Answer: Pumpkins and cherries are both fruits, unlike sweet potatoes.
- Communicate the lesson objectives (unless withholding this information for a while is part of your overall plan).

Provide information effectively.

- Determine the basic information and organize it. Use this basic structure as scaffolding for the lesson.
- Present information clearly and simply. Use familiar terms, examples, illustrations.
- Model what you mean. If appropriate, demonstrate or use analogies—"If the basketball Ann is holding were the sun, how far away do you think I would have to hold this pea to represent Pluto…?"

Check for understanding, and give guided practice.

- Ask a question, and have every student signal an answer—"Thumbs up if this statement is true, down if it's false."
- Ask for a choral response: "Everyone, is this a dependent or an independent clause?"
- Sample individual responses: "Everyone, think of an example of a closed system. Jon, what's your example?"

Allow for independent practice.

- Get students started right by doing the first few questions together.
- Make independent practice brief. Monitor responses, giving feedback quickly.

Source: From Anita Woolfolk, *Educational Psychology, 8/e.* Copyright © 2001. Reprinted by permission of Allyn & Bacon.

snapshot of the students' thinking and of their misconceptions, so these can be addressed directly as misconceptions rather than simply as "wrong answers."

Criticisms of Direct Instruction. Critics say that direct instruction is limited to lower-level objectives, and that it is based on traditional teaching methods, ignores innovative models, and discourages students' independent thinking. Some researchers claim that the direct instruction model is based on the *wrong* theory of learning. Teachers break material into small segments, present each segment clearly, and reinforce or correct, thus *transmitting* accurate understandings from teacher to student. The student is seen as an "empty vessel" waiting to be filled with knowledge, rather than an active constructor of knowledge (Anderson, 1989a; Berg & Clough, 1991; Davis, Maher, & Noddings, 1990). These criticisms of direct instruction echo the criticisms of behavioral learning theories.

But there is ample evidence that direct instruction and explanation can help students learn actively, not passively. For younger and less-prepared learners, student-controlled learning without teacher direction and instruction can lead to systematic deficits in the students' knowledge. Without guidance, the understandings that students construct can be incomplete and misleading (Weinert & Helmke, 1995). Deep understanding and fluid performance—whether in dance or mathematical problem solving or reading—require models of expert performance and extensive practice with feedback (Anderson, Reder, & Simon, 1995). Guided and independent practice with feedback are at the heart of the direct instruction model.

What direct instruction cannot do is *ensure* that students understand. If badly done, it may encourage students to memorize and mimic but never to "own" the knowledge. To help students reach this goal, Eleanor Duckworth believes that teachers must pay very close attention to understanding their students' understandings (Meek, 1991). In the next two sections we look at teaching for understanding. The first section focuses on the subject and the second on the learning.

Teaching for Understanding: Focus on the Subject

In middle and high schools, academic subjects become more complex and more important than basic skills in teaching. It is clear that a teacher's knowledge of the subject is critical for teaching (Borko & Putnam, 1996). Part of that knowledge is **pedagogical content knowledge,** or knowing how to teach a subject to your particular students (Shulman, 1987). In the last decade, psychologists have made great progress understanding how students learn different subjects (Mayer, 1992). Based on these findings, many approaches have been developed to teach reading, writing, science, mathematics, social studies, and all the other subjects. Below we look at a few key subjects and the controversies surrounding how to teach them.

Learning to Read and Write

For years, educators have debated whether students should be taught to read and write through code-based (phonics, skills) approaches that relate letters to sounds and sounds to words or through meaning-based (whole-language, literature-based, emergent literacy) approaches that do not dissect words and sentences into pieces, but instead focus on the meaning of the text (Goodman, 1986; Smith, 1994; Stahl & Miller, 1989; Symons, Woloshyn, & Pressley, 1994; Vellutino, 1991).

Whole Language.   Advocates of **whole-language approaches** believe that learning to read is a natural process, very much like mastering your native language. The whole-language argument is that reading is a kind of guessing game in which students sample words and make predictions and guesses about meaning based on the context of other words in the passage and on their prior knowledge. Thus, words should not be presented out of context, and "sounding out" words and "breaking whole (natural) language into bite-size abstract little pieces" should be avoided (Goodman, 1986, p. 7). Rather, children should be immersed in a print-rich environment, surrounded by books worth reading and adults who read—to the children and for themselves.

Do Students Need Skills and Phonics?   On the other side of the argument, there are now two decades of research demonstrating that skill in recognizing sounds and words supports reading. Advocates of code-based approaches cite research showing that being able to identify many words as you read does not depend on using context to guess meaning. In fact, it is almost the other way around—knowing words helps you make sense of context. Identifying words as you read is a highly automatic process. The more fluent and automatic you are in identifying words, the more effective you will be in getting meaning from context (Vellutino, 1991). It is the poorest readers who resort to using context to help them understand meaning (Pressley, 1996).

Many studies support the code-based position. For example, three different groups reported similar findings in the *Journal of Educational Psychology* (December, 1991). Summarizing the results of these investigations, Frank Vellutino states:

> I think it is fair to say that the major theoretical assumptions on which whole-language approaches to instruction are based have simply not been verified in relevant research testing those assumptions. Aside from the fact that there are very sound reasons to reject the "natural" parallel between spoken and written language drawn by whole-language theorists, the research supports the following generalizations: (a) The most basic skill in learning to read is word identification; (b) an adequate degree of fluency in word identification is a basic prerequisite to successful reading comprehension; (c) word identification in skilled readers is a fast-acting, automatic, and in effect modular process that depends little on contextual information for execution; (d) even skilled readers can predict not more than one word out of four in sentence contexts, indicating that the predictive role of context must be extremely limited; (e) because of limited facility in word identification, beginning and poor readers are much more dependent on context than are more advanced readers. (p. 442)

Vellutino goes on to list two more generalizations, that alphabetic coding and awareness of letter sounds are essential skills for acquiring word identification, so some direct teaching of the alphabet and phonics is helpful in learning to read. The best approach probably makes sensible use of both phonics and whole language. After all, we want our students to be fluent *and* enthusiastic readers and writers (Bus & van IJzendoorn, 1999; Pressley, 1998)

Being Sensible about Reading and Writing.   The results of high-quality studies suggest that:

- Whole-language approaches to reading and writing are most effective in preschool and kindergarten. Whole language gives children a good conceptual basis for reading and writing. The social interactions around reading and writing—reading big books, writing shared stories, examining pictures, discussing meaning—are activities that support literacy and mirror the early home experiences of children who come to school prepared to learn. Whole-language approaches seem to improve students' motivation, interest, and attitude toward reading and help children understand the nature and purposes of reading and writing (Graham & Harris, 1994; Morrow, 1992; Neuman & Roskos, 1992).

- **Phonemic awareness**—the sense that words are composed of separate sounds and that sounds are combined to say words—in kindergarten and first grade predicts literacy in later grades. If children do not have phonemic awareness in the early grades, direct teaching can dramatically improve their chances of long-term achievement in literacy. Earlier is better—preschoolers tend to profit more from phonological training than kindergarten or primary grade students. (Bus & van IJzendoorn, 1999; Pressley, 1998).
- Excellent primary school teachers use both explicit decoding-skills teaching and whole-language instruction. Reading teachers should use a balanced approach rather than stressing either a literature-based whole-language or a skills-first approach (Adams, Trieman, & Pressley, 1998; Bus & van IJzendoorn, 1999; Vellutino, 1991).

If students need help cracking the code—give them what they need. Don't let ideology get in the way. You will just send more students to private tutors—if their families can afford it. But don't forget that reading and writing are for a purpose. Surround students with good literature and create a community of readers and writers. The Center for Early Reading describes 10 principles that capture this balanced approach to teaching, as shown in Table 5.5 on the next page.

The above discussion applies to reading and writing in the early grades, but what about the later years when comprehending difficult texts becomes important? Here learning strategies (Chapter 3) can be helpful.

Learning and Teaching Mathematics

Some of the most compelling support for constructivist approaches to teaching comes from mathematics education. Critics of direct instruction believe that traditional mathematics instruction often teaches students an unintended lesson—that they "cannot understand mathematics," or worse, that mathematics doesn't have to make sense, you just have to memorize the formulas. Arthur Baroody and Herbert Ginsburg (1990, p. 62) give this example:

> Sherry, a junior high student, explained that her math class was learning how to convert measurements from one unit to another. The interviewer gave Sherry the following problem:
>
> > To feed data into the computer, the measurements in your report have to be converted to one unit of measurement: feet. Your first measurement, however, is 3 feet 6 inches. What are you going to feed into the computer?
>
> Sherry recognized immediately that the conversion algorithm taught in school applied.... However, because she really did not understand the rationale behind the conversion algorithm, Sherry had difficulty in remembering the steps and how to execute them. After some

**TABLE 5.5   Improving the Reading Achievement of America's Children:
CIERA's 10 Research-Based Principles**

CIERA (the Center for the Improvement of Early Reading Achievement) has reviewed the
research on learning to read and distilled the best findings into these 10 principles. You can read
the expanded version of the principles on their website—www.ciera.org—under free information.
Reprinted by permission of CIERA.

1. **Home language and literacy experiences** support the development of key print concepts and a range of knowledge prepares students for school-based learning. Programs that help families initiate and sustain these experiences show positive benefits for children's reaching achievement.

   Examples: Joint reading with a family member, parental modeling of good reading habits, monitoring homework and television viewing.

2. **Preschool programs** are particularly beneficial for children who do not experience informal learning opportunities in their homes. Such preschool experiences lead to improved reading achievement, with some effects lasting through grade 3.

   Examples: Listening to and examining books, saying nursery rhymes, writing messages, and seeing and talking about print.

3. **Skills that predict later reading** success can be promoted in kindergarten and grade 1. The two most powerful of these predictors are letter-name knowledge and phonemic awareness. Instruction in these skills has demonstrated positive effects on primary grade reading achievement, especially when it is coupled with letter-sound instruction.

   Examples: Encourage children to hear and blend sound through oral renditions of rhymes, poems, and songs, as well as writing messages and in journals.

4. **Primary-level instruction** that supports successful reading acquisition is consistent, well-designed, and focused.

   Examples: Systematic word recognition instruction on common, consistent letter-sound relationships and important but often unpredictable high-frequency words, such as *the* and *what;* teaching children to monitor the accuracy of their reading as well as their understanding of texts through strategies such as predicting, in-

ferencing, clarifying misunderstandings, and summarizing; promoting word recognition and comprehension through repeated reading of text, guided reading and writing, strategy lessons, reading aloud with feedback, and conversations about texts children have read.

5. **Primary-level classroom environments** in successful schools provide opportunities for students to apply what they have learned in teacher-guided instruction to everyday reading and writing.

   Examples: Teachers read books aloud and hold follow-up discussions, children read independently every day, and children write stories and keep journals. These events are monitored frequently by teachers, ensuring that time is well spent and that children receive feedback on their efforts. Teachers design and revise these events based on information from ongoing assessment of children's strengths and needs.

6. **Cultural and linguistic diversity** among America's children reflects the variations within their communities and homes. This diversity is manifest in differences in the children's dispositions toward and knowledge about topics, language, and literacy.

   Examples: Effective instruction includes assessment, integration, and extension of relevant background knowledge and the use of texts that recognize diverse backgrounds. Build on the children's language when children are learning to speak, listen to, write, and read English. When teachers capitalize on the advantages of bilingualism or biliteracy, second language reading acquisition is significantly enhanced.

7. **Children who are identified as having reading disabilities** profit from the same sort of well-balanced instructional programs that benefit all children who are learning to read and

TABLE 5.5 Continued

write, including systematic instruction *and* meaningful reading and writing.

Examples: Intensive one-on-one or small-group instruction, attention to both comprehension and word recognition processes, thoroughly individualized assessment and instructional planning, and extensive experiences with many types of texts.

8. **Proficient reading in third grade** and above is sustained and enhanced by programs that adhere to four fundamental features:

Features: (1) deep and wide opportunities to read, (2) acquiring new knowledge and vocabulary, through wide reading and through explicit instruction about networks of new concepts, (3) emphasizing the influence on understanding of kinds of text (e.g., stories versus essays) and the ways writers organize particular texts, and (4) assisting students in reasoning about text.

9. **Professional opportunities** to improve reading achievement are prominent in successful schools and programs.

Examples: Opportunities for teachers and administrators to analyze instruction, assessment,

and achievement; to set goals for improvement; to learn about effective practices; and to participate in ongoing communities that deliberately try to understand both successes and persistent problems.

10. **Entire school staffs,** not just first-grade teachers, are involved in bringing children to high levels of achievement.

Examples: In successful schools, reading achievement goals are clear, expectations are high, instructional means for attaining goals are articulated, and shared assessments monitor children's progress. Even though they might use different materials and technologies, successful schools maintain a focus on reading and writing and have programs to involve parents in their children's reading and homework. Community partnerships, including volunteer tutoring programs, are common.

---

time she came up with an improbable answer (it was less than 3 feet). Sherry knew she was in trouble and became flustered. At this point, the interviewer tried to help by asking her if there was any other way of solving the problem. Sherry responded sharply, "No!" She explained, "That's the way it has to be done." The interviewer tried to give Sherry a hint: "Look at the numbers in the problem, is there another way we can think about them that might help us figure out the problem more easily?" Sherry grew even more impatient, "This is the way I learned in school, so it has to be the way."

Sherry believed that there was only one way to solve a problem. Though Sherry knew that 6 inches was one-half a foot and that the fraction one-half was equivalent to the decimal expression .5, she did not use this knowledge to solve the problem informally and quickly ("3 feet 6 inches is 3½ feet, or 3.5 feet"). Her beliefs prevented her from effectively using her existing mathematical knowledge to solve the problem.

Sherry had probably been taught to memorize the steps to convert one measurement to another. How would a constructivist approach teach the same material?

Jere Confrey (1990) analyzed an expert mathematics teacher in a class for high school girls who had difficulty with mathematics. Confrey identified five components in a model of this teacher's approach to teaching. These components are summarized in Table 5.6.

TABLE 5.6   A Constructivist Approach to Mathematics: Five Components

1. Promote students' autonomy and commitment to their answers.
   Examples:
   - Question both right and wrong student answers.
   - Insist that students at least try to solve a problem and be able to explain what they tried.
2. Develop students' reflective processes.
   Examples:
   - Question students to guide them to try different ways to resolve the problem.
   - Ask students to restate the problem in their own words; to explain what they are doing and why; and to discuss what they mean by the terms they are using.
3. Construct a case history of each student.
   Examples:
   - Note general tendencies in the way the student approaches problems, as well as common misconceptions and strengths.
4. If the student is unable to solve a problem, intervene to negotiate a possible solution with the student.
   Examples:
   - Based on the case study and your understanding of how the student is thinking about a problem, guide the student to think about a possible solution.
   - Ask questions such as "Is there anything you did in the last one that will help you here?" or "Can you explain your diagram?"
   - If the student is becoming frustrated, ask more direct, product-oriented questions.
5. When the problem is solved, review the solution.
   Examples:
   - Encourage students to reflect on what they did and why.
   - Note what students did well and build confidence.

Source: From "What Constructivism Implies for Teaching," by J. Confrey, 1990, in *Constructivist Views on the Teaching and Learning of Mathematics* by R. Davis, C. Maher, and N. Noddings (Eds.). Monograph 4 of the National Council of Teachers of Mathematics, Reston, VA. Copyright © 1990 National Council of Teachers of Mathematics. Adapted with permission.

Learning Science

If you have worked with adolescents, you know that by high school many students have "learned" some unfortunate lessons. Like Sherry, described in the preceding section, they have learned that math is impossible to understand and you just have to memorize the rules to get the answers. Or they may have developed some misconceptions about the world, such as the belief that the Earth is warmer in the summer because it is closer to the sun.

Many educators note that the key to understanding in science is for students to directly examine their own theories and confront the shortcomings (Hewson, Beeth, & Thorley, 1998). Only then can true learning and conceptual change happen. For change to take place, students must go through six stages: initial discomfort with their own ideas and beliefs, attempts to explain away inconsistencies between their theories and evidence presented to them, attempts to adjust measurements or observations to fit personal theories, doubt, vacillation, and finally conceptual change (Nissani & Hoefler-Nissani, 1992). You can see Piaget's notions of assimilation, disequilibrium, and accommodation operating here. Students try to make new information fit existing ideas (assimilation), but when the fit simply won't work and disequilibrium occurs, then accommodation or changes in cognitive structures follow.

The goal of **conceptual change teaching** in science is to help students pass through these six stages of learning. The two central features of conceptual change teaching are:

- Teachers are committed to teaching for student understanding rather than "covering the curriculum."
- Students are encouraged to make sense of science using their current ideas—they are challenged to describe, predict, explain, justify, debate, and defend the adequacy of their understanding. Dialogue is key. Only when intuitive ideas prove inadequate can new learning take hold (Anderson & Roth, 1989).

Conceptual change teaching has much in common with cognitive apprenticeships and inquiry learning described in Chapter 3—with scaffolding and dialogue playing key roles (Shuell, 1996). The following Theory into Action Guidelines, adapted from Hewson, Beeth, and Thorley (1998), give some ideas that principals can suggest for teaching that encourages conceptual change.

How would these guidelines look in practice? One answer comes from Michael Beeth's study of a fifth-grade classroom. Table 5.7 (page 179) is a list of learning goals that the teacher presents to her students.

In this classroom, the teacher typically began instruction with question such as, "Do you have ideas? Can you talk about them? Bring them out in to the open? Why do you like your ideas? Why are you attracted to them?" (Beeth, 1998, p. 1095). During her teaching she constantly ask question that require explanation and justifications. She summarizes the students' answers, and sometimes challenges, "But do you really believe what you say?" Studies of the students in the teacher's classroom over the years show that they have a sophisticated understanding of science concepts.

TABLE 5.7 One Teacher's Learning Goals for Conceptual Change Teaching

The teacher in one fifth-grade class gives these questions to her students to support their thinking about science.

---

1. Can you state your own ideas?
2. Can you talk about why you are attracted to your ideas?
3. Are your ideas consistent?
4. Do you realize the limitations of your ideas and the possibility they might need to change?
5. Can you try to explain your ideas using physical models?
6. Can you explain the difference between understanding an idea and believing in an idea?
7. Can you apply intelligible and plausible to your own ideas?

Source: Adapted from "Teaching Science in Fifth Grade: Instructional Goals that Support Conceptual Change," by M. E. Beeth, 1998, *Journal of Research in Science Teaching, 35,* p. 1093. Reprinted by permission of Wiley-Liss, Inc., a subsidiary of John Wiley & Sons, Inc.

THEORY INTO ACTION GUIDELINES

Conceptual Change Teaching

Encourage students to make their ideas explicit.

Examples
1. Ask students to make predictions that might contradict their naive conceptions.
2. Ask students to state their ideas in their own words, including the attractions and limitations of the ideas for them.
3. Have students explain their ideas using physical models or illustrations.

Help students see the differences among ideas.

Examples
1. Have students summarize or paraphrase each other's ideas.
2. Encourage comparing ideas by presenting and comparing evidence.

Encourage metacognition.

Examples
1. Give a pretest before starting a unit, then have students discuss their own responses to the pretest.
2. Group similar pretest responses together and ask students to discover a more general concept underlying the responses.
3. At the end of lessons, ask students: "What did you learn? What do you understand? What do you believe about the lesson? How have your ideas changed?"

Explore the status of ideas. Status is an indication of how much students know and accept ideas and find them useful.

Examples
1. Ask direct questions about how intelligible, plausible, and fruitful an idea is—that is, do you know what the idea means, do you believe it, and can you achieve some valuable outcome using the idea
2. Plan activities and experiments that support and question the students' ideas, such as showing successful applications or pointing out contradictions.

Ask students for justifications of their ideas.

Examples
1. Teach students to use terms such as "consistent," "inconsistent," "coherent" in giving justifications.
2. Ask students to share and analyze each other's justifications.

A Model for Good Subject Matter Teaching

There is less accumulated evidence about teaching for understanding in school subjects, but a few some initial findings point to some common elements in successful programs (Brophy, 1997). The emphasis is on the role of the students in constructing useful understandings as they assume more and more responsibility for learning. Brophy identified 10 keys to successful teaching for understanding:

1. The curriculum emphasizes knowledge, skills, and values that will be useful outside as well as inside school.
2. Students become more expert by actually using knowledge in practical applications so that conceptual understanding and self-regulation develop simultaneously.

3. A few important topics are addressed in depth instead of "covering" the curriculum. Supporters of the constructivist approach believe (with Howard Gardner) that coverage is the enemy of understanding.
4. The content to be learned is organized around a small set of powerful or "big" ideas.
5. The teacher presents information but also scaffolds students' efforts to learn.
6. The students' role is to actively work to make sense of the information and make it their own.
7. Teaching begins with the students' prior knowledge, even if that understanding includes some misunderstanding and conceptual change must be the goal.
8. Class activities include authentic tasks that call for critical thinking and problem solving, not just memorizing.
9. Higher-order thinking skills are taught and applied as students learn subject matter, not during separate, stand-alone "thinking" activities.
10. The teacher's goal is to create a learning community where dialogue and cooperation promote student understanding of content.

For an example of a teaching model that includes these 10 elements, see the **Community of Learners** model developed by Ann Brown and Joe Campione (1994). In this model, first used in the schools of Oakland, California, students are organized into small collaborative groups to research an important topic in depth. Reciprocal teaching is used to give students strategies for understanding difficult texts and other learning material. Students receive direct instruction, modeling, and coaching in the learning and research strategies they will need and practice the strategies in context of doing the actual research. Jigsaw cooperative learning groups divide the material to be learned and each student becomes an expert resource on one aspect of the topic. Students demonstrate their growing understandings in learning performances for real audiences. Evaluations of this model are very promising.

Criticisms of Constructivist Approaches to Subject Teaching

Constructivist approaches have done much to correct the excesses of tell and drill teaching. Some positive outcomes from constructivist teaching are better understanding of the material, greater enjoyment of literature, more positive attitudes toward school, better problem solving, and greater motivation (Harris & Graham, 1996; Palincsar, 1998). But total reliance on constructivist approaches that ignores direct teaching of skills can be detrimental for some children. For example, Harris and Graham describe the experiences of their daughter Leah in a whole-language/progressive education school, where the teachers successfully developed their daughter's creativity, thinking, and understanding.

> Skills, on the other hand, have been a problem for our daughter and for other children. At the end of kindergarten, when she had not made much progress in reading, her teacher said she believed Leah had a perceptual problem or a learning disability. Leah began asking what was wrong with her, because other kids were reading and she wasn't. Finally, an assessment was done. (p. 26)

The testing indicated no learning disability, strong comprehension abilities, and poor word attack skills. Luckily, Leah's parents knew how to teach word attack skills. Direct teaching of these skills helped Leah become an avid and able reader in about six weeks.

Leah's experience is not unique. Whole-language and constructivist approaches alone may not work for *all* children (Airasian & Walsh, 1997; Harris & Graham, 1996; Smith, 1994) or all kinds of learning (Weinert & Helmke, 1995). Susan Stodolsky (1988) cautions that constructivist methods may not be equally successful across all subject areas. If students fall behind because they lack specific skills, it would be unethical to withhold teaching and wait for those skills to "develop naturally," simply to be true to a particular philosophy. We agree with Jere Brophy (1997) that some constructivists "are being unrealistic, even romantic, in suggesting that teachers should routinely avoid transmitting knowledge and instead function only as discussion facilitators and scaffolders of learning...." (p. 231).

Ernst von Glasersfeld (1995), a strong advocate of constructivist teaching in mathematics, believes that it is a misunderstanding of constructivism to say that memorization and rote learning always are useless. "There are, indeed, matters that can and perhaps must be learned in a purely mechanical way" (p. 5). Classrooms that integrate constructivist teaching with needed direct teaching of skills are especially good learning environments for students with special needs. Careful ongoing assessment of each student's abilities, knowledge, and motivations followed by appropriate support should insure that no students are lost or left behind (Graham & Harris, 1994).

The research on teaching for understanding brings us again to a focus on balance and quality teaching.

Beyond Models to Outstanding Teaching

We have looked at teaching from the perspectives of the teacher, the subject, and the student. In spite of the debates and different viewpoints, there is no one best way to teach. Different goals require different methods. Teacher-centered instruction leads to better performance on achievement tests, while the open, informal methods like discovery learning or inquiry approaches are associated with better performance on tests of creativity, abstract thinking, and problem solving. In addition, the open methods are better for improving attitudes toward school and for stimulating curiosity, cooperation among students, and lower absence rates (Walberg, 1990). According to these conclusions, when the goals of teaching involve problem solving, creativity, understanding, and mastering processes, many approaches besides direct instruction should be effective.

These guidelines are in keeping with Tom Good's conclusion that teaching should become less direct as students mature and when the goals involve affective development and problem solving or critical thinking (Good, 1983). Of course, every subject, even college English or chemistry, can require some direct instruction. In teaching when to use "who" and "whom," or how to set up laboratory apparatus, direct instruction may be the best approach. Noddings (1990) reminds teachers that students may need some direct instruction in how to use various manipulative materials to get the possible benefits from them. Students working in cooperative groups may need guidance, modeling, and practice in how to ask questions and give explanations. And to solve difficult problems, students may need some direct instruction in possible problem-solving strategies.

The message for teachers is to match instructional methods to learning goals. In the early stages of learning, when students have little prior knowledge or even relevant personal experiences to provide a basis for discussion and analysis, it makes little sense to spend class time discussing and analyzing. Reading, researching, even memorizing may be needed to develop a common base of information to support discussion (Brophy, 1997).

Cautions: Where's the Learning?

As an instructional leader, you will be bombarded with claims and counterclaims about teaching innovations. Many of these programs and techniques will look promising. But it makes sense to ask, "Where's the evidence for learning? Have these innovations been tested in situations similar to your own? Do the strategies improve the bottom line—student learning and motivation? What's the evidence? How large are the gains and do they last? If the teaching approaches have not been tested, are they at least consistent with what we know about student learning and motivation. Will the teaching methods encourage student attention, cognitive investment, and long-term memory?

The research support for teacher effects and direct instruction is strong and based on large-scale, carefully conducted studies. As we have seen, this work is not without its critics, but if we focus on the learning of explicit information, the research on direct instruction offers good guidance.

Turning to higher-level objectives, we would expect that the newer models of teaching for subject understanding would be best. But be aware that the research base for these approaches is thin so far. As Brophy (1997) noted, many of the instructional models advocated by intellectual leaders and position statements published by professional organizations "have yet to be tested empirically, let alone enjoy a rich accumulation of systematic evidence of effects on student outcomes" (p. 226). In other words, there is no clear evidence (beyond testimonials of advocates) that these models have worked once, much less in many different schools and settings. Slavin and Fashola (1998) are even more blunt:

> Educational innovation lacks the respect for scientific evidence and independent replication that has characterized the most productive and progressive aspects of our society and economy, from medicine, technology, and engineering to agriculture. We know far more about the safety and effectiveness of our children's shampoo than we do about the reading or math programs their teachers use. Our children, our teachers, and our society deserve much better. (p. ix).

Advocates for many widely marketed practices such as whole language, integrated curriculum models, learning styles, developing multiple intelligences, and eliminating ability grouping base their arguments on their strong commitments to theories but do not have evidence that these approaches lead to learning. There is probably value in all these ideas, but be aware that clear evidence of strong connections to student learning is not readily available.

Summary

It takes time and experience to become an expert teacher. These teachers have a rich store of well-organized knowledge about the many specific situations of teaching. This includes knowledge about the subjects they teach, their students, general teaching strategies, subject-specific ways of teaching, settings for learning, curriculum materials, and the goals of education.

Learning to teach is a gradual process. The concerns and problems of teachers change as they progress. During the beginning years, attention tends to be focused on survival. Maintaining discipline, motivating students, evaluating students' work, and dealing with parents are universal concerns for beginning teachers. The more experienced teacher can move on to concerns about professional growth and effectiveness with a wide range of students.

The first step in teaching is planning. Teachers engage in several levels of planning—by the year, term, unit, week, and day. All the levels must be coordinated. Accomplishing the year's plan requires breaking the work into terms, the terms into units, and the units into weeks and days. The plan determines how time and materials will be turned into activities for students. There is no single model of planning, but all plans should allow for flexibility. Most plans include instructional objectives.

An instructional objective is a clear and unambiguous description of your educational intentions for your students. Mager's influential system for writing behavioral objectives states that objectives ought to describe what students will be doing when demonstrating their achievement and how you will know they are doing it. A good objective has three parts—the intended student behavior, the conditions under which the behavior will occur, and the criteria for acceptable performance. Gronlund's alternative approach suggests that an objective should be stated first in general terms, then the teacher should clarify by listing sample behaviors that would provide evidence that the student has attained the objective.

Bloom and others have developed taxonomies categorizing basic objectives in the cognitive, affective, and psychomotor domains. In real life, of course, behaviors from these three domains occur simultaneously. A taxonomy encourages systematic thinking about relevant objectives and ways to evaluate them. Six basic objectives are listed in the cognitive domain: knowledge, comprehension, application, analysis, synthesis, and evaluation. A recent revision of this taxonomy keeps the same cognitive processes, but adds that these processes can act on four kinds of knowledge—factual, conceptual, procedural, and metacognitive.

In teacher-centered approaches, teachers select learning objectives and plan how to get students to meet those objectives. Teachers control the "what" and "how" of learning. In contrast, planning is shared and negotiated in student-centered, or constructivist, approaches. The teacher and students together make decisions about content, activities, and approaches. Rather than having specific student behaviors as objectives, the teacher has overarching goals or "big ideas" that guide planning. Integrated content and teaching with themes are often part of the planning. Assessment of learning is ongoing and mutually shared by teacher and students.

After planning is the teaching itself. For years, researchers have tried to unravel the mystery of effective teaching. Researchers have used a variety of methods including classroom observation, case studies, interviews, experimentation with different methods, and other approaches to study teaching in real classrooms. Results of research on teacher characteristics indicate that thorough and expert knowledge of a subject, organization and clarity in presentation, and enthusiasm all play important parts in effective teaching. But no one way of teaching has been found to be right for each class, lesson, or day.

Teacher knowledge of the subject is necessary—because being more knowledgeable helps teachers be clearer and more organized—but not sufficient for effective teaching; organization and clarity are important characteristics of good teaching. Teachers who provide clear presentations and explanations tend to have students who learn more and who rate their teachers more positively. Clarity begins with planning. Tell students what they will be learning and how they could approach it. During the lesson, avoid vague language, make clear connections between facts or concepts by using explanatory links, and check often for understanding. Finally, teacher warmth, friendliness, and understanding seem to be the traits most strongly related to positive student attitudes.

In direct instruction, the teacher gives well-organized presentations, clear explanations, carefully delivered prompts, and feedback. These actions can be resources for students as they construct understanding. In student-centered approaches, the teacher designs authentic tasks, monitors student thinking, ask questions, and prods inquiry. Both kinds of teaching may be appropriate at different times.

Today there is an ongoing debate between advocates of whole-language approaches to reading and writing and balanced approaches that include direct teaching of skills and phonics. Advocates of whole language believe children learn best when they are surrounded by good literature and read and write for authentic purposes. Advocates of a balanced approach cite extensive research indicating that skill in recognizing sounds and words—phonemic awareness—is fundamental in learning to read. Excellent primary teachers use a balanced approach combining authentic reading with skills instruction when needed.

Constructivist approaches to mathematics and science emphasize deep understanding of concepts (as opposed to memorization), discussion and explanation, and exploration of students' implicit understandings. Success with any innovative approach to teaching often requires gaining and maintaining the cooperation of families. Many educators note that the key to understanding in science is for students to directly examine their own theories and confront the shortcomings. For change to take place, students must go through six stages: initial discomfort with their own ideas and beliefs, attempts to explain away inconsistencies between their theories and evidence presented to them, attempts to adjust measurements or observations to fit personal theories, doubt, vacillation, and finally conceptual change.

Many educators feel that the careful use of direct instruction methods—well-organized presentations, clear explanations, carefully delivered prompts, and guided discovery—can be a resource for students as they construct understanding. In all cases, teaching methods should match learning. There is more research evidence for the value of direct instruction than for constructivist approaches, but the ideas from student-centered, constructivist models of teaching can be useful. To evaluate new approaches, ask if they match the principles of learning and motivation described in Chapters 3 and 4.

KEY TERMS

affective domain   (161)
behavioral objectives   (157)
cognitive domain   (159)
cognitive objectives   (157)
Community of Learners   (179)
conceptual change
   teaching   (177)

constructivist approach   (162)
direct instruction   (168)
explanatory links   (166)
instructional objective   (156)
pedagogical content
   knowledge   (171)
phonemic awareness   (173)

psychomotor domain   (162)
taxonomy   (159)
whole-language
   approaches   (171)

SOME IDEAS FOR YOUR PORTFOLIO

1. Develop a classroom observation form to provide feedback to teachers about the teaching
   and learning in the classroom. Consider each
   of the following:

   ■ Teacher behavior
   ■ Student behavior
   ■ Classroom climate
   ■ Teacher and principal attitudes
   ■ Innovations
   ■ Other important aspects of teaching and
     learning in the classroom.

   Then plan a discussion of your observations
   with the teacher. Be sure to describe the discussion in terms of its:

   ■ Place—where will you talk with the teacher?
   ■ Structure—what will be the format and
     structure of your conversation?
   ■ Goals—what are the objectives and expected
     outcomes?

2. Prepare a 45-minute PTO talk about direct
   instruction.

   ■ Start by describing direct instruction.

   ■ Consider the pros and cons of direct instruc-
     tion.
   ■ Contrast direct instruction with a construc-
     tivist approach to teaching.
   ■ Under what situations is each approach
     appropriate?
   ■ Propose and defend a balance approach to
     teaching.

   Remember you are speaking to parents as well
   as your teachers.

3. As principal, develop an induction plan for beginning teachers. Describe the elements of the
   plan, for example:

   ■ Mentors
   ■ In-service orientation
   ■ Recognition awards and activities
   ■ Rookie roundtables
   ■ Social activities
   ■ Relations with experienced teachers
   ■ Social and resource support.

INSTRUCTIONAL LEADER'S TOOLBOX

Readings

Airasian, P. W., & Walsh, M. E. (1997). Constructivist
   cautions. *Phi Delta Kappan, 78,* 444–449.
Anderson, L. W., & Krathwohl, D. R. (Eds.) (2001). *A
   taxonomy of teaching and learning: A revision of
   Bloom's taxonomy of educational objectives.* New
   York: Addison, Wesley, Longman.
Magnusson, S. J., & Palincsar, A. S. (1995). The learning
   environment as a site of science reform. *Theory Into
   Practice, 34,* 43–50.

Nuthall, G., & Alton-Lee, A. (1990). Research on teaching and learning: Thirty years of change. *Elementary School Journal, 90,* 546–570.
Pressley, M. (1998). *Reading instruction that works: The
   case for balanced teaching.* New York: The Guilford Press.

Videos

How to make homework more meaningful by involving parents, 15 minutes. Educational Consultant: Joyce Epstein. Use homework to strengthen students' skills and make learning more meaningful. This video shows

- Assignments that help students establish regular schedules, and demonstrate and discuss what they've learned
- Strategies for initiating and encouraging family participation

- Ways to follow-up assignments with class discussion and demonstration.

Order from: Association for Supervision and Curriculum Development (ASCD), 125 N. West St., Alexandria, VA 22314-2798. Telephone: (703) 549-9110; FAX: (703) 549-3891. http://shop.ascd.org/category.cfm?categoryid=video

Websites

Constructivism in Teacher Education: Considerations for Those Who Would Link Practice to Theory	http:www.ed.gov/databases/ERIC_Digests/ed426986.html
The Project Approach	http:www.ed.gov/databases/ERIC_Digests/ed368509.html
Teaching Science through Inquiry	http:www.ed.gov/databases/ERIC_Digests/ed359048.html
Active Learning: Creating Excitement in the Classroom	http:www.ed.gov/databases/ERIC_Digests/ed340272.html
Thinking in Outdoor Inquiry	http:www.ed.gov/databases/ERIC_Digests/ed348198.html
The Essential Elements of Cooperative Learning in the Classroom	http:www.ed.gov/databases/ERIC_Digests/ed370881.html
Cooperative Learning	http:www.ed.gov/databases/ERIC_Digests/ed346999.html
Peer-Tutoring: Toward a New Model	http:www.ed.gov/databases/ERIC_Digests/ed362506.html
Cross-Age and Peer Tutoring	http:www.ed.gov/databases/ERIC_Digests/ed350598.html
Using "Think-Time" and "Wait-Time" Skillfully in the Classroom	http:www.ed.gov/databases/ERIC_Digests/ed370885.html
Classroom Questions	http:www.ed.gov/databases/ERIC_Digests/ed422407.html

Organizations

American Educational Research Association	http://www.aera.net

National Educational Technology Standards for Teachers	www.iste.org/TeacherStandards.html
National Council of Teachers of Mathematics Standards	http://www.nctm.org
National Science Education	http://www.nse.org
National Science Teachers Association	http://www.nsta.org
National Council for the Social Studies	http://www.ncss.org
National Council of Teachers of English	http://www.ncte.org
International Reading Association (IRA)	http://www.reading.org
Council for Exceptional Children (CEC)	http://www.cec.sped.org
National Association for Bilingual Education	http://www.nabe.org
Interstate New Teacher Assessment and Support Consortium. Model Standards for Beginning Teacher Licensing and Development: A Resource for State Dialogue	http://www.ccsso.org/intascst.html

6 Classroom Management

Preview: Key Points

Leadership Challenge

Organizing the Learning Environment
The Basic Task: Gain Their Cooperation
Managing The Learning Environment

**Creating a Positive Learning Environment:
Some Research Results**
Rules and Procedures
Theory into Action Guidelines: Rules
and Procedures
Planning Spaces for Learning
Theory into Action Guidelines: Designing
Learning Spaces

Getting Started: The First Weeks of Class
Effective Classroom Managers for Elementary
Students
Effective Classroom Managers for Secondary
Students

Creating a Learning Community
The Three Cs of Classroom Management
Getting Started on Community

Maintaining a Good Learning Environment
Encouraging Engagement
Theory into Action Guidelines: Encouraging
Student Accountability
Prevention Is the Best Medicine

Dealing with Discipline Problems
Special Problems with Secondary Students

Theory into Action Guidelines: Penalties
Special Programs for Classroom Management

The Need for Communication
Message Sent—Message Received
Diagnosis: Whose Problem Is It?
Counseling: The Student's Problem
Confrontation and Assertive Discipline
Student Conflicts and Confrontations
Communicating with Families about Classroom
Management
Theory into Action Guidelines: Working
with Families

**Designing Motivating Learning Environment
on Target for Learning**
Authentic Tasks
Supporting Autonomy
Recognizing Accomplishment
Grouping
Evaluation
Time

Summary

Key Terms

Some Ideas for Your Portfolio

Instructional Leader's Toolbox
Readings
Videos
Websites
Organizations

PREVIEW: KEY POINTS

- A main task of teaching is to enlist students' cooperation in activities that will lead to learning and a first step in accomplishing this task is to organize the learning environment.
- The goals of good classroom management are to make more time for learning, give all students access to learning, and support the development of self-management in students.
- Research on effective elementary and secondary class managers shows that these teachers have carefully planned rules and procedures (including consequences) for their classes; they teach these rules and procedures early, using explanations, examples, practice, correction, and student involvement.
- To create supportive learning contexts, teachers design flexible room arrangements that match their teaching goals and the learning activities of the class.
- Once a good class environment is established, it must be maintained by encouraging student engagement and preventing management problems; withitness, overlapping, group focus, and movement management are the skills of good preventers.
- For special or more difficult situations, group consequences, token systems, or contingency contracts may be helpful.
- When conflicts arise, teachers can deal more effectively with the situation if they first determine who "owns" the problem, then respond appropriately with empathetic listening or problem solving.
- Conflicts between students, though potentially dangerous, can be the occasions for learning conflict negotiation and peer mediation strategies.
- Establishing a positive learning context also includes attention to the factors that support motivation to learn—tasks, autonomy, recognition, grouping, evaluation, and time.

Leadership Challenge

You were hired in July as principal of Samuel Proctor Elementary School. This is your first job as principal after having been a teacher for six years. It is only the second week of school and you hear screaming when you are still halfway down the hall. "Give it back, it's MINE!" "No way—come and get it!" "I hate you." A crashing sound follows as a table full of books hits the floor. You are surprised to hear one of your first-year teachers desperately trying to get control of the situation. You subsequently learn that the teacher has no management system—no order. Students walk around the room while the teacher is talking to the class, students interrupt when the teacher is working with a group, other students torment the class goldfish, and still others open their lunches (or other students') for a self-determined, mid-morning snack. Some students listen, but ask a million questions off the topic. Simply taking roll and introducing the first activity is a major project. Your new teacher is trying hard, but seems completely overwhelmed.

- How would you approach the situation?
- Which problem behaviors should the teacher tackle first?
- Would giving rewards or administering punishments be useful in this situation? Why or why not?

- What specific suggestions would you give to this teacher?
- What action would you take?

Organizing the Learning Environment

Classrooms are particular kinds of environments. They have distinctive features that influence their inhabitants no matter how the students or the desks are organized for learning or what the teacher believes about education (Doyle, 1986). Classrooms are multidimensional. They are crowded with people, tasks, and time pressures. Many individuals, all with differing goals, preferences, and abilities, must share resources, accomplish various tasks, use and reuse materials without losing them, move in and out of the room, and so on. In addition, actions can have multiple effects. Calling on low-ability students may encourage their participation and thinking but may slow the discussion and lead to management problems if the students cannot answer. And events occur simultaneously—everything happens at once and the pace is fast. Teachers have literally hundreds of exchanges with students during a single day. In this rapid-fire existence, events are unpredictable. Even when plans are carefully made, the overhead projector is in place, and the demonstration is ready, the lesson can still be interrupted by a burned-out bulb in the projector or a loud, angry discussion right outside the classroom. Because classrooms are public, the way the teacher handles these unexpected intrusions is seen and judged by all. Students are always noticing if the teacher is being "fair." Is there favoritism? What happens when a rule is broken? Finally, classrooms have histories. The meaning of a particular teacher's or student's actions depends in part on what has happened before. The 15th time a student arrives late requires a different response from the teacher than the first late arrival. In addition, the history of the first few weeks of school affects life in the class all year.

The Basic Task: Gain Their Cooperation

No productive activity can take place in a group without the cooperation of all members. This obviously applies to classrooms. Even if some students don't participate, they must allow others to do so. (We all have seen one or two students bring an entire class to a halt.) So the basic management task for teachers is to achieve order and harmony by gaining and maintaining student cooperation in class activities (Doyle, 1986). Given the multidimensional, simultaneous, fast-paced, unpredictable, public, and historical nature of classrooms, this is quite a challenge.

Gaining student cooperation means much more than dealing effectively with misbehavior. It means planning activities, having materials ready, making appropriate behavioral and academic demands on students, giving clear signals to students, accomplishing transitions smoothly, foreseeing problems and stopping them before they start, selecting and sequencing activities so that flow and interest are maintained—and much more. Also, different activities require different managerial skills. For example, a new or complicated activity may be a greater threat to classroom management than a familiar or simple activity.

Obviously, gaining the cooperation of kindergartners is not the same task as gaining the cooperation of high school seniors. Jere Brophy and Carolyn Evertson (1978) identified four general stages of classroom management, defined by age-related needs. During kindergarten and the first few years of elementary school, children are learning how to go to school. They are being socialized into a new role. Direct teaching of classroom rules and procedures is important during this stage. Little learning will take place until the children master these basics. Children in the middle elementary years are usually familiar with the student role, even if they are not always perfect examples of it. Many school and classroom routines have become relatively automatic. Specific new rules and procedures for a particular activity may have to be taught directly, however. Still, at this stage teachers will spend more time monitoring and maintaining the management system than teaching it directly.

Toward the end of elementary school and the beginning of middle school, friendships and status within peer groups take on tremendous importance. Pleasing the teacher may be replaced by pleasing peers. Some students begin to test and defy authority. The management challenges at this stage are to deal productively with these disruptions and to motivate students who are becoming less concerned with teachers' opinions and more interested in their social lives. By the end of high school, the focus of most students returns to academics. By this time, unfortunately, many of the students with overwhelming behavioral problems have dropped out. At this stage the challenges are to manage the curriculum, fit academic material to students' interests and abilities, and help students become more self-managing in their learning. The first few classes each semester may be devoted to teaching particular procedures for using materials and equipment, or for keeping track of and submitting assignments. But most students know what is expected.

Managing the Learning Environment

The aim of **classroom management** is to maintain a positive, productive learning environment, relatively free of behavior problems. But order for its own sake is an empty goal. There are at least three reasons why management is important.

More Time for Learning.   Obviously, students will learn only the material they have a chance to learn. Almost every study examining time and learning has found a significant relationship between time spent on content and student learning (Berliner, 1988). In fact, the correlations between content studied and student learning are usually larger than the correlations between specific teacher behaviors and student learning (Rosenshine, 1979). But if you time all the different activities throughout the school day, you might be surprised by how little actual teaching takes place. Many minutes each day are lost through interruptions, disruptions, late starts, and rough transitions (Karweit, 1989; Karweit & Slavin, 1981). So one important goal of classroom management is to expand the sheer number of minutes available for learning. This is sometimes called *allocated time.*

But simply making more time for learning will not automatically lead to achievement. To be valuable, time must be used effectively. The way students process information is a central factor in what they learn and remember. Think back to Chapter 3. To learn, students must pay attention and process information. Basically, students will learn what they do, practice, and think about (Doyle, 1983). Time spent actively involved in specific learning tasks is often called *engaged time,* or sometimes **time on task.** Again, however, engaged time doesn't guarantee learning. Students may be struggling with material that is too difficult or using the wrong learning strategies. When students are working with a high rate of success—really learning and understanding—the time spent is called **academic learning time.** Figure 6.1 shows how the 1,000+ hours of time mandated for school in most states can become only about 333 hours of quality academic learning time for a typical student. Good class management increases academic learning time by keeping students actively engaged in worthwhile, appropriate learning activities.

Access to Learning. Each classroom activity has its own rules for participation. Sometimes these rules are clearly stated by the teacher, but often they are implicit and unstated. Teacher and students may not even be aware that they are following different rules for different activities (Berliner, 1983). And the differences are sometimes quite subtle. For

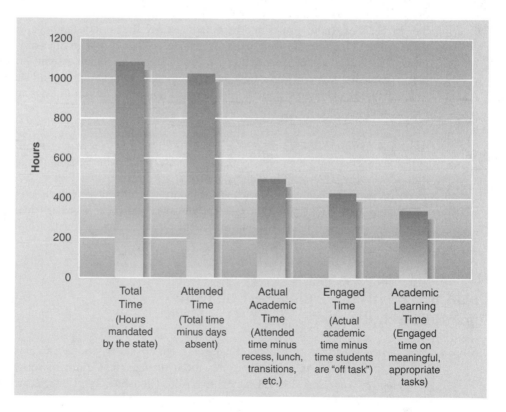

FIGURE 6.1 Who Knows Where the Time Goes? The over 1,000 hours per year of instruction mandated by most states can represent only 300 or 400 hours of quality academic learning time.

Source: From C. S. Weinstein and A. J. Mignano, Jr. *Elementary Classroom Management.* Copyright © 1993 by The McGraw-Hill Companies. Adapted with permission of The McGraw-Hill Companies.

example, in a reading group students may have to raise their hands to make a comment, but in a show-and-tell circle in the same class they may simply have to catch the teacher's eye. As we saw in Chapter 2, the rules defining who can talk; what they can talk about; and when, to whom, and how long they can talk are often called *participation structures*. In order to participate successfully in a given activity, students must understand the participation structure. Some students, however, seem to come to school less able to participate than others. The participation structures they learn at home in interactions with siblings, parents, and other adults do not match the participation structures of school activities (Tharp, 1989). But teachers are not necessarily aware of this conflict. Instead, the teachers see that a child doesn't quite fit in, always seems to say the wrong thing at the wrong time, or is very reluctant to participate, and the teachers are not sure why. Often they blame the students for being disruptive or uncooperative, and the students conclude that the teacher or the school is simply against them.

What can be done? In order to involve all students, teachers must make sure that everyone knows *how* to participate in each specific activity. The key is awareness. What are the teacher's or school's rules and expectations? Are they understandable, given the students' cultural backgrounds and home experiences? What unspoken rules or values may be operating? Is the teacher clear and consistent in signaling students about how to participate? To reach the second goal of good classroom management—giving all students access to learning—teachers must make sure everyone knows how to join in class activities. This means teaching, practicing, and signaling appropriate ways to participate.

Management for Self-Management.   The third goal of any management system is to help students become better able to manage themselves. Encouraging self-management requires extra time, but teaching students how to take responsibility is an investment well worth the effort. When elementary and secondary teachers have very effective class management systems but neglect to set student self-management as a goal, their students often find that they have trouble working independently after they graduate from these "well-managed" classes.

Creating a Positive Learning Environment: Some Research Results

What can teachers do to be good managers? For several years, researchers at the University of Texas at Austin studied classroom management quite thoroughly (Emmer, Evertson, & Anderson, 1980; Emmer, Evertson, Clements, Worsham, & Murray, 2000; Evertson, 1988; Evertson, Emmer, Clements, Worsham, & Murray, 2000). Their general approach was to study a large number of classrooms, making frequent observations the first weeks of school and less-frequent visits later in the year. After several months there were dramatic differences among the classes. Some had very few management problems, while others had many. The most and least effective teachers were identified based on the quality of classroom management and student achievement in their classrooms later in the year.

Next, the researchers looked at their observation records of the first weeks of class to see how the effective teachers got started. Other comparisons were made between the teachers who ultimately had harmonious, high-achieving classes and those whose classes were fraught with problems. On the basis of these comparisons, management principles were developed. The researchers then taught these principles to a new group of teachers; the results were quite positive. Teachers who applied the principles had fewer problems; their students spent more time learning and less time disrupting; and achievement was higher. The findings of these studies are detailed in two books on classroom management (Emmer et al., 2000; Evertson et al., 2000). Many of the ideas in the following pages are from these books.

Rules and Procedures

At the elementary school level, teachers must lead 20 to 30 students of varying abilities through many different activities each day. Without efficient rules and procedures, a great deal of time is wasted answering the same question over and over. "My pencil broke. How can I do my math? I'm finished with my story. What should I do now? Jason hit me!" At the secondary school level, teachers must deal daily with over 100 students who use dozens of materials and often change rooms for each class. Secondary school students are also more likely to challenge teachers' authority. The effective managers studied by Emmer and Evertson and their respective colleagues (2000) had planned procedures and rules for coping with these situations.

Procedures.   How will materials and assignments be distributed and collected? Under what conditions can students leave the room? How will grades be determined? What are the special routines for handling equipment and supplies in science, art, or vocational classes? **Procedures** describe how activities are accomplished in classrooms, but they are seldom written down; they are simply the ways of getting things done in class. Weinstein (1996) and Weinstein and Mignano (1997) suggest that teachers establish procedures to cover the following areas:

- Administrative routines, such as taking attendance
- Student movement, such as entering and leaving or going to the bathroom
- Housekeeping, such as watering plants or storing personal items
- Routines for accomplishing lessons, such as how to collect assignments or return homework
- Interactions between teacher and student, such as how to get the teacher's attention when help is needed
- Talk among students, such as giving help or socializing

If teachers, particularly beginning teachers, are having trouble with class management, check these six areas. You might use these six areas as a framework for helping teachers think through their procedures and routines. The Theory into Action Guidelines on page 194 should help principals coach their teachers.

THEORY INTO ACTION GUIDELINES

Rules and Procedures

Determine procedures for student upkeep of desks, classroom equipment, and other facilities.

Examples

1. Some teachers set aside a cleanup time each day or once a week in self-contained classes.
2. You might demonstrate and have students practice how to push chairs under the desk, take and return materials stored on shelves, sharpen pencils, use the sink or water fountain, assemble lab equipment, etc.
3. In some classes a rotating monitor is in charge of equipment or materials.

Decide how students will be expected to enter and leave the room.

Examples

1. How will students know what they should do as soon as they enter the room? Some teachers have a standard assignment ("Have your homework out and be checking it over" or "Do the problem of the day.").
2. Under what conditions can students leave the room? When do they need permission?
3. If students are late, how do they gain admission to the room?
4. Many teachers require students to be in their seats and quiet before they can leave at the end of class. The teacher, not the bell, dismisses class.

Establish a signal and teach it to your students.

Examples

1. In the classroom, some teachers flick the lights, sound a chord on a piano or recorder, move to the podium and stare silently at the class, use a phrase like "Eyes, please," take out their grade books, or move to the front of the class.

2. In the halls, a raised hand, one clap, or some other signal may mean "Stop."
3. On the playground, a raised hand or whistle may mean "Line up."

Set procedures for student participation in class.

Examples

1. Will you have students raise their hands for permission to speak or simply require that they wait until the speaker has finished?
2. How will you signal that you want everyone to respond at once? Some teachers raise a cupped hand to their ear. Others preface the question with "Everyone...."
3. Make sure you are clear about differences in procedures for different activities: reading group, learning center, discussion, teacher presentation, seatwork, film, peer learning group, library, and so forth.
4. How many students at a time can be at the pencil sharpener, teacher's desk, learning center, sink, bookshelves, reading corner, or bathroom?

Determine how you will communicate, collect, and return assignments.

Examples

1. Some teachers reserve a particular corner of the board for listing assignments. Others write assignments in colored chalk. For younger students it may be better to prepare assignment sheets or folders, color-coding them for math workbook, reading packet, and science kit.
2. Some teachers collect assignments in a box or bin; others have a student collect work while they introduce the next activity.

Rules

Statements specifying the expected and forbidden actions in class are called **rules.** They are the do's and don'ts of classroom life. Unlike procedures, rules are often written down and posted. In establishing rules, teachers should consider what kind of atmosphere they want to create. What student behaviors will help them teach effectively? What limits do the students need to guide their behavior? The rules teachers set should be consistent with school rules, and also in keeping with principles of learning. For example, we know from the research on small-group learning that students benefit when they explain work to peers. They learn as they teach. A rule that forbids students to help each other may be inconsistent with good learning principles. Or a rule that says, "No erasures when writing" may make students focus more on preventing mistakes than on communicating clearly in their writing (Burden, 1995; Weinstein & Mignano, 1997). Having a few general rules that cover many specifics is better than listing all the do's and don'ts. But, if specific actions are forbidden, such as chewing gum in class or smoking in the bathrooms, then a rule should make this clear.

Rules for Elementary School.   Evertson and her colleagues (2000) give five examples of general rules for elementary school classes:

1. *Be polite and helpful.* This applies to behavior toward adults (including substitute teachers) and children. Examples of polite behavior include waiting your turn, saying "please" and "thank you," and not fighting or calling names.
2. *Respect other people's property.* This might include picking up litter; returning library books; not marking on walls, desks, or buses; and getting permission before using other people's things.
3. *Listen quietly while others are speaking.* This applies to the teacher and other students, in large-class lessons or small-group discussions.
4. *Do not hit, shove, or hurt others.* Make sure you give clear explanations of what you mean by "hurt." Does this apply to hurt feelings as well as hurt bodies?
5. *Obey all school rules.* This reminds students that all school rules apply in every classroom. Then students cannot claim, for example, that they thought it was OK to chew gum or listen to a radio in your class, even though these are against school rules, "because you never made a rule against it for us."

Whatever the rule, students need to be taught the behaviors that the rule includes and excludes. Examples, practice, and discussion will be needed before learning is complete. Many teachers you work with may think that their job is done when the rule is made or posted, then wonder why there are so many problems. Chances are that these teachers have not taught and practiced the rules. And as you've seen, different activities often require different rules. This can be confusing for elementary students until they have thoroughly learned all the rules. To prevent confusion, some teachers have signs that list the rules for each activity. Then, before the activity, they post the appropriate sign as a reminder. This provides clear and consistent cues about participation structures so all students, not just the "well-behaved," know what is expected. Of course, these rules must be explained, discussed, and practiced before the signs can have their full effect.

Rules for Secondary School.   Emmer and colleagues (2000) suggest six examples of rules for secondary students:

1. *Bring all needed materials to class.* The teacher must specify the type of pen, pencil, paper, notebook, texts, and so on.
2. *Be in your seat and ready to work when the bell rings.* Many teachers combine this rule with a standard beginning procedure for the class, such as a warm-up exercise on the board or a requirement that students have paper with a proper heading ready when the bell rings.
3. *Respect and be polite to everyone.* This covers fighting, verbal abuse, and general troublemaking.
4. *Respect other people's property.* This means property belonging to the school, the teacher, or other students.
5. *Listen and stay seated while someone else is speaking.* This applies when the teacher or other students are talking.
6. *Obey all school rules.* As with the elementary class rules, this covers many behaviors and situations, so teachers do not have to repeat every school rule for your class. It also reminds the students that their teachers will be monitoring them inside and outside your class.

Consequences.   Teachers must decide on consequences as soon as they determine their rules and procedures. It is too late to make this decision after the rule has been broken or the procedure not followed. For many infractions, the logical consequence is having to go back and "do it right." Students who run in the hall may have to return to where they started and walk properly. Incomplete papers can be redone. Materials left out should be put back (Charles, 1996). Sometimes consequences are more complicated. In their case studies of four expert elementary-school teachers, Weinstein and Mignano (1997) found that the teachers' negative consequences fell into seven categories, as shown in Table 6.1.

The main point here is that planning about penalties (and rewards) must happen early on, so students know before they break a rule or use the wrong procedure what this will mean for them.

Who Sets the Rules and Consequences?   Not all rules have to be stated as rules. For example, Ken, the sixth-grade teacher described in Chapter 5, works with his students to develop his class rules at the beginning of the year. Rather than specifying dos and don'ts, Ken and his students devise a "Bill of Rights" for the class, describing the rights of the students and of the teacher. These rights cover most of the situations that might need a "rule." The rights for one recent year's class are listed in Table 6.2 on page 198. Developing rights and responsibilities rather than rules makes a very important point to students. "Teaching children that something is wrong *because there is a rule against it* is not the same as teaching them that there is a rule against it *because it is wrong,* and helping them to understand why this is so" (Weinstein, 1999, p. 154). Students should understand that the rules are developed so that everyone can live and learn together.

Another kind of planning that affects the learning environment is the physical arrangement of the class furniture, materials, and learning tools. Here again, principals can help teachers be aware of the implications of classroom designs for learning.

TABLE 6.1   Seven Categories of Penalties for Students

1. *Expressions of disappointment.* If students like and respect their teacher, then a serious, sorrowful expression of disappointment may cause students to stop and think about their behavior.

2. *Loss of privileges.* Students can lose free time. If they have not completed homework, for example, they can be required to do it during a free period or recess.

3. *Exclusion from the group.* Students who distract their peers or fail to cooperate can be separated from the group until they are ready to cooperate. Some teachers give a student a pass for 10 to 15 minutes. The student must go to another class or study hall, where the other students and teachers ignore the offending student for that time.

4. *Written reflections on the problem.* Students can write in journals, write essays about what they did and how it affected others, or write letters of apology—if this is appropriate. Another possibility is to ask students to describe objectively what they did; then the teacher and the student can sign and date this statement. These records are available if parents or administrators need evidence of the students' behavior.

5. *Detentions.* Detentions can be very brief meetings after school, during a free period, or at lunch. The main purpose is to talk about what has happened. (In high school, detentions are often used as punishments; suspensions and expulsions are available as more extreme measures.)

6. *Visits to the principal's office.* Expert teachers tend to use this penalty rarely, but they do use it when the situation warrants. Some schools require students to be sent to the office for certain offenses, such as fighting. If a student is told to go to the office and refuses, the teacher might call the office saying the student has been sent. Then the student has the choice of either going to the office or facing the principal's penalty for "disappearing" on the way.

7. *Contact with parents.* If problems become a repeated pattern, most teachers contact the student's family. This is done to seek support for helping the student, not to blame the parents or punish the student.

Source: From C. S. Weinstein and A. J. Mignano, Jr. *Elementary Classroom Management.* Copyright © 1993 by The McGraw-Hill Companies. Adapted with permission of the McGraw-Hill Companies.

Planning Spaces for Learning

There are two basic ways of organizing space: interest areas and personal territories. These are not mutually exclusive; many teachers use a design that combines interest areas and personal territories. Individual students' desks—their territories—are placed in the center, with interest areas in the back or around the periphery of the room. This allows the flexibility needed for both large- and small-group activities. Figure 6.2 on page 199 shows an elementary classroom that combines interest area and personal territory arrangements.

Interest-Area Arrangements.   The design of interest areas can influence the way the areas are used by students. For example, working with a classroom teacher, Weinstein (1977) was able to make changes in interest areas that helped the teacher meet her objectives of having more girls involved in the science center and having all students experiment more with a variety of manipulative materials. In a second study, changes in a library corner led to more involvement in literature activities throughout the class (Morrow & Weinstein, 1986).

To plan classroom space, first decide what activities the classroom should accommodate. For example, if the teacher is in a self-contained elementary classroom, you might set

TABLE 6.2   A Bill of Rights for Students and Teachers

Students' Bill of Rights

Students in this class have the following rights:

> To whisper when the teacher isn't talking or asking for silence.
> To celebrate authorship or other work at least once a month.
> To exercise outside on days there is no physical education class.
> To have 2-minute breaks.
> To have healthy snacks during snack time.
> To participate in choosing a table.
> To have privacy. Get permission to touch anyone else's possessions.
> To be comfortable.
> To chew gum without blowing bubbles or making a mess.
> To make choices about the day's schedule.
> To have free work time.
> To work with partners.
> To talk to the class without anyone else talking.
> To work without being disturbed.

Teacher's Bill of Rights

The Teacher has the following rights:

> To talk without anyone else talking, moving about, or disturbing the class.
> To work without being disturbed.
> To have everyone's attention while giving directions.
> To punish someone who is not cooperating.
> To send someone out of the group or room, or to the office.

Source: From C. S. Weinstein and A. J. Mignano, Jr. *Elementary Classroom Management.* Copyright © 1993 by The McGraw-Hill Companies. Adapted with permission of The McGraw-Hill Companies.

up interest areas for reading, arts and crafts, science, and math. If the teacher handles one particular subject on the junior or senior high level, you might divide the room into several areas, perhaps for audiovisual activities, small-group instruction, quiet study, and projects.

The next step is to draw several possible floor plans. Use graph paper if possible, and draw to scale. The Theory into Action Guidelines on page 200 help principals and teachers think through their decisions about design.

Personal Territories. Can the physical setting influence teaching and learning in class-rooms organized by territories? Adams and Biddle (1970) found that verbal interaction be-tween teacher and students was concentrated in the center front of the classroom and in a line directly up the center of the room. The data were so dramatic that Adams and Biddle coined the term "action zone" to refer to this area of the room. Later research modified this finding. Even though most rooms have an **action zone** where participation is greatest, this

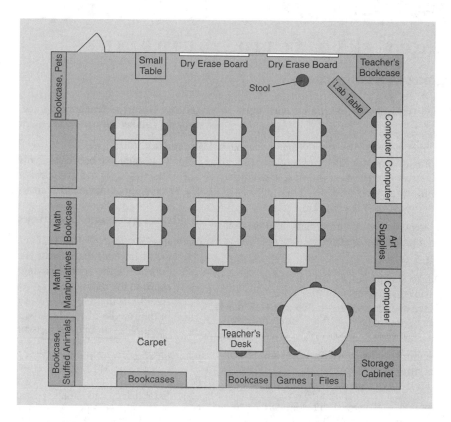

FIGURE 6.2   An Elementary Classroom Arrangement   This 4th-grade teacher has designed a space that allows teacher presentations and demonstrations, small group work, computer interactions, math manipulatives activities, informal reading, art, and other projects without constant rearrangements required.

Source: From C. S. Weinstein and A. J. Mignano, Jr. *Elementary Classroom Management.* Copyright © 1993 by The McGraw-Hill Companies. Reproduced with permission of The McGraw-Hill Companies.

area may be on one side, or near a particular learning center, not necessarily front and center (Good, 1983).

Front-seat location does seem to increase participation for students who are predisposed to speak in class, whereas a seat in the back will make it more difficult to participate and easier to sit back and daydream (Woolfolk & Brooks, 1983). To "spread the action around," Weinstein and Mignano (1997) suggest that teachers move around the room when possible, establish eye contact with students seated far away, and direct comments to students seated at a distance.

Many teachers vary the seating so the same students are not always assigned to the back of the room or to make the arrangement more appropriate for particular objectives

THEORY INTO ACTION GUIDELINES

Designing Learning Spaces

Note the fixed features and plan accordingly.

Examples

1. Remember that the audiovisual center and computers need an electrical outlet.
2. Keep art supplies near the sink, small-group work by a blackboard.

Create easy access to materials and a well-organized place to store them.

Examples

1. Make sure materials are easy to reach and visible to students.
2. Have enough shelves so that materials need not be stacked.

Provide students with clean, convenient surfaces for studying.

Examples

1. Put bookshelves next to reading area, games near game table.
2. Prevent fights by avoiding crowded workspaces.

Make sure work areas are private and quiet.

Examples

1. Make sure there are no tables or work areas in the middle of traffic lanes; a person should not have to pass through one area to get to another.
2. Keep noisy activities as far as possible from quiet ones. Increase the feeling of privacy by placing partitions, such as bookcases or pegboards, between areas or within large areas.

Arrange things so teachers can see students and students can see all instructional presentations.

Examples

1. Make sure teachers can see over partitions.
2. Design seating so that students can see instruction without moving their chairs or desks.

Avoid dead spaces and "racetracks."

Examples

1. Don't have all the interest areas around the outside of the room, leaving a large dead space in the middle.
2. Avoid placing a few items of furniture right in the middle of this large space, creating a "racetrack" around the furniture.

Provide choices and flexibility.

Examples

1. Establish closed, small spaces, private cubicles for individual work; open tables for group work; and cushions on the floor for whole-class meetings.
2. Give students a place to keep their personal belongings. This is especially important if students don't have personal desks.

Try new arrangements, then evaluate and improve.

Examples

1. Have a "two-week arrangement," then evaluate.
2. Enlist the aid of students. They have to live in the room, too, and designing a classroom can be a very challenging educational experience.

and activities. Figure 6.3 is a high school mathematics class with a seating arrangement that allows focus on teacher demonstration as well as small-group work.

Horizontal rows (like the front and back rows in Figure 6.3) share many of the advantages of the traditional row and column arrangements. Both are useful for independent

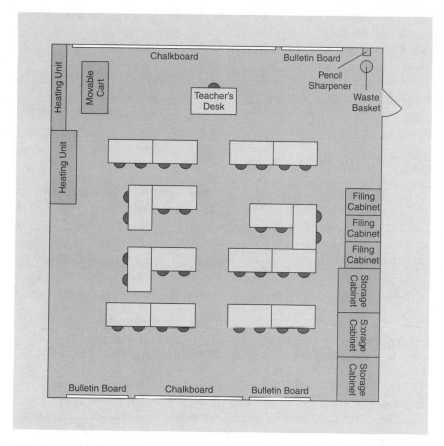

FIGURE 6.3 A High School Math Classroom   This high school teacher has designed a math classroom that allows teacher presentations and demonstrations as well as small-group work. By moving 4 tables, the room can be transformed into 4 horizontal rows for independent work or testing.

Source: From C. S. Weinstein and A. J. Mignano, Jr. *Elementary Classroom Management.* Copyright © 1993 by The McGraw-Hill Companies. Reproduced with permission of The McGraw-Hill Companies.

seatwork and teacher, student, or media presentations; they encourage students to focus on the presenter and simplify housekeeping, so they are good arrangements for the beginning of the school year—especially for new teachers. Horizontal rows also permit students to work more easily in pairs. However, this is a poor arrangement for large-group discussion.

Clusters of four or circle arrangements are best for student interaction. Circles are especially useful for discussions but still allow for independent seatwork. Clusters permit students to talk, help one another, share materials, and work on group tasks. Both arrangements, however, are poor for whole-group presentations or tests and may make class management more difficult. The stack special formation, where students sit close together near the focus of attention (the back row may even be standing), should be used only for short periods of time, because it is not comfortable and can lead to discipline problems. On the other hand, the fishbowl can create a feeling of group cohesion and is helpful when the teacher wants students to watch a demonstration, brainstorm on a class problem, or see a small visual aid. The point is that instructional leaders can help teachers design spaces for learning that match the teachers' goals and activities. If there are problems with an activity, maybe the physical design is getting in the way rather than supporting learning.

Getting Started: The First Weeks of Class

Determining a room design, rules, and procedures are first steps toward having a well-managed class—but how do effective teachers gain students' cooperation in those first critical days and weeks? One study carefully analyzed the first weeks' activities of effective and ineffective elementary teachers, and found striking differences (Emmer, Evertson, & Anderson, 1980).

Effective Classroom Managers for Elementary Students

In the effective teachers' classrooms, the very first day was well organized. Name tags were ready. There was something interesting for each child to do right away. Materials were set up. The teachers had planned carefully to avoid any last-minute tasks that might take them away from their students. These teachers dealt with the children's pressing concerns first. "Where do I put my things? How do I pronounce my teacher's name? Can I whisper to my neighbor? Where is the bathroom?" The effective teachers had a workable, easily understood set of rules and taught the students the most important rules right away. They taught the rules like any other subject, with lots of explanation, examples, and practice.

Throughout the first weeks, the effective managers continued to spend quite a bit of time teaching rules and procedures. Some used guided practice to teach procedures; others used rewards to shape behavior. Most taught students to respond to a bell or some other signal to gain their attention. These teachers worked with the class as a whole on enjoyable academic activities. They did not rush to get students into small groups or to get them started in readers. This whole-class work gave the teachers a better opportunity to continue monitoring all students' learning of the rules and procedures. Misbehavior was stopped quickly and firmly, but not harshly.

In the poorly managed classrooms, the first weeks were quite different. Rules were not workable; they were either too vague or very complicated. For example, one teacher made a rule that students should "be in the right place at the right time." Students were not told what this meant, so their behavior could not be guided by the rule. Neither positive nor negative behaviors had clear, consistent consequences. After students broke a rule, ineffective managers might give a vague criticism, such as "Some of my children are too noisy," or issue a warning, but not follow through with the threatened consequence.

In the poorly managed classes, procedures for accomplishing routine tasks varied from day to day and were never taught or practiced. Instead of dealing with these obvious needs, ineffective managers spent time on procedures that could have waited. For example, one teacher had the class practice for a fire drill the first day, but left unexplained other procedures that would be needed every day. Students wandered aimlessly and had to ask each other what they should be doing. Often the students talked to one another because they had nothing productive to do. Ineffective teachers frequently left the room. Many became absorbed in paperwork or in helping just one student. They had not made plans for how to deal with late-arriving students or interruptions. One ineffective manager tried to teach students to respond to a bell as a signal for attention, but later let the students ignore it. All in all, the first weeks in these classrooms were disorganized and filled with surprises for teachers and students alike.

Effective Classroom Managers for Secondary Students

What about getting started in a secondary school class? It appears that many of the differences between effective and ineffective elementary school teachers hold at the secondary level as well. Again, effective managers focus on establishing rules, procedures, and expectations on the first day of class. These standards for academic work and class behavior are clearly communicated to students and consistently enforced during the first weeks of class. Student behavior is closely monitored, and infractions of the rules are dealt with quickly. In classes with lower-ability students, work cycles are shorter; students are not required to spend long, unbroken periods on one type of activity. Instead, during each period they are moved smoothly through several different tasks. In general, effective teachers carefully follow each student's progress, so students cannot avoid work without facing consequences (Emmer & Evertson, 1982).

With all this close monitoring and consistent enforcement of the rules, you may wonder if effective secondary teachers have to be grim and humorless. Not necessarily. The effective managers in one study also smiled and joked more with their students (Moskowitz & Hayman, 1976). As any experienced teacher knows, there is much more to smile about when the class is cooperative. In fact, there is another requirement for getting started, one that was evident in the sixth-grade class run by the "class constitution"—establishing a climate of trust and respect that creates a community for learning

Creating a Learning Community

Nel Noddings (1992, 1995) has written about the need to create caring educational environments where students take more responsibility for governing their school and classroom. As we saw in Chapter 4 when we discussed the need for social support, students are more intrinsically motivated when they feel that their teachers care about them (Grolnick, Ryan, & Deci, 1991). Historically, however, American schools have emphasized regulating students' behavior through rules, not through relationships. But this is not true in every culture. For example, in the book, *Learning to Teach in Two Cultures*, Shimahara and Sakai (1995) observe that the Japanese approach to classroom management emphasizes such interpersonal bonds as emotional ties, relationships, and character. Success of the Japanese system "does not depend on many rules, but on a sense of trust and interdependency between the classroom teacher and his or her students and among the students" (Shimahara & Sakai, 1995, p. 79). One approach to developing this kind of caring and mutually trusting community is David and Roger Johnson's "Three Cs" of school and classroom management.

The Three Cs of Classroom Management

The three Cs for safe and productive schools are cooperative community, constructive conflict resolution, and civic values (Johnson & Johnson, 1999). Classroom management begins by establishing a learning community based on cooperative approaches such as those described in Chapter 3. At the heart of the community is the idea of positive interdependence—individuals working together to achieve mutual goals. Constructive conflict resolution is essential in the community because conflicts are inevitable and even necessary for learning. Piaget's theory of development and the research on conceptual change teaching tell us that true learning requires cognitive conflict. And individuals trying to exist in groups will have interpersonal conflict—these can lead to learning too. Table 6.3 shows how academic and interpersonal conflicts can be positive forces in a learning community. At the end of this chapter we will talk more about conflict resolution in schools.

The last C is civic values—the understandings and beliefs that hold the community together. Values are learned through direct teaching, modeling, literature, group discussions, the sharing of concerns. Some teachers have a "Concerns Box," where student can put written concerns and comments. The box is opened once a week at a class meeting and the concerns are discussed. Johnson and Johnson (1999) give an example of a class meeting about respect. One student tells her classmates that she felt hurt during recess the day before be-

TABLE 6.3 Academic and Interpersonal Conflict and Learning

Conflict, if handled well, can support learning. Academic conflicts can lead to critical thinking and conceptual change. Conflicts of interest are unavoidable, but can be handled so no one is the loser.

Academic Controversy	Conflicts of Interest
One person's ideas, information, theories, conclusions, and opinions are incompatible with those of another, and the two seek to reach an agreement.	The actions of one person attempting to maximize benefits prevents, blocks or interferes with another person maximizing her or his benefits.
Controversy Procedure	*Integrative (Problem-Solving) Negotiations*
Research and prepare positions	Describe wants
Present and advocate positions	Describe feelings
Refute opposing position and refute attacks on own position	Describe reasons for wants and feelings
Reverse perspectives	Take other's perspective
Synthesize and integrate best evidence and reasoning from all sides	Invent three optional agreements that maximize joint outcomes
	Choose one and formalize agreement

Source: From "The Three Cs of School and Classroom Management," by D. Johnson and R. Johnson, 1999, in H. J. Freiberg (Ed.), *Beyond Behaviorism: Changing the Classroom Management Paradigm* (p. 133), Boston: Allyn & Bacon. Copyright © 1999 by Allyn & Bacon. Adapted by permission.

cause no one listened when she was trying to teach them the rules to a new game. The students discussed what it means to be respectful and why respect is important. Then the students shared personal experiences of times when they felt respected versus not respected.

Getting Started on Community

Here is how a seventh-grade teacher described her experiences working with one English class to establish rules and procedures together (Freiberg, 1999, p. 171):

> I began with my first period class. We started slowly, with my asking them about what it would take for the class to work for them. I told them what it would take for the class to work for me. I was amazed at the overlap. They wanted to know up front what I expected of them in terms of tests, quantity and quality of work, late assignments, talking in class, and amount and how often they would have homework, where they could sit, grading and whether classroom participation counted. We talked about the best classes and the worst classes. We talked about respect and the need to respect each other, to listen, to be willing to be an active participant without [verbally] running over other people in the class or being run over. I talked about "my teacher time" and their "student time." Well, this was five months ago and I am amazed at their level of cooperation. I am well ahead of last year in the curriculum; we have class meeting once a week to see how things are going and to adjust as needed. We created a classroom constitution and had a constitutional convention when we felt it needed to be changed. I didn't believe it would make a difference, the students really surprised me with their level of maturity and responsibility and I surprised myself with my own willingness to change. This has been a great year and I am sorry to see it end and my students leave to another grade level. I am considering asking my principal to move me to the eighth grade so I could have the same students again. I have been teaching for fourteen years and this has been my best year ever. I feel supported by my students and my students told me that they feel supported by me.

Maintaining a Good Learning Environment

A good start is just that—a beginning. Effective teachers build on this beginning. They maintain their management system by preventing problems and keeping students engaged in productive learning activities.

Encouraging Engagement

The format of a lesson affects student involvement. In general, as teacher supervision increases, students' engaged time also increases (Emmer & Evertson, 1981). For example, Frick (1990) found that elementary students working directly with a teacher were on task 97% of the time, while students working on their own were on task only 57% of the time. This does not mean that teachers should eliminate independent work for students. It simply means that this type of activity usually requires careful monitoring.

When the task provides continuous cues for the student about what to do next, involvement will be greater. Activities with clear steps are likely to be more absorbing, because one step leads naturally to the next. When students have all the materials they need to complete a task, they tend to stay involved (Kounin & Doyle, 1975). If their curiosity is piqued, students will be motivated to continue seeking an answer. And students tend to be more engaged if they are involved in authentic tasks—activities that have connections to real life.

Of course, teachers can't supervise every student all the time or rely on curiosity. Something else must keep students working on their own. In their study of elementary and secondary teachers, Evertson, Emmer, and their colleagues found that effective class managers at both levels had well-planned systems for encouraging students to manage their own work (Evertson et al., 2000; Emmer et al., 1997). The Theory into Action Guidelines should help principals and teachers plan strategies for effective classroom management.

THEORY INTO ACTION GUIDELINES

Encouraging Student Accountability

Make basic work requirements clear.

Examples
1. Specify and post the routine work requirements for headings, paper size, pen or pencil use, and neatness.
2. Establish and explain rules about late or incomplete work and absences. If a pattern of incomplete work begins to develop, deal with it early; speak with parents if necessary.
3. Make due dates reasonable, and stick to them unless the student has a very good excuse for lateness.

Communicate the specifics of assignments.

Examples
1. With younger students, have a routine procedure for giving assignments, such as writing them on the board in the same place each day. With older students, assignments may be dictated, posted, or given in a syllabus.
2. Remind students of coming assignments.
3. With complicated assignments, give students a sheet describing what to do, what resources are available, due dates, and so on. Older students should also be told about grading criteria.
4. Demonstrate how to do the assignment, do the first few questions together, or provide a sample worksheet.

Monitor work in progress.

Examples
1. When you make an assignment in class, make sure each student gets started correctly. If you check only students who raise their hands for help, you will miss those who think they know what to do but don't really understand, those who are too shy to ask for help, and those who don't plan to do the work at all.
2. Check progress periodically. In discussions, make sure everyone has a chance to respond.

Give frequent academic feedback.

Examples
1. Elementary students should get papers back the day after they are handed in.
2. Good work can be displayed in class and graded papers sent home to parents each week.
3. Students of all ages can keep records of grades, projects completed, and extra credits earned.
4. For older students break up long-term assignments into several phases, giving feedback at each point.

Prevention Is the Best Medicine

What else can teachers do to maintain their management system? The ideal way to manage problems, of course, is to prevent them in the first place. In a classic study, Jacob Kounin (1970) examined classroom management by comparing effective teachers, whose classes were relatively free of problems, with ineffective teachers, whose classes were continually plagued by chaos and disruption. Observing both groups in action, Kounin found that they were not very different in the way they handled discipline once problems arose. The difference was that the successful managers were much better at preventing problems. Kounin concluded that effective classroom managers were especially skilled in four areas: "with-it-ness," overlapping activities, group focusing, and movement management (Doyle, 1977). More recent research confirms the importance of these factors (Emmer & Evertson, 1981; Evertson, 1988).

Withitness.   It is important to demonstrate **withitness,** communicating to students that you are aware of everything that is happening in the classroom, that you aren't missing anything. "With-it" teachers seem to have eyes in the back of their heads. They avoid becoming absorbed or interacting with only a few students, because this encourages the rest of the class to wander. They are always scanning the room, making eye contact with individual students, so the students know they are being monitored (Brooks, 1985).

These teachers prevent minor disruptions from becoming major. They also know who instigated the problem, and they make sure the right people are dealt with. In other words, they do not make what Kounin called *timing errors* (waiting too long before intervening) or *target errors* (blaming the wrong student and letting the real perpetrators escape responsibility for their behavior). If two problems occur at the same time, effective managers deal with the more serious one first. For example, a teacher who tells two students to stop whispering but ignores even a brief shoving match at the pencil sharpener communicates to students a lack of awareness. Students begin to believe they can get away with almost anything if they are clever (Charles, 1996).

Overlapping and Group Focus.   Effective teachers are good at **overlapping**—keeping track of and supervising several activities at the same time. For example, a teacher may have to check the work of an individual and at the same time keep a small group working by saying, "Right, go on," and stop an incident in another group with a quick "look" or reminder (Burden, 1995; Charles, 1996).

Maintaining a **group focus** means keeping as many students as possible involved in appropriate class activities and avoiding narrowing in on just one or two students. All students should have something to do during a lesson. For example, the teacher might ask everyone to write the answer to a question, then call on individuals to respond while the other students compare their answers. Choral responses might be required while the teacher moves around the room to make sure everyone is participating (Charles, 1996). Some teachers have their students use small blackboards or colored cards for responding in groups. This lets the teacher check for understanding as well. For example, during a grammar lesson the teacher might say, "Everyone who thinks the answer is 'have run,' hold up the red side of your card. If you think the answer is 'has run,' hold up the green side" (Hunter, 1982). This is one way teachers can ensure that all students are involved and check that they all understand the material.

Movement Management.   Effective teachers are good at **movement management**—keeping lessons and the group moving at an appropriate (and flexible) pace, with smooth transitions and variety. The effective teacher avoids abrupt transitions, such as announcing a new activity before gaining the students' attention or starting a new activity in the middle of something else. In these situations, one third of the class will be doing the new activity, many will be on the old lesson, several will be asking other students what to do, some will be taking the opportunity to have a little fun, and most will be confused.

Another transition problem Kounin noted is *slowdown,* or taking too much time to start a new activity. Sometimes teachers give too many directions. Problems also arise when teachers have students work one at a time while the rest of the class waits and watches. Charles (1985, p. 26) gives this example:

> During a science lesson the teacher began, "Row 1 may get up and get their beakers. Row 2 may get theirs. Now Row 3. Now, Row 1 may line up to put some bicarbonate of soda in their beakers. Row 2 may follow them," and so forth. When each row had obtained their bicarbonate of soda the teacher had them go row by row to add water. This left the remainder of the class sitting at their desks with no direction, doing nothing or else beginning to find something with which to entertain themselves.

A teacher who successfully demonstrates withitness, overlapping activities, group focus, and movement management tends to have a class filled with actively engaged students who do not escape his or her all-seeing eye. This need not be a grim classroom. It is more likely a busy place where students are actively learning and gaining a sense of self-worth rather than misbehaving in order to get attention and achieve status.

Dealing with Discipline Problems

In 2001, *Phi Delta Kappa* published the 33st annual Gallup Poll of the public's attitude toward public schools. In 1999, as in almost every year since 1969, "lack of discipline" was named as the number one problem facing the schools (Rose & Gallup, 1999). In 2000, the biggest problem named was lack of financial support, but discipline was a close second. Then in 2001, lack of discipline and lack of financial support tied as the top problems facing public school schools (Rose, & Gallup, 2001). Clearly, the public sees discipline as an important challenge for teachers.

Being an effective manager does not mean publicly correcting every minor infraction of the rules. This kind of public attention may actually reinforce the misbehavior. Teachers who frequently correct students do not necessarily have the best-behaved classes (Irving & Martin, 1982). The key is to know what is happening and what is important so you can prevent problems. Emmer and colleagues (2000) and Levin and Nolan (2000) suggest seven simple ways teachers can stop misbehavior quickly, moving from least to most intrusive:

- *Make eye contact* with, or move closer to, the offender. Other nonverbal signals, such as pointing to the work students are supposed to be doing, might be helpful. Make sure the student actually stops the inappropriate behavior and gets back to work. If you do not, students will learn to ignore your signals.

- Try *verbal hints* such as "name-dropping" (simply insert the student's name into the lecture), asking the student a question, or making a humorous (not sarcastic) comment such as, "I must be hallucinating. I swear I heard someone shout out an answer, but that can't be because I haven't called on anyone yet!"
- You might also ask students *if they are aware* of the negative effects of their actions or send an "I message," described later in the chapter.
- If they are not performing a class procedure correctly, *remind the students* of the procedure and have them follow it correctly. You may need to quietly collect a toy, comb, magazine, or note that is competing with the learning activities, while privately informing the students that their possessions will be returned after class.
- In a calm, unhostile way, *ask the student to state the correct rule or procedure* and then to follow it. Glasser (1969) proposes three questions: "What are you doing? Is it against the rules? What should you be doing?"
- Tell the student in a clear, assertive, and unhostile way to *stop the misbehavior.* (Later in the chapter we will discuss assertive messages to students in more detail.) If students "talk back," simply repeat your statement.
- *Offer a choice.* For example, when a student continued to call out answers no matter what the teacher tried, the teacher said, "John, you have a choice. Stop calling out answers immediately and begin raising your hand to answer or move your seat to the back of the room and you and I will have a private discussion later, You decide" (Levin & Nolan, 2000, p. 177).

If teachers or principals must impose penalties, the Theory into Action Guidelines on page 210, taken from Weinstein and Mignano (1997, Weinstein, 1996), give ideas about how to do it. The examples are taken from the actual words of the expert teachers described in their book.

Special Problems with Secondary Students

Many secondary students never complete their work. Besides encouraging student responsibility, what else can teachers do to deal with this frustrating problem? Because students at this age have many assignments and teachers have many students, both teacher and students may lose track of what has and has not been completed. It often helps to teach students how to use a daily planner. In addition, the teacher must keep accurate records. But the most important thing is to enforce the established consequences for incomplete work. Teachers should not pass a student because they know that he or she is "bright enough" to pass. Teachers should make it clear to these students that the choice is theirs: do the work and pass, or refuse to do the work and face the consequences.

There is also the problem of students who continually break the same rules, always forgetting materials, for example, or getting into fights. What should teachers do? Teachers should seat these students away from others who might be influenced by them; try to catch them before they break the rules. If, however, rules are broken, the teacher must be consistent in applying established consequences. Teachers should not accept promises to do better next time (Levin & Nolan, 2000). Students must be taught how to monitor their own behavior; some of the learning strategies described in Chapter 3 should be helpful. Finally, the teacher

THEORY INTO ACTION GUIDELINES

Penalties

Delay the discussion of the situation until you and the students involved are calmer and more objective.

Examples

1. Say calmly to a student, "Sit there and think about what happened. I'll talk to you in a few minutes," or, "I don't like what I just saw. Talk to me during your free period today."
2. Say, "I'm really angry about what just happened. Everybody take out journals; we are going to write about this." After a few minutes of writing, the class can discuss the incident.

Impose penalties privately.

Examples

1. Make arrangements with students privately. Stand firm in enforcing arrangements.
2. Resist the temptation to "remind" students in public that they are not keeping their side of the bargain.
3. Move close to a student who must be disciplined and speak so that only the student can hear.

After imposing a penalty, reestablish a positive relationship with the student immediately.

Examples

1. Send the student on an errand or ask him or her for help.
2. Compliment the student's work or give a real or symbolic "pat on the back" when the student's behavior warrants. Look hard for such an opportunity.

Set up a graded list of penalties that will fit many occasions.

Example

1. For not turning in homework: (1) receive reminder; (2) receive warning; (3) hand homework in before close of school day; (4) stay after school to finish work; (5) participate in a teacher–student–parent conference to develop an action plan.

should remain friendly with the students and try to catch them in a good moment so he or she can talk to the students about something other than their rule breaking.

The defiant, hostile student can pose serious problems. If there is an outbreak, the teacher should try to get out of the situation as soon as possible; everyone loses in a public power struggle. One possibility is for the teacher to give the student a chance to save face and cool down by saying, "It's your choice to cooperate or not. You can take a minute to think about it." If the student complies, they can talk later about controlling the outbursts. If the student refuses to cooperate, the teacher can tell him or her to wait in the hall until he or she gets the class started on work, and can then step outside for a private talk. If the student refuses to leave, teachers should know that they can send another class member for help from the principal or the assistant principal. Again, follow through. If the student complies before help arrives, the teacher should not let him or her off the hook. If outbursts occur frequently, the teacher might arrange a conference with the counselor, parents, or other teachers. If the problem is an unreconcilable clash of personalities, the student should be transferred to another teacher.

It sometimes is useful to keep records of the incidents by logging the student's name, words and actions, date, time, place, and teachers' response. These records may help identify patterns and can prove helpful in meeting with administrators, parents, or special services personnel (Burden, 1995). Some teachers have students sign each entry to verify the incidents.

Violence or destruction of property is a difficult and potentially dangerous problem. For teachers, the first step is to send for help and get the names of participants and witnesses. Then get rid of any crowd that may have gathered; an audience will only make things worse. The teacher should not try to break up a fight without help. Tell teachers to make sure the school office is aware of the incident; the school should have a policy for dealing with these situations.

Special Programs for Classroom Management

In some situations your teachers may want to consider using a much more formal classroom management system. Three possibilities, all based on behavioral principles, are group consequences, contingency contracts (described in Chapter 3), and token programs.

Group Consequences. A teacher can base reinforcement for the class on the cumulative behavior of all members of the class, usually by adding each student's points to a class or a team total. The **good behavior game** is an example of this approach. A class is divided into two teams. Specific rules for good behavior are cooperatively developed. Each time a student breaks one of the rules, that student's team is given a mark. The team with the fewest marks at the end of the period receives a special reward or privilege (longer recess, first to lunch, and so on). If both teams earn fewer than a preestablished number of marks, both teams receive the reward. Most studies indicate that even though the game produces only small improvements in academic achievement, it can produce definite improvements in the behaviors listed in the good behavior rules.

Teachers can also use **group consequences** without dividing the class into teams, that is, they can base reinforcement on the behavior of the whole class. Wilson and Hopkins (1973) conducted a study using group consequences to reduce noise levels. Radio music served effectively as the reinforcer for students in a home economics class. Whenever noise in the class was below a predetermined level, students could listen to the radio; when the noise exceeded the level, the radio was turned off. Given the success of this simple method, such a procedure might be considered in any class where music does not interfere with the task at hand or distract the students.

However, caution is needed in group approaches. The whole group should not suffer for the misbehavior or mistakes of one individual if the group has no real influence over that person (Epanchin, Townsend, & Stoddard, 1994; Jenson, Sloane, & Young, 1988). We have seen an entire class break into cheers when the teacher announced that one boy was transferring to another school. The chant "No more points! No more points!" filled the room. The "points" referred to the teacher's system of giving one point to the whole class each time anyone broke a rule. Every point meant 5 minutes of recess lost. The boy who was transferring had been responsible for many losses. He was not very popular to begin with, and the point system, though quite effective in maintaining order, had led to rejection and even greater unpopularity.

Peer pressure in the form of support and encouragement, however, can be a positive influence. Group consequences are recommended for situations in which students care about the approval of their peers. If the misbehavior of several students seems to be encouraged by the attention and laughter of other students, then group consequences could be helpful. Teachers might show students how to give support and constructive feedback to classmates. If a few students seem to enjoy sabotaging the system, those students may need separate arrangements.

Token Reinforcement Programs.   Often it is difficult to provide positive consequences for all the students who deserve them. A **token reinforcement system** can help solve this problem by allowing all students to earn tokens for both academic work and positive classroom behavior. The tokens may be points, checks, holes punched in a card, chips, play money, or anything else that is easily identified as the student's property. Periodically the students exchange the tokens they have earned for some desired reward (Martin & Pear, 1992).

Depending on the age of the student, the rewards could be small toys, school supplies, free time, special class jobs, or other privileges. When a "token economy," as this kind of system is called, is first established, the tokens should be given out on a fairly continuous schedule, with chances to exchange the tokens for rewards often available. Once the system is working well, however, tokens should be distributed on an intermittent schedule and saved for longer periods of time before they are exchanged for rewards.

Another variation is to allow students to earn tokens in the classroom and then exchange them for rewards at home. These plans are very successful when parents are willing to cooperate. Usually a note or report form is sent home daily or twice a week. The note indicates the number of points earned in the preceding time period. The points may be exchanged for minutes of television viewing, access to special toys, or private time with parents. Points can also be saved up for larger rewards such as trips. Have teachers avoid using this procedure, however, if they suspect a child might be harmed for poor reports.

Token reinforcement systems are complicated and time-consuming. Generally, they should be used in only three situations: to motivate students who are completely uninterested in their work and have not responded to other approaches; to encourage students who have consistently failed to make academic progress; and to deal with a class that is out of control, such as the one described in the leadership challenge at the beginning of this chapter. Some groups of students seem to benefit more than others from token economies. Students who are developmentally delayed or have mental retardation, children who have failed often, students with few academic skills, and students with behavior problems all seem to respond to the concrete, direct nature of token reinforcement.

Before you try a token system, you should be sure that the teacher's methods and materials are right for the students. Sometimes class disruptions or lack of motivation indicate that teaching practices need to be changed. Maybe the class rules are unclear or are enforced inconsistently. Maybe the text is too easy or too hard. Maybe the pace is wrong. If these problems exist, a token system may improve the situation temporarily, but the students will still have trouble learning the academic material (Jenson, Sloane, & Young, 1988).

The few pages devoted here to group consequences and token reinforcement and contingency contracts can offer only an introduction to these programs. If you want to allow a large-scale reward program in your school, you should probably seek more information. In addition, remember that, applied inappropriately, external rewards can undermine the students' motivation to learn (Deci, 1975; Lepper & Greene, 1978).

The Need for Communication

Communication between teacher and students is essential when problems arise. Communication is more than "teacher talks—student listens." It is more than the words exchanged between individuals. We communicate in many ways. Actions, movements, voice tone, facial expressions, and many other nonverbal behaviors send messages to the students. Many times the messages the teacher intends to send are not the messages that students receive.

Message Sent—Message Received

TEACHER: Carl, where is your homework?

CARL: I left it in my dad's car this morning.

TEACHER: Again? You will have to bring me a note tomorrow from your father saying that you actually did the homework. No grade without the note.

MESSAGE CARL RECEIVES: I can't trust you. I need proof you did the work.

TEACHER: Sit at every other desk. Put all your things under your desk. Jane and Laurel, you are sitting too close together. One of you move!

MESSAGE JANE AND LAUREL RECEIVE: I expect you two to cheat on this test.

A new student comes to Ms. Lincoln's kindergarten. The child is messy and unwashed. Ms. Lincoln puts her hand lightly on the girl's shoulder and says, "I'm glad you are here." Her muscles tense, and she leans away from the child.

MESSAGE STUDENT RECEIVES: I don't like you.

In all interactions, a message is sent and a message is received. Sometimes teachers or principals believe they are sending one message, but their voices, body positions, choices of words, and gestures may communicate a different message. Students may hear the hidden message and respond to it. For example, a student may respond with hostility if she or he feels insulted by the teacher (or by another student), but may not be able to say exactly where the feeling of being insulted came from. Perhaps it was in the teacher's tone of voice, not the words actually spoken. In such cases, the teacher may feel attacked for no reason. "What did I say? All I said was…." The first principle of communication is that people respond to what they think was said or meant, not necessarily to the speaker's intended message or actual words.

Diagnosis: Whose Problem Is It?

Teachers may find many student behaviors unacceptable, unpleasant, or troubling. It is often difficult to stand back from these problems, take an objective look, and decide on an appropriate response. According to Thomas Gordon (1981), the key to good teacher–student relationships is determining why the teacher is troubled by a particular behavior and whose problem it is. The teacher must begin by asking who "owns" the problem. The answer to this question is critical. If it is really the student's problem, the teacher must become a counselor and supporter, helping the student find his or her own solution. But if the teacher "owns" the problem, it is the teacher's responsibility to find a solution through problem solving with the student.

Diagnosing who owns the problem is not always straightforward. Let's look at three troubling situations to get some practice in this skill:

1. A student writes obscene words and draws sexually explicit illustrations in a school encyclopedia.
2. A student tells you that his parents had a bad fight and he hates his father.
3. A student quietly reads a magazine in the back of the room.

Why are these behaviors troubling? If the teacher cannot accept the student's behavior because it has a serious effect on the teacher—if the teacher is blocked from reaching his or her goals by the student's action—then the teacher owns the problem. It is the teacher's responsibility to confront the student and seek a solution. A teacher-owned problem appears to be present in the first situation described above—the young pornographer—because teaching materials are damaged.

If teachers feel annoyed by the behavior because it is getting in the student's own way or because they are embarrassed for the child, but the behavior does not directly interfere with teaching, then it is probably the student's problem. The test question is: Does this student's action tangibly affect the teacher or prevent the teacher from fulfilling the role of teaching? The student who hates his father would not prevent a teacher from teaching, even though he or she might wish the student felt differently. The problem is really the student's, and he must find his own solution.

Situation 3 is more difficult to diagnose. One argument is that the teacher is not interfered with in any way, so it is the student's problem. Another argument is that teachers might find reading the paper distracting during a lecture, so it is their problem, and they must find a solution. In a gray area such as this, the answer probably depends on how the teacher actually experiences the student's behavior. Having decided who owns the problem, it is time to act.

Counseling: The Student's Problem

Let's consider a situation in which a student finds a reading assignment "dumb." How might a teacher handle this positively?

STUDENT: This book is really dumb! Why did we have to read it?

TEACHER: You're pretty upset. This seemed like a worthless assignment to you. [Teacher paraphrases the student's statement, trying to hear the emotions as well as the words.]

STUDENT: Yeah! Well, I guess it was worthless. I mean, I don't know if it was. I couldn't exactly read it.

TEACHER: It was just too hard to read, and that bothers you.

STUDENT: Sure, I felt really dumb. I know I can write a good report, but not with a book this tough.

TEACHER: I think I can give you some hints that will make the book easier to understand. Can you see me after school today?

STUDENT: Okay.

Here the teacher used *empathetic listening* to allow the student to reach a solution. By trying to hear the student and by avoiding the tendency to jump in too quickly with advice, solutions, criticisms, reprimands, or interrogations, the teacher keeps the communication lines open. Here are a few <u>unhelpful</u> responses the teacher might have made:

I chose the book because it is the best example of a coming-of-age novel in our library. You will need to have read it before your English II class next year. (The teacher justifies the choice; this prevents the student from admitting that this "important" assignment is too difficult.)

Did you really read it? I bet you didn't do the work, and now you want out of the assignment. (The teacher accuses; the student hears, "The teacher doesn't trust me!" and must defend herself or himself or accept the teacher's view.)

Your job is to read the book, not ask me why. I know what's best. (The teacher pulls rank, and the student hears, "You can't possibly decide what is good for you!" The student can rebel or passively accept the teacher's judgment.)

Empathetic, active listening can be a helpful response when students bring problems to teachers (or teachers bring problems to you). You (or the teacher) must reflect back to the person what you hear him or her saying. This reflection is more than a parroting of the words; it should capture the emotions, intent, and meaning behind them. Sokolove, Garrett, Sadker, and Sadker (1986) have summarized the components of active listening: (1) blocking out external stimuli; (2) attending carefully to both the verbal and nonverbal messages; (3) differentiating between the intellectual and the emotional content of the message; and (4) making inferences regarding the speaker's feelings.

When students realize they really have been heard and not evaluated negatively for what they have said or felt, they feel freer to trust the teacher and to talk more openly. Sometimes the true problem surfaces later in the conversation, as in the example above where reading level was the real problem for the student.

Confrontation and Assertive Discipline

Now let's assume a student is doing something that actively interferes with teaching. The teacher decides the student must stop. The problem is the teacher's. Confrontation, not counseling, is required.

"I" Messages.   Gordon (1974) recommends sending an "I message in order to intervene and change a student's behavior. An "**I**" **message** tells a student in a straightforward, assertive, and nonjudgmental way what she or he is *doing,* how it *affects the teacher* as a teacher, and *how the teacher feels* about it. The student is then free to change voluntarily, and often does so. Here are two "I" messages:

> If you leave your book bags in the aisles, I might trip and hurt myself.

> When you all call out, I can't concentrate on each answer, and I'm frustrated.

Assertive Discipline.   Lee and Marlene Canter (1992; Canter, 1989) suggest other approaches for dealing with a teacher-owned problem. They call their method **assertive discipline**—teachers must make their expectations clear and must follow through with established consequences. Students then have a straightforward choice: they can follow the rules or accept the consequences. Many teachers are ineffective with students because they are either wishy-washy and passive or hostile and aggressive.

The *passive style* can take several forms. Instead of telling the student directly what to do, the teacher tells, or often asks, the student to try or to think about the appropriate action. The passive teacher might comment on the problem behavior without actually telling the child what to do differently: "Why are you doing that? Don't you know the rules?" or "Sam, are you disturbing the class?" Or teachers may clearly state what should happen, but never follow through with the established consequences, giving the students "one more chance" every time. Finally, teachers may ignore behavior that should receive a response or may wait too long before responding.

A *hostile response style* involves different mistakes. Teachers may make "you" statements that condemn the student without stating clearly what the student should be doing: "You should be ashamed of the way you're behaving!" or "You never listen!" or "You are acting like a baby!" Teachers may also threaten students angrily but follow through too seldom, perhaps because the threats are too vague—"You'll be very sorry you did that when I get through with you!"—or too severe. For example, a teacher tells a student in a physical education class that he will have to sit on the bench for three weeks. A few days later the team is short one member and the teacher lets the student play, never returning him to the bench to complete the three-week sentence. Often a teacher who has been passive becomes hostile and explodes when students persist in misbehaving.

In contrast with both the passive and hostile styles, an assertive response communicates to the students that you care too much about them and the process of learning to allow inappropriate behavior to persist. Assertive teachers clearly state what they expect. To be most effective, the teachers often look into a student's eyes when speaking and address the student by name. Assertive teachers' voices are calm, firm, and confident. They are not sidetracked by accusations such as "You just don't understand!" or "You don't like me!" Assertive teachers do not get into a debate about the fairness of the rules. They expect changes, not promises or apologies.

Even though many teachers and school administrators have given enthusiastic testimonies about the assertive discipline approach, others question its effectiveness. But for some of the teachers you work with, these ideas could be helpful.

Confrontations and Negotiations. If "I" messages or assertive responses fail and a student persists in misbehaving, teacher and student are in a conflict. Several pitfalls now loom. The two individuals become less able to perceive each other's behavior accurately. Research has shown that the angrier you get with another person, the more you see the other as the villain and yourself as an innocent victim. Because you feel the other person is in the wrong, and he or she feels just as strongly that the conflict is all your fault, very little mutual trust is possible. A cooperative solution to the problem is almost impossible. In fact, by the time the discussion has gone on a few minutes, the original problem is lost in a sea of charges, countercharges, and self-defense (Johnson & Johnson, 1994).

There are three methods of resolving a conflict between teacher and student. One is for the teacher to impose a solution. This may be necessary during an emergency, as when a defiant student refuses to go to the hall to discuss a public outbreak, but it is not a good solution for most conflicts. The second method is for the teacher to give in to the student's demands. Teachers might be convinced by a particularly compelling student argument, but again, this should be used sparingly. It is generally a bad idea to be talked out of a position, unless the position was wrong in the first place. Problems arise when either the teacher or the student gives in completely.

Gordon recommends a third approach, which he calls the "no-lose method." Here the needs of both the teacher and the students are taken into account in the solution. No one person is expected to give in completely; all participants retain respect for themselves and each other. The no-lose method is a six-step, problem-solving strategy:

1. Define the problem. What exactly are the behaviors involved? What does each person want? (Use active listening to help students pinpoint the real problem.)
2. Generate many possible solutions. Brainstorm, but remember, don't allow any evaluations of ideas yet.
3. Evaluate each solution. Any participant may veto any idea. If no solutions are found to be acceptable, brainstorm again.
4. Make a decision. Choose one solution through consensus—no voting. In the end, everyone must be satisfied with the solution.
5. Determine how to implement the solution. What will be needed? Who will be responsible for each task? What is the timetable?
6. Evaluate the success of the solution. After trying the solution for a while, ask, "are we satisfied with our decision? How well is it working? Should we make some changes?"

Many of the conflicts in classrooms are between students. These can be important learning experiences for all concerned.

Student Conflicts and Confrontations

Handling conflict is difficult for most of us—for young people it can be even harder. Given the public's concern about violence in schools, it is surprising how little we know about conflicts among students (Johnson, Johnson, Dudley, Ward, & Magnuson, 1995).

Conflicts: Goals and Needs.   When people are in conflict, they have two major concerns. The first is to satisfy their needs and meet their goals. This usually is the source of the conflict—the needs or goals of one person or group clash with the needs or goals of others. The second concern is to maintain an appropriate relationship with the other party in the conflict. Both of these concerns can be placed on a continuum from not very important to critically important. Different strategies are called for, depending on the importance of the goals and the relationships, as shown in Table 6.4 (Johnson & Johnson, 1994).

The message here is that different strategies make sense in different situations. Without guidance and practice, however, teachers and students may always use the same strategy— they may not be able to fit strategy to situation.

Violence in the Schools.   Violence among youth is a growing problem. Young people ages 12 to 24 are the most likely victims of nonfatal violence in American society, and many of these attacks happen on school property. This problem has many causes; it is a challenge for every element of society. What can the schools do?

One answer is prevention. Some Chicano gang members in Chicago reported that they turned to gang activities when their teachers insulted them, called them names, humiliated them publicly, belittled their culture, ignored them in class, or blamed all negative incidents on particular students. The students reported joining gangs for security and to escape teachers who treated them badly or expected little of them because they were Latino (Padilla, 1992; Parks, 1995). Another two-year study in Ohio found that gang members re-

---

TABLE 6.4 Strategies for Managing Conflict

Different situations call for different strategies. But any strategy can be used inappropriately. For example, withdrawing may be used inappropriately to avoid all conflict or appropriately to postpone confrontation until constructive discussions are possible.

Goal Important?	Relationship Important?	Strategy	Appropriate Uses	Inappropriate Uses
No	No	Withdraw	Postpone until constructive discussion is possible	Avoid conflict, hide
No	Yes	Smooth/Give in	When other's needs are more important	Give in just to be liked
Yes	No	Force	Seldom appropriate, perhaps when others' safety is your responsibility	To intimidate, win at all costs, overpower
Yes	Yes	Confront	Resolve conflict— strengthen relationship— protect both parties' goals	Generally appropriate
Moderately	Moderately	Compromise	When mutual sacrifices are required for the common good	When confrontation could satisfy both parties' goals

Source: From Anita Woolfolk, *Educational Psychology, 8/e.* Copyright © 2001. Reprinted by permission of Allyn & Bacon.

spected teachers who insisted on academic performance in a caring way (Huff, 1989). We once asked a gifted educator in an urban New Jersey high school which teachers were most effective with the really tough students. He said there are two kinds, teachers who can't be intimidated or fooled and expect their students to learn, and teachers who really care about the students. When we asked, "Which kind are you?" and he answered "Both!"

Besides prevention, schools can also establish mentoring programs, conflict resolution training, social skills training, more relevant curricula, and parent and community involvement programs (Padilla, 1992; Parks, 1995). One intervention that seems to be helpful is peer mediation.

Peer Mediation.   David Johnson and his colleagues provided conflict resolution training—**peer mediation**—to 227 students in second through fifth grade. Students learned a five-step negotiating strategy:

1. Jointly define the conflict. Separate the person from the problem and the actions involved, avoid win–lose thinking, get both parties' goals clear.
2. Exchange positions and interests. Present a tentative proposal and make a case for it; listen to the other person's proposal and feelings; and stay flexible and cooperative.
3. Reverse perspectives. See the situation from the other person's point of view and reverse roles and argue for that perspective.
4. Invent at least three agreements that allow mutual gain. Brainstorm, focus on goals, think creatively, and make sure everyone has power to invent solutions.
5. Reach an integrative agreement. Make sure both sets of goals are met. If all else fails, flip a coin, take turns, or call in a third party—a mediator.

In addition to learning conflict resolution, all students in Johnson and Johnson's study were trained in mediation strategies. The role of the mediator was rotated—every day the teacher chose two students to be the class mediators and to wear the mediator's T-shirt. Johnson and his colleagues found that students learned the conflict resolutions and mediation strategies and used them successfully, both in school and at home, to handle conflicts in a more productive way. For details of the strategies, see Johnson and Johnson (1994), Miller (1994), or Smith (1993).

Peer mediation has also been successful with older students and serious problems (Sanchez & Anderson, 1990). In one program, selected gang members are given mediation training, then all members are invited to participate voluntarily in the mediation process, supervised by school counselors. Strict rules governed the process leading to written agreements signed by gang representatives. Sanchez and Anderson (1990) found that gang violence in the school was reduced to a bare minimum—"The magic of the mediation process was communication" (p. 56).

Communicating with Families about Classroom Management

As we have seen throughout this book, families are important partners in education. This statement applies to classroom management as well. When parents and teachers share the same expectations and support each other, they can create a more positive classroom environment and more time for learning. The Theory into Action Guidelines provide ideas for principals and teachers as they work with families and the community.

Designing Motivating Learning Environments on Target for Learning

So far we have examined how to establish an orderly and organized learning environment that makes time and space for learning. But there is more to a classroom than order. The learning environment also includes the tasks and social relationships that affect learning by

---

THEORY INTO ACTION GUIDELINES

Working with Families

Make sure families know the expectations and rules of your class and school.

Examples

1. At a Family Fun Night, have your students do skits showing the rules—how to follow them and what breaking them "looks like" and "sounds like."
2. Make a poster for the refrigerator at home that describes, in a light way, the most important rules and expectations.
3. For older students, give families a list of due dates for the major assignments, along with tips about how to encourage quality work by pacing the effort—avoiding last-minute panic.
4. Communicate in appropriate ways—use the family's first language when possible. Tailor messages to the reading level of the home.

Make families partners in recognizing good citizenship.

Examples

1. Send positive notes home when students, especially students who have had trouble with classroom management, work well in the classroom.
2. Give ideas for ways any family, even those with few economic resources, can celebrate

accomplishment—a favorite food; the chance to choose a video to rent; a comment to a special person such as an aunt, grandparent, or minister; the chance to read to a younger sibling.

Identify talents in the community to help build a learning environment in your class.

Examples

1. Have students write letters to carpet and furniture stores asking for donations of remnants to carpet a reading corner.
2. Find family members who can build shelves or room dividers, paint, sew, laminate manipulative materials, write stories, repot plants, or network computers.
3. Contact businesses for donations of computers, printers, or other equipment.

Seek cooperation from families when behavior problems arise

Examples

1. Talk to families over the phone or in their home. Have good records about the problem behavior.
2. Listen to family members and solve problems with them.

influencing motivation to learn. We discussed motivation to learn in Chapter 4. Here we explore ways to create learning contexts—classrooms and schools—that support motivation to learn.

Carol Ames (1990, 1992) has identified six areas where teachers make decisions that can influence student motivation to learn: the nature of the task that students are asked to do, the autonomy students are allowed in working, how students are recognized for their accomplishments, grouping practices, evaluation procedures, and the scheduling of time in the classroom. Epstein (1989) coined the acronym **TARGET** to organize these areas of possible teacher influence. Table 6.5 on page 222 summarizes the model. In the following pages we will examine each of these areas more closely.

Authentic Tasks

Recently there has been a great deal written about the use of authentic tasks in teaching. An authentic task is one that has some connection to the real-life problems and situations that students will face outside the classroom, now and in the future. If the tasks are authentic, students are more likely to see the genuine utility value of the work and are also more likely to find the tasks meaningful and interesting.

Problem-based learning is one example of the use of authentic tasks in teaching. According to William Stepien and Shelagh Gallagher (1993), "problem-based learning turns instruction topsy-turvy. Students meet an ill-structured problem before they receive any instruction. In place of covering the curriculum, learners probe deeply into issues searching for connections, grappling with complexity, and using knowledge to fashion solutions" (p. 26). An example problem presented to one group of seventh and eighth graders in Illinois is, "What should be done about a nuclear waste dump site in our area?" The students soon learn that this real problem is not a simple one. Scientists disagree about the dangers. Environmental activists demand that the materials be removed, even if this bankrupts the company involved—one that employs many local residents. Some members of the state assembly want the material taken out of state, even though no place in the country is licensed to receive the toxic materials. The company believes the safest solution is to leave the materials buried. The students must research the situation, interview parties involved, and develop recommendations to be presented to state experts and community groups. "In problem-based learning students assume the roles of scientists, historians, doctors, or others who have a real stake in the proposed problem. Motivation soars because students realize it's their problem" (Stepien & Gallagher, 1993, p. 26).

Supporting Autonomy

The second area in the TARGET model involves how much choice and autonomy students are allowed. We saw in Chapter 4 that the need for self-determination—the need to be an origin not a pawn—is an important factor in motivation. There is no intrinsic motivation without self-determination. Classroom environments that support student autonomy are associated with greater student interest, sense of competence, self-esteem, creativity, conceptual learning, and preference for challenge. These relationships appear to hold from first grade through graduate school (Ryan & Grolnick, 1986; Williams, Wiener, Markakis,

TABLE 6.5 The TARGET Model for Supporting Student Motivation to Learn

Teachers make decisions in many areas that can influence motivation to learn. The TARGET acronym highlights task, autonomy, recognition, grouping, evaluation, and time.

TARGET Area	Focus	Objectives	Examples of Possible Strategies
Task	How learning tasks are structured—what the student is asked to do	Enhance intrinsic attractiveness of learning tasks Make learning meaningful	Encourage instruction that relates to students' backgrounds and experience Avoid payment (monetary and other) for attendance, grades, or achievement Foster goal setting and self-regulation
Autonomy/ Responsibility	Student participation in learning/school decisions	Provide optimal freedom for students to make choices and take responsibility	Give alternatives in making assignments Ask for student comments on school life— and take them seriously Encourage students to take initiatives and evaluate their own learning Establish leadership opportunities for *all* students
Recognition	The nature and use of recognition and reward in the school setting	Provide opportunities for *all* students to be recognized for learning Recognize *progress* in goal attainment Recognize challenge seeking and innovation	Foster "personal best" awards Reduce emphasis on "honor rolls" Recognize and publicize a wide range of school-related activities of students
Grouping	The organization of school learning and experiences	Build an environment of acceptance and appreciation of all students Broaden the range of social interaction, particularly of at-risk students Enhance social skills development	Provide opportunities for cooperative learning, problem solving, and decision making Encourage multiple group membership to increase range of peer interaction Eliminate ability-grouped classes

Evaluation	The nature and use of evaluation and assessment procedures	Grading and reporting processes Practices associated with use of standardized tests Definition of goals and standards	Reduce emphasis on social comparisons of achievement Give students opportunities to improve their performance (e.g., study skills, classes) Establish grading/reporting practices that portray student progress in learning Encourage student participation in the evaluation process
Time	The scheduling of the school day	Allow the learning task and student needs to dictate scheduling Provide opportunities for extended and significant student involvement in learning tasks	Allow students to *progress at their own rate* whenever possible Encourage flexibility in the scheduling of learning experiences Give teachers greater control over time usage through, for example, block scheduling Give all students the chance to revise and improve their work

Source: From "Reinventing Schools for Early Adolescents: Emphasizing Task Goals," by M. L. Maehr and E. M. Anderman, 1993, *The Elementary School Journal, 93,* pp. 604–605. Copyright © 1993 by The University of Chicago Press. Adapted with permission.

Reeve, & Deci, 1993). In autonomy-oriented classrooms, students are more likely to believe that the work is important, even if it is not "fun." Thus they tend to internalize educational goals and take them as their own. For example, the problem-based project described above might encourage autonomy and self-determination as the students made choices about how best to solve the problem of toxic-waste dumps.

What else can teachers do to support choice without creating chaos?

Supporting Choices.   Like totally unguided discovery or aimless discussions, unstructured or unguided choices can be counterproductive for learning (Garner, 1998). For example, Dyson (1997) found that children became anxious and upset when directed by teachers to draw or write about anything they want in anyway they want. Dyson says that students see this unbounded choice as a "scary void." We know that adults in our classes also find it disconcerting if we ask them to design a final project that will determine their grade. The alternative is **bounded choice**—giving students a range of options that set valuable tasks for them but also allow them to follow personal interests. The balance must be just right: "too much autonomy is bewildering and too little is boring" (Guthrie et al., 1998, p. 185).

Students also can exercise autonomy about how they receive feedback from the teacher or from classmates. Figure 6.4 describes a strategy called "Check it Out" in which

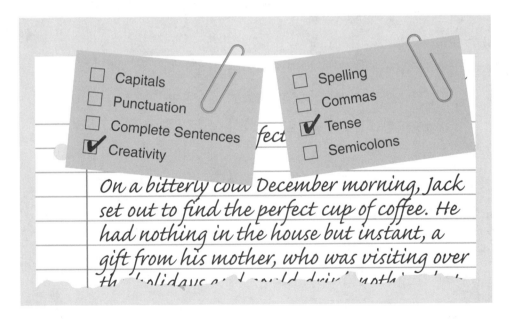

FIGURE 6.4   Student Autonomy: Check It Out   Using this technique to support autonomy, the teacher decides on a set of skills that will be developed over a unit, but the student decides which skill(s) will be evaluated on any given assignement. Over the course of the unit, all the skills have to be "checked out." This student has indicated that she wants the teacher to "check out" her creativity and verb tense.

Source: From *150 Ways to Increase Intrinsic Motivation in the Classroom* (pp. 33–34) by J. P. Raffini, 1996, Boston: Allyn & Bacon. Copyright © 1996 Allyn & Bacon, Inc. Adapted with permission.

students specify the skills that they want to have evaluated in a particular assignment. Over the course of a unit, all the skills have to be "checked out," but students choose when each one is evaluated.

Beyond these ideas, what can teachers do to support student self-determination in everyday interactions? A study by Reeve, Bolt, and Cai (1999) found that, compared to controlling teachers, autonomy-supporting teachers listened more, held instructional materials less, resisted giving solutions to problems, gave fewer directives, and asked more questions about what students wanted to do.

Autonomy-Supporting Class Climates.   What can teachers do to support student autonomy? An obvious first step is to limit their controlling messages to their students and make sure the information they provide highlights students' growing competence. Unfortunately, when teachers are under pressure and "controlled" by the school administration, they are likely to treat students the same way. In one study, teachers told to "make sure" their students performed well in solving problems were more critical and gave students more hints and less time for independent work than teachers who were told that their job was to "help" the students learn how to solve the problems themselves. And the students of the pressured teachers actually performed worse (Boggiano, Flink, Shields, Seelbach, & Barrett, 1993).

Recognizing Accomplishment

The third TARGET area is recognition. How should students' accomplishments be acknowledged and rewarded? Authentic praise focuses on progress, growing competence, and independence. But nothing in teaching is simple. We have also seen that giving students rewards for activities that they already enjoy can undermine intrinsic motivation. Students should be recognized for improving on their own personal best, for tackling difficult tasks, for persistence, and for creativity—not just for performing better than others. The next section explains one way to use personal progress as a basis for recognition in classrooms.

Grouping

The fourth element of the TARGET is grouping. You may remember a teacher who made you want to work hard—someone who made a subject come alive. Or you may remember how many hours you spent practicing as a member of a team, orchestra, choir, or theater troupe. If you do, then you know the motivational power of relationships with other people. David and Roger Johnson (1985) describe the power this way:

> Motivation to learn is inherently interpersonal. It is through interaction with other people that students learn to value learning for its own sake, enjoy the process of learning, and take pride in their acquisition of knowledge and development of skill. Of the interpersonal relationships available in the classroom, peers may be the most influential on motivation to learn. (p. 250)

The ways that students relate to peers are influenced by the group structures created by the teacher. Several studies have shown that when the task involves complex learning and problem-solving skills, cooperation leads to higher achievement than competition, especially for low-ability students (Johnson & Johnson, 1985; Slavin, 1995). In addition, well-designed cooperative learning seems to result in improved ability to see the world from another person's point of view, better relations among different ethnic groups in schools and classrooms, increased self-esteem, greater willingness to help and encourage fellow students, and greater acceptance of handicapped and low-achieving students (Slavin, 1995; Stipek, 1996; Webb & Palincsar, 1996). Students learn to set attainable goals and to negotiate. They become more altruistic. The interaction with peers that students enjoy so much becomes a part of the learning process. The result? The need for belonging described by Maslow is more likely to be met and motivation is increased.

There are many approaches to peer learning or group learning, as you saw in Chapter 3. Some approaches, such as STAD, are designed specifically to enhance motivation.

STAD.   Robert Slavin and his associates have developed a system for overcoming the disadvantages of the cooperative goal structure (lack of focus, off-task behaviors, unfair division of work) while maintaining its advantages. The system is called **Student Teams–Achievement Divisions,** or **STAD** (Slavin, 1995). Each team has about five members with a mix of abilities, ethnic backgrounds, and sexes. The teacher calculates an individual learning expectation (ILE) score, or base score, for each team member. This score represents the student's average level of performance. Details about how to determine the base scores are given in Table 6.6.

TABLE 6.6   Using Individual Learning Expectations

The idea behind individual learning expectations, or ILEs, is that students ought to be judged in relation to their own abilities and not compared to others. The focus is on improvement, not on comparisons among students.

To calculate an ILE score, the teacher simply averages the student's grades or test scores from previous work. These scores are usually on a 100-point scale. Letter grades can be converted to points based on the school's system—for example, A = 90 points, B = 80 points, and so on. The student's average score is her or his initial base score. The ILE score becomes the standard for judging each student's work.

If the teacher is using the STAD system of cooperative learning, then students earn points for their group based on the following system:

Test Score	Points Earned for Group
A perfect score	3
10 or more points above ILE score	3
5 to 9 points above ILE score	2
4 points below to 4 points above ILE score	1
5 or more points below ILE score	0

Source: From Anita Woolfolk, *Educational Psychology, 8/e.* Copyright © 2001. Reprinted by permission of Allyn & Bacon.

Students work in their teams to study and prepare for twice-weekly quizzes, but they take the quizzes individually, just as in a regular class. Based on test performance, each team member can earn from one to three points for the group. Table 6.6 shows how points are awarded by comparing each student's current test score to his or her base (ILE) score (Slavin, 1995). As you can see from the table, every student has an equal chance to contribute the maximum number of points to the team total. Thus, every student, not just the most able or motivated, has reason to work hard. This system avoids the problem of students' unequal contributions to a group project. Every week the group earning the greatest number of points is declared the winner. Team accomplishments should be recognized in a class newsletter or a bulletin board display. Every few weeks the teams can be changed so that students have a chance to work with many different class members. Every two weeks or so the teacher must recompute each student's ILE score by averaging the old base score with grades on the recent tests. With this system, improvement pays off for all students. Those with less ability can still earn the maximum for their team by scoring 10 or more points above their own base score. Those with greater ability are still challenged because they must score well above their own average or make a perfect score to contribute the maximum to the group total.

Evaluation

The next TARGET area is evaluation. The greater the emphasis on competitive evaluation and grading, the more students will focus on performance goals rather than learning goals and the more they will be ego-involved as opposed to task-involved. Students must take tests, answer questions in class, and complete assignments, and they must perform within certain time limits. Doyle (1983) suggests that students look upon most classroom work as "an exchange of performance for grades" (p. 181). Grading here refers to more than marks on a report card. It includes both the formal and informal evaluations made by teachers.

Of course, not all students are caught up in an exchange of performance for grades. Low-achieving students who have little hope of either "making the grade" or mastering the task may simply want to finish. One study of first graders found that low-achieving students made up answers, filled in the page with patterns, or copied from other students, just to get through their seatwork. As one student said when she finished a word/definition matching exercise, "I don't know what it means, but I did it" (Anderson, Brubaker, Alleman-Brooks, & Duffy, 1985, p. 132). On closer examination, the researchers found that the work was much too hard for these students, so they connected words at random.

How can teachers prevent students from simply focusing on the grade or doing the work "just to get finished"? The most obvious answer is to de-emphasize grades and emphasize learning in the class. Students need to understand the value of the work. Instead of saying, "You will need to know this for the test," tell students how the information will be useful in solving problems they want to solve. Suggest that the lesson will answer some interesting questions. Communicate that understanding is more important than finishing.

Unfortunately, many teachers do not follow this advice. Brophy (1988) reports that when he and several colleagues spent about 100 hours observing how six teachers introduced their lessons, they found that most introductions were routine, apologetic, or unenthusiastic.

The introductions described procedures, made threats, emphasized finishing, or promised tests on the material. A few examples are:

"You don't expect me to give you baby work to do every day, do you?"

"My talkers are going to get a third page to do during lunch."

"If you are done by 10 o'clock, you can go outside." (Brophy, 1988, p. 204)

During 100 hours, only nine introductions included statements that described the value of the work or suggested that it would be interesting, and these often were brief. One example is, "Answer the comprehension questions with complete sentences. All these stories are very interesting. You'll enjoy them" (Brophy, 1988, p. 203).

While many teachers are similar to the six Brophy studied, there are exceptions. Hermine Marshall (1987) described a few elementary school teachers who seemed to establish a learning orientation in their classrooms. They stressed understanding instead of performing, being graded, or finishing work.

Time

The final TARGET element is time. How does the use of time affect student motivation? Most experienced teachers know that there is too much work and not enough time in the school day. Students seldom have the opportunity to stick with an activity. Even if they become engrossed in a project, students must stop and turn their attention to another subject when the bell rings or the schedule demands. Furthermore, students must progress as a group. If particular individuals can move faster or if they need more time, they may still have to follow the pace of the whole group. So scheduling often interferes with motivation by making students move faster or slower than would be appropriate or by interrupting their involvement. It is difficult to develop persistence and a sense of efficacy in the face of difficulties when students are not allowed to stick with an activity. Block scheduling is one attempt to make more connected (and motivated) time for learning.

Summary

Classrooms are by nature multidimensional, full of simultaneous activities, fast-paced and immediate, unpredictable, public, and affected by the history of students' and teachers' actions. A manager must juggle all these elements every day.

Productive classroom activity requires students' cooperation. Maintaining cooperation is different for each different age group. Young students are learning how to "go to school" and need to learn the general procedures of school. Older students need to learn the specifics required for working in different subjects. Working with adolescents requires teachers to understand the power of the adolescent peer group.

The goals of effective classroom management are to make ample time for learning; improve the quality of time use by keeping students actively engaged; make sure participation structures are clear, straightforward, and consistently signaled; and encourage student self-management.

The most effective teachers set rules and establish procedures for handling predictable problems. Procedures should cover administrative tasks, student movement, housekeeping, routines for running lessons, interactions between students and teachers, and interactions among students. Consequences should be established for following and breaking the rules and procedures so that the teacher and the students know what will happen.

There are two basic kinds of spatial organization, territorial (the traditional classroom arrangement) and functional (dividing space into interest or work areas). Flexibility is often the key. Access to materials, convenience, privacy when needed, ease of supervision, and a willingness to reevaluate plans are important considerations in the teacher's choice of physical arrangements.

For effective classroom management, it is essential to spend the first days of class teaching basic rules and procedures. Students should be occupied with organized, enjoyable activities and learn to function cooperatively in the group. Quick, firm, clear, and consistent responses to infractions of the rules characterize effective teachers. To create a positive environment and prevent problems, teachers must take individual differences into account, maintain student motivation, and reinforce positive behavior. Successful problem preventers are skilled in four areas described by Kounin: "withitness," overlapping, group focusing, and movement management. When penalties have to be imposed, teachers should impose them calmly and privately.

There are several special procedures that may be helpful in maintaining positive management, including group consequences, token economies, and contingency contracts. A teacher must use these programs with caution, emphasizing learning and not just "good" behavior.

Communication between teacher and student is essential when problems arise. All interactions between people, even silence or neglect, communicate some meaning. Techniques such as empathetic listening, determining whether the teacher or the student "owns" the problem, assertive discipline, avoidance of passive and hostile responses, and active problem solving with students help teachers open the lines of positive communication. Students need guidance in resolving conflicts. Different strategies are useful, depending on whether the goal, the relationship, or both are important to those experiencing conflict. It can help to reverse roles and see the situation through the eyes of the other. In dealing with serious problems, prevention and peer mediation might be useful. No matter what the situation, the cooperation of families can help to create a positive learning environment in your classroom and school.

TARGET is an acronym for the six areas where teachers make decisions that can influence student motivation to learn: the nature of the *task* that students are asked to do, the *autonomy* students are allowed in working, how students are *recognized* for their accomplishments, *grouping* practices, *evaluation* procedures, and the scheduling of *time* in the classroom. The tasks that teachers set affect motivation. When students encounter tasks that are related to their interests, stimulate their curiosity, or are connected to real-life situations, the students are more likely to be motivated to learn.

Like totally unguided discovery or aimless discussions, unstructured or unguided choices can be counterproductive for learning. The alternative is bounded choice—giving students a range of options that set valuable tasks for them but also allow them to follow personal interests. The balance must be just right so that students are not bewildered by too much choice or bored by too little. The more competitive the grading, the more students set performance goals and focus on "looking competent"; that is, the more they are ego-involved. When the focus is on performing rather than learning, students often see the goal of classroom tasks as simply finishing, especially if the work is difficult.

In order to foster motivation to learn, teachers should be flexible in their use of time in the classroom. Students who are forced to move faster or slower than they should or who are interrupted as they become involved in a project are not likely to develop persistence for learning.

KEY TERMS

academic learning time   (191)
action zone   (198)
assertive discipline   (216)
bounded choice   (224)
classroom management   (190)
empathetic (active)
    listening   (215
good behavior game   (211)

group consequences   (211)
group focus   (207)
"I" message   (216)
movement management   (208)
overlapping   (207)
peer mediation   (219)
procedures   (193)
rules   (193)

Student Teams–Achievement
    Divisions (STAD)   (226)
TARGET   (221)
time on task   (190)
token reinforcement
    system   (212)
withitness   (207)

SOME IDEAS FOR YOUR PORTFOLIO

1. Reread the case at the beginning of this chapter and assume you are the principal in the school. Develop a plan for first working with this teacher and then consider a general policy on classroom management for Samuel Procter Elementary School. Be sure to consider the following issues:

   ■ How would you approach the situation? Who should be involved?

   ■ Which problem behaviors should the teacher tackle first?

   ■ Would giving rewards or administering punishments be useful in this situation? Why or why not?

   ■ What specific suggestions would you give to this teacher?

   ■ What action would you take?

   ■ Should there be a school-wide policy?

   ■ Who should be involved in the development the school policy, if needed?

2. Write a first-of-the-year newsletter for families describing your school's rules, procedures, and discipline actions. Be sure to include:

   ■ General school rules

   ■ Policy on teacher rules in the classroom

   ■ Homework requirements

   ■ Policies on tardiness and absences

   ■ Behavior on school property

   ■ Policy on suspension and expulsion

   ■ Other key aspects of a good citizen policy

   Your challenge is to be clear, firm, precise, and yet humanistic and open—not an easy task.

3. Draw a floor plan of a classroom in your school—one that could be improved in its physical arrangement.

   ■ Interview the teacher about her or his learning objectives and management issues.

■ With the teacher, redesign the classroom space (furniture, workstations, storage, etc.) so that the design supports both learning and management goals.

Your final project should include both before and after maps of the classroom, with an explicit rationale for each change.

INSTRUCTIONAL LEADER'S TOOLBOX

Readings

Emmer, E. T., Evertson, C. M., & Worsham, M. E. (2000). *Classroom management for secondary teachers* (5th ed.). Boston: Allyn & Bacon.

Evertson, C. M., Emmer, E. T., & Worsham, M. E. (2000*). Classroom management for elementary teachers* (5th ed.). Boston: Allyn & Bacon.

Herbert, E. A. (1998). Design matters: How school environment affects children. *Educational Leadership, 56*(1), 69–71.

Johnson, D., & Johnson, R. (1999). The three Cs of school and classroom management. In H. J. Freiberg (Ed.), *Beyond behaviorism: Changing the classroom management paradigm* (pp. 119–144). Boston: Allyn & Bacon.

Weinstein, C. S. (1999). Reflections on best practices and promising programs: Beyond assertive classroom discipline. In H. J. Freiberg (Ed.), *Beyond behaviorism: Changing the classroom management paradigm* (pp. 147–163). Boston: Allyn & Bacon.

Videos

Classroom management: A proactive approach to creating an effective learning environment, 1 hour. This video shows how teachers can minimize student behavior problems—and maximize learning—with a three-stage management plan. Planning: how to arrange a classroom, direct students' attention, and present rules. Implementing: how to provide time for practicing classroom rules and procedures including homework assignments. Maintaining: how teachers can evaluate their own management systems. #614-160ER. Association for Supervision and Curriculum Development, 125 N. West St., Alexandria, VA 22314-2798.

Discipline and the law, 29 minutes. Addresses legal questions about teachers' rights to discipline children. Available from Insight Media, 2162, Broadway, New York, NY 10024

Websites

Classroom Management	http://scholar.coe.uwf.edu/pacee/steps/tutorial/classmanagement/main.htm#section4
The Nova Scotia Teachers' Union has organized a set of resources on anti-violence, including reference to resources on anger management, conflict resolution, and peer mediation.	http://www.nstu.ns.ca/violence/intro.html
Excellent tutorial on classroom management.	http://scholar.coe.uwf.edu/pacee/steps/tutorial/classmanagement/main.thm#section4

Phi Delta Kappan (see the September issue for the Annual PDK/Gallup Poll of the Public's Attitudes Toward the Public Schools)	http://www.pdkintl.org/
Comprehensive guide to behavior management for bus drivers.	http://www.state.ia.us/educate/programs/transportation/special_needs/behavmod.html

Organizations

Consistency Management and Cooperative Discipline H. Jerome Freiberg University of Houston College of Education Houston, TX 77204-5872 713-743-8663	http://www.coc.uh.edu/~Freiberg/cm/cover.html
Learning Together Roger T. Johnson and David W. Johnson The Cooperative Learning Center 60 Peik Hall University of Minnesota Minneapolis, MN 55455 612-624-7031	www.clcrc.com

Preview: Key Points

Leadership Challenge

Evaluation, Measurement, and Assessment
Norm-Referenced Tests
Criterion-Referenced Tests

What Do Test Scores Mean?
Basic Concepts
Types of Scores
Interpreting Test Scores

Types of Standardized Tests
Achievement Tests: What Has the Student
Learned?
Diagnostic Tests: What Are the Student's
Strengths and Weaknesses?
Aptitude Tests: How Well Will the Student Do
in the Future?
Theory into Action Guidelines: Family
Partnerships for Using Test Results

Issues in Standardized Testing
The Uses of Testing in American Society
Advantages in Taking Tests—Fair and Unfair
Theory into Action Guidelines: Becoming an
Expert Test-Taker

**New Directions in Standardized Testing and
Classroom Assessment**
Authentic Assessment
Authentic Classroom Tests
Performance in Context: Portfolios and Exhibitions
Theory into Action Guidelines: Student Portfolios
Evaluating Portfolios and Performances
Theory into Action Guidelines: Developing
a Rubric
Getting the Most from Traditional Tests

Effects of Grades and Grading on Students
Effects of Failure
Effects of Feedback
Grades and Motivation
Theory into Action Guidelines: Grading

Summary

Key Terms

Some Ideas for Your Portfolio

Instructional Leader's Toolbox
Readings
Websites
Organizations

PREVIEW: KEY POINTS

- All teaching involves assessing and evaluating learning, that is, collecting information and making judgments about student performance.
- There are two general types of tests: norm-referenced and criterion-referenced.
- Criterion-referenced tests are scored using a fixed standard or minimum passing score whereas norm-referenced tests are scored by comparing individuals with others who have taken the same test; that is, group *norms* are used to evaluate performance.
- When norms are used, test scores are standardized as a percentile score, grade-equivalent score, or as a standard score such as a *z*-score, *T*-score, or stanine scores.

- All good tests are reliable and valid.
- There are three broad categories of standardized tests: achievement, diagnostic, and aptitude, each with a different purpose.
- Achievement tests measure how much a student has learned in specific content areas; diagnostic tests identify specific learning problems; and aptitude tests measure abilities developed over many years and are used to predict how well a student will do in the future at learning unfamiliar material.
- Students can be prepared for standardized testing in several ways that improve their performance.
- Criticisms have led to new approaches that avoid some of the problems of standardized testing.
- Authentic assessment, portfolios, and exhibitions are alternative ways to assess and evaluate student performance in a realistic context.
- Grades and high standards have both positive and negative consequences for students.

Leadership Challenge

You are the principal of Washington Middle School. April, one of your beginning seventh-grade teachers, has come to you with a question. First, she shares a computer printout with you showing the results of the fall testing, including scores on a group test of intelligence for all the seventh-grade students in her class. The printouts have been distributed to all teachers in the school by the guidance department. Then she shows you notes from two parents. They want to meet with April to see their child's scores, and especially, as one parent put it, "To find out how smart Jason really is." You look at the printouts and at the parental requests, as April asks you for advice on what to do?

- What do the intelligence test scores tell you about these students?
- How do you suggest that April respond to the request from the parents?
- Do you need to talk to the guidance department about the purpose of the data?
- Do you need a school policy on testing results?

All teaching involves assessing and evaluating learning. At the heart of assessment is judgment, making decisions based on values. In the process of evaluation, we compare outcomes and information to some set of criteria and then make judgments. Principals and teachers must make all kinds of judgments. "Should we use a different text this year? Will Sarah do better if she repeats the first grade? Should Terry get a B– or a C+ on the project? How well do the students know how to solve quadratic equations?"

Evaluation, Measurement, and Assessment

Measurement is evaluation put in quantitative terms—the numeric description of an event or characteristic. Measurement tells how much, how often, or how well by providing scores, ranks, or ratings. Instead of saying, "Sarah doesn't seem to understand addition," a teacher might say, "Sarah answered only 2 of the 15 problems correctly in her addition homework." Measurement also allows a school to compare one student's performance on one particular task with a standard or with the performances of the other students. When we think of measurement, we often think of paper-and-pencil tests. Not all the evaluative decisions made by teachers and principals involve measurement. Some decisions are based on information that is difficult to express numerically: student preferences, information from parents, previous experiences, even intuition. But measurement does play a large role in many school and classroom decisions, and properly done, it can provide unbiased data for evaluations.

Increasingly, evaluation and measurement specialists are using the term **assessment** to describe the process of gathering information about students' learning. Assessment is broader than testing and measurement. Assessment is "any of a variety of procedures used to obtain information about student performance" (Linn & Gronlund, 2000, p. 32). Assessments can be formal, such as unit tests, or informal, such as observing who emerges as a leader in a group of teachers or students. Assessments can be designed by classroom teachers or by local, state, or national agencies such as school districts or the Educational Testing Service. And today, assessments can go well beyond paper-and-pencil exercise to observations of performances and the development of portfolios and artifacts. In this chapter, we examine formal assessments designed by groups and agencies outside the school as well as teacher-made assessment devices. Many of these assessments techniques usually involve testing and the reporting of scores, so we will start by examining two types of tests.

The answers given on any type of test have no meaning by themselves; we must make some kind of comparison to interpret test results. There are two basic types of comparison: In the first, a test score is compared to the scores obtained by other people who have taken the same test—a norm-referenced comparison. The second type is criterion-referenced. Here, the comparison is to a fixed standard or minimum passing score.

Norm-Referenced Tests

In **norm-referenced testing,** the people who have taken the test provide the *norms* for determining the meaning of a given individual's score. You can think of a norm as being the typical level of performance for a particular group. By comparing the individual's raw score (the actual number correct) to the norm, we can determine if the score is above, below, or around the average for that group. There are at least three types of **norm groups** (comparison groups) in education—the class or school itself, the school district, and national samples.

Norm-referenced tests cover a wide range of general objectives rather than assessing a limited number of specific objectives. Norm-referenced tests are especially useful in measuring the overall achievement of students who have come to understand complex material by different routes. Norm-referenced tests are also appropriate when only the top few candidates can be admitted to a program.

However, norm-referenced measurement has its limitations. The results of a norm-referenced test do not tell you whether students are ready to move on to more advanced material. For instance, knowing that a student is in the top 3% of the class on a test of algebraic concepts will not tell you if he or she is ready to move on to geometry; everyone in the class may have a limited understanding of the algebraic concepts.

Nor are norm-referenced tests particularly appropriate for measuring affective and psychomotor objectives. To measure individuals' psychomotor learning, you need a clear description of standards. (Even the best gymnast in school performs certain exercises better than others and needs specific guidance about how to improve.) In the affective area, attitudes and values are personal; comparisons among individuals are not really appropriate. For example, how could we measure an "average" level of political values or opinions? Finally, norm-referenced tests tend to encourage competition and comparison of scores. Some students compete to be the best. Others, realizing that being the best is impossible, may compete to be the worst. Either goal has its casualties.

Criterion-Referenced Tests

When test scores are compared, not to those of others, but to a given criterion or standard of performance, this is **criterion-referenced testing.** To decide who should be allowed to drive a car, it is important to determine just what standard of performance is appropriate for selecting safe drivers. It does not matter how your test results compare to the results of others. If your performance on the test was in the top 10% but you consistently ran through red lights, you would not be a good candidate for receiving a license, even though your score was high.

Criterion-referenced tests measure the mastery of very specific objectives. The results of a criterion-referenced test should tell parents, teachers, and principals exactly what the students can and cannot do, at least under certain conditions. For example, a criterion-referenced test would be useful in measuring the ability to add three-digit numbers. A test could be designed with 20 different problems, and the standard for mastery could be set at 17 correct out of 20. (The standard is often somewhat arbitrary and may be based on such things as the teacher's experience.) If two students receive scores of 7 and 11, it does not matter that one student did better than the other because neither met the standard of 17. Both need more help with addition.

Criterion-referenced tests, however, are not appropriate for every situation. Many subjects cannot be broken down into a set of specific objectives. Moreover, although standards are important in criterion-referenced testing, they can often be arbitrary, as you have already seen. When deciding whether a student has mastered the addition of three-digit numbers comes down to the difference between 16 or 17 correct answers, it seems difficult to justify one particular standard over another. Finally, at times it is valuable to know how the students in your school compare to other students at their grade level both locally and nationally. Table 7.1 offers a comparison of norm-referenced and criterion-referenced tests. You can see that each type of test is well suited for certain situations, but each also has its limitations.

What Do Test Scores Mean?

On the average, more than 1 million standardized tests are given per school day in classes throughout this country (Lyman, 1986). Most of these are norm-referenced standardized tests. **Standardized tests** are called standardized because "the same directions are used for administering them in all classrooms and standard procedures are used for scoring and in-

TABLE 7.1   Deciding on the Type of Test to Use

Norm-referenced tests may work best when you are
- Measuring general ability in certain areas, such as English, algebra, general science, or American history.
- Assessing the range of abilities in a large group.
- Selecting top candidates when only a few openings are available.

Criterion-referenced tests may work best when you are
- Measuring mastery of basic skills.
- Determining if students have prerequisites to start a new unit.
- Assessing affective and psychomotor objectives.
- Grouping students for instruction.

Source: From Anita Woolfolk, *Educational Psychology, 8/e.* Copyright © 2001. Reprinted by permission of Allyn & Bacon.

terpreting them" (Carey, 1994, p. 443). Standard methods of developing items, administering the test, scoring it, and reporting the scores are all implied by the term *standardized test*.

Basic Concepts

In standardized testing the test items and instructions have been tried out to make sure they work and then rewritten and retested as necessary. The final version of the test is administered to a **norming sample,** a large sample of subjects as similar as possible to the students who will be taking the test in school systems throughout the country. This norming sample serves as a comparison group for all students who take the test. Hence, standardized tests typically come with norms. Let's look at some of the measurements on which normative comparisons and interpretations are based.

Measurements of Central Tendency and Standard Deviation.   You have probably had a great deal of experience with means. A **mean** is simply the arithmetical average of a group of scores. The mean offers one way of measuring **central tendency,** the score that is typical or representative of the whole distribution of scores.

Two other measures of central tendency are the median and the mode. The **median** is the middle score in the distribution, the point at which half the scores are larger and half are smaller. The **mode** is the score that occurs most often. If two scores tie for the most frequent, we have a bimodal distribution.

The measure of central tendency gives a score that is representative of the group of scores, but it does not tell you anything about how the scores are distributed. Two groups of scores may both have a mean of 50 but be alike in no other way. One group might contain the scores 50, 45, 55, 55, 45, 50, 50; the other group might contain the scores 100, 0, 50, 90, 10, 50, 50. In both cases the mean, median, and mode are all 50, but the distributions are quite different.

The **standard deviation** is a measure of how widely the scores vary from the mean. The larger the standard deviation, the more spread out the scores in the distribution. The smaller the standard deviation, the more the scores are clustered around the mean. For example, in the distribution 50, 45, 55, 55, 45, 50, 50, the standard deviation is much smaller than in the distribution 100, 0, 50, 90, 10, 50, 50. Another way of saying this is that distributions with very small standard deviations have less variability in their scores.

Knowing the mean and the standard deviation of a group of scores gives you a better picture of the meaning of an individual score. For example, suppose you received a score of 78 on a test. You would be very pleased with the score if the mean of the test were 70 and the standard deviation were 4. In this case, your score would be 2 standard deviations above the mean, a score well above average.

Consider the difference if the mean of the test had remained at 70 but the standard deviation had been 20. In the second case, your score of 78 would be less than 1 standard deviation from the mean. You would be much closer to the middle of the group, with a score above average, but not that high. Knowing the standard deviation tells you much more than simply knowing the **range** of scores. No matter how the majority scored on the tests, one or two students may do very well or very poorly and thus make the range very large.

The Normal Distribution.   Standard deviations are very useful in understanding test results. They are especially helpful if the results of the tests form a normal distribution. You have encountered the **normal distribution** before. It is the bell-shaped curve, the most famous frequency distribution because it describes many naturally occurring physical and social phenomena. Many scores fall in the middle, giving the curve its bell shape. You find fewer and fewer scores as you look out toward the end points, or *tails,* of the distribution. The normal distribution has been thoroughly analyzed by statisticians. The mean of a normal distribution is also its midpoint. Half the scores are above the mean, and half are below it. In a normal distribution, the mean, median, and mode are all the same point.

Another convenient property of the normal distribution is that the percentage of scores falling within each area of the curve is known, as you can see in Figure 7.1. A person scoring within 1 standard deviation of the mean obviously has company. Many scores pile up here. In fact, 68% of all scores are located in the area from 1 standard deviation below to 1 standard deviation above the mean. About 16% of the scores are higher than 1 standard deviation above the mean. Of this higher group, only 2% are better than 2 standard deviations above the mean. Similarly, only about 16% of the scores are less than 1 standard deviation below the mean, and of that group only about 2% are worse than 2 standard deviations below. At 2 standard deviations from the mean in either direction, the scorer has little company.

The SAT college entrance exam and the GRE test are examples of exams with normal distributions. The mean is 500 and the standard deviation is 100. If you know people who made scores in the 700s, you know they did very well. Only about 2% of the people who take the test do that well, because only 2% of the scores are better than 2 standard deviations above the mean in a normal distribution.

Types of Scores

Now you have enough background for a discussion of the different kinds of scores you may encounter in reports of results from standardized tests.

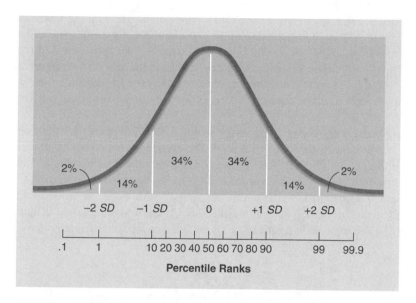

FIGURE 7.1   The Normal Distribution   The normal distribution or bell-shaped curve has certain predictable characteristics. For example, 68% of the scores are clustered between 1 standard deviation below and 1 standard deviation above the mean.

Source: From Anita Woolfolk, *Educational Psychology, 8/e.* Copyright © 2001. Reprinted by permission of Allyn & Bacon.

Percentile Rank Scores.   The concept of ranking is the basis for one very useful kind of score reported on standardized tests, a **percentile rank** score. In percentile ranking, each student's raw score is compared with the raw scores of the students in the norming sample. The percentile rank shows the percentage of students in the norming sample that scored at or below a particular raw score. If a student's score were the same as or better than three quarters of the students in the norming sample, the student would score in the 75th percentile or have a percentile rank of 75. You can see that this does *not* mean that the student had a raw score of 75 correct answers or even that the student answered 75% of the questions correctly. Rather, the 75 refers to the percentage of people in the norming sample whose scores on the test were equal to or below this student's score. A percentile rank of 50 means that a student has scored as well as or better than 50% of the norming sample and has achieved an average score.

A Caution Interpreting Percentile Scores.   Differences in percentile ranks do not mean the same thing in terms of raw score points in the middle of the scale as they do at the fringes. The graph in Figure 7.2 shows Joan's and Alice's percentile scores on the fictitious Test of Excellence in Language and Arithmetic. Both students are about average in arithmetic skills. One equaled or surpassed 50% of the norming sample; the other, 60%. However, because their scores are in the middle of the distribution, this difference in percentile ranks means a raw score difference of only a few points. Their raw scores were actually 75 and 77. In the language test, the difference in percentile ranks seems to be about the same as the difference in arithmetic, because one ranked at the 90th percentile and the other at the 99th. But the difference in their raw scores on the language test is much greater. It takes a greater difference in raw score points to make a difference in percentile rank at the extreme ends of the scale. On the language test the difference in raw scores is about 10 points.

Grade-Equivalent Scores.   Generally, **grade-equivalent scores** are obtained from separate norming samples for each grade level. The average of the scores of all the 10th graders in the norming sample defines the 10th-grade equivalent score. Suppose the raw-score average of the 10th-grade norming sample is 38. Any student who attains a raw score of 38 on that test will be assigned a grade-equivalent score of 10th grade. Grade-equivalent scores are generally listed in numbers such as 8.3, 4.5, 7.6, 11.5, and so on. The whole number gives the grade. The decimals stand for tenths of a year, but they are usually interpreted as months.

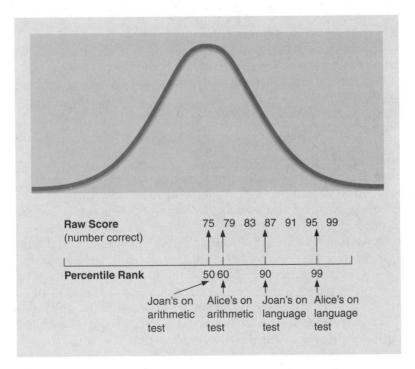

FIGURE 7.2   Percentile Ranking on a Normal Distribution Curve
Percentile scores have different meanings at different places on the scale. For example, a difference of a few raw score points near the mean might translate into a 10-point percentile difference, while it would take 6 or 7 points to make a 10 point percentile difference farther out of the scale.

Source: From Anita Woolfolk, *Educational Psychology, 8/e.* Copyright © 2001. Reprinted by permission of Allyn & Bacon.

Suppose a student with the grade-equivalent score of 10 is a 7th grader. Should this student be promoted immediately? Probably not. Different forms of tests are used at different grade levels, so the 7th grader may not have had to answer items that would be given to 10th graders. The high score may represent superior mastery of material at the 7th-grade level rather than a capacity for doing advanced work. Even though an average 10th grader could do as well as our 7th grader on this particular test, the 10th grader would certainly know much more than this test covered. Also, grade-equivalent score units do not mean the same thing at every grade level. For example, a 2nd grader reading at the 1st-grade level would have more trouble in school than an 11th grader who reads at the 10th-grade level.

Because grade-equivalent scores are misleading and are so often misinterpreted, especially by parents, most educators and psychologists strongly believe they should not be used at all. There are several other forms of reporting available that are more appropriate.

Standard Scores. As you may remember, one problem with percentile ranks is the difficulty in making comparisons among ranks. A discrepancy of a certain number of raw-score points has a different meaning at different places on the scale. With standard scores, on the other hand, a difference of 10 points is the same everywhere on the scale.

Standard scores are based on the standard deviation. A very common standard score is called the **z score.** A z score tells how many standard deviations above or below the average a raw score is. In the example described earlier, in which you were fortunate enough to get a 78 on a test where the mean was 70 and the standard deviation was 4, your z score would be +2, or 2 standard deviations above the mean. If a person were to score 64 on this test, the score would be 1.5 standard deviation units *below* the mean, and the z score would be –1.5. A z score of 0 would be no standard deviations above the mean—in other words, right on the mean.

To calculate the z score for a given raw score, subtract the mean from the raw score and divide the difference by the standard deviation. The formula is:

$$z = \frac{X - \bar{X}}{SD}$$

Because it is often inconvenient to use negative numbers, other standard scores have been devised to eliminate this difficulty. The ***T* score** has a mean of 50 and uses a standard deviation of 10. Thus a *T* score of 50 indicates average performance. If you multiply the z score by 10 (which eliminates the decimal) and add 50 (which gets rid of the negative number), you get the equivalent *T* score as the answer. The person whose z score was –1.5 would have a *T* score of 35.

First multiply the z score by 10: $-1.5 \times 10 = -15$

Then add 50: $-15 + 50 = 35$

The scoring of the SAT or GRE test is based on a similar procedure. The mean of the scores is set at 500, and a standard deviation of 100 is used.

Before we leave this section on types of scores, we should mention one other widely used method. **Stanine scores** (the name comes from "standard nine") are standard scores.

There are only nine possible scores on the stanine scale, the whole numbers 1 through 9. The mean is 5, and the standard deviation is 2. Each unit from 2 to 8 is equal to half a standard deviation.

Stanine scores provide a method of considering a student's rank, because each of the nine scores includes a specific range of percentile scores in the normal distribution. For example, a stanine score of 1 is assigned to the bottom 4% of scores in a distribution. A stanine of 2 is assigned to the next 7%. Of course, some raw scores in this 7% range are better than others, but they all get a stanine score of 2.

Each stanine score represents a wide range of raw scores. This has the advantage of encouraging teachers and parents to view a student's score in more general terms instead of making fine distinctions based on a few points. Figure 7.3 compares the four types of standard scores we have considered, showing how each would fall on a normal distribution curve.

Interpreting Test Scores

One of the most common problems with the use of tests is misinterpretation of scores. This often happens because of the belief that numbers are precise measurements of a student's

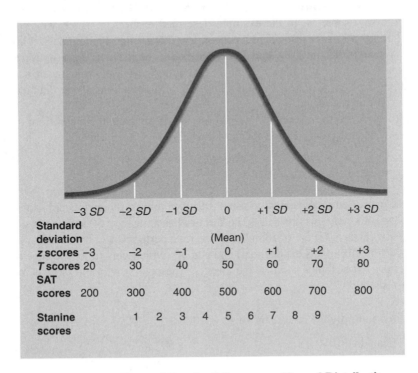

FIGURE 7.3   Four Types of Standard Scores on a Normal Distribution Curve   Using this figure, you can translate one type of standard into another.

Source: From Anita Woolfolk, *Educational Psychology, 8/e.* Copyright © 2001. Reprinted by permission of Allyn & Bacon.

ability. No test provides a perfect picture of a person's abilities; a test is only one small sample of behavior. Two factors are important in developing good tests and interpreting results: reliability and validity.

Reliability. If you took a standardized test on Monday, then took the same test again a week later, and you received about the same score each time, you would have reason to believe the test was reliable. If 100 people took the test one day, then repeated it the following week, and the ranking of the individual scores was about the same for both tests, you would be even more certain the test was reliable. (Of course, this assumes that no one looks up answers or studies before the second test.) A reliable test gives a consistent and stable "reading" of a person's ability from one occasion to the next, assuming the person's ability remains the same. A reliable thermometer works in a similar manner, giving you a reading of 100°C each time you measure the temperature of boiling water. Measuring a test's **reliability** in this way, by giving the test on two different occasions, indicates *stability* or *test–retest reliability*. If a group of people takes two equivalent versions of a test and the scores on both tests are comparable, this indicates *alternate-form reliability*.

Reliability can also refer to the internal consistency or the precision of a test. This type of reliability, known as *split-half reliability,* is calculated by comparing performance on half of the test questions with performance on the other half. If, for example, someone did quite well on all the odd-numbered items and not at all well on the even-numbered items, we could assume that the items were not very consistent or precise in measuring what they were intended to measure. The most effective way to improve reliability is to add more items to a test. Generally speaking, longer tests are more reliable than shorter ones.

True Score. All tests are imperfect estimators of the qualities or skills they are trying to measure. There are errors in every testing situation. Sometimes the errors are in the students' favor and they score higher than their ability might warrant, because, for example, they reviewed a key section just before the test. Sometimes the errors go against students—they are sick, sleepy, or focused on the wrong material in their review. But if students could be tested over and over again without becoming tired and without memorizing the answers, their good luck and bad luck would even out, and the average of the test scores would be close to a true score. In other words, we can think of a student's true score as the mean of all the scores the student would receive if the test were repeated many times.

In reality, however, students take a test only once. That means that the score each student receives is made up of the hypothetical true score plus some amount of error. How can error be reduced so that the actual score can be brought closer to a true score? As you might guess, this returns us to the question of reliability. The more reliable the test, the less error in the score actually obtained. On standardized tests, test developers take this into consideration and make estimations of how much the students' scores would probably vary if they were tested repeatedly. This estimation is called the **standard error of measurement.** It represents the *standard deviation* of the distribution of scores from our hypothetical repeated testings. Thus a reliable test can also be defined as a test with a small standard error of measurement. In their interpretation of tests, principals and teachers must also take into consideration the margin for error.

Confidence Interval. Never base an opinion of a student's ability or achievement on the exact score the student obtains. Many test companies now report scores using a **confidence interval,** or "standard error band," that encloses the student's actual score. This makes use of the standard error of measurement and allows a teacher to consider the range of scores that might include a student's true score.

Let us assume, for example, that two students in your school take a standardized achievement test in Spanish. The standard error of measurement for this test is 5. One student receives a score of 79 and the other, a score of 85. At first glance, these scores seem quite different. But when you consider the standard error bands around the scores, not just the scores alone, you see that the bands overlap. The first student's true score might be anywhere between 74 and 84 (that is, the actual score of 79 plus and minus the standard error of 5). The second student's true score might be anywhere between 80 and 90. It is crucial to keep in mind the idea of standard error bands when selecting students for special programs. No child should be rejected simply because the obtained score missed the cutoff by one or two points. The student's true score might well be above the cutoff point.

Validity. If a test is sufficiently reliable, the next question is whether it is valid, that is, does the test measure what it is suppose to measure? To have **validity,** the decisions and inferences based on the test must be supported by evidence. This means that validity is judged in relation to a particular use or purpose, that is, in relation to the actual decision being made and the evidence for that decision (Linn & Gronlund, 2000).

A test must be reliable in order to be valid. For example, if, over a few months, an intelligence test yields different results each time it is given to the same child, then by definition it is not reliable. Certainly it couldn't be a valid measure of intelligence because intelligence is assumed to be fairly stable, at least over a short period of time. However, reliability will not guarantee validity. If that intelligence test gave the same score every time for a particular child but didn't predict school achievement, speed of learning, or other characteristics associated with intelligence, then performance on the test would not be a true indicator of intelligence. The test would be reliable—but invalid.

Types of Standardized Tests

Several kinds of standardized tests are used in schools today. One look in the cumulative folders that include testing records for individual students over several years shows the many ways students are tested in this country. There are three broad categories of standardized tests: achievement, diagnostic, and aptitude (including interest). As an instructional leader, you will probably encounter achievement and aptitude tests most frequently.

Achievement Tests: What Has the Student Learned?

The most common standardized tests given to students are **achievement tests,** which are meant to measure how much a student has learned in specific content areas such as reading comprehension, language usage, computation, science, social studies, mathematics, and logical reasoning. There are achievement tests for both individuals (for example, the Wide-

Range Achievement Test; Peabody Individual Achievement Test; KeyMath Diagnostic Tests) and groups (the California, Metropolitan, SRA, or Stanford Achievement Tests; the TerraNova [Comprehensive Test of Basic Skills]; and the Iowa Tests). These tests vary in their reliability and validity. Group tests can be used for screening—to identify children who might need further testing or as a basis for grouping students according to achievement levels. Individual achievement tests are given to determine a child's academic level more precisely, or to help diagnose learning problems.

Using Information from a Norm-Referenced Achievement Test. What specific information can principals and teachers expect from achievement test results? Test publishers usually provide individual profiles for each student, showing scores on each subtest. Figure 7.4 on page 246 is an example of an individual profile for a fifth grader, whom they have called "Ken Allen," on the *California Achievement Test,* Fifth Edition.

Note that the Individual Test Record reports the scores in many different ways. At the top of the form, after the identifying information about Ken's grade and birthday, is a list of the various tests—Reading Vocabulary, Reading Comprehension, Total Reading (Vocabulary and Comprehension combined), Language Mechanics, and so on. Beside each test are several different ways of reporting Ken's score:

NS: Ken's National Stanine Score (his stanine score based on a national norming sample comparison group).

NCE: Ken's Normal Curve Equivalent Score (a score used mostly for research purposes to evaluate certain compensatory education programs).

SS: Ken's Scale Score. This describes growth in achievement that typically occurs as a student progresses through the grades—the higher the grade the higher the expected scale score.

NCR: Ken's actual number correct—his raw score.

NP: Ken's National Percentile Score, telling us where he stands in relation to students at his grade level across the country.

RANGE: The range of national percentile scores in which Ken's *true score* is likely to fall. You may remember from our discussion of true scores that this range, or confidence interval, is determined by adding and subtracting the standard error of the test from Ken's actual score. There is a 95% chance that Ken's true score is within this range.

Beside the scores is a graph showing Ken's national percentile and stanine scores, with the standard error bands indicated around the scores. Bands that show any overlap are probably not significantly different. When there is no overlap between bands for two test scores, we can be reasonably certain that Ken's achievement levels in these two areas are actually different.

Interpreting Achievement Test Scores. Let's look at Ken's scores more carefully. In language mechanics he has a stanine score of 5, which is equal to a scale score of 717. This

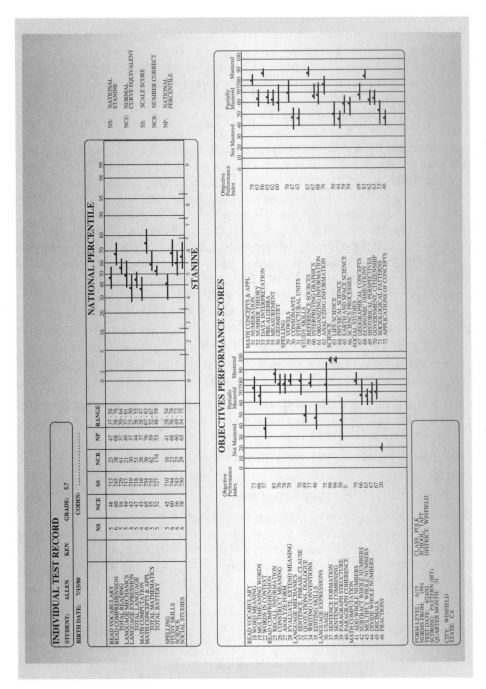

FIGURE 7.4   An Individual Test Record   Test publishers provide several kinds of report forms for individual students and for entire classes. The form above gives both norm-referenced and criterion-referenced information about a fifth-grade boy.

Source: Reproduced from the *California Achievement Test*, 5th edition, by permission of the publisher, CTB/McGraw-Hill. Copyright © 1992 CTB by Macmillan/McGraw-Hill School Publishing Company. All rights reserved.

is at the 49th percentile nationally. His true national percentile score is probably in the range from 37 to 61 (that is, plus and minus 1 standard error of measurement from the actual score of 49, so the standard error of the language mechanics test must be 12). By looking at the graph, we can see that Ken's language mechanics and language expression score bands overlap. His achievement in these areas is probably similar, even though there seems to be a difference when you look at the NP scores alone. Comparing language expression with reading comprehension, on the other hand, we see that the bands do not overlap. Ken is stronger in reading comprehension than in language expression.

The profile in Figure 7.4 tells us a number of things. First, we can see that all Ken's scores are within the average range compared to the national norming sample. Ken's highest score is in math concepts and applications. However, this score band overlaps several other score bands, so we cannot say for sure that this is his strongest area. Ken's strength in math concepts and applications raises his total math battery score to a percentile of 59, but his math computation score is significantly lower than his math concepts score (the bands do not overlap). With some work on math computations, Ken would probably improve his overall math performance. We can also see that Ken is weak in spelling. Improving his spelling might improve his vocabulary score and vice versa.

The scores we have just described are all norm-referenced. However, results from standardized tests like the one Ken took can also be interpreted in a criterion-referenced way. The bottom portion of Ken's Individual Test Record in Figure 7.4 breaks down the larger categories of the top section (reading vocabulary, reading comprehension, etc.) and shows criterion-referenced scores that indicate mastered, partially mastered, or not mastered for specific skills. These include reading vocabulary skills such as the use of word meanings and words in context and study skills such as using reference sources and interpreting graphics. The *Objective Performance Index* score is an estimate of the percentage of all possible items that Ken could be expected to answer correctly in each performance area. In other words, based on his performance on these test items, what percentage of all possible questions in this area (at his level) should he get right? Teachers can use these results to get an idea of Ken's strengths and weaknesses with these specific skills and thus determine his progress toward objectives in a given subject. Be aware, though, that some of these specific skill areas may be measured with only a few items each, and the fewer the items, the more potential problems there can be with reliability.

Diagnostic Tests: What Are the Student's Strengths and Weaknesses?

If teachers want to identify specific learning problems, they may need to refer to results from the various diagnostic tests that have been developed. Most **diagnostic tests** are given to students individually by a highly trained professional. The goal is usually to identify the specific problems a student is having. Achievement tests, both standardized and teacher-made, identify weaknesses in academic content areas like mathematics, computation, or reading. Individually administered diagnostic tests identify weaknesses in learning processes. There are diagnostic tests to assess the ability to hear differences among sounds, remember spoken words or sentences, recall a sequence of symbols, separate figures from their background, express relationships, coordinate eye and hand movements, describe objects orally, blend sounds to form words, recognize details in a picture, coordinate move-ments, and many other abilities needed to learn, remember, and communicate learning. Elementary school students are more likely than secondary school students to take diag-nostic tests. High school students are more likely to take aptitude tests.

Aptitude Tests: How Well Will the Student Do in the Future?

Both achievement and aptitude tests measure developed abilities. Achievement tests may measure abilities developed over a short period of time, such as during a week-long unit on map reading, or over a longer period of time, such as a semester. **Aptitude tests** are meant to measure abilities developed over many years and to predict how well a student will do in the future at learning unfamiliar material. The greatest difference between the two types of tests is that they are used for different purposes. Achievement tests measure final perfor-mance (and perhaps give grades), and aptitude tests predict how well people will do in par-ticular programs like college or professional school (Anastasi, 1988).

Scholastic Aptitude.   The purpose of a scholastic aptitude test, such as the SAT (Scholas-tic Assessment Test) or ACT (American College Testing Program) is to predict how well a student is likely to do in college. Colleges use such scores to help decide on acceptances and rejections. The SAT may have seemed like an achievement test to you, measuring what you had learned in high school. Although the test is designed to avoid drawing too heavily on spe-cific high school curricula, the questions are very similar to achievement test questions.

Standardized aptitude tests—such as the SAT, the School and College Ability Tests (SCAT), and the Preliminary Scholastic Assessment Test (PSAT) for younger students—seem to be reliable in predicting future achievement. Because standardized tests are less open to teacher bias, they may be even fairer predictors of future achievement than high school grades. Indeed, some psychologists believe grade inflation in high schools has made tests like the SAT even more important. Others believe that the SATs are not good predictors of success in college, particularly for women or members of cultural or ethnic minority groups. The controversy continues with some critics demanding that colleges drop tests as criteria for admission and supporters calling for improved testing.

IQ and Scholastic Aptitude.   In Chapter 2 we discussed one of the most influential apti-tude tests of all, the IQ test. The IQ test as we know it could well be called a test of scholastic aptitude. The IQ score is really a standard score with a mean of 100 and a standard deviation of 15 or 16, depending on the test. Thus about 68% of the general population would score be-tween +1 and –1 standard deviations from the mean, or between about 85 and 115.

A difference of a few points between two students' IQ scores should not be viewed as important. Scores between 90 and 109 are within the average range. In fact, scores be-tween 80 and 119 are considered within the range of low average to high average. To see the problems that may arise, consider the following conversation:

> PARENT: We came to speak with you today because we are shocked at our son's IQ score. We can't believe he has only a 99 IQ when his sister scored much higher on the same test. We know they are about the same. In fact, Sam has better marks than Lauren did in the fifth grade.

PRINCIPAL: What was Lauren's score?

PARENT: Well, she did much better. She scored a 103!

Clearly, brother and sister have both scored within the average range. While the standard error of measurement on the WISC-III (Weschler Intelligence Scale for Children, third edition) varies slightly from one age to the next, the average standard error for the total score is 3.2. So the bands around Sam's and Lauren's IQ scores—about 96 to 102 and 100 to 106—are overlapping. Either child could have scored 100, 101, or 102.

Discussing Test Results with Families.   At times, you and your teachers will be expected to explain or describe test results to your students' families. The following Theory into Action guidelines (page 250) will give principals and teachers direction.

Issues in Standardized Testing

Today, many important decisions about students, teachers, and schools are based in part on the results of standardized tests. Test scores may affect admission to first grade, promotion from one grade to the next, high school graduation, access to special programs, placement in special education classes, teacher certification and tenure, and school funding. Because the decisions affected by test scores are so critical, many educators call this process **high-stakes testing.** By 1991, 47 states had some form of statewide mandated testing for public school students (Ziomek & Maxey, 1993). Some groups are working to increase the role of testing—by establishing national examination requirements, for example—while others are working to cut back the use of standardized tests in schools (Linn & Gronlund, 2000; Madaus & Kellaghan, 1993).

In the next few pages we will consider two basic questions: What role should testing play in making decisions about people? Do some students have an unfair advantage in taking tests?

The Uses of Testing in American Society

Tests are not simply procedures used in research. Every day, there are many decisions made about individuals that are based on the results of tests. Should Liz be issued a driver's license? How many and which students from the eighth grade would benefit from an accelerated program in science? Who belongs in a remedial class? Who will be admitted to college or professional school? Who will get a teaching or principal's certificate? In answering these questions, it is important to distinguish between the quality of the test itself and how the test is used. Even the best instruments can be, and have been, misused. In earlier years, for example, using otherwise valid and reliable individual intelligence tests, many students were inappropriately identified as having mental retardation. The problem was not with the tests, but with the fact that the test score was the only information used to classify students. Much more information must be considered.

Behind all the statistics and terminology are issues related to values and ethics. Who will be tested? What are the consequences of choosing one test over another for a particular purpose with a given group? What is the effect of the testing on the students? How will the test scores of minority group students be interpreted? What do we really mean by intelligence,

THEORY INTO ACTION GUIDELINES

Family Partnerships for Using Test Results

Be ready to explain, in nontechnical terms, what each type of score on the test report means.

Examples

1. If the test is norm-referenced, know if the comparison group was national or local. Explain that the child's score shows how he or she performed *in relation to* the other students in the comparison group.
2. If the test is criterion-referenced, explain that the child's scores show how well he or she performs in specific areas.

If the test is norm-referenced, focus on the percentile scores. They are the easiest to understand.

Examples

1. Percentile scores tell what percent of students in the comparison group made the same score or lower—higher percentiles are better and 99 is as high as you can get. 50 is average.
2. Remind parents that percentile scores do not tell the "percent correct" so scores that would be bad on a classroom test (say 65% to 75% or so) are above average—even good—as percentile scores.

Avoid using grade-equivalent scores.

Examples

1. If parents want to focus on the "grade level" of their child, tell them that high grade-

equivalent scores reflect a thorough understanding of the current grade level and NOT the capacity to do higher grade-level work.
2. Tell parents that the same grade-equivalent score has different meanings in different subjects—reading versus mathematics, for example.

Be aware of the error in testing.

Examples

1. Encourage parents to think of the score not as a single point but as a range or band that includes the score.
2. Ignore small differences between scores.
3. Note that sometimes individual skills on criterion-referenced tests are measured with just a few (2 or 3) items. Compare test scores to actual class work in the same areas.

Use conference time to plan a learning goal for the child, one that families can support.

Examples

1. Have example questions, similar to those on the test, to show parents what their child can do easily and what kinds of questions he or she found difficult.
2. Be prepared to suggest an important skill to target.

---

competence, and scholastic aptitude? Do our views agree with those implied by the tests we use to measure these constructs? How will test results be integrated with other information about the individual to make judgments? Answering these questions requires choices based on values as well as accurate information about what tests can and cannot tell us.

Readiness Testing.   In 1988, Georgia became the first state to require that children pass a test before moving from kindergarten to first grade (Fiske, 1988; Linn, 1986). The test quickly became a symbol of the misuse of tests. Public outcry led to modifications of the policy and spurred many educators to reform the **readiness testing** process. In fact, the uproar over this group-administered, machine-scored, norm-referenced test for kindergarten children "probably did more to advance readiness assessment reform in this country than all other causes combined" (Engel, 1991, p. 41).

Critics of readiness tests (Meisels, 1989; Shepard & Smith, 1989) believe:

1. Group-administered paper-and-pencil tests are inappropriate for preschool children and thus should not be the basis for decisions about school entry. Readiness tests do not have sufficient predicative validity to be used alone to make screening or placement decisions (Linn & Gronlund, 2000).
2. The use of readiness tests narrows the preschool curriculum, making it more academic and less developmentally appropriate.
3. The evidence shows that delaying entry into first grade or retaining students in kindergarten is not effective. Students who are retained do no better than similar students who are not held back.

In spite of these criticisms, today almost every state uses testing at the state or district level to determine if a child is "ready" for first grade or to place a child in a special "developmental kindergarten" (Kirst, 1991). Several states, as well as a few test publishers, are trying to develop appropriate ways to determine readiness. Engel (1991) suggests that such procedures could be ongoing assessments about many different aspects of readiness—cognitive, social/emotional, physical, and so on. These assessments would be indirect, that is, they would be completed by adults rather than requiring the children to answer questions directly on paper. The observations would provide useful information for teaching; they would be conducted in a comfortable natural setting, often as part of the preschool program itself.

Minimum and World-Class Standards. In many studies comparing the United States with other industrialized nations, American students have placed low in academic achievement. For example, in the Third International Mathematics and Science Study (TIMSS), the students in the United States did not do well compared to students from other developed countries. Even though these conclusions have been questioned (Berliner & Biddle, 1997; Bracey, 1997), policymakers are concerned. One suggestion to improve student performance is minimum competency testing. A **minimum competency test** is a standardized test meant to determine whether an individual meets the minimum standard for moving to the next level or graduating. Almost every state in the United States has some kind of high school competency testing program. Some people have even suggested that a national examination would be helpful (O'Neil, 1991).

The push for a national test slowed, replaced by the idea of *national standards* (Lewis, 1995; Ziomek & Maxey, 1993). There are several kinds of standards.

- *Content standards* define what should be learned in particular subject areas such as mathematics or history.
- *Performance standards* specify the level or quality of student learning expected.

■ *Opportunity-to-learn standards* describe the conditions and resources necessary to give every student an equal chance to meet the content and performance standards.

■ *World-class standards* refer to the level of content and performance expected in other countries.

National educational groups such as the National Council of Teachers of Mathematics (NCTM, 1991) have led the way in establishing standards (Hambleton, 1996; Lewis, 1995; Resnick & Nolan, 1995). At this point, standards are voluntary, but the debate continues about the value of adopting national standards. The public is divided on the standards question. In the 1999 Phi Delta Kappa/Gallup Poll of the Public's Attitude Toward the Public Schools (Rose & Gallup, 1999), 57% of the respondents said current standards were "about right" while 33% said standards were too low (but 43% of people in urban centers felt standards were too low).

Advantages in Taking Tests—Fair and Unfair

In this section we will consider three basic issues: Are standardized tests biased against minority students? Can students gain an advantage on admissions tests through coaching? Can they be taught test-taking skills?

Bias and Fairness in Testing.   Are tests such as the individual measures of intelligence or college admissions tests fair assessments for minority group students? This is a complex question. Research on test bias shows that most standardized tests predict school achievement equally well across all groups of students. Items that might appear on the surface to be biased against minorities are not necessarily more difficult for minorities to answer correctly (Sattler, 1992). Even though standardized aptitude and achievement tests are not biased against minorities in predicting school performance, many people believe that the tests still can be unfair. Tests may not have *procedural fairness,* that is, some groups may not have an equal opportunity to show what they know on the test: Here are a few examples:

1. The language of the test and the tester is often different from the languages of the students.
2. Answers that support middle class values are often rewarded with more points.
3. On individually administered intelligence tests, being very verbal and talking a lot is rewarded.

The above three factors favor students who feel comfortable in that particular situation. Also, tests may not be fair, because different groups have had different *opportunities to learn* the material tested. The questions asked tend to center on experiences and facts more familiar to the dominant culture than to minority group students.

Stereotype Threat.   When stereotyped individuals are in situations where the stereotype applies, they bear an extra emotional and cognitive burden. The burden is the possibility of confirming the stereotype, in the eyes or others or in their own eyes. Thus when girls are asked to solve complicated mathematics problems, for example, they are at risk of confirming widely held stereotypes that girls are inferior to boys in mathematics. It is not necessary that the individual even believe the stereotype. All that matters is that the person is *aware* of the stereotype and *cares about performing* well enough to disprove its unflattering implications (Aronson, Lustina, Good, Keough, Steele, & Brown, 1999). What are the results of stereotype threat? Recent research provides answers that should interest all educators.

In the short run, the fear that you might confirm a negative stereotype can induce test anxiety and undermine performance. In a series of experiments, Joshua Aronson, Claude Steele and their colleagues have demonstrated that when African American or Latino college students are put situations that induce stereotype threat, their performance suffers (Aronson & Salinas, 1998; Aronson, Steele, Salinas, & Lustina, 1999; Steele & Aronson, 1995). For example, African American and white undergraduate subjects in an experiment at Stanford University were told that the test they were about to take would precisely measure their verbal ability. A similar group of subjects was told that the purpose of the test was to understand the psychology of verbal problem solving and not to asses individual ability. When the test was presented as diagnostic of verbal ability, the African American students solved about half as many problems as the white students. In the nonthreat situation, the two groups solved about the same number of problems. Other studies found that anxiety and distraction were the main impediments. The African American students were more likely to be thinking about the stereotypes as they tried to work.

As you saw in Chapter 4, students often develop self-defeating strategies to protect their self-esteem about academics. They withdraw, claim to not care, exert little effort— they *disidentify* or psychologically disengage from success in the domain and claim "math is for nerds" or "school is for losers." There is evidence that African Americans are more likely than whites to reject identifying with academics (Major & Schmader, 1998; Ogbu, 1997). Once students define academics as "uncool" it is unlikely they will exert the effort needed for real learning.

Combating Stereotype Threat. Stereotypes are pervasive and difficult to change. Rather than wait for changes, it may be better to acknowledge that these images exist, at least in the eyes of many, and give students ways of coping with the stereotypes. Aronson and Fried (in press) demonstrated the powerful effects of changing beliefs about intelligence. In their study, African American and white undergraduates were asked to write letters to "at-risk" middle school students to encourage them to persist in school. Some of the undergraduates were given evidence that intelligence is *improvable* and encouraged to communicate this information to their pen pals. Others were given information about multiple intelligences, but not told that these multiple abilities can be improved. The middle school students were not real, but the process of writing persuasive letters about improving intelligence proved powerful. The African American college students, and the white students to a lesser extent, who were encouraged to believe that intelligence can be improved had higher grade point averages and reported greater enjoyment of and engagement in school when contacted at the end of the next school quarter. Thus, believing that intelligence can be improved might inoculate students against the effects of stereotype threat when they take high-pressure tests.

Concern about cultural bias in testing has led some psychologists to try to develop **culture-fair** or **culture-neutral tests.** These efforts have not been very successful. On many of the so-called culture-fair tests, the performance of students from lower socioeconomic backgrounds and minority groups has been the same as or worse than their performance on the standard Wechsler and Binet Intelligence scales (Sattler, 1992).

Coaching and Test-Taking Skills.

Courses to prepare students for college entrance exams are becoming more popular. As you probably know from experience, both commercial and public school coaching programs are available. In general, research has indicated that short high school training programs yield average gains of 10 points in SAT verbal scores and 15 points in SAT math scores, whereas longer commercial programs show gains of anywhere from 50 to as much as 200 points for some people (Owen, 1985). Kulik, Kulik, and Bangert (1984) analyzed the results of 40 different studies on aptitude and achievement test training and found that there were more substantial gains when students practiced on a parallel form of a test for brief periods. The design of the coaching program, therefore, may be the critical factor.

Two other types of training can make a difference in test scores. One is simple familiarity with the procedures of standardized tests. Students who have extensive experience with standardized tests do better than those who do not. Some of this advantage may be the result of greater self-confidence, less tendency to panic, familiarity with different kinds of questions (for example, analogies such as "house: garage: _____: car"), and practice with the various answer sheets (Anastasi, 1988). Even brief orientations about how to take tests can help students who lack familiarity and confidence.

A second type of training that appears to be very promising is instruction in general cognitive skills such as solving problems, carefully analyzing questions, considering all alternatives, noticing details and deciding which are relevant, avoiding impulsive answers, and checking work. These are the kinds of metacognitive and study skills we have discussed before. Training in these skills is likely to generalize to many tasks (Anastasi, 1988).

Preparing Students for Testing.

We recently read about a sixth-grade class that used their statewide testing as an opportunity for problem-based learning (Ewy with student authors, 1997). This class read a newspaper article about the upcoming test and the less than stellar performance of the sixth graders in previous years. They took on the following problem: How could they improve their own test scores on the IGAP (Illinois Goal Assessment Program). The students talked about why the problem was important and how to solve it, generating the problem analysis chart in Figure 7.5.

Then they divided into groups to do different tasks: schedule practice times, look for resources, make up questions and interview experts, and set up a tutoring program. The result? The students met or exceeded the state reading, writing and mathematics goals. When they moved to junior high and had to take the math placement test, these students researched the test. What are cutoff points, possible the range of scores, evaluation criteria? Perhaps you can take on a similar problem in your school. Instructional leaders can use the following guidelines to give teachers suggestions for helping students take tests.

FIGURE 7.5   Taking on "The Test": Problem-Based Learning

Students in a sixth-grade classroom produced this chart as they designed a program for improving their own test performance.

Problem Analysis Chart

Problem: How can we improve our performance on the IGAP test in such a way that we (1) keep improving each year, (2) set a good example for our school, (3) make preparing for IGAP more fun?

Our Ideas	Facts We Know	Our Questions	Our Action Plan
■ Pay attention in class ■ Hold fundraiser to get books and computer program ■ Look at actual IGAP book format ■ Practice: Use computer games ■ Get someone who knows how to coach IGAP: teacher, parent, friend, brother/sister ■ Tackle one subject at a time ■ Find out who wants to know	■ Test on reading, writing, and math ■ You get better when you practice ■ You might read questions wrong ■ Fill in circles ■ Writing is scored by time, spelling, sentence structure	■ When is IGAP? ■ How long is the test? ■ How long should we practice? ■ What should we practice (math, reading, writing)? ■ How many problems? ■ How is the test scored (math, reading, writing)? ■ How much time is given for math, reading, writing? ■ How did I do on the last IGAP test?	■ Ask principal, teacher, tutor ■ Ask person who made test ■ Work with teacher to set up schedule ■ Look for resources for practice ■ Ask parents and principal to help

Source: Adapted from "Kids Take on 'the Test,'" by C. Ewy & student authors, *Educational Leadership, 54*(4), p. 77. Copyright © 1997 by the Association for Supervision and Curriculum Development. Reprinted with permission. All rights reserved.

New Directions in Standardized Testing and Classroom Assessment

As the public and government demanded greater accountability in education in the 1980s and 1990s and as traditional standardized tests became the basis for high-stakes decisions, pressure to do well led many teachers and schools to "teach to the test." This tended to focus student learning on basic skills and facts. Even more troubling, say critics, the traditional tests assess skills that have no equivalent in the real world. Students are asked to solve problems or answer questions they will never encounter again; they are expected to do so alone, without relying on any tools or resources and while working under extreme time limits. Real life just isn't like this. Important problems take time to solve and often require using resources, consulting other people, and integrating basic skills with creativity and high-level thinking (Kirst, 1991; Wolf, Bixby, Glenn, & Gardner, 1991).

THEORY INTO ACTION GUIDELINES

Becoming an Expert Test-Taker

Use the night before the test effectively.

Examples

1. Study the night before the exam, ending with a final look at a summary of the key points, concepts, and relationships.
2. Get a good night's sleep. If you know you generally have trouble sleeping the night before an exam, try getting extra sleep on several previous nights.

Set the situation so you can concentrate on the test.

Examples

1. Give yourself plenty of time to eat and get to the exam room.
2. Don't sit near a friend. It may make concentration difficult. If your friend leaves early, you may be tempted to do so too.

Make sure you know what the test is asking.

Examples

1. Read the directions carefully. If you are unsure, ask the instructor or proctor for clarification.
2. Read each question carefully to spot tricky words, such as *not, except, all of the following but one.*
3. On an essay test, read every question first, so you know the size of the job ahead of you and can make informed decisions about how much time to spend on each question.
4. On a multiple-choice test, read every alternative, even if an early one seems right.

Use time effectively.

Examples

1. Begin working right away and move as rapidly as possible while your energy is high.
2. Do the easy questions first.
3. Don't get stuck on one question. If you are stumped, mark the question so you can return to it easily later, and go on to questions you can answer more quickly.
4. If you are unsure about a question, answer it but mark it so you can go back if there is time.
5. On a multiple-choice test, if you know you will not have time to finish, fill in all the remaining questions with the same letter if there is no penalty for guessing.
6. If you are running out of time on an essay test, do not leave any questions blank. Briefly outline a few key points to show the instructor you "knew" the answer but needed more time.

Know when to guess on multiple-choice or true-false tests.

Examples

1. Always guess when only right answers are scored.
2. Always guess when you can eliminate some of the alternatives.
3. Don't guess if there is a penalty for guessing, unless you can confidently eliminate at least one alternative.
4. Are correct answers always longer? shorter? in the middle? more likely to be one letter? more often true than false?
5. Does the grammar give the right answer away or eliminate any alternatives?

Check your work.

Examples

1. Even if you can't stand to look at the test another minute, reread each question to make sure you answered the way you intended.
2. If you are using a machine-scored answer sheet, check occasionally to be sure the number of the question you are answering corresponds to the number of the answer on the sheet.

On essay tests, answer as directly as possible.

Examples

1. Avoid flowery introductions. Answer the question in the first sentence and then elaborate.
2. Don't save your best ideas till last. Give them early in the answer.
3. Unless the instructor requires complete sentences, consider listing points, arguments, and so on by number in your answer. It will help you organize your thoughts and concentrate on the important aspects of the answer.

Learn from the testing experience.

Examples

1. Pay attention when the teacher reviews the answers. You can learn from your mistakes, and the same question may reappear in a later test.
2. Notice if you are having trouble with a particular kind of item; adjust your study approach next time to handle this type of item better.

Authentic Assessment

In response to these criticisms, the **authentic assessment** movement was born. The goal was to create standardized tests that assess complex, important, real-life outcomes. The approach is also called *direct assessment, performance assessment,* or *alternative assessment.* These terms refer to procedures that are alternatives to traditional multiple-choice standardized tests because they directly assess student performance on "real-life" tasks (Hambleton, 1996; Worthen, 1993). Some states are developing procedures to conduct authentic assessments. For example, in 1990, Kentucky passed the Educational Reform Act. The act identifies six objectives for students, including such goals as applying knowledge from mathematics, the "hard" sciences, arts, humanities, and the social sciences to problems the students will encounter throughout their lives as they become self-sufficient individuals and responsible members of families, work groups, and communities.

It is important to be sensible about authentic assessment. Just being different from traditional standardized tests will not guarantee that the alternative tests are better. Many questions have to be answered. Assume, for example, that a new assessment requires students to complete a hands-on science project. If the student does well on one science project, does this mean the student "knows" science and would do well on other projects? One study found that students' performance on three different science tasks was quite variable: a student who did well on the absorbency experiment, for example, might have trouble with the electricity task. Thus, it was hard to generalize about a student's knowledge of science based on just the three tasks. Many more tasks would be needed to get a good sense of science knowledge. Because authentic assessment is a new area, it will take time to develop high-quality alternative assessments for use by whole school districts or states. Until more is known, it may be best to focus on authentic assessment at the classroom level.

One of the main criticisms of standardized tests—that they control the curriculum, emphasizing recall of facts instead of thinking and problem solving—is a major criticism of classroom tests as well. Few educators would dispute these criticisms. What can be done? Should innovations in classroom assessment make traditional testing obsolete? One solution that has been proposed to solve the testing dilemma is to apply the concept of authentic assessment to classroom testing.

Authentic Classroom Tests

Authentic tests ask students to apply skills and abilities as they would in real life. For example, they might use fractions to enlarge or reduce recipes. If our instructional goals for students include the abilities to write, speak, listen, create, think critically, solve problems, or apply knowledge, then our tests should ask students to write, speak, listen, create, think, solve, and apply. How can this happen?

Many educators suggest we look to the arts and sports for analogies to solve this problem. If we think of the "test" as being the recital, exhibition, game, mock court trial, or other performance, then teaching to the test is just fine. All coaches, artists, and musicians gladly "teach" to these "tests" because performing well on these tests is the whole point of instruction. Authentic assessment asks students to perform. The performances may be thinking performances, physical performances, creative performances, or other forms.

It may seem odd to talk of thinking as a performance, but there are many parallels. Serious thinking is risky, because real-life problems are not well defined. Often the outcomes of our thinking are public—others evaluate our ideas. Like a dancer auditioning for a Broadway show, we must cope with the consequences of being evaluated. Like a sculptor looking at a lump of clay, a student facing a difficult problem must experiment, observe, redo, imagine and test solutions, apply both basic skills and inventive techniques, make interpretations, decide how to communicate results to the intended audience, and often accept criticism and improve the solution (Eisner, 1999; Herman, 1997). Table 7.2 lists some characteristics of authentic tests.

Performance in Context: Portfolios and Exhibitions

The concern with authentic assessment has led to the development of several new approaches based on the goal of *performance in context*. Instead of circling answers to "factual" questions on nonexistent situations, students are required to solve real problems. Facts are used in a context where they apply—for example, the student uses grammar facts to write a persuasive letter to a software company requesting donations for the class computer center. The following example of a test of performance is taken from the Connecticut Core of Common Learning:

> Many local supermarkets claim to have the lowest prices. But what does this really mean? Does it mean that every item in their store is priced lower, or just some of them? How can you really tell which supermarket will save you the most money? Your assignment is to design and carry out a study to answer this question. What items and prices will you compare and why? How will you justify the choice of your "sample"? How reliable is the sample, etc.? (Wolf, Bixby, Glenn, & Gardner, 1991, p. 61)

Students completing this "test" will use mathematical facts and procedures in the context of solving a real-life problem. In addition, they will have to think critically and write persuasively.

Portfolios and exhibitions are two new approaches to assessment that require performance in context. With these new approaches, it is difficult to tell where instruction stops and assessment starts because the two processes are interwoven.

TABLE 7.2   Characteristics of Authentic Tests

A. Structure and Logistics

1. Are more appropriately public; involve an audience, a panel, and so on.
2. Do not rely on unrealistic and arbitrary time constraints.
3. Offer known, not secret, questions or tasks.
4. Are more like portfolios or a *season* of games (not one-shot).
5. Require some collaboration with others.
6. Recur—and are *worth* practicing for, rehearsing, and retaking.
7. Make assessment and feedback to students so central that school schedules, structures, and policies are modified to support them.

B. Intellectual Design Features

1. Are "essential"—not needlessly intrusive, arbitrary, or contrived to "shake out" a grade.
2. Are "enabling"—constructed to point the student toward more sophisticated use of the skills or knowledge.
3. Are contextualized, complex intellectual challenges, not "atomized" tasks, corresponding to isolated "outcomes."
4. Involve the student's own research or use of knowledge, for which "content" is a means.
5. Assess student habits and repertoires, not mere recall or plug-in skills.
6. Are *representative* challenges—designed to emphasize *depth* more than breadth.
7. Are engaging and educational.
8. Involve somewhat ambiguous ("ill-structured") tasks or problems.

C. Grading and Scoring Standards

1. Involve criteria that assess essentials, not easily counted (but relatively unimportant) errors.
2. Are graded not on a "curve" but in reference to performance standards (criterion-referenced, not norm-referenced).
3. Involve demystified criteria of success that appear to *students* as inherent in successful activity.
4. Make self-assessment a part of the assessment.
5. Use a multifaceted scoring system instead of one aggregate grade.
6. Exhibit harmony with shared schoolwide aims—a *standard.*

D. Fairness and Equity

1. Ferret out and identify (perhaps hidden) strengths.
2. Strike a *constantly* examined balance between honoring achievement and native skill or fortunate prior training.
3. Minimize needless, unfair, and demoralizing comparisons.
4. Allow appropriate room for student learning styles, aptitudes, and interests.
5. Can be—should be—attempted by *all* students, with the test "scaffolded up," not "dumbed down," as necessary.

Source: From "Teaching to the Authentic Test," by G. W. Wiggins, 1989, *Educational Leadership,* 45(7), p. 44. Copyright © 1989 by the Association of Supervision and Curriculum Development. Reprinted with permission. All rights reserved.

Portfolios.   According to Paulson, Paulson, and Meyer (1991), a **portfolio** is a purposeful collection of student work that demonstrates the student's efforts, progress, and achievements. The collection should include student participation in selecting contents, the criteria for judging merit, and evidence of student self-reflection. Portfolios often include work in progress, revisions, student self-analyses, and reflections on what the student has learned. For example, one student's self-reflection is presented in Figure 7.6.

Written work or artistic pieces are common contents of portfolios, but students might also include graphs, diagrams, snapshots of displays, peer comments, audio- or videotapes,

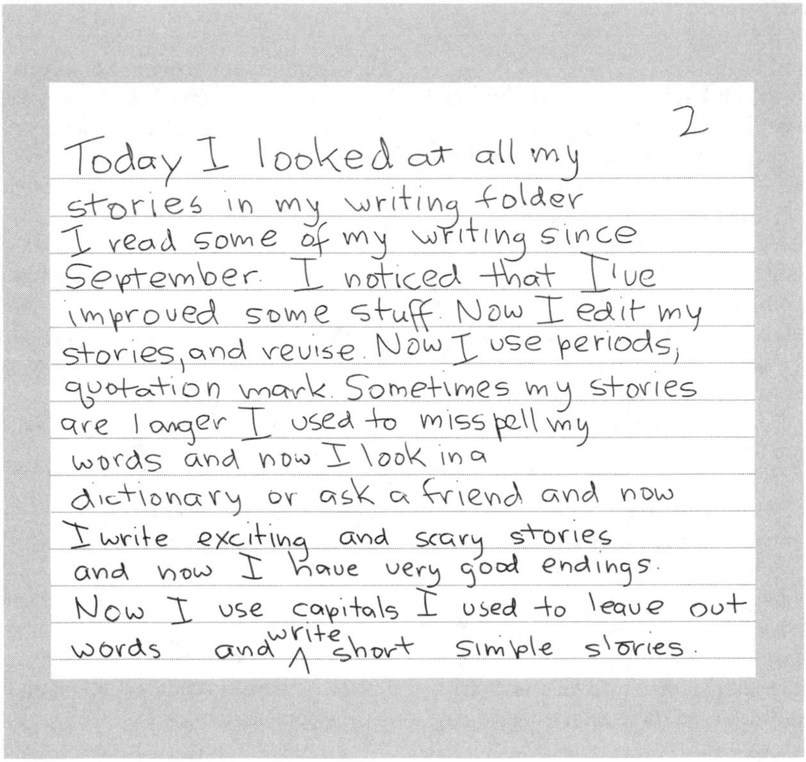

> Today I looked at all my stories in my writing folder I read some of my writing since September. I noticed that I've improved some stuff. Now I edit my stories, and revise. Now I use periods, quotation mark. Sometimes my stories are longer I used to miss pell my words and now I look in a dictionary or ask a friend and now I write exciting and scary stories and now I have very good endings. Now I use capitals I used to leave out words and write short simple stories.
>
> 2

FIGURE 7.6   A Student Reflects on Learning: Self-Analysis of Work in a Portfolio   Not only has this student's writing improved, but the student has become a more self-aware and self-critical writer.

Source: From "What Makes a Portfolio a Portfolio?" by F. L. Paulson, P. Paulson, and C. Meyers, 1991, *Educational Leadership, 48, 5,* p. 63. Copyright © 1991 by the Association for Supervision and Curriculum Development. Reprinted with permission. All rights reserved.

laboratory reports, computer programs—anything that demonstrates learning in the area being taught and assessed (Belanoff & Dickson, 1991; Camp, 1990; Wolf, Bixby, Glenn, & Gardner, 1991). The Vermont Mathematics Portfolio, for example, has (a) five to seven of the student's "best pieces," including at least one puzzle, one investigation, one application, and no more than two examples of group work; (b) a letter to the portfolio examiner; and (c) a collection of other pieces of mathematics work (Abruscato, 1993). The Guidelines on the following page should give principals some ideas for helping teachers use portfolios in their teaching.

Exhibitions.   An **exhibition** is a performance test that has two additional features. First, it is public, so students preparing exhibitions must take the audience into account; communication and understanding are essential. Second, an exhibition often requires many hours

THEORY INTO ACTION GUIDELINES

Student Portfolios

Students should be involved in selecting the pieces that will make up the portfolio.

Examples

1. During the unit or semester, ask each student to select work that fits certain criteria, such as "my most difficult problem," "my best work," "my most improved work," or "three approaches to...."
2. For their final submissions, ask students to select pieces that best show how much they have learned.

A portfolio should include information that shows student self-reflection and self-criticism.

Examples

1. Ask students to include a rationale for their selections.
2. Have each student write a "guide" to his or her portfolio, explaining how strengths and weaknesses are reflected in the work included.
3. Include self- and peer critiques, indicating specifically what is good and what might be improved.
4. Model self-criticism of your own productions.

The portfolio should reflect the students' activities in learning.

Examples

1. Include a representative selection of projects, writings, drawings, and so forth.

2. Ask students to relate the goals of learning to the contents of their portfolios.

The portfolio can serve different functions at different times of the year.

Examples

1. Early in the year, it might hold unfinished work or "problem pieces."
2. At the end of the year, it should contain only what the student is willing to make public.

Portfolios should show growth.

Examples

1. Ask students to make a "history" of their progress along certain dimensions and to illustrate points in their growth with specific works.
2. Ask students to include descriptions of activities outside class that reflect the growth illustrated in the portfolio.

Teach students how to create and use portfolios.

Examples

1. Keep models of very well done portfolios as examples, but stress that each portfolio is an individual statement.
2. Examine your students' portfolios frequently, especially early in the year when they are just getting used to the idea. Give constructive feedback.

of preparation, because it is the culminating experience of a whole program of study. Ted Sizer (1984) proposed that "exhibitions of mastery" replace traditional tests in determining graduation or course completion requirements. Grant Wiggins (1989) believes that an exhibition of mastery "is meant to be more than a better test. Like the thesis and oral examination in graduate school, it indicates whether a student has earned a diploma, is ready to leave high school" (p. 47).

Evaluating Portfolios and Performances

Checklists, rating scales, and scoring rubrics are helpful when you assess performances, because assessments of performances, portfolios, and exhibitions are criterion-referenced, not norm-referenced. In other words, the students' products and performances are compared to established public standards, not ranked in relation to other students' work (Cambourne & Turbill, 1990; Wiggins, 1991). For example, Figure 7.7 gives three alternatives—numerical, graphic, and descriptive—for rating an oral presentation.

Scoring Rubrics.   A checklist or rating scale gives specific feedback about elements of a performance. **Scoring rubrics** are rules that are used to determine the quality of a student performance (Mabry, 1999). For example, a rubric describing an excellent oral presentation might be:

> Pupil consistently faces audience, stands straight, and maintains eye contact; voice projects well and clearly; pacing and tone variation appropriate; well-organized; points logically and completely presented; brief summary at end. (Airasian, 1996, p. 155)

It is often helpful to have students join in the development of rating scales and scoring rubrics. When students participate, they are challenged to decide what quality work looks or sounds like in a particular area. They know in advance what is expected. As students gain practice in designing and applying scoring rubrics, their work and their learning often improve. Figure 7.8 is an evaluation form for self- and peer assessment of contributions to cooperative learning groups.

Performance assessment requires careful judgment on the part of teachers and clear communication to students about what is good and what needs improving. In some ways the approach is similar to the clinical method first introduced by Binet to assess intelligence: It is based on observing the student perform a variety of tasks and comparing his or her performance to a standard. Just as Binet never wanted to assign a single number to represent the child's intelligence, teachers who use authentic assessments do not try to assign one score to the student's performance. Even if rankings, ratings, and grades have to be given, these judgments are not the ultimate goals—improvement of learning is. Here are Guidelines for principals to help teachers develop rubrics, taken from Goodrich (1997).

Reliability, Validity, and Equity.   Because judgment plays such a central role in evaluating performances, issues of reliability, validity, and equity are critical considerations. When raters are experienced and scoring rubrics are well developed and refined, however, reliability may improve (Herman & Winters, 1994; LeMahieu, Gitomer, & Eresh, 1993).

Some of this improvement in reliability occurs because a rubric focuses the raters' attention on a few dimensions of the work and gives limited scoring levels to chose from. If scorers can give only a rating of 1, 2, 3, or 4, they are more likely to agree than if they could score based on a 100-point scale. So the rubrics may achieve reliability not because they capture underlying agreement among raters, but because the rubrics limit options and thus limit variability in scoring (Mabry, 1999).

FIGURE 7.7   Three Ways of Rating an Oral Presentation

Numerical Rating Scale

Directions: Indicate how often the pupil performs each of these behaviors while giving an oral presentation. For each behavior circle **1** if the pupil **always** performs the behavior, **2** if the pupil **usually** performs the behavior, **3** if the pupil **seldom** performs the behavior, and **4** if the pupil **never** performs the behavior.

Physical Expression

A. Stands straight and faces audience.

   1   2   3   4

B. Changes facial expression with change in the tone of the presentation.

   1   2   3   4

Graphic Rating Scale

Directions: Place an **X** on the line which shows how often the pupil did each of the behaviors listed while giving an oral presentation.

Physical Expression

A. Stands straight and faces the audience.

   always   **usually**   **seldom**   **never**

B. Changes facial expressions with change in tone of the presentation.

   always   **usually**   **seldom**   **never**

Descriptive Rating Scale

Directions: Place an **X** on the line at the place which best describes the pupil's performance on each behavior.

Physical Expression

A. Stands straight and faces audience.

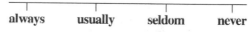

stands straight, always looks at audience	**weaves, fidgets, eyes roam from audience to ceiling**	**constant, distracting movements, no eye contact with audience**

B. Changes facial expressions with change in tone of the presentation.

matches facial expressions to content and emphasis	**facial expressions usually appropriate, occasional lack of expression**	**no match between tone and facial expression; expression distracts**

Source: From *Assessment in the Classroom* (p. 153), by P. W. Airasian, 1996, New York: McGraw-Hill. Copyright © by The McGraw-Hill Companies. Adapted with permission.

FIGURE 7.8   Self- and Peer Evaluation of Group Learning

Student Self- and Peer Evaluation Form

This form will be used to assess the members of your learning group. Fill one form out on yourself. Fill one form out on each member of your group. During the group discussion, give each member the form you have filled out on them. Compare the way you rated yourself with the ways your groupmates have rated you. Ask for clarification when your rating differs from the ratings given you by your groupmates. Each member should set a goal for increasing his or her contribution to the academic learning of all group members.

Person Being Rated: _____

Write the number of points earned by the group member:
(4 = Excellent, 3 = Good, 2 = Poor, 1 = Inadequate)

_____ On time for class.

_____ Arrives prepared for class.

_____ Reliably completes all assigned work on time.

_____ Work is of high quality.

_____ Contributes to groupmates' learning daily.

_____ Asks for academic help and assistance when it is needed.

_____ Gives careful step-by-step explanations (doesn't just tell answers).

_____ Builds on others' reasoning.

_____ Relates what is being learned to previous knowledge.

_____ Helps draw a visual representation of what is being learned.

_____ Voluntarily extends a project.

Source: From "The Role of Cooperative Learning in Assessing and Communicating Student Learning," by D. W. Johnson and R. T. Johnson. In *ASCD 1996 Yearbook: Communicating Student Learning* (p. 41), T. Guskey (Ed.). Copyright © 1996 by the Association for Supervision and Curriculum Development. Reprinted with permission. All rights reserved.

In terms of validity, there is some evidence that students who are classified as "master" writers on the basis of portfolio assessment are judged less capable using standard writing assessment. Which form of assessment is the best reflection of enduring qualities? There is so little research on this question, it is hard to say. (Herman & Winters, 1994). In addition, when rubrics are developed to assess specific tasks, the results of applying the rubric may not predict performance on anything except very similar tasks, so what do we actually know about students' learning more generally (Haertel, 1999; Herman, 1997)?

Equity is an issue in all assessment and no less so with performances and portfolios. With a public performance there could be bias effects based on a student's appearance and speech or the student's access to expensive audio, video, or graphic resources. Performance assessments have the same potential as other tests to discriminate unfairly against students who are not wealthy or who are culturally different (McDonald, 1993). And the extensive group work, peer editing, and out-of-class time devoted to portfolios means that some students may have access to more extensive networks of support and outright help.

THEORY INTO ACTION GUIDELINES

Developing a Rubric

1. **Look at models:** Show students examples of good and not-so-good work. Identify the characteristics that make good ones good and the bad ones bad.
2. **List criteria:** Use the discussion of models to begin a list of what counts in quality work.
3. **Articulate gradations of quality:** Describe the best and worst levels of quality, then fill in the middle levels based on your knowledge of common problems and the not-so-good work.
4. **Practice on models:** Have your students use the rubrics to evaluate the models that you gave them in Step 1.
5. **Use self- and peer assessment:** Give students their task. As they work, stop them occasionally for self- and peer assessment.

6. **Revise:** Always give students time to revise their work based on the feedback they get in Step 5.
7. **Use teacher assessment:** use the same rubrics students used to access their work.

Step 1 may be necessary only when you are asking students to engage in a task with which they are unfamiliar. Steps 3 and 4 are useful but time-consuming; you can do these on your own especially when you've been using rubrics for a while. A class experienced in rubric-based assessment can streamline the process so that it begins with listing criteria, after which the teacher writes out the gradations of quality, check them with the students, makes revisions, then uses the rubrics for self-, peer, and teacher assessments.

Many students in your school will have families with sophisticated computer graphic and desktop publishing capabilities. Others may have little support from home. These differences can be sources of bias and inequity.

Getting the Most from Traditional Tests

Even though there are many new ways of testing, students can still benefit from traditional tests. Both instruction and assessment are most effective when they are well organized and planned. When you have a good plan, you are in a better position to judge the tests provided in teacher's manuals and texts and those developed by teachers.

When to Test?   Frank Dempster (1991) examined the research on reviews and tests and reached these useful conclusions for teachers:

1. Frequent testing encourages the retention of information and appears to be more effective than a comparable amount of time spent reviewing and studying the material.
2. Tests are especially effective in promoting learning if you give students a test on the material soon after they learn it, then retest on the material later. The retestings should be spaced farther and farther apart.
3. The use of cumulative questions on tests is a key to effective learning. Cumulative questions ask students to apply information learned in previous units to solve a new problem.

Unfortunately, the curriculum in many schools is so full that there is little time for frequent tests and reviews. Dempster argues that students will learn more if we "teach them less," that is, if the curriculum includes fewer topics, but explores those topics in greater depth and allows more time for review, practice, testing, and feedback (Dempster, 1993).

Judging Textbook Tests.   Most elementary and secondary school texts today come complete with supplemental materials such as teaching manuals, handout masters, and ready-made tests. Using these tests can save time, but is this good teaching practice? The answer depends on your objectives for your students, the way you taught the material, and the quality of the tests provided (Airasian, 1996). If the textbook test matches your testing plan and the instruction you actually provided for your students, then it may be the right test to use. Table 7.3 gives key points to consider in evaluating textbook tests.

One aspect of assessment that affects every school is grading. Teachers are more directly involved with grading than parents, but everyone in a school is concerned about how grades affect students.

Effects of Grades and Grading on Students

There is some evidence that high standards, a competitive class atmosphere, and a large percentage of lower grades are associated with increased absenteeism and dropout rates (Moos & Moos, 1978). This seems especially likely with disadvantaged students (Wessman, 1972). Highly competitive classes may be particularly hard on anxious students or students who lack self-confidence. So, while high standards and competition do tend gen-

---

TABLE 7.3   Key Points to Consider in Judging Textbook Tests

The decision to use a textbook test must come *after* a teacher identifies the objectives that he or she taught and now wants to assess.

Textbook tests are designed for the typical classroom, but since few classrooms are typical, most teachers deviate somewhat from the text in order to accommodate their pupils' needs.

The more classroom instruction deviates from the textbook objectives and lesson plans, the less valid the textbook tests are likely to be.

The main consideration in judging the adequacy of a textbook test is the match between its test questions and what pupils were taught in their classes:

- Are questions similar to the teacher's objectives and instructional emphases?
- Do questions require pupils to perform the behaviors they were taught?
- Do questions cover all or most of the important objectives taught?
- Is the language level and terminology appropriate for pupils?
- Does the number of items for each objective provide a sufficient sample of pupil performance?

Source: From *Assessment in the Classroom* (p. 190), by P. Airasian, 1996, New York: McGraw-Hill. Copyright © 1996 by The McGraw-Hill Companies. Adapted with permission.

erally to be related to increased academic learning, it is clear that a balance must be struck between high standards and a reasonable chance to succeed.

Effects of Failure

It may sound as though low grades and failure should be avoided in school. But the situation is not that simple. After reviewing many years of research on the effects of failure from several perspectives, Margaret Clifford (1990, 1991) concluded that failure can have both positive and negative effects on subsequent performance, depending on the situation and the personality of the students involved.

For example, one study required subjects to complete three sets of problems. On the first set, the experimenters arranged for subjects to experience either zero, 50, or 100% success. On the second set, it was arranged for all subjects to fail completely. On the third set of problems, the experimenters merely recorded how well the subjects performed. Those who had succeeded only 50% of the time before the failure experience performed the best. It appears that a history of complete failure or 100% success may be bad preparation for learning to cope with failure, something we must all learn. Some level of failure may be helpful for most students, especially if teachers help the students see connections between hard work and improvement. Efforts to protect students from failure and guarantee success may be counterproductive. Clifford (1990) gives this advice to teachers:

> It is time for educators to replace easy success with challenge. We must encourage students to reach beyond their intellectual grasp and allow them the privilege of learning from mistakes. There must be a tolerance for error-making in every classroom, and gradual success rather than continual success must become the yardstick by which learning is judged. (p. 23)

So far, we have been talking about the effects of failing a test or perhaps a course. But what about the effect of failing an entire grade—that is, of being held back? Almost 20% of seniors have repeated at least one grade since kindergarten, usually in the earlier grades (Kelly, 1999). Some researchers believe that being held back injures students' self-esteem and increases the chances that they will drop out of school (Grissom & Smith, 1989; Roderick, 1994). In their view, students generally do better academically when promoted. Other researchers have found some advantage for more emotionally immature children of average or above average ability who are retained in first, second, or third grade (Kelly, 1999; Pierson & Connell, 1992), but the advantage may not last. In one study that followed many students for several years, children who could have been retained, but who were promoted, did about as well as similar children who were held back, and sometimes better (Reynolds, 1992).

No matter what, students who have trouble should get help, whether they are promoted or retained. Just covering the same material again in the same way won't solve the students' academic or social problems. As Jeannie Oakes (1999) has said, "No sensible person advocates social promotion as it is currently framed—simply passing incompetent students on to the next grade" (p. 8). The best approach may be to promote the students along with their peers, but to give them special remediation during the summer or the next year (Mantzicopoulos & Morrison, 1992; Shepard & Smith, 1989). An even better approach would be to prevent the problems before they occur by providing extra resources such as tutoring, as happens in the Reading Recovery program or Slavin's Success for All (Oakes, 1999).

Effects of Feedback

The results of several studies of feedback fit well with the notion of "successful" or constructive failure. These studies have concluded that it is more helpful to tell students *why* they are wrong so they can learn more appropriate strategies (Bangert-Drowns, Kulik, Kulik, & Morgan, 1991). Students often need help figuring out why their answers are incorrect. Without such feedback, they are likely to make the same mistakes again. Yet this type of feedback is rarely given. In one study, only about 8% of the teachers noticed a consistent type of error in a student's arithmetic computation and informed the student (Bloom & Bourdon, 1980).

What are the identifying characteristics of effective written feedback? With older students (late elementary through high school), written comments are most helpful when they are personalized and when they provide constructive criticism. This means the teacher should make specific comments on errors or faulty strategies, but balance this criticism with suggestions about how to improve, and with comments on the positive aspects of the work (Butler & Nisan, 1986; Elawar & Corno, 1985). Working with sixth-grade teachers, Elawar and Corno (1985) found that feedback was dramatically improved when the teachers used these four questions as a guide: "What is the key error? What is the probable reason the student made this error? How can I guide the student to avoid the error in the future? What did the student do well that could be noted?" (p. 166). Here are some examples of teachers' written comments that proved helpful (Elawar & Corno, 1985, p. 164):

> Juan, you know how to get a percent, but the computation is wrong in this instance.... Can you see where? (Teacher has underlined the location of errors.)

> You know how to solve the problem—the formula is correct—but you have not demonstrated that you understand how one fraction multiplied by another can give an answer that is smaller than either ($\frac{1}{2} \times \frac{1}{2} = \frac{1}{4}$).

These comments should help students correct errors and should recognize good work, progress, and increasing skill.

Grades and Motivation

Is there really a difference between working for a grade and working to learn? The answer depends in part on how a grade is determined. If your teachers test only at a simple but detailed level of knowledge, they may force their students to choose between higher aspects of learning and a good grade. But when a grade reflects meaningful learning, working for a grade and working to learn become the same thing. Finally, although high grades may have some value as rewards or incentives for meaningful engagement in learning, low grades generally do not encourage greater efforts. Students receiving low grades are more likely to withdraw, blame others, decide that the work is "dumb," or feel responsible for the low grade but helpless to make improvements. Rather than give a failing grade, your teachers might consider the work incomplete and give students support in revising or improving. Maintain high standards and give students a chance to reach them (Guskey, 1994). Principals can help teachers with grading by suggesting the following Theory into Action Guidelines.

THEORY INTO ACTION GUIDELINES

Grading

Avoid reserving high grades and high praise for answers that simply conform to those in the textbook.

Examples

1. Give extra points for correct and creative answers.
2. Withhold your opinions until all sides of an issue have been explored.
3. Reinforce students for disagreeing in a rational, productive manner.
4. Give partial credit for partially correct answers.

Make sure each student has a good chance to be successful, especially at the beginning of a new task.

Examples

1. Pretest students to make sure they have prerequisite abilities.
2. When appropriate, provide opportunities for students to retest to raise their grades, but make sure the retest is as difficult as the original.
3. Consider failing efforts as "incomplete" and encourage students to revise and improve.

Balance written and oral feedback.

Examples

1. Consider giving short, lively written comments with younger students and more extensive written comments with older students.

2. When the grade on a paper is lower than the student might have expected, be sure the reason for the lower grade is clear.
3. Tailor comments to the individual student's performance; avoid writing the same phrases over and over.
4. Note specific errors, possible reasons for errors, ideas for improvement, and work done well.

Make grades as meaningful as possible.

Examples

1. Tie grades to the mastery of important objectives.
2. Give ungraded assignments to encourage exploration.
3. Experiment with performances and portfolios.

Base grades on more than just one criterion.

Examples

1. Use essay questions as well as multiple-choice items on a test.
2. Grade oral reports and class participation.

Summary

All teaching involves assessing and evaluating student learning. At the heart of assessment is judgment, making decisions based on values and goals. In the process of evaluation, we measure results and compare outcomes to some set of criteria. Test results have no meaning by themselves; we must make some kind of comparison to interpret them. There are two basic types of comparison: in the first, a test score is compared to the scores obtained by other people who have taken the same test—a norm-referenced comparison. The second type is criterion-referenced. Here, the comparison is to a fixed standard or minimum passing score.

Increasingly, standardized tests are given to students. These test are called standardized because they have standard methods of developing items, administering the test, scoring it, and reporting the scores. The final version of the test is administered to a large sample of subjects as similar as possible to the students who will be taking the test in school systems throughout the country. This norming sample serves as a comparison group for all students who take the test. Test scores of individuals and groups are compared to the mean (average score) and distribution in the norming sample. To make comparisons easy the scores are also standardized using percentile scores, z scores, stanine scores or T scores. For example, a T score of 60 for an individual means that the person has scored one standard deviation above the mean score for the normative sample. Other comparisons such as grade-equivalent scores are useful to principals and teachers as they make assessments about progress.

No test provides a perfect picture of a person's or group's ability or progress. Two critical features of any test are its reliability and validity; that is, does the test measure the results consistently and does it measure what it is suppose to measure? At a minimum all tests should be reliable and valid. Achievement tests are designed to measure what a student has learned in a specific content area whereas diagnostic tests measure a student's strengths and weaknesses, often to plan a course of action that will help the student learn and progress. Elementary school students are more likely than secondary school students to take diagnostic tests. High school students are more likely to take aptitude tests such as the SAT or IQ tests, which are meant to measure abilities developed over many years and to predict how well a student will do in the future.

Today, many important decisions about students, teachers, and schools are based in part on the results of standardized tests. Because the decisions affected by test scores are so critical, many educators call this process high-stakes testing. One suggestion to improve student performance is minimum competency testing, which is a standardized test meant to determine whether an individual meets the minimum standard for moving to the next level or graduating. Almost every state in the United States has some kind of high school competency testing program; in fact, there is some pressure for standardized national examinations. But most standardized test have been criticized as being biased against minority students. Culture-fair tests are difficult to find. There is, however, evidence that students can prepare for standardized tests and learn test-taking skills. Another criticism of traditional forms of testing is that such tests are merely samples of performance at one particular point in time; they fail to capture the student's potential for future learning. An alternative view of cognitive assessment is based on the assumption that the goal of assessment is to reveal potential for learning and to identify the psychological and educational interventions that will help the person realize this potential.

As the public and government demanded greater accountability in education and as traditional standardized tests became the basis for high-stakes decisions, pressure to do well led many teachers and schools to "teach to the test." Even more troubling, say critics, the traditional tests assess skills that have no equivalent in the real world. In response to these criticisms, the authentic assessment movement was born. The goal was to create standardized tests that assess complex, important, real-life outcomes. The approach is also called direct assessment, performance assessment, or alternative assessment. Similarly, new approaches to classroom assessment include authentic classroom tests that ask students to apply skills and abilities as they would in real life. The concern with authentic assessment has led to the development of several new approaches based on the goal of performance in context. For example, a portfolio is a purposeful collection of student work that demonstrates the student's efforts, progress, and achievements. The collection usually includes student participation in selecting contents, the criteria for judging merit, and evidence of student self-reflection. Portfolios include work in progress, revisions, student self-analyses, and reflections on what the student has learned, but the issues of reliability, validity, and equity remain important in assessment using such alternative means of testing.

High standards, a competitive class atmosphere, and a large percentage of lower grades are associated with increased absenteeism and dropout rates, especially for disadvantaged students. It may sound as though low grades and failure should be avoided in school, but the situation is not that simple. Failure can have both positive and negative effects on subsequent performance, depending on the situation and the personality of the students. For example, it is helpful to tell students *why* they are wrong so they can learn more appropriate strategies. Without such feedback, students are likely to make the same mistakes again, yet this type of feedback is rarely given. If teachers test only at a simple but detailed level of knowledge, they may force their students to choose between higher aspects of learning and a good grade; however, when a grade reflects meaningful learning, working for a grade and working to learn become the same thing. Finally, although high grades may have some value as rewards or incentives for meaningful engagement in learning, low grades generally do not encourage greater efforts.

KEY TERMS

achievement test (244)
aptitude tests (248)
assessment (235)
authentic assessment (257)
authentic tests (258)
central tendency (237)
confidence interval (244)
criterion-referenced
   testing (236)
culture-fair (culture-neutral)
   tests (254)
diagnostic tests (247)
exhibition (260)

grade-equivalent scores (240)
high-stakes testing (249)
mean (237)
measurement (234)
median (237)
minimum competency test (251)
mode (237)
normal distribution (238)
norm groups (235)
norming sample (237)
norm-referenced testing (235)
percentile rank (239)
portfolio (259)

range (238)
readiness testing (251)
reliability (243)
scoring rubric (262)
standard deviation (237)
standard error of
   measurement (243)
standard score (241)
standardized tests (236)
stanine score (241)
T score (241)
validity (244)
z score (241)

SOME IDEAS FOR YOUR PORTFOLIO

1. Based on the case at the beginning of this chapter, work with your teachers to develop a policy on sharing standardized test results with parents. Be sure that your policy is clear, precise, and can be included in a written statement to the parents of students in your school.

As you draft your statement, address the following issues:

- School philosophy on the meaning and use of standardized test scores
- Brief description of the tests taken
- Guidance for interpreting the scores appropriately
- Parent's role in preparing their children for testing
- The role of teachers and the principal in meeting with parents about test results
- Any other information useful to the parents in your school

2. Analyze the state report card results for your school over the past few years (or, if there are no report card results, compile and use standardized test scores).

- Identify specific areas of students' strengths and weaknesses.

- Develop a report to your faculty that is informative but not accusatory
- Then jointly devise a plan with your teachers for capitalizing on the strengths and improving the areas of weakness.

3. Investigate how four other schools are using authentic assessment. Work with a teacher to develop a supplemental authentic assessment plan for a unit of study in your curriculum.

- Specify the components of the assessment process, for example, portfolios, exhibitions, projects, presentations, and so on.
- Specify the rubrics for evaluating each component.
- Discuss how your plan for authentic assessment will be used in grading.

INSTRUCTIONAL LEADER'S TOOLBOX

Readings

Aschbacher, P. (1997). New directions in student assessment [Special Issue]. *Theory Into Practice, 36*(4), 194–272.

Ewy, C., & student authors (1997). Kids take on "the test." *Educational Leadership, 54*(4), 76–78.

Goodrich, H. (1997). Understanding rubrics. *Educational Leadership, 54*(4), 14–17.

Haertel, E. H. (1999). Performance assessment and educational reform. *Phi Delta Kappa, 80,* 662–666.

Kelly, K. (1999). Retention vs. social promotion: Schools search for alternatives. *Harvard Education Letter, 15*(1), 1–3.

Websites

Helping Children Master the Tricks and Avoid the Traps of Standardized Tests	http://www.ed.gov/databases/ERIC_Digests/ed429987.html
On Standardized Testing	http://www.ed.gov/databases/ERIC_Digests/ed338445.html
Performance Assessment Links in Science,	http://www.ctls.sri.com/pals
Pathways to School Improvement—Assessment	http://www.ncrel.org/skrs/areas/as0cont.htm
Guidelines for the Development and Management of Performance Assessments	http://www.ed.gov/databases/ERIC_Digests/ed410229.html

Norm- and Criterion-Referenced Testing	http://www.ed.gov/databases/ERIC_Digests/ed410316.html
A Developmental Approach to Assessment of Young Children	http://www.ed.gov/databases/ERIC_Digests/ed407172.html
Grading Students	http://www.ed.gov/databases/ERIC_Digests/ed398239.html
Portfolios for Assessment and Instruction	http://www.ed.gov/databases/ERIC_Digests/ed388890.html
Assessment and Testing: Measuring Up to Expectations	http://www.ed.gov/databases/ERIC_Digests/ed391559.html
Making the A: How to Study for Tests	http://www.ed.gov/databases/ERIC_Digests/ed385613.html
Creating Meaningful Performance Assessments	http://www.ed.gov/databases/ERIC_Digests/ed381985.html
Authentic Mathematics Assessment	http://www.ed.gov/databases/ERIC_Digests/cd354245.html
TIMSS	http://nces.ed.gov/timss/
The Case for Authentic Assessment	http://www.ed.gov/databases/ERIC Digests/ed328611.html

Organizations

Educational Testing Service	www.ets.org
Educational Resources Information Center (ERIC) Clearing House on Assessment and Evaluation. The site provides extensive information about a wide array of standardized tests.	http://ericae.net
National Center for Research on Evaluation, Standards, and Student Testing. The center conducts research on educational testing	http://cresst96.cse.ucla.edu/index.htm
Performance Assessment Links in Science	http://www.ctl.sri.com/pals/.
Pathways to School Improvement—Assessment	http://www.ncrel.org/skrs/pathways.htm

Assessing and Changing School Culture and Climate

Preview: Key Points

Leadership Challenge

The School Workplace

Organizational Culture
    Levels of Culture
    Functions of Culture
    Common Elements of Culture
    Some General Propositions about School Culture

Organizational Climate
    Organizational Climate: Open to Closed
    A Revised OCDQ
    Climate Types
    The OCDQ: Some Implications

Organizational Climate: Healthy To Unhealthy
    Dimensions of Organizational Health
    Organizational Health Inventory (OHI-S)
    The OHI: Some Implications

Collective Efficacy

Changing School Climate
    Some Assumptions about Change in Schools
    The Case of Martin Luther King, Jr. High School:
        An Example
    A Problem
    An Organizational Development Model
    Back to Martin Luther King, Jr. High School

Summary

Key Terms

Some Ideas for Your Portfolio

Instructional Leader's Toolbox
    Readings
    Websites
    Organizations

PREVIEW: KEY POINTS

- School culture and school climate are two ways to capture the feel or atmosphere of the school workplace.
- Organizational culture is a pattern of shared orientations that binds the unit together and gives it a distinctive identity.
- School culture can be examined at four levels: tacit assumptions, core values, shared norms, artifacts.
- Schools can create cultures that encourage learning and improvement among all participants.
- School climate is a relatively enduring quality of the school environment that is experienced by teachers, influences their behavior, and is based on their collective perceptions of behavior.
- School climate can be viewed using a personality metaphor and measured in terms of the openness of interactions among teachers and between teachers and the principal.
- School climate can also be examined using a health metaphor and measured in terms of healthy interactions between students, teachers, and administrators.

- The collective efficacy of a school is another important property of the school environment.
- Change is characteristic of all organizations, but change can be random or directed.
- Schools have the potential to become learning organizations that solve their own problems.
- An organizational development model can provide guidelines for changing school climate.

Leadership Challenge

You are the principal of an urban high school in the Northeast. About one third of your students are minority and another 14% are newly arrived immigrants to this "ethnically rich" community. The diversity of the school and community makes your job a challenging one. You are committed to improving the school; among your goals are increasing the graduation rates, increasing the number of students heading to college, and in general, making the high school a place where students want to be rather than have to be. You are in the middle of your third year, and although the job is difficult and demands long hours, you feel like you are making a difference. Most of the teachers seem reasonably content and you believe that they are receptive to your initiatives. Yet, you have a nagging suspicion that things are not quite right at Martin Luther King, Jr. High School. Little things keep happening that give you pause—teachers leaving early, teachers skipping meetings, teachers not attending extracurricular activities. You decide to systematically examine the climate of your school. What you find is shocking to you. The teachers describe the school work environment in much more negative terms than you do. They question your leadership. Morale is low. The academic emphasis in the school is poor. The climate is closed. At least that is what your teachers say.

- You are dismayed and surprised, but what do you do?
- Where do you begin?

Think about it. Later in the chapter we will describe what principal Elbert Gibbs did.

The School Workplace

A collective sense of identity emerges in organizations as members interact and transform the workplace into a distinctive institution. There are many common terms used to refer to this indigenous feel of the organization—ecology, milieu, setting, tone, field, character, atmosphere, culture, and climate. All are used to refer to the internal quality of the organization as experienced by its members, but *organizational culture* and *organizational climate* are the two concepts that have captured the attention of scholars and researchers.

These two approaches to examining the collective identity of the workplace, culture and climate, come from different intellectual traditions. Scholars of organizational culture tend to use the qualitative and ethnographic techniques of anthropology and sociology to examine the character or atmosphere of organizations. They are interested in thick, rich descriptions and understanding how the elements of culture fit together. In contrast, scholars of climate use quantitative techniques and multivariate analyses to find patterns of perceived behavior in organizations. Their background and training are more likely to be in multivariate statistics and psychology or social psychology rather than in ethnography and anthropology or sociology. Moreover, these researchers tend to be more interested in how climate influences organizational outcomes. The goal of studying climate is often to determine effective strategies of change and the impact that organizations have on groups and individuals.

Both perspectives, climate and culture, are attempts to understand the influence of social context on organizational life. Thus, both should be useful to instructional leaders as they grapple with how social conditions in the school affect teaching and learning. Which perspective is better? You be the judge. Our position is that both frameworks are useful; the concepts are complements rather than alternatives.

Organizational Culture

There is no single accepted definition of organizational culture. At one level everyone agrees that culture refers to the social context of the organization and that different organizations have different cultures. The idea that groups and organizations have certain things that are shared or held in common that make them distinctive is also generally accepted. But what are the critical shared elements? Some argue that they are the customs, rituals, and traditions of the organizations; others argue they are the implicit values and norms that evolve in work groups; and still others maintain they are the shared meanings that are created as members interact with each other in organizations. Indeed organizational culture has been defined from all these perspectives. The notion of culture accentuates the need for stability, consistency, and meaning in organizational life (Schein, 1992). It's useful to think of **organizational culture** as a pattern of shared orientations that binds the organization together and gives it a distinctive identity (Hoy & Miskel, 2001).

Levels of Culture

Culture manifests itself at different levels of abstraction. One way to begin to disentangle the concept is to examine these levels of culture. The levels range from very visible and tangible aspects that are concrete to deeply held, basic assumptions that are unconscious, tacit, and abstract (Schein, 1992). In between the fairly concrete artifacts and the abstract basic assumptions are informal norms and core values. The levels of analysis at which culture can be analyzed are pictured in Figure 8.1.

Culture as Tacit Assumptions.   At its most abstract level, culture is the collective manifestation of **tacit assumptions.** Such assumptions have become unconscious, basic premises about human nature, social relationships, truth, reality, and environment; they are taken for granted—and they are highly resistant to change. The pattern of basic assumptions that has developed within the organization to cope with its problems of external adaptation and internal integration is its culture. When the pattern has worked well enough to be considered valid, it is taught to new members as the correct way to perceive, think, feel, and solve fundamental organizational problems.

Culture as a set of tacit assumptions defines for its members what to pay attention to, what things mean, how to react emotionally to what is going on, and what actions to take

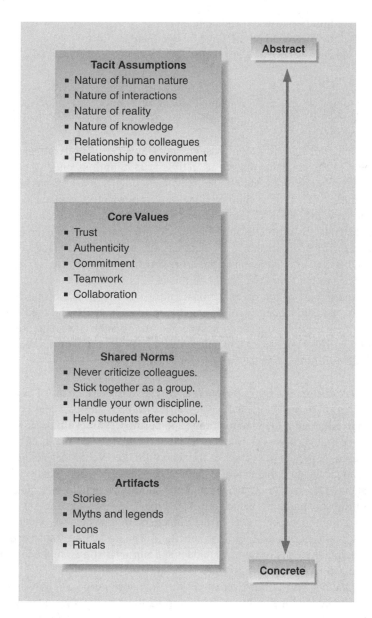

FIGURE 8.1   Levels of Culture

in different situations (Schein, 1992). Consider a school that has a strong culture with the following basic assumptions:

- Relationships among teachers are primarily group oriented and shared.
- Decisions are determined through debate, which necessitates conflict and the testing and sharing of ideas.

- Teachers are highly motivated and competent.
- All teachers are evaluated by the same fair standards.
- Teachers view the school as a big family; they accept, respect, and take care of each other.

These basic assumptions give rise to shared values of cooperation, expertise, openness, fairness, and respect—a school culture where an effective program of instructional improvement is possible.

Any challenge or questioning of basic assumptions can lead to anxiety and defensiveness. Schein (1992) explains that the shared basic assumptions making up the culture of a group can be conceived of—at both the individual and group levels—as psychological defense mechanisms that protect the individual and group and permit them to function. Thus change is very difficult. Moreover, because the basic assumptions of an organization are often unconscious, distortions of information are quite possible. For example, if we believe that people will take advantage of us whenever they have a chance, we interpret events in ways that confirm that assumption. A principal's visit is seen as an opportunity to exploit weaknesses rather than help. Further if this belief is not only a personal one but one that is shared and is part of the organizational culture, teachers will discuss with others how they have been taken advantage of during the principal's visits, and the beliefs are reconfirmed. If beliefs are individual and idiosyncratic, they can be corrected more easily because the group will not reinforce them. But when the beliefs are part of the culture, they become mutually reinforced and the culture is validated.

Culture as Core Values.   As groups emerge, they also develop a set of common, core values that are central to behavior; such values define, in broad terms, ideas organizational members need to embrace if they are to "fit in" and be successful. **Values** are abstract conceptions of the desirable. If we ask teachers to explain why they do the things they do, we may begin to discover the central values of the school. Shared values define the basic character of the school and give the school a distinctive identity. When teachers know what their school stands for, they know what standards should be upheld and make decisions consistent with those standards. Values are on a higher level of abstraction than norms, which are also common expectations of how teachers should behave. Values deal with ideals and ends, while norms deal with the specific means to achieve those ends. In other words, values define the ends of human conduct and norms distinguish the legitimate and illegitimate means to accomplish those ends.

William Ouchi's (1981) book on successful Japanese corporations was one of the first analyses of organizational culture. Ouchi argued that the key to success in organizations was not so much a matter of technology as it was culture; in fact, he identified the core values of successful American and Japanese organizations, which included the following: trust, commitment, cooperation, teamwork, egalitarianism, and intimacy. Notice that these are fairly abstract values of the organization. There are competing values that are embodied in organizational actions such as competition, loyalty, democracy, expertise, innovation, and impersonality. Schools develop their own culture; that is, schools develop a core of common values that members embrace and that guide their behavior.

We expect, for example, that instructional leadership will be most effective in a culture that is imbued with such values as openness, authenticity, cooperation, collegiality, and innovation. On the other hand, a school culture that values competition, impersonality, correctness, and hierarchy will likely make the improvement of teaching and learning more difficult. But how do shared values develop in schools? There is no easy or simple answer. Leadership can help. If a principal, for example, can convince teachers to act based on trust and collegiality and if such actions are perceived as successful, then the perceived value that trust and collegiality are "good" gradually starts a process of cognitive transformation. Over time this transformation can lead to a common set of shared values or beliefs, but the process will proceed only if the actions continue to work well. (Schein, 1992).

In strong cultures, core values are held intensely, shared widely, and guide organizational behavior; however, the content as well as the strength of culture are important. Each school has a set of core values that undergirds behavior. If improvement is to be successful, the core values must be consistent with authentic principal practices.

Culture as Shared Norms.

Culture as Shared Norms.   The next level of analysis for culture is in terms of the informal norms. **Norms** are the unwritten and informal expectations that teachers learn as they become socialized into the school. Norms are expectations, not behavior. Becoming a member of a group means learning the important informal expectations of behavior for the group. Norms are universal and guide group activity. Make no mistake; norms affect behavior. The stronger the norms, the more constraining they are on behavior. Although norms are less abstract than values and tacit assumptions, they often are not obvious. In fact, it is sometimes difficult to surface the important norms of a group because members are reluctant talk about them unless they are confident the information will not be held against them: in fact, many groups have a norm against revealing the important unofficial expectations to outsiders.

Norms are communicated to members by stories and significant events in the history of the school that vividly depict what the organization stands for. New teachers quickly learn the shared norms of the group, which are critical elements of the informal organization. Norms influence the way teachers dress and interact, the way they respond to authority, and the way they balance their own interests with those of the organization. In brief, norms are the informal rules that govern behavior in schools.

Although there are few, if any, universal norms for teachers, common ones exist in many schools. For example, "Handle your own discipline problems," and "Don't criticize other teachers to students," are two typical norms found in many schools. Examples of other norms that are more idiosyncratic are: "Don't rock the boat," "Innovate, try new ideas," "Support your fellow teachers even when they are wrong," "Never let students out of class before the bell rings," "Change your bulletin boards frequently," and "Don't criticize the principal in public." Norms are enforced by such informal sanctions as invitations to participate in special events (positive) and ostracism (negative). Teachers develop their own distinctive expectations for each other in their schools. Do teachers prize contentious debate or courteous restraint? Are playful and relaxed interactions appropriate or are interactions structured and formal? Groups develop norms to answer such questions (Bolman & Deal, 1997). In brief, the shared norms of the work group define a major slice of the culture of a school.

Culture as Artifacts.

Culture as Artifacts.   At the most basic and concrete level, the shared perspectives of which we speak are the things that members see, hear, and feel that make the organization distinctive. **Artifacts** include aspects of the physical environment (buildings, layout, classrooms, lounges, etc.) as well as the language, activities, and ceremonies that have become a routine part of organizational life. Although artifacts are easy to observe, they are sometimes difficult to decipher (Schein, 1999) because they are infused with meanings that come from that special group. For example, in one school informality may be a sign of inefficiency and fooling around, but in another school informality represents independent and efficient interaction among committed professionals.

There are many artifacts that are useful in understanding the culture of a school. Stories are narratives that become part of the school culture; they are based on true events, but often combine truth and fiction. The story of the heroic principal who supports a teacher even at risk of losing his or her job becomes retold and elaborated to embody the supportive norms that exist between the principal and teacher. Some stories are **myths;** that is, they communicate an unquestioned belief that cannot be demonstrated by the facts. Legends are stories that have become institutionalized. They have been repeated and elaborated in ways that add to the importance of the event. They capture what the organization has come to value. People who do extraordinary things that capture the essence of the culture become legends and heroes. The principal who stood by his teacher and overcame great pressure from parents becomes the focus for cohesiveness, loyalty, and commitment in a school. The stories of heroes and legends provide insight into the core values of an organization.

Icons and rituals are important artifacts because they also indirectly communicate the culture of the school. Logos, mottoes, and trophies are icons that offer a glimpse of the school culture. **Rituals** are the routine ceremonies and rites that are visible examples of what is valued in the school. Beyer and Trice (1987) identify four rites that are typical of most organizations: rites of passage, degradation, enhancement, and integration. For example, the faculty lounge, coffee groups, and parties provide activities that bind the group together and make it a unique whole. Rites of enhancement are often seen in formal assemblies as the school recognizes the teacher of the year or the debate team champions. Such ceremonies reinforce appropriate behavior and signal what the school values. New teachers go through a series of rites of passage as they are assigned difficult classes, lunch duty, and after-school detention. They quickly learn to cope and discover the appropriate "way to do things around here."

Artifacts are observable and fairly concrete, but their meanings are often obscured. Only with time in the organization can one learn the meanings of the artifacts of a particular school. Stories, myths, legends, rituals, and icons typically embody the informal norms, core values, and basic assumptions of the organization. These latter elements of school culture are less obvious, but provide a fuller picture.

In summary, a school's culture can be examined at four levels—artifacts, shared norms, core values, and tacit assumptions. Although artifacts are most concrete, they sometimes are difficult to decipher. At the other extreme, tacit assumptions are most abstract and difficult to identify, but they most clearly capture the meanings of events and relationships in organizations. Core values and shared norms are at the middle range of abstraction and also give meaning and understanding to the culture of the school. A thorough understanding of culture requires a comprehension of all four levels. In other words, to understand the culture of a school, one must comprehend the meanings and the shared orientations of the school—its artifacts, norms, values, and basic assumptions.

Functions of Culture

Although there is no one best culture for all schools, strong cultures promote cohesiveness, loyalty, and commitment, which in turn reduce the propensity for members to leave the organization (Mowday, Porter, & Steers, 1982). Moreover, Robbins (1998) summarizes a number of important functions performed by the organization's culture:

- Culture has a boundary-defining function; it creates distinctions among organizations.
- Culture provides the organization with a sense of identity.
- Culture facilitates the development of commitment to the group.
- Culture enhances stability in the social system.
- Culture is the social glue that binds the organization together; it provides the appropriate standards for behavior.
- Culture serves to guide and shape the attitudes and behavior of organizational members.

It is important to remember, however, that a strong culture can be either functional or dysfunctional—that is, it can promote or impede effectiveness.

Common Elements of Culture

At the core on any organizational culture is a set of shared values. Several studies (O'Reilly, Chatman, & Caldwell, 1991; Chatman & Jehn, 1994) have suggested that there are seven basic elements that shape the culture of most organizations:

- *Innovation:* the degree to which employees are expected to be creative and take risks
- *Stability:* the degree to which activities focus on the status quo rather than change
- *Attention to detail:* the degree to which there is concern for precision and detail
- *Outcome orientation:* the degree to which management emphasizes results
- *People orientation:* the degree to which management decisions are sensitive to individuals
- *Team orientation:* the degree of emphasis on collaboration and teamwork
- *Aggressiveness:* the degree to which employees are expected to be competitive rather than easygoing

The culture of most organizations can be mapped by using these elements to describe the values that are dominant. Schein (1999), however, provides three cautions. First, cultures are deep, not superficial; thus if you assume that you can manipulate it, you are likely to fail. Second, culture is broad because it is formed by beliefs and assumptions about daily life in organizations; hence, deciphering culture is a challenge. Third, culture is stable because it provides meaning and makes life predictable; consequently, changing it is difficult.

Some General Propositions about School Culture

Without question school culture is a complex, symbolic, and contextual. Much of what occurs in schools can only be understood and interpreted in the unique context of the school's culture. Bolman and Deal (1997) summarize the complexities and difficulties of understanding organizational activities.

■ The most important aspect of any organizational event is not what happened but what it means. *Events are often not what they seem.*

■ What an event means is often not clear because the activity must be interpreted in the context, and events have multiple meanings because people interpret them differently. *Meaning is elusive.*

■ Because events are typically ambiguous or uncertain, it is difficult to understand what happened, why it happened, and what will happen next. *Events are often puzzles: the future is problematic.*

■ The greater the ambiguity and uncertainty in events, the more difficult it is to use rational approaches to solve problems. *Rational decision making is limited as a process to solve organizational problems.*

■ When organizational members are confronted with ambiguity and uncertainty, they create symbols and stories to resolve conflict, provide understanding, and create hope. *Explanations are invented both to resolve conflict and to create positive outcomes.*

■ The importance of many organizational events rests with what the event expresses not what it produces. *Myths, rituals, ceremonies, and sagas often give people the meanings that they seek.*

The implications of these propositions for principals are clear. The principal must be part of the culture in order to understand it. Significant events should never be accepted at face value; their meanings must be interpreted in terms of the values and norms of the school and from the points of view of different organizational members. Given the uncertainty and ambiguity of school life, rational responses to school problems are only part of the solution. The symbolic aspects of actions are often more important than the content of the action. For example, it is not so much what a principal says or does when working with teachers but how it is done and what it means. A talk to a teacher about a difficult student can be seen as a judgment of poor teaching or an opportunity to solve a mutual problem; the meaning of the event depends on the shared norms and values of the group. Principals need to be creative in their ability to develop stories and explanations that ameliorate conflict. Humor and play are also important aspects of instructional leadership that reduce tension and encourage creativity (Bolman & Deal, 1997). Finally, the rituals, stories, and sagas of a school are important to help teachers give meaning and value to their work.

Although there is no one culture that is best for every school, there are some tacit assumptions that facilitate the process of improvement of instruction. Consider the following set of basic assumptions that Schein (1992) suggests is at the heart of a learning culture.

■ Teachers and students are proactive problem solvers and learners.

■ Solutions to problems derive from a pragmatic search; knowledge is found in many forms—scientific research, experience, trial and error, and clinical research in which teachers and principals work things out together.

■ Teachers have good intentions and are amenable to change and improvement.

■ Creativity and innovation are central to student learning.

- Both individualism and teamwork are important aspects of human interaction.
- Information and communication are central to the well-being of the school.
- Diversity is a resource that has the potential to enhance learning.
- Productive learning is enhanced by both challenge and support.
- The world is a complex field of interconnected forces in which multiple causation is more likely than simple causation.

Schools anchored with such assumptions have created learning cultures that encourage improvement among all participants.

Organizational Climate

Another aspect of the school context that sets the scene for effective instructional leadership is organizational climate. Teachers' performances in schools are in part determined by the climate in which they work. **Organizational climate** is a general concept that refers to teachers' perceptions of the school's work environment; it is affected by the formal organization, informal organization, and politics, all of which, including climate, affect the motivations and behavior of teachers. Simply stated, the set of internal characteristics that distinguishes one school from another and influences the behavior of its members is the organizational climate of the school. More specifically, climate is a relatively enduring quality of the school environment that is experienced by teachers, influences their behavior, and is based on their collective perceptions (Hoy & Miskel, 2001).

As we have suggested earlier, climate and culture both refer to the atmosphere of the school. Culture is a broader construct than climate, and exists at a higher level of abstraction than climate; indeed, climate can be considered a manifestation of culture. Culture refers to shared *beliefs* and climate refers to basic patterns of *behavior* that exist in organizations. Admittedly there is not a huge difference between shared assumptions, values, and norms and shared perceptions of behavior, but the distinction is a useful one. School climate is a little more manageable in some respects. For example, climate can be conceived and measured from a variety of perspectives, several of which are described and discussed in this chapter. Each provides the principal with a valuable set of conceptual capital to analyze, understand, and improve teaching and learning.

Organizational Climate: Open to Closed

Probably the most best-known conceptualization and measurement of the organizational climate of a school was developed by Andrew W. Halpin and Don B. Croft (1962) in their pioneering study of elementary schools. As they visited and observed schools they were struck by the dramatic differences they found in the "feel" of the schools. Halpin (1966) described the marked contrasts as follows:

> In one school the teachers and the principal are zestful and exude confidence in what they are doing. They find pleasure in working with each other; this pleasure is transmitted to students.... In a second school the brooding discontentment of teachers is palpable; the

principal tries to hide his incompetence and his lack of direction behind a cloak of authority.... And the psychological sickness of such a faculty spills over on the students who, in their own frustration, feed back to teacher a mood of despair. A third school is marked by neither joy nor despair, but by hollow ritual...in a strange way the show doesn't seem to be for real." (p. 131)

These stark differences in the feel of schools led Halpin and Croft (1962) to a systematic attempt to conceptualize and measure school climate. They viewed the climate of the school in terms of its personality, that is, just as individuals have personalities, schools have organizational climates. Two general sets of social behavior were mapped: principal–teacher interactions and teacher–teacher interactions. The principal's leadership can influence teacher behavior, but so can group behavior affect the principal's behavior; hence, the leadership of the principal, the nature of the teacher group, and their mutual interaction became the key components for identifying the social climate of schools. In all, eight dimensions of teacher–teacher and teacher–principal behavior were identified as Halpin and Croft (1962) developed an instrument to measure the organizational climate of elementary schools, the Organizational Climate Description Questionnaire (**OCDQ**).

A Revised OCDQ

The original OCDQ spawned hundreds of studies in the 1960s and 70s (Anderson, 1982). But times and conditions have changed dramatically since the first appearance of the OCDQ. Many of the items no longer measure what they were intended to measure; some of the subtests are no longer valid; the reliabilities of some of the subtests are low; and time has rendered many of the items irrelevant to contemporary school organizations (Hoy & Miskel, 2001). Consequently, it should come as no surprise that the OCDQ has been revised and updated for use in today's schools. The original OCDQ was designed for use only in elementary schools, but revised versions have been formulated and tested for elementary (Hoy & Clover, 1986), middle (Hoy & Sabo, 1998), and high schools (Hoy, Tarter, & Kottkamp, 1991). Regardless of level, the conceptual foundations of the instruments are similar; they are based upon the openness of professional interactions. Although we will describe only the revised Organizational Climate Description Questionnaire for elementary schools (OCDQ-RE), reliable versions for use in middle and high schools are available. All the climate instruments describe the behavior of principals as they interact with their teachers and the behavior of teachers as they interact with their colleagues.

Principal Behavior.   The first element of school climate is the principal's style of interacting with teachers. Three key aspects of principal–teacher interactions set the tone for life in schools—supportive, directive, and restrictive principal behavior.

- *Supportive* behavior reflects genuine concern for teachers. Principals respect the professional expertise of their teachers and treat them as colleagues. Assisting teachers, complimenting teachers, providing constructive criticism, and concern for their personal welfare are examples of supportive behavior.
- *Directive* behavior is starkly task-oriented with little attention to the personal needs of teachers. The principal's behavior is direct and controlling: teachers are closely

observed, criticized, and constrained. Communication is downward with little attention to feedback from teachers. In brief, directive principal behavior is autocratic, rigid, and controlling.

■ *Restrictive* behavior is burdensome. Principals overload teachers with unnecessary work—too many committees, too much paperwork, and too much busywork. The principal hinders rather than facilitates teachers' work.

Teachers' Behavior. The second key element of school climate is the teachers' behavior in school. Teachers do not react to the school organization as isolated individuals but as members of a teacher work group; they are part of the informal organization. As they work in school, they interact with other teachers and form ideas that have important consequences for their behavior. Three important dimensions of teacher interactions are postulated to have major influence on the climate of the school—collegial, intimate, and disengaged teacher behavior.

■ *Collegial* behavior is supportive professionalism among teachers. Teachers are pleased with their school; they accept and support each other and feel a sense of accomplishment in their teaching. Above all, teachers are professionals who respect the competence and dedication of their colleagues.

■ *Intimate* behavior is close personal relations among teachers both inside and outside the school. Teachers' closest friends are often teachers in their school; they talk and confide in each other.

■ *Disengaged* behavior is a general sense of alienation and separation among teachers in the school. There is little cohesiveness among teachers. They bicker with each other and ramble when they talk in meetings. Teachers are simply going through the motions; they are not productive in group efforts or team building.

These six features are the key elements for developing school climates. But specifically how are these dimensions of climate measured? How are the profiles determined? What do the profiles mean?

Interpreting the OCDQ-RE. All items are simple descriptive statements of interactions in schools. Teachers are asked to describe the extent to which each item characterizes his or her school. The responses to each item are made on a four-point scale: rarely occurs, sometimes occurs, often occurs, and very frequently occurs. Sample items for each of the dimensions of the OCDQ-RE are summarized in Table 8.1 and a copy of the instrument is found in the Appendix (p. 328).

Using factor-analytic techniques and a sample of 70 elementary schools, 44 items were identified that measured six dimensions of school climate (Hoy, Tarter, & Kottkamp, 1991). The six aspects, taken together, map a profile of the climate of each school. Scores for all subtests and schools were standardized so that the mean score was 500 and the standard deviation was 100. Then the scores are interpreted as one would SAT or GRE scores. A score of 500 is a school with average openness whereas one with a score of 600 is quite open—more than one standard deviation better than an average school. For example, the profiles of the climates for two hypothetical schools might be plotted as indicated in Figure 8.2. The school climate profiled with the gray line in the figure reflects an open

TABLE 8.1 Sample Items for Each Dimension of the OCDQ-RE

Principal Behavior	Teacher Behavior

Principal Behavior

Supportive Behavior
- The principal uses constructive criticism.
- The principal compliments teachers.
- The principal listens to and accepts teachers' suggestions.

Directive Behavior
- The principal monitors everything teachers do.
- The principal rules with an iron fist.
- The principal checks lesson plans.

Restrictive Behavior
- Teachers are burdened with busywork.
- Routine duties interfere with the job of teaching.
- Teachers have too many committee requirements.

Teacher Behavior

Collegial Behavior
- Teachers help and support each other.
- Teachers respect the professional competence of their colleagues.
- Teachers accomplish their work with vim, vigor, and pleasure.

Intimate Behavior
- Teacher socialize with each other.
- Teachers' closest friends are other faculty members at this school.
- Teachers have parties for each other.

Disengaged Behavior
- Faculty meetings are useless.
- There is a minority group of teachers who always oppose the majority.
- Teachers ramble when they talk at faculty meetings.

A copy of the entire instrument is found in the Appendix.

school climate with a supportive, nondirective, and nonrestrictive principal and a collegial, engaged, intimate faculty committed to the teaching–learning task. The other school, indicated by the black line, represents a closed school climate with a directive, restrictive, and nonsupportive principal and suspicious (noncollegial), disengaged, and distant teachers.

Elementary school climate rests on two general factors of openness (Hoy & Clover, 1986; Hoy & Tarter, 1997b). Specifically, openness in faculty relations is characterized by teacher interactions that are meaningful and tolerant (low disengagement); that are friendly, close, and supportive (high intimacy); and that are enthusiastic, accepting, and mutually respectful (high collegial relations). Openness in principal behavior is characterized by avoiding the assignment of meaningless routines and burdensome duties to teachers (low restrictiveness); by giving flexibility and freedom to teachers to act independently (low directiveness); and by giving teachers respect and support in both personal and professional matters (high supportiveness). In general, this factor depicts a functional flexibility and openness in the principals' leadership behavior.

The conceptual underpinnings of the OCDQ-RE are consistent and clear. The instrument has two general factors—one a measure of openness of teacher interactions and the other a measure of openness of teacher–principal relations. Organizational climate is a description of the perceptions of the faculty. Some may question whether a climate is open or closed just because the teachers perceive it to be. Whether or not it really is cannot be answered and is probably irrelevant. Teachers' perceptions of what is "out there" motivate their behavior.

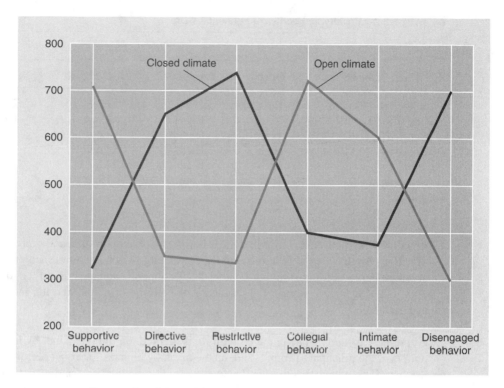

FIGURE 8.2   Contrasting School Climate Profile

Climate Types

These two openness factors are relatively independent. That is, it is quite possible to have open faculty interactions and closed principal ones or vice versa. Thus, theoretically, four contrasting types of school climate are possible. First, both factors can be open, producing a congruence between the principal's and teachers' behavior. Second, both factors can be closed, producing a congruence of closedness. Moreover, there are two incongruent patterns. The principal's behavior can be open with the faculty, but teachers may be closed with each other; or the principal may be closed with teachers, while the teachers are open with each other (see Figure 8.2 earlier). Table 8.2 provides a summary of the patterns of the four climate prototypes. Using this information, it is possible to sketch a behavioral picture of each climate.

Open Climate.   The distinctive features of the **open climate** are the cooperation and re- spect that exist within the faculty and between the faculty and principal. This combination suggests a climate in which the principal listens and is open to teacher suggestions, gives genuine and frequent praise, and respects the professional competence of the faculty (high supportiveness). Principals also give their teachers freedom to perform without close scru- tiny (low directiveness) and provide facilitating leadership behavior devoid of bureaucratic

TABLE 8.2   Prototypic Profiles of School Climate

Climate Dimension	Climate Type			
	Open	**Engaged**	**Disengaged**	**Closed**
Supportive	High	Low	High	Low
Directive	Low	High	Low	High
Restrictive	Low	High	Low	High
Collegial	High	High	Low	Low
Intimate	High	High	Low	Low
Disengaged	Low	Low	High	High

trivia (low restrictiveness). Similarly, teacher behavior supports open and professional interactions (high collegial relations) among the faculty. Teachers know each other well and are close personal friends (high intimacy). They cooperate and are committed to their work (low disengagement). In brief, the behavior of both the principal and the faculty is open and authentic.

Engaged Climate.   The **engaged climate** is marked, on the one hand, by ineffective attempts of the principal to control and, on the other, by high professional performance of the teachers. The principal is rigid and autocratic (high directiveness) and respects neither the professional competence nor the personal needs of the faculty (low supportiveness). Moreover, the principal hinders the teachers with burdensome activities and busywork (high restrictiveness). The teachers, however, ignore the principal's behavior and conduct themselves as professionals. They respect and support each other, are proud of their colleagues, and enjoy their work (highly collegial). Moreover, the teachers not only respect each other's competence but they like each other as people (high intimacy), and they cooperate with each other as they engage in the task at hand (high engagement). In short, the teachers are productive professionals in spite of weak principal leadership; the faculty is cohesive, committed, supportive, and open.

Disengaged Climate.   The **disengaged climate** stands in stark contrast to the engaged climate. The principal's behavior is open, concerned, and supportive. The principal listens and is open to teachers (high supportiveness), gives the faculty freedom to act on their professional knowledge (low directiveness), and relieves teachers of most of the burdens of paperwork and committee assignments (low restrictiveness). Nonetheless, the faculty is unwilling to accept the principal. At worst, the faculty actively works to immobilize and sabotage the principal's leadership attempts; at best, the faculty simply ignores the principal. Teachers not only do not like the principal but they neither like nor respect each other as friends (low intimacy) or as professionals (low collegial relations). The faculty is simply disengaged from the task. In sum, although the principal is supportive, concerned, flexible, facilitating, and noncontrolling (i.e., open), the faculty is divisive, intolerant, and uncommitted (i.e., closed).

Closed Climate.   The **closed climate** is virtually the antithesis of the open climate. The principal and teachers simply appear to go through the motions, with the principal stressing routine trivia and unnecessary busywork (high restrictiveness) and the teachers responding minimally and exhibiting little commitment (high disengagement). The principal's ineffective leadership is further seen as controlling and rigid (high directiveness) as well as unsympathetic, unconcerned, and unresponsive (low supportiveness). These misguided tactics are accompanied not only by frustration and apathy but also by a general suspicion and lack of respect of teachers for each other as either friends or professionals (low intimacy and noncollegial relations). Closed climates have principals who are nonsupportive, inflexible, hindering, and controlling and a faculty that is divisive, intolerant, apathetic, and uncommitted. These four school climate types are pictured in Figure 8.3.

The OCDQ: Some Implications

A basic assumption of our analysis of instructional leadership is that a school's organizational climate is closely related to its improvement practices. The collective perceptions of teachers about their work environment influence their motivations and behaviors in the classroom. An open climate, with its authentic interpersonal relations, seems likely to produce a situation where constructive change can succeed. The closed climate, on the other hand, presents an environment of hostility, suspicion, and inauthenticity where the improvement of instruction is doomed to failure. Improving teaching and learning simply will not work in a closed climate; in fact, in such schools it seems futile to attempt to improve the teaching-learning process. If the climate of a school is closed, the first task is to change it. Such change requires a cooperative effort between the teachers and principal; in fact, the principal's leadership is a key to improving the climate. Trust and openness are necessary conditions for effective school improvement.

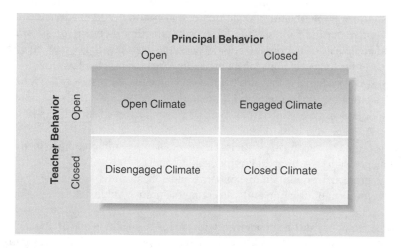

FIGURE 8.3   Typology of School Climates

Research on school climates consistently supports the conclusion that the school's openness and its emotional tone are related in predictable ways. Openness is associated with less student alienation, a lower student dropout rates, and more student satisfaction with schools (Hoy, 1972; Mullins, 1986, Finkelstein, 1998). Moreover, open schools are generally more effective than closed ones, and teachers are more involved in decision making (Hoy, Tarter, & Kottkamp, 1991; Hoy & Sabo, 1998). Openness and teacher commitment and teacher loyalty (Hoy, Tarter, & Kottkamp, 1991; Reiss & Hoy, 1998) are also positively associated.

Open organizational relations also have positive consequences in schools because they facilitate the process of improving instruction. No climate can guarantee effective teaching and learning because school climate in and of itself it cannot make a poor program good or a weak teacher strong, but an open school climate can provide the necessary atmosphere for reflection, cooperation, change, and improvement. There are three separate OCDQ measures for school climates—one for elementary schools (Hoy & Tarter, 1997b), another for middle schools (Hoy & Tarter, 1997b), and one for high schools (Hoy, Tarter, & Kottkamp, 1991, Hoy & Tarter, 1997a). There are no copyright restrictions for the use of any of instruments for research or school improvement; in fact, they are all available at www.coe.ohio-state.edu/whoy. Simply log on, download the instrument, and use it.

Organizational Climate: Healthy to Unhealthy

Another framework for defining and measuring the social climate of a school is the organizational health of a school. The idea of positive health in an organization is not new, and it calls attention to factors that facilitate growth and development as well as to conditions that impede positive organizational dynamics. It is likely that the state of health of a school can tell us much about the probable success of change initiatives.

Matthew Miles (1969) defines a healthy organization as one that survives and adequately copes over the long haul as it continuously develops and extends its surviving and coping abilities. Implicit in this definition is that healthy organizations deal successfully with disruptive outside forces while effectively directing their energies toward the major goals and objectives of the organization. Operations on a given day may be effective or ineffective, but the long-term prognosis in healthy organizations is favorable.

All social systems, if they are to grow and develop, must satisfy the four basic conditions of adaptation, goal attainment, integration, and latency (Parsons, Bales, & Shils, 1953). In other words, organizations must successfully solve four basic problems:

- The problem of acquiring sufficient resources and accommodating to their environments
- The problem of setting and implementing goals
- The problem of maintaining solidarity and cohesiveness within the system
- The problem of creating and preserving the unique values of the system

Thus, organizations must be concerned with the instrumental needs of goal achievement as well as the expressive and developmental needs of its participants. Healthy organizations meet both sets of needs. All formal organizations, including schools, exhibit three distinct levels of responsibility and control over these needs—the technical, managerial, and institutional levels.

The technical level produces the basic organizational product. In schools, the technical function is the teaching–learning process. Teachers and principals are professionals who are directly responsible for student learning. Educated students are the product of schools, and the entire technical function revolves around the problems associated with effective teaching and student learning.

The managerial level mediates and controls the internal efforts of the organization. The chief managerial function is the administrative process, a process that is qualitatively different from teaching. Principals are the prime administrative officers in schools. They must find ways to develop teacher loyalty and trust, motivate teacher effort, coordinate their work, and improve their instruction. The administration services the technical system in two important ways: first, it mediates between the teachers and students and parents; and second, it procures the necessary resources for effective teaching. Thus, teacher needs should be a basic concern of the administration.

The institutional level connects the organization with its environment. It is important for schools to have legitimacy and backing in the community. Principals and teachers need this support to perform their respective functions in a harmonious fashion without undue pressure and interference from individuals and groups outside the school.

This broad framework provides the integrative scheme for conceptualizing and measuring the **organizational health** of a school. Specifically, a healthy organization is one in which the technical, managerial, and institutional levels are in harmony; the organization meets its needs and successfully copes with disruptive outside forces as it directs its energies toward its mission.

Dimensions of Organizational Health

Seven specific aspects of organizational health are viewed as crucial dimensions of the interaction patterns of life in schools—institutional integrity, principal influence, consideration, initiating structure, resource support, morale, and academic emphasis. These critical components meet both the task and social needs of the social system, and they represent each of the three levels of responsibility and control within the school.

- **Institutional integrity** refers to the school's ability to adapt to its environment in a way that maintains the educational integrity of its programs. Teachers are protected from unreasonable community and parental demands. The school is not vulnerable to the whims of the public. Neither a few vocal parents nor select citizens' groups can affect the operation of the school when their demands are not consistent with the educational programs. The board of education and the administration are successful in enabling the school to cope with destructive outside forces.
- **Principal influence** refers to the principal's ability to affect the decisions of superiors. Being able to persuade superiors, get additional support, and not be impeded by the hierarchy are important facets of leadership. In fact, a key to effective leadership is the ability to influence superiors while at the same time not becoming overly dependent upon them.

- **Consideration** refers to the principal's leader behavior that is friendly and open. This aspect of behavior reflects behavior indicative of respect, mutual trust, colleagueship, and support. Consideration does not denote a superficial or calculative affability; it expresses a genuine concern for teachers as colleagues and professionals.
- **Initiating structure** refers to the principal's behavior in specifying the work relationships with teachers. The principal clearly defines the work expectations, the standards of performance, and the methods of procedure. The principal's behavior is task-oriented, and the work environment is structured and achievement-oriented. Like consideration, initiating structure is a major dimension of effective leadership performance.
- **Resource support** refers to providing teachers with the basic materials they need to do an outstanding teaching job. Instructional materials and supplies are readily available. If extra or supplementary materials are needed or requested, they are quickly supplied. In brief, teachers have access to the materials that they need.
- **Morale** refers to a collective sense of friendliness, openness, and trust within the faculty. The teachers form a cohesive unit that is enthusiastic about teaching. They like each other, they like their jobs, they help each other, and they are proud of their school.
- **Academic emphasis** refers to the extent to which the school is driven by a quest for academic excellence. High but attainable standards of academic performance are set, and an orderly, serious learning environment exists. The press for academic achievement is supported by administrators, teachers, and students alike. Teachers believe in their students, and students respond with vigor. Academic success is respected as a major accomplishment among students themselves. Good grades and scholarship earn praise and admiration from students as well as teachers.

These seven aspects of teacher and principal patterns of interaction form the framework for defining and measuring the organizational health of schools. The elements of the organizational health framework are summarized in Table 8.3.

TABLE 8.3   The Dimensions and Levels of Organizational Health Inventory

Institutional Level—School–Community Relations
- Institutional integrity

Managerial Level—Administrators
- Principal influence
- Consideration
- Initiating structure
- Resource support

Technical Level—Teachers
- Morale
- Academic emphasis

Organizational Health Inventory (OHI-S)

The Organizational Health Inventory is a descriptive questionnaire, not unlike the OCDQ, that measures these seven patterns of behavior. The **OHI** is administered to the professional staff of the school, and teachers are asked to describe the extent to which each item characterizes their school along a four-point scale: rarely occurs, sometimes occurs, often occurs, and very frequently occurs. Examples of the items of the health inventory for high schools (OHI-S), grouped by subtest, are listed in Table 8.4.

The OHI-S is a valid and the reliable instrument to measure the organizational health of secondary schools (Hoy, Tarter, & Kottkamp, 1991). To facilitate the interpretation of school health, school scores are standardized so the mean score is 500 and the standard deviation was 100. Then the scores are interpreted as one would SAT or GRE scores. A climate

---

TABLE 8.4 Sample Items for Each Dimension of the OHI

Institutional Level (School)
Institutional Integrity
- Teachers are protected from unreasonable community and parental demands.
- The school is open to the whims of the public.*

Managerial Level (Administration)
Principal Influence
- The principal is able to influence the actions of his or her superiors.
- The principal is impeded by superiors.*

Consideration
- The principal is friendly and approachable.
- The principal looks out for the personal welfare of faculty members.

Initiating Structure
- The principal lets faculty members know what is expected of them.
- The principal maintains definite standards of performance.

Resource Support
- Teachers receive necessary classroom supplies.
- Supplementary materials are available for classroom use.

Technical Level (Teachers)
Morale
- There is a feeling of trust and confidence among the staff.
- Teachers in this school are cool and aloof to each other.*

Academic Emphasis
- The learning environment is orderly and serious.
- This school set high standards for academic performance.

A copy of the entire instrument is found in the Appendix.
*These items are scored in reverse.

score of 500 is a school with average health while one with a score of 610 is quite healthy—more than one standard deviation better than an average school. Profiles for three schools are graphed in Figure 8.4. School A represents a school with a healthy climate—all dimensions of health are substantially above the mean; School C, in contrast, is below the mean in all aspects of health; and School B is a typical school—about average on all dimensions.

The subtests of the OHI-S are modestly correlated with each other; that is, if a school scores high on one subtest, there is some tendency to score higher on some of the other subtests. Furthermore, factor analysis of the subtests demonstrated that one general factor explained most of the variation among the subtests—a factor we called school health. High schools array themselves along a continuum with a few schools having profiles of very healthy organizations, a few having very unhealthy profiles, and most schools having somewhat mixed profiles in between the extremes. An index of health can be developed by simply adding the standard scores of the seven subtests; the higher the sum, the healthier the school dynamics.

We sketch below a behavioral picture for each of the poles of the continuum—that is, the prototypes for very healthy and unhealthy school climates.

Healthy School Climate.   Where there is a **healthy school climate,** the school is protected from unreasonable community and parental pressures. The board successfully resists

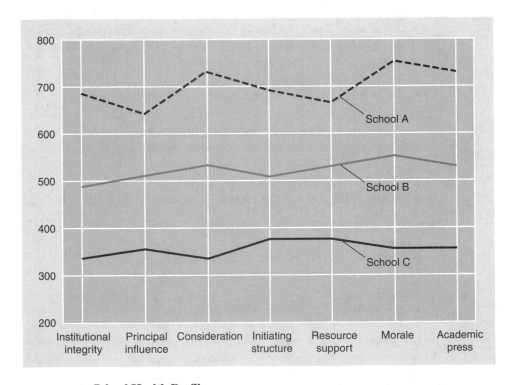

FIGURE 8.4   School Health Profiles

all narrow efforts of vested interest groups to influence policy. The principal of a healthy school provides dynamic leadership, leadership that is both task-oriented and relations-oriented. Such behavior is supportive of teachers and yet provides direction and maintains high standards of performance. Moreover, the principal has influence with his or her superiors as well as the ability to exercise independent thought and action. Teachers in a healthy school are committed to teaching and learning. They set high but achievable goals for students; they maintain high standards of performance; and the learning environment is orderly and serious. Furthermore, students work hard on academic matters, are highly motivated, and respect other students who achieve academically. Classroom supplies and instructional materials are accessible if needed. Finally, in a healthy school, teachers like each other, trust each other, are enthusiastic about their work, and identify positively with the school. They are proud of their school.

Unhealthy School Climate. When there is an unhealthy school climate, the school is vulnerable to destructive outside forces. Teachers and administrators are bombarded by unreasonable demands from parental and community groups. The school is buffeted by the whims of the public. The principal does not demonstrate leadership; that is, the principal provides little direction or structure, exhibits limited consideration and support for teachers, and has virtually no ability to influence the action of superiors. Morale of teachers is low. Teachers feel good neither about each other nor about their jobs. They act aloof, suspicious, and defensive. Finally, there is little press for academic excellence. Neither students nor teachers believe that academic matters are serious and important. Indeed, academically oriented students are ridiculed by their peers and are viewed as threats by their teachers.

The OHI: Some Implications

The OHI is a useful tool for several reasons. First, it reliably measures seven key dimensions of the organizational health of schools. Second, the conceptual underpinnings of the OHI are consistent with setting an atmosphere for improving teaching and learning. Third, a healthy school climate facilitates student achievement in schools (Hoy & Hannum, 1997; Hoy & Sabo, 1998).

Research findings using the OHI are encouraging. As one would expect, the healthier the organizational dynamics, the greater the degree of faculty trust in the principal, trust in colleagues, and trust in the organization itself. Not surprisingly, too, there is a strong correlation between the openness and health of schools; open schools are healthy schools and healthy schools are open ones (Hoy, Tarter, & Kottkamp, 1991, Hoy & Sabo, 1998). The research also strongly supports the importance of the organizational health as a pivotal aspect of school life. In general, school health is positively associated with student achievement, school quality, overall school effectiveness, teacher participation, effective leadership, and a strong culture (Hoy, Tarter, & Kottkamp, 1991, Hoy & Sabo, 1998).

Healthy organizational dynamics also have positive consequences because they facilitate teaching and learning. Although such an environment cannot guarantee high achievement, it does provide an atmosphere conducive to improvement of instruction. Moreover, the characteristics of healthy schools have many of the attributes stressed in the effective-school literature: an orderly and serious environment; high but attainable goals;

visible rewards for academic achievement; principals who are dynamic leaders, and a cohesive unit based on mutual trust.

In sum, organizational health is another functional framework for analyzing important aspects of the character of life in schools. The OHI is a practical tool for assessing the health of a school. Like openness in school climate, healthy organizational dynamics are necessary conditions for an effective program of improvement. The principal must first have a positive climate; if it is lacking, it must be developed. Although we have described the OHI for high schools (see Appendix, p. 335), there are versions of the instruments for elementary and middle schools (Hoy & Tarter, 1997b). There are no copyright restrictions for use of any of the instruments for research or school improvement; in fact, they are available at www.coe.ohio-state.edu/whoy. Simply log on, download the instrument, copy it, and use it.

Collective Efficacy

Another way of looking at the school context for learning is through the lens of collective efficacy of the school. **Collective efficacy** is the shared perception of teachers in a school that the efforts of the faculty as a whole will have a positive effect on student learning. Collective efficacy is an important school property (Bandura 1993, 1997). Just as teacher efficacy partially explains the effect of teachers on student achievement at the individual level, collective efficacy helps explain the differential effect that schools have on student achievement. Bandura (1997) observes that because schools present teachers with a host of unique challenges involving such things as public accountability, shared responsibility for student outcomes, and minimal control over work environments, the task of developing high levels of collective efficacy is difficult but possible. The rest of this section draws heavily on Goddard, Hoy, & Woolfolk Hoy (2000) and on Hoy & Miskel (2001).

At the collective level, efficacy beliefs are social perceptions, which are strengthened rather than depleted through their use. To the extent that collective efficacy is positively associated with student achievement, there is strong reason to lead schools in a direction that will systematically develop teacher efficacy; such efforts may indeed be rewarded with continuous growth in not only collective teacher efficacy but also student achievement (Goddard, Hoy, & Woolfolk Hoy, 2000).

Organizations, like people, learn (Cohen & Sproull, 1996); in fact, organizations use processes similar to learning in individuals (Cook & Yanon, 1996). Schools act purposefully in pursuit of their educational goals. For example, one school may be working to raise student achievement scores whereas another is trying to increase parental involvement. Organizational functioning depends on the knowledge, vicarious learning, self-reflection, and self-regulation of individual members. For example, a school that responds to falling achievement scores by implementing a curricular reform that was effective in another district is engaged in a self-regulatory process that is informed by the vicarious learning of its members. Such examples demonstrate the importance of vicarious learning and self-regulation at the school level, even though we must remember that organizations act through individuals. Four primary sources of self-efficacy information are mastery experience, vicarious experience, social persuasion, and emotional arousal (Bandura, 1997). Just as these sources are critical for individuals, they are also basic in the development of collective efficacy.

- *Mastery experiences* are important for organizations. Teachers as a group experience successes and failures. Successes enhance strong beliefs in the faculty's sense of collective efficacy, while failures erode it. If success, however, is frequent and easy, failure is likely to produce discouragement. A resilient sense of collective efficacy requires overcoming difficulties through persistent effort. Organizations learn by experience whether they are likely to succeed in attaining their goals (Huber, 1996; Levitt & March, 1996).

- *Vicarious experience* is also important for schools. Direct experience is not the only source of information for a faculty about its collective efficacy. Teachers listen to stories about the accomplishment of their colleagues and success stories of other schools. Further, the effective-schools research describes characteristics of exemplary schools. So just as vicarious experience and modeling serve as effective sources of personal teacher efficacy, so too do they promote a sense of collective efficacy. Organizations learn by observing other organizations (Huber, 1996).

- *Verbal persuasion* is another means of strengthening the faculty's conviction that it has the capability to achieve what it seeks. Teachers can be changed by talks, workshops, professional development, and feedback about achievement. In fact, the more cohesive the faculty, the more likely the group as a whole will be persuaded by sound argument. Although verbal persuasion alone is a powerful change agent, when it is coupled with models of success and positive direct experience, it can greatly influence the sense of collective efficacy. Persuasion can promote extra effort and persistence, both of which can lead to the solution of problems and thus to mastery experiences.

- Organizations have *affective states.* Just as individuals react to stress, so do organizations. Efficacious organizations tolerate pressure and crises and continue to function effectively. Such organizations learn how to adapt and cope with disruptive forces. Less efficacious organizations, when confronted by such problems, often react in dysfunctional ways that reinforce their basic dispositions of failure by misinterpreting stimuli—sometimes overreacting, at other times underreacting, and at still other times not reacting at all. The affective state of an organization has much to do with how challenges are interpreted by the organizations.

Although all four of these sources of information are significant in the creation of collective teacher efficacy, it is the processing and interpretation of the information that is critical. Two key elements in the development of collective efficacy are the *analysis of the teaching task* and the *assessment of teaching competence.*

Teachers assess what will be required as they engage in teaching—the analysis of the teaching task. The assessment occurs at two levels—the individual and the school. At the school level, inferences about the challenges of teaching in that school are made, that is, what it would take for the school to be successful. Teachers consider the abilities and motivations of students, availability of instructional materials, community constraints, the quality of physical facilities, and a general optimism about the capability of the school to deal with negative factors both in the students' home and in the school. Teachers analyze what the school needs to be successful, the barriers that need to be overcome, and available resources.

Teachers analyze the teaching task in conjunction with their assessment of the teaching competency of the faculty. That is, they make explicit judgments of the teaching competence of their colleagues in light of an analysis of the teaching task in their specific school. At the school level, the analysis of the general teaching competence of the faculty leads to inferences about the faculty's teaching skills, methods, training, and expertise. Judgments of teaching competence might include faculty beliefs in the ability of all children in their school to succeed. Because the analyses of task and competence occur simultaneously, it is difficult to separate these two domains of collective efficacy, but as they interact with each other collective efficacy in the school develops.

There is emerging support for the impact of collective efficacy on student achievement. In this seminal study of collective teacher efficacy and student achievement, Bandura (1993) uncovered two important findings: (a) student achievement (aggregated to the school level) was significantly and positively related to collective efficacy, and (b) collective efficacy had a greater effect on student achievement than did student socioeconomic status (aggregated to the school level). Roger Goddard and colleagues (Goddard, Hoy, & Woolfolk Hoy, 2000; Goddard, Sweetland, & Hoy, 2000) also found strong support for the model and again confirmed the significance of collective teacher efficacy in facilitating high student achievement.

In sum, the major influences on collective teacher efficacy are assumed to be the analysis and interpretation of the four sources of information—mastery experience, vicarious experience, social persuasion, and affective state. In these processes, the organization focuses its attention on two related domains: the teaching task and teaching competence. Both domains are assessed in terms of whether the organization has the capacities to succeed in teaching students. The interactions of these assessments lead to the shaping of collective teacher efficacy in a school. The consequences of high collective teacher efficacy will be the acceptance of challenging goals, strong organizational effort, and a persistence that leads to better performance. Of course, the opposite is also true. Lower collective efficacy leads to less effort, the propensity to give up, and a lower level of performance. The process and components of collective teacher efficacy, similar to those of teacher efficacy (Tschannen-Moran, Woolfolk Hoy, & Hoy, 1998), are shown in Figure 8.5: the proficiency of performance provides feedback to the organization, which provides new information that will further shape the collective teacher efficacy of the school. Beliefs about both the task of teaching and the teaching competence, however, are likely to remain unchanged unless something dramatic occurs; hence, once established, the collective efficacy of a school is a relatively stable property that requires substantial effort to change.

You can determine the collective efficacy of your school by using the Collective Efficacy Scale (CE-Scale) found in the Appendix (p. 332). Strategies for improving the collective efficacy of your schools are linked to the model found in Figure 8.5. The first key is to provide direct experiences through which teachers succeed in improving student performance because success enhances strong beliefs in the faculty's sense of collective efficacy, while failures erode it. It is also useful to provide actual examples of schools and school programs that are highly effective. Verbal persuasion is likely to be successful if the teachers and the principal work together on in-service activities specifically designed to improve

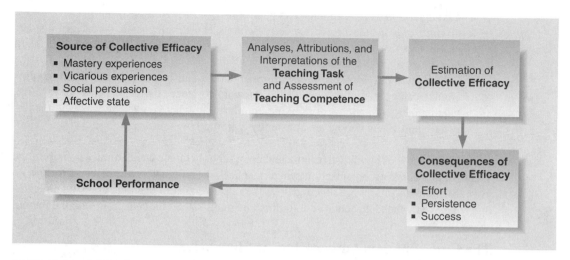

FIGURE 8.5   A Model of Collective Efficacy

student learning. Finally, building an open and healthy school climate, one in which teachers are not threatened by mistakes but view them as learning opportunities, creates an affective state for the school that is functional to improving teaching and learning.

Changing School Climate

We have described several frameworks for examining school context. It should be clear that improvement of instruction is most likely in school climates that are open in interactions and healthy in organizational dynamics and where there is strong collective efficacy. Moreover, we have offered a set of instruments that enables teachers and principals to assess the organizational climate of their schools. What happens when the climates are closed, unhealthy, or inefficacious? Embarking immediately on a program of improvement of instruction with teachers working cooperatively with principals is difficult and usually counterproductive. Indeed, it seems futile for principals and teachers to attempt any authentic plan to improve instruction that involves cooperation, trust, and respect in such climates. At best, such attempts will be meaningless rituals, and at worst, they provide opportunities for the administration and teachers to punish and blame each other. If the school setting is inappropriate, changing *it* is the first business of the day.

Some Assumptions about Change in Schools

Before we proceed any further, we think it is useful to examine some basic assumptions about organizations and change to which we subscribe (Hoy & Tarter, 1997a).

- *Change is a characteristic of all organizations.* Organizations are in a constant state of flux. Change can be random or a resource harnessed for improvement, but it cannot be eliminated.

- *Change has direction.* Change can be progressive or regressive or aimless.
- *Organizational learning is possible.* Schools can develop their own learning processes to solve their problems. Principals and teachers have the potential to learn how to solve problems together.
- *Schools can be learning organizations.* Schools can become places where professionals can continually expand their capacity to create the results that they desire, where emergent patterns of thinking are nurtured, where collective aspiration is liberated, and where people are constantly learning how to learn (Senge, 1990).

The process of building a healthy and open school climate can naturally transform the school into a learning organization where teacher professionals continually learn how to learn. Such organizations are functional for the improvement of teaching and student learning. We have included an actual case to illustrate one strategy for changing school climate.

The Case of Martin Luther King, Jr. High School: An Example

Martin Luther King, Jr. High School is on an old campus in an urban community in the northeast on the corridor between New York City and Philadelphia. It is the only high school in Urban Park and enrolls a little over 1200 students. Other potential students in the town are enrolled in Orthodox Jewish schools, and there is a large Catholic population that sends many of its children to St. Polycarp High School. While the school has it supporters in the town, it doesn't lack detractors. Urban Park is an ethnically rich small city of 45,000. The African American population has remained a stable population of about a quarter of the district. About 14% of the population is newly-arrived Russians and Indians, and another 8% or so are Hispanic. A unique aspect of this urban community is its proximity to a major public university; consequently, about 20% of the students in the school are children of faculty, graduate students, and staff. By and large, however, this is a working class community with great diversity and financially pressed to support it schools.

Elbert Gibbs is a dynamic and youthful administrator. People meeting him are struck by his physical fitness; he jogs daily on the high school track, usually with student athletes after school. Gibbs was a former high school football player who earned athletic scholarships through college. After college he became a successful high school teacher for several years before returning to the state university to pursue his master's degree in educational administration. He earned his principalship by dint of hard work as an assistant principal for three years in a nearby urban center. Elbert is on the fast track. In his course work at the university, Gibbs found the literature on school climate, culture, and change intriguing. He decided to do a systematic analysis of his high school.

Let's take a look at King High. First, we examine the climate profiles as described by Gibbs. In other words, the following profile is the way Gibbs and his teachers responded to the OHI and the OCDQ-RS. He sought to maintain his objectivity in filling out the forms. Gibbs also had his teachers answer the same instruments at a faculty meeting. He took pains to get a frank response from the teachers by absenting himself from the meeting and insisting that teachers provide candid responses to the anonymous questionnaires. They rather enjoyed the activity. A comparison of the climate profiles as perceived by the teachers and Gibbs found is summarized below:

	Principal	**Faculty**
Institutional Integrity	540	420
Initiating Structure	560	555
Consideration	540	505
Principal Influence	510	465
Resources Allocation	500	445
Academic Emphasis	530	455
Morale	520	480
Overall Health	529	485
Supportive	555	490
Directive	480	540
Engaged	510	515
Frustrated	465	542
Overall Openness	533	481

A Problem

A quick glance at the profiles signals discrepancy. Gibbs describes a much healthier and open school climate than his teachers. Who is right? It doesn't matter; the problem is the discrepancy in views. Gibbs see his behavior as much more positive and open than his teachers do. For example, on every dimension of health he describes the school higher than the teachers. Similarly, on every OCDQ measure, he describes the school as more open than his teachers. Starkly, the difference between Gibbs and the faculty is that he sees an above average climate and they see one below average. What's happening?

Identifying and solving a problem call for different strategies. Gibbs has used climate instruments to identify the problem. That's the easy part. What to do and how to change the organization are other matters. Gibbs has to discover the root of the discrepancy: that is, why the teachers describe his behavior as more directive and less supportive than he thinks it is. There are only two aspects of school climate on which Gibbs and his faculty agree. Both judge the teachers to be slightly above average in their engagement, and both agree that the principal initiates structure and action to solve problems. But after that, there is not much agreement. Why does the faculty perceive most interactions in the school as much less positive than Gibbs? For example, why is it that the faculty doesn't see the supportive leadership that Gibbs is trying to model? Why does the faculty describe the climate as basically unhealthy when Gibbs sees it as healthy? Does Gibbs suffer from unrealistic optimism? The principal cannot solve this problem alone because it is an inter-action issue. It may be a question of misperception. But who is misperceiving?

An Organizational Development Model

What is a good strategy for developing healthy and open learning organizations? One po-tentially useful way to change school climate is a collaborative effort on the part of all those concerned, often called an **organizational development model.** This approach ad-dresses both individual and organizational needs, and is a planned effort to make both the individual and institution more productive (Hanson & Lubin, 1995). The approach is useful for principals who want to improve the climate of their school. In order to be suc-cessful, this strategy requires that administrators and teachers recognize difficulties, take responsibility for their solution, and develop and implement actions plans. In the case at hand, the objective is to have teachers and the principal recognize that a challenge exists. Identifying a problem—discrepancies between the principal's and the teachers' perception of the social interactions in the workplace—was made possible by using the climate instru-ments described earlier in this chapter.

Before proceeding further, we outline and begin to apply the steps in an organiza-tional development approach (Hoy & Tarter, 1997a):

1. *Identify the problem*—discrepancies in the climate profiles.
2. *Establish a problem-solving team*—usually the teachers in the school. To change cli-mate, teachers must be involved.
3. *The team takes on the problem*—the teachers and principal come to an understanding of the difficulty. Teachers examine the data with the principal and express a willing-ness to resolve the troubling issues. They must understand the situation and see the need for change.
4. *Diagnosis of the problem*—the team diagnoses the causes of the problem.
5. *Develop an action plan*—the team develops an action plan by examining alterna-tives, consequences, and then selecting a course of action.
6. *Implement action plan*—put the plan into action.
7. *Evaluate*—assess the consequences of the plan by collecting new data and evaluat-ing discrepancies.

Back to Martin Luther King, Jr. High School

Principal Elbert Gibbs was startled by the school climate data. The teachers view the school as much more negative than he does. This discrepancy in perceptions defines the problem, which Gibbs has identified. Now, he needs to join forces with his teachers and in-volve them in organizational problem solving. Does this mean that he should involve all the teachers in the school? Perhaps. But especially those who want to be part of the process and have something to say should be involved. Over the long run, the goal is to routinely have all teachers participate in decision making and organizational problem solving; that is, to create a learning organization. Over the short run, however, the problem is to put to-gether a team to begin the process.

One way to get interested teachers involved is to use an in-service workshop. Most schools have a day or two throughout the year for such activities, and Martin Luther King, Jr. High School (MLKHS) is no exception.

First, teachers need to understand the ideas of health and openness and how they are measured. In a faculty this large, the information can be presented efficiently at the workshop with accompanying overheads and handouts to simplify the explanation. Our own experience is that teachers are very receptive to the climate ideas, especially because data about their school are available; the results of the OCDQ and the OHI are intriguing. An explanation of school climate and its measures can be done in a half day. That is, by the end of the morning of an in-service day, teachers should be able interpret overheads of profiles of school climates.

Next, teachers are ready to look at the profile of their own school as they have described it. In this school the teachers' score for general health is 485 (below average) and school openness is 481 (below average). From the teachers' vantage point, this is an unhealthy school and its climate is closed. There are major discrepancies between the teachers and principal on institutional integrity (420 | 540), on principal's influence (465 | 510), on resource support (445 | 500), on academic emphasis (455 | 530), on supportiveness (490 | 555), and on directiveness (540 | 480). These are major differences in views. What's happening here? Both the teachers and principal need to know.

The principal must discover why the teachers saw his behavior as less supportive and more directive than he did. Gibbs admitted to the faculty that he was puzzled by the results because he thought his relationship with the faculty was better than the teacher data suggested. Although he was perplexed, he was willing to examine his own values and choices in this open forum. This is not to say he was comfortable in doing so. Most principals are not and he was no exception, but he felt he needed to continue what he started—an analysis of the school climate. There was no turning back. He believed that he needed to have an open mind toward his own as well as to his faculty's behavior. He knew there were risks, but he wanted a platform of openness and trust to build a more effective school—one in which the improvement of instruction was a primary goal.

Actually, the problem-solving process seemed daunting. There were, after all, almost 60 professionals on the faculty and the faculty had judged the school climate to be deficient. The thing that bothered Gibbs more than anything else was the low academic emphasis that the teachers believed existed in the school. While troubled by the teacher frustration and his reported directive leadership, the lack of academic emphasis hurt his professional pride. He wanted this school to be an important sequence in the education of all students, but minorities especially. Gibbs and the teachers must seek explanations and avoid blaming or scapegoating. Was the problem real or imagined? Of course it was real, and the teachers recognized it.

At the next faculty meeting, Gibbs and his teachers had an open conversation about the causes of the discrepancies. With overheads and charts at his disposal, Gibbs took 20 minutes to review the health profiles of MKLHS and then opened the meeting for discussion. Let's listen in:

GIBBS: I was surprised that you believe that parents are too obtrusive and there is too much community pressure. I don't just let people wander the halls, but I do want a lot of parental involvement in the school. I think it helps us to do our work.

FACULTY MEMBER: I have spent a considerable part of my adult life learning the skills of teaching. I appreciate help, but generally parents interfere; they don't help, they get in the way.

GIBBS: What do you mean? Give me an example.

FACULTY MEMBER: I have a master's in history from the university and I have taught history for fourteen years. I am interested in teaching students how to evaluate evidence, how to think. Parents want me to talk about the unique contributions of their group. Do you think the Multicultural Fair idea was our idea?

GIBBS: Well, I think multiculturalism is a good idea. After all, we have a multicultural school.

FACULTY MEMBER: We know that! But, it's outside interference we resent. We think we should control those kinds of decisions, not outsiders. That's why our scores on institutional integrity differ from yours.

GIBBS: What do you think I can do? Parents have a right to come into the school.

FACULTY MEMBER: Of course they have a right to come in. But they are not here to write curriculum.

(Long period of silence)

GIBBS: Well, well…we need to talk about this some more. I am beginning to understand why we responded to the items on institutional integrity differently. That's useful. But what really surprised me, and I don't understand, was our wholly different views of my leadership. I think of myself as being a lot more supportive and more open than you give me credit for.

(Long period of silence)

FACULTY MEMBER: Well, we do think of you as supportive, but we get too many directives. You are always dropping in on our classes unannounced. You are always telling us what to do like we are students not teachers. It's just too much.

GIBBS: Give me an example.

FACULTY MEMBER: We need more freedom to make the decisions that we need to make. You're an old history teacher, and I am a veteran English teacher. Why do you think you know more about teaching composition than I do?

GIBBS: I never said I did.

FACULTY MEMBER: Maybe, but you sure act like it. Here's what I mean: I am struggling in class with one of the slower students trying to teach him the skills of writing simple sentences, and I am making progress. And, you suggest that I should give the students more freedom to develop their ideas. That's not a bad idea in itself. But, you just don't understand what's happening in the class. To be candid, I sometimes find your supervision obtrusive and irritating.

GIBBS: We need to talk about this later.

ANOTHER FACULTY MEMBER: I agree with Wally. You need to treat us more as colleagues and less as employees. We like you and you work hard. But so do we. You don't see us equals. We feel like hired help.

GIBBS: I don't want to hurt your feelings, but when things go wrong, I take the heat. I am sorry you feel as you do, but I do respect you.

FACULTY MEMBER: You asked for some examples, and you got them. What are you going to do?

GIBBS: Well, I'll have to think about this. I asked for your interpretations, you have given them—but frankly, it's hard for me not to be defensive. We have some work to do.

This little exchange should give you a flavor of the kind of conversation that may occur. A close analysis of the conversation shows that the principal himself sees a difference in his status and he indirectly communicates it ("I'm the one accountable"). Teachers are seeking more autonomy and some teachers feel the principal doesn't respect their abilities. In other parts of the dialogue, it also became obvious that teachers felt that occasionally Gibbs's observations of their performance were critical but neither insightful nor constructive. These were some of the reasons for the discrepancies between Gibbs's perception of his leadership style and the faculty's perceptions.

At this point, Gibbs needs a plan of action. Sixty professionals in a faculty meeting just is not the right format to get at the root causes of the discrepancies. Gibbs decided to ask for volunteers to work on the problems surfaced by the climate analysis. Between volunteers (and all were included) and appointees the principal put together a task force of 12 veteran teachers who were willing to work to improve the climate of the school. After the task force was appointed, Gibbs went to the superintendent and requested a modest stipend for the teachers. Gibbs argued that use of the climate measures served two important purposes. First, it got the faculty to engage in organizational problem solving, and second it provided a useful vehicle for administrative assessment. The superintendent agreed to support Gibbs's foray into school improvement and organizational problem solving. To that end, she underwrote the cost for three Saturday-morning work sessions.

What are the causes of the discrepancies? The first Saturday, the principal and teachers decided to develop a series of rival explanations for the differences in perceptions. The teachers had to be willing to take some risks in articulating their position without fear of reprisal. The teachers were divided into three groups and each developed an explanation of what was happening. The principal and his assistant were not part of any group. But nonetheless, Gibbs and his assistant also developed a tentative explanation of the data. After a couple of hours, the group as a whole reassembled and the four explanations were presented and compared. After comparing the explanations, the faculty agreed to devote the next session trying to reconcile differences.

The next session opened with a brief recapitulation of the teachers' perspective on the climate data. The teachers saw the parents as having entirely too much access to the school; ultimately, they claimed that the parents interfered rather than helped. The faculty didn't mind parent participation in education, but they expected the principal to be a better gatekeeper. Parents were going directly to the teachers with their concerns and demands.

There was agreement that Gibbs needed to serve as a buffer between community groups and the teachers. Growing out of conversations of the kind that we have just heard, the teachers suggested that if Gibbs were less directive, they would be less frustrated. The teachers saw themselves being drafted for too many activities. In fact, many were suspicious of his latest climate venture; they saw it as just another drain on their time that would be fruitless. A number of teachers also offered that busywork, such as written, formal lesson plans that go unreviewed, be eliminated. They suggested a committee on paperwork whose charge was to reduce paperwork wherever feasible. For his part, Gibbs still did not agree with the explanation of his faculty, but he respected the faculty's judgment and agreed that something needed to be done and he would do it.

Although Gibbs believed he had adequate support from central, the teachers complained that he had little influence in getting them the things that they needed to improve their work. Making copies was always a problem; it took a long time to get class sets of materials; supplementary materials were simply not forthcoming. Gibbs saw it differently. He almost always got what he requested from the superintendent, as long as it was within reason. He believed that she respected his opinions and efforts. Gibbs was not sure the teachers understood the limited resources of the district; this was not a wealthy suburban district.

The teachers agreed that academic emphasis at MLKHS was below average. They saw little respect among students for academics. Football was king closely followed by indifference. The teachers felt they were only being realistic in lowering their expectations of student performance. In fact, a good many teachers believed that most students simply couldn't do the work. They had difficulty getting students to do homework, not to mention classroom discipline problems. Gibbs, however, was unaware that for at least half the teachers, student homework and apathy were problems. Gibbs was probably misled by the orderly appearances of the halls and the good relations he had with students. It was not that Gibbs thought MKLHS was an academic powerhouse. Clearly, it was not. But, he believed that compared to other urban high schools, his was above average.

On the measures of both directive and frustrated behavior of the principal, there were sharp discrepancies between Gibbs and the faculty. By and large, the teachers believed that his observations of their classroom teaching were intrusive and authoritarian. He didn't visit the classrooms often, but when he did, he always had many directives for improvement. The teachers resented the style if not the substance of his comments. The teachers resented the formal sign-in and sign-out required of all teachers. The teachers resented the extreme formalization in the school—forms for parking, for library materials, for audiovisual equipment, about grade distribution, and more: repetitive absentee forms, lateness forms, lunch forms, and a form for virtually anything out of the ordinary was required. Teachers believed the forms for the most part unnecessary. Gibbs saw the forms as a necessary way to monitor things.

If nothing else, the teachers and Gibbs were now communicating openly with each other and explaining their positions. Gibbs was interested but he was unconvinced on many issues. The teachers, for their part, enjoyed letting Gibbs know how they felt. They believed that he was interested in them and the school and eventually would come around. At least he was open and not too defensive.

How do we develop constructive plans for reducing discrepancies and improving climate? This is the time for the teachers and the principal to work together to forge a realistic plan. There is no one best way to do this, but in the current case the principal and teachers decided to each work on the plan independently and then come back together (much in the same manner as they had framed the causes of the problem) to propose a school improvement plan.

The faculty task force met on yet another Saturday morning to discuss and formulate an improvement plan. In response to the analysis of problem causes, the principal offered the following:

1. Gibbs suggested that the teachers report all instances of parental interference to his office. Gibbs would monitor the reports and try to buffer the teachers from the parents.
2. Gibbs was genuinely concerned about the appearance of a heavy-handedness in his administration, and he proposed two immediate actions. He would review the amount of paperwork and reduce it dramatically, if possible. He respected his faculty and conceded that they should have more independence in decision making. In fact, he proposed that a leadership cabinet be formed composed of all the department chairs and administrators to share in decision making in the school.
3. Gibbs was still perplexed by the faculty's low student expectation; he rationalized that if it was as bad as his teachers said, the school needed some strong direct leadership. Here was his dilemma: How could he work with teachers to improve the academic climate and simultaneously remain indirect? He turned to his teachers for advice in this matter.
4. Gibbs promised that he would make himself more readily available to the faculty. He also pledged that in the future, his criticism would be constructive and helpful. He concluded by reaffirming confidence and admiration for his faculty and pointed out the one area in which there was virtual agreement was the commitment of the teachers to the school.
5. Finally, Gibbs was concerned about the academic seriousness of the school. This was a good school in a community that supported education. He was shocked to find his teachers did not share his perception of the academic climate. He vowed to address the issue on a number of fronts. First, a series of meetings with his faculty were necessary to discover the origin of the faculty's mediocre assessment of the academic emphasis at MLK.

The faculty for its part came in with the following set of recommendations:

1. The teachers proposed that Gibbs become involved as a liaison between teachers and parents. They recommended that department chairs together with Gibbs and the executive committee of the PTA meet regularly to address and mollify parental concerns.
2. The teachers proposed a system of peer coaching to improve the teaching–learning process. They also asked that they be given more input into future in-service meetings. They wanted teachers to be more directly involved, and administrators less, in improving instruction. After all, they reasoned, their job was teaching, and the principal's job was administration.
3. Because MLKJHS was not a large school, the faculty asked for more informal consultation. They didn't want more meetings, just more influence and information.

4. The teachers recommended that a committee of teachers be appointed to streamline the bureaucratic procedures—eliminate forms.
5. The teachers recommended that a schoolwide policy be established on homework and tutorials. The honor society would be approached and asked to do volunteer tutoring a few afternoons a week.
6. Finally, the faculty commended the principal for his concern and action in trying to improve the school workplace.

After the suggestions and recommendations were enumerated and discussed, Gibbs and the faculty were concerned about the number of different issues that surfaced and the time needed to confront them. Gibbs for his part admitted that he was unrealistically optimistic and the whole exercise provided him with a reality check. The teachers, on the other hand, were a little afraid that if they tried to do too much, nothing would be accomplished. They needed a reasonable plan that was realistic and attainable. There was, however, an inherent dilemma in their suggestions: they wanted greater involvement and more interaction but fewer meetings and less administrative work. They agreed to be idealistic and yet pragmatic. The following aspects were key elements of their eventual plan:

1. A committee of teachers would work with the principal to find ways to reduce administrative trivia and paperwork.
2. Gibbs and the teachers agreed that department chairs, the executive committee of the PTA, and Gibbs would meet regularly to address community concerns.
3. Gibbs agreed with the teachers that a system of peer coaching should be initiated. Teachers agreed to combine classes on occasion so that they could serve as teaching models and coaches for each other. Department chairs would work out the details. Gibbs turned over the next three professional in-service days to the teachers and department chairs—they would plan and conduct the in-service days.
5. The faculty and Gibbs agreed that a leadership cabinet composed of department chairs and elected teachers should be formed to share in the governance of the school. Gibbs agreed to consult with the faculty cabinet concerning all matters in which teachers had a personal stake and professional knowledge.
6. Gibbs suggested and the teachers agreed that the faculty would have complete independence in planning the programs for the three in-service days of professional development next year.

Clearly, this plan is not a set of step-by-step procedures to be accomplished in a rigid way. To the contrary, the plan is a set of accepted guidelines and commitments. The teachers and principal realize that their plan requires increased effort. It is ironic that a major goal of the plan is to reduce unnecessary busywork, yet the cost of involvement, professional control, and autonomy is more work to do. The faculty is committed to the plan even though they know it will be more work, but they believe meaningful work.

How successful would this plan be? That is an empirical question. In six months two activities would occur to assess its effectiveness. First, the OCDQ and OHI would be administered and scored, and then the principal and faculty would revisit the climate and changes at MLKHS.

Just to keep things in perspective, let us review what has happened at MLKHS. The morning of the first day was spent explaining, discussing, and interpreting the climate frameworks, their measures, and the school profiles. In the afternoon, the teachers were confronted with the openness and health profiles of MLKHS. After some discussion of those profiles and agreement on what they meant, the principal introduced his perception of the school profile, which diverged dramatically from that of the faculty. The discrepancies led to a frank and open discussion between the principal and teachers culminating in the formation of three teacher groups to develop tentative explanations about the causes of the discrepancies in perceptions. After working in small groups for an hour or so, the teachers reconvened and shared their explanations coming to a rough consensus about the causes of the discrepancy.

The next day was spent formulating a plan to reduce the discrepancies and improve the health and openness of the school. These two in-service days should be thought of as a beginning of a continuous program of improvement and problem solving. Even if these educators are successful in developing the school climate they all desire, periodic monitoring of climate is a wise course. The two goals of this process were: first, the climate of the school is improved and the stage is set for effective supervision, and second, group problem solving and organizational learning become natural elements of school life.

Summary

Organizational culture and climate are two complementary ways to capture the feel or working atmosphere of schools. Culture is the shared set of beliefs and values that binds the organization together and gives it a distinctive identity. The culture of the school can be viewed from four vantage points—tacit assumptions, core values, shared norms, artifacts— all of which contribute to a full understanding of school culture. Schools can create cultures that encourage learning and improvement of instruction or those that discourage such outcomes. Significant events should never be accepted at face value; their meanings must be interpreted in terms of the values and norms of the school and from the points of view of different organizational members.

School climate is a relatively enduring quality of the school environment that is experienced by teachers, influences their behavior, and is based on their collective perceptions of dominant patterns of school behavior. Whereas culture is the shared beliefs and values of the school, climate refers to perceptions of the basic patterns of behavior that exist in schools. Although values and behavior should be related, they are not the same. School climate was conceptualized and measured from two perspectives—the openness and health of interpersonal relations. The OCDQ-RE is an instrument to measure the openness of interactions among teachers and administrators, while the OHI is an inventory to gauge the health of the interactions among students, teachers, and administrators. Both instruments give a reliable snapshot of school climate and are useful in attempts to improve the teaching–learning environment. In addition, the Collective Efficacy Scale (CE-Scale) is another instrument that can give an important picture of the teaching and leaning environment of the school. Does the faculty believe that it has the capacity to organize and execute its actions and overcome student difficulties and increase student learning?

Organizations are in a constant state of flux. Their change can be progressive, regressive, or aimless. Schools can develop their own learning procedures to solve their problems. They can become places where teachers and principals can continually expand their capacity to create the results that they desire, where emergent patterns of thinking are nurtured, where collective aspiration is liberated, and where people are constantly learning how to learn (Senge, 1990).

We concluded this chapter with an example of how to use the climate frame and measures as bases for organizational change. Using an organizational development approach, we identified a climate problem, established a problem-solving team, diagnosed the potential problem causes, developed an action plan, and set the stage for effective school improvement.

KEY TERMS

academic emphasis   (292)
artifacts   (280)
closed climate   (289)
collective efficacy   (296)
consideration   (292)
disengaged climate   (288)
engaged climate   (288)
healthy school climate   (294)
initiating structure   (292)

institutional integrity   (291)
morale   (292)
myths   (280)
norms   (279)
OCDQ   (284)
OHI   (293)
open climate   (287)
organizational climate   (283)
organizational culture   (276)

organizational development
    model   (302)
organizational health   (291)
principal influence   (291)
resource support   (292)
rituals   (280)
tacit assumptions   (276)
values   (278)

SOME IDEAS FOR YOUR PORTFOLIO

1. Determine the organizational climate of your school by using both the OHI and OCDQ.
   - First you respond to each instrument.
   - Then have the faculty of your school respond to each.
   - Develop two profiles of the climate: yours and the faculty's.
   - Compare the two profiles and speculate on the reasons for on any differences.
   - Then develop a two-year plan of action for improving the school climate.

2. Describe the organizational culture of your school.
   - Be sure and include a description of the norms and values for each of the following areas: innovation, stability, attention to detail, outcome orientation, people orientation,

team orientation, and aggressiveness. Provide examples of the consequences of each.
   - Also identify any other shared values that make your school distinctive and give examples.
   - Critique your school's organizational culture; that is, discuss its strengths and weaknesses.
   - Finally, develop a two-year plan of action for improving the school culture.

3. Over a two-year period, develop a series of inservice activities to improve the collective efficacy of the school. In particular, make sure that your activities are directed toward developing
   - mastery experiences
   - vicarious experiences

- verbal persuasion
- affective states

Clearly explain how your plan will address each of these sources of collective efficacy.

Then develop an evaluation plan to assess the effectiveness of your inservice activities.

INSTRUCTIONAL LEADER'S TOOLBOX

Readings

Bandura, A. (1997). *Self-Efficacy: The Exercise of Control.* New York: Freeman.

Cohen, M. D., & Sproull, L. S. (Eds.). (1996). *Organizational Learning.* Thousand Oaks, CA: Sage.

Hoy, W. K., & Sabo, D. (1998). *Quality Middle Schools: Open and Healthy.* Thousand Oaks, CA: Corwin Press.

Hoy, W. K., & Tarter, C. J. (1997). *The Road to Open and Healthy Schools: A Handbook for Change, Elementary Edition.* Thousand Oaks, CA: Corwin Press.

Hoy, W. K., Tarter, C. J., & Kottkamp, R. (1991). *Open Schools/Healthy Schools: Measuring Organizational Climate.* Beverly Hills, CA: Sage.

Ouchi, W. (1981). *Theory Z.* Reading, MA: Addison-Wesley.

Senge, P. M. (1990). *The Fifth Discipline: The Art and Practice of the Learning Organization.* New York: Doubleday.

Schein, E. H. (1992). *Organizational Culture and Leadership* (2nd ed.). San Francisco: Jossey-Bass.

Schein, E. H. (1999). *The Corporate Culture.* San Francisco: Jossey-Bass.

Websites

Climate instruments	http://www.coe.ohio-state.edu/whoy
Learning organizations	http://www.stanford.edu/group/SLOW
Organizational culture	http://www.leadership-development.com/c-culture
Resources for educators in rural areas	http://www.ncrel.org/rural/
Pathways to School Improvement	http://www.ncrel.org/skrs/pathwayg.htm

Organizations

Academy of Management	http://www.aom.pace.edu
University Council for Educational Administration	http://www.ucea.org

A P P E N D I C E S

Council of Chief State School Officers Interstate School Leaders Consortium

Film and Video Resources

Web Resources for Teaching Content

Conducting a Job Interview

Guidelines for Helping Beginning Teachers

Guidelines for Observing Classroom Behavior

OCDQ-RE

CE-Scale

OHI-S

Teacher's Sense of Efficacy Scale (long form)

Teacher's Sense of Efficacy Scale (short form)

Council of Chief State School Officers Interstate School Leaders Consortium

Standards for School Leader

Available at http://www.ccsso.org/standrds.html

Standard 1: A school administrator is an educational leader who promotes the success of all students by **facilitating the development, articulation, implementation, and stewardship of a vision of learning that is shared and supported by the school community.**

Knowledge

The administrator has knowledge and understanding of:

- Learning goals in a pluralistic society
- The principles of developing and implementing strategic plans
- Systems theory
- Information sources, data collection, and data analysis strategies
- Effective communication
- Effective consensus-building and negotiation skills

Dispositions

The administrator believes in, values, and is committed to:

- The educability of all
- A school vision of high standards of learning
- Continuous school improvement
- The inclusion of all members of the school community
- Ensuring that students have the knowledge, skills, and values needed to become successful adults
- A willingness to continuously examine one's own assumptions, beliefs, and practices
- Doing the work required for high levels of personal and organization performance

Performances

The administrator facilitates processes and engages in activities ensuring that:

- The vision and mission of the school are effectively communicated to staff, parents, students, and community members
- The vision and mission are communicated through the use of symbols, ceremonies, stories, and similar activities
- The core beliefs of the school vision are modeled for all stakeholders
- The vision is developed with and among stakeholders
- The contributions of school community members to the realization of the vision are recognized and celebrated
- Progress toward the vision and mission is communicated to all stakeholders
- The school community is involved in school improvement efforts
- The vision shapes the educational programs, plans, and actions
- An implementation plan is developed in which objectives and strategies to achieve the vision and goals are clearly articulated
- Assessment data related to student learning are used to develop the school vision and goals
- Relevant demographic data pertaining to students and their families are used in developing the school mission and goals
- Barriers to achieving the vision are identified, clarified, and addressed
- Needed resources are sought and obtained to support the implementation of the school mission and goals
- Existing resources are used in support of the school vision and goals
- The vision, mission, and implementation plans are regularly monitored, evaluated, and revised

Standard 2: A school administrator is an educational leader who promotes the success of all students by **advocating, nurturing, and sustaining a school culture and instructional program conducive to student learning and staff professional growth.**

Knowledge

The administrator has knowledge and understanding of:

- Student growth and development
- Applied learning theories
- Applied motivational theories
- Curriculum design, implementation, evaluation, and refinement
- Principles of effective instruction
- Measurement, evaluation, and assessment strategies
- Diversity and its meaning for educational programs
- Adult learning and professional development models
- The change process for systems, organizations, and individuals

- The role of technology in promoting student learning and professional growth
- School cultures

Dispositions

The administrator believes in, values, and is committed to:

- Student learning as the fundamental purpose of schooling
- The proposition that all students can learn
- The variety of ways in which students can learn
- Lifelong learning for self and others
- Professional development as an integral part of school improvement
- The benefits that diversity brings to the school community
- A safe and supportive learning environment
- Preparing students to be contributing members of society

Performances

The administrator facilitates processes and engages in activities ensuring that:

- All individuals are treated with fairness, dignity, and respect
- Professional development promotes a focus on student learning consistent with the school vision and goals
- Students and staff feel valued and important
- The responsibilities and contributions of each individual are acknowledged
- Barriers to student learning are identified, clarified, and addressed
- Diversity is considered in developing learning experiences
- Lifelong learning is encouraged and modeled
- There is a culture of high expectations for self, student, and staff performance
- Technologies are used in teaching and learning
- Student and staff accomplishments are recognized and celebrated
- Multiple opportunities to learn are available to all students
- The school is organized and aligned for success
- Curricular, co-curricular, and extra-curricular programs are designed, implemented, evaluated, and refined
- Curriculum decisions are based on research, expertise of teachers, and the recommendations of learned societies
- The school culture and climate are assessed on a regular basis
- A variety of sources of information is used to make decisions
- Student learning is assessed using a variety of techniques
- Multiple sources of information regarding performance are used by staff and students
- A variety of supervisory and evaluation models is employed
- Pupil personnel programs are developed to meet the needs of students and their families

Standard 3: A school administrator is an educational leader who promotes the success of all students by **ensuring management of the organization, operations, and resources for a safe, efficient, and effective learning environment.**

Knowledge

The administrator has knowledge and understanding of:

- Theories and models of organizations and the principles of organizational development
- Operational procedures at the school and district level
- Principles and issues relating to school safety and security
- Human resources management and development
- Principles and issues relating to fiscal operations of school management
- Principles and issues relating to school facilities and use of space
- Legal issues impacting school operations
- Current technologies that support management functions

Dispositions

The administrator believes in, values, and is committed to:

- Making management decisions to enhance learning and teaching
- Taking risks to improve schools
- Trusting people and their judgments
- Accepting responsibility
- High-quality standards, expectations, and performances
- Involving stakeholders in management processes
- A safe environment

Performances

The administrator facilitates processes and engages in activities ensuring that:

- Knowledge of learning, teaching, and student development is used to inform management decisions
- Operational procedures are designed and managed to maximize opportunities for successful learning
- Emerging trends are recognized, studied, and applied as appropriate
- Operational plans and procedures to achieve the vision and goals of the school are in place
- Collective bargaining and other contractual agreements related to the school are effectively managed
- The school plant, equipment, and support systems operate safely, efficiently, and effectively

- Time is managed to maximize attainment of organizational goals
- Potential problems and opportunities are identified
- Problems are confronted and resolved in a timely manner
- Financial, human, and material resources are aligned to the goals of schools
- The school acts entrepreneurally to support continuous improvement
- Organizational systems are regularly monitored and modified as needed
- Stakeholders are involved in decisions affecting schools
- Responsibility is shared to maximize ownership and accountability
- Effective problem-framing and problem-solving skills are used
- Effective conflict resolution skills are used
- Effective group-process and consensus-building skills are used
- Effective communication skills are used
- A safe, clean, and aesthetically pleasing school environment is created and maintained
- Human resource functions support the attainment of school goals
- Confidentiality and privacy of school records are maintained

Standard 4: A school administrator is an educational leader who promotes the success of all students by **collaborating with families and community members, responding to diverse community interests and needs, and mobilizing community resources.**

Knowledge

The administrator has knowledge and understanding of:

- Emerging issues and trends that potentially impact the school community
- The conditions and dynamics of the diverse school community
- Community resources
- Community relations and marketing strategies and processes
- Successful models of school, family, business, community, government, and higher education partnerships

Dispositions

The administrator believes in, values, and is committed to:

- Schools operating as an integral part of the larger community
- Collaboration and communication with families
- Involvement of families and other stakeholders in school decision-making processes
- The proposition that diversity enriches the school
- Families as partners in the education of their children
- The proposition that families have the best interests of their children in mind
- Resources of the family and community needing to be brought to bear on the education of students
- An informed public

Performances

The administrator facilitates processes and engages in activities ensuring that:

- High visibility, active involvement, and communication with the larger community is a priority
- Relationships with community leaders are identified and nurtured
- Information about family and community concerns, expectations, and needs is used regularly
- There is outreach to different business, religious, political, and service agencies and organizations
- Credence is given to individuals and groups whose values and opinions may conflict
- The school and community serve one another as resources
- Available community resources are secured to help the school solve problems and achieve goals
- Partnerships are established with area businesses, institutions of higher education, and community groups to strengthen programs and support school goals
- Community youth family services are integrated with school programs
- Community stakeholders are treated equitably
- Diversity is recognized and valued
- Effective media relations are developed and maintained
- A comprehensive program of community relations is established
- Public resources and funds are used appropriately and wisely
- Community collaboration is modeled for staff
- Opportunities for staff to develop collaborative skills are provided

Standard 5: A school administrator is an educational leader who promotes the success of all students by **acting with integrity, fairness, and in an ethical manner.**

Knowledge

The administrator has knowledge and understanding of:

- The purpose of education and the role of leadership in modern society
- Various ethical frameworks and perspectives on ethics
- The values of the diverse school community
- Professional codes of ethics
- The philosophy and history of education

Dispositions

The administrator believes in, values, and is committed to:

- The ideal of the common good
- The principles in the Bill of Rights

- The right of every student to a free, quality education
- Bringing ethical principles to the decision-making process
- Subordinating one's own interest to the good of the school community
- Accepting the consequences for upholding one's principles and actions
- Using the influence of one's office constructively and productively in the service of all students and their families
- Development of a caring school community

Performances

The administrator:

- Examines personal and professional values
- Demonstrates a personal and professional code of ethics
- Demonstrates values, beliefs, and attitudes that inspire others to higher levels of performance
- Serves as a role model
- Accepts responsibility for school operations
- Considers the impact of one's administrative practices on others
- Uses the influence of the office to enhance the educational program rather than for personal gain
- Treats people fairly, equitably, and with dignity and respect
- Protects the rights and confidentiality of students and staff
- Demonstrates appreciation for and sensitivity to the diversity in the school community
- Recognizes and respects the legitimate authority of others
- Examines and considers the prevailing values of the diverse school community
- Expects that others in the school community will demonstrate integrity and exercise ethical behavior
- Opens the school to public scrutiny
- Fulfills legal and contractual obligations
- Applies laws and procedures fairly, wisely, and considerately

Standard 6: A school administrator is an educational leader who promotes the success of all students by **understanding, responding to, and influencing the larger political, social, economic, legal, and cultural context.**

Knowledge

The administrator has knowledge and understanding of:

- Principles of representative governance that undergird the system of American schools
- The role of public education in developing and renewing a democratic society and an economically productive nation
- The law as related to education and schooling
- The political, social, cultural and economic systems and processes that impact schools

- Models and strategies of change and conflict resolution as applied to the larger political, social, cultural and economic contexts of schooling
- Global issues and forces affecting teaching and learning
- The dynamics of policy development and advocacy under our democratic political system
- The importance of diversity and equity in a democratic society

Dispositions

The administrator believes in, values, and is committed to:

- Education as a key to opportunity and social mobility
- Recognizing a variety of ideas, values, and cultures
- Importance of a continuing dialogue with other decision makers affecting education
- Actively participating in the political and policy-making context in the service of education
- Using legal systems to protect student rights and improve student opportunities

Performances

The administrator facilitates processes and engages in activities ensuring that:

- The environment in which schools operate is influenced on behalf of students and their families
- Communication occurs among the school community concerning trends, issues, and potential changes in the environment in which schools operate
- There is ongoing dialogue with representatives of diverse community groups
- The school community works within the framework of policies, laws, and regulations enacted by local, state, and federal authorities
- Public policy is shaped to provide quality education for students
- Lines of communication are developed with decision makers outside the school community

Film and Video Resources

- *Insight Media.* The website has video and CD-ROM resources for teacher education, special education, and psychology http://www.insight-media.com/.
- *Films for the Humanities and Sciences* www.films.com
- *Association for Supervision and Curriculum Development (ASCD)* has many videos for professional development. Order from: Association for Supervision and Curriculum Development (ASCD), 125 N. West St., Alexandria, VA 22314-2798. Telephone: (703) 549-9110; FAX: (703) 549-3891. http://shop.ascd.org/category.cfm?categoryid=video
- A complete catalog of audio- and videotape resources for critical thinking can be obtained by writing *The Foundation for Critical Thinking,* 4655 Sonoma Mountain Road, Santa Rosa, CA 95404 or the Center for Critical Thinking and Moral Critique, Sonoma State University, Rohnert Park, CA 94928.

Web Resources
for Teaching Content

Science	http://www.scitrek.org/
	http://discovery.skywalk.com/science.html
	http://wise.berkeley.edu/WISE/
	http://dpls.dacc.wisc.edu/whyfiles/index.html
Mathematics	http://forum.swarthmore.edu/
Social Studies	http://www.historyhouse.com
English	http://cela.albany.edu/
	http://www.ciera.org/ciera

Conducting a Job Interview

Here is a collection of questions* to use in selecting teachers. We have grouped the questions around a number of typical topics.

Questions about why applicant wants a position in your school system

1. Why do you want this position?
2. Why do you want to work in this district?
3. What do you know about our school/school system?

Questions about the applicant's conceptions of good teaching

1. Do you remember your favorite or best elementary or high school teacher? Tell me what there was about him/her that you admire.
2. What makes a good teacher?
3. Why would you be a good teacher? What are your strengths? Weaknesses?

Questions about the applicant's beliefs/goals/philosophy

1. What do you hope to achieve with your students?
2. If there were only one skill or concept that you could get them to learn, what would it be and why?
3. Why did you want to become a teacher?
4. What is your stance on (be familiar with the initiatives of the school or district to identify issues that might come up):
   - Inclusion?
   - Whole language versus phonics?
   - Using concrete rewards to motivate students?
   - Involving families and the community in your classroom?
   - Integrated curriculum?
5. If you were to be on an advisory committee for your college to improve the preparation of teachers, what would you suggest and why?
6. What current trends in public education please you? Displease you?

---

*Thanks to Dr. Harry Galinsky, former superintendent of Paramus, NJ, and Superintendent of the Year and Dr. Michael DiPaola, former superintendent of Pitman, NJ, and Associate Professor of Education at the College of William and Mary for their questions and suggestions.

Questions about the applicant's skills/abilities

1. What is the best lesson you have taught? What made it good?
2. What has been your best experience in the classroom so far? What made it good?
3. What support do you need to make you successful?
4. Tell me about all your experiences in working with children in addition to your student teaching.
5. What has happened in your student teaching experience that you felt you were not well prepared for and how did you handle it? What would you do differently now that you have had this experience?

Questions about the applicant's classroom management skills

1. What are the challenging aspects of classroom management for you?
2. What was your most challenging discipline problem so far and how did you handle it?
3. Here is a specific situation (interviewer describes a student who challenges your authority or refuses to follow rules or do work). What would you do?
4. How will you establish rapport with students and motivate them?

Questions about the applicant's instructional strategies

1. How do you accommodate different student abilities and learning styles in your teaching?
2. How do you make accommodations for students with special needs and challenges?
3. How would you involve families and the community in your classroom?
4. Based on what you know so far, would you prefer to work alone and be responsible for smaller numbers of students or collaborate with other teachers and be responsible for larger numbers of students?
5. What role does technology play in your teaching?

Guidelines for Helping Beginning Teachers

- Schedule an orientation for beginning teachers.
- Develop a mentoring system for beginning teachers.
- Provide teachers with an appropriate mix of courses, students, and facilities; beginning teachers deserve good classrooms and the requisite supplies.
- If possible, provide a light load for beginning teachers. For example, keep the number of preparations for new high school teachers to two or three at most.
- Make sure that extra-curricular duties are not overly demanding for beginning teachers. Protect your beginning teachers.
- Provide both social and work-related activities (e.g., team teaching, cooperative instruction, etc.) for beginning teachers. Encourage beginning teachers to interact with each other. Develop a "Rookie Roundtable," a regular meeting of beginning teachers focused on typical problems.
- Develop a newsletter that reports on the accomplishments of all teachers, but highlight those of beginning teachers.
- Avoid formal classroom evaluation by the principal of beginning teachers, and instead have colleagues coach, monitor, provide feedback on strengths and weaknesses, and develop opportunities for practice and feedback in a non-threatening environment.
- Plan some in-service programs specifically for beginning teachers; find out what your beginning teachers need and want and help them get it.
- Have beginning teachers meet regularly with their mentors to identify and share problems before they become serious.
- Celebrate accomplishments. Plan and schedule events for experienced and beginning teachers such as luncheons, parties, and award recognition.
- Provide for joint planning, cooperative teaching, committee assignments, and other cooperative activities between new and experienced teachers.
- Provide opportunities for new teachers to observe master teachers at work.

Guidelines for Observing Classroom Behavior

Student–Teacher Relations

- What is the evidence of organization and clarity in teacher presentations?
- How enthusiastic is the teacher?
- How does the teacher demonstrate care, warmth, and empathy, and how does he or she nurture students?
- How does the teacher motivate students?
- What is the evidence that the teacher listens to and responds to individual student's needs, interests, and concerns?
- How does the teacher encourage respect for other students and their views?
- How does the teacher encourage and build on student discussions?
- What is the evidence that the teacher is concerned with the social–emotional development of students?

The Teaching–Learning Process

- To what extent is the teacher concerned with comprehension and application of knowledge? Analysis, synthesis, and evaluation?
- To what extent does the teacher use inquiry approaches?
- Which instructional methods did the students find most interesting?
- What is the evidence of student learning?
- How does the teacher use real-life examples to stimulate interest, illustrate, and integrate the concepts being taught?
- What instructional techniques are used to motivate divergent thinking?
- How does the teacher integrate different instructional activities?
- How does the teacher prevent frustration and confusion?
- To what extent and how is learning reinforced?
- To what extent and how does the teacher use groups?

Classroom Management

- What student behaviors were acceptable and unacceptable in class?
- How does the teacher effectively use classroom space?
- What did you like and dislike about the physical environment of the classroom?
- How does the teacher enlist student cooperation?

- Are the rules of the classroom known and used by students?
- What activities encourage student engagement? Prevent management problems?
- How is conflict managed?
- What is the evidence that a positive leaning context exists?
- What is the evidence that students are developing responsibly and managing themselves?

OCDQ-RE

DIRECTIONS:
The following are statements about your school. Please indicate the extent to which each statement characterizes your school by circling the appropriate response.

RO = Rarely Occurs   SO = Sometimes Occurs
O = Often Occurs   VFO = Very Frequently Occurs

1.	The teachers accomplish their work with vim, vigor, and pleasure	RO SO O VFO
2.	Teachers' closest friends are other faculty members at this school	RO SO O VFO
3.	Faculty meetings are useless	RO SO O VFO
4.	The principal goes out of his/her way to help teachers	RO SO O VFO
5.	The principal rules with an iron fist	RO SO O VFO
6.	Teachers leave school immediately after school is over	RO SO O VFO
7.	Teachers invite faculty members to visit them at home	RO SO O VFO
8.	There is a minority group of teachers who always oppose the majority	RO SO O VFO
9.	The principal uses constructive criticism	RO SO O VFO
10.	The principal checks the sign-in sheet every morning	RO SO O VFO
11.	Routine duties interfere with the job of teaching	RO SO O VFO
12.	Most of the teachers here accept the faults of their colleagues	RO SO O VFO
13.	Teachers know the family background of other faculty members	RO SO O VFO
14.	Teachers exert group pressure on nonconforming faculty members	RO SO O VFO
15.	The principal explains his/her reasons for criticism to teachers	RO SO O VFO
16.	The principal listens to and accepts teachers' suggestions	RO SO O VFO
17.	The principal schedules the work for the teachers	RO SO O VFO
18.	Teachers have too many committee requirements	RO SO O VFO
19.	Teachers help and support each other	RO SO O VFO
20.	Teachers have fun socializing together during school time	RO SO O VFO
21.	Teachers ramble when they talk at faculty meetings	RO SO O VFO
22.	The principal looks out for the personal welfare of teachers	RO SO O VFO
23.	The principal treats teachers as equals	RO SO O VFO
24.	The principal corrects teachers' mistakes	RO SO O VFO
25.	Administrative paperwork is burdensome at this school	RO SO O VFO
26.	Teachers are proud of their school	RO SO O VFO
27.	Teachers have parties for each other	RO SO O VFO
28.	The principal compliments teachers	RO SO O VFO

29.	The principal is easy to understand	RO	SO	O	VFO
30.	The principal closely checks classroom (teacher) activities	RO	SO	O	VFO
31.	Clerical support reduces teachers' paperwork	RO	SO	O	VFO
32.	New teachers are readily accepted by colleagues	RO	SO	O	VFO
33.	Teachers socialize with each other on a regular basis	RO	SO	O	VFO
34.	The principal supervises teachers closely	RO	SO	O	VFO
35.	The principal checks lesson plans	RO	SO	O	VFO
36.	Teachers are burdened with busy work	RO	SO	O	VFO
37.	Teachers socialize together in small, select groups	RO	SO	O	VFO
38.	Teachers provide strong social support for colleagues	RO	SO	O	VFO
39.	The principal is autocratic	RO	SO	O	VFO
40.	Teachers respect the professional competence of their colleagues	RO	SO	O	VFO
41.	The principal monitors everything teachers do	RO	SO	O	VFO
42.	The principal goes out of his/her way to show appreciation to teachers	RO	SO	O	VFO

*OCDQ instruments for all levels are available at: http://www.coe.ohio-state.edu/whoy

Administering the OCDQ-RE Instrument

The OCDQ-RE is best administered as part of a faculty meeting. It is important to guarantee the anonymity of the teacher respondent; teachers are not asked to sign the questionnaire and no identifying code is placed on the form. Most teachers do not object to responding to the instrument, which takes less than ten minutes to complete. It is probably advisable to have someone other than an administrator collect the data. It is important to create a nonthreatening atmosphere where teachers give candid responses. All of the health and climate instruments follow the same pattern of administration.

Scoring

The responses vary along a four-point scale defined by the categories "rarely occurs," "sometimes occurs," "often occurs," and "very frequently occurs" (1 through 4, respectively).

Step 1: Score each item for each teacher with the appropriate number (1, 2, 3, or 4). Be sure to reverse-score items 6, 31, 37.

Step 2: Calculate an average school score for each item. For example, if the school had 15 teachers, one would add all 15 scores on each item and then divide by 15. Round the scores to the nearest hundredth. This score represents the average school item score. You should have 42 average school item scores before proceeding.

Step 3: Sum the average school item scores as follows:

Supportive Behavior (S)=4+9+15+16+22+23+28+29+42
Directive Behavior (D)=5+10+17+24+30+34+35+39+41

Restrictive Behavior (R)=11+18+25+31+36
Collegial Behavior (C)=1+6+12+19+26+32+37+40
Intimate Behavior (Int)=2+7+13+20+27+33+38
Disengaged Behavior (Dis)=3+8+14+21

These six scores represent the climate profile of the school.

How does your school compare with others? We have supplied information on a large and diverse sample of New Jersey elementary schools, which gives a rough basis for comparing your school with others. The average scores and standard deviations for each climate dimension are summarized below. Standard deviations tell us how close most schools are to the average; the smaller the standard deviation, the closer most schools are to the typical school.

	Mean *(M)*	Standard Deviation *(SD)*
Supportive Behavior (S)	23.34	7.16
Directive Behavior (D)	19.34	5.43
Restrictive Behavior (R)	12.98	3.42
Collegial Behavior (C)	23.11	4.20
Intimate Behavior (Int)	17.23	4.10
Disengaged Behavior (Dis)	6.98	2.38

To make the comparisons easy, we recommend you standardize each of your subtest scores. Standardizing the scores gives them a "common denominator" that allows direct comparisons among all schools.

Computing Standardized Scores of the OCDQ-RE

Convert the school subtest scores to standardized scores with a mean of 500 and a standard deviation of 100, which we call SdS scores. Use the following formulas:

SdS for S=100 × (S–23.34)/7.16+500

First compute the difference between your school score on S and the mean of 23.34 for the normative sample (S–23.34). Then multiply the difference by 100 [100 × (S–23.34)]. Next divide the product by standard deviation of the normative sample (7.16). Then add 500 to the result. You have computed a standardized score (SdS) for the supportive behavior subscale (S).

Next: Repeat the process for each dimension as follows:

SdS for D=100 × (D–19.34)/5.43+500
SdS for R=100 × (R–12.98)/3.42+500
SdS for C=100 × (C–23.11)/4.20+500
SdS for Int=100 × (Int–17.23)/4.10+500
SdS for Dis=100 × (Dis–6.98)/2.38+500

You have standardized your school scores against the normative data provided in the New Jersey sample. For example, if your school score is 600 on supportive behavior, it is one standard deviation above the average score on supportive behavior of all schools in the sample; that is, the principal is more supportive than 84% of the other principals. A score of 300 represents a school that is two standard deviations below the mean on the subtest. You may recognize this system as the one used in reporting individual scores on the SAT, CEEB, and GRE. The range of these scores is presented below:

If the score is 200, it is lower than 99% of the schools.
If the score is 300, it is lower than 97% of the schools.
If the score is 400, it is lower than 84% of the schools.
If the score is 500, it is average.
If the score is 600, it is higher than 84% of the schools.
If the score is 700, it is higher than 97% of the schools.
If the score is 800, it is higher than 99% of the schools.

There are two other scores that can be easily computed and are usually of interest to teachers and principals. Recall that two openness dimensions were determined in the second-order factor analysis of the OCDQ-RE. Accordingly, the two openness measures can be computed as follows:

$$\text{Principal Openness} = \frac{(\text{SdS for S}) + (1000\text{-SdS for D}) + (1000\text{-SdS for R})}{3}$$

$$\text{Teacher Openness} = \frac{(\text{SdS for C}) + (\text{SdS for Int}) + (1000\text{-SdS for Dis})}{3}$$

These openness indices are interpreted the same way as the subtest scores, that is, the mean of the "average" school is 500. Thus, a score of 650 on teacher openness represents a highly open faculty. We have changed the numbers into categories ranging from high to low by using the following conversion table:

Above 600 VERY HIGH
551–600 HIGH
525–550 ABOVE AVERAGE
511–524 SLIGHTLY ABOVE AVERAGE
490–510 AVERAGE
476–489 SLIGHTLY BELOW AVERAGE
450–475 BELOW AVERAGE
400–449 LOW
Below 400 VERY LOW

We recommend using all the dimensions of OCDQ-RE to gain a finely tuned picture of school climate.

Computer Scoring Program

A computer scoring program is available from Arlington Writers, 1881 Marblecliff Crossing Ct., Columbus, OH 43204. The program, which runs on Windows, will score each subtest, standardize school scores, and provide indices of openness. For further information, contact Arlington Writers (fax 614-488-5075).

CE-Scale

DIRECTIONS:
Indicate your level of agreement with each of the following statements from STRONGLY DISAGREE (1) to STRONGLY AGREE (6).

	Strongly Disagree					Strongly Agree
1. Teachers in the school are able to get through to the most difficult students	1	2	3	4	5	6
2. Teachers here are confident they will be able to motivate their students	1	2	3	4	5	6
3. If a child doesn't want to learn teachers here give up	1	2	3	4	5	6
4. Teachers here don't have the skills needed to produce meaningful student learning	1	2	3	4	5	6
5. If a child doesn't learn something the first time, teachers will try another way	1	2	3	4	5	6
6. Teachers in this school are skilled in various methods of teaching	1	2	3	4	5	6
7. Teachers here are well-prepared to teach the subjects they are assigned to teach	1	2	3	4	5	6
8. Teachers here fail to reach some students because of poor teaching methods	1	2	3	4	5	6
9. Teachers in this school have what it takes to get the children to learn	1	2	3	4	5	6
10. The lack of instructional materials and supplies makes teaching very difficult	1	2	3	4	5	6
11. Teachers in this school do not have the skills to deal with student disciplinary problems	1	2	3	4	5	6
12. Teachers in this school think there are some students whom no one can reach	1	2	3	4	5	6
13. The quality of school facilities here really facilitates the teaching and learning process	1	2	3	4	5	6
14. The students here come in with so many advantages they are bound to learn	1	2	3	4	5	6
15. These students come to school ready to learn	1	2	3	4	5	6
16. Drugs and alcohol abuse in the community make learning difficult for students here	1	2	3	4	5	6
17. The opportunities in this community help ensure that these students will learn	1	2	3	4	5	6

18. Students here just aren't motivated to learn	1 2 3 4 5 6	
19. Learning is more difficult at this school because students are worried about their safety	1 2 3 4 5 6	
20. Teachers here need more training to know how to deal with these students	1 2 3 4 5 6	
21. Teachers in this school truly believe every child can learn	1 2 3 4 5 6	

Source: Roger Goddard, University of Michigan. Reprinted by permission.

Scoring Directions for the CE-Scale

The Collective Efficacy Scale (CE-Scale) is a 21-item scale. Ten of the items in this scale are reversed scored, that is, "1" is scored "6," "2" is scored "5," etc. For example, the item, "If a child doesn't want to learn, teachers here give up," is scored in reverse. Thus, a strongly agree "6" would be scored "1," suggesting low efficacy.

To score the scale:

1. First reverse scores on the following items: 3, 4, 8, 10, 11, 12, 16, 18, 19, 20.
2. Then add the scores for all 21 items: the greater the sum, the higher the collective efficacy.
3. Average all the individual teacher scores to find a collective efficacy score of the school.

Validity and Reliability Evidence for the Collective Efficacy Scale

The development of the 21-item collective efficacy scale included several phases. Scale development began initially by modifying items from the original Gibson and Dembo (1984) teacher efficacy scale to reflect collective efficacy (i.e., changing the object of the efficacy items from "I" to "We"). Next, additional items were written in response to a review by a panel of experts with experience in teacher efficacy research. Following this review, the items were subjected to a field test and then a pilot test with 46 teachers in 46 schools (1 teacher from each school). Results from the pilot study suggested that the 21 items did indeed offer a valid and reliable measure of collective efficacy (for a detailed discussion of the pilot study results see Goddard, Hoy, and Woolfolk Hoy, 2000).

Based on the promise of the results from the initial phases of our study, we decided to test the criterion-related validity, predictive validity, and reliability of scores on the collective efficacy scale in a more comprehensive sample. A sample of 452 teachers in 47 randomly selected elementary schools in a large urban district in the Midwest completed the collective efficacy survey. At the school level (for a rationale see Goddard, 2001), the 21 collective efficacy items were submitted to a principal axis factor analysis. All items loaded strongly on a single factor and explained 57.89 percent of the item variation. The alpha coefficient of reliability was strong (.96).

Criterion-related validity of the school collective efficacy scores was tested in several ways. The criterion variables examined were personal teaching efficacy (Hoy & Woolfolk, 1993), faculty trust in colleagues (Hoy & Kupersmith, 1985), and environmental press (Hoy & Sabo, 1998). Personal teaching efficacy is a measure of a teacher's self-perceptions of capability to educate students. It was predicted that when aggregated to the school level, teachers' perceptions of personal efficacy would be moderately and positively related to collective teacher efficacy; a high correlation was not expected because personal and collective teacher efficacy have different referents (self versus group). Moreover, the collective teacher efficacy measure directly assesses perceptions of both perceived competence and task whereas the personal teacher efficacy measure includes only items about competence. As predicted, there was a moderate and positive ($r = .54$, $p < .01$) correlation between personal teacher efficacy aggregated at the school level and collective teacher efficacy.

A positive relationship between faculty trust in colleagues and collective teacher efficacy was predicted, and similar to the pilot results, trust in colleagues was positively and significantly related to collective teacher efficacy ($r = .62$, $p < .01$).

Finally, we predicted no relationship between collective teacher efficacy and environmental press or the extent to which teachers experience "unreasonable community demands" (Hoy & Sabo, 1998). There is no a priori reason to expect that teachers' assessments of group capabilities would be associated with their perceptions of external demands. In other words, a demanding task and external pressures do not necessarily make people feel more or less capable. It is how they handle the pressure that determines capability. As predicted, the observed relationship between collective teacher efficacy and environmental press was not statistically significant ($r = .05$, n.s.).

As a test of predictive validity, we employed hierarchical linear modeling to show that scores on the collective efficacy scale were significant predictors of the mathematics and reading achievement (measured by the 7th Edition of Metropolitan Achievement Test) of 7016 second-, third-, and fifth-grade students who attended the 47 sampled schools.

Taken together, these results provide, content, criterion-related, and predictive validity evidence for scores on the collective efficacy scale as well as strong reliability evidence.

REFERENCES

Gibson, S., & Dembo, M. (1984). Teacher efficacy: A construct validation. *Journal of Educational Psychology, 76,* 569–582.

Goddard, R. D., Hoy, W. K., & Woolfolk Hoy, A. (2000). Collective teacher efficacy: Its meaning, measure, and impact on student achievement. *American Education Research Journal, 37,* 479–507.

Goddard, R. D. (2001). A theoretical and empirical analysis of the measurement of collective efficacy: The development of a short form. *Educational and Psychological Measurement, 61*(6), 1071–1084.

Hoy, W. K., & Kupersmith, W. J. (1985). The meaning and measure of faculty trust. *Educational and Psychological Research, 5,* 1–10.

Hoy, W. K., & Sabo, D. J. (1998). *Quality middle schools: Open and healthy.* Thousand Oaks, CA: Corwin Press, Inc.

Hoy, W. K., & Woolfolk, A. E. (1993). Teachers' sense of efficacy and the organizational health of schools. *The Elementary School Journal, 93,* 356–372.

OHI-S

DIRECTIONS:

The following are statements about your school. Please indicate the extent to which each statement characterizes your school by circling the appropriate response.

RO = Rarely Occurs   SO = Sometimes Occurs
O = Often Occurs   VFO = Very Frequently Occurs

1. Teachers are protected from unreasonable community and parental demands	RO	SO	O	VFO
2. The principal gets what he or she asks for from superiors	RO	SO	O	VFO
3. The principal is friendly and approachable	RO	SO	O	VFO
4. The principal asks that faculty members follow standard rules and regulations	RO	SO	O	VFO
5. Extra materials are available if requested	RO	SO	O	VFO
6. Teachers do favors for each other	RO	SO	O	VFO
7. The students in this school can achieve the goals that have been set for them	RO	SO	O	VFO
8. The school is vulnerable to outside pressures	RO	SO	O	VFO
9. The principal is able to influence the actions of his or her superiors	RO	SO	O	VFO
10. The principal treats all faculty members as his or her equal	RO	SO	O	VFO
11. The principal makes his or her attitudes clear to the school	RO	SO	O	VFO
12. Teachers are provided with adequate materials for their classrooms	RO	SO	O	VFO
13. Teachers in this school like each other	RO	SO	O	VFO
14. The school sets high standards for academic performance	RO	SO	O	VFO
15. Community demands are accepted even when they are not consistent with the educational program	RO	SO	O	VFO
16. The principal is able to work well with the superintendent	RO	SO	O	VFO
17. The principal puts suggestions made by the faculty into operation	RO	SO	O	VFO
18. The principal lets faculty know what is expected of them	RO	SO	O	VFO
19. Teachers receive necessary classroom supplies	RO	SO	O	VFO
20. Teachers are indifferent to each other	RO	SO	O	VFO
21. Students respect others who get good grades	RO	SO	O	VFO
22. Teachers feel pressure from the community	RO	SO	O	VFO
25. Administrative paperwork is burdensome at this school	RO	SO	O	VFO
26. Teachers are proud of their school	RO	SO	O	VFO
27. Teachers have parties for each other	RO	SO	O	VFO

(continued)

Continued

RO = Rarely Occurs   SO = Sometimes Occurs
O = Often Occurs   VFO = Very Frequently Occurs

28.	The principal compliments teachers	RO	SO	O	VFO
29.	The principal is easy to understand	RO	SO	O	VFO
30.	The principal closely checks classroom (teacher) activities	RO	SO	O	VFO
31.	Clerical support reduces teachers' paperwork	RO	SO	O	VFO
32.	New teachers are readily accepted by colleagues	RO	SO	O	VFO
33.	Teachers socialize with each other on a regular basis	RO	SO	O	VFO
34.	The principal supervises teachers closely	RO	SO	O	VFO
35.	The principal checks lesson plans	RO	SO	O	VFO
36.	Teachers are burdened with busy work	RO	SO	O	VFO
37.	Teachers socialize together in small, select groups	RO	SO	O	VFO
38.	Teachers provide strong social support for colleagues	RO	SO	O	VFO
39.	The principal is autocratic	RO	SO	O	VFO
40.	Teachers respect the professional competence of their colleagues	RO	SO	O	VFO
41.	The principal monitors everything teachers do	RO	SO	O	VFO
42.	The principal goes out of his/her way to show appreciation to teachers	RO	SO	O	VFO

*All versions of the OHI are available at: http://www.coe.ohio-state.edu/whoy

Administering the OHI-S Instrument

The OHI-S is best administered as part of a faculty meeting. It is important to guarantee the anonymity of the teacher respondent; teachers are not asked to sign the questionnaire and no identifying code is placed on the form. Most teachers do not object to responding to the instrument, which takes less than ten minutes to complete. It is probably advisable to have someone other than an administrator collect the data. It is important to create a non-threatening atmosphere where teachers give candid responses. All of the health and climate instruments follow the same pattern of administration.

Scoring

The responses vary along a four-point scale defined by the categories "rarely occurs," "sometimes occurs," "often occurs," and "very frequently occurs." (1 through 4, respectively). When an item is reversed scored, "rarely occurs" receives a 4, "sometimes occurs" a 3, and so on. Each item is scored for each respondent, and then an average school score for each item is computed by averaging the item responses across the school because the school is the unit of analysis.

Step 1: Score each item for each respondent with the appropriate number (1, 2, 3, or 4). Be sure to reverse score items 8, 15, 20, 22, 29, 30, 34, 36, 39.

Step 2: Calculate an average school score for each item. If the school has 60 teachers, one would add all 60 scores on each item and then divide the sum by 60. Round the scores to the nearest hundredth. This score represents the average school item score. You should have 44 school item scores before proceeding.

Step 3: Sum the average school item scores as follows:

Institutional Integrity (II)=1+8+15+22+29+36+39
Initiating Structure (IS)=4+11+18+25+32
Consideration (C)=3+10+17+24+31
Principal Influence (PI)=2+9+16+23+30
Resource Support (RS)=5+12+19+26+33
Morale (M)=6+13+20+27+34+37+40+42+44
Academic Emphasis (AE)=7+14+21+28+35+38+41+43

These seven scores represent the health profile of the school. You may wish to compare your school profile with other schools. To do so, we recommend that you standardize each school score. The current data base on secondary schools is drawn from a large, diverse sample of schools from New Jersey. The average scores and standard deviations for each health dimension are summarized below:

	Mean *(M)*	Standard Deviation *(SD)*
Institutional Integrity (II)	18.61	2.66
Initiating Structure (IS)	14.36	1.83
Consideration (C)	12.83	2.03
Principal Influence (PI)	12.93	1.79
Resource Support (RS)	13.52	1.89
Morale (M)	25.05	2.64
Academic Emphasis (AE)	21.33	2.76

Computing the Standardized Scores for the OHI-S

Convert the school subtest scores to standardized scores with a mean of 500 and a standard deviation of 100, which we call SdS score. Use the following formulas:

SdS for II=100(II–18.61)/2.66+500

First compute the difference between your school score on II and the mean for the normative sample (II–18.61). Then multiply the difference by one hundred [100(II–18.61)]. Next divide the product by the standard deviation of the normative sample (2.66). Then add 500 to the result. You have computed a standardized score (SdS) for the institutional integrity subscale.

Repeat the process for each dimension as follows:

SdS for IS=100(IS–14.36)/1.83+500
SdS for C=100(C–12.83)/2.03+500
SdS for PI=100(PI–12.93)/1.79+500
SdS for RS=100(RS–13.52)/1.89+500

SdS for M=100(M–25.05)/2.64+500
SdS for AE=100(AE–21.33)/2.76+500

You have standardized your school scores against the normative data provided in the New Jersey sample. For example, if your school score is 700 on institutional integrity, it is two standard deviations above the average score on institutional integrity of all schools in the sample; that is, the school has more institutional integrity than 97% of the schools in the sample. You may recognize this system as the one used in reporting individual scores on the SAT, CEEB, and GRE. The range of these scores is presented below:

If the score is 200, it is lower than 99% of the schools.
If the score is 300, it is lower than 97% of the schools.
If the score is 400, it is lower than 84% of the schools.
If the score is 500, it is average.
If the score is 600, it is higher than 84% of the schools.
If the score is 700, it is higher than 97% of the schools.
If the score is 800, it is higher than 99% of the schools.

Health Index

An overall index of school health can be computed as follows:

$$\text{Health} = \frac{(\text{SdS for II}) + (\text{Sds for IS}) + (\text{Sds for C}) + (\text{SdS for PI}) + (\text{SdS for RS}) + (\text{SdS for M}) + (\text{SdS for AE})}{7}$$

This health index is interpreted the same way as the subtest scores, that is, the mean of the "average" school is 500. Thus, a score of 650 on the health index represents a very healthy school, one that is one and a half standard deviations above the average school, and a score lower than 400 represents a very sick school climate. Most school scores, however, fall between these extremes and can only be diagnosed by carefully comparing all elements of the climate.

Computer Scoring Program

A computer scoring program for the OHI-S is available from Arlington Writers, 1881 Marblecliff Crossing Ct., Columbus, Ohio 43204. The program, which runs on Windows, will score each subtest, standardize school scores, and provide index of health. Further information on the scoring program can be obtained from Arlington Writers (Fax 614-488-5075).

Teacher's Sense of Efficacy Scale (long form)

Directions: This questionnaire is designed to help us gain a better understanding of the kinds of things that create difficulties for teachers in their school activities. Please indicate your opinion about each of the statements below. Your answers are confidential.

Teacher Beliefs	How much can you do?								
	Nothing		Very Little		Some Influence		Quite A Bit		A Great Deal
1. How much can you do to get through to the most difficult students?	(1)	(2)	(3)	(4)	(5)	(6)	(7)	(8)	(9)
2. How much can you do to help your students think critically?	(1)	(2)	(3)	(4)	(5)	(6)	(7)	(8)	(9)
3. How much can you do to control disruptive behavior in the classroom?	(1)	(2)	(3)	(4)	(5)	(6)	(7)	(8)	(9)
4. How much can you do to motivate students who show low interest in school work?	(1)	(2)	(3)	(4)	(5)	(6)	(7)	(8)	(9)
5. To what extent can you make your expectations clear about student behavior?	(1)	(2)	(3)	(4)	(5)	(6)	(7)	(8)	(9)
6. How much can you do to get students to believe they can do well in school work?	(1)	(2)	(3)	(4)	(5)	(6)	(7)	(8)	(9)
7. How well can you respond to difficult questions from your students?	(1)	(2)	(3)	(4)	(5)	(6)	(7)	(8)	(9)
8. How well can you establish routines to keep activities running smoothly?	(1)	(2)	(3)	(4)	(5)	(6)	(7)	(8)	(9)
9. How much can you do to help your students value learning?	(1)	(2)	(3)	(4)	(5)	(6)	(7)	(8)	(9)
10. How much can you gauge student comprehension of what you have taught?	(1)	(2)	(3)	(4)	(5)	(6)	(7)	(8)	(9)
11. To what extent can you craft good questions for your students?	(1)	(2)	(3)	(4)	(5)	(6)	(7)	(8)	(9)
12. How much can you do to foster student creativity?	(1)	(2)	(3)	(4)	(5)	(6)	(7)	(8)	(9)
13. How much can you do to get children to follow classroom rules?	(1)	(2)	(3)	(4)	(5)	(6)	(7)	(8)	(9)

(continued)

Continued

Teacher Beliefs	How much can you do?								
	Nothing	*Very Little*		*Some Influence*		*Quite A Bit*		*A Great Deal*	
14. How much can you do to improve the understanding of a student who is failing?	(1)	(2)	(3)	(4)	(5)	(6)	(7)	(8)	(9)
15. How much can you do to calm a student who is disruptive or noisy?	(1)	(2)	(3)	(4)	(5)	(6)	(7)	(8)	(9)
16. How well can you establish a classroom management system with each group of students?	(1)	(2)	(3)	(4)	(5)	(6)	(7)	(8)	(9)
17. How much can you do to adjust your lessons to the proper level for individual students?	(1)	(2)	(3)	(4)	(5)	(6)	(7)	(8)	(9)
18. How much can you use a variety of assessment strategies?	(1)	(2)	(3)	(4)	(5)	(6)	(7)	(8)	(9)
19. How well can you keep a few problem students from ruining an entire lesson?	(1)	(2)	(3)	(4)	(5)	(6)	(7)	(8)	(9)
20. To what extent can you provide an alternative explanation or example when students are confused?	(1)	(2)	(3)	(4)	(5)	(6)	(7)	(8)	(9)
21. How well can you respond to defiant students?	(1)	(2)	(3)	(4)	(5)	(6)	(7)	(8)	(9)
22. How much can you assist families in helping their children do well in school?	(1)	(2)	(3)	(4)	(5)	(6)	(7)	(8)	(9)
23. How well can you implement alternative strategies in your classroom?	(1)	(2)	(3)	(4)	(5)	(6)	(7)	(8)	(9)
24. How well can you provide appropriate challenges for very capable students?	(1)	(2)	(3)	(4)	(5)	(6)	(7)	(8)	(9)

*This instrument is commonly called the "Ohio State Teacher Efficacy Scale" because it was created while the developers were at The Ohio State University.

Teacher's Sense of Efficacy Scale* (short form)

Directions: This questionnaire is designed to help us gain a better understanding of the kinds of things that create difficulties for teachers in their school activities. Please indicate your opinion about each of the statements below. Your answers are confidential.

		How much can you do?								
Teacher Beliefs		*Nothing*		*Very Little*		*Some Influence*		*Quite A Bit*		*A Great Deal*
1. How much can you do to control disruptive behavior in the classroom?	(1)	(2)	(3)	(4)	(5)	(6)	(7)	(8)	(9)
2. How much can you do to motivate students who show low interest in school work?	(1)	(2)	(3)	(4)	(5)	(6)	(7)	(8)	(9)
3. How much can you do to get students to believe they can do well in school work?	(1)	(2)	(3)	(4)	(5)	(6)	(7)	(8)	(9)
4. How much can you do to help your students value learning?	(1)	(2)	(3)	(4)	(5)	(6)	(7)	(8)	(9)
5. To what extent can you craft good questions for your students?	(1)	(2)	(3)	(4)	(5)	(6)	(7)	(8)	(9)
6. How much can you do to get children to follow classroom rules?	(1)	(2)	(3)	(4)	(5)	(6)	(7)	(8)	(9)
7. How much can you do to calm a student who is disruptive or noisy?	(1)	(2)	(3)	(4)	(5)	(6)	(7)	(8)	(9)
8. How well can you establish a classroom management system with each group of students?	(1)	(2)	(3)	(4)	(5)	(6)	(7)	(8)	(9)
9. How much can you use a variety of assessment strategies?	(1)	(2)	(3)	(4)	(5)	(6)	(7)	(8)	(9)
10. To what extent can you provide an alternative explanation or example when students are confused?	(1)	(2)	(3)	(4)	(5)	(6)	(7)	(8)	(9)
11. How much can you assist families in helping their children do well in school?	(1)	(2)	(3)	(4)	(5)	(6)	(7)	(8)	(9)
12. How well can you implement alternative strategies in your classroom?	(1)	(2)	(3)	(4)	(5)	(6)	(7)	(8)	(9)

*This instrument is commonly called the "Ohio State Teacher Efficacy Scale" because it was created while the developers were at The Ohio State University.

Directions for Scoring the Teacher's Sense of Efficacy Scales

Developers: Megan Tschannen-Moran, College of William and Mary and Anita Woolfolk Hoy, the Ohio State University.

Construct Validity

For information on the construct validity, see Teacher Efficacy: Capturing an Elusive Construct, Megan Tschannen-Moran and Anita Woolfolk Hoy, in the journal of *Teaching and Teacher Education,* 2001, Vol. 17, pp. 783–805. These instruments should never be used to make decisions about individual teachers.

Factor Analysis

It is important to conduct a factor analysis to determine how your subjects respond to the questions. We have consistently found three moderately correlated factors: *Efficacy for Student Engagement, Efficacy for Instructional Practices,* and *Efficacy for Classroom Management,* but at times the makeup of the scales varies slightly. With preservice teachers we recommend that the full 24-item scale (or the 12-item short form) be used, because the factor structure often is less distinct for these respondents.

Subscale Scores:

To determine the Efficacy in Student Engagement, Efficacy in Instructional Practices, and Efficacy in Classroom Management subscale scores, we compute unweighed means of the items that load on each factor. Generally these groupings are:

Long Form
Efficacy in Student Engagement: Items 1, 2, 4, 6, 9, 10, 12, 14, 22
Efficacy in Instructional Strategies: Items 7, 10, 11, 17, 18, 20, 23, 24
Efficacy in Classroom Management: Items 3, 5, 8, 13, 15, 16, 19, 21

Short Form
Efficacy in Student Engagement: Items 2, 3, 4, 11
Efficacy in Instructional Strategies: Items 5, 9, 10, 12
Efficacy in Classroom Management: Items 1, 6, 7, 8

Reliabilities

In "Teacher Efficacy: Capturing an Elusive Construct," Tschannen-Moran and Woolfolk Hoy (2001). *Teaching and Teacher Education,* the following were found:

	Long Form			Short Form		
	Mean	*SD*	*alpha*	*Mean*	*SD*	*alpha*
Total	7.1	.94	.94	7.1	.98	.90
Engagement	7.3	1.1	.87	7.2	1.2	.81
Instruction	7.3	1.1	.91	7.3	1.2	.86
Management	6.7	1.1	.90	6.7	1.2	.86

REFERENCES

Abi-Nader, J. (1991). Creating a vision of the future: Strategies for motivating minority students. *Phi Delta Kappan, 72,* 546–549.

Abruscato, J. (1993). Early results and tentative implications from the Vermont Portfolio Project. *Phi Delta Kappan, 74,* 474–477.

Adams, M. J., Treiman, R., & Pressley, M. (1998). Reading, writing, and literacy. In I. Sigel & A. Renninger (Eds.), *Handbook of child psychology: Child psychology in practice* (Vol. 4, pp. 275–355). New York: Wiley.

Adams, R. S., & Biddle, B. J. (1970). *Realities of teaching: Exploration with videotape.* New York: Holt, Rinehart, & Winston.

Airasian, P. W. (1996). *Assessment in the classroom.* New York: McGraw-Hill.

Airasian, P. W. (2001). Types, uses, and critiques of objectives. In L. Anderson & D. Krathwohl (Eds.), *A taxonomy of teaching and learning: A revision of Bloom's taxonomy of educational objectives.* New York: Addison, Wesley, Longman.

Airasian, P. W., & Walsh, M. E. (1997). Constructivist cautions. *Phi Delta Kappan, 78,* 444–449.

Alderman, M. K. (1985). Achievement motivation and the preservice teacher. In M. Alderman & M. Cohen (Eds.), *Motivation theory and practice for preservice teachers* (pp. 37–49). Washington, DC: ERIC Clearinghouse on Teacher Education.

Alexander, P. A. (1996). The past, present, and future of knowledge research: A reexamination of the role of knowledge in learning and instruction. *Educational Psychologist, 31,* 89–92.

Alexander, P. A., & Murphy, P. K. (1998). The research base for APA's learner-centered psychological principles. In N. Lambert & B. McCombs (Eds.), *How students learn: Reforming schools through learner-centered education.* Washington, DC: American Psychological Association.

Alloy, L. B., & Seligman, M. E. P. (1979). On the cognitive component of learned helplessness and depression. *The Journal of Learning and Motivation, 13,* 219–276.

Allport, G. (1954). *The nature of prejudice.* Cambridge, MA: Addison-Wesley.

American Association for the Advancement of Science (AAAS). (1993). *Benchmarks for science literacy.* Washington, DC: Author.

Ames, C. (1990). Motivation: What teachers need to know. *Teachers College Record, 91,* 409–421.

Ames, C. (1992). Classrooms: Goals, structures, and student motivation. *Journal of Educational Psychology, 84,* 261–271.

Ames, R., & Lau, S. (1982). An attributional analysis of student help-seeking in academic settings. *Journal of Educational Psychology, 74,* 414–423.

Anastasi, A. (1988). *Psychological testing* (6th ed.). New York: Macmillan.

Anderman, E. M., & Maehr, M. L. (1994). Motivation and schooling in the middle grades. *Review of Educational Research, 64,* 287–310.

Anderson, C. S. (1982). The search for school climate: A review of the research. *Review of Educational Research, 52,* 368–420.

Anderson, C. W., Holland, J. D., & Palincsar, A. S. (1997). Canonical and sociocultural approaches to research and reform in science education: The story of Juan and his group. *The Elementary School Journal, 97,* 359–384.

Anderson, C. W., & Roth, K. J. (1989). Teaching for meaningful and self-regulated learning of science. In J. Brophy (Ed.), *Advances in research on teaching* (Vol. 1, pp. 265–306). Greenwich, CT: JAI Press.

Anderson, J. R. (1993). Problem solving and learning. *American Psychologist, 48,* 35–44.

Anderson, J. R., Reder, L. M., & Simon, H. A. (1995). Applications and misapplication of cognitive psychology to mathematics education. Unpublished manuscript. [www document] URL http://www.psy.cmu.edu/~mm4b/misapplied.html

Anderson, J. R., Reder, L. M., & Simon, H. A. (1996). Situated learning and education. *Educational Researcher, 25,* 5–11.

Anderson, L. M. (1989a). Learners and learning. In M. Reynolds (Ed.), *Knowledge base for beginning teachers* (pp. 85–100). New York: Pergamon.

Anderson, L. M. (1989b). Classroom instruction. In M. Reynolds (Ed.), *Knowledge base for beginning teachers* (pp. 101–116). New York: Pergamon.

Anderson, L. M., Brubaker, N. L., Alleman-Brooks, J., & Duffy, G. G. (1985). A qualitative study of seatwork in first-grade classrooms. *Elementary School Journal, 86,* 123–140.

Anderson, L. W., & Krathwohl, D. R. (Eds.). (2001). *A taxonomy for learning, teaching, and assessing: A revision of Bloom's taxonomy of educational objectives.* New York: Addison, Wesley, Longman.

Anderson, L. W., & Sosniak, L. A. (Eds.). (1994). *Bloom's Taxonomy: A forty-year retrospective. Ninety-third yearbook for the National Society for the Study of Education: Part II.* Chicago: University of Chicago Press.

Armbruster, B. B., & Anderson, T. H. (1981). Research synthesis on study skills. *Educational Leadership, 39,* 154–156.

Aronson, E. (in press). Building empathy, compassion and achievement in the jigsaw classroom. In J. Aronson & D. Cordova, *Improving education: Classic and contemporary lessons from psychology.* Mahwah, NJ: Erlbaum.

Aronson, E., & Patnoe, S., (1997). *Cooperation in the classroom: The Jigsaw method.* New York: Longman.

Aronson, J., & Fried, C. B. (in press). Reducing the effects of stereotype threat on African American college students: The role of theories of intelligence. *Journal of Experimental Social Psychology.*

Aronson, J., Lustina, M. J., Good, C., Keough, K., Steele, C. M., & Brown, J. (1999). When White men can't do math: Necessary and sufficient factors in stereotype threat. *Journal of Experimental Social Psychology, 35,* 29–46.

Aronson, J., & Salinas, M. F. (1998). Stereotype threat, attributional ambiguity, and Latino underperformance. Unpublished manuscript, University of Texas at Austin.

Aronson, J., Steele, C. M., Salinas, M. F., & Lustina, M. J. (1999). The effect of stereotype threat on the standardized test performance of college students. In E. Aronson (Ed.), *Readings About the Social Animal* (8th ed.). New York: Freeman.

Ashcraft, M. H. (2001). *Cognition* (3rd ed.). Upper Saddle River, NJ: Prentice-Hall.

Atkinson, J. W. (1964). *An introduction to motivation.* Princeton, NJ: Van Nostrand.

Atkinson, R. K., Levin, J. R., Kiewra, K. A., Meyers, T., Atkinson, L. A., Renandya, W. A., & Hwang, Y. (1999). Matrix and mnemonic text-processing adjuncts: Comparing and combining their components. *Journal of Educational Psychology, 91,* 242–257.

Au, K. H. (1980). Participation structures in a reading lesson with Hawaiian children: Analysis of a culturally appropriate instructional event. *Anthropology and Education Quarterly, 11,* 91–115.

Ausubel, D. P. (1963). *The psychology of meaningful verbal learning.* New York: Grune and Stratton.

Baddeley, A. D. (1986). *Working memory.* Oxford, UK: Clarendon Books.

Bailey, S. M. (1993). The current status of gender equity research in American schools. *Educational Psychologist, 28,* 321–339.

Baker, D. (1986). Sex differences in classroom interaction in secondary science. *Journal of Classroom Interaction, 22,* 212–218.

Bandura, A. (1982). Self-efficacy mechanisms in human agency. *American Psychologist, 37,* 122–147.

Bandura, A. (1986). *Social foundations of thought and action.* Englewood Cliffs, NJ: Prentice-Hall.

Bandura, A. (1993). Perceived self-efficacy in cognitive development and functioning. *Educational Psychologist, 28,* 117–148.

Bandura, A. (1997). *Self-efficacy: The exercise of control.* New York: Freeman.

Bangert-Drowns, R. L., Kulik, C. C., Kulik, J. A., & Morgan, M. (1991). The instructional effect of feedback in test-like events. *Review of Educational Research, 61,* 213–238.

Banks, J. A. (1993). Multicultural education: Characteristics and goals. In J. Banks & C. McGee Banks (Eds.), *Multicultural education: Issues and perspectives* (2nd ed.) (pp. 2–26). Boston: Allyn & Bacon.

Banks, J. A. (1994). *Multiethnic education: Theory and practice.* Boston: Allyn & Bacon.

Banks, J. A. (1997). *Teaching strategies for ethnic studies* (6th ed.). Boston: Allyn & Bacon.

Baron, R. A. (1998). *Psychology* (4th ed.). Boston: Allyn & Bacon.

Baroody, A. R., & Ginsburg, H. P. (1990). Children's learning: A cognitive view. In R. Davis, C. Maher, & N. Noddings (Eds.), *Constructivist views on the teaching and learning of mathematics* (pp. 51–64). Monograph 4 of the National Council of Teachers of Mathematics, Reston, VA.

Bartlett, F. C. (1932). *Remembering: A study in experimental and social psychology.* New York: Macmillan.

Baumeister, R. F., & Leary, M. R. (1995). The need to belong: Desire for interpersonal attachments as a fundamental human motivation. *Psychological Bulletin, 117,* 497–529.

Becker, W. C., Engelmann, S., & Thomas, D. R. (1975). *Teaching 1: Classroom management.* Chicago: Science Research Associates.

Beeth, M. E. (1998). Teaching science in fifth grade: Instructional goals that support conceptual change. *Journal of Research in Science Teaching, 35,* 1091–1101.

Belanoff, P., & Dickson, M. (1991). *Portfolios: Process and product.* Portsmouth, NH: Heinemann, Boynton/Cook.

Bennett, C. I. (1999). *Comprehensive multicultural education: Theory and practice* (4th ed.). Boston: Allyn & Bacon.

Berg, C. A., & Clough, M. (1991). Hunter lesson design: The wrong one for science teaching. *Educational Leadership, 48*(4), 73–78.

Berk, L. (2002). *Infants, children, and adolescents* (4th ed.). Boston: Allyn & Bacon.

Berliner, D. (1983). Developing concepts of classroom environments: Some light on the T in studies of ATI. *Educational Psychologist, 18,* 1–13.

Berliner, D. (1987). But do they understand? In V. Richardson-Koehler (Ed.), *Educators' handbook: A research perspective* (pp. 259–293). New York: Longman.

Berliner, D. (1988). Simple views of effective teaching and a simple theory of classroom instruction. In D. Berliner & B. Rosenshine (Eds.), *Talks to teachers* (pp. 93–110). New York: Random House.

Berliner, D., & Biddle, B. (1997). *The manufactured crisis: Myths, frauds, and the attack on America's public schools.* White Plains: Longman.

Berlyne, D. (1966). Curiosity and exploration. *Science, 153,* 25–33.

Betancourt, H., & Lopez, S. R. (1993). The study of culture, ethnicity, and race in American psychology. *American Psychologist, 48,* 629–637.

Beyer, J. M., & Trice, H. M. (1987). How an organization's rites reveal its culture. *Organizational Dynamics, 15,* 4–24.

Bjorklund, D. F. (1989). *Children's thinking: Developmental function and individual differences.* Pacific Grove, CA: Brooks/Cole.

Bloom, B. S., Engelhart, M. D., Frost, E. J., Hill, W. H., & Krathwohl, D. R. (1956). *Taxonomy of educational objectives. Handbook I: Cognitive domain.* New York: David McKay.

Bloom, R., & Bourdon, L. (1980). Types and frequencies of teachers' written instructional feedback. *Journal of Educational Research, 74,* 13–15.

Blumenfeld, P. C., Puro, P., & Mergendoller, J. R. (1992). Translating motivation into thoughtfulness. In H. Marshall (Ed.), *Redefining student learning: Roots of educational change* (pp. 207–240). Norwood, NJ: Ablex.

Boggiano, A. K., Flink, C., Shields, A., Seelbach, A., & Barrett, M. (1993). Use of techniques promoting students' self-determination: Effects on students' analytic problem-solving skills. *Motivation and Education, 17,* 319–336.

Bolman, L. G., & Deal, T. E. (1997). *Reframing organizations: Artistry, choice, and leadership* (2nd ed.). San Francisco, CA: Jossey-Bass.

Borko, H., & Putnam, R. (1996). Learning to teach. In D. Berliner & R. Calfee (Eds.), *Handbook of educational psychology* (pp. 673–708). New York: Macmillan.

Borko, H., & Livingston, C. (1989). Cognition and improvisation: Differences in mathematics instruction by expert and novice teachers. *American Educational Research Journal, 26,* 473–498.

Borkowski, J. G., Johnston, M. B., & Reid, M. K. (1986). Metacognition, motivation, and the transfer of control processes. In S. J. Ceci (Ed.), *Handbook of cognition: Social and neurological aspects of learning disabilities.* Hillsdale, NJ: Erlbaum.

Bracey, G. W. (1997). *The truth about America's schools: The Bracey Reports, 1991–97.* Bloomington, IN.: Phi Delta Kappa Educational Foundation.

Brooks, D. (1985). Beginning the year in junior high: The first day of school. *Educational Leadership, 42,* 76–78.

Brophy, J. E. (1983). Conceptualizing student motivation to learn. *Educational Psychologist, 18,* 200–215.

Brophy, J. E. (1985). Teacher-student interaction. In J. Dusek (Ed.), *Teacher expectancies.* Hillsdale, NJ: Erlbaum.

Brophy, J. E. (1988). On motivating students. In D. Berliner & B. Rosenshine (Eds.), *Talks to teachers* (pp. 201–245). New York: Random House.

Brophy, J. E. (1997). Effective teaching. In H. Walberg & G. Heartel (Eds.), *Psychology and educational practice* (pp. 212–232). Berkeley, CA: McCutchan.

Brophy, J. E., & Evertson, C. (1978). Context variables in teaching. *Educational Psychologist, 12,* 310–316.

Brophy, J. E., & Good, T. (1986). Teacher behavior and student achievement. In M. Wittrock (Ed.), *Handbook of research on teaching* (3rd ed.) (pp. 328–375). New York: Macmillan.

Brophy, J. E., & Kher, N. (1986). Teacher socialization as a mechanism for developing student motivation to learn. In R. Feldman (Ed.), *Social psychology applied to education* (pp. 256–288). New York: Cambridge University Press.

Brown, A. L. (1987). Metacognition, executive control, self-regulation, and other more mysterious mechanisms. In F. Weinert & R. Kluwe (Eds.), *Metacognition, motivation, and understanding* (pp. 65–116). Hillside, NJ: Erlbaum.

Brown, A. L. (1992). Design experiments: Theoretical and methodological challenges in creating complex interventions in classroom settings. *Journal of the Learning Sciences, 2,* 141–178.

Brown, A. L., Bransford, J., Ferrara, R., & Campione, J. (1983). Learning, remembering, and understanding. In P. Mussen (Ed.), *Handbook of child psychology* (Vol. 3). New York: Wiley.

Brown, A. L., & Campione, J. C. (1996). Psychological theory and the design of innovative learning environments: On procedures, principles, and systems. In L. Schauble & R. Glaser (Eds.), *Innovations in learning: New environments for education* (pp. 289–325). Mahwah, NJ: Lawrence Erlbaum Associates.

Bruner, J. S. (1966). *Toward a theory of instruction.* New York: Norton.

Bruner, J. S., Goodnow, J. J., & Austin, G. A. (1956). *A study of thinking.* New York: Wiley.

Bruning, R. H., Schraw, G. J., & Ronning, R. R. (1999). *Cognitive psychology and instruction* (3rd ed.). Columbus, OH: Merrill.

Burden, P. R. (1995). *Classroom management and discipline: Methods to facilitate cooperation and instruction.* White Plains, NY: Longman.

Bus, A. G., & van IJzendoorn, M. H. (1999). Phonological awareness and early reading: A meta-analysis of experimental training studies. *Journal of Educational Psychology, 91,* 403–414.

Buss, D. M. (1995). Psychological sex differences: Origin through sexual selection. *American Psychologist, 50,* 164–168.

Butler, R., & Neuman, O. (1995). Effects of task and ego achievement goals on help-seeking behaviors and attitudes. *Journal of Educational Psychology, 87,* 261–271.

Butler, R., & Nisan, M. (1986). Effects of no feedback, task-related comments, and grades on intrinsic motivation and performance. *Journal of Educational Psychology, 78,* 210–224.

Byrnes, J. P. (1996). *Cognitive development and learning in instructional contexts.* Boston: Allyn & Bacon.

Byrnes, J. P., & Fox, N. A. (1998). The educational relevance of research in cognitive neuroscience. *Educational Psychology Review, 10,* 297–342.

Calderhead, J. (1996). Teacher: Beliefs and knowledge. In D. Berliner & R. Calfee (Eds.), *Handbook of educational psychology* (pp. 709–725). New York: Macmillan.

Calderhead, J., & Robson, M. (1991). Images of teaching: Student teachers' early conceptions of classroom practice. *Teaching and Teacher Education, 7,* 1–8.

Callahan, C. M., Tomlinson, C. A., & Plucker, J. (1997). *Project STATR using a multiple intelligences model in identifying and promoting talent in high-risk students.* Storrs, CT: National Research Center for Gifted and Talented, University of Connecticut Technical Report.

Cambourne, B., & Turbill, J. (1990). Assessment in whole-language classrooms: Theory into practice. *Elementary School Journal, 90,* 337–349.

Camp, R. (1990, Spring). Thinking together about portfolios. *The Quarterly of the National Writing Project, 27,* 8–14.

Canfield, J. (1990). Improving students' self-concepts. *Educational Leadership, 48*(1), 48–50.

Cangelosi, J. S. (1990). *Designing tests for evaluating student achievement.* New York: Longman.

Canter, L. (1989). Assertive discipline—More than names on the board and marbles in a jar. *Phi Delta Kappan, 71*(1), 41–56.

Canter, L., & Canter, M. (1992). *Lee Canter's assertive discipline: Positive behavior management for today's classroom.* Santa Monica: Lee Canter and Associates.

Carey, L. M. (1994). *Measuring and evaluating school learning* (2nd ed.). Boston: Allyn & Bacon.

Carroll, J. (1993). *Human cognitive abilities: A survey of factor analytic studies.* Cambridge, England: Cambridge University Press.

Cartwright, G. P., Cartwright, C. A., & Ward, M. E. (1989). *Educating special learners.* Belmont, CA: Wadsworth.

Ceci, S. J. (1991). How much does schooling influence intelligence and its cognitive components? A reassessment of the evidence. *Developmental Psychology, 27,* 703–720.

Chamot, A. U., & O'Malley, J. M. (1996). The cognitive academic language learning approach: A model for linguistically diverse classrooms. *The Elementary School Journal, 96,* 259–274.

Chance, P. (1993). Sticking up for rewards. *Phi Delta Kappan, 74,* 787–790.

Charles, C. M. (1985). *Building classroom discipline: From models to practice* (2nd ed.). New York: Longman.

Charles, C. M. (1996). *Building classroom discipline* (5th ed.). White Plains, NY: Longman.

Chatman, J. A., & Jehn, K. A. (1994). Assessing the relationship between industry characteristics and organizational culture: How different can you be? *Academy of Management Journal, 37*(3), 522–553.

Clark, C. M. (1983). Personal communication.

Clark, C. M., & Peterson, P. L. (1986). Teachers' thought processes. In M. Wittrock (Ed.), *Handbook of research on teaching* (3rd ed.) (pp. 255–296). New York: Macmillan.

Clark, C. M., & Yinger, R. (1988). Teacher planning. In D. Berliner & B. Rosenshine (Eds.), *Talks to teachers* (pp. 342–365). New York: Random House.

Clarke, J. H., & Agne, R. M. (1997). *Interdisciplinary high school teaching.* Boston: Allyn & Bacon.

Clifford, M. M. (1990). Students need challenge, not easy success. *Educational Leadership, 48*(1), 22–26.

Clifford, M. M. (1991). Risk taking: Empirical and educational considerations. *Educational Psychologist, 26,* 263–298.

Cobb, P., & Bowers, J. (1999). Cognitive and situated learning: Perspectives in theory and practice. *Educational Researcher, 28*(2), 4–15.

Cognition and Technology Group at Vanderbilt (CTGV). (1990). Anchored instruction and its relations to situated cognition. *Educational Researcher, 19*(6) 2–10.

Cognition and Technology Group at Vanderbilt (CTGV). (1993). Anchored instruction and situated learning revisited. *Educational Technology, 33*(3), 52–70.

Cognition and Technology Group at Vanderbilt (CTGV). (1996). Looking at technology in context: A framework for understanding technology and educational research. In D. Berliner & R. Calfee (Eds.), *Handbook of educational psychology* (pp. 807–840). New York: Macmillan.

Cohen, M. D., & Sproull, L. S. (Eds.). (1996). *Organizational learning.* Thousand Oaks, CA: Sage.

Cole, M. (1985). The zone of proximal development: Where culture and cognition create each other. In J. V. Wertsch (Ed.), *Culture, communication, and cognition: Vygotskian perspectives* (pp. 146–161). Cambridge: Cambridge University Press.

Collins, A., Brown, J. S., & Holum, A. (1991). Cognitive apprenticeship: Making thinking visible. *American Educator, 15*(3), 38–39.

Collins, A., Brown, J. S., & Newman, S. E. (1989). Cognitive apprenticeship: Teaching the crafts of reading, writing, and mathematics. In L. B. Resnick (Ed.), *Knowing, learning, and instruction: Essays in honor of Robert Galser* (pp. 453–494). Hillsdale, NJ: Lawrence Erlbaum.

Confrey, J. (1990). What constructivism implies for teaching. In R. Davis, C. Maher, & N. Noddings (Eds.), *Constructivist views on the teaching and learning of mathematics* (pp. 107–122). Monograph 4 of the National Council of Teachers of Mathematics, Reston, VA.

Cook, S. D. N., & Yanon, D. (1996). Culture and organizational learning. In M. D. Cohen & L. S. Sproull (Eds.), *Learning.* Thousand Oaks, CA: Sage.

Cooke, B. L., & Pang, K. C. (1991). Recent research on beginning teachers: Studies of trained and untrained novices. *Teaching and Teacher Education, 7,* 93–110.

Cordova, D. I., & Lepper, M. R. (1996). Intrinsic motivation and the process of learning: Beneficial effects of contextualization, personalization, and choice. *Journal of Educational Psychology, 88,* 715–730.

Corno, L., & Snow, R. E. (1986). Adapting teaching to individual differences in learners. In M. Wittrock (Ed.), *Handbook of research on teaching* (3rd ed.) (pp. 605–629). New York: Macmillan.

Council of Chief State School Officers. (1996). *Interstate School Leader Licensure Consortium: Standards for school leaders.* Washington, DC: Author.

Covington, M. V. (1992). *Making the grade: A self-worth perspective on motivation and school reform.* New York: Holt, Rinehart, & Winston.

Covington, M. V., & Omelich, C. L. (1984). An empirical examination of Weiner's critique of attribution research. *Journal of Educational Psychology, 76,* 1214–1225.

Covington, M. V., & Omelich, C. L. (1987). "I knew it cold before the exam": A test of the anxiety-blockage hypothesis. *Journal of Educational Psychology, 79,* 393–400.

Cowley, G., & Underwood, A. (1998, June 15). Memory. *Newsweek, 131*(24), 48–54.

Craik, F. I. M., & Lockhart, R. S. (1972). Levels of processing: A framework for memory research. *Journal of Verbal Learning and Verbal Behavior, 11,* 671–684.

Cummins, J. (1994). The acquisition of English as a second language. In K. Spangenberg-Urbschat & R. Prichard (Eds.), *Kids come in all languages: Reading instruction for ESL students* (pp. 36–62). Newark, DE: International Reading Association.

Current Directions in Psychological Science. (1993). Special Section: Controversies, 2, 1–12.

Dansereau, D. F. (1985). Learning strategy research. In J. Segal, S. Chipman, & R. Glaser (Eds.), *Thinking and learning skills. Vol. I: Relating instruction to research.* Hillsdale, NJ: Erlbaum.

Darley, J. M., Glucksberg, S., & Kinchla, R. (1991). *Psychology* (5th ed.). Englewood Cliffs, NJ: Prentice-Hall.

Davis, J. K. (1991). Educational implications of field-dependence–independence. In S. Wapner & J. Demick (Eds.), *Field-dependence–independence: Cognitive styles across the life span* (pp. 149–176). Hillsdale, NJ: Lawrence Erlbaum.

Davis, R. B., Maher, C. A., & Noddings, N. (Eds.). (1990). *Constructivist views on the teaching and learning of mathematics.* Monograph 4 of the National Council of Teachers of Mathematics, Reston, VA.

deCharms, R. (1976). *Enhancing motivation.* New York: Irvington.

Deci, E. L. (1975). *Intrinsic motivation.* New York: Plenum.

Deci, E. L., & Ryan, R. M. (1985). *Intrinsic motivation and self-determination in human behavior.* New York: Plenum.

Deci, E. L., Vallerand, R. J., Pelletier, L. G., & Ryan, R. M. (1991). Motivation and education: The self-determination perspective. *Educational Psychologist, 26,* 325–346.

Dempster, F. N. (1991). Synthesis of research on reviews and tests. *Educational Leadership, 48*(7), 71–76.

Dempster, F. N. (1993). Exposing our students to less should help them learn more. *Phi Delta Kappan, 74,* 432–437.

Derry, S. J. (1989). Putting learning strategies to work. *Educational Leadership, 47*(5), 4–10.

Derry, S. J. (1992). Beyond symbolic processing: Expanding horizons for educational psychology. *Journal of Educational Psychology, 84,* 413–419.

Deshler, D. D., & Schumaker, J. B. (1986). Learning strategies: An instructional alternative for low-achieving adolescents. *Exceptional Children, 52,* 583–590.

Deutsch, M. (1949). An experimental study of the effects of cooperation and competition upon group processes. *Human Relations, 2,* 199–231.

Dewey, J. (1910). *How we think.* Boston: D. C. Heath.

Diller, L. (1998). *Running on ritalin.* New York: Bantam books.

DiVesta, F. J., & Gray, G. S. (1972). Listening and notetaking. *Journal of Educational Psychology, 63,* 8–14.

Dole, J. A., Duffy, G. G., Roehler, L. R., & Pearson, P. D. (1991). Moving from the old to the new: Research on reading comprehension instruction. *Review of Educational Research, 61,* 239–264.

Doyle, W. (1977). The uses of nonverbal behaviors: Toward an ecological model of classrooms. *Merrill-Palmer Quarterly, 23,* 179–192.

Doyle, W. (1983). Academic work. *Review of Educational Research, 53,* 159–200.

Doyle, W. (1986). Classroom organization and management. In M. C. Wittrock (Ed.), *Handbook of research on teaching* (3rd ed.) (pp. 392–431). New York: Macmillan.

Driscoll, M. P. (1994). *Psychology of learning for instruction.* Boston: Allyn & Bacon.

Driscoll, M. P. (1998). *Psychology of learning for instruction* (2nd ed.) Boston: Allyn & Bacon.

Duchastel, P. (1979). Learning objectives and the organization of prose. *Journal of Educational Psychology, 71,* 100–106.

Duffy, G., Roehler, L. R., Meloth, M. S., & Vavrus, L. G. (1986). Conceptualizing instructional explanation. *Teaching and Teacher Education, 2,* 197–214.

Duke, D. L. (1993). How a staff development program can rescue at-risk students. *Educational Leadership, 50,* 28–30.

Dunn, K., & Dunn, R. (1978). *Teaching students through their individual learning styles.* Reston, VA: National Council of Principals.

Dunn, K., & Dunn, R. (1987). Dispelling outmoded beliefs about student learning. *Educational Leadership, 44*(6), 55–63.

Dunn, R. (1987). Research on instructional environments: Implications for student achievement and attitudes. *Professional School Psychology, 2,* 43–52.

Dunn, R., Beaudry, J. S., & Klavas, A. (1989). Survey of research on learning styles. *Educational Leadership, 47*(7), 50–58.

Dunn, R., Dunn, K., & Price, G. E. (1984). *Learning Style Inventory.* Lawrence, KS: Price Systems.

Dweck, C. S., & Bempechat, J. (1983). Children's theories on intelligence: Consequences for learning. In S. Paris, G. Olson, & W. Stevenson (Eds.), *Learning and motivation in the classroom* (pp. 239–256). Hillsdale, NJ: Erlbaum.

Dyson, A. H. (1997). *Writing superheroes: Contemporary childhood, popular culture, and classroom literacy.* New York: Teachers College Press.

Eccles, J., & Wigfield, A. (1985). Teacher expectations and student motivation. In J. Dusek (Ed.), *Teacher expectancies* (pp. 185–226). Hillsdale, NJ: Erlbaum.

Eisner, E. W. (1999). The uses and limits of performance assessments. *Phi Delta Kappan, 80,* 658–660.

Elawar, M. C., & Corno, L. (1985). A factorial experiment in teachers' written feedback on student homework: Changing teacher behavior a little rather than a lot. *Journal of Educational Psychology, 77,* 162–173.

Emmer, E. T., & Evertson, C. M. (1981). Synthesis of research on classroom management. *Educational Leadership, 38,* 342–345.

Emmer, E. T., & Evertson, C. M. (1982). Effective classroom management at the beginning of the school year in junior high school classes. *Journal of Educational Psychology, 74,* 485–498.

Emmer, E. T., Evertson, C. M., & Anderson, L. M. (1980). Effective classroom management at the beginning of the school year. *Elementary School Journal, 80,* 219–231.

Emmer, E. T., Evertson, C., Clements, B., & Worsham, M. (2000). *Classroom management for secondary teachers* (5th ed.). Boston: Allyn & Bacon.

Engel, P. (1991). Tracking progress toward the school readiness goal. *Educational Leadership, 48*(5), 39–42.

Epanchin, B. C., Townsend, B., & Stoddard, K. (1994). *Constructive classroom management: Strategies for creating positive learning environments.* Pacific Grove, CA: Brooks/Cole.

Epstein, J. L. (1989). Family structure and student motivation. In R. E. Ames & C. Ames (Eds.), *Research on motivation in education: Vol 3. Goals and cognitions* (pp. 259–295). New York: Academic Press.

Espe, C., Worner, C., & Hotkevich, M. (1990). Whole language—What a bargain. *Educational Leadership, 47*(6), 45.

Evertson, C. M. (1988). Managing classrooms: A framework for teachers. In D. Berliner & B. Rosenshine (Eds.), *Talks to teachers* (pp. 54–74). New York: Random House.

Evertson, C. M., Emmer, E. T., Clements, B. S., & Worsham, M. E. (2000). *Classroom management for elementary teachers* (5th ed.). Boston: Allyn & Bacon.

Ewy, C., & student authors. (1997). Kids take on "the test." *Educational Leadership, 54*(4), 76–78.

Farnham-Diggory, S. (1994). Paradigms of knowledge and instruction. *Review of Educational Research, 64,* 463–477.

Feiman-Nemser, S. (1983). Learning to teach. In L. Shulman & G. Sykes (Eds.), *Handbook of teaching and policy* (pp. 150–170). New York: Longman.

Fennema, E., & Peterson, P. (1988). Effective teaching for boys and girls: The same or different? In D. Berliner & B. Rosenshine (Eds.), *Talks to teachers* (pp. 111 127). New York: Random House.

Ferguson, D. L., Ferguson, P. M., & Bogdan, R. C. (1987). If mainstreaming is the answer, what is the question? In V. Richardson-Koehler (Ed.), *Educators' handbook: A research perspective* (pp. 394–419). New York: Longman.

Finkelstein, R. (1998). *The effects of organizational health and pupil control ideology on the achievement and alienation of high school students.* Unpublished Doctoral Dissertation, St Johns University, Queens, NY.

Fiske, E. B. (1988, April 10). America's test mania. New York Times (Education Life Section), pp. 16–20.

Fitzgerald, J. (1995). English-as-a-second-language learners' cognitive reading process: A review of the research in the United States. *Review of Educational Research, 62,* 145–190.

Flammer, A. (1995). Developmental analysis of control beliefs. In A. Bandura, (Ed.). *Self-efficacy in changing societies* (pp. 69–113). New York: Cambridge University Press.

Flavell, J. H. (1985). *Cognitive development* (2nd ed.). Englewood Cliffs, NJ: Prentice-Hall.

Flavell, J. H., Green, F. L., & Flavell, E. R. (1995). *Young children's knowledge about thinking.* Monographs of the Society for Research in Child Development, 60(1) (Serial No. 243).

Floden, R. E., & Klinzing, H. G. (1990). What can research on teacher thinking contribute to teacher preparation? A second opinion. *Educational Researcher, 19*(4), 15–20.

Fox, L. H. (1981). Identification of the academically gifted. *American Psychologist, 36,* 1103–1111.

Freiberg, H. J. (Ed.). (1999). *Beyond behaviorism: Changing the classroom management.* Boston: Allyn & Bacon.

Frick, T. W. (1990). Analysis of patterns in time: A method of recording and quantifying temporal relations in education. *American Educational Research Journal, 27,* 180–204.

Friend, M., & Bursuck, W. (2002). *Including students with special needs: A practical guide for classroom teachers.* (2nd ed.). Boston: Allyn & Bacon.

Fuller, F. G. (1969). Concerns of teachers: A developmental conceptualization. *American Educational Research Journal, 6,* 207–226.

Gagné, E. D. (1985). *The cognitive psychology of school learning.* Boston: Little Brown.

Gagné, E. D., Yekovich, C. W., & Yekovich, F. R. (1993). *The cognitive psychology of school learning* (2nd ed.). New York: HarperCollins.

Gardner, H. (1983). *Frames of mind: The theory of multiple intelligences.* New York: Basic Books.

Gardner, H. (1993). *Multiple intelligences: The theory in practice.* New York: Basic Books.

Gardner, H. (1998). Reflections on multiple intelligences: Myths and messages. In A. Woolfolk (Ed.), *Readings in educational psychology* (2nd ed.) (pp. 61–67). Boston: Allyn & Bacon.

Gardner, H. (1999, August). Who owns intelligence? Invited address at the Annual Meeting of the American Psychological Association, Boston.

Gardner, R., Brown, R., Sanders, S., & Menke, D. J. (1992). "Seductive details" in learning from text. In K. A. Renninger, S. Hidi, & A. Krapp (Eds.), *The role of interest in learning and development* (pp. 239–254). Hillsdale, NJ: Erlbaum.

Garmon, A., Nystrand, M., Berends, M., & LePore. P. C. (1995). An organizational analysis of the effects of ability grouping. *American Educational Research Journal, 32,* 687–715.

Garner, R. (1990). When children and adults do not use learning strategies: Toward a theory of settings. *Review of Educational Psychology, 60,* 517–530.

Garner, R. (1992). Learning from school tests. *Educational Psychologist, 27,* 53–63.

Garner, R. (1998). Choosing to learn and not-learn in school. *Educational Psychology Review, 10,* 227–238.

Garrison, J. (1995). Deweyan pragmatism and the epistemology of contemporary social constructivism. *American Educational Research Journal, 32,* 716–741.

Gartner, A., & Lipsky, D. K. (1987). Beyond special education: Toward a quality system for all students. *Harvard Educational Review, 57,* 367–395.

Geary, D. C. (1995a). Reflections of evolution and culture in children's cognition: Implications for mathematical development and instruction. *American Psychologist, 50,* 24–37.

Geary, D. C. (1995b). Sexual selection and sex differences in spatial cognition. *Learning and Individual Differences, 7,* 289–303.

Geary, D. C. (1999). Evolution and developmental sex differences. *Current Directions in Psychological Science, 8,* 115–120.

Gergen, K. J. (1997). Constructing constructivism: Pedagogical potentials. *Issues in Education: Contributions from Educational Psychology, 3,* 195–202.

Gersten, R. (1996a). The language-minority students in transition: Contemporary instructional research. *The Elementary School Journal, 96,* 217–220.

Gersten, R. (1996b). Literacy instruction for language-minority students: The transition years. *The Elementary School Journal, 96,* 217–220.

Gillett, M., & Gall, M. (1982, March). The effects of teacher enthusiasm on the at-task behavior of students in the elementary grades. Paper presented at the annual meeting of the American Educational Research Association, New York.

Glasser, W. (1969). *Schools without failure.* New York: Harper & Row.

Goals 2000. Available online at http://www.edgov/G2K/teachers/negs.html

Goddard, R. D. (2001). A theoretical and empirical analysis of the measurement of collective efficacy: The development of a short form. *Educational and Psychological Measurement, 61*(6), 1071–1084.

Goddard, R. D., Hoy, W. K., & Woolfolk Hoy, A. (2000). Collective teacher efficacy: Its meaning, measure, and impact on student achievement. *American Educational Research Journal, 37,* 479–507.

Goddard, R. D., Sweetland S. R., & Hoy, W. K. (2000). Academic emphasis of urban elementary schools and student achievement: A multi-level analysis. *Educational Administration Quarterly, 36,* 683–702.

Goldenberg, C. (1996). The education of language-minority students: Where are we, and where do we need to go? *The Elementary School Journal, 96,* 353–361.

Goleman, D. (1995). *Emotional intelligence.* New York: Bantam.

Good, T. L. (1983). Classroom research: A decade of progress. *Educational Psychologist, 18,* 127–144.

Good, T. L., & Brophy, J. E. (1997). *Looking in classrooms* (7th ed.). New York: Longman.

Good, T. L., & Marshall, S. (1984). Do students learn more in heterogeneous or homogeneous groups? In P. Peterson, L. C. Wilkinson, & M. Hallinan (Eds.), *The social context of instruction: Group organization and group processes* (pp. 15–38). Orlando, FL: Academic Press.

Goodenow, C. (1993). Classroom belonging among early adolescents: Relationships to motivation and achievement. *Journal of Early Adolescence, 13,* 21–43.

Goodman, K. S. (1986). *What's whole in whole language: A parent-teacher guide.* Portsmouth, NH: Heinemann.

Goodrich, H. (1997). Understanding rubrics. *Educational Leadership, 54*(4), 14–17.

Gordon, E. W. (1991). Human diversity and pluralism. *Educational Psychologist, 26,* 99–108.

Gordon, T. (1974). *Teacher effectiveness training.* New York: Peter H. Wyden.

Gordon, T. (1981). Crippling our children with discipline. *Journal of Education, 163,* 228–243.

Graham, S. (1991). A review of attribution theory in achievement contexts. *Educational Psychology Review, 3,* 5–39.

Graham, S. (1994). Motivation in African Americans. *Review of Educational Research, 64,* 55–117.

Graham, S. (1995). Narrative versus meta-analytic reviews of race differences in motivation. *Review of Educational Research, 65,* 509–514.

Graham, S. (1996). How causal beliefs influence the academic and social motivation of African-American children. In G. G. Brannigan (Ed.), *The enlightened educator: Research adventures in the schools* (pp. 111–126). New York: McGraw-Hill.

Graham, S., & Harris, K. R. (1994). The effects of whole language on children's writing: A review of literature. *Educational Psychologist, 29,* 187–192.

Graham, S., & Weiner, B. (1996). Theories and principles of motivation. In D. Berliner & R. Calfee (Eds.), *Handbook of educational psychology* (pp. 63–84). New York: Macmillan.

Grant, C. A., & Sleeter, C. E. (1989). Race, class, gender, exceptionality, and educational reform. In J. Banks & C. McGee Banks (Eds.), *Multicultural education: Issues and perspectives* (pp. 49–66). Boston: Allyn & Bacon.

Greeno, J. G., Collins, A. M., & Resnick, L. B. (1996). Cognition and learning. In D. Berliner & R. Calfee (Eds.), *Handbook of educational psychology* (pp. 15–46). New York: Macmillan.

Gregorc, A. F. (1982). *Gregorc style delineator: Development, technical, and administrative manual.* Maynard, MA: Gabriel Systems.

Grissom, J. B., & Smith, L. A. (1989). Repeating and dropping out of school. In L. Shepard & M. Smith (Eds.), *Flunking grades: Research and policies on retention* (pp. 34–63). Philadelphia: Falmer Press.

Grolnick, W. S., & Ryan, R. M. (1989). Parent styles associated with children's self-regulation and competence in school. *Journal of Educational Psychology, 81,* 143–154.

Grolnick, W. S., Ryan, R. M., & Deci, E. L. (1991). Inner resources for school achievement: Motivational mediators of children's perceptions of their parents. *Journal of Educational Psychology, 83,* 508–517.

Gronlund, N. E. (2000). *How to write and use instructional objectives* (6th ed.). Columbus: OH: Merrill.

Gross, M. U. M. (1992). The use of radical acceleration in cases of extreme intellectual precocity. *Gifted Child Quarterly, 36,* 91–99.

Grossman, H., & Grossman, S. H. (1994). *Gender issues in education.* Boston: Allyn & Bacon.

Guilford, J. P. (1988). Some changes in the Structure-of-Intellect model. *Educational and Psychological Measurement, 48,* 1–4.

Guitierrez, R., & Slavin, R. E. (1992). Achievement effects of the nongraded elementary school: A best evidence synthesis. *Review of Educational Research, 62,* 333–376.

Guskey, T. R. (1994). Making the grade: What benefits students? *Educational Leadership, 52*(2), 14–21.

Gustafsson, J-E., & Undheim, J. O. (1996) Individual differences in cognitive functioning. In D. Berliner & R. Calfee (Eds.), *Handbook of educational psychology* (pp. 186–242). New York: Macmillan.

Guthrie, J. T., Cox, K. E., Anderson, E., Harris, K., Mazzoni, S., & Rach, L. (1998). Principles of integrated instruction for engagement in reading. *Educational Psychology Review, 10,* 227–238.

Haertel, E. H. (1999). Performance assessment and educational reform. *Phi Delta Kappan, 80,* 662–666.

Hakuta, K., & Gould, L. J. (1987). Synthesis of research on bilingual education. *Educational Leadership, 44*(6), 38–45.

Halford, J. M. (1999). A different mirror: A conversation with Ronald Takaki. *Educational Leadership, 56*(7), 8–13.

Hall, J. W. (1991). More on the utility of the keyword method. *Journal of Educational Psychology, 83,* 171–172.

Hallahan, D. P., & Kauffman, J. M. (2000). *Exceptional learners: Introduction to special education* (8th ed.). Boston: Allyn & Bacon.

Hallahan, D. P., Kauffman, J. M., & Lloyd, J. W. (1999). *Introduction to learning disabilities* (2nd ed.). Boston: Allyn & Bacon.

Hallowell, E. M., & Ratey, J. J. (1994). *Driven to distraction.* New York: Pantheon Books.

Halpern, D. F. (1996). Changing data, changing minds: What the data on cognitive sex differences tell us and what we hear. *Learning and Individual Differences, 8,* 73–82.

Halpin, A. W. (1966). *Theory and research in administration.* New York: Macmillan.

Halpin, A. W., & Croft, D. B. (1962). *The organization climate of schools.* Contract #SAE 543-8639. U.S. Office of Education, Research Project.

Hambleton, R. K. (1996). Advances in assessment models, methods, and practices. In D. C. Berliner & R. C. Calfee (Eds.), *Handbook of educational psychology* (pp. 899–925). New York: Macmillan.

Hamilton, R. J. (1985). A framework for the evaluation of the effectiveness of adjunct questions and objectives. *Review of Educational Research, 55,* 47–86.

Hansen, R. A. (1977). Anxiety. In S. Ball (Ed.), *Motivation in education.* New York: Academic Press.

Hanson, P. G., & Lubin (1995). *Answers to questions most frequently asked about organizational development.* Thousand Oaks, CA: Sage.

Harris, K. R., & Graham, S. (1996). Memo to constructivist: Skills count too. *Educational Leadership, 53*(5), 26–29.

Herman, J. (1997). Assessing new assessments: How do they measure up? *Theory Into Practice, 36,* 197–204.

Herman, J., & Winters. L. (1994). Portfolio research: A slim collection. *Educational Leadership, 52*(2), 48–55.

Hernshaw, L. S. (1987). *The shaping of modern psychology: A historical introduction from dawn to present day.* London: Routledge & Kegan Paul.

Hewson, P. W., Beeth, M. E., & Thorley, N. R. (1998). Teaching for conceptual change. In B. J. Fraser & K. G. Tobin (Eds.), *International handbook of science education* (pp. 199–218). New York: Kluwer.

Hilgard, E. R. (1996). Perspectives on educational psychology. *Educational Psychology Review, 8,* 419–431.

Hill, K. T., & Eaton, W. O. (1977). The interaction of test anxiety and success-failure experiences in determining children's arithmetic performance. *Developmental Psychology, 13,* 205–211.

Hill, K. T., & Wigfield, A. (1984). Test anxiety: A major educational problem and what can be done about it. *Elementary School Journal, 85,* 105–126.

Hines, C. V., Cruickshank, D. R., & Kennedy, J. J. (1982, March). Measures of teacher clarity and their relationships to student achievement and satisfaction. Paper presented at the annual meeting of the American Educational Research Association, New York.

Hines, C. V., Cruickshank, D. R., & Kennedy, J. J. (1985). Teacher clarity and its relation to student achievement and satisfaction. *American Educational Research Journal, 22,* 87–99.

Hiroto, D. S., & Seligmen, M. E. P. (1975). Generality of learned helplessness in man. *Journal of Personality and Social Psychology, 31,* 311–327.

Horgan, D. D. (1995). *Achieving gender equity: Strategies for the classroom.* Boston: Allyn & Bacon.

Hoy, W. K. (1972). Dimensions of student alienation and characteristics of public high schools. *Interchange, 3,* 38–51.

Hoy, W. K., & Clover, S. I. R. (1986). Elementary school climate: A revision of the OCDQ. *Educational Administration Quarterly, 22,* 93–110.

Hoy, W. K., & Hannum, J. (1997). Middle school climate: An empirical assessment of organizational health and student achievement. *Educational Administration Quarterly, 33,* 290–311.

Hoy, W. K., & Miskel, C. G. (1996). *Educational administration: Theory, research, and practice* (5th ed.). New York: McGraw-Hill.

Hoy, W. K., & Miskel, C. G. (2001). *Educational administration: Theory, research, and practice* (6th ed.). New York: McGraw-Hill.

Hoy, W. K., & Sabo, D. J. (1998). *Quality middle schools: Open and healthy.* Thousand Oaks, CA: Corwin Press.

Hoy, W. K., & Tarter, C. J. (1995). *Administrators solving the problems of practice: Decision-making concepts, cases, and consequences.* Boston: Allyn & Bacon.

Hoy, W. K., & Tarter, C. J. (1997a). *The road to open and healthy schools: A handbook for change, secondary edition.* Thousand Oaks, CA: Corwin Press.

Hoy, W. K., & Tarter, C. J. (1997b). *The road to open and healthy schools: A handbook for change, elementary edition.* Thousand Oaks, CA: Corwin Press.

Hoy, W. K., Tarter, C. J., & Kottkamp, R. (1991). *Open schools/healthy schools: Measuring organizational climate.* Beverly Hills, CA: Sage.

Hoy, W. K., & Woolfolk, A. E. (1990). Organizational socialization of student teachers. *American Educational Research Journal, 27,* 279–300.

Hoy, W. K., & Woolfolk, A. E. (1993). Teachers' sense of efficacy and the organizational health of schools. *Elementary School Journal, 93,* 355–372.

Huber, G. P. (1996). Organizational learning: The contributing processes and literatures. In M. D. Cohen & L. S. Sproull (Eds.), *Organizational learning* (pp. 124–162). Thousand Oaks, CA: Sage.

Huff, C. R. (1989). Youth gangs and public policy. *Crime & Delinquency, 35,* 524–537.

Hunter, M. (1982). *Mastery teaching.* El Segundo, CA: TIP Publications.

Hunter, M. (1995). Mastery teaching. In J. H. Block, S. T. Evertson, & T R. Guskey (Eds.), *School improvement programs* (pp. 181–204). New York: Scholastic.

Iran-Nejad, A. (1990). Active and dynamic self-regulation of learning processes. *Review of Educational Research, 60,* 573–602.

Irving, O., & Martin, J. (1982). Withitness: The confusing variable. *American Educational Research Journal, 19,* 313–319.

Irwin, J. W. (1991). *Teaching reading comprehension* (2nd ed.). Boston: Allyn & Bacon.

Jagacinski, C. M., & Nicholls, J. G. (1987). Competence and affect in task involvement and ego involvement: The impact of social comparison information. *Journal of Educational Psychology, 76,* 107–114.

Jenson, W. R., Sloane, H. N., & Young, K. R. (1988). *Applied behavior analysis in education: A structured teaching approach.* Englewood Cliffs, NJ: Prentice-Hall.

Johnson, D. W., & Johnson, R. (1985). Motivational processes in cooperative, competitive, and individualistic learning situations. In C. Ames & R. Ames (Eds.), *Research on motivation in education. Vol. 2: The classroom milieu.* (pp. 249–286). New York: Academic Press.

Johnson, D. W., & Johnson, R. (1994). *Learning together and alone: Cooperation, competition, and individualization* (4th ed.). Boston: Allyn & Bacon.

Johnson, D. W., & Johnson, R. (1999). The three Cs of school and classroom management. In H. J. Freiberg (Ed.), *Beyond behaviorism: Changing the classroom management paradigm* (pp. 119–144). Boston: Allyn & Bacon.

Johnson, D. W., Johnson, R., Dudley, B., Ward, M., & Magnuson, D. (1995). The impact of peer mediation training on the management of school and home conflicts. *American Educational Research Journal, 32,* 829–844.

Jones, E. D., & Southern, W. T. (1991). Conclusions about acceleration: Echoes of a debate. In W. Southern & E. Jones (Eds.), *The academic acceleration of gifted chil-*

dren. (pp. 223–228). New York: Teachers College Press.

Jurden, F. H. (1995). Individual differences in working memory and complex cognition. *Journal of Educational Psychology, 87,* 93–102.

Kagan, S. (1994). *Cooperative learning.* San Juan Capistrano, CA: Kagan Cooperative Learning.

Karweit, N. (1989). Time and learning: A review. In R. E. Slavin (Ed.), *School and classroom organization* (pp. 69–95). Hillsdale, NJ: Erlbaum.

Karweit, N., & Slavin, R. (1981). Measurement and modeling choices in studies of time and learning. *American Educational Research Journal, 18,* 157–171.

Keefe, J. W. (1982). Assessing student learning styles: An overview. In *Student learning styles and brain behavior.* Reston, VA: National Association of Secondary School Principals.

Keefe, J. W., & Monk, J. S. (1986). *Learning style profile examiner's manual.* Reston, VA: National Association of Secondary School Principals.

Kelly, K. (1999). Retention vs. social promotion: Schools search for alternatives. *Harvard Education Letter, 15*(1), 1–3.

Keogh, B. K., & MacMillan, D. L. (1996). Exceptionality. In D. Berliner & R. Calfee (Eds.), *Handbook of educational psychology* (pp. 311–330). New York: Macmillan.

Keyser, V., & Barling, J. (1981). Determinants of children's self-efficacy beliefs in an academic environment. *Cognitive Therapy and Research, 5,* 29–40.

Kiewra, K. A. (1985). Investigating notetaking and review: A depth of processing alternative. *Educational Psychologist, 20,* 23–32.

Kiewra, K. A. (1988). Cognitive aspects of autonomous note taking: Control processes, learning strategies, and prior knowledge. *Educational Psychologist, 23,* 39–56.

Kiewra, K. A. (1989). A review of note-taking: The encoding storage paradigm and beyond. *Educational Psychology Review, 1,* 147–172.

Kindsvatter, R., Wilen, W., & Ishler, M. (1988). *Dynamics of effective teaching.* New York: Longman.

King, A. (1990). Enhancing peer interaction and learning in the classroom through reciprocal questioning. *American Educational Research Journal, 27,* 664–687.

Kirst, M. (1991). Interview on assessment issues with Lorrie Shepard. *Educational Researcher, 20*(2), 21–23.

Kogan, N. (1983). Stylistic variation in childhood and adolescence: Creativity, metaphor, and cognitive style. In P. Mussen (Ed.), *Handbook of child psychology* (4th ed.) (Vol. 3, pp. 630–706). New York: Wiley.

Kohn, A. (1993). Rewards versus learning: A response to Paul Chance. *Phi Delta Kappan, 74,* 784–785.

Kolata, G. B. (1980). Math and sex: Are girls born with less ability? *Science, 210,* 1234–1235.

Kounin, J. S. (1970). *Discipline and group management in classrooms.* New York: Holt, Rinehart & Winston.

Kounin, J. S., & Doyle, P. H. (1975). Degree of continuity of a lesson's signal system and task involvement of children. *Journal of Educational Psychology, 67,* 159–164.

Kozulin, A., & Falik, L. (1995). Dynamic cognitive assessment of the child. *Current Directions, 4,* 192–195.

Krathwohl, D. R., Bloom, B. S., & Masia, B. B. (1964). *Taxonomy of educational objectives. Handbook II: Affective domain.* New York: David McKay.

Kreitzer, A. E., & Madaus, G. F. (1994). Empirical investigations of the hierarchical structure of the taxonomy. In L. W. Anderson & L. A. Sosniak (Eds.), *Bloom's taxonomy: A forty-year retrospective. Ninety-third yearbook for the National Society for the Study of Education: Part II* (pp. 64–81). Chicago: University of Chicago Press.

Kulik, C. C., & Kulik, J. A. (1982). Effects of ability grouping on secondary school students: A meta-analysis of evaluation findings. *American Educational Research Journal, 19,* 415–428.

Kulik, J. A., & Kulik, C. C. (1984). Effects of accelerated instruction on students. *Review of Educational Research, 54,* 409–425.

Kulik, J. A., Kulik, C. C., & Bangert, R. L. (1984, April). Effects of practice on aptitude and achievement test scores. *American Educational Research Journal, 21,* 435–447.

Land, M. L. (1987). Vagueness and clarity. In M. Dunkin (Ed.), *The international encyclopedia of teaching and teacher education* (pp. 392–397). New York: Pergamon.

Language Development and Hypermedia Group. (1992). "Open" software design: A case study. *Educational Technology, 32,* 43–55.

Larrivee, B. (1985). *Effective teaching behaviors for successful mainstreaming.* New York: Longman.

Lave, J. (1988). *Cognition in practice: Mind, mathematics, and culture in everyday life.* New York: Cambridge University Press.

Lave, J., & Wenger, E. (1991). *Situated learning: Legitimate peripheral participation.* Cambridge, MA: Cambridge University Press.

Leavy, J. (1996, March 18). Mother's little helper. *Newsweek, 127,* 51–56.

Leinhardt, G. (1986). Expertise in mathematics teaching. *Educational Leadership, 43,* 28–33.

Leinhardt, G. (1988). Situated knowledge and expertise in teaching. In J. Calderhead (Ed.), *Teachers' professional learning* (pp. 146–168). London: Farmer Press.

LeMahieu, P., Gitomer, D. H., & Eresh, J. T. (1993). Portfolios in large-scale assessment: Difficult but not impossible. Unpublished manuscript, University of Delaware.

Lepper, M. R. (1988). Motivational considerations in the study of instruction. *Cognition and Instruction, 5,* 289–309.

Lepper, M. R., & Greene, D. (1978). *The hidden costs of rewards: New perspectives on the psychology of human motivation.* Hillsdale, NJ: Erlbaum.

Levin, J. R. (1994). Mnemonic strategies and classroom learning: A twenty-year report card. *Elementary School Journal, 94,* 235–254.

Levin, J. R., & Nolan, J. F. (2000). *Principles of classroom management: A professional decision-making model.* Boston: Allyn & Bacon.

Levitt, B. L., & March, J. G. (1996). In M. D. Cohen & L. S. Sproull (Eds.), *Organizational learning* (pp. 124–162). Thousand Oaks, CA: Sage.

Lewis, A. C. (1995). An overview of the standards movement. *Phi Delta Kappan, 76,* 744–750.

Liben, L. S., & Signorella, M. L. (1993). Gender-schematic processing in children: The role of initial interpretations of stimuli. *Developmental Psychology, 29,* 141–149.

Linn, M. C., & Hyde, J. S. (1989). Gender, mathematics, and science. *Educational Researcher, 18,* 17–27.

Linn, R. L. (1986). Educational testing and assessment: Research needs and policy issues. *American Psychologist, 41,* 1153–1160.

Linn, R. L., & Gronlund, N. E. (2000). *Measurement and assessment in education* (8th ed.). Columbus, OH: Merrill.

Locke, E. A., & Latham, G. P. (1990). *A theory of goal setting and task performance.* Englewood Cliffs, NJ: Prentice-Hall.

Lohman, D. L. (1989). Human intelligence: An introduction to advances in theory and research. *Review of Educational Research, 59,* 333–374.

Lowenstein, G. (1994). The psychology of curiosity: A review and reinterpretation. *Psychological Bulletin, 117,* 75–98.

Lyman, H. B. (1986). *Test scores and what they mean* (4th ed.). Englewood Cliffs, NJ: Prentice-Hall.

Mabry, L. (1999). Writing to the rubrics: Lingering effects of traditional standardized testing on direct writing assessment. *Phi Delta Kappan, 80,* 673–679.

Madaus, G. F., & Kellaghan, T. (1993). Testing as a mechanism of public policy: A brief history. *Measurement and Evaluation in Counseling and Development, 26,* 6–10.

Mager, R. (1975). *Preparing instructional objectives* (2nd ed.). Palo Alto, CA: Fearon.

Magnusson, S. J., & Palincsar, A. S. (1995). The learning environment as a site of science reform. *Theory Into Practice, 34,* 43–50.

Major, B., & Schmader, T. (1998). Coping with stigma through psychological disengagement. In J. Swim & C. Stangor (Eds.), *Stigma: The target's perspective* (pp. 219–241). New York: Academic Press.

Maker, C. J. (1987). Gifted and talented. In V. Richardson-Koehler (Ed.), *Educators' handbook: A research perspective* (pp. 420–455). New York: Longman.

Mantzicopoulos, P., & Morrison, D. (1992). Kindergarten retention: Academic and behavioral outcomes through the end of second grade. *American Educational Research Journal, 29,* 182–198.

Marsh, H. W., Walker, R., & Debus, R. (1991). Subject-specific components of academic self-concept and self-efficacy. *Contemporary Educational Psychology, 16,* 331–345.

Marshall, H. H. (1996). Implications of differentiating and understanding constructivist approaches. *Journal of Educational Psychology, 31,* 235–240.

Marshall, H. H. (1987). Motivational strategies of three fifth-grade teachers. *Elementary School Journal, 88,* 135–150.

Marshall, H. H. (Ed.). (1992). *Redefining student learning: Roots of educational change.* Norwood, NJ: Ablex.

Martin, C. L., & Little, J. K. (1990). The relation of gender understanding to children's sex-typed preferences and gender stereotypes. *Child Development, 61,* 1427–1439.

Martin, G., & Pear, J. (1992). *Behavior modification: What it is and how to do it* (4th ed.). Englewood Cliffs, NJ: Prentice-Hall.

Maslow, A. H. (1968). *Toward a psychology of being* (2nd ed.). New York: Van Nostrand.

Maslow, A. H. (1970). *Motivation and personality* (2nd ed.). New York: Harper and Row.

Mason, D. A., & Good, T. L. (1993). Effects of two-group and whole-class teaching on regrouped elementary students' mathematics achievement. *American Educational Research Journal, 30,* 328–360.

Mayer, J. D., & Salovey, P. (1993). The intelligence of emotional intelligence. *Intelligence, 17,* 433–442.

Mayer, J. D., & Salovey, P. (1997). What is emotional intelligence? In P. Salovey & D. Sluyter (Eds.), *Emotional development, emotional literacy, and emotional intelligence.* New York: Basic Books.

Mayer, R. E. (1992). Cognition and instruction: Their historic meeting within educational psychology. *Journal of Educational Psychology, 84,* 405–412.

Mayer, R. E. (1996). Learners as information processors: Legacies and limitations of educational psychology's second metaphor. *Journal of Educational Psychology, 31,* 151–161.

McClelland, D. C. (1985). *Human motivation.* Glenview, IL: Scott, Foresman.

McClelland, D., Atkinson, J. W., Clark, R. W., & Lowell, E. L. (1953). *The achievement motive.* New York: Appleton-Century-Crofts.

McClelland, D., & Pilon, D. (1983). Sources of adult motives in patterns of parent behavior in early childhood. *Journal of Personality and Social Psychology, 44,* 564–574.

McClelland, D. C. (1993). Intelligence is not the best predictor of job performance. *Current Directions in Psychological Science, 2,* 5–6.

McCormick, C. B., & Levin, J. R. (1987). Mnemonic prose-learning strategies. In M. Pressley & M. McDaniel (Eds.), *Imaginary and related mnemonic processes* (pp. 407–427). New York: Springer-Verlag.

McDonald, J. P. (1993). Three pictures of an exhibition: Warm, cool, and hard. *Phi Delta Kappan, 6,* 480–485.

McLoyd, V. C. (1998). Economic disadvantage and child development. *American Psychologist, 53,* 185–204.

McNemar, Q. (1964). Lost: Our intelligence? Why? *American Psychologist, 19,* 871–882.

Medley, D. M. (1979). The effectiveness of teachers. In P. Peterson & H. Walberg (Eds.), *Research on teaching: Concepts, findings, and implications* (pp. 11–27). Berkeley, CA: McCutchan.

Meek, A. (1991). On thinking about teaching: A conversation with Eleanor Duckworth. *Educational Leadership, 48*(6), 30–34.

Meichenbaum, D., Burland, S., Gruson, L., & Cameron, R. (1985). Metacognitive assessment. In S. Yussen (Ed.), *The growth of reflection in children* (pp. 1–30). Orlando, FL: Academic Press.

Meisels, S. J. (1989). High-stakes testing in kindergarten. *Educational Leadership, 46*(7), 16–22.

Mendell, P. R. (1971). Retrieval and representation in long-term memory. *Psychonomic Science, 23,* 295–296.

Messick, S. (1994). The matter of style: Manifestations of personality in cognition, learning, and teaching. *Educational Psychologist, 29,* 121–136.

Miles, M. B. (1969). Planned change and organizational health: Figure and ground. In F. D. Carver & T. J. Sergiovanni (Eds.), *Organizations and Human Behavior* (pp. 375–391). New York: McGraw-Hill.

Miller, E. (1994). Peer mediation catches on, but some adults don't. *Harvard Education Letter, 10*(3), 8.

Miller, G. A. (1956). The magical number seven, plus or minus two: Some limits on our capacity for processing information. *Psychological Review, 63,* 81–97.

Miller, G. A., Galanter, E., & Pribram, K. H. (1960). *Plans and the structure of behavior.* New York: Holt, Rinehart & Winston.

Miller, P. H. (2002). *Theories of developmental psychology* (4th ed.). New York: Worth.

Mills, J. R., & Jackson, N. E. (1990). Predictive significance of early giftedness: The case of precocious reading. *Journal of Educational Psychology, 82,* 410–419.

Mitchell, B. M. (1984). An update on gifted and talented education in the U.S. *Roeper Review, 6,* 161–163.

Moos, R. H., & Moos, B. S. (1978). Classroom social climate and student absences and grades. *Journal of Educational Psychology, 70,* 263–269.

Morris, C. G. (1991). *Psychology: An introduction* (7th ed.). Englewood Cliffs, NJ: Prentice-Hall.

Morris, P. F. (1990). Metacognition. In M. W. Eysenck, (Ed.), *The Blackwell dictionary of cognitive psychology* (pp. 225–229). Oxford, UK: Basil Blackwell.

Morrow, L. M. (1992). The impact of a literature-based program on literacy achievement, use of literature, and attitudes of children from minority backgrounds. *Reading Research Quarterly, 27,* 251–275.

Morrow, L. M., & Weinstein, C. (1986). Encouraging voluntary reading: The impact of a literature program on children's use of library centers. *Reading Research Quarterly, 21,* 330–346.

Moshman, D. (1997). Pluralist rational constructivism. *Issues in Education: Contributions from Educational Psychology, 3,* 229–234.

Moskowitz, G., & Hayman, M. L. (1976). Successful strategies of inner-city teachers: A year-long study. *Journal of Educational Research, 69,* 283–289.

Mowday, R. T., Porter, L. W., & Steers, R. M. (1982). *Employee-organizational linkages: The psychology of commitment, absenteeism, and turnover.* New York: Academic Press.

Mullins, T. (1983). *Relations among teachers' perceptions of the principal's style, teachers' loyalty to the principal, and teachers' zone of acceptance.* Unpublished Doctoral Dissertation, Rutgers University, New Brunswick, NJ.

Murphy, P. K., & Alexander, P. A. (2000). A motivated exploration of motivation terminology. *Contemporary Educational Psychology, 25,* 3–53.

Murray, H. G. (1983). Low inference classroom teaching behavior and student ratings of college teaching effectiveness. *Journal of Educational Psychology, 75,* 138–149.

National Council of Teachers of Mathematics (NCTM). (1989). *Curriculum and evaluation standards for school mathematics.* Reston, VA: Author.

National Council of Teachers of Mathematics (NCTM). (1991). *Professional standards for teaching mathematics.* Reston, VA: Author.

National Joint Committee on Learning Disabilities (NJCLD). (1989). *Letter from NJCLD to member organizations. Topic: Modifications to the NJCLD definition of learning disabilities.* Washington, DC: Author.

Naveh-Benjamin, M. (1991). A comparison of training programs intended for different types of test-anxious students: Further support for an information-processing model. *Journal of Educational Psychology, 83,* 134–139.

Naveh-Benjamin, M., McKeachie, W. J., & Lin, Y. (1987). Two types of test-anxious students: Support for an information processing model. *Journal of Educational Psychology, 79,* 131–136.

Needles, M., & Knapp, M. (1994). Teaching writing to children who are undeserved. *Journal of Educational Psychology, 86,* 339–349.

Neisser, U., Boodoo, G., Bouchard, A., Boykin, W., Brody, N., Ceci, S. J., Halpern, D. F., Loehlin, J. C., Perloff, R., Sternberg, R. J., & Urbina, S. (1996). Intelligence: Knowns and unknowns. *American Psychologist, 51,* 77–101.

Nelson, K. (1986). *Event knowledge.* Hillsdale, NJ: Erlbaum.

Nelson, T. O. (1996). Consciousness and metacognition. *American Psychologist, 51,* 102–116.

Nestor-Baker, N. S. (1999). Tacit knowledge in the superintendency: An exploratory analysis. Unpublished doctoral dissertation, The Ohio State University, Columbus, OH.

Neuman, S. B., & Roskos, K. (1992). Literacy objects as cultural tools: Effects on children's literacy behaviors in play. *Reading Research Quarterly, 27,* 255–275.

Newby, T. J. (1991). Classroom motivation: Strategies of first-year teachers. *Journal of Educational Psychology, 83,* 195–200.

Newcombe, N., & Baenninger, M. (1990). The role of expectations in spatial test performance: A meta-analysis. *Sex Roles, 16,* 25–37.

Nicholls, J. G., & Miller, A. (1984). Conceptions of ability and achievement motivation. In R. Ames & C. Ames (Eds.), *Research on motivation in education. Vol. 1: Student Motivation* (pp. 39–73). New York: Academic Press.

Nissani, M., & Hoefler-Nissani, D. M. (1992). Experimental studies of belief dependence of observations and of resistance to conceptual change. *Cognition and Instruction, 9,* 97–111.

Noddings, N. (1990). Constructivism in mathematics education. In R. Davis, C. Maher, & N. Noddings (Eds.), *Constructivist views on the teaching and learning of mathematics* (pp. 7–18). Monograph 4 of the National Council of Teachers of Mathematics, Reston, VA.

Noddings, N. (1992). *The challenge to care in schools: An alternative approach to education.* New York: Teachers College Press.

Noddings, N. (1995). Teaching themes of care. *Phi Delta Kappan, 76,* 675–679.

Norman, D. P. (1982). *Learning and memory.* San Francisco: Freeman.

Oakes, J. (1999). Promotion or retention: Which one is social? *Harvard Education Letter, 15*(1), 8.

O'Donnell, A. M., & O'Kelly, J. (1994). Learning from peers: Beyond the rhetoric of positive results. *Educational Psychology Review, 6,* 321–350.

Ogbu, J. U. (1987). Variability in minority school performance: A problem in search of an explanation. *Anthropology and Education Quarterly, 18,* 312–334.

Ogbu, J. U. (1997). Understanding the school performance of urban blacks: Some essential background knowledge. In H. Walberg, O. Reyes, & R. P. Weissberg (Eds.), *Children and youth: Interdisciplinary perspectives* (pp. 190–140). Norwood, NJ: Ablex.

Ogbu, J. U. (1999). Beyond language: Ebonics, Proper English, and identity in a Black-American speech community. *American Educational Research Journal, 36,* 147–184.

O'Leary, K. D. (1980). Pills or skills for hyperactive children? *Journal of Applied Behavior Analysis, 13,* 191–204.

O'Neil, J. (1990). Link between style, culture proves divisive. *Educational Leadership, 48*(2), 8.

O'Neil, J. (1991). Drive for national standards picking up steam. *Educational Leadership, 48*(5), 4–8.

O'Reilly, C. A. I., Chatman, J. A., & Caldwell, D. (1991). People and organizational culture: A Q-sort approach to assessing person-organization fit. *Academy of Management Journal, 34*(3), 487–516.

Ormrod, J. E. (1999). *Human learning* (3rd ed.). Upper Saddle River: NJ: Merrill/Prentice-Hall.

Ortony, A., Clore, G. L., & Collins, A. (1988). *The cognitive structure of emotions.* Cambridge: Cambridge University Press.

Ouchi, W. (1981). *Theory Z.* Reading, MA: Addison-Wesley.

Ovando, C. J. (1989). Language diversity and education. In J. Banks & C. McGee Banks (Eds.), *Multicultural education: Issues and perspectives* (pp. 208–228). Boston: Allyn & Bacon.

Owen, L. (1985). *None of the above: Behind the myth of scholastic aptitude.* Boston: Houghton Mifflin.

Padilla, F. M. (1992). *The gang as an American enterprise.* New Brunswick, NJ: Rutgers University Press.

Pajares, F. (1997). Current directions in self-efficacy research. In M. L. Maehr & P. R. Pintrich (Eds.), *Advances in motivation and achievement* (Vol. 10, pp. 1–49). Greenwich, CT: JAI Press.

Palincsar, A. S. (1998). Social constructivist perspectives on teaching and learning. In J. T. Spence, J. M. Darley, & D. J. Foss (Eds.), *Annual Review of Psychology* (pp. 345–375). Palo Alto, CA: Annual Reviews.

Palincsar, A. S., & Brown, A. L. (1989). Classroom dialogues to promote self-regulated comprehension. In J. Brophy (Ed.), *Advances in research on teaching* (Vol. 1, pp. 35–67). Greenwich, CT: JAI Press.

Palincsar, A. S., Magnusson, S. J., Marano, N., Ford, D., & Brown, N. (1998). Designing a community of practice: Principles and practices of the GIsML community. *Teaching and Teacher Education, 14,* 5–19.

Panksepp, J. (1998). Attention deficit hyperactivity disorders, psychostimulants, and intolerance of playfulness: A tragedy in the making? *Current Directions in Psychological Science, 7,* 91–98

Paris, S. (1988, April). Fusing skill and will: The integration of cognitive and motivational psychology. Paper presented at the annual meeting of the American Educational Research Association, New Orleans.

Paris, S. G., & Cunningham, A. E. (1996). Children becoming students. In D. Berliner & R. Calfee, (Eds.), *Handbook of Educational Psychology* (pp. 117–146). New York: Macmillan.

Paris, S. G., Lipson, M. Y., & Wixson, K. K. (1983). Becoming a strategic reader. *Contemporary Educational Psychology, 8,* 293–316.

Parks, C. P. (1995). Gang behavior in the schools: Myth or reality? *Educational Psychology Review, 7,* 41–68.

Parsons, T., Bales, R. F., & Shils, E. A. (1953). *Working papers in the theory of action.* New York: Free Press.

Pasch, M., Sparks-Langer, G., Gardner, T. G., Starko, A. J., & Moody, C. D. (1991). *Teaching as decision making: Instructional practices for the successful teacher.* New York: Longman.

Pate, P. E., McGinnis, K., & Homestead, E. (1995). Creating coherence through curriculum integration. In M. Harmin, *Inspiring active learning: A handbook for teachers* (pp. 62–70). Alexandria, VA: Association for Supervision and Curriculum Development.

Paulman, R. G., & Kennelly, K. J. (1984). Test anxiety and ineffective test taking: Different names, same construct? *Journal of Educational Psychology, 76,* 279–288.

Paulson, F. L., Paulson, P. R., & Meyer, C. A. (1991). What makes a portfolio a portfolio? *Educational Leadership, 48*(5), 60–63.

Payne, K. J., & Biddle, B. J. (1999). Poor school funding, child poverty, and mathematics achievement. *Educational Researcher, 28*(6), 4–12.

Pelham, W. E. (1981). Attention deficits in hyperactive and learning-disabled children. *Exceptional Education Quarterly, 2,* 13–23.

Perrone, V. (1994). How to engage students in learning. *Educational Leadership, 51*(5), 11–13.

Perry, N. E., VandeKamp, K., & Mercer, L. (2000, April). Investigating teacher–student interactions that foster self-regulated learning. In N. E. Perry (Chair), Symposium conducted at the meeting of the American Educational Research Association, New Orleans.

Peterson, P. L., & Comeaux, M. A. (1989). Assessing the teacher as a reflective professional: New perspectives on teacher evaluation. In A. Woolfolk (Ed.), *Research perspectives on the graduate preparation of teachers* (pp. 132–152). Englewood Cliffs, NJ: Prentice-Hall.

Phillips, D. (1997). How, why, what, when, and where: Perspectives on constructivism and education. *Issues in Education: Contributions from Educational Psychology, 3,* 151–194.

Piaget, J. (1985). *The equilibrium of cognitive structures: The central problem of intellectual development* (T. Brown & K. L. Thampy, Trans.). Chicago: University of Chicago Press.

Pierson, L. H., & Connell, J. P. (1992). Effect of grade retention on self-system processes, school engagement, and academic performance. *Journal of Educational Psychology, 84,* 300–307.

Pintrich, P. R., Marx, R. W., & Boyle, R. A. (1993). Beyond cold conceptual change: The role of motivational beliefs and classroom contextual factors in the process of conceptual change. *Review of Educational Research, 63,* 167–199.

Pintrich, P. R., & Schrauben, B. (1992). Students' motivational beliefs and their cognitive engagement in academic tasks. In D. Schunk & J. Meece (Eds.), *Students' perceptions in the classroom: Causes and consequences* (pp. 149–183). Hillsdale, NJ: Erlbaum.

Pintrich, P. R., & Schunk, D. H. (2002). *Motivation in education: Theory, research, and applications* (2nd ed.). Columbus, OH: Merrill.

Popham, W. J. (1993). *Educational evaluation* (3rd ed.). Boston: Allyn & Bacon.

Powell, R. R., Garcia, J., & Denton, J. J. (1985, March). The portrayal of minorities and women in selected elementary science series. Paper presented at the annual meeting of the American Educational Research Association, Chicago.

Prawat, R. S. (1992). Teachers beliefs about teaching and learning: A constructivist perspective. *American Journal of Education, 100,* 354–395.

Prawat, R. S. (1996). Constructivism, modern and postmodern. *Issues in Education: Contributions from Educational Psychology, 3,* 215–226.

Pressley, M. (1986). The relevance of the good strategy user model to the teaching of mathematics. In J. Levin & M. Pressley (Eds.), *Educational Psychologist, 21* (Special issue on learning strategies), 139–161.

Pressley, M. (1991). Comparing Hall (1988) with related research on elaborative mnemonics. *Journal of Educational Psychology, 83,* 165–170.

Pressley, M. (1996, August). Getting beyond whole language: Elementary reading instruction that makes sense in light of recent psychological research. Paper presented at the Annual meeting of the American Psychological Association, Toronto.

Pressley, M. (1998). *Reading instruction that works: The case for balanced teaching.* New York: The Guilford Press.

Pressley, M., Levin, J., & Delaney, H. D. (1982). The mnemonic keyword method. *Review of Research in Education, 52,* 61–91.

Purcell, P., & Stewart, L. (1990). Dick and Jane in 1989. *Sex Roles, 22,* 177–185.

Rachlin, H. (1991). *Introduction to modern behaviorism* (3rd ed.), New York: W. H. Freeman.

Raffini, J. P. (1996). *150 ways to increase intrinsic motivation in the classroom.* Boston: Allyn & Bacon.

Recht, D. R., & Leslie, L. (1988). Effect of prior knowledge on good and poor readers' memory of text. *Journal of Educational Psychology, 80,* 16–20.

Reeve, J. (1996). *Motivating others: Nurturing inner motivational resources.* Boston: Allyn & Bacon.

Reeve, J., Bolt, E., & Cai, Y. (1999). Autonomy-supportive teachers: How they teach and motivate students. *Journal of Educational Psychology, 91,* 537–548.

Reid, M. K., & Borkowski, J. G. (1987). Causal attributions of hyperactive children: Implications for teaching strategies and self-control. *Journal of Educational Psychology, 79,* 296–307.

Reiss, F., & Hoy, W. K. (1998). Faculty loyalty: An important but neglected concept in the study of schools. *Journal of School Leadership, 8,* 4–21.

Reisberg, D., & Heuer, F. (1992). Remembering the details of emotional events. In E. Winograd & U. Neisser (Eds.), *Affect and accuracy in recall: Studies of "flashbulb" memories.* Cambridge, England: Cambridge University Press.

Rennie, L. J., & Parker, L. H. (1987). Detecting and accounting for gender differences in mixed-sex and single-sex groupings in science lessons. *Educational Review, 39*(1), 65–73.

Renninger, K. A., Hidi, S., & Krapp, A. (Eds.). (1992). *The role of interest in learning and development.* Hillsdale, NJ: Lawrence Erlbaum.

Renzulli, J. S., & Reis, S. M. (1991). The schoolwide enrichment model: A comprehensive plan for the development of creative productivity. In N. Colangelo & G. Davis (Eds.), *Handbook of gifted education.* (pp. 111–141). Boston: Allyn & Bacon.

Renzulli, J. S., & Smith, L. H. (1978). *The Learning Styles Inventory: A measure of student preferences for instructional techniques.* Mansfield Center, CT: Creative Learning Press.

Resnick, L. B. (1981). Instructional psychology. *Annual Review of Psychology, 32,* 659–704.

Resnick, L. B. (1987). Learning in school and out. *Educational Researcher, 16*(9), 13–20.

Resnick, L. B., & Nolan, K. (1995). Where in the world are world-class standards? *Educational Leadership, 52*(6), 6–11.

Reynolds, A. (1992). Grade retention and school adjustment: An explanatory analysis. *Educational Evaluation and Policy Analysis, 14*(2), 101–121.

Reynolds, M. C., & Birch, J. W. (1988). *Adaptive mainstreaming: A primer for teachers and principals* (3rd ed.). New York: Longman.

Richardson, T. M., & Benbow, C. P. (1990). Long-term effects of acceleration on the social-emotional adjustment of mathematically precocious youths. *Journal of Educational Psychology, 82,* 464–470.

Robbins, S. P. (1998). *Organizational behavior: Concepts, controversies, applications.* Upper Saddle River, NJ: Allyn & Bacon.

Robinson, D. H. (1998). Graphic organizers as aids to test learning. *Reading Research and Instruction, 37,* 85–105.

Robinson, D. H., & Kiewra, K. A. (1995). Visual argument: Graphic outlines are superior to outlines in improving learning from text. *Journal of Educational Psychology, 87,* 455–467.

Roderick, M. (1994). Grade retention and school dropout: Investigating an association, *American Educational Research Journal, 31,* 729–760.

Rogers, C. R., & Freiberg, H. J. (1994). *Freedom to learn* (3rd ed.). Columbus, OH: Charles E. Merrill.

Rose, L. C., & Gallup, A. M. (1999). The 31st annual Phi Delta Kappa/Gallup Poll of the public's attitude toward the public schools. *Phi Delta Kappan, 81*(1), 41–58.

Rose, L. C., & Gallup, A. M. (2001). The 33st annual Phi Delta Kappa/Gallup Poll of the public's attitude toward the public schools. *Phi Delta Kappan, 83*(1), 41–58.

Rosenshine, B. (1979). Content, time, and direct instruction. In P. Peterson & H. Walberg (Eds.), *Research on teaching: Concepts, findings, and implications* (pp. 28–56). Berkeley, CA: McCutchan.

Rosenshine, B. (1988). Explicit teaching. In D. Berliner & B. Rosenshine (Eds.), *Talks to teachers* (pp. 75–92). New York: Random House.

Rosenshine, B., & Furst, N. (1973). The use of direct observation to study teaching. In R. Travers (Ed.), *Second handbook of research on teaching.* Chicago: Rand McNally.

Rosenshine, B., & Stevens, R. (1986). Teaching functions. In M. Wittrock (Ed.), *Handbook of research on teaching* (3rd ed.) (pp. 376–391). New York: Macmillan.

Rosenthal, R., & Jacobson, L. (1968). *Pygmalion in the classroom.* New York: Holt, Rinehart, Winston.

Roskos, K., & Neuman, S. B. (1995). Two beginning kindergarten teachers' planning for integrated literacy instruction. *Elementary School Journal, 96,* 195–215.

Rumelhart, D., & Ortony, A. (1977). The representation of knowledge in memory. In R. Anderson, R. Spiro, & W. Montague (Eds.), *Schooling and the acquisition of knowledge* (pp. 99–135). Hillsdale, NJ: Erlbaum.

Ruopp, F., & Driscoll, M. (1990, January/February). Access to algebra. *Harvard Education Letter, 6*(A), 4–5.

Ryan, R. M. (1991). The nature of the self in autonomy and relatedness. In G. R. Goethals & J. Strauss (Eds.), *Multidisciplinary perspectives on the self.* New York: Springer-Verlag.

Ryan, R. M., & Deci, E. L. (1996). When paradigms clash: Comments on Cameron and Pierce's claim that rewards do not undermine intrinsic motivation. *Review of Educational Research, 66,* 33–38.

Ryan, R. M., & Grolnick, W. S. (1986). Origins and pawns in the classroom: Self-report and projective assessments of individual differences in the children's perceptions. *Journal of Personality and Social Psychology, 50,* 550–558.

Ryans, D. G. (1960). *Characteristics of effective teachers, their descriptions, comparisons and appraisal: A research study.* Washington, DC: American Council on Education.

Sabers, D. S., Cushing, K. S., & Berliner, D. C. (1991). Differences among teachers in a task characterized by simultaneity, multidimensionality, and immediacy. *American Educational Research Journal, 28,* 68–87.

Sadker, M., & Sadker, D. (1986). Sexism in the classroom: From grade school to graduate school. *Phi Delta Kappan, 68,* 512.

Sadker, M., Sadker, D., & Klein, S. (1991). The issue of gender in elementary and secondary education. *Review of Research in Education, 17,* 269–334.

Salovey, P., & Mayer, J. D. (1990). Emotional intelligence. *Imagination, Cognition, and Personality, 9,* 185–211.

Sanchez, F., & Anderson, M. L. (1990, May). Gang mediation: A process that works. *Principal,* 54–56.

Sattler, J. (2001). *Assessment of children* (4th ed. rev.). San Diego: Jerome M. Sattler.

Sawyer, R. J., Graham, S., & Harris, K. R. (1992). Direct teaching, strategy instruction, and strategy instruction with explicit self-regulation: Effects on the composition skills and self-efficacy of learning disabled students. *Journal of Educational Psychology, 84,* 340–352.

Scales, P., & McEwin, C. K. (1994). *Growing pains: The making of America's middle school teachers.* Columbus, OH: National Middle School Association and the Center for Early Adolescence.

Schein, E. H. (1992). *Organizational culture and leadership* (2nd ed.). San Francisco: Jossey-Bass.

Schein, E. H. (1999). *The corporate culture.* San Francisco: Jossey-Bass.

Schiefele, U. (1991). Interest, learning, and motivation. *Educational Psychologist, 26,* 299–324.

Schraw, G., & Moshman, D. (1995). Metacognitive theories. *Educational Psychology Review, 7,* 351–371.

Schunk, D. H. (2000). *Learning theories: An educational perspective* (3rd ed.). Columbus, OH: Merrill/Prentice-Hall.

Schwartz, B., & Reisberg, D. (1991). *Learning and memory.* New York: Norton.

Seddon, G. M. (1978). The properties of Bloom's taxonomy of educational objectives for the cognitive domain. *Review of Educational Research, 48,* 303–323.

Seligman, M. E. P. (1975). *Helplessness: On depression, development, and death.* San Francisco: Freeman.

Semb, G. B., & Ellis, J. A. (1994). Knowledge taught in school: What is remembered? *Review of Educational Research, 64,* 253–286.

Senge, P. M. (1990). *The fifth discipline: The art and practice of the learning organization.* New York: Doubleday.

Serbin, L., & O'Leary, D. (1975, January), How nursery schools teach girls to shut up. *Psychology Today,* 56–58.

Serpell, R. (1993). Interface between sociocultural and psychological aspects of cognition. In E. Forman, N. Minick, & C. A. Stone (Eds.), *Contexts for learning: Sociocultural dynamics in children's development* (pp. 357–368). New York: Oxford University Press.

Shavelson, R. J. (1987). Planning. In M. Dunkin (Ed.), *The international encyclopedia of teaching and teacher education* (pp. 483–486). New York: Pergamon Press.

Shepard, L. A., & Smith, M. L. (1989). Academic and emotional effects of kindergarten retention. In L. Shepard & M. Smith (Eds.), *Flunking grades: Research and policies on retention* (pp. 79–107). Philadelphia: Falmer Press.

Shimahara, N. K., & Sakai, A. (1995). *Learning to teach in two cultures.* New York: Garland.

Shoda, Y., Mischel, W., & Peake, P. K. (1990). Predicting adolescent cognitive and self-regulatory competencies from preschool delay of gratification. *Developmental Psychology, 26,* 978–986.

Shuell, T. J. (1986). Cognitive conceptions of learning. *Review of Educational Research, 56,* 411–436.

Shulman, L. S. (1987). Knowledge and teaching: Foundations of the new reform. *Harvard Educational Review, 19*(2), 4–14.

Shultz, J., & Florio, S. (1979). Stop and freeze: The negotiation of social and physical space in a kindergarten/first grade classroom. *Anthropology and Education Quarterly, 10,* 166–181.

Sisk, D. A. (1988). Children at risk: The identification of the gifted among the minority. *Gifted Education International, 5,* 138–141.

Sizer, T. (1984). *Horace's compromise: The dilemma of the American high school* (updated ed.). Princeton, NJ: Houghton Mifflin.

Skinner, B. F. (1950). Are theories of learning necessary? *Psychological Review, 57,* 193–216.

Slavin, R. E. (1987). Ability grouping and student achievement in elementary schools: A best-evidence synthesis. *Review of Educational Research, 57,* 293–336.

Slavin, R. E. (1990). Achievement effects of ability grouping in secondary schools: A best-evidence synthesis. *Review of Educational Research, 60,* 471–500.

Slavin, R. E. (1995). *Cooperative learning* (2nd ed.). Boston: Allyn & Bacon.

Slavin, R. E., & Fashola, O. S. (1998). *Show me the evidence: Proven and promising programs for America's schools.* Thousand Oaks, CA: Corwin.

Slavin, R. E., & Karweit, N. (1985). Effects of whole class, ability grouped, and individualized instruction on mathematics achievement. *American Educational Research Journal, 22,* 351–368.

Smith, C. B. (Moderator) (1994). *Whole language: The debate.* Bloomington, IN: EDINFO Press.

Smith, F. (1975). *Comprehension and learning: A conceptual framework for teachers.* New York: Holt, Rinehart & Winston.

Smith, J. D., & Caplan, J. (1988). Cultural differences in cognitive style development. *Developmental Psychology, 24,* 46–52.

Smith, M. (1993). Some school-based violence prevention strategies. *NASSP Bulletin, 77*(557), 70–75.

Snider, V. E. (1990). What we know about learning styles from research in special education. *Educational Leadership, 48*(2), 53.

Snow, C. E. (1987). Beyond conversation: Second language learners' acquisition of description and explanation. In J. P. Lantolf & A. Labarca (Eds.), *Research in second language learning: Focus on the classroom* (pp. 3–16). Norwood, NJ: Ablex.

Snow, R. E., Corno, L., & Jackson, D. (1996). Individual differences in affective and cognitive functions. In D. Berliner & R. Calfee (Eds.), *Handbook of educational psychology* (pp. 243–310). New York: Macmillan.

Snowman, J. (1984). Learning tactics and strategies. In G. Phye & T. Andre (Eds.), *Cognitive instructional psychology* (pp. 243–275). Orlando, FL: Academic Press.

Soar, R. S., & Soar, R. M. (1979). Emotional climate and management. In P. Peterson & H. Walberg (Eds.), *Research on teaching: Concepts, findings, and implications* (pp. 97–119). Berkeley, CA: McCutchan.

Sokolove, S., Garrett, J., Sadker, D., & Sadker, M. (1986). Interpersonal communications skills. In J. Cooper (Ed.), *Classroom teaching skills: A handbook* (pp. 233–278). Lexington, MA: D. C. Heath.

Spearman, C. (1927). *The abilities of man: Their nature and measurement.* New York: Macmillan.

Spiro, R. J., Feltovich, P. J., Jacobson, M. L., & Coulson, R. L. (1991). Cognitive flexibility, constructivism, and hypertext: Random access instruction for advanced knowledge acquisition in ill-structured domains. *Educational Technology, 31*(5), 24–33.

Stahl, S. A., & Miller, P. D. (1989). Whole language and language experience approaches for beginning reading: A quantitative research synthesis. *Review of Educational Research, 59,* 87–116.

Stainback, S., & Stainback, W. (1992). Schools as inclusive communities. In W. Stainback & S. Stainback (Eds.), *Controversial issues confronting special education: Divergent perspectives* (pp. 29–43). Boston: Allyn & Bacon.

Stanovich, K. E. (1991). Reading disability: Assessment issues. In H. Swanson (Ed.), *Handbook of assessment of learning disabilities: Theory, research, and practice* (pp. 147–175). Austin, TX: Pro-Ed.

Stanovich, K. E. (1998). Cognitive neuroscience and educational psychology: What season is it? *Educational Psychology Review, 10,* 419–426.

Steele, C. M., & Aronson, J. (1995). Stereotype threat and the intellectual test performance of African Americans. *Journal of Personality and Social Psychology, 69,* 797–811.

Stepien, W., & Gallagher, S. (1993). Problem-based learning: As authentic as it gets. *Educational Leadership, 50*(7), 25–28.

Sternberg, R. J. (1985). *Beyond IQ: A triarchic theory of human intelligence.* New York: Cambridge University Press.

Sternberg, R. J. (1990). *Metaphors of mind: Conceptions of the nature of intelligence.* New York: Cambridge University Press.

Sternberg, R. J., & Detterman, D. L. (Eds.). (1986). *What is intelligence? Contemporary viewpoints on its nature and definition.* Norwood, NJ: Ablex.

Sternberg, R. J., & Wagner, R. K. (1993). The g-ocentric view of intelligence and job performance is wrong. *Current Directions in Psychological Science, 2,* 1–5.

Sternberg, R. J., Wagner, R. K., Williams, W. M., & Horvath, J. A. (1995). Testing common sense. *American Psychologist, 50,* 912–927.

Stevenson, H. W., & Stigler, J. (1992). *The learning gap.* New York: Summit Books.

Stipek, D. J. (2002). *Motivation to learn* (3rd ed.). Boston: Allyn & Bacon.

Stipek, D. J. (1996). Motivation and instruction. In D. Berliner & R. Calfee (Eds.), *Handbook of educational psychology* (pp. 85–109). New York: Macmillan.

Stodolsky, S. S. (1988). *The subject matters: Classroom activity in math and social studies.* Chicago: University of Chicago Press.

Stumpf, H. (1995). Gender differences on tests of cognitive abilities: Experimental design issues and empirical results. *Learning and Individual Differences, 7,* 275–288.

Swanson, H. L. (1990). The influence of metacognitive knowledge and aptitude on problem solving. *Journal of Educational Psychology, 82,* 306–314.

Swanson, H. L., O'Conner, J. E., & Cooney, J. B. (1990). An information processing analysis of expert and novice teachers' problem solving. *American Educational Research Journal, 27,* 533–556.

Symons, S., Woloshyn, V., & Pressley, M. (1994). The scientific evaluation of the whole language approach to literacy development [Special issue]. *Educational Psychologist, 29*(4).

Tait, H., & Entwistle, N. J. (in press). Identifying students at risk through ineffective study strategies. *Higher Education.*

Taylor, J. B. (1983). Influence of speech variety on teachers' evaluation of reading comprehension. *Journal of Educational Psychology, 75,* 662–667.

Teacher Magazine (1991, April). You and the system: Who you will teach, p. 32H.

Tharp, R. G. (1989). Psychocultural variables and constants: Effects on teaching and learning in schools. *American Psychologist, 44,* 349–359.

Thompson, G. (1991). *Teaching through themes.* New York: Scholastic.

Thurstone, L. L. (1938). Primary mental abilities. *Psychometric Monographs,* No. 1.

Tobias, S. (1985). Text anxiety: Interference, defective skills, and cognitive capacity. *Educational Psychologist, 20,* 135–142.

Tobin, K. (1990, April). Metaphors in the construction of teacher knowledge. Paper presented at the Annual Meeting of the American Educational Research Association, Boston.

Tochon, F., & Munby, H. (1993). Novice and expert teachers' time epistemology: A wave function from didactics to pedagogy. *Teaching and Teacher Education, 9,* 205–218.

Tomlinson-Keasey, C. (1990). Developing our intellectual resources for the 21st century: Educating the gifted. *Journal of Educational Psychology, 82,* 399–403.

Torrance, E. P. (1986). Teaching creative and gifted learners. In M. Wittrock (Ed.), *Handbook of research on teaching* (3rd ed.) (pp. 630–647). New York: Macmillan.

Tschannen-Moran, M., & Woolfolk Hoy, A. (2001). Designing, implementing, and improving collaborative learning: A memorable model. *Teacher Educator, 37.*

Tschannen-Moran, M., Woolfolk Hoy, A., & Hoy, W. K. (1998). Teacher efficacy: Its meaning and measure. *Review of Educational Research, 68,* 202–248.

Urdan, T. C., & Maehr, M. L. (1995). Beyond a two-goal theory of motivation and achievement: A case for social goals. *Review of Educational Research, 65,* 213–243.

Van Meter, P., Yokoi, L., & Pressley, M. (1994). College students' theory of note-taking derived from their perceptions of note-taking. *Journal of Educational Psychology, 86,* 323–338.

Veenman, S. (1984). Perceived problems of beginning teachers. *Review of Educational Research, 54,* 143–178.

Vellutino, F. R. (1991). Introduction to three studies on reading acquisition: Convergent findings on theoretical foundations of code-oriented versus whole-language approaches to reading instruction. *Journal of Educational Psychology, 83,* 437–443.

Vera, A. H., & Simon, H. A. (1993). Situated action: A symbolic interpretation. *Cognitive Science, 17,* 7–48.

Vispoel, W. P., & Austin, J. R. (1995). Success and failure in junior high school: A critical incident approach to understanding students' attributional beliefs. *American Educational Research Journal, 32,* 377–412.

von Glaserfeld, E. (1990). An exposition of constructivism: Why some like it radical. In R. Davis, C. Maher, & N Noddings (Eds.), *Constructivist views on the teaching and learning of mathematics* (pp. 19–30). Monograph 4 of the National Council of Teachers of Mathematics, Reston, VA.

von Glaserfeld, E. (1995). A constructivist approach to teaching. In L. Steffe & J. Gale (Eds.), *Constructivism in education* (p. 5). Hillsdale, NJ: Lawrence Erlbaum.

von Glaserfeld, E. (1997). Amplification of a constructivist perspective. *Issues in Education: Contributions from Educational Psychology, 3,* 203–210.

Vroom, V. (1964). *Work and motivation.* New York: Wiley.

Vygotsky, L. S. (1978). *Mind in society: The development of higher mental process.* Cambridge, MA: Harvard University Press.

Walberg, H. J. (1990). Productive teaching and instruction: Assessing the knowledge base. *Phi Delta Kappan, 72,* 470–478.

Walton, G. (1961). Identification of the intellectually gifted children in the public school kindergarten. Unpublished doctoral dissertation, University of California, Los Angeles.

Wang, A. Y., & Thomas, M. H. (1995). Effects of keywords on long-term retention: Help or hindrance? *Journal of Educational Psychology, 87,* 468–475.

Wang, A. Y., Thomas, M. H., & Ouellette, J. A. (1992). Keyword mnemonic and retention of second-language vocabulary words. *Journal of Educational Psychology, 84,* 520–528.

Wang, M. C., Haertel, G. D., & Walberg, H. J. (1993). Toward a knowledge base for school learning. *Review of Educational Research, 63,* 249–294.

Wang, M. C., Haertel, G. D., & Walberg, H. J. (1997). Learning influences. In H. Walberg & G. Heartel (Eds.), *Psychology and educational practice* (pp. 199–211). Berkeley, CA: McCutchan.

Webb, N. (1985). Verbal interaction and learning in peer-directed groups. *Theory Into Practice, 24,* 32–39.

Webb, N., & Palincsar, A. (1996). Group processes in the classroom. In D. C. Berliner & R. C. Calfee (Eds.), *Handbook of educational psychology* (pp. 841–876). New York: Macmillan.

Weinberg, R. A. (1989). Intelligence and IQ. *American Psychologist, 44,* 98–104.

Weiner, B. (1979). A theory of motivation for some classroom experiences. *Journal of Educational Psychology, 71,* 3–25.

Weiner, B. (1980). The role of affect in rational (attributional) approaches to human motivation. *Educational Researcher, 9,* 4–11.

Weiner, B. (1986). *An attributional theory of motivation and emotion.* New York: Springer.

Weiner, B. (1992). *Human motivation: Metaphors, theories, and research.* Newbury Park, CA: Sage.

Weiner, B. (1994). Ability versus effort revisited: The moral determinants of achievement evaluation an achievement as a moral system. *Educational Psychologist, 29,* 163–172.

Weiner, B., & Graham, S. (1989). Understanding the motivational role of affect: Life span research from an attributional perspective. *Cognition and Emotion, 4,* 401–419.

Weiner, B., Russell, D., & Lerman, D. (1978). Affective consequences of causal ascriptions. In J. H. Harvey, W. J. Ickes, & R. F. Kidd (Eds.), *New directions in attribution research* (Vol. 2). Hillsdale, NJ: Erlbaum.

Weinert, F. E., & Helmke, A. (1995). Learning from wise mother nature or big brother instructor: The wrong choice as seen from an educational perspective. *Educational Psychologist, 30,* 135–143.

Weinstein, C. S. (1977). Modifying student behavior in an open classroom through changes in the physical design. *American Educational Research Journal, 14,* 249–262.

Weinstein, C. S. (1996). *Secondary classroom management: Lessons from research and practice.* New York: McGraw-Hill.

Weinstein, C. S. (1999). Reflections on best practices and promising programs: Beyond assertive classroom discipline. In H. J. Freiberg (Ed.), *Beyond behaviorism: Changing the classroom management paradigm* (pp. 147–163). Boston: Allyn & Bacon.

Weinstein, C. S., & Mignano, A. J., Jr. (1997). *Elementary classroom management: Lessons from research and practice* (2nd ed.) New York: McGraw-Hill.

Weiss, G., & Hechtman, L. T. (1993). *Hyperactive children grow up: ADHD in children, adolescents, and adults* (2nd ed.). New York: Guilford Press.

Wentzel, K. R. (1999). Social-motivational processes and interpersonal relations: Implications for understanding motivation in school. *Journal of Educational Psychology, 91,* 76–97.

Wessman, A. (1972). Scholastic and psychological effects of a compensatory education program for disadvantaged high school students: Project A B C. *American Educational Research Journal, 9,* 361–372.

White, S., & Tharp, R. G. (1988, April). Questioning and wait-time: A cross cultural analysis. Paper presented at the annual meeting of the American Educational Research Association, New Orleans.

Whitehead, A. N. (1929). *The aims of education.* New York: Macmillan.

Whitmore, J. R., & Maker, C. J. (1985). *Intellectual giftedness in disabled persons.* Rockville: MD: Aspen.

Wigfield, A., & Eccles, J. (1989). Test anxiety in elementary and secondary school students. *Educational Psychologist, 24,* 159–183.

Wiggins, G. (1989). Teaching to the authentic test. *Educational Leadership, 46*(7), 41–47.

Wiggins, G. (1991). Assessment, authenticity, context, and validity. *Phi Delta Kappan, 75,* 200–214.

Williams, G. C., Wiener, M. W., Markakis, K. M., Reeve, J., & Deci, E. L. (1993). Medical student motivation for internal medicine. *Annals of Internal Medicine.*

Willig, A. C. (1985). A meta-analysis of selected studies on the effectiveness of bilingual education. *Review of Educational Research, 55,* 269–317.

Willingham, W. W., & Cole, N. S. (1997). *Gender and fair assessment.* Mahwah, NJ: Lawrence Erlbaum Associates.

Wilson, C. W., & Hopkins, B. L. (1973). The effects of contingent music on the intensity of noise in junior high home economics classes. *Journal of Applied Behavior Analysis, 6,* 269–275.

Wingate, N. (1986). Sexism in the classroom. *Equity and Excellence, 22,* 105–110.

Witkin, H. A., Moore, C. A., Goodenough, D. R., & Cox, R. W. (1977). Field-dependent and field-independent cognitive styles and their educational implications. *Review of Educational Research, 47,* 1–64.

Wittrock, M. C. (1992). An empowering conception of educational psychology. *Educational Psychologist, 27,* 129–142.

Wolf, D., Bixby, J., Glenn, J., III, & Gardner, H. (1991). To use their minds well: New forms of student assessment. *Review of Research in Education, 17,* 31–74.

Wolters, C. A., Yu, S. L., & Pintrich, P. R. (1996). The relation between goal orientation and students' motivational beliefs and self-regulated learning. *Learning and Individual Differences, 8,* 211–238.

Women on Words and Images. (1975). *Dick and Jane as victims: Sex stereotyping in children's readers.* Available from author, P.O. Box 2163, Princeton, NJ.

Wood, S. E., & Wood, E. G. (1999). *The world of psychology* (3rd ed.). Boston: Allyn & Bacon.

Woolfolk, A. E., & Brooks, D. (1983). Nonverbal communication in teaching. In E. Gordon (Ed.), *Review of research in education* (Vol. 10, pp. 103–150). Washington, DC: American Educational Research Association.

Woolfolk, A. E., & Hoy, W. K. (1990). Prospective teachers' sense of efficacy and beliefs about control. *Journal of Educational Psychology, 82,* 81–91.

Woolfolk, A. E., Rosoff, B., & Hoy, W. K. (1990). Teachers' sense of efficacy and their beliefs about managing students. *Teaching and Teacher Education, 6,* 137–148.

Woolfolk Hoy, A., & Tschannen-Moran, M. (1999). Implications of cognitive approaches to peer learning for teacher education. In A. O'Donnell & A. King (Eds.), *Cognitive perspectives on peer learning* (pp. 257–284). Mahwah, NJ: Lawrence Erlbaum.

Worthen, B. R. (1993). Critical issues that will determine the future of alternative assessment. *Phi Delta Kappan, 74,* 444–457.

Wright, S. C., & Taylor, D. M. (1995). Identity and the language of the classroom: Investigating the impact of heritage versus second language instruction on personal and collective self-esteem. *Journal of Educational Psychology, 87,* 241–252.

Yee, A. H. (1992). Asians as stereotypes and students: Misperceptions that persist. *Educational Psychology Review, 4,* 95–132.

Yerkes, R. M., & Dodson, J. D. (1908). The relation of strength of stimulus to rapidity of habit formation. *Journal of Comparative Neurology, 18,* 459–482.

Yetman, N. R. (1999). *Majority and minority: The dynamics of race and ethnicity in American life.* (6th ed.). Boston: Allyn & Bacon.

Young, A. J. (1997). I think, therefore I'm motivated: The relations among cognitive strategy use, motivational orientation, and classroom perceptions over time. *Learning and Individual Differences, 9,* 249–283.

Zeidner, M. (1995). Adaptive coping with test situations. *Educational Psychologist, 30,* 123–134.

Zigmond, N., Jenkins, J., Fuchs, D., Deno, S., & Fuchs, L. S. (1995). When students fail to achieve satisfactorily: A reply to Leskey and Waldron. *Phi Delta Kappan, 77,* 303–306.

Zimmerman. B. J. (1995). Self-efficacy and educational development. In A. Bandura (Ed.), *Self-efficacy in changing societies* (202–231). New York: Cambridge University Press.

Ziomek, R. L., & Maxey, J. M. (1993). To nationally test or not to nationally test: That is the question! *Measurement and Evaluation in Counseling and Development, 26,* 64–68.

INDEX

Ability differences, 38–42
Ability grouping, 38–39, 40
Abi-Nader, J., 141–142
Abruscato, J., 260
Academic learning time, 190–191
Accountability, 206
Achievement
    anxiety and, 136–137
    intelligence and, 37–38, 130–131
Achievement motivation, 120
Achievement tests, 244–247
    interpreting, 245–247
    norm-referenced, 245
Action zones, 198–199
Adams, M. J., 173
Adams, R. S., 198
Affective domain, 161–162
Affective states, 297
Agne, R. M., 164
Airasian, P. W., 156, 180, 262, 263, 266
Alderman, M. K., 130–131
Alexander, P. A., 72, 117, 132
Alleman-Brooks, J., 227
Allocated time, 190
Alloy, L. B., 125
Allport, G., 102
American Association for the Advancement of Science, 94
Americans with Disabilities Act (ADA), 48
Ames, C., 125, 221
Ames, R., 125
Anastasi, A., 248, 254
Anchored instruction, 100
Anderman, E. M., 118, 126, 222–223
Anderson, C. S., 177, 284
Anderson, C. W., 118
Anderson, E., 224
Anderson, J. R., 80, 94, 95–96, 171
Anderson, L. M., 169, 171, 192, 202, 227
Anderson, L. W., 159, 160, 161
Anderson, M. L., 219
Anderson, T. H., 86–87, 90
Antecedents, 65
Anxiety, 136–137, 138
Aptitude tests, 248–249
Arends, R. E., 101
Armbruster, B. B., 86–87, 90
Aronson, E., 102, 104–105
Aronson, J., 253

Arousal, 134–137
    anxiety and, 136–137, 138
    curiosity and, 134–135
    defined, 134
Artifacts, 279–280
Ashcraft, M. H., 80
Assertive discipline, 216
Assessment, 8–9, 233–273
    achievement tests in, 244–247
    advantages of tests, 252–255
    aptitude tests in, 248–249
    criterion-referenced tests in, 236
    defined, 235
    diagnostic tests in, 247–248
    grades and grading in, 266–269
    leadership challenge of, 234
    measurement, 234–235
    new directions in, 255–266
    norm-referenced tests in, 235–236, 245
    test scores in, 236–244
    uses of tests in, 249–252
Atkinson, J. W., 120
Atkinson, L. A., 87
Atkinson, R. K., 87
Attainment value of learning, 140, 141
Attention, capturing, 76
Attention deficit-hyperactive disorder (ADHD), 42–44, 83
Attribution theory, 123–126, 130–131
    cues and causes in, 125–126
    dimensions, 123–124
    learned helplessness, 124–125
    motivation and, 125
Au, K. H., 22–23, 26
Austin, G. A., 72
Austin, J. R., 132–133
Ausubel, D. P., 72
Authentic assessment, 257–265
    authentic tests in, 10, 258, 259
    exhibitions in, 258, 260–261, 262–265
    portfolios in, 258, 259–260, 261, 262–265
    standardized tests versus, 257
Authentic tasks, 97, 221, 222
Authentic tests, 10, 258, 259
Autonomy, 221–225

Baddeley, A. D., 77
Baenninger, M., 29

Bailey, S. M., 28
Baker, D., 29
Bales, R. F., 290
Bandura, A., 127–128, 296, 298
Bangert, R. L., 254
Bangert-Downs, R. L., 268
Banks, J. A., 18, 19
Barling, J., 128
Baron, R. A., 35
Baroody, A. R., 173
Barrett, M., 225
Bartlett, F. C., 81, 89
Baumeister, R. F., 121
Beane, J. A., 164
Beaudry, J. S., 25
Becker, W. C., 67
Beeth, M. E., 176, 177, 179
Behavioral objectives, 157
Behavioral views of learning, 4, 63–70, 95–96
    antecedents and behavior change, 65–67
    teaching applications of, 67–70
    types of consequences and, 63–65
Behavioral views of motivation, 5, 113–114, 115
Being needs, 119
Belanoff, P., 260
Beliefs, 126–130
    about ability, 126–127
    about self-efficacy, 127–130
Bempechat, J., 126
Benbow, C. P., 42
Bennett, Christine I., 20
Berends, M., 39
Berg, C. A., 171
Berliner, D. C., 154, 166, 190, 191, 251
Berlyne, D., 134
Betancourt, H., 18
Between-class ability grouping, 38–39
Beyer, J. M., 280
Bias, in testing, 252
Biddle, B. J., 18, 198, 251
Bilingualism, 20–21, 22, 152
Birch, J. W., 42
Bixby, J., 255, 258, 260
Bjorklund, D. F., 23
Black, H., 87
Black English, 19–20
Bloom, B. S., 159–161

Bloom, R., 268
Blumenfeld, P. C., 116
Bodily-kinesthetic intelligence, 33
Bogdan, R. C., 49–52
Boggiano, A. K., 225
Bolman, L. G., 279, 281–282
Bolt, E., 225
Boodoo, G., 30, 38
Borko, H., 153, 154, 171
Borkowski, J. G., 44, 84
Bouchard, A., 30, 38
Bounded choice, 224–225
Bourdon, L., 268
Bowers, J., 93
Boykin, W., 30, 38
Boyle, R. A., 112, 132
Bracey, G. W., 251
Bransford, J., 83
Brody, N., 30, 38
Brooks, D., 199, 207
Brophy, J. E., 39, 113, 115–116, 125,
    134, 137, 138, 141, 167–168,
    177–178, 180, 181, 189–190,
    227–228
Brown, A. L., 83, 85, 165, 178–179
Brown, J., 253
Brown, J. S., 100–101
Brown, N., 98
Brown, R., 84
Brubaker, N. L., 227
Bruner, J. S., 4, 72, 89, 97
Bruning, R. H., 89
Burden, P. R., 195, 207, 211
Burland, S., 81
Bursuck, W., 48, 53, 88
Bus, A. G., 172, 173
Buss, D. M., 29
Butler, R., 117, 268
Byrnes, J. P., 25, 85

Cai, Y., 225
Calderhead, J., 155, 156
Caldwell, D., 281
Callahan, C. M., 35
Cambourne, B., 262
Cameron, R., 81
Camp, R., 260
Campione, J. C., 83, 178–179
Cangelosi, J. S., 162
Canter, L., 216
Canter, M., 216
Caplan, J., 24
Carey, L. M., 236–237
Carroll, J., 31
Cartwright, C. A., 44
Cartwright, G. P., 44
Causal attribution, 123–124
Ceci, S. J., 30, 37, 38

Central tendency, 237
Chamot, A. U., 21
Chance, P., 114
Change
    behavior, 65–67
    conceptual change teaching, 177,
        178, 179
    in school climate, 299–309
Charles, C. M., 196, 207, 208
Chatman, J. A., 281
Chunking, 77
Clarity, 165–167
    during the lesson, 166–167
    organization and, 165
    planning for, 166
Clark, C. M., 155–156
Clark, R. W., 120
Clarke, J. H., 164
Classroom conditions, 137–139
Classroom management, 7–8,
        187–232
    aim of, 190
    communication and, 213–220
    discipline problems and, 208–213
    for elementary students, 195,
        202–203
    leadership challenge of, 188–189
    learning community and, 203–205
    learning environment and,
        189–203, 205–208, 220–228
    for secondary students, 196, 203
    special programs for, 211–213
    stages of, 189–190
    three Cs of, 204–205
Clements, B. S., 166, 192–193, 195,
    196, 208
Clifford, M. M., 10, 137, 267
Clore, G. L., 115
Closed climate, 289
Clough, M., 171
Clover, S. I. R., 284, 286
Coaching, for taking tests, 254,
    256–257
Cobb, P., 93
Cognition and Technology Group at
    Vanderbilt University (CTGV),
    94, 100
Cognitive apprenticeships, 100–101
Cognitive domain, 159–161
Cognitive objectives, 157
Cognitive styles, 3, 23, 24–25
Cognitive views of learning, 4,
    70–89, 95–96
    information processing model in,
        73–74, 82
    knowledge and, 72–73
    learning strategies and tactics,
        83–89

long-term memory in, 77–81
metacognition in, 81–83,
    160–161
sensory memory in, 74–75
working memory in, 75–77
Cognitive views of motivation, 5,
    114–115
Cohen, M. D., 296
Cold cognition, 131–132
Cole, M., 91–92
Cole, N. S., 29
Collaborative consultation, 52
Collective efficacy, 296–299
Collective Efficacy Scale
    (CE-Scale), 298–299
Collins, A. M., 72, 94, 100–101,
    115, 165
Comeaux, M. A., 154
Communication, 213–220
    assertive discipline in, 216
    conflict management in,
        217–219
    confrontations in, 217–219
    counseling in, 214–215
    diagnosis in, 213–214
    with families about classroom
        management, 219–220
    "I" messages in, 209, 216
    message sent–message received,
        213
    negotiations in, 217
Community of Learners, 178–179
Community partnerships, 119
Conceptual change teaching, 177,
    178, 179
Conditional knowledge, 73, 84
Confidence, 139–140
Confidence interval, 244
Confidentiality, 49
Conflict management, 217–219
Confrey, J., 175, 176
Confrontations, 217–219
Connell, J. P., 267
Consequences, 196–197
Constructivist views of learning, 4, 7,
    89–105
    knowledge and, 93–94
    nature of, 89–91
    planning and, 162–164
    teaching applications of, 94–105
    types of, 89–93
Context, 80
Contingency contract programs,
    67–70, 71
Continuous improvement, 2
Cook, S. D. N., 296
Cooke, B. L., 155
Cooney, J. B., 154

Cooperation
    classroom management and, 7–8,
        189–190
    in constructivist approach, 101–105
Cooperative learning, 101–105,
    162–164, 225–227, 262–264
Cooperative teaching, 52
Coping, with anxiety, 137
Cordova, D. I., 133
Corno, L., 24, 39, 268
Coulson, R. L., 91
Council of Chief State School
    Officers, 1
Counseling, 214–215
Covington, M. V., 127, 130, 136
Cowley, G., 132
Cox, K. E., 224
Cox, R. W., 23
Craik, F. I. M., 77, 80
Criterion-referenced tests, 236
Croft, D. B., 283
Cross-grade grouping, 39
Cruickshank, D. R., 165, 166
Cues and cuing, 66, 125–126
Cultural diversity, 18–19
Culturally compatible classrooms,
    21–27, 28
    cognitive and learning styles in,
        23–25
    participation structures in, 26
    social organization in, 22–23
    sources of misunderstandings in,
        26–27
Culture-fair tests, 254
Culture-neutral tests, 254
Cummins, J., 21
Cunningham, A. F., 72
Curiosity, 134–135, 141
Curriculum, 67–70, 83–90, 94–105,
    171–179, 186
Curriculum, gender bias in, 27
Curriculum planning, 155–165
    constructivist perspective on,
        162–164
    learning spaces, 197–202
    mathematics
    constructivist approach in, 7,
        173–176, 180
    examples of good teachers, 153
    gender bias in, 30
    learning disabilities and, 45
    sex differences in mental abilities,
        29
    teaching for understanding,
        173–176
objectives for learning, 156–159
reading
    learning disabilities and, 45, 46

strategies for, 88–89
    teaching for understanding,
        171–173, 174–175
science
    constructivist approach in, 7,
        176–177
    teaching for understanding,
        176–177
    taxonomies in, 159–162
Cushing, K. S., 154
Cylert, 44

Dansereau, D. F., 84
Darley, J. M., 118
Davis, J. K., 23
Davis, R. B., 171
Deal, T. E., 279, 281–282
Debus, R., 127
Decay, 81
deCharms, R., 121
Deci, E. L., 5, 70, 112–114, 120–121,
    203, 212–213, 221–223
Deciding what is important, 84–86
Declarative knowledge, 72–73
Decoding skills, 173
Defense mechanisms, 278
Deficiency needs, 119
Delaney, H. D., 88
Delgardelle, M., 106
Dempster, F. N., 265–266
Deno, S., 48
Denton, J. J., 27
Derry, S. J., 83–85, 91, 93, 94
Deshler, D. D., 46
Detterman, D. L., 30
Deutsch, M., 102
Dewey, J., 4, 89, 97, 102
Dexedrine, 44
Diagnosis, of communication
    problems, 213–214
Diagnostic tests, 247–248
Dialects, 19–20
Dickson, M., 260
Diller, L., 44
Direct instruction, 168–171
Discipline, assertive, 216
Discipline problems, 208–213
    penalties and, 210
    with secondary students, 209–211
Disengaged climate, 288
DiVesta, F. J., 86
Dodson, J. D., 134, 136
Dole, J. A., 84, 85
Domain-specific knowledge, 72
Doyle, P. H., 205–206
Doyle, W., 7, 155, 189, 190, 207, 227
Driscoll, M. P., 91, 94, 97, 102,
    152–153

Drug therapy, 44
Duchastel, P., 158
Duckworth, E., 171
Dudley, B., 217
Duffy, G. G., 84, 85, 166, 227
Duke, D. L., 155
Duncker, 89
Dunn, K., 24, 25
Dunn, R., 24, 25
Dweck, C. S., 126
Dyson, A. H., 224

Eaton, W. O., 136
Eccles, J., 136, 138, 140
Education for All Handicapped
    Children Act (Public Law
    94–142), 48
Effective teaching
    characteristics of effective
        teachers, 165–167, 168
    classroom management in,
        202–203
    concerns of teachers, 155
    examples of, 151–153
    in inclusive classrooms, 49–52
    nature of, 6–7
    teacher effects on student
        learning, 167–171
Efficacy, 12
Ego-involved learners, 117
Eisner, E. W., 258
Elaboration, 79–80
Elaborative rehearsal, 77
Elawar, M. C., 268
Elementary students
    classroom management for, 195,
        202–203
organizational climate and, 285, 286
Ellis, J. A., 81
Emmer, E. T., 166, 192–193, 195,
    196, 202, 203, 205, 207, 208
Emotional intelligence, 35
Engaged climate, 288
Engaged time, 190–191
Engagement, 205–206
Engel, P., 251
Engelhart, M. D., 159–160
Engelmann, S., 67
English as a Second Language
    (ESL), 21, 22
Enthusiasm, of teacher, 167
Entity view of ability, 126–127
Entwistle, N. J., 24
Epanchin, B. C., 211
Episodic memory, 78
Epstein, J. L., 221
EQ, 35
Equity, 264–265

Eresh, J. T., 262
Espe, C., 99
Evaluation, 83. *See also* Assessment
   in TARGET model, 223, 227–228
Evertson, C. M., 166, 189–190,
   192–193, 195, 196, 202, 203,
   205, 207, 208
Ewy, C., 254, 255
Excellence, 2
Executive control processes, 77,
   81–83
Exhibitions, 10, 259, 260–261,
   262–265
Existential intelligence, 32
Expectancy-value theories, 115
Expert teachers, 153–154
Explanatory links, 166–167
Extrinsic motivation, 112–113
Eye contact, 208

Failure, 267
Failure-accepting students, 130, 131
Failure-avoiding students, 130, 131
Fairness, in testing, 252
Familiarity, 141
Families, 51, 119, 220, 250
Family conferences, 51
   about aptitude test results, 249,
     250
   about classroom management,
     219–220
Family partnerships, 119
Fantasy, 133
Farnaham-Diggory, S., 72
Fashola, O. S., 181
Feedback, from grades, 268
Feiman-Nemser, S., 155
Feltovich, P. J., 91
Fennema, E., 30
Ferguson, D. L., 49–52
Ferguson, P. M., 49–52
Ferrara, R., 83
Field dependence, 23–25
Field independence, 23–25
Finkelstein, R., 290
Fiske, E. B., 250
Fitzgerald, J., 21
Flammer, A., 128
Flavell, E. R., 83
Flavell, J. H., 83
Flink, C., 225
Floden, R. E., 154
Florio, S., 26
Focus on task, 142–143
Ford, D., 98
Forgetting, 81
Fox, L. H., 41
Fox, N. A., 25

Freiberg, H. J., 205
Frick, T. W., 205
Fried, C. B., 253
Friend, M., 48, 53, 88
Frost, E. J., 159–160
Fuchs, D., 48
Fuchs, L. S., 48
Fuller, F. G., 155
Furst, N., 165, 167

Gagné, E. D., 73, 78, 80
Galanter, E., 72, 115
Gall, M., 167
Gallagher, S., 221
Gallup, A. M., 208, 252
Garcia, J., 27
Gardner, H., 32–34, 40, 55, 255,
   258, 260
Gardner, R., 84
Gardner, T. G., 97
Garmon, A., 39
Garner, R., 83, 133–134, 224
Garrett, J., 215
Garrison, J., 91, 94
Gartner, A., 45
Geary, D. C., 29, 93
Gender bias
   in curriculum, 27
   eliminating, 30, 31
   sex differences in mental abilities,
     29
Gender differences, 3, 27–30
Gender schemas, 27
General intelligence, 31
Gergen, K. J., 92
Gersten, R., 20–22
Gifted and talented students, 39–42
Gillett, M., 167
Ginsburg, H. P., 173
Gitomer, D. H., 262
Glasser, W., 209
Glenn, J. III, 255, 258, 260
Glucksberg, S., 118
Goals, 116–118
   conflicts and, 218
   defined, 116
   lessons for teachers and
     principals, 118
   types of, 116–118
Goddard, R. D., 2, 296, 298
Goldenberg, C., 21
Goleman, D., 35
Good, C., 253
Good, T. L., 39, 40, 134, 167–168,
   180, 198–199
Good behavior game, 211–212
Goodenough, D. R., 23
Goodenow, C., 121

Goodman, K. S., 171, 172
Goodnow, J. J., 72
Goodrich, H., 262
Gordon, E. W., 25
Gordon, T., 214, 216, 217
Gould, L. J., 21
Grade-equivalent scores, 240–241
Grades and grading, 10, 142,
   266–269
Graham, S., 46, 112, 123, 125, 126,
   128, 129, 173, 179, 180
Grant, C. A., 18
Gray, G. S., 86
Green, F. L., 83
Greene, D., 70, 121, 212–213
Greeno, J. G., 72, 94, 165
Gregorc, A. F., 24
Grissom, J. B., 267
Grolnick, W. S., 121, 203, 221–222
Gronlund, N. E., 156–158, 160, 235,
   244, 249, 251
Gross, M. U. M., 42
Grossman, H., 26, 29
Grossman, S. H., 26, 29
Group focus, 207
Grouping, in TARGET model, 222,
   225–227
Group IQ tests, 36, 41
Group work, 101–105
Gruson, L., 81
Guilford, J. P., 32, 35–36, 40
Guitierrez, R., 39
Guskey, T. R., 268
Gustafsson, J-E., 31
Guthrie, J. T., 224

Haertel, E. H., 264
Haertel, G. D., 3
Hakuta, K., 21
Halford, J. M., 18
Hall, J. W., 88
Hallahan, D. P., 45, 50, 83
Hallowell, E. M., 43–44
Halpern, D. F., 29, 30, 38
Halpin, A. W., 283–284
Hambleton, R. K., 252, 257
Hamilton, R. J., 158
Hannum, J., 295
Hansen, R. A., 136
Hanson, P. G., 302
Harris, K. R., 46, 173, 179, 180, 224
Hatch, T., 33
Hayman, M. L., 203
Healthy school climate, 294–295
Hechtman, L. T., 44
Helmke, A., 168, 171, 180
Herman, J., 258, 262, 264
Hernshaw, L. S., 70

Heuer, F., 132
Hewson, P. W., 176, 177
Hidi, S., 132
Hierarchy of needs, 118–120
Highlighting, 86
High-stakes testing, 9
Hilgard, E. R., 38
Hill, K. T., 136
Hill, W. H., 159–160
Hines, C. V., 165, 166
Hiroto, D. S., 124
Hoefler-Nissani, D. M., 176
Holland, J. D., 118
Holum, A., 100
Homestead, E., 164
Hopkins, B. L., 211
Horgan, D. D., 30
Horvath, J. A., 36
Hostile response style, 216
Hot cognition, 131–132
Hotkevich, M., 99
Hoy, W. K., 2, 62, 129, 130, 276, 283–286, 290, 293, 295, 296, 298–300, 302
Huber, G. P., 297
Huff, C. R., 218–219
Humanistic approaches to motivation, 5, 114, 115
Humanist psychology, 5, 114, 115
Hunter, M., 169, 207
Hunter Mastery Teaching Program, 169, 170
Hwang, Y., 87
Hyde, J. S., 29
Hyperactivity and attention disorders, 42–44, 83

Images, 78
"I" messages, 209, 216
Impulsive cognitive styles, 24
Incentives, 113–114, 142
Inclusion, 48, 49–52
Incremental view of ability, 126–127
Individual differences, 3–4, 16–59, 83. *See also* Ability differences; Gender differences; Intelligence; Multicultural classrooms
Individual education program (IEP), 48–49, 50
Individual IQ tests, 36, 41
Individuals with Disabilities Education Act (IDEA), 48
Individual Test Record, 245, 246
Information processing model, 73–74, 82
Innovations, 106
Inquiry learning, 97–99

Instructional leadership. *See also* Principals
  good teaching and, 6–7
  leadership challenges of, 17–18, 61–62, 111–112, 151, 188–189, 234, 275
  role of, 2–3
Instructional objectives, 156–159
Instrumental value of learning, 141–142
Intelligence, 30–38
  achievement and, 37–38, 130–131
  defined, 30
  emotional, 35
  general intelligence, 31
  heredity versus environment and, 38
  IQ and, 36–38, 39, 41
  multiple intelligences, 32–35
  nature of, 30–36
  as process, 35–36
Interest-area arrangements, 197–198
Interests, 131–134
  building on students', 133
  tapping, 132–134
Interest value of learning, 140, 141
Interference, 81
Internalization, 113
Interpersonal dynamics, 12
Interpersonal intelligence, 33
Interstate School Licensure Consortium (ISLLC), 313–320
Intrapersonal intelligence, 33
Intrinsic motivation, 112–113
IQ, 36–38, 39, 41
  scholastic aptitude and, 248–249
Iran-Nejad, A., 91
Irving, O., 208
Irwin, J. W., 86
Ishler, M., 99

Jackson, D., 24
Jackson, N. E., 40
Jacobson, L., 38
Jacobson, M. L., 91
Jagacinski, C. M., 117
Jehn, K. A., 281
Jenkins, J., 48
Jenson, W. R., 211, 212
Jigsaw, 104–105
Johnson, D. W., 103, 116, 203–204, 217–219, 225–226, 264
Johnson, R. T., 103, 116, 203–204, 217–219, 225–226, 264
Johnston, M. B., 84
Jones, E. D., 42
Jurden, F. H., 77

Kagan, S., 105
Kansas Learning Strategies Curriculum, 46
Karweit, N., 39, 155, 190
Kauffman, J. M., 45, 50, 54, 83
Keefe, J. W., 24–25
Kellaghan, T., 249
Kelly, K., 267
Kennedy, J. J., 165, 166
Kennelly, K. J., 136
Keogh, B. K., 42
Keogh, K., 253
Keyser, V., 128
Kher, N., 138
Kiewra, K. A., 86, 87
Kinchla, R., 118
Kindsvatter, R., 99
King, A., 104
Kirst, M., 251, 255
Klavas, A., 25
Klein, S., 28–29
Klinzing, H. G., 154
Knapp, M., 97
Knowledge
  learning and, 72–73, 93–94
  teachers', 165
Kogan, N., 24
Kohler, 89
Kohn, A., 114
Kolata, G. B., 30
Kottkamp, R., 2, 284, 285, 290, 293, 295
Kounin, J. S., 205–208
Krapp, A., 132
Krathwohl, D. R., 159–161
Kreitzer, A. E., 160
Kulik, C. C., 39, 42, 254, 268
Kulik, J. A., 39, 42, 254, 268

Land, M. L., 165
Language Development and Hypermedia Group, 97
Language differences, 19–21
Larrivee, B., 49
Latham, G. P., 115, 116
Lau, S., 125
Lave, J., 94
Learned helplessness, 45, 124–125
Learning, 60–109
  access to, 191–192
  behavioral views of, 4, 63–70, 95–96
  cognitive views of, 4, 70–89, 95–96
  constructivist views of, 4, 7, 89–105
  defined, 62
  leadership challenge of, 61–62

Learning *(continued)*
    motivation to learn in school,
        115–116
    nature of, 62–63
    significant influences on, 3
    teacher effects on, 167–171
    theories of, 4–5
    time for, 190–191
Learning community, 203–205
    getting started on, 205
Learning disabilities, 44–46, 47, 83
Learning environment
    authentic tasks in, 221
    autonomy in, 221–225
    cooperation in, 7–8, 189–190
    engagement in, 205–206
    learning spaces in, 197–202
    managing, 190–192
    prevention and, 207–208
    procedures in, 193
    recognizing accomplishment in,
        221–225
    rules in, 193–197
    TARGET model, 221–228
Learning goals, 117
Learning preferences, 24–25
Learning spaces, 197–202
    designing, 200
    interest-area arrangements,
        197–198
    personal territories, 198–202
Learning strategies and tactics,
        83–89, 90
    deciding what is important, 84–86
    mnemonics, 87–88
    reading strategies, 88–89
    visual tools, 86–87
Learning Style Inventory, 24–25
Learning Style Profile, 24–25
Learning styles, 3, 23, 24–25
Leary, M. R., 121
Least restrictive placement, 48
Leinhardt, G., 154
LeMahieu, P., 262
LePore, P. C., 39
Lepper, M. R., 70, 114, 121, 133,
        137, 212–213
Lerman, D., 125
Leslie, L., 72
Levin, J. R., 87, 88, 208–209
Levitt, B. L., 297
Lewis, A. C., 251–252
Liben, L. S., 27
Limited English proficiency
        (LEP), 21
Lin, Y., 137
Linguistic intelligence, 33
Linn, M. C., 29

Linn, R. L., 235, 244, 249, 250, 251
Lipsky, D. K., 45
Lipson, M. Y., 72
Little, J. K., 27
Livingston, C., 153, 154
Lloyd, J. W., 45
Locke, E. A., 115, 116
Lockhart, R. S., 77, 80
Locus of causality, 113
Loehlin, J. C., 30, 38
Logical-mathematical intelligence,
        33
Lohman, D. L., 31
Long-term memory, 73–74, 77–81
    capacity and duration of, 77–78
    contents of, 78–79
    storing and retrieving information
        in, 79–81
Lopez, S. R., 18
Lowell, E. L., 120
Lowenstein, G., 134
Lubin, 302
Lustina, M. J., 253
Lyman, H. B., 236

Mabry, L., 262
MacMillan, D. L., 42
Madaus, G. F., 160, 249
Maehr, M. L., 117, 118, 126,
        222–223
Mager, R., 157
Magnuson, D., 217
Magnusson, S. J., 98
Maher, C. A., 171
Mainstreaming, 48
Maintenance rehearsal, 77
Major, B., 253
Maker, C. J., 41
Mantzicopoulos, P., 267
Marano, N., 98
March, J. G., 297
Markakis, K. M., 221–223
Marsh, H. W., 127
Marshall, H. H., 91, 94–96, 228
Marshall, S., 39
Martin, C. L., 27
Martin, G., 212
Martin, J., 208
Martin Luther King, Jr. High School,
        300–309
Marx, R. W., 112, 132
Masia, B. B., 161
Maslow, A. H., 5, 114, 118–120,
        135, 226
Maslow's hierarchy of needs,
        118–120
Mason, D. A., 40
Mastery experiences, 128, 297

Mastery-oriented students, 130–131
Mathematics
    constructivist approach in, 7,
        173–176, 180
    examples of good teachers, 153
    gender bias in, 30
    learning disabilities and, 45
    sex differences in mental abilities,
        29
    teaching for understanding,
        173–176
Maxey, J. M., 249, 251–252
Mayer, G. R., 68, 71
Mayer, J. D., 35
Mayer, R. E., 91, 171
Mazzoni, S., 224
McClelland, D. C., 37, 120, 130–131
McCormick, C. B., 87
McDonald, J. P., 264
McEwin, C. K., 101
McGinnis, K., 164
McKeachie, W. J., 137
McLoyd, V. C., 18
McNemar, Q., 31
Mean, 237
Measurement, 234–235.
        See also Assessment
Median, 237
Medley, D. M., 165
Meece, J. L., 46
Meek, A., 171
Meichenbaum, D., 81
Meisels, S. J., 251
Meloth, M. S., 166
Mendell, P. R., 78
Menke, D. J., 84
Mental abilities, sex differences in,
        29
Mercer, C. D., 47
Mercer, L., 83
Mergendoller, J. R., 116
Message sent–message received, 213
Messick, S., 23
Metacognition, 81–83, 160–161
Meyer, C. A., 259
Meyer, M., 106
Meyers, T., 87
Middleton, J., 106
Mignano, A. J., Jr., 151, 152, 191,
        193, 195–199, 201, 209
Miles, M. B., 290
Miller, A., 117, 126
Miller, E., 219
Miller, G. A., 72, 75, 115
Miller, P. D., 171
Miller, P. H., 91, 132
Mills, J. R., 40
Minimum competency testing, 251

Mischel, W., 35
Miskel, C. G., 276, 283, 284, 296
Mitchell, B. M., 42
Mnemonics, 87–88
Mode, 237
Monitoring, 83
Monk, J. S., 24–25
Moody, C. D., 97
Moore, C. A., 23
Moos, B. S., 266
Moos, R. H., 266
Morgan, M., 268
Morris, P. F., 83, 130–131
Morrison, D., 267
Morrow, L. M., 173, 197
Moshman, D., 83, 91–93
Moskowitz, G., 203
Motivation, 5–6, 110–149
    achievement, 120, 130–131
    arousal and, 134–137
    attribution theory and, 123–126,
        130–131
    beliefs and, 126–130, 131
    defined, 112
    efficacy and, 128 129
    extrinsic, 112–113
    general approaches to, 113–115
    goals and, 116–118
    grades and, 268
    interests and, 132–134
    intrinsic, 112–113
    leadership challenge of,
        111–112
    to learn, 115–116
    needs and, 118–123
    strategies to encourage, 137–143
Movement management, 208
Mowday, R. T., 281
Mullins, T., 290
Multicultural classrooms, 18–27
    cultural diversity and, 18–19
    culturally compatible classrooms,
        21–27, 28
    language differences in, 19–21
Multiple intelligences, 32–35
Multiple representations, 97
Munby, H., 154
Murphy, P. K., 117, 132
Murray, H. G., 167
Musical intelligence, 33
Myths, 280

National Council of Teachers of
    Mathematics (NCTM), 94, 252
National Joint Committee on
    Learning Disabilities, 44
National Middle School Association,
    101

National standards, 251–252
Naturalist intelligence, 33
Naveh-Benjamin, M., 136, 137
Needles, M., 97
Needs, 118–123
    achievement motivation, 120
    conflicts and, 218
    defined, 118
    lessons for teachers and
        principals, 121–123
    Maslow's hierarchy of, 118–120
    self-determination, 120–121,
        122
    social support, 121
Negative reinforcement, 64–65, 66
Negotiations, 217
Neisser, U., 30, 38
Nelson, K., 79
Nelson, T. O., 83
Nestor-Baker, N. S., 35
Neuman, O., 117
Neuman, S. B., 164, 173
Newby, T. J., 143, 144
Newcombe, N., 29
Newman, S. E., 100 101
Nicholls, J. G., 117, 126
Nissani, M., 176, 268
Noddings, N., 171, 180, 203
Nolan, J. F., 208–209
Nolan, K., 252
Normal distribution, 238
Norman, D. P., 84
Norm groups, 235
Norming sample, 237
Norm-referenced tests, 235–236,
    245
Norms, 279
Note taking, 86, 87
Novelty, 141
Nystrand, M., 39

Oakes, J., 267
Objectives for learning, 156–159
    developing, 159
    general, 157–158
    specific, 157
    usefulness of, 158
O'Conner, J. E., 154
O'Donnell, A. M., 103, 104
Ogbu, J. U., 20, 118, 253
O'Kelly, J., 103, 104
O'Leary, D., 28
O'Leary, K. D., 42, 43
O'Malley, J. M., 21
Omelich, C. L., 127, 130, 136
O'Neil, J., 25, 251
Open climate, 287–288
Openness, 12

O'Reilly, C. A. I., 281
Organization, 79–80, 165–167
Organizational climate, 10–12,
    283–296
    changing, 299–309
    defined, 283
    healthy to unhealthy, 290–296
    open to closed, 283–284
    Organizational Culture
        Description Questionnaire
        (OCDQ), 284–286, 289–290
    types of, 287–289
Organizational Climate Description
    Questionnaire (OCDQ),
    284–286, 289–290
Organizational culture, 10–12,
    276–283
    common elements of, 281
    defined, 276
    functions of, 281
    general propositions and, 281–283
    levels of, 276–280
    school workplace and, 275–276
Organizational health, 290–296
    dimensions of, 291 292
    Organizational Health Inventory
        (OHI-S), 293–296
Organizational Health Inventory
    (OHI-S), 293–296
Ormond, J. E., 85
Ortony, A., 78, 115
Ouchi, W., 278
Ouellette, J. A., 88
Outstanding teaching, 180–181
Ovando, C. J., 21
Overlapping, 207
Owen, L., 254

Padilla, F. M., 218, 219
Pajares, F., 127
Palincsar, A. S., 85, 89, 91, 98, 102,
    104, 105, 118, 179, 226
Pang, K. C., 155
Panksepp, J., 44
Paris, S. G., 44, 72
Parker, L. H., 29
Parks, C. P., 218, 219
Parks, S., 87
Parsons, T., 290
Participation structures, 26, 192
Pasch, M., 97
Passive style, 216
Pate, P. E., 164
Patnoe, S., 102, 104
Paulman, R. G., 136
Paulson, F. L., 259, 260
Paulson, P. R., 259, 260
Payne, K. J., 18

Peake, P. K., 35
Pear, J., 212
Pearson, P. D., 84, 85
Pedagogical content knowledge, 171–180
Peer mediation, 219
Pelham, W. E., 83
Pelletier, L. G., 5, 114, 120–121
Penalties, 197, 210
Percentile rank, 239–240
Performance goals, 117
Performance in context, 10
Perloff, R., 30, 38
Perrone, V., 162–164
Perry, N. E., 83
Personal territories, 198–202
Peterson, P. L., 30, 154, 155–156
Phillips, D., 91, 92
Phonemic awareness, 173
Phonics, 7, 172
Piaget, J., 4, 89, 91, 95–96, 102, 134, 176
Pierson, L. H., 267
Pilon, D., 120
Pintrich, P. R., 24, 112, 115–117, 128, 132
Planning, 83, 155–164
    constructivist perspective on, 162–164
    learning spaces, 197–202
    objectives for learning, 156–159
    taxonomies in, 159–162
Plato, 30
Plucker, J., 35
Popham, W. J., 158
Porter, L. W., 281
Portfolios, 258, 259–260, 261, 262–265
    of principals, 13–14
    student, 10
Positive expectations, 139–140
Positive reinforcement, 64
Powell, R. R., 27
Prawat, R. S., 91, 94
Preliminary Scholastic Aptitude Test (PSAT), 248
Presentation punishment, 65
Pressley, M., 84, 86, 88, 171–173
Prevention, 207–208
Pribram, K. H., 72, 115
Price, G. E., 24
Principals
    attributions and, 131
    beliefs and, 131
    goals and, 118
    leadership challenges of, 17–18, 61–62, 111–112, 151
    needs and, 121–123

in Organizational Climate Description Questionnaire (OCDQ), 284–285, 286
    perspectives of, 6
    portfolios of, 13–14
    role of, 2–3
Problem-based learning, 99–100, 101, 221
Procedural knowledge, 73
Procedural memory, 78
Procedures
    classroom management and, 7–8
    defined, 193
    in learning environment, 193
    rules versus, 193–194
Productions, 78
Prompting, 67, 68
Psychological constructivism, 91
Psychomotor domain, 162
Pullen, P. L., 54
Punishment, 65, 66, 69–70
Purcell, P., 27
Puro, P., 116
Putnam, R., 171

Rach, L., 224
Rachlin, H., 64
Radical constructivism, 92–93
Raffini, J. P., 112, 122, 133, 224
Range, 238
Ratey, J. J., 43–44
Readiness testing, 250–251
Reading
    learning disabilities and, 45, 46
    strategies for, 88–89
    teaching for understanding, 171–173, 174–175
Reading wars, 7
Recht, D. R., 72
Recognition, in TARGET model, 222, 225
Reconstruction, 80–81
Reder, L. M., 94, 171
Reeve, J., 112, 122, 221–223, 225
Referrals, 52, 54
Reflective cognitive styles, 24
Regular education initiative, 48
Rehearsal, 77
Reid, M. K., 44, 84
Reinforcement, 63–65, 66, 69–70
Reinforcers, 63–65
Reis, S. M., 40, 41
Reisberg, D., 63, 81, 132
Reiss, F., 290
Relatedness, 121
Reliability, 243, 262
Removal punishment, 65
Renandya, W. A., 87

Rennie, L. J., 29
Renninger, K. A., 132
Renzulli, J. S., 24, 40, 41
Resnick, L. B., 72, 79, 94, 97, 165, 252
Rewards, 113–114, 142
Reynolds, A., 267
Reynolds, M. C., 42
Richardson, T. M., 42
Ritalin, 44
Rituals, 280
Robbins, S. P., 281
Robinson, D. H., 86
Robson, M., 155
Roderick, M., 267
Roehler, L. R., 84, 85, 166
Rogers, C., 5, 114
Ronning, R. R., 89
Rose, L. C., 208, 252
Rosenshine, B., 165, 167–169, 190
Rosenthal, R., 38
Roskos, K., 164, 173
Rosoff, B., 129
Roth, K. J., 177
Rubrics, 265
Rules
    classroom management and, 7–8, 193–197
    consequences and, 196–197
    for elementary students, 195
    procedures versus, 193–194
    for secondary students, 196
Rumelhart, D., 78
Ruopp, F., 152–153
Russell, D., 125
Ryan, R. M., 5, 112–114, 120–121, 203, 221–222
Ryans, D. G., 167

Sabers, D. S., 154
Sabo, D. J., 2, 284, 290, 295
Sadker, D., 28–29, 215
Sadker, M., 28–29, 215
Sakai, A., 203
Salinas, M. F., 253
Salovey, P., 35
Sanchez, F., 219
Sanders, S., 84
Sattler, J., 37, 252, 254
Sawyer, R. J., 46
Scales, P., 101
Schein, E. H., 11, 276–278, 280–283
Schemas, 78–79
Schematic knowledge, 84
Schiefele, U., 141
Schmader, T., 253
Scholastic aptitude tests, 248–249
School and College Ability Tests (SCAT), 248

School climate. *See* Organizational climate
School culture. *See* Organizational culture
School restructuring, 3
Schrauben, B., 24
Schraw, G. J., 83, 89
Schumaker, J. B., 46
Schunk, D. H., 79, 91, 93, 115–117, 120, 124, 128, 136
Schwartz, B., 63, 81
Science
    constructivist approach in, 7, 176–177
    teaching for understanding, 176–177
Scoring rubrics, 262
Secondary students
    classroom management for, 196, 203
    discipline problems and, 209–211
Seddon, G. M., 160
Seelbach, A., 225
Self-actualization, 114, 118–120
Self-comparison, 140
Self-concept, 127
Self-determination, 5, 120–121, 122, 221–225
Self-efficacy, 127–130, 132
Self-esteem, 127
Self-management, 192
Self-motivation, 35
Self-worth, 132
Seligman, M. E. P., 45, 124, 125
Semantic memory, 78
Semb, G. B., 81
Senge, P. M., 12, 300, 310
Sensory memory, 74–75
Serbin, L., 28
Serpell, R., 92
Sex discrimination, 27–29
Shavelson, R. J., 156
Shepard, L. A., 251, 267
Shields, A., 225
Shils, E. A., 290
Shimahara, N. K., 203
Shoda, Y., 35
Short-term memory, 73–74
Shuell, T. J., 72, 177
Shulman, L. S., 171
Shultz, J., 26
Signorella, M. L., 27
Simon, H. A., 91, 94, 171
Sisk, D. A., 41
Sizer, T., 10, 261
Skinner, B. F., 4, 63, 95–96

Slavin, R. E., 39, 104, 105, 181, 190, 226, 227
Sleeter, C. E., 18
Sloane, H. N., 211, 212
Smith, C. B., 171, 180
Smith, F., 75
Smith, J. D., 24
Smith, L. A., 267
Smith, L. H., 24
Smith, M., 219
Smith, M. L., 251, 267
Snider, V. E., 25
Snow, C. E., 21
Snow, R. E., 24, 39
Snowman, J., 86
Soar, R. M., 167
Soar, R. S., 167
Social constructivism, 91–92, 93
Social goals, 117–118
Social learning approaches to motivation, 6, 115
Social negotiation, 97
Social organization, 22–23
Social persuasion, 128
Social support, 121
Sociocultural views of motivation, 115
Sociological constructivism, 92
Sokolove, S., 215
Sosniak, L. A., 159, 160
Southern, W. T., 42
Sparks-Langer, G., 97
Spatial intelligence, 33
Spearman, C., 31, 35–36, 55
Spiro, R. J., 91, 97
Sproull, L. S., 296
Stahl, S. A., 171
Stainback, S., 48
Stainback, W., 48
Standard deviation, 237–238, 243
Standard English, 19–20
Standard error of measurement, 243
Standardized tests, 9–10
    basic concepts of, 236–238
    bias and fairness in, 252
    coaching and, 254
    defined, 236–237
    getting the most from, 265–266
    interpreting scores for, 242–244
    new directions in, 255–265
    preparing students for, 254
    stereotype threat and, 252–254
    test-taking skills and, 254
    types of, 244–249
    types of scores for, 238–242
    uses of, 249–252
Standard scores, 241–242

Stanford-Binet, 36
Stanine scores, 241–242
Stanovich, K. E., 25, 45
Starko, A. J., 97
State anxiety, 136
Steele, C. M., 253
Steers, R. M., 281
Stepien, W., 221
Stereotype threat, 252–254
    combating, 253–254
    nature of, 252–253
Stereotyping
    gender-based, 29
    learning style and, 25
Sternberg, R. J., 30, 32, 36, 38, 55
Stevens, R., 168–169
Stevenson, H. W., 38
Stewart, L., 27
Stigler, J., 38
Stipek, D. J., 115–117, 120, 121, 126, 133, 134, 138, 141, 142, 226
Stoddard, K., 211
Stodolsky, S. S., 180
Story grammar, 78–79
Student-centered instruction, 97
Students with learning challenges, 42–52
    hyperactivity and attention disorders, 42–44, 83
    integration of, 46–49
    learning disabilities, 44–46, 47, 83
Student-Teams Achievement Division (STAD), 226–227
Stumpf, H., 29
Subject matter teaching, 177–180
Sulzer-Azaroff, B., 68, 71
Summaries, 85
Swanson, H. L., 83, 154
Sweetland, S. R., 2, 298
Symons, S., 171

Tacit assumptions, 276–278
Tait, H., 24
Taking notes, 86, 87
Target errors, 207
TARGET model, 221–228
Tarter, C. J., 2, 284–286, 290, 293, 295, 296, 299–300, 302
Tarter, J., 62
Task-involved learners, 117
Taxonomies, 159–162
    in affective domain, 161–162
    in cognitive domain, 159–161
    defined, 159
    in psychomotor domain, 162
Taylor, D. M., 21
Taylor, J. B., 19–20

Teacher efficacy, 12, 296–299, 341–343
Teachers
  analysis of teaching task by, 297–298
  assessment of student learning, 9
  attributions and, 131
  beginning, and motivation of students, 143, 144
  beliefs and, 131
  classroom management and, 7–8
  efficacy of, 129–130
  expert, 153–154
  goals and, 118
  knowledge of, 165
  needs and, 121–123
  in Organizational Climate Description Questionnaire (OCDQ), 285, 286
  perspectives of, 6
Teaching, 150–186. *See also* Effective teaching
  behaviorial theories in, 67–70
  cautions concerning, 181
  leadership challenge of, 151
  outstanding, 180–181
  planning and, 155–164
  for understanding, 171–180
Teaching methods, for gifted and talented students, 41–42
Textbook tests, 266
Tharp, R. G., 21, 26, 192
Theory of multiple intelligences, 32–35
Thomas, D. R., 67
Thomas, M. H., 88
Thompson, G., 164
Thorley, N. R., 176, 177
Thurstone, L. L., 32, 35–36
Time, in TARGET model, 223, 228
Time on task, 190–191
Timing errors, 207
Tobias, S., 136
Tobin, K., 91
Tochon, F., 154
Token reinforcement system, 212–213
Tomlinson, C. A., 35
Tomlinson-Keasey, C., 39
Torrance, E. P., 25, 41
Townsend, B., 211
Tracking, 38–39
Trait anxiety, 136
Treiman, R., 173
Triarchic theory of intelligence, 36
Trice, H. M., 280
True score, 243

Tschannen-Moran, M., 104, 105, 129, 298
Turbill, J., 262

Underlining, 86
Underwood, A., 132
Undheim, J. O., 31
Unhealthy school climate, 295
Urbina, S., 30, 38
Urdan, T. C., 117, 118
Utility value of learning, 140

Validity, 244, 264
Vallerand, R. J., 5, 114, 120–121
Value of learning, 140–142
Values, 278–279
VandeKamp, K., 83
van Ijzendoorn, M. H., 172, 173
Van Meter, P., 86
Vavrus, L. G., 166
Veenman, S., 155
Vellutino, F. R., 171–173
Vera, A. H., 91
Verbal hints, 209
Verbal persuasion, 297
Vicarious experiences, 128, 297
Violence, 211, 218–219
Vispoel, W. P., 132–133
Visual tools, 86–87
von Glasersfeld, E., 89, 91, 180
Vroom, V., 115
Vygotsky, L., 4, 89, 91–92, 95–96, 102

Wagner, R. K., 36, 38
Walberg, H. J., 3, 180
Walker, R., 127
Walsh, M. E., 180
Walton, G., 41
Wang, A. Y., 88
Wang, M. C., 3
Ward, M. E., 44, 217
Warmth, of teacher, 167
Webb, N., 102, 104, 226
Wechsler scales, 36, 37
Weinberg, R. A., 38
Weiner, B., 112, 115, 123–125, 129
Weinert, P. E., 168, 171, 180
Weinstein, C. S., 151, 152, 191, 193, 195–199, 201, 209
Weiss, G., 44
Wenger, E., 94
Wentzel, K. R., 118
Wessmann, A., 266
White, S., 26
Whitehead, A. N., 100
Whitmore, J. R., 41

Whole-language approaches, 7, 171–172, 180
Wiener, M. W., 221–223
Wigfield, A., 136, 138, 140
Wiggins, G. W., 10, 259, 261, 262
Wilen, W., 99
Williams, G. C., 221–223
Williams, W. M., 36
Willig, A. C., 21
Willingham, W. W., 29
Wilson, C. W., 211
Wingate, N., 28
Winters, L., 262, 264
Within-class ability grouping, 39
Withitness, 207
Witkin, H. A., 23
Wittrock, M. C., 91
Wixson, K. K., 72
Wolf, D., 255, 258, 260
Woloshyn, V., 171
Wolters, C. A., 117
Women on Words and Images, 27
Wood, E. G., 35
Wood, S. E., 35
Woolfolk, A. E., 66, 73, 74, 129, 130, 135, 139, 170, 199, 218, 226, 237, 239, 240, 242
Woolfolk Hoy, A., 104, 105, 129, 296, 298
Work-avoidant learners, 117
Working memory, 75–77
Worner, C., 99
Worsham, M., 166, 192–193, 195, 196, 208
Worthen, B. R., 257
Wright, S. C., 21
Writing, teaching for understanding, 171–173

Yanon, D., 296
Yee, A. H., 29
Yekovich, C. W., 73, 78, 80
Yekovich, F. R., 73, 78, 80
Yerkes, R. M., 134, 136
Yetman, N. R., 21
Yinger, R., 155–156
Yokoi, L., 86
Young, A. J., 117
Young, K. R., 211, 212
Yu, S. L., 117

Zeidner, M., 136, 137
Zigmond, N., 48
Zimmerman, B. J., 128
Ziomek, R. L., 249, 251–252
Z score, 241